Serious Games and Edutainment Applications

Minhua Ma · Andreas Oikonomou · Lakhmi C. Jain
Editors

Serious Games and Edutainment Applications

Springer

Editors
Minhua Ma
The Glasgow School of Art
Digital Design Studio
The Hub
G51 1EA Glasgow
UK
m.ma@gsa.ac.uk

Andreas Oikonomou
University of Derby
E514
School of Computing and Mathematics
Kedleston Road
DE22 1GB Derby
UK
a.oikonomou@derby.ac.uk

Lakhmi C. Jain
University of South Australia
School of Electrical and Information Engineering
Adelaide South Australia
Australia
Lakhmi.Jain@unisa.edu.au

ISBN 978-1-4471-5811-0 ISBN 978-1-4471-2161-9 (eBook)
DOI 10.1007/978-1-4471-2161-9
Springer London Dordrecht Heidelberg New York

British Library Cataloguing in Publication Data
A catalogue record for this book is available from the British Library

© Springer-Verlag London Limited 2011
Softcover reprint of the hardcover 1st edition 2011
Apart from any fair dealing for the purposes of research or private study, or criticism or review, as permitted under the Copyright, Designs and Patents Act 1988, this publication may only be reproduced, stored or transmitted, in any form or by any means, with the prior permission in writing of the publishers, or in the case of reprographic reproduction in accordance with the terms of licenses issued by the Copyright Licensing Agency. Enquiries concerning reproduction outside those terms should be sent to the publishers.
The use of registered names, trademarks, etc., in this publication does not imply, even in the absence of a specific statement, that such names are exempt from the relevant laws and regulations and therefore free for general use.
The publisher makes no representation, express or implied, with regard to the accuracy of the information contained in this book and cannot accept any legal responsibility or liability for any errors or omissions that may be made.

Printed on acid-free paper

Springer is part of Springer Science+Business Media (www.springer.com)

Preface

My interest in the serious games began in 2005 with work on virtual reality games for post-stroke rehabilitation but was rekindled in 2009 when experimenting Second Life as a learning and teaching environment for computer game design and working with Nottingham University Hospitals on computer games intervention with mucus clearing devices for Cystic Fibrosis. *Serious Games and Edutainment Applications* arose from the First International Workshop on Serious Games Development and Applications at University of Derby in 2010. The event has now becomes an annual conference and is supported by the Gala European Network of Excellence in Serious Games, the TARGET project which is partially funded by the European Community under the Seventh Framework Programme, and a number of partners such as the Glasgow School of Art, University of Derby, INESC ID, and Technical University of Lisbon. This year, the annual conference (SGDA 2011) is hosted by the Technical University of Lisbon (IST/UTL), and the conference proceedings will be published by Springer-Verlag as part of the LNCS series.

Serious Games and Edutainment Applications offers an insightful introduction to the development and applications of games technologies in educational settings, with cutting edge academic research and industry updates which will inform readers current and future advances in the area. The book is divided into five parts: introduction, theories and reviews, custom-made games and case studies, use of Commercial-off-the-shelf (COTS) games in education, and social aspects and gamification.

The book will benefit academics, researchers, graduates, and undergraduates in the fields of computer games and education, educators who wish to use games technologies in their teaching, game designers and developers, game publishers, and entrepreneurs in the games industry. For academics delivering taught modules in any fields, this book can serve as a good collection of related articles to facilitate a broad understanding of this subject and as such it can become one of the handbook to help educators to select, plan, and carry out teaching using commercial or custom-made games. Professional game designers and developers who adapt off-the-shelf virtual environment for teaching and learning purposes will find some interesting examples of using

COTS games in educational settings and guidelines on choosing a suitable game for the classroom in Part IV. The custom-made edutainment applications presented in Part III of the book may be of particular interest to those who create new edutainment applications using video games technologies and game design processes.

Glasgow, UK Minhua Ma

Contents

Part I Introduction

1 **Innovations in Serious Games for Future Learning** 3
Minhua Ma, Andreas Oikonomou, and Lakhmi C. Jain

2 **Serious Games: A New Paradigm for Education?** 9
Sara de Freitas and Fotis Liarokapis

3 **Origins of Serious Games** 25
Damien Djaouti, Julian Alvarez, Jean-Pierre Jessel, and Olivier Rampnoux

4 **Serious Learning in Serious Games** 45
Konstantin Mitgutsch

Part II Theories and Reviews

5 **Social Flow and Learning in Digital Games: A Conceptual Model and Research Agenda** 61
Christine M. Bachen and Chad Raphael

6 **A Formalism to Define, Assess and Evaluate Player Behaviour in Mobile Device Based Serious Games** 85
Hanno Hildmann and Jule Hildmann

7 **Serious Games for Health and Safety Training** 107
Rafael J. Martínez-Durá, Miguel Arevalillo-Herráez, Ignacio García-Fernández, Miguel A. Gamón-Giménez, and Angel Rodríguez-Cerro

8 **Augmenting Initiative Game Worlds with Mobile Digital Devices** . 125
Jule Hildmann and Hanno Hildmann

Part III Custom-Made Games and Case Studies

9 Enhancing Learning in Distributed Virtual Worlds through Touch: A Browser-based Architecture for Haptic Interaction . . . 149
Sylvester Arnab, Panagiotis Petridis, Ian Dunwell, and Sara de Freitas

10 Operation ARIES!: A Serious Game for Teaching Scientific Inquiry 169
Keith Millis, Carol Forsyth, Heather Butler, Patty Wallace, Arthur Graesser, and Diane Halpern

11 From Global Games to Re-contextualized Games: The Design Process of TekMyst 197
Carolina Islas Sedano, Jan Pawlowski, Erkki Sutinen, Mikko Vinni, and Teemu H. Laine

12 Using Serious Games for Assessment 225
Aidan Sliney and Dave Murphy

13 Designing and Evaluating Emotional Student Models for Game-Based Learning 245
Karla Muñoz, Paul Mc Kevitt, Tom Lunney, Julieta Noguez, and Luis Neri

14 Fun *and* Learning: Blending Design and Development Dimensions in Serious Games through Narrative and Characters 273
Tim Marsh, Li Zhiqiang Nickole, Eric Klopfer, Chuang Xuejin, Scot Osterweil, and Jason Haas

Part IV Use of Commercial-Off-the-Shelf (COTS) Games in Education

15 Choosing a Serious Game for the Classroom: An Adoption Model for Educators 291
Kae Novak and Rurik Nackerud

16 Learning Narratives with Harry Potter. "Manuel de Fallas's The Prophet Newspaper" 309
Sara Cortés Gómez, Rut Martínez Borda, and Pilar Lacasa

17 Using *Dungeons and Dragons* to Integrate Curricula in an Elementary Classroom 329
Alexandra Carter

18 Modding in Serious Games: Teaching Structured Query Language (SQL) Using NeverWinter Nights 347
Mario Soflano

19 Expanding a VLE-Based Integration Framework Supporting Education in Second Life 369
Peter R. Bloomfield

Part V Social Aspects and Gamification

20 Casual Social Games as Serious Games: The Psychology of Gamification in Undergraduate Education and Employee Training . . . 399
Richard N. Landers and Rachel C. Callan

21 Experiences of Promoting Student Engagement Through Game-Enhanced Learning . . . 425
Therese Charles, David Bustard, and Michaela Black

22 What Computing Students Can Learn by Developing Their Own Serious Games . . . 447
Matt Smith

23 Social Interactive Learning in Multiplayer Games . . . 481
Vanessa Camilleri, Leonard Busuttil, and Matthew Montebello

Index . . . 503

Contributors

Julian Alvarez Ludoscience, France, julian@ludoscience.com

Miguel Arevalillo-Herráez Universidad de Valencia, Computing Department, Burjassot, Spain, miguel.arevalillo@uv.es

Sylvester Arnab Serious Games Institute, Coventry University, Coventry, UK, s.arnab@coventry.ac.uk

Christine M. Bachen Communication Department, Santa Clara University, Santa Clara, CA 95053-0277, USA, cbachen@scu.edu

Michaela Black University of Ulster, Coleraine BT52 1SA, UK, mm.black@ulster.ac.uk

Peter R. Bloomfield School of Computing, University of the West of Scotland, Paisley, Scotland, UK, peter.bloomfield@uws.ac.uk

Rut Martínez Borda Department of Psychology, Education and Physical Education, University of Alcala, Madrid, Spain, rut.martinez@uah.es

David Bustard University of Ulster, Coleraine BT52 1SA, UK, dw.bustard@ulster.ac.uk

Leonard Busuttil University of Malta, Msida, Malta, leonard.busuttil@um.edu.mt

Heather Butler Claremont Graduate University, Claremont, CA, USA, heather.butler@cgu.edu

Rachel C. Callan Old Dominion University, Norfolk, VA, USA, rjohn104@odu.edu

Vanessa Camilleri University of Malta, Msida, Malta, vanessa.camilleri@um.edu.mt

Alexandra Carter University of California, Los Angeles, CA, USA, alexcarter@ucla.edu

Therese Charles University of Ulster, Coleraine BT52 1SA, UK, theresecharles@gmail.com

Sara de Freitas Serious Games Institute (SGI), Coventry University, Coventry, UK, s.defreitas@coventry.ac.uk

Damien Djaouti IRIT, Toulouse III University, Toulouse, France; Ludoscience, France, Damien.Djaouti@irit.fr

Ian Dunwell Serious Games Institute, Coventry University, Coventry, UK, idunwell@cad.coventry.ac.uk

Carol Forsyth University of Memphis, Memphis, TN, USA, carol_forsyth@yahoo.com

Miguel A. Gamón-Giménez Instituto IRTIC, Universidad de Valencia, Paterna, Spain, Miguel.A.Gamon@uv.es

Ignacio García-Fernández Instituto IRTIC, Universidad de Valencia, Paterna, Spain, Ignacio.garcia@uv.es

Sara Cortés Gómez Department of Psychology, Education and Physical Education, University of Alcala, Madrid, Spain, sara.cortesg@uah.es

Arthur Graesser University of Memphis, Memphis, TN, USA, art.graesser@gmail.com

Jason Haas Comparative Media Studies, Massachusetts Institute of Technology, Cambridge, MA, USA, jhaas@mit.edu

Diane Halpern Claremont McKenna College, Claremont, CA, USA, diane.halpern@claremontmckenna.edu

Hanno Hildmann Etisalat BT Innocation Centre (EBTIC), Khalifa University, Abu Dhabi, UAE; University of the West of Scotland (UWS), Scotland, UK, hanno@cypherpunx.org

Jule Hildmann Centrum für Erlebnispädagogik Volkersberg, Volkersberg, Germany, jule.hildmann@gmx.de

Carolina Islas Sedano University of Eastern Finland, FI-80101 Joensuu, Finland, carolina.islas@uef.fi

Lakhmi C. Jain School of Electrical and Information Engineering, University of South Australia, Adelaide, SA, Australia, Lakhmi.Jain@unisa.edu.au

Jean-Pierre Jessel IRIT, Toulouse III University, Toulouse, France, Jean-Pierre.Jessel@irit.fr

Paul Mc Kevitt University of Ulster, Derry/Londonderry, BT48 7JL, UK, p.mckevitt@ulster.ac.uk

Eric Klopfer The Education Arcade, Massachusetts Institute of Technology, Cambridge, MA, USA, klopfer@mit.edu

Pilar Lacasa Department of Psychology, Education and Physical Education, University of Alcala, Madrid, Spain, p.lacasa@uah.es

Teemu H. Laine University of Eastern Finland, FI-80101 Joensuu, Finland, teemu.laine@uef.fi

Richard N. Landers Old Dominion University, Norfolk, VA, USA, rnlanders@odu.edu

Fotis Liarokapis Serious Games Institute (SGI), Coventry University, Coventry, UK, f.liarokapis@coventry.ac.uk

Tom Lunney Faculty of Computing and Engineering, School of Computing and Intelligent Systems, University of Ulster, Derry/Londonderry BT48 7JL, UK, tf.lunney@ulster.ac.uk

Minhua Ma Digital Design Studio, Glasgow School of Art, Glasgow G51 1EA, UK, m.ma@gsa.ac.uk

Tim Marsh James Cook University, QLD, Australia, tim.marsh@jcu.edu.au

Rafael J. Martínez-Durá Instituto IRTIC, Universidad de Valencia, Paterna, Spain, Rafael.Martinez@uv.es

Keith Millis Department of Psychology, Northern Illinois University, DeKalb, IL 60115, USA, kmillis@niu.edu

Konstantin Mitgutsch Singapore-MIT Gambit Game Lab, Massachusetts Institute of Technology, Cambridge, MA 02139, USA, k_mitgut@mit.edu

Matthew Montebello University of Malta, Msida, Malta, matthew.montebello@um.edu.mt

Karla Muñoz Faculty of Computing and Engineering, School of Computing and Intelligent Systems, Intelligent Systems Research Centre, University of Ulster, Derry/Londonderry, UK, Munoz_Esquivel-K@email.ulster.ac.uk

Dave Murphy University College Cork, Cork, Ireland, d.murphy@cs.ucc.ie

Rurik Nackerud Oregon Virtual Academy, North Bend, OR 97459, USA, Rurik.Nackerud@gmail.com

Luis Neri Engineering School, Tecnológico de Monterrey (ITESM), Mexico City C.P. 14380, Mexico, neri@itesm.mx

Li Zhiqiang Nickole Ubisoft & National University of Singapore, Singapore, Singapore, fenris_nightwolf@hotmail.com

Julieta Noguez Computer Department, Engineering School, Tecnológico de Monterrey (ITESM), Mexico City C.P. 14380, Mexico, jnoguez@itesm.mx

Kae Novak Front Range Community College, Westminster, CO, USA, que.jinn@gmail.com

Andreas Oikonomou School of Computing and Mathematics, University of Derby, Derby DE22 1GB, UK, a.oikonomou@derby.ac.uk

Scot Osterweil The Education Arcade, Massachusetts Institute of Technology, Cambridge, MA, USA, scot_o@mit.edu

Jan Pawlowski University of Jyväskylä, FI-40014 Jyväskylä, Finland, jan.pawlowski@jyu.fi

Panagiotis Petridis Serious Games Institute, Coventry University, Coventry, UK, ppetridis@cad.coventry.ac.uk

Olivier Rampnoux European Centre for Children's Products (CEPE), Poitiers University, Poitiers, France, olivier.rampnoux@univ-poitiers.fr

Chad Raphael Communication Department, Santa Clara University, Santa Clara, CA 95053-0277, USA, craphael@scu.edu

Angel Rodríguez-Cerro Instituto IRTIC, Universidad de Valencia, Paterna, Spain, angel.rodriguez@uv.es

Aidan Sliney University College Cork, Cork, Ireland, aidansliney@gmail.com

Matt Smith Department of Informatics, Institute of Technology Blanchardstown, Dublin 15, Republic of Ireland, matt.smith@itb.ie

Mario Soflano School of Computing, University of the West of Scotland, Paisley, Scotland, UK, Mario.Soflano@uws.ac.uk

Erkki Sutinen University of Eastern Finland, FI-80101 Joensuu, Finland, erkki.sutinen@uef.fi

Mikko Vinni University of Eastern Finland, FI-80101 Joensuu, Finland, mikko.vinni@uef.fi

Patty Wallace Northern Illinois University, DeKalb, IL, USA, pwallace@niu.edu

Chuang Xuejin National University of Singapore, Singapore, Singapore, kleken@gmail.com

About the Editors

Dr. Minhua Ma is the Head of Academic Programmes at Digital Design Studio, The Glasgow School of Art. Before joining Glasgow School of Art, she was Reader in Visualisation & Virtual Reality and Programme Leader for MSc Computer Games Production at the School of Computing and Mathematics, University of Derby. She completed her Doctorate in Computer Science from the University of Ulster in 2005, MSc in Computing Science from the University of Newcastle upon Tyne in 2001, and MA and BA in linguistics in 1998 and 1995 respectively. Her research areas include serious games, 3D visualisation, Virtual Reality, and Natural Language Processing. Her principal lines of work have been published in 50 peer-reviewed books, journals as well as conference proceedings. She has received grants from EU and East Midlands Development Agency for her work on computer games intervention with mucus clearing devices for cystic fibrosis; the Northern Ireland Chest, Heart and Stroke Association for her work on Virtual Reality in stroke rehabilitation, and a number of other grants for her research in visualisation and games.

She has been supervising 4 Ph.D. students (one completed) in video games and e-learning. With her team she has been developing serious games for healthcare and natural language 3D visualisation systems with broad impact in intelligent multimedia, serious games, forensic visualisation and other areas. Dr. Ma is the Accepting Associate Editor responsible for the serious games section of the Elsevier journal *Entertainment Computing*. She has been editing two books on games technology with Springer, and special issues for a couple of journals. She also authored some book chapters and organised a number of conferences and workshops in serious games and 3D visualisation. Dr. Ma is serving on the Editorial Board for the *Journal of Intelligent Decision Technologies* and numerous conference programme committees.

Dr. Andreas Oikonomou is Subject Co-ordinator and lecturer for Computer Games at the University of Derby. Prior to this appointment Dr. Oikonomou was the head of Derby Games Studio, the university's commercial games development division and has also worked as Project and Quality Assurance manager for the university's Business Development Unit. Previously to the above roles Dr. Oikonomou was multimedia and game development lecturer at Coventry University for 5 years and worked as a research assistant for the same institution for 2 years. He holds a PhD in Educational Multimedia Development, a Master's degree in Information Technology for Management and a BSc in Engineering. His current interests include game design, game based learning and assessment, real-time rendering, interactive multimedia, biomedical engineering and business management. Dr. Oikonomou has published 14 journal and conference papers in many aspects of biomedical computing, educational multimedia, computer games and e-learning systems development.

Prof. Lakhmi C. Jain is a Director/Founder of the Knowledge-Based Intelligent Engineering Systems (KES) Centre, located in the University of South Australia. He is a fellow of the Institution of Engineers Australia. His interests focus on the artificial intelligence paradigms and their applications in complex systems, art-science fusion, e-education, e-healthcare, unmanned air vehicles and intelligent agents.

Part I
Introduction

Chapter 1
Innovations in Serious Games for Future Learning

Minhua Ma, Andreas Oikonomou, and Lakhmi C. Jain

1.1 Introduction

The recent emergence of serious games as a branch of video games has introduced the concept of games designed for a serious purpose other than pure entertainment. To date the major applications of serious games include education and training, engineering, healthcare (Garcia-Ruiz et al., 2011), military applications, city planning, production, crisis response, just to name a few. Serious games have primarily been used as a tool that gives players a novel way to interact with games in order to learn skills and knowledge, promote physical activities, support social-emotional development, and treat different types of psychological and physical disorders amongst others. Many recent studies have identified the benefits of using video games in a variety of serious—even critical—contexts. Games technology is inexpensive, widely available, fun and entertaining for people of all ages. If utilised alongside, or combined with conventional training and educational approaches it could provide a more powerful means of knowledge transfer in almost every application domain.

This book *Serious Games and Edutainment Applications* offers an insightful introduction to the development and applications of games technologies in educational settings. It includes cutting edge academic research and industry updates that will inform readers of current and future advances in the area. The book is suitable for both researchers and educators who are interested in using games for educational purposes as well as game professionals who are trying to gain a thorough understanding of issues involved in the application of video games technology into educational settings.

M. Ma (✉)
Digital Design Studio, Glasgow School of Art, Glasgow G51 1EA, UK
e-mail: m.ma@gsa.ac.uk

M. Ma et al. (eds.), *Serious Games and Edutainment Applications*,
DOI 10.1007/978-1-4471-2161-9_1, © Springer-Verlag London Limited 2011

1.2 Chapters Included in the Book

This book includes 23 chapters. Chapter 1 provides an introduction to serious games and simulation in education. It presents brief abstracts of all chapters included in the book. The book is divided into five parts: introduction, theories and reviews, custom-made games and case studies, use of Commercial-off-the-shelf (COTS) games in education, and social aspects and gamification.

Part I includes three other chapters. Chapter 2 explores the context for the new paradigm of learning in relation to key critical concepts that centre around gamification, immersion, interface, and social interactivity. Chapter 3 reviews the history and nature of serious games and compares statistics, market and economical models of serious games before and after 2002. In Chapter 4 three different levels of learning processes in serious games are discussed, i.e. learning in, through, and beyond games. The authors argue that most studies research the transfer of behaviour, of knowledge, competences and skills whilst not much is known about deep and meaningful transformative learning processes. They then derive conclusions from theoretical and empirical evidence of previous studies and several case studies on commercial serious games.

Part II covers concepts and theoretical research of game based learning and serious game study. Chapter 5 provides a comprehensive review of game flow and learning in educational game play. A conceptual model of social game flow is presented and the comparison of game flow for traditional, e-learning and social games is discussed. Finally, a research agenda for further studies in serious games is laid out. Chapter 6 proposes using propositional logic to formally define and evaluate game play behaviours in mobile device based serious games. Statements constructed by propositional logic provide an unambiguous way for an interface within a game to enable researchers to define the behaviour of interest for the game and evaluate player behaviours automatically. Chapter 7 reviews applications of serious games in health and safety training and discusses design, evaluation, and technological aspects related to the development of this type of serious games. Chapter 8 proposes to combine initiative games with mobile technologies to accurately monitor and evaluate the learning progress of participants and enrich the gaming experience for players. A number of technical and educational considerations are discussed. The authors argue that mobile devices can be implemented to augment initiative games in order to intensify the training effect on social and personal skills in players.

Part III includes reviews of six custom-made serious games for various educational and training purposes and case studies. Chapter 9 investigates the impact of haptics in a virtual learning environment and describes a framework for integrating tactile interaction in learning over the web. An application in the Roma Nova project on cultural heritage is demonstrated as a case study of enhancing learning through haptic interaction. Chapter 10 describes a game called Operation ARIES! which teaches the player critical thinking and scientific reasoning within scientific inquiry. It discusses how the game design incorporates various principles of learning found in cognitive psychology and the learning sciences. Next a hyper-contextualised game design model and two case studies of employing this model to re-contextualise the game SciMyst, a riddle-solving game designed for a science festival and a new learning context (a museum of technology) are presented in Chapter 11. Chapter 12 investigates the benefits of using serious games for formative assessment. Two 3D simulations for assessment are reviewed in term of assessment information, assessor, and implementation methods. Chapter 13 describes the design and implementation of a serious game PlayPhysics, which is an emotional game-based learning environment for teaching Physics. It focuses on the player emotional model of the player using observable behaviours and self-reported emotions during game play. Finally, another educational game 'Waker' for students to learn about aspects of physics in high schools is presented in Chapter 14. The authors compare four versions of the game and carry out a study in a Singapore high school to investigate the effectiveness of game features (puzzle, narrative, and voiceover) in engaging students, their play experience and achieving learning objectives.

Adopting Commercial-off-the-shelf (COTS) games or game mods for teaching and learning significantly reduces the development cost and improves quality of serious games. Part IV provides guidelines and case studies of using COTS games in educational settings. Firstly, Chapter 15 proposes an evaluative framework, which enables faculties from multiple disciplines to effectively incorporate COTS games into their curriculum. Chapter 16 investigates why and how COTS games can be used to improve literacy at school through an experiment of bringing the game Harry Potter and the Order of the Phoenix into a language class to develop students' narrative thinking while they reconstruct the actions experienced in the game as a narrative. Chapter 17 describes a case study of using *Dungeons and Dragons* based game design projects to integrate curricula including mathematics, social studies, research skills, written and oral communication, artistic and creative development, and social and emotional development, in a primary school. The conclusions and recommendations are supported by empirical experiments and would be helpful for teachers who plan to adopt similar approaches in primary and secondary education. Chapter 18 describes a work-in-progress project which integrates web-based VLEs activities (discussion boards, course structures, and wikis) within the Second Life virtual environment. Finally, the author of Chapter 19 reports the use of a NeverWinter Nights mod to teach SQL in a fun and challenging way.

Part V is on social aspects and gamification. Chapters 20 and 21 both explore gamification in undergraduate education. Chapter 22 discusses a broad range of theories relating to the advantages of teaching computing students by asking them to develop their own serious games, e.g. enquiry-based learning, instructionist vs. constructionist serious games, and intelligent tutors. The final chapter investigates social interactive learning in multiplayer games.

1.3 Conclusion and Future Trends of Serious Games

This chapter gives an overview of the book. The chapters in this book also give the reader a perspective of future trends of serious games.

1.3.1 Pervasive Serious Games

Emerging and pervasive technologies bring lots of potential for pervasive games (a.k.a. *ubiquitous computing games*, or *mixed reality games*), especially Live Action Role Playing Games (LARPS) that take place both virtually in game worlds and in the real world, as people run around in physical space to accomplish game-related missions that register only in cyberspace, e.g. location-based games like *Geocaching* and *Botfighter*. Chapters 8 and 11 discuss theories and experiments on using mobile technology for serious games. Besides these applications, Waern (2009) shares his experiences of developing a pervasive game for the iPhone.

1.3.2 Alternative Input Devices for Serious Games

The traditional keyboard and mouse combination as the primary input devices, now mainly for video games on PC platform, predates the growing popularity of video game input devices like Xbox 360, Wii Remote, and recently released controller free interface–Microsoft Kinect and PlayStation Move. Thorpe et al. (2011) review mainstream and alternative input devices for video games including dance mat, haptics, camera-based input and so on, and compare them in a two-player game. To date, most serious games still use traditional keyboard and mouse input, very few attempts have been made to use alternative game interfaces in serious games. Through a browser-based architecture for haptic interaction, Chapter 9 argues that by stimulating multiple perceptions, learning experiences may be more accurately replicated in a virtual world. This may be one of the future trends for serious game applications especially for medical training.

1.3.3 Social Media and Learning

Using social media to improve learning is becoming more important due to the popularity of social gaming and the effectiveness of social interaction in the learning process. The community aspect of serious games is explored and experimented with in Chapters 5, 20, and 23. We believe that putting social psychology into serious game would be another direction for future development of edutainment applications.

References

Annetta, L.A., Folta, E., Klesath, M.: V-learning: Distance Education in the 21st Century Through 3D Virtual Learning Environments. Springer, Berlin (2010)

Baldwin, M.W., Dandeneau, S.D.: Putting social psychology into serious games. Soc. Personality Psychol. Compass **3**(4), 547–565, July 2009. Blackwell (2009)

Bergeron, B.: Developing Serious Games, Game Development Series. Charles River Media, Hingham, MA (2006)

Connolly, T., Stansfield, M., Boyle, L.: Games-Based Learning Advancement for Multi-Sensory Human Computer Interfaces: Techniques and Effective Practices. IGI Global, Hershey, PA (2009)

Egenfeldt-Nielsen, S.: Third generation educational use of computer games. J. Educ. Multimedia Hypermedia **16**(3), 263–281 (2007)

Garcia-Ruiz, M.A., Tashiro, J., Kapralos, B., Martin, M.V.: Crouching Tangents, Hidden Danger: Assessing Development of Dangerous Misconceptions within Serious Games for Healthcare Education. Gaming and Simulations: Concepts, Methodologies, Tools and Applications, pp. 1712–1749. Information Resources Management Association, Hershey, PA (2011)

Kankaanranta, M., Neittaanmaki, P.: Design and Use of Serious Games (International Series on Intelligent Systems, Control and Automation: Science and Engineering). Springer, Berlin (2010)

Ritterfeld, U., Cody, M., Vorderer, P.: Serious Games Mechanisms and Effects. Routledge, New York (2009)

Thorpe, A., Ma, M., Oikonomou, A.: Alternative input methods for video games. In Mehdi, Q. et al. (eds.) Proceedings of the 16th IEEE Conference on Computer Games: AI, Animation, Mobile, Interactive Multimedia, Educational and Serious Games (CGames 2011), Galt House Hotel, Louisville, KY, 27–30 Jul 2011.

Waern: Technology rant: Hardcore use of the IPhone. Pervasive Games: Theory and Design. Experiences on the Boundary between Life and Play [Online]. http://pervasivegames.wordpress.com/2009/07/16/technology-rant-hardcore-use-of-the-iphone/ (2009)

Chapter 2
Serious Games: A New Paradigm for Education?

Sara de Freitas and Fotis Liarokapis

2.1 Introduction: Serious Games: A New Paradigm for Education?

The pervasiveness of gaming, the widespread use of the internet and the need to create more engaging educational practices have led to the emergence of serious games as a new form for education and training. While many have begun to see the potential of serious games to supplement and augment traditional formal education and informal non-curriculum training, the authors consider the potential of serious games to offer a paradigm shift in how education and training are delivered in the twenty-first century. The implications of this transition to a new paradigm of game-based learning will be broadly to adopt metaphors of games, or the 'gamification' of learning. The shift will include the adoption of: distributed tutoring models using avatar-driven scaffolded approaches, models of assessment and accreditation towards peer- and personalised modelling of the learner and provide an emphasis upon social interactive learning based upon dialogue and social interactions rather than tutor-based and individual study. This will increase opportunities for synchronous feedback and feedback loops, and mean the integration of multimodal interfaces including brain-computer interfaces (BCIs) and haptics.

Research work being undertaken by the authors and Research team at the Serious Games Institute (SGI) in the UK is bringing together different lines of research in educational research, computer science and neuropsychology to evaluate how this new paradigm might look and feel testing the principles outlined in this chapter in a model of ancient Rome populated by virtual agents and being evaluated with school children aged 11–14 years old.

To illustrate the conceptual basis of this shift, this chapter will explore the context for the new paradigm of learning in relation to the key critical concepts that centre around gamification, immersion and social interactivity, in this chapter we analyse these base critical concepts firstly in relation to the notion of 'gamification'

S. de Freitas (✉)
Serious Games Institute (SGI), Coventry University, Coventry, UK
e-mail: s.defreitas@coventry.ac.uk

M. Ma et al. (eds.), *Serious Games and Edutainment Applications*,
DOI 10.1007/978-1-4471-2161-9_2, © Springer-Verlag London Limited 2011

through the lens of an historical overview of serious games and secondly in a section exploring the need for an overall model for serious game design based upon four models and frameworks developed in past research work: the four dimensional framework (de Freitas and Oliver, 2006), exploratory learning model (de Freitas and Neumann, 2009), multimodal interface architecture model (White et al., 2007) and the game-based learning framework (Staalduinen and de Freitas, 2011). The chapter aims to set out the key conceptual territory for serious game design and bring together the main theoretical areas under consideration for future development of effective serious game content.

2.2 Historical Overview of Serious Games: The Gamification of Learning

The notion of ‘gamification’ has recently come to the fore as an expression of the pervasiveness of gaming in everyday. At the beginning of 2010 the games industry posted total sales of $1.17 billion just for the month of January. The value of serious games in 2008 was between $1 and 2 billion, recent reports circulating in US and Europe are talking about $9–11 billion. A recent study on gaming behaviour in Europe by the International Software Federation of Europe (ISFE, 2010) found that 74% of those aged 16–19 considered themselves gamers (n = 3000), 60% of those 20–24, 56% 25–29 and 38% 30–44. While 32% of the total UK population consider themselves gamers (n = 3000). Thirty one percent of females described themselves as gamers and 34% of males. These recent demographic studies show that the introduction of casual gaming and the wider appeal of online games have extended gaming audiences from the more traditional game-players of young males out to female audiences. Further, far from being age limited, the recent appeal of online games is extending games out to older game players.

Over the past decade there have been tremendous advances in entertainment computing technology and the gaming industry grew enormously ranging from console, PC and mobile based games. Real-time computer graphics can achieve near-photorealism and virtual game worlds are usually populated with considerable amounts of high quality content, creating a rich user experience, as well as reducing development costs considerably. As games in entertainment and leisure time increases its hold on us, so too does the power of games for non-entertainment purposes begin to take a more central role, and increasingly we begin to more clearly understand the mechanics that underpin its success. One of the best examples of ‘gamification’ – or how games are pervading our lives – is the example of serious games, educational gaming as well as games and virtual worlds that are specifically developed for educational purposes reveal the potential of these technologies to engage and motivate beyond leisure time activities (Anderson et al., 2009). A broad definition refers to serious games as computer games that have an educational and learning aspect and are not used just for entertainment purposes. Serious games are currently being used in a range of different contexts and two survey papers regarding of serious games have been recently documented (Susi et al., 2007; Anderson et al., 2009).

While arguments against serious games have centred upon a lack of empirical evidence in support of its efficacy, two large studies in the UK and US respectively have demonstrated positive results in large sample groups, in one study on *Triage Trainer* considerable efficacy of game-based approaches over traditional learning techniques were demonstrated (Knight et al., 2010), while in another study on the game *Re:Mission* behavioural change in children with respect to medication adherence was proven in clinical trials (Kato et al., 2008). These studies have shown the ability for serious games to engage young and older learners, by targeting specific groups, and in both cases of experienced gamers and non-gamers have shown the efficacy of the game format for behavioural and attitudinal change. In another recent study, attitudinal change was found in a game *Floodsim* designed to raise awareness about flooding issues (Rebolledo-Mendez et al., 2009). Together the power of 'immersive experiences' is proving more engaging and motivating than standard approaches to training and education and more evidence of this efficacy is growing in the literature. The notion of 'immersion' itself is becoming considered as a central design tool as we move towards considering learning not only as knowledge construction but also as socialization, in our work we regard immersion as critical to good game design because it engages and motivates, and often includes components of interactivity, narrativity, 'flow' and fidelity (Csikszentmihalyi, 1990; de Freitas and Oliver, 2006).

In a recent book by the game designer Jane McGonigal, the author argues that reality is in general very unsatisfying for many, and how many people are finding happiness increasingly in games environments (McGonigal, 2011). Her thesis advances the notion that game elements could be used to engage and motivate more 'real world' activities, such as work and education. Her premise starts from a positive psychology as opposed to traditional psychology perspective, which aims to look at human behaviour not in terms of illness and depression, but in terms of happiness and wellness. Psychologists such as Mihaly Csikszentmihalyi have opened up this area of psychology that aims to express positive behaviours such as happiness, and these McGonigal argues are aspects that are mirrored in good game play (Csikszentmihalyi, 1990). In work examining animal play undertaken by Stuart Brown, he draws upon a synthesis study of psychopaths, the studies revealed that 'normal play behaviour was virtually absent throughout the lives of highly violent, anti-social men, regardless of demography' (Brown, 1998, p. 249). The work underlines the argument that the traditional approach to games and game play as being without value, and as being addictive or violent, is in fact the opposite of the truth. Games and play are incredibly powerful tools for socialization and collaboration and in fact indicate real potential for therapy and rehabilitation. McGonigal's work shows that the 'fixes' of games can be overlaid upon real world activities to motivate and engage, and that play can be used effectively for socialization as well as therapy.

Previous studies illustrated that games can promote learning (e.g. van Eck, 2006). Spatial abilities can be also improved by playing arcade games (de Lisi and Wolford,

2002). Further potential benefits of games include improved self-monitoring, problem recognition and problem-solving, decision-making, better short-term and long-term memory, and increased social skills such as collaboration, negotiation, and shared decision-making (Rieber, 1996; Mitchell and Savill-Smith, 2004). *Mingoville* (Sørensen and Meyer, 2007) is a serious game based on the idea that children learn and are motivated by problem-solving and game activities rather than traditional skills-based and textbook based material focusing on reading, writing, spelling and listening. The project intends to explore, build and implement prototypes in collaboration with companies, using their products and experience to develop knowledge about serious game challenges, educational design and assessment with the aim of innovation. In another study, a multi-player educational gaming platform that was designed for students combined content with pedagogy showing potentials to advance gaming theories and problem-based solving approaches in multi-player educational gaming platforms (Annetta et al., 2006).

The success of serious computer games in educational scenarios is based on the combination of audiovisual media that is prevalent in these games, which enhances the absorption of information in the learner's memory (Paivio, 1990; Baddeley, 2000). This has been found to considerably improve the process of learning (Fadel, 2008). Different learners will have different preferential learning styles, so a serious game cannot automatically guarantee success, and there is some evidence of the learner's gender playing a role in this (Hodgins, 2005), however the available evidence generally suggests that the visual medium that serious games employ has a positive effect (Solanki, 2009). Another factor for the success of educational serious games is the actual presentation of the subject matter in the form of computer games, which have been found to improve the players' concentration and attention levels (Kirriemuir and McFarlane, 2006). This not only benefits the retention of information as such, but also increases the learners' motivation, thereby improving the learning experience.

A popular platform for serious games is online gaming on virtual worlds for greater open-ended exploration and on games engines designed for more quests and missions and narrative-based games. The availability of various virtual world platforms such as Second Life (Linden Research, 2008), Active Worlds (Active Words, 2008) and the OLIVE platform (Forterra Systems, 2008), allows for a number of operations in virtual environments. Some of them include: social networking, collaboration, learning, training, experimentation as well as custom-based applications. A characteristic application is the Stanford Medical School project which used the Olive platform to practice innovation through supporting training for cardio-pulmonary resuscitation (CPR), mass casualty and assessment in acute-care medicine (de Freitas and Neumann, 2009). An example of a serious game application developed on a game engine, is one used to train traffic accident investigators how to attend a virtual traffic accident (BinSubaih et al., 2006). To measure the system's effectiveness it was empirically evaluated with 56 police officers. The SG-ETS project developed three serious games demonstrators and results showed distinct gender and age differences with respect to game type favoured and levels of gaming (de Freitas and Jarvis, 2008). Another example is a serious game that allows users to interact with 3D Web content (Web3D) using virtual and augmented reality (AR) in engineering education and learning (Liarokapis et al., 2004).

This trend towards using games technologies in non-leisure as well as in entertainment contexts constitutes a gamification of our everyday lives. Games are becoming more pervasive and this pervasiveness which in the past was regarded negatively taking up valuable recreation time and making children addictive, is now being seen in a more balanced light, as a means for educating children, for providing therapy and enriching our everyday lives with greater happiness and fulfilment. Gamification here includes the use of games not only as a cultural form, but can be used effectively as metaphors for achieving behavioural and attitudinal changes. As we have seen in *Re:Mission* where games were used for supporting behavioural change in children taking treatment for cancer, or as in *Triage Trainer* where games can be used to simulate reality to support learning transfer or as in *Floodsim* where games were used effectively for supporting attitudinal change about environmental issues. Other cultural forms of games such as mixed reality games that blend real and virtual world activities together have real capabilities for informing behavioural change as well. In the mixed reality game, *Chore Wars* for example, the game elements of competition and scoreboards encourage players to do the vacuuming and cleaning in their homes. *World Without Oil* is a game used to envisage the world when oil has run out and *Quest to Learn* is a US public school using games to transform the curriculum and education. These, and other examples, show the range of ways that gamification is changing many activities in our lives, increasing the fun in our lives, making us more aware of social and environmental issues and providing a new paradigm for curriculum-based education. But how can this capability be harnessed for future serious game design and how can we create more engaging and motivating experiences in a more replicable way?

2.3 Serious Game Design: A New Model for Experience Design?

At the heart of the challenge of designing effective serious games, there is a significant debate between game designers and instructional designers as to the exact role of pedagogy in serious games. While the authors have argued in their work that pedagogy needs to be a central aspect of serious game design (e.g. de Freitas and Oliver, 2006), others including Zyda argue pedagogy must be subordinate to story and that the entertainment component comes first (Zyda, 2005). Getting a balance between the demands of good game design with the requirements to measure and show learning outcomes has driven much of the conceptual work in the field. At the SGI it has led to the development of four models and frameworks that are being adapted in current evaluation work, and tested in the Roma Nova test-bed project.

Over the last 3 years the SGI has been examining the implementation of theory-predicated serious game design, work has aimed to bring together a theoretical basis for serious game design, including developing and testing the following models and frameworks, which placed pedagogy at the centre of serious game design:

- The four dimensional framework (4DF) which brought together four dimensions of the learner, the context of learning, the representation of the game and the pedagogies adopted (for example, associative, cognitive, situative learning theories) (de Freitas and Oliver, 2006). Work here has centred upon using the framework for evaluating games and for developing games leading to the exploratory learning game design model (below).
- The exploratory learning model (ELM) (de Freitas and Neumann, 2009) was a learning model extending exploratory learning from Kolb's experiential learning cycle (Kolb, 1984), where social interaction becomes the heart of more interactive and engaging learning processes.
- The work of the 4DF and ELM led broadly to developments in the SG-ETS project that led to the exploratory learning game design model, which aimed to bring together game and product design together with participatory design models for enhancing more learner-centred design and evaluation strategies (e.g. de Freitas and Jarvis, 2008; Jarvis and de Freitas, 2009).
- The game-based learning framework, which aimed to bring together a number of different learning frameworks and models, including the 4DF and the Garris model of game motivation (Staalduinen and de Freitas, 2011). See Fig. 2.1.

In general, this work can be demonstrated to show the necessity of bringing together game design and pedagogic modelling strategies however the approach is not always a seamless one – and the work has led to a paradigm change in evaluation and learning design that has crystallised in the Roma Nova test-bed project. From

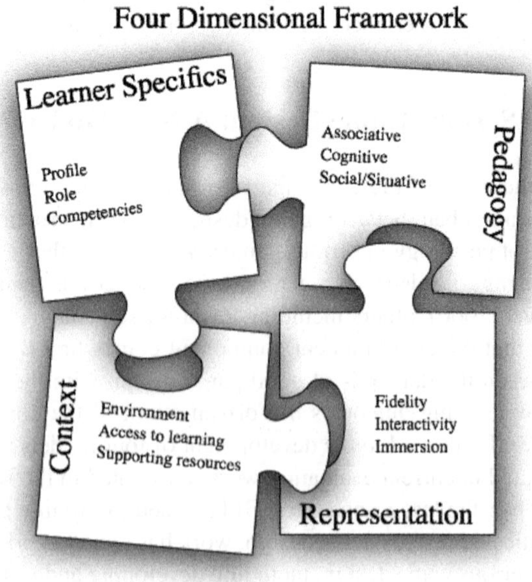

Fig. 2.1 Game-based learning framework
Source: Staalduinen & de Freitas (2011)

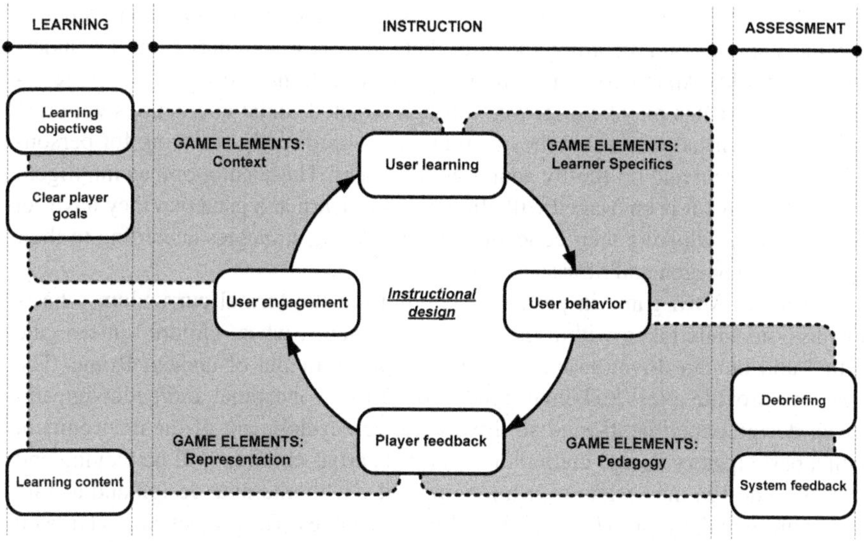

Fig. 2.2 Exploratory game design model
Source: de Freitas and Jarvis (2008)

the outset, and in all research projects, researchers have deployed a participatory design methodology that centres upon learner profiling and modelling, and involvement in all the design phases. See Fig. 2.2. This method has allowed for incremental advances in the development of serious game design approaches that have led to the *Roma Nova* implementation (Panzoli et al., 2010).

The research work has found varied outcomes, in particular the importance of feedback and the need for more sophisticated measures of in-game feedback (e.g. Dunwell and de Freitas, 2011), in addition the wider use of social interactive learning – in need of a model for evaluation – and the general pedagogic drive towards 'situative learning theories' that centre upon social learning and interactions. Based upon these research findings and considerations, the *Roma Nova* implementation sought to bring together agent technologies within a high-fidelity virtual environment, with the use of serious games elements. Through social interactions within the environment, both though questing and with the use of dialogic-based interactions with the avatars a greater sense of immersion and interactivity could, we hypothesised, be produced with the benefit of increased knowledge through experience-based learning.

We asserted that this might lead to greater retention of knowledge learnt in this way – an aspect still to be proven in the ongoing evaluation work (results forthcoming). In an attempt to frame this evaluation drive, we are considering the neuropsychological aspects of learning and so one line of ongoing research is focusing upon neuropsychological studies with children using the system. The migration of education and training from the physical world to the virtual world in the *Roma Nova* instance is being supported by a game-based environment which supports a range of functionality including social interactions, modelling real environments, document sharing and recording facilities that allow users to replay activities undertaken in-world. Apart from the provision of educational content, the student's learning experience may be improved through targeted social interactions with real and realistic virtual tutors that they can interact with directly, allowing for personalised assessment and on-the-fly adaption of content. These autonomous intelligent tutoring systems it is envisaged will allow users to learn at a pace that they have set themselves by adjusting their educational and learning strategies according to their needs (Groenewegen and Strassner, 2004).

The *Roma Nova* game in particular builds from the formal curriculum a basis for missions undertaken within dialogic environments, where children interrogate virtual and human driven avatars in an exploratory model of ancient Rome. The idea is to provide a test-bed environment for testing conceptual and pedagogically driven design experiments, and so drive iterative development of the environment with a participatory design methodology at its heart as children will be playing and helping to design the system over a long period – with alternate design and testing phases through the year to fit around teaching timetables. The project has so far been developed and two testing phases are planned for March for usability testing using heuristics with computer science students, and in Malta in April with 200 school children for usability, as well as educational research methods for establishing the learning objectives and favoured feedback mechanisms. In the future, we envisage a socially driven and participatory model for developing all interactive exploratory learning environments, and argue that the four dimensional framework (see Fig. 2.3, de Freitas and Oliver, 2006) and the exploratory learning model (de Freitas and Neumann, 2009) will be used as a conceptual basis for designing and testing these environments and approaches.

Other more development focused work being undertaken in the Research & Development Group is developing multimodal architectures to allow human computer interfaces to be easily incorporated in the environments. See Fig. 2.4. The MIM model proposed by White et al. (2007) and being developed in current work by Petridis and colleagues, outlines an architecture for achieving this integration and we are currently testing the model using BCIs, haptics and other input devices (Arnab et al., 2010).

The idea of serious games design has led us to a hybrid approach to design that incorporates both pedagogic and game design principles and blends elements of games with simulation and modelling. The main outcome for the work is the evaluation-based approaches that have led to iterative design strategies, heuristics and educational research methods when combined with social network analysis. In another project, the game *Code of Everand* has been evaluated. 90,000 children in the UK have played the game and initial data analysis using clique percolation social network analysis methodology have found interesting correlations between game play and social interactivity, correlations that could be used to inform game design for supporting more collaborative learning approaches, when combined with real-time on-the-fly adaptivity will open even greater capabilities for providing personalised feedback and content retrieval.

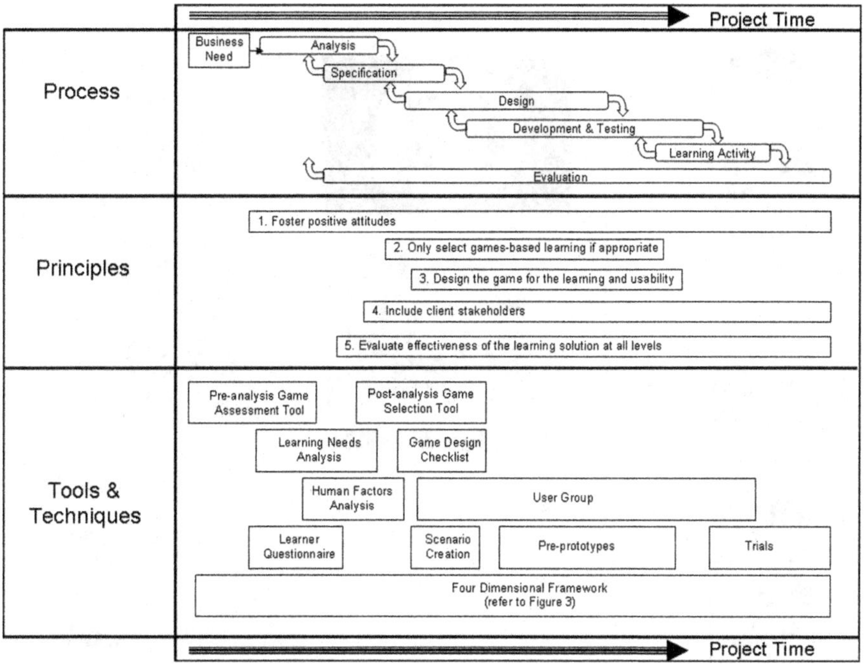

Fig. 2.3 Four dimensional framework
Source: de Freitas (2010)

Through the holistic approach to research and design, and through the inductive method of bringing together a range of different methods for data collection and analysis, it is envisaged that future uses of data coming from the user may be used to inform the 'play' of the gamer within the learning environment. Just as more sophisticated feedback mechanisms will be integrated in the virtual environment, so too will the ability for us to create more advanced methods for the feedback loop in the game and during game play. We postulate that two elements are in need of more research in advance of better deployment of serious games towards the end of greater immersion: the learner model, and this will be more detailed, dynamic and able to change on-the-fly and second, the game responsiveness, and this will be through different and varied data capture of the learner, possibly through biofeedback mechanisms or other interface devices, e.g. haptics, virtual reality interaction devices. Through the learner model and greater game responsiveness the serious game mechanisms can be improved and consolidated as part of the more immersive and interactive environment. Realism and fidelity may be controlled to greater or lesser extent depending upon budgets and target user groups, but improved learner modelling and game responsiveness can together alter the level of interaction of the user and support a more multidimensional journey of user in the virtual (and real) environments that they are playing within.

Game design in this new paradigm therefore will need to reflect better the learner and their requirements through engagement with their changing user model, but

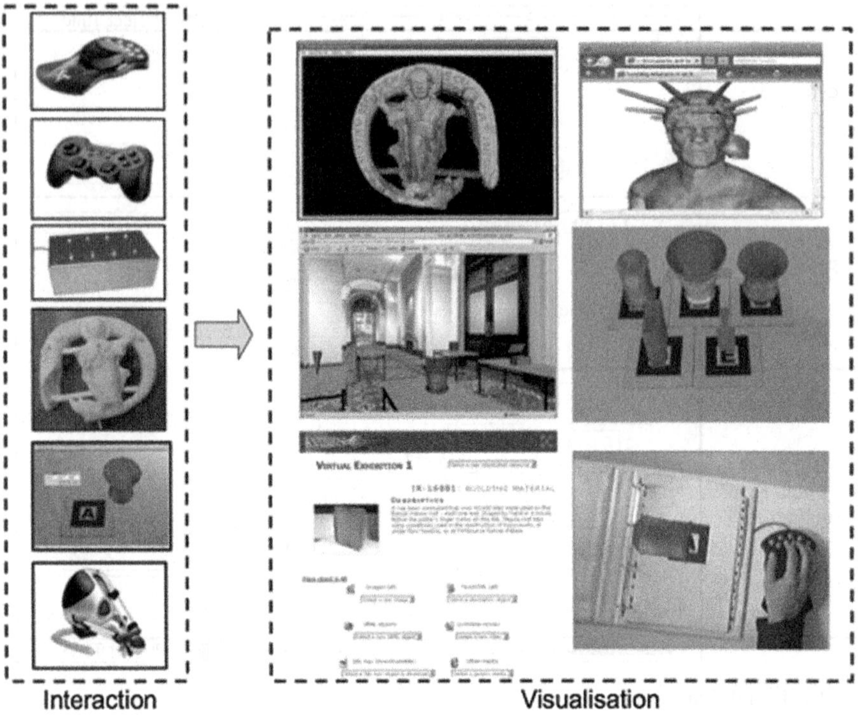

Fig. 2.4 Integrating different multimodal interface devices
Source: White et al. (2007)

will also need to respond on-the-fly to changes with respect to missions, narrative, flow and feedback levels in a multimodal way, adapting to the position, context and previous behaviour, as well as to their physiological state and mental attention and affect. The next version of the exploratory game design model therefore, outlined in previous work (see Fig. 2.2) will need to bring together more closely the dynamic learner/user model, the physiological measures of the user and the serious game design elements. Using the level of interaction model within the environment, a more adaptive and sensitised set of interactions between the user and the environment may be then effected (Panzoli et al., 2010).

The main learning point from the varied studies of existing serious games included in this chapter has been a move in pedagogic terms from a constructivist or cognitive-centred theoretical basis towards a more social and interactive position. In particular, it is worth here noting the importance of social networks and communities in current learning practices. The growth of social networks has been a significant phenomenon, and has led many in society, not just students, to substantially change their communicational behaviours. The use of Skype in business contexts and Facebook in educational environments shows the pervasiveness not just of games but of social networking, and increasingly these modes are being considered for marketing, training and product testing, amongst other uses.

As social network tools become more central to our lives, a deeper socialization goes in tandem with the blurring between domains of work and leisure, physical and virtual spaces, therefore social and cultural elements, as well as technological issues are becoming major drivers for a greater reliance upon a socialization based increasingly upon community-based models, not just of communication, but also for business models and social organisation. Online virtual communities are particularly popular among the younger generation as they enable discussion around shared interests (communities of interest), developing social relationships (communities of relationships) and exploring new identities (communities of fantasy) (Hagel and Armstrong, 1997). Several of these also provide access to games and serious games, however, not all online virtual communities that propose serious games are successful in attracting large numbers of users due to issues of engagement and complexities with building long lasting communities (Losh, 2008). The power of immersive experiences seems to be predicated upon the level of interaction and the social interconnections within the game environment, where building and engagement with the users is central like in *World of Warcraft* is manifest communities seem to have greater strength and longevity (MacCallum-Stewart, 2011). However there is still very little research to demonstrate the tipping points of these gaming communities and in general it is fair to say that it is the communities and community models that hold the environments together.

To support more social interactive learning, we have been developing a game-based exploratory learning model, which places greater emphasis upon exploration in virtual environments and gives greater emphasis to social interactions taking place in-world (extending from work based upon Jarvis and de Freitas, 2009). This exploratory learning model is based upon Kolb's experiential learning cycle, but while Kolb encourages reflection upon real world interactions, the exploratory learning model focuses upon explorations of the virtual and real spaces, and centres upon dialogic exchanges as a basis for learning (from Socrates). Alongside the social interactions built into the game environment through dialogues between the learners and the human and virtual driven characters in the game, we are taking the best designs from commercial entertainment games and bringing these advanced artificial intelligence and multimodal interactions together with curriculum based objectives in an engaging and high fidelity environment. The *Roma Nova* project is the beginning of a new approach to serious games design that provides high quality interactions, provides full feedback and adapts to the learners requirements on-the-fly. It supports a social interactive learning approach and operates using a distributed model of tutoring within a hybrid environment that blends virtual world exploration with gaming elements and structure in terms of narrative and quests. Through using the participatory design model as a core design tool in the development process we are altering the way development and evaluation are considered. In the future all games will be designed iteratively like this, and we hope to set a new benchmark for good design within the education area of game design.

2.4 Conclusions: Future of Serious Games

The work to date has led us rather unexpectedly to a vision for future learning, and that is a vision that in the future all learning will involve game-based and immersive, social and interactive elements. While our initial research never intended this outcome, as many researchers the world over appreciate research is not an exact science and often we do not find what we set out to find. In the *Roma Nova* project we see the confluence of the three elements of gamification, serious games elements and social interactive pedagogies. Together the power of immersive experiences has the potential to change how we learn, by creating immersive and distributed tutoring environments where the environment is a wrapper for a range of different e-learning resources and materials all brought into a single interface of a physically engaging environment that can be traversed and engaged with through games, narratives and missions. Social interactive learning models underpinning exploratory learning of the environments and populated with virtual agents that can provide customised and personalised information when needed and adapted to the user's requirements to scaffold the processes of learning.

The *Roma Nova* project has allowed us to experiment with different methods of feedback and interaction, aspects which will be the bedrock of successful systems for education in the future. Not only can data be presented more meaningfully, but also a context for peer interactions can be presented through collaborative missions and objectives. Shared goals and outcomes can be designed through simple scenario editing and players can be monitored and assessed seamlessly through performance in the environment and levelling up through the game. As we have seen in the *Code of Everand* evaluation, a large amount of data can be collected from the user, and as a method of analysis of performance and in terms of reduced workload for the tutor, game-based assessment has substantial benefits over traditional methods. More sophisticated measures and assessment can be built into the system through feedback mechanisms, and in addition the scope for collecting and using biofeedback and physiological measures can also help to assess and more objectively validate and benchmark performance against previous performance or in relation to others in the same class or category, or just as a relative measure.

The future of serious gaming includes three significant aspects: convergent technologies, widening application areas and efficacy proofs that together will power the wider uptake of these applications over the next 3–5 years. Particular emphasis will be given to the value of immersive applications in serious games which offer the potential of transforming the way we perceive training and multimodal learning. Moreover, serious games in the future will have many new capabilities and we are only just beginning to scrape the surface of the real capabilities that will exist. However there is a need for continued and sustained research, development and assessment of the efficacy of game-based approaches, a requirement for standards and a drive towards greater iterations of evaluation and design cycles. The new paradigm for learning therefore will continue to drive innovation across education, and it is important to involve all the stakeholders: educationalists, game designers and developers, researchers and centrally the learner in all stages of the design and implementation process. Serious games are a new and emerging sector of the games industry, but they are here to stay and could solve many of our key problems and challenges with engaging learners as well as supporting social learning long into the twenty-first century.

References

Active Words Inc.: Active Words. http://www.activeworlds.com (2008). Accessed 18 Sept 2008

Anderson, E.F., McLoughlin, L., et al.: Serious games in cultural heritage. In: Proceedings of the 10th VAST International Symposium on Virtual Reality, Archaeology and Cultural Heritage – STARs session, Eurographics, Malta, pp. 29–48, 22–25 September 2009

Annetta, L.A., Murray, M.R., et al.: Serious games: Incorporating video games in the classroom. Educause Rev. **3**, 16–22 (2006)

Arnab, S., Petridis, P., Dunwell, I., de Freitas, S.: Touching artefacts in an ancient world on a browser-based platform. IADIS International Conference: Web Virtual Reality and Three-Dimensional Worlds 2010, Freiburg, Germany, 27–29 July (2010)

Baddeley, A.D.: The episodic buffer: A new component of working memory? Trends Cogn. Sci. **4**(11), 417–423 (2000)

BinSubaih, A., Maddock, S., Romano, D.M.: An architecture for portable serious games. In: Doctoral Symposium hosted at the 20th European Conference on Object-Oriented Programming ECOOP 2006, Nantes, France (2006)

Brown, S.: Play as an organizing principle. In: Bekoff, M., Byers, J.A. (eds.) Animal Play: Evolutionary, Comparative, and Ecological Perspectives, pp. 243–259. Cambridge University Press, Cambridge (1998)

Csikszentmihalyi, M.: Flow: The Psychology of Optimal Experience. Harper and Row, New York (1990)

de Freitas, S., Jarvis, S.: Towards a development approach for serious games. In: Connolly, T.M., Stansfield, M., Boyle, E. (eds.) Games-Based Learning Advancements for Multi-Sensory Human-Computer Interfaces: Techniques and Effective Practices, pp. 215–231. IGI Global, Hershey, PA (2008)

de Freitas, S., Neumann, T.: The use of 'exploratory learning' for supporting immersive learning in virtual environments. Comput. Educ. **52**(2), 343–352 (2009)

de Freitas, S., Oliver, M.: How can exploratory learning with games and simulations within the curriculum be most effectively evaluated? Comput. Edu. **46**(3), 249–264 (2006)

de Lisi, R., Wolford, J.L.: Improving children's mental rotation accuracy with computer game playing. J. Genet. Psychol. **163**(3), 172–182 (2002)

Dunwell, I., de Freitas, S.: Four-dimensional consideration of feedback in serious games. In: de Freitas, S., Maharg, P. (eds.) Digital Games and Learning, pp. 42–62. Continuum Publishing, London (2011)

Fadel, C.: Multimodal learning through media: What the research says, White Paper, Cisco. http://www.cisco.com/web/strategy/docs/education/Multimodal-Learning-Through-Media.pdf (2008). Accessed 30 Oct 2009

Forterra Systems Inc.: OLIVE – Purpose driven virtual worlds for everyone. http://www.forterrainc.com/images/stories/pdf/OLIVE_Dec07_Final_Rev.pdf (2008). Accessed 18 Sep 2008

Groenewegen, S., Strassner, J.: Virtuelle Charaktere in Lehrsituationen: Ein Konzept zur Nachbildung von realem Unterricht. In: Groenewegen S., Strassner, J. (eds.) 1.Workshop AR VR, im Tagungsband Graphiktag 2004, GI Chemnitz (2004)

Hagel, H., Armstrong, A.: Net Gain: Expanding Markets through Virtual Communities. Business School Press, Boston, MA (1997)

Hodgins, D.: Coordinator early childhood education. Male and female differences. languagelog.ldc.upenn.edu/myl/llog/Hodgins1.pdf (2005). Accessed 13 Feb 2009

Interactive Software Federation of Europe: Video gamers in Europe 2010 report. http://www.isfe.eu/sites/isfe.eu/files/isfe_final_combined.pdf (2010). Accessed 24 Nov 2011

Jarvis, S., de Freitas, S.: Evaluation of an immersive learning programme to support triage training. In Proceedings of the 1st IEEE International Conference in Games and Virtual Worlds for Serious Applications, IEEE Computer Society, Coventry, UK, 23–24 March 2009

Kato, P.M., Cole, S.W., Bradlyn, A.S., Pollock, B.H.: A video game improves behavioral outcomes in adolescents and young adults with cancer: A randomized trial. Pediatrics **122**, 305–317 (2008)

Kirriemuir, J., McFarlane, C.A.: Literature review in games and learning, White Paper, Future Lab. http://www.futurelab.org.uk/resources/documents/lit_reviews/Games_Review.pdf (2006). Accessed 30 Oct 2009

Knight, J., Carly, S., Tregunna, B., Jarvis, S., Smithies, R., de Freitas, S., Mackway-Jones, K., Dunwell, I.: Serious gaming technology in major incident triage training: A pragmatic controlled trial. Resuscitation J. **81**(9), 1174–1179 (2010)

Kolb, D.A.: Experiential Learning: Experience as the Source of Learning and Development. Prentice Hall, Englewood Cliffs, NJ (1984)

Liarokapis, F., Mourkoussis, N., et al.: Web3D and augmented reality to support engineering education, World Trans. Eng. Technol. Educ. UICEE **3**(1), 11–14 (2004)

Linden Research: Second life. http://www.secondlife.com (2008). Accessed 18 Sep 2008

Losh, E.: Polite company: Rules of play in five Facebook games. In: Proceedings of the 2008 International Conference on Advances in Computer Entertainment Technology, pp. 345–351. ACM Press, Yokohama, Japan (2008)

MacCallum-Stewart, E.: Stealth learning in online learning. In: de Freitas, S., Maharg, P. (eds.) Digital Games and Learning, pp. 107–218. Continuum Press, London & New York (2011)

McGonigal, J.: Reality is Broken. Jonathan Cape, London (2011)

Mitchell, A., Savill-Smith, C.: The Use of Computer and Video Games for Learning: A Review of the Literature. Learning and Skills Development Agency, London. http://www.lsda.org.uk/ (2004). Accessed 10 Oct 2008

Paivio, A.: Mental Representations: A Dual Coding Approach. Oxford University Press, New York, NY (1990)

Panzoli, D., Peters, C., Dunwell, I., Sanchez, S., Petridis, P., Protopsaltis, A., Scesa, V., de Freitas, S.: Levels of interaction: A user-guided experience in large-scale virtual environments. In: IEEE 2nd International Conference in Games and Virtual Worlds for Serious Applications (VS GAMES10), pp. 87–90. IEEE, Braga, Portugal, 26–27 March 2010

Rebolledo-Mendez, G., Avramides, K., de Freitas, S., Memarzia, K.: Societal impact of a Serious Game on raising public awareness: The case of FloodSim. In: Proceedings of the 2009 ACM SIGGRAPH Symposium on Video Games, pp. 15–22. New Orleans, Louisiana (2009)

Rieber, L.P.: Seriously considering play: Designing interactive learning environments based on the blending of microworlds, simulations, and games. Educ. Technol. Res. Dev. **44**(2), 43–58 (1996)

Solanki, D.: Do E-learning and Serious Games help students to revise more effectively rather than the traditional approach of using Textbooks? Bachelors Dissertation, Coventry University (2009)

Sørensen, B.H., Meyer, B.: Serious games in language learning and teaching – a theoretical perspective. In: Proceedings of the 3rd International Conference of the Digital Games Research Association, pp. 559–566, Tokyo, Japan (2007)

Staalduinen, J.P.v., de Freitas, S.: A game-based learning framework: Linking game design and learning outcomes. In: Khyne, M.S. (ed.) Learning to Play: Exploring the Future of Education with Video Games, pp. 29–54. Peter Lang, New York (2011)

Susi, T., Johannesson, M., Backlund, P.: Serious games – an overview. Technical Report HS-IKI-TR-07-001. http://www.his.se/upload/19354/HS-%20IKI%20-TR-07-001.pdf (2007). Accessed 10 Oct 2008

van Eck, R.: Digital game-based learning: It's not just the digital natives who are restless. Educause Rev. **41**(2), 16–30 (2006, March)

White, M., Petridis, P., Liarokapis, F., Plecinckx, D.: Multimodal mixed reality interfaces for visualizing digital heritage. Int. J. Architectural Comput. (IJAC), Special Issue on Cultural Heritage 5, 2, Multi-Science Publishing Co Ltd, 322–337 (June, 2007)

Zyda, M.: From visual simulation to virtual reality to games. Computer **38**(9), 25–32 (2005)

Chapter 3
Origins of Serious Games

Damien Djaouti, Julian Alvarez, Jean-Pierre Jessel, and Olivier Rampnoux

3.1 Introduction

At a glance, "Serious Games" appear to be a recent phenomenon. A market study shows that the worldwide Serious Games market is worth 1.5 billion € in 2010 (Alvarez et al., 2010). If we consider this statistic as an indicator of the success of "Serious Games", we can question whether they really represent the "first attempt" at using video games for serious purposes.

The current definition of "Serious Games" appears to follow the lead set by Sawyer and Rejeski (2002). However, the oxymoron "Serious Games" was used with a similar meaning before the publication of this white paper. Therefore, we will first review the origins of this term and analyse how it evolved to designate "games that do not have entertainment, enjoyment or fun as their primary purpose" (Michael and Chen, 2005).

Moreover, the idea of using games, and more specifically video games, to deal with serious matters is also older than we would at first think. According to Sawyer: "[America's Army] was the first successful and well-executed serious game that gained total public awareness" (Gudmundsen, 2006). But games matching the definition drawn by Sawyer were released long before *America's Army* (2002). Actually, we can even suppose that some of the first video games were designed to serve serious purposes. We will review these pioneer video games in detail before broadening the scope of our study to analyse the variations of "Serious Games" releases from 1951 to 2011.

We hope that this information will help the reader to understand the origins of the current wave of "Serious Games."

D. Djaouti (✉)
IRIT, Toulouse III University, Toulouse, France

Ludoscience, France
e-mail: Damien.Djaouti@irit.fr

M. Ma et al. (eds.), *Serious Games and Edutainment Applications*,
DOI 10.1007/978-1-4471-2161-9_3, © Springer-Verlag London Limited 2011

3.2 Origins of the "Serious Game" Oxymoron

Current research on the use of games outside of entertainment may raise a debate about "Serious Games" being an oxymoron. Indeed, video games have been demonstrated to be useful in education (ELSPA, 2006; Gee, 2005, 2007; Klopfer et al., 2009; Robertson, 2009; Shaffer, 2007), defence (Caspian Learning, 2008; Smith, 2009), healthcare (Lieberman, 2001; Robertson and Miller, 2008)... and so on. According to these references, we could argue that all games are "serious" and that the "Serious Games" term is not really an oxymoron.

However, if we consider the historical origins of this term and how it reached the gaming field, we believe it was meant to be an oxymoron. For example, we can trace the use of this term back to the Renaissance. Neo-Platonists used the term "serio ludere" to refer to the use of light-hearted humour in literature dealing with serious matters (Manning, 2004). A similar idea can be found in the Swedish novel "*Den allvarsamma leken*", whose English title is "The Serious Game" (Soderberg, 2001). Written in 1912, this novel tackles the delicate topic of adultery. The "playful" side of cheating is put in opposition with the "serious" consequences of adultery. Here, the "Serious Game" oxymoron stresses the differences between adultery and the usual definition of games, such as the one coined by Huizinga (1951) : "a free activity standing quite consciously outside 'ordinary' life as being 'not serious', but at the same time absorbing the player intensely and utterly."

A similar use of the "Serious Game" oxymoron can be used to describe the professional practice of games and sports. For example, in the autobiographical "Not Dark Yet: A Very Funny Book About a Very Serious Game", Mike Harfield (2008) tells about his 30 year long career as a professional cricket player.

The first use of the "Serious Game" oxymoron with a meaning close to its current use seems to be in "Serious Games", a book written by Clark Abt (1970). Abt is a researcher who worked in an U.S. research laboratory during the cold war (Abt Associates, 2005). One of his goals was to use games for training and education. He actually designed several computer games such as *T.E.M.P.E.R.* (Raytheon, 1961). This game was used by military officers to study the Cold War conflict on a worldwide scale. But in his book, Abt also provides examples of "non-digital" Serious Games, such as math-related games to be used in schools. Abt also gives a clear definition of "Serious Games": "Games may be played seriously or casually. We are concerned with serious games in the sense that these games have an explicit and carefully thought-out educational purpose and are not intended to be played primarily for amusement. This does not mean that serious games are not, or should not be, entertaining."

Another example of a "non-digital" game explicitly labelled as "Serious Game" is presented in the book "The New Alexandria Simulation: A Serious Game of State and Local Politics" (Jansiewicz, 1973). This book explains how to play a game designed to teach the basics of the U.S. political mechanisms. Despite its age, this game is still used in classrooms, thanks to several reissues since 2004. It is also interesting to note that Jansiewicz kept his game in a non-digital format, because he thinks that only human interactions can convey the complexity of politics

(Jansiewicz, 2011). Kahn and Perez (2009) have conducted a study on this game and observed that it improved the learning outcome for students in an "Introduction to American Politics" course.

Another example of "Serious Games" used as an oxymoron is the title of an artistic exhibition held in the Barbican Art Gallery from 1996 to 1997. The companion book of this exhibition (Graham, 1996) presents the work of eights artists who sought to make a link between video games and modern art. One of these artists, Regina Corwell, created an interactive art piece to ask if video games can be used as a mean of artistic expression: "If we shift from the fun of games with their overt or covert messages about power, speed, command and control to those same messages delivered for expediency and with urgency by the military and to the efficiency of the office workplace and the various heritage in consumer culture, are art and culture ready to squarely face this complex mosaic?"

This latter example limits the scope of "Serious Games" to video games, in a similar fashion to most current definitions of Serious Games (Michael and Chen, 2005; Zyda, 2005). Indeed, all these definitions seem to be influenced by the vision of Ben Sawyer and his white paper entitled "Serious Games: Improving Public Policy through Game-based Learning and Simulation" (Sawyer and Rejeski, 2002). As the title suggests, this paper is a call to use the technology and knowledge from the entertainment video game industry to improve game-based simulations in public organisations. However, this paper does not mention the oxymoron "Serious Games" one single time apart from in its title. Indeed, Sawyer first wrote his paper under the title "Improving Public Policy through Game Based Learning and Simulations." But his colleague David Rejeski felt that this title lacked something. Rejeski was aware of a book entitled "Serious Play" (Schrage, 1999), which details how private companies use simulations to stimulate innovation. In reference to this book, Rejeski decided to modify the title of Sawyer's white paper to include the oxymoron "Serious Games." This paper was quickly followed by the creation of the "Serious Games Initiative", an association to promote the use of games for serious purposes. Thus, the oxymoron "Serious Games" was gaining some momentum in the minds of many people (Sawyer, 2009). By chance, 2002 was also the release date of America's Army, a game that Sawyer considers as "[...] the first successful and well-executed serious game that gained total public awareness" (Gudmundsen, 2006). The conjunction of *America's Army*'s popular success and Sawyer and Rejeski's efforts to promote such games, makes us identify 2002 as the starting point of the "current wave" of Serious Games.

Later, Sawyer refined his definition of "Serious Games" to "any meaningful use of computerized game/game industry resources whose chief mission is not entertainment" (Sawyer, 2007). Michael Zyda, who participated in the development of *America's Army*, proposed a similar definition (Zyda, 2005) : "A mental contest, played with a computer in accordance with specific rules, that uses entertainment, to further government or corporate training, education, health, public policy, and strategic communication objectives." Nowadays, most Serious Games that are released tend to follow this line by sticking to the use of digital games, instead of following the broader definition of "Serious Games" for both digital and non-digital games introduced in the 1970s.

3.3 Were Video Games Solely Meant for Entertainment?

Although the current wave of "Serious Games" appears to begin in 2002, many games were designed for serious purposes before this date. Abt's book features many earlier "Serious Games", including some examples of computer-based games. If we stick to current definitions, any digital game that was "designed for a purpose going beyond entertainment" can be considered a Serious Game. In popular culture, *Pong* (Atari, 1972) is usually considered as the first video game. If it is unquestionably the first video game to have embraced a massive commercial success, it is not "the" first video game per se (Barton and Loguidice, 2009a). Among the video games invented before *Pong*, some titles are not designed for entertainment but for serious purposes. In the chronological order of their appearance, these serious purposes are: **to illustrate a scientific research study**, **to train professionals** and **to broadcast a message**.

3.3.1 Early Digital Games Designed to Illustrate a Scientific Research Study

The first example in this category comes from England during the invention of the first computers. Created in 1951 by Ferranti, the *Manchester Mark I* is the first computer to have been publicly commercialized. It supports several programs created by researchers in computer science (Copeland, 2000). For example, Dietrich Prinz programmed a chess game that can "play" against a human, at least for the latter moves before checkmate (Wall, 2009). The first game able to play a full game of chess was released in 1958 for the *IBM 704* computer (Bernstein et al., 1958). In a similar vein, Christopher Stratchey developed a checkers game in 1951 for the *Pilot ACE* computer. Unfortunately, this game required too much memory for the *Pilot ACE* to be able to run it properly. Stratchey then recreated his program for the *Manchester Mark I* (Jackson, 2000). All of these computer games were created by scientists to do research in computer science, especially in the artificial intelligence field (Newell et al., 1958).

Last but not least, the United Kingdom is also the birthplace of what is currently considered as the first video game in history, *OXO* (Donovan, 2010). Also known as *Noughts and Crosses*, it is a tic-tac-toe game created by Alexander Douglas for the Cambridge University's *EDSAC* computer. The particularity of this game lies in its input and output devices. Unlike aforementioned examples, this game displays a tic-tac-toe grid on a CRT screen. This screen was originally built as a memory monitor for the *EDSAC*. But by manipulating the memory of the computer with his program, Douglas succeeded in displaying a tic-tac-toe grid on it. He also used the rotary phone dial plugged into the computer as a rudimentary "gamepad." Each cell in the grid is numbered from 1 to 9. To select a cell and place a nought or a cross, the human player simply has to dial the corresponding number on the phone. This game was designed to illustrate a research thesis in computer science on "human-computer interface" (Cohen, 2009).

Additional examples of such games for research can be found in the neighbourhood of *Spacewar!*. This game is widely regarded as the first video game solely designed for entertainment (Barton and Loguidice, 2009b; Chaplin and Ruby, 2006; Fleming, 2007; Graetz, 1981; Herz, 1997; Kent, 2001; Levy, 1984). It was created by a group of hackers at the MIT. Alongside this game, other programs were created, such as *Qubic*, a game that looks like a three-dimensional tic-tac-toe. It was programmed by Bill Daly in order support his masters thesis in computer science (Daly, 1961).

3.3.2 Early Video Games Designed to Train Professionals

During the Cold War, the U.S. army invested a lot of money in research. Numerous projects from this period led to technologies that are now widespread in our daily lives, such as computers or the Internet. However, many of the first computer programs were created to serve military purposes. From ballistics computations to resource management, the U.S. army was very familiar with computer simulations. Meanwhile, military officers around the world were using "war games" for training purposes (Halter, 2006). These two influences formed the idea of creating computer-based war games in research departments (Montfort, 2005).

HUTSPIEL is a very good example of such games. Created in 1955, this strategy war game allows two human players to experiment with the impact of nuclear weapons on a global battlefield. The OTAN fights against the URSS in a fictional – but highly probable at the time – battle along the Rhine. This game is highly detailed. It simulates ammunition and fuel supply for each unit controlled by the two players (Harrison Jr., 1964). *HUTSPIEL* was invented by the Operations Research Office (ORO), a research centre conducted by the John Hopkins University. This centre was closed down in 1961 in favour of the Research Analysis Corporation (RAC), which pursued most of its research projects. These two research centres conducted many studies on the use of computer games for training purposes (Research Analysis Corporation, 1965). Besides *HUTSPIEL, NEWS (Naval Electronic Warfare Simulator)* was designed in 1958 to simulate naval battles. In the early 1960s, the RAC built *THEATERSPIEL*, an improved version of *HUTSPIEL* (Harrison Jr., 1964).

Several similar games were created during the 1960s, mainly under the command of the Joint War Games Agency (Banister, 1967). This section of the U.S. Army was dedicated to the use of games for military purposes. *T.E.M.P.E.R.*, the Cold-War simulation game created in 1961 by a team led by Clark Abt, was created for this agency. Abt later founded his own company, Abt Associates, to create similar games. For instance, *ARPA-AGILE COIN GAME* simulates an internal revolutionary conflict in a country (Abt Associates, 1965). These strategy games represent the first step to more complex simulation models used for tactical evaluation, such as *CARMONETTE* (Dondero, 1973).

Alongside such military-related games, the RAC also designed training computer games for civilians. For example, in 1956 they built a series of games called

American Management Association Games. This collection of turn-based strategy games casts the players as managers of a product firm. They compete against each other in order to earn as much money as possible within 40 turns of play (Harrison Jr., 1964).

Obviously, none of these games was available to the general public, and the little information we can find about them today comes from unclassified military documents. We can however consider them as being the ancestors of the simulation video games that appeared on personal computers in the 1980s, either with military topics (Dunnigan, 1992) or not (Wolf, 2007).

3.3.3 Early Video Games Designed to Broadcast a Message

Games can also convey a particular message. In 1951, Ferranti built a computer called *NIMROD* that could play only one single game: the game of *NIM*. In this math-based game, each player picks matches from a pile. The player who takes the last one looses. While *NIMROD* represents an important step for computer science, it was not designed to do scientific research. Its sole purpose was to be a live advertisement for its constructor. Indeed, this large computer was built to be shown during the "Festival of Britain" (Montfort, 2005). It was an impressive piece, but it did not use a CRT display. Instead, the current state of play was displayed through a set of coloured lights. A first set of lights was built into a small control panel, so players could see the remaining number of matches whilst pressing buttons to play. Another set of lights was built into the front part of the computer itself, so that visitors could watch the game even if they were far away from the control panel. This computer was so successful during the festival that it was also shown during industrial fairs in Germany and in Toronto (Smillie, 2010). However, despite its popular success during these three events, this game failed to broadcast its message about the technical expertise of Ferranti. As told by John Makepeace Bennet, the inventor of *NIMROD* (Bennett et al., 1994): "The machine was a great success but not quite in the way intended, as I discovered during my time as spruiker on the Festival stand. Most of the public were quite happy to gawk at the flashing lights and be impressed. A few took an interest in the algorithm and even persisted to the point of beating the machine at the game. Only occasionally did we receive any evidence that our real message about the basics of programming had been understood."

In a similar vein, *Tennis for Two also* aims to broadcast a message to the general public. This tennis game is played from a side view with simulated gravity. It was created in 1958 by William Higinbotham, an American nuclear physicist working at the Brookhaven National Laboratory (Poole, 2001). During this cold war era, the general public was not really at ease with scientific research, especially with laboratories working on nuclear projects. In order to reassure the neighbouring population, the Brookhaven National Laboratory regularly organized guided tours. However, Higinbotham found these tours quite boring. He then decided to create a computer game to improve these guided tours (Anderson, 1983): "It might liven up the place to have a game that people could play, and which would convey the message that our scientific endeavors have relevance for society." This game was successfully displayed for 2 years at the laboratory before being dismantled. Although it would later be used as a reference during legal battles for the paternity of the invention of video games (Kent, 2001), its sole purpose was to broadcast a reassuring message to the civilians living near the nuclear research laboratory. We can also note that Higinbotham was a recognized physicist in the scientific community. Like other researchers involved in the Manhattan project, he spent most of his life fighting against the proliferation of nuclear weapons. Besides the quality of his scientific works and his ethical engagement, Higinbotham illustrates the close relationship between the technological progress due to the Cold War and the field of video games (A. Wilson, 1968).

3.3.4 Did Serious Games Appear Before Entertainment Video Games?

All the games presented thus far were non-commercial. However, some of the first video games available in stores were also designed for purposes that went beyond entertainment. The first home video game console, the *Magnavox Odyssey* (Ralph Baer, 1972), was shipped with both entertainment games (*Tennis, Haunted House, Roulette*...) and educational games (*Analogic, States, Simon Says*...). Its inventor, Ralph Baer, was working for an U.S. defence contractor, Sanders Associates. While Sanders accepted to let his employee release a console for the entertainment market, Baer quickly imagined "serious" applications of his technology. He improved his "light-gun" technology to design gun-shooting games for training purposes. His *Interactive Video Training System* series uses real weapons – such as LAW or STINGER rocket launchers – as devices to play with rail-shooting games. These games were proposed for training to military forces, but also to police departments (Baer, 2005).

Nowadays, most video games are solely designed for entertainment purposes (ESA, 2010). But in the light of all these examples, it can be argued that entertainment video games only appeared after the first digital "Serious Games."

3.4 The Ancestors of Current "Serious Games"

Following these pioneering experiences, many video games were released to support serious purposes before the current wave of "Serious Games." Below are six examples of such games for a wide range of domains.

3.4.1 Education

One of the most famous ancestors of current "Serious Games" can be found in the field of Education. *The Oregon Trail* (MECC, 1971) started as a text-only game created by three History teachers: Don Rawitsch, Bill Heinemann and Paul Dillenberger. It casts the player as an American pilgrim in 1848, whose goal is to reach Oregon in order to settle down. The road to Oregon is full of traps, but the game is enriched with information related to this period of American History. This game was "published" by the Minnesota Educational Computing Consortium (MECC). This institution helped teachers from Minnesota to use computers for teaching. *The Oregon Trail* was so popular with students (and teachers) that many upgrades have been released. In 1978 a graphical version of the game was released in open-source format. It was improved and released commercially in 1985. This game was followed by several sequels – *The Oregon Trail II* (MECC, 1996), *The Oregon Trail: 3rd Edition* (MECC, 1997) – and spin-offs – *The Amazon Trail* (MECC, 1993), *The Africa Trail* (MECC, 1997). But the original game is still popular today thanks to mobile phone versions and a Facebook application. Ultimately, this game clearly shows that an "educational" or "serious" game is not necessarily the opposite to a "popular and commercially successful" game.

3.4.2 Healthcare

Captain Novolin (Raya Systems, 1992) is designed to teach kids how to manage diabetes. This game lets you play as a diabetic superhero, who must take care of the glucose-level in his blood while beating evil junk food aliens. This platform game "hijacks" the well-know "collectable bonuses" mechanism to broadcast a message. The bonuses that the hero can collect are all food items. So, if the hero collects too many of them he risks feeling sick due to a high level of glucose in his blood. Hopefully, before each level, a nutritionist tells players how many food items they are allowed to eat. Players also have to manage their insulin. This game and three other health-related titles were released for the Super Nintendo console by the same company, *Raya Systems*. While they were not labelled as "Serious Games", several research studies have been conducted to analyse their effects on children (Lieberman, 2001). For example, the game *Packy & Marlon* (Raya Systems, 1994), similar to *Captain Novolin* with a two-player mode, was analysed in a clinical trial (Brown et al., 1997). The group of children who were presented with this game was observed to be better at managing their diabetes. The number of cases where these children had to go to the hospital due to a glucose crisis decreased by 77% compared with the group who did not play it. The study concludes that the games helped the children to learn how to manage insulin and to have healthy meals in order to prevent glucose-related crises.

3.4.3 Defence

Apart from the games produced for the Joint War Games Agency and before the release of *America's Army*, the U.S. army showed a high interest in entertainment video games for its training purposes. One of the most famous examples is *The Bradley Trainer* (Atari, 1981). Also known as *Military Battlezone* or *Army*

Battlezone, this game is a customised version of *Battlezone* (Atari, 1980). The original game casts the player as a tank in a 3D world, and asks him to shoot down opposing vehicles. The U.S. Army hired Atari to create a more realistic version of this game so they could use it as a training tool. Instead of a fictional tank, the player is now controlling the *Bradley Fighting Vehicle*, a military ground vehicle armed with a chain-gun and a canon. The player must shoot down opposing helicopters and tanks by firing the weapons of this real vehicle. The realism of the ballistics simulation has been improved to match the training purpose of this game (James, 1997). Although Atari accepted to create this customized version of its game for the U.S. Army, several of its employees were clearly against it, including Ed Rotberg, the designer of *Battlezone* (Kent, 2001): "We didn't want anything to do with the military. I was doing games. I didn't want to train people to kill." Though anecdotal, this reaction illustrates the cultural differences between the field of entertainment video games and the current "Serious Games" industry.

3.4.4 Art and Culture

Versailles 1685 (Cryo, 1997) is the flagship of the "cultural entertainment" video games wave. Such games merge entertainment and cultural education. This example is set in Versailles during the reign of Louis XIV. The player must investigate to identify who is threatening to destroy Versailles. They can freely move inside this beautiful place, talk with historical characters, and learn about the paintings and arts of this era. This title received a warm reception in Europe with more than 300,000 copies sold. It opened the way for similar titles with different historical periods, such as *Egypt 1156 BC Tomb of the pharaoh* (Cryo, 1997), *Byzantine: The Betrayal* (Discovery Channel Multimedia, 1997), *China the Forbidden City* (Cryo, 1998), *Pilgrim Faith As A Weapon* (Axel Tribe, 1998), *Vikings* (Index+, 1998), *Rome: Caesar's Will* (Montparnasse Multimedia, 2000)...

3.4.5 Religion

Captain Bible in the dome of Darkness (BridgeStone Multimedia Group, 1994) is an adventure-action video game designed to teach Christian religion. In a distant future, the player is cast as a hero in a city full of robots telling "lies" (e.g. "*You don't have to serve either God or the devil, you can be your own master.*"). The player must navigate through the city and seek verses from the Bible. These verses can counter the "lies" told by the robots in order to defeat them. Like many entertainment titles of the same period, this game was distributed both as shareware and retail versions.

3.4.6 Corporate Training and Advertising

Last but not least, *Pepsi Invaders* (Atari, 1983) is an original example of a video game used as a corporate management tool. This game plays exactly in the same way as *Space Invaders* (Taito, 1978), but aliens are replaced by the letters P-E-P-S-I.

This game was created for the sales employees of Coca-Cola. Play sessions are limited to 3 min, in order to prevent them spending too much time playing. Coca-Cola thought this game would be a good motivational tool for its employees, and a way to strengthen its competitiveness against Pepsi. Besides this unique example, many food-related brands also used video games as advertising tools, especially with console-based titles. For instance, *Kool Aid Man* (Mattel Electronics, 1983) promotes Kool Aid drinks; *M.C. Kids* (Virgin Interactive, 1991) is a platform game set in the famous fast-food universe; *Chex Quest* (Digital Café, 1996) is a first-person shooter that helped to sell many Chex cereal boxes…

3.4.7 The Numerous Ancestors of "Serious Games"

As we can see, these six examples clearly match the current definitions of "Serious Games", though they were not using this label. We can complete these illustrative examples by some quantitative data about the number of such ancestors of "Serious Games." While far from complete, we have referenced a total number of 2218 "Serious Games." To check whether a video game can be considered a "Serious Game", we simply verified that it matches the definitions coined by Sawyer (2007, 2002), Zyda (2005) and Chen and Michael (2005).

As seen in Fig. 3.1, the number of games released each year regularly increases, with a high peak at the end of the 2000s. As we consider that 2002 is the starting point of the current wave of "Serious Games", it means that we have a corpus of 1265 "Serious Games." We also have a total of 953 ancestors of "Serious Games" (43% of our total corpus).

Out of the 953 ancestors of Serious Games, 65.8% were designed for the educational market, as seen in Fig. 3.2. We also note that 10.7% of them were created for advertising and 8.1% for ecology. The ancestors of "Serious Games" show a clear dominance of educational games. The situation is very different when we look at the current wave of "Serious Games" in Fig. 3.3. Though Education is still a major market, it represents only 25.7%. As the size of Education decreased, all the others market have grown. Advertising reaches the top with 30.6% of the games, and all others markets that were often below 2% are now between 4 and 10%.

Overall, we can observe that most of the ancestors of "Serious Games" are in fact "educational games" – edutainment, edugames, etc. According to these figures, we can argue that the current wave of "Serious Games" allows video games to embrace a wider variety of themes. Their ancestors were mostly meant for education while current "Serious Games" can be found in different markets with a more homogenous breakdown. This may be due to the fact that "Serious Games" are far more numerous than their ancestors. Indeed, 1265 "Serious Games" were released between 2002 and 2010 (8 years), while only 926 of their ancestors were published between 1980 and 2001 (21 years). Although "Serious Games" and their ancestors match the same definitions, here we can see a difference between them. "Serious Games" are different from their ancestors not as individual games, but as a group of games which targets a wider range of topics thanks to a larger population.

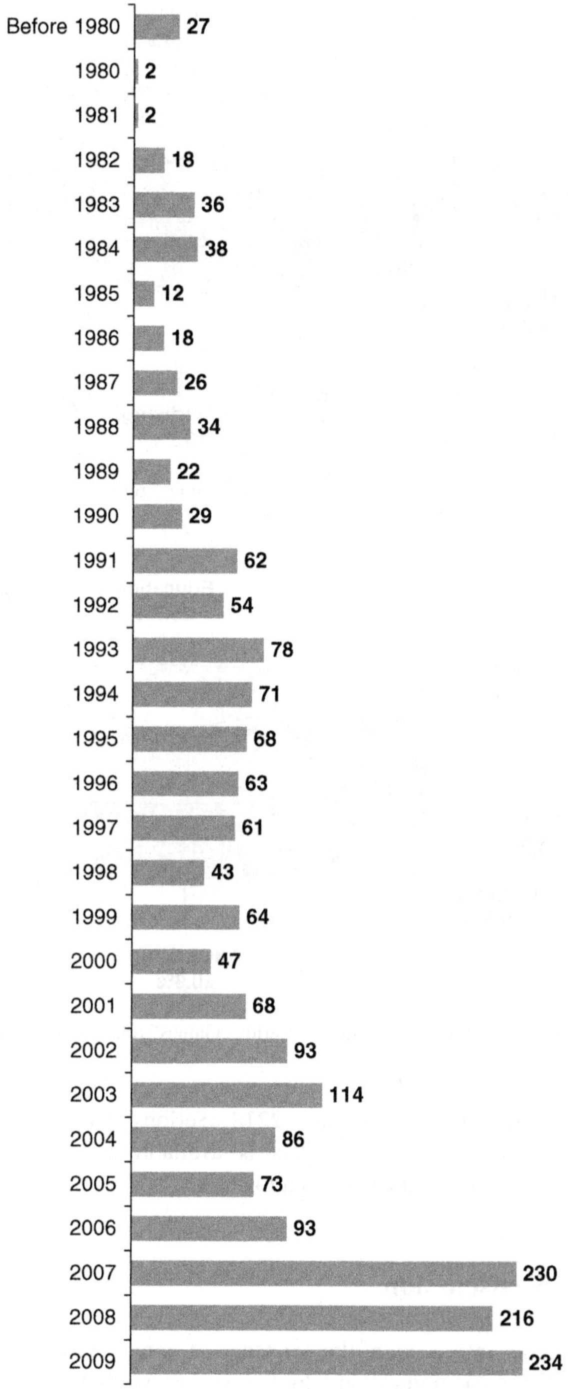

Fig. 3.1 Number of "Serious Games" released each year [2218 games]

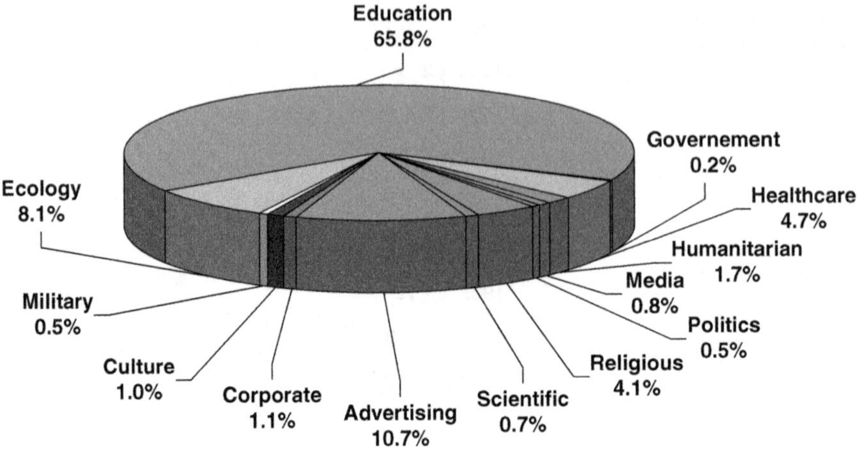

Fig. 3.2 Market repartition of "Serious Games" released before 2002 [953 games]

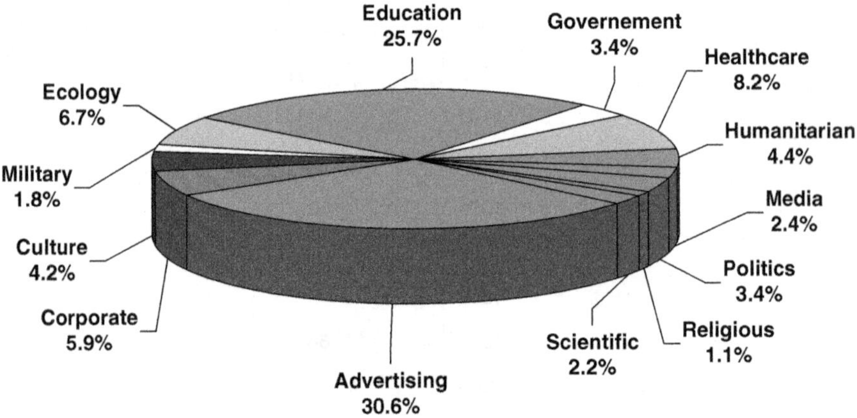

Fig. 3.3 Market repartition of "Serious Games" released after 2002 [1265 games]

The full list of the 2218 Serious Games that we used as a reference corpus for these data is available in an online collaborative database: http://serious.gameclassification.com/

3.5 Discussion

Taking into account the existence of games designed for serious purposes before 2002, we can question why the oxymoron "Serious Games" has only been widely used since the beginning of 2002. Indeed, if such games are available since the beginning of video games, why wait 40 years to name them with a specific term?

Several elements can explain this fact. The main one seems to be the dominance of "entertainment" games in the market, and the bad reputation from which they sometimes suffer. As we noted earlier, the current wave of "Serious Games" mainly originates from the USA. Games like *America's Army* and the work of Sawyer through the *Serious Game Initiative* were the driving forces of the current wave of "Serious Games." Our conviction is that U.S. designers of "Serious Games" had to invent a new label to convince people that their games were "not just for entertainment." But why did video games have such a "negative" image that these designers wanted to emphasize how different they are from "entertainment video games"?

The history of video games can shed some light on this topic. More specifically, we think that two factors explain the quite "negative" image of video games in the USA at the beginning of the 2000s:

- The marketing strategies of video game manufacturers that targeted children's entertainment.
- Several controversies about the content of video games, especially their violence and the possible impact they may have on children.

3.5.1 Leisure for Children?

Historically, two economical models co-existed for video games. In the first one, players pay for each play session, for instance with arcade games. In the second, players buy a retail copy of the video game and play it on a home console or computer. With such economic models, it seems logical that the most profitable games are the ones that players enjoy the most. The more fun a game is, the more likely players are willing to pay for it. Moreover, with arcade games the place in which you play matters. Therefore, the first arcade cabinets were set up in bars, restaurants, shopping malls and amusement parks. Games located in such places are designed to entertain people, and not to make them learn something. This fact is far from being anecdotal. The first home video game console, the *Odyssey* (Magnavox, 1972), is sold as a system with both leisure and educational games (see Section 3.2.4). However, manufacturers realised that the home video games that sold the most were the ones based on successful arcade titles. For example, many home version of *Pong* were released between 1975 and 1977 (Herman, 1997). Later on the best-selling titles on the *VCS 2600* (Atari, 1977) were adaptations of popular arcade titles like *Space Invaders* (1978) and *Pac-Man* (1980). So, while educational titles were available on home consoles, they quickly faded away because entertainment titles sold more copies. However until this time, games were not targeted at a specific age range. Adults were often seen playing video games in TV advertising.

Then came the 1983 crash of the video game industry in the USA. Due to this huge crisis, retailers believed that "video games were a fad", and refused to sell new consoles or cartridges, fearing people would no longer buy them. This was a huge problem for Nintendo, who successfully launched the *Famicom* in Japan and was looking for a way to sell it in the U.S. In order to convince American retailers that its home console was different from previous ones, Nintendo disguised it as a toy. The name was changed from "Family Computer" to "Nintendo Entertainment System", and the console was shipped with a robot toy. Moreover, Nintendo's advertising campaign solely focused on children, hoping it would sell better. And this strategy was very successful. But to convince parents that the *N.E.S.* and its games were "safe for children", Nintendo created a very restrictive system to control which games were published for its console. In order to release a game for the *N.E.S.*, game developers had to adhere to some limitations, such as to pay Nintendo royalties and to avoid publishing more than a few games per year. But they also had to follow the "Nintendo Content Policy", which explicitly states that video games must not deal with "topics inappropriate for children", such as violence, sex, religion or politics (Kent, 2001). Ultimately, though the video game industry became a very profitable market again, it was now bearing the image of being "a leisure activity for children."

3.5.2 Leisure for Children with Inappropriate Content?

Such an image can explain why many people were shocked to discover the existence of rather violent video games. For example, *Mortal Kombat* (Acclaim, 1992) raised so much concern among politicians that the video game industry had to create a way to rate games. Created in 1994, the *Entertainment Software Rating Board* (*ESRB*) rates video games by adding logos on video games boxes. These logos warn parents about the content of the video games, and display recommended age limitations. But this rating system was not enough to put an end to the debate over video game violence. In 1999, the Columbine tragedy initiated a new controversy, as the two killers were apparently avid players of *Doom* (id Software, 1993). The full details of this very complex and sensitive debate is not within the scope of this chapter. But we can at least cite Dave Grossman, who clearly accuses *Doom* of being dangerous in his book titled "Stop Teaching Our Kids to Kill" (Grossman and Degaetano, 1999): "Doom is being marketed and has been licensed to the United State Marine Corps. The Marine Corps is using it as an excellent tactical training device. How can the same device be provided indiscriminately to children over the internet, and yet the Marine Corps continues to use this device?"

Whilst his opinion has been later criticized, this retired military officer clearly illustrates what many people in the U.S. were thinking at the time. On one hand, video games "are a leisure activity for children." On the other, many video games feature violent and war-themed content. The existence of *Marine Doom* (U.S. Army, 1996), a modified version of *Doom II* (id Software, 1994) created and used by the U.S. Army for training purposes, emphasized this apparent contradiction between the video games audience and their content.

Apart from the ethical and moral considerations on this topic, we can appreciate that in 1999, the image of video games in the U.S. was not very positive. So, when the colonel E. Casey Wardy proposed the *America's Army* project to his hierarchy, we can understand that it would have been a bad idea to call it a "video game" (America's Army, 2010). Although it appears to be a coincidence, this game was publicly launched in 2002, when Sawyer and Rejeksi published their white paper on "Serious Games." So, this oxymoron was used as a label to emphasize the difference between *America's Army*, which is designed for serious purposes and not for children's leisure, and entertainment video games. This label must have seemed quite relevant, as many other video games designed for serious purposes used it too, thus launching the current wave of "Serious Games."

3.5.3 U.S. Video Games Market as the Birthplace for "Serious Games"?

It is also interesting to note that the two other historical video games markets, Europe and Japan, did not rely on such a label to release video games for serious purposes. Video game historians always observed that the Japanese video games market was not focused on a child audience (Ashcraft, 2009; Kohler, 2004). Though many games are available for children, games for adults and/or serious purposes also get published in Japan without raising public controversy. Therefore, to release *Dr Kawashima's Brain Training* (Nintendo, 2005), Nintendo did not need to use the "Serious Game" label.

Regarding the European video game market, it is very similar to the U.S. game market with one historical exception: a better balance between the home console and home computer markets, especially during the 1980s and 1990s (Donovan, 2010; Railton, 2005). At the time, the European market was always the last market segment to receive home console games. This delay between the international releases of games produced by big studios allowed several smaller companies to thrive on the home computer market. These smaller companies often designed games that addressed different themes than those created by big studios. For example, the wave of "cultural entertainment" video games is a European phenomenon.

To summarize, we can identify that the U.S. video games market was the one that most needed to use a different label in order to be able to produce video games dealing with serious purposes and/or targeting an adult audience.

3.5.4 "Serious Games" as a Label for a New Economic Model?

These few aspects from the history of video games can help us to understand why we had to wait until the beginning of the 2000s to see a specific term to label video games designed for serious purposes. But the current wave of "Serious Games" is more than just a new label. Current "Serious Games" are also based on a new economic model. While the ancestors of "Serious Games" were based on the same economic model as entertainment video games (people buying retail copies), it is no longer the case for most current "Serious Games." Instead, they are now funded by "clients", who hire a development studio to create a video game tailored to their needs. The studio is paid once to create the game, so "clients" can use it as they wish. If the game is intended to broadcast a message, it is likely that it will be available free of charge on the Internet. If the game is designed for training purpose, "clients" will probably use it for the internal training sessions of their employees. As the game's success is no longer tied to its retail performance, we can identify that this different economic model is better suited to games dealing with serious purposes. As we have noted earlier, ancestors of "Serious Games" were greatly focused on Education while the newer games embrace a wide variety of themes. This may be due to the fact that educational games were easier to sell with the previous economic model than games dealing with other topics. Hence, this new economic model is likely to enable the current wave of "Serious Games" to last longer and embrace more public recognition than their ancestors.

3.6 Conclusion

At first sight, "Serious Games" may seem to be a new phenomenon that appeared from nowhere. Whilst there is unquestionably some novelty in the current wave of "Serious Games", we can identify several sources of their historical origins.

First, we observe that the very first video games were not designed purely for entertainment. We can also note that these early video gaming experiments coincide with the first use of the "Serious Game" oxymoron to name games designed to serve purposes other than purely entertainment. But the first "Serious Games" were not necessarily based on a digital support. For example, Clark Abt and his colleagues designed several "Serious Games" using a wide range of supports, from board games to sports to early computer simulations.

Meanwhile, video games flourished as an industry focused on entertainment. However, some of the titles released in the video games market were designed to serve serious purposes, such as education, healthcare, defence... Whilst they were not labelled as "Serious Games", these video games are the closest ancestors to the "Serious Games" we know today. Apart from public awareness, the main difference between these ancestors and current "Serious Games" is their economic model. However, to be able to use an economic model better suited to video games dealing with serious matters and/or targeting an adult audience, designers had to mark their difference from "entertainment" video games and their sometimes negative image. We think that this is the main reason that explains why the label "Serious Games" was used again, 40 years after its creation, to name a new generation of video games designed for serious purposes.

Nevertheless, history is a rich and complex resource, and these elements are just a little information relating to Serious Games. While we do not pretend to have reached completeness, we hope that the historical elements proposed in this chapter will help the reader to understand the origins of the current wave of "Serious Games."

Acknowledgements Authors would like to thank Maxine Johnson for proof-reading this chapter and correcting many of its English language errors.

References

Abt Associates: Counter-Insurgency Game Design Feasibility and Evaluation Study. ARPA, Pentagon (1965)

Abt Associates: Biography of Clark C. Abt. http://www.abtassociates.com/page.cfm?PageID=104 (2005). Accessed 26 Oct 2010

Abt, C.C.: Serious Games. Viking Press, New York (1970)

Alvarez, J., Alvarez, V., Djaouti, D., Michaud, L.: Serious Games: Training & Teaching – Healthcare – Defence & Security – Information & Communication. IDATE, France (2010)

America's Army: The making of America's Army. *America's Army Official Website*. http://www.americasarmy.com/aa/about/makingof.php#3 (2010, July 4). Accessed 17 Nov 2010

Anderson, J.: Who really invented the video game? Creat. Comput. Video Arcade Games **1**(1), 8 (1983)

Ashcraft, B.: Arcade Mania: The Turbo-charged World of Japan's Game Centers. Editions Pix'N Love, France (2009)

Baer, R.H.: Videogames: In the Beginning. Rolenta Press, Springfield, NJ (2005)

Banister, A.W.: The case for cold war gaming in the military services. *Air University Review*. http://www.airpower.au.af.mil/airchronicles/aureview/1967/jul-aug/banister.html (1967, July)

Barton, M., Loguidice, B.: The history of pong: Avoid missing game to start industry. http://www.gamasutra.com/view/feature/3900/the_history_of_pong_avoid_missing_.php?print=1 (2009a, January 9). Accessed 27 Oct 2010

Barton, M., Loguidice, B.: The history of spacewar!: The best waste of time in the history of the universe. http://www.gamasutra.com/view/feature/4047/the_history_of_spacewar_the_best_.php?print=1 (2009b, June 10). Accessed 27 Oct 2010

Bennett, J.M., Broomham, R., Murton, P., Pearcey, T., Rutledge, R.: Computing in Australia: The Development of a Profession. Hale & Iremonger, Sydney (1994)

Bernstein, A., Roberts, M.D.V., Arbuckle, T., Belsky, M.A.: A chess playing program for the IBM 704. In: Managing Requirements Knowledge, International Workshop on, vol. 0, p. 157. IEEE Computer Society, Los Alamitos, CA (1958). doi: http://doi.ieeecomputersociety.org/10.1109/AFIPS.1958.1

Brown, S.J., Lieberman, D.A., Gemeny, B.A., Fan, Y.C., Wilson, D.M., Pasta, D.J.: Educational video game for juvenile diabetes: Results of a controlled trial. Inform. Health Soc. Care **22**(1), 77–89 (1997)

Caspian Learning: Serious Games in Defence Education. Caspian Learning, Royaume-Uni (2008)

Chaplin, H., Ruby, A.: Smartbomb: The Quest for Art, Entertainment, and Big Bucks in the Videogame Revolution. Algonquin Books, Chapel Hill, NC (2006)

Cohen, D.: OXO aka Noughts and Crosses – The First Video Game. About.com: Classic Video Games. http://classicgames.about.com/od/computergames/p/OXOProfile.htm (2009, October 30). Accessed 27 Oct 2010

Copeland, J.: A Brief History of Computing. http://www.alanturing.net/turing_archive/pages/Reference%20Articles/BriefHistofComp.html (2000, June). Accessed 17 Nov 2010

Daly, W.G.: Computer Strategies for the Game of Qubic (Master thesis). Massachusetts Institute of Technology, Cambridge, MA (1961, February)

Dondero, L.J.: A Hierarchy of Combat Analysis Models. General Research Corporation, USA (1973)

Donovan, T.: Replay: The History of Video Games. Yellow Ant Media Ltd, United Kingdom (2010)

Dunnigan, J.F.: The Complete Wargames Handbook: How to Play, Design, and Find Them (Rev Sub.). Quill, New York. http://www.hyw.com/books/wargameshandbook/contents.htm (1992)

ELSPA: Unlimited Learning: Computer and Videogames in the Learning Landscape. ELSPA, Royaume-Uni (2006)
ESA: Essential Facts About the Computer and Video Game Industry. ESA, Washington, DC (2010)
Fleming, J.: Down the Hyper-Spatial Tube: Spacewar and the Birth of Digital Game Culture. http://www.gamasutra.com/view/feature/1433/down_the_hyperspatial_tube_.php?print=1 (2007, June 1). Accessed 27 Oct 2010
Gee, J.P.: Learning by design: Good video games as learning machines. E-Learning **2**(1), 5 (2005). doi:10.2304/elea.2005.2.1.5
Gee, J.P.: What Video Games Have to Teach Us About Learning and Literacy. Second Edition: Revised and Updated Edition (2nd ed.). Palgrave Macmillan, New York (2007)
Graetz, M.: The origin of spacewar! Creat. Comput. 56–67, USA (1981, June)
Graham, B.: Serious Games: Art, Interaction, Technology. Barbican Art Gallery in association with Tyne & Wear Museums, London (1996)
Grossman, D., Degaetano, G.: Stop Teaching Our Kids to Kill: A Call to Action Against TV, Movie and Video Game Violence (1er ed.). Crown Archetype, USA (1999)
Gudmundsen, J.: Movement aims to get serious about games. USA Today. http://www.usatoday.com/tech/gaming/2006-05-19-serious-games_x.htm (2006, May 19)
Halter, E.: From Sun Tzu to Xbox: War and Video Games. Thunder's Mouth Press, New York (2006)
Harfield, M.: Not Dark Yet: A Very Funny Book About a Very Serious Game. Loose Chippings Books, United Kingdom (2008)
Harrison Jr., J.O.: Computer-Aided Information Systems for Gaming. Research Analysis Corporation, USA (1964)
Herman, L.: Phoenix: The Fall & Rise of Videogames, 2nd edn. Rolenta Press, USA (1997)
Herz, J.C.: Joystick Nation: How Videogames Ate Our Quarters, Won Our Hearts, and Rewired Our Minds, 1er edn. Little, Brown and Company, Boston, MA (1997)
Huizinga, J.: Homo ludens. Gallimard, Paris (1951)
Jackson, M.: Christopher Strachey: A personal recollection. Higher Order Symbol. Comput. **13**, 73–74 (2000). doi:10.1023/A:1010005808988
James, H.: Halcyon Days. http://www.dadgum.com/halcyon/ (1997)
Jansiewicz, D.R.: The New Alexandria Simulation: A Serious Game of State and Local Politics. Canfield Press, San Francisco, CA (1973)
Jansiewicz, D.R.: The game of politics – frequently asked questions. http://www.gameofpolitics.com/f__a__q_.htm (2011). Accessed 8 Feb 2011
Kahn, M.A., Perez, K.M.: The game of politics simulation: An exploratory study. J. Political Sci. Educ. **5**(4), 332 (2009). doi:10.1080/15512160903253707
Kent, S.L.: The Ultimate History of Video Games, 1er edn. Three Rivers Press, New York (2001)
Klopfer, E., Osterweil, S., Salen, K.: Moving Learning Games Forward. The Education Arcade, Massachusetts Institute of Technology, USA (2009)
Kohler, C.: Power-Up: How Japanese Video Games Gave the World an Extra Life. BRADY GAMES, USA (2004)
Levy, S.: Hackers: Heroes of the Computer Revolution. Anchor Press, USA (1984)
Lieberman, D.A.: Management of chronic pediatric diseases with interactive health games: Theory and research findings. J. Ambulatory Care Manage. **24**(1), 26–38 (2001)
Manning, J.: The Emblem. Reaktion Books, United Kingdom (2004)
Michael, D., Chen, S.: Serious Games: Games That Educate, Train, and Inform, 1er edn. Course Technology PTR, USA (2005)
Montfort, N.: Twisty Little Passages: An Approach to Interactive Fiction. The MIT Press, Cambridge, MA (2005)
Newell, A., Shaw, J., Simon, H.A.: Chess-Playing Program and the Problem of Complexity. RAND Corporation, USA (1958)
Poole, S.: Trigger Happy. Fourth Estate, London (2001)

Railton, J.: The A to Z of Cool Computer Games (illustrated edition.). Allison & Busby, London (2005)
Research Analysis Corporation: RAC Publications List. Research Analysis Corporation, USA (1965)
Robertson, D.: The Games in Schools – Community of Practice. European Schoolnet, Brussels (2009)
Robertson, D., Miller, D.: Using Dr Kawashima's Brain Training in Primary Classrooms: A Randomised Controlled Study. A Summary for the BBC. Learning and Teaching Scotland, Scotland (2008)
Sawyer, B.: The "Serious Games" landscape. Presented at the Instructional & Research Technology Symposium for Arts, Humanities and Social Sciences, Camden (2007)
Sawyer, B.: Foreword : From virtual U to serious game to something bigger. In: Ritterfeld, U., Cody, M., Vorderer, P. (eds.) Serious Games: Mechanisms and Effects, 1er edn. pp. XI–XVI Routledge, New York (2009)
Sawyer, B., Rejeski, D.: Serious Games: Improving Public Policy Through Game-Based Learning and Simulation. Woodrow Wilson International Center for Scholars, Washington, DC (2002)
Schrage, M.: Serious Play: How the World's Best Companies Simulate to Innovate, 1er edn. Harvard Business Press, Boston, MA (1999)
Shaffer, D.W.: How Computer Games Help Children Learn (Reprint.). Palgrave Macmillan, New York (2007)
Smillie, K.: Some Topics in Computing. http://webdocs.cs.ualberta.ca/~smillie/Topics/Topics.html (2010)
Smith, R.D.: Military Simulation & Serious Games: Where We Came From and Where We are Going. Modelbenders LLC, USA (2009)
Soderberg, H.: The Serious Game, 1er edn. Marion Boyars Publishers Ltd, United Kingdom (2001)
Wall, B.: Biography of Dietrich Prinz (2009, February)
Wilson, A.: The Bomb and the Computer, 1st edn. Barrie & Rockliff the Cresset P., London (1968)
Wolf, M.J.: The Video Game Explosion: A History from Pong to Playstation and Beyond. Greenwood Press, Westport, CT (2007)
Zyda, M.: From visual simulation to virtual reality to games. Computer **38**(9), 25–32 (2005)

Chapter 4
Serious Learning in Serious Games

Learning In, Through, and Beyond Serious Games

Konstantin Mitgutsch

4.1 Introduction

In the musical film "Mary Poppins" (1964) the nanny, played by Julie Andrews, explains to Mr. Banks' children, Jane and Michael, how to transform something as bitter as medicine into a sweet and joyful game. She performs the song "A Spoonful of Sugar", the children learn to enjoy taking their medicine with the addition of a sweet treat, and the game is completed. One could argue that this is what serious games are all about – designing a spoonful of sugar and filling it with "serious" content. The idea of using games for serious and educational purposes beyond entertainment reaches back to institutional forms of play in general (cf. Locke, 1689; Rousseau, 1762; Fröbel, 1826; Montessori, 1909). Games are extraordinary learning tools and motivate players to explore the edges of their competence, their skills, and their knowledge. Playing is a voluntary activity that relates to the needs and values of the players. It is contextualized in its own space, time, and by its affinity group. Playing can be defined as the voluntary attempt to confront ourselves with unnecessary challenges in a satisfying way (cf. Suits, 2005). But what if these *unnecessary challenges* are designed to be serious and overcoming them has a meaningful impact on our everyday lives and those of others? What if games are intentionally designed to "empower us to change the world in meaningful ways"? (McGonigal, 2011, p. 14). Games are learning tools, but are they *serious* learning instruments and what does *serious learning* in serious games mean?

In the 1970s the term *serious game* was introduced by Clark Abt (1970), but the technical term was not made dominant until the *Serious Game Initiative*[1] coined it in 2002 (cf. Wu, 2008). Although an established definition of serious games is lacking, Abt's understanding of games aiming at explicit educational purposes is still in use: "We are concerned with serious games in the sense that these games

[1] http://www.seriousgames.org/

K. Mitgutsch (✉)
Singapore-MIT Gambit Game Lab, Massachusetts Institute of Technology, Cambridge, MA 02139, USA
e-mail: k_mitgut@mit.edu

M. Ma et al. (eds.), *Serious Games and Edutainment Applications*,
DOI 10.1007/978-1-4471-2161-9_4, © Springer-Verlag London Limited 2011

have an explicit and carefully thought-out educational purpose and are not intended to be played primarily for amusement" (Abt, 1970, p. 9). This does not mean that serious games should not be entertaining – they must be engaging to capture the learners' attention (cf. Klimmt, 2009) – but their primary aim is to have an educational impact. This aim can be described as the intention to design a playful environment that provides *serious* content, topics, narratives, rules and goals to foster a specific purposeful learning process. Serious games are intentionally designed playful learning experiences. Serious games do not simply teach their rules, narrative, fictions, metaphors or goals, but they teach the players something about the world, themselves, and their own values, beliefs and behaviors (cf. Peng et al., 2010). From an educational and learning theoretical perspective, it can be argued that *serious* games, compared to entertainment-orientated games, aim at teaching something *beyond* the game play experience itself. Because if the learning process would stay exclusively related to the game space, the educational impact is in question. Although, the idea to use games for *serious* learning appears appealing, we still lack an educational, theoretically founded and evidence-based framework that helps us understand how learning in serious games takes place (cf. Clark, 2007). In particular, we lack a framework that helps us understand how *serious* learning – learning that changes players' perspectives on themselves, others and the world, – takes place.

The following chapter traces the question, what forms of *serious* learning in serious games can be identified. To answer this question a theoretical inquiry into different learning levels in games based on Gregory Bateson's (1972) concept of learning will be outlined and exemplified. On its basis the theory of "transformative learning" (Mezirow, 1996) as a form of *serious* learning will be introduced and applied to serious games. To support this theoretical approach, empirical studies and examples of serious games will be analyzed and compared. Furthermore, the conditions under which transformative learning processes could be fostered, and where the possibility space of games reaches their limits will be discussed. So what does *serious learning* in serious games mean?

4.2 Learning in Serious Games

The combination of playing and learning based on digital technology has been identified as a major task of twenty-first century investigation on learning (cf. Shaffer et al., 2005). The fact *that* we learn in games appears indisputable considering recent studies and theoretical argumentations (cf. Gee, 2003; Salen, 2007; Ritterfeld et al., 2009; Gee and Hayes, 2010) but when it comes to the question of *what* and *how* players learn through playing games, controversial answers can be found. Particularly on an empirical level, we still need to learn more about *how* learning takes place in games. As Richard Clark (2007, p. 56) states: "The widespread interest in learning and motivation of serious video games has not been balanced by a robust discussion about evidence for their pedagogical effectiveness." But what does *pedagogical effectiveness* in regard to the impact of purposeful game design mean? Before these questions can be answered on an educational or empirical level, the learning theoretical assumptions underlying serious games need to be explored.

When we are playing games, our learning abilities are challenged. We need to understand the controls of the game and its goals, perform within its rules and its fiction, make meaning of the narrative and characters, and explore the provided game space. Furthermore, we are acquiring information that we need to memorize, and we solve problems while we are forced to take actions. Sometimes we role play, cooperate with or fight against others, or interpret the actions of the simulated others. In video games, learning takes place on different levels and in a variety of ways. From an entertainment-oriented approach to games, it might be reasonable to reduce the complexity of the learning processes taking place in a game to the obvious problem: Are the players understanding *how to play* the game, or not? But if games are intentionally designed to foster serious, meaningful and deep learning, the question of what kind of learning is taking place *in*, *through* and *beyond* the game appears fundamental. As we are learning, we "always learn something" (Gee, 2008, p. 23) – but in serious games this *something* reaches beyond the game itself. Although computer games have multiple potentials to foster learning, the knowledge and abilities learned in games do not always seem to be transferable to real life contexts. Even if players change their habits and routines after playing a game on a short-term scale (cf. Klimmt, 2009), we still do not have evidence of players' thinking changing substantially. How can we differentiate between these different levels of learning in games?

4.3 Levels of Learning in Serious Games

The differentiation of learning levels, stages and modes had a high peak as developmental theorists (Piaget, 1974) and the Cognitivists (Bloom, 1956; Gagné, 1987) began exploring the ways people learn. A theorist seldom related to levels of learning in games is the anthropologist and cyberneticist, Gregory Bateson (cf. Egenfeldt-Nielsen et al., 2006). Bateson's concept of learning levels (cf. Bateson, 1972) is a functional framework to differentiate three fundamental levels of learning in, through and beyond playing serious games. The advantage of Bateson's concept of learning is that he approaches learning not only as a developmental, emotional, or cognitive process but also as an activity of change in relation to the context that is framing this change. Thereby his concept allows us to compare basic learning processes, contextualized forms of learning, and serious and transformative learning in different settings:

While Bateson's theory of framing in the process of playing has been widely adopted in the field of game studies (Wolf and Perron, 2003), his understanding of learning is rarely applied to computer game studies. Bateson defines learning as a phenomenon, which is inherently relational and involves multiple logical levels. Bateson regards learning as an action of change: "The word 'learning' undoubtedly denotes change of some kind. To say what kind of change is a delicate matter"

(Bateson, 1972, p. 283). In his hierarchical model of learning levels, he divides this "delicate matter" into five different learning processes (Bateson, 1972). In this chapter, I want to highlight three of the most essential aspects of these levels that I will apply to serious games. Without outlining Bateson's complex concept in detail,[2] I will apply his concept to games and compare between learning *in*, *through* and *beyond* serious games. As an example, I will analyze a serious game designed by Egenfeldt-Nielsen "Global Conflicts: Sweatshops" (Serious Game Interactive/Global Conflicts, 2009). The game can be described as a 3D text adventure that focuses on the problem of child labor in developing countries and uses techniques of investigative journalism to engage the player with this topic.

4.3.1 Learning in Serious Games

Gregory Bateson argued that every learning processes starts on a basic level he calls learning *zero,* as a linear reaction to an external stimulus or as Bateson suggests: "The simple receipt of information from an external event" (Bateson, 1972, p. 284). On this first learning level the players receive information, memorize it and react to it without reflecting the context or reasons – like a rat in the t-maze or a robot analysing data. For example, the binary code of a computers and its "reaction" within learning *zero* can be regarded as an example of learning on this first basic level. The process of learning *zero* is linear. It can be understood as a specific behaviour in relation to information. This first basic level that behaviourists focus on in their approach (Pavlov, 1928; Skinner, 1974; Thorndike, 1932), is for Bateson a starting point for every further learning levels. At this first and very basic level of learning, players of serious games collect certain input, data and information and react to it – but they do not *make sense* out of it yet. Learning *in* games in this sense is all about linear interactions, collecting, reacting, and memorizing.

So what data and information do players acquire on a first basic learning level in *Global Conflicts: Sweatshops* (Fig. 4.1)? In the beginning, the players learn that their character is a male company co-owner of the European Leather Industry (ELI) who is asked to go to Bangladesh to investigate if claims of child labour in one of the supplying tanneries in Dhaka are true. Two assignments are given: "First, I should seek proof of children working at the tannery. Second, I must find a solution that will not be harmful to ELI nor to the people working at the tannery."[3] The task is to collect information, prepare a well-founded argument and confront the head of the company, *Rodro Raihan*. The players find themselves in territory labelled "Bangladesh" in front of a building. Players can take actions such as interacting with specific virtual characters by "talking" to them. By "talking", they can choose from given dialogue patterns and see how the characters react and answer questions. For example, the first interview partner called *Maxine* informs the player, "In

[2] He distinguishes between zero-, proto- and deutero-learning (Bateson, 1972, pp. 248–287).

[3] www.globalconflicts.eu

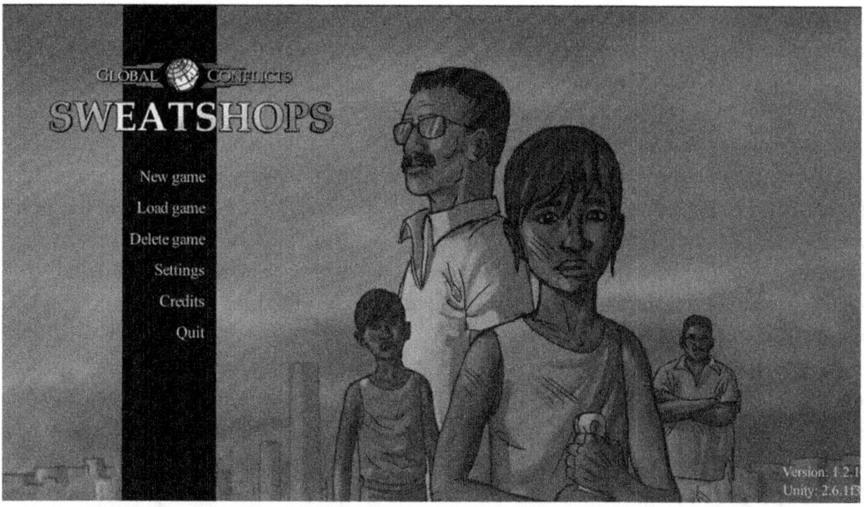

Fig. 4.1 Global Conflicts: Sweatshops (2006): www.globalconflicts.eu
Source: http://inthanatos.egloos.com/4675622

Bangladesh alone, there are about five million children working all day and never getting any schooling"[4].

On a first basic level of learning, the players react to input, but they do not contextualize or value it yet. They are collecting facts and act inside a neutral possibility space. Thereby the players gather information about chemicals, child labour, pollution and the working conditions in the leather tannery through interviewing people. The players are reacting to the algorithms provided by the game and acquire the information that is achieved by the game. The conversations are small riddles that have to be solved. All learning taking place in this first level of learning in the game could also be performed by a computer – and the computer would be more efficient than a human player. But to succeed in *Global Conflict: Sweatshop* the players need to take a further step and contextualize the information and make sense out of it.

4.3.2 Learning Through Serious Games

To relate the collected data and information acquired on the first learning level to a particular meaning and action, it needs to be framed and contextualised by the players. On this second learning level, that Bateson labels *learning one* (Bateson, 1972), the players discover responses to repeatable contexts. By framing their perception and the collected data (first level), the players enrich the neutral data with meaningful interpretations. Bateson defines a frame as "a class or set of messages

[4] www.globalconflicts.eu

(or meaningful actions)" (p. 186). The players are thereby enabled to choose whether certain information should be included or excluded, judged as meaningful or useless, or necessary or unnecessary for their game play. The process of learning that occurs at this second level can be described as a choice of given alternatives in special contexts and as a process of change and repetition, which alters the relation of information to the context. Bateson talks of framing when individuals consider the specific frame, i.e. the specific context of their behavioural response. On the first learning level (zero) players do not consider how to act – they react like rats in the T-maze to a stimulus –, but by framing they choose between alternatives and analyse what to do in the particular situation. The learning *through* playing the game can be defined as *contextual* learning.

Returning to the example of *Global Conflicts: Sweatshops,* the players on this second level start make sense of what is going on in the game. The territory is Bangladesh, the characters the players are interviewing behave in a specific way and they mirror the players' questions. By framing the situation, the players' learn through playing the game that there is a forceful power relationship between the working children, their parents, their poverty and the boss of the company. The fact that the players have to choose their questions and answers carefully relates to the context of a game. In addition, the accent of the interviewees, the atmosphere of the territory and the aesthetics of the graphics are now also related to the learning in the game. For example, we learn that the father of one of the children is sick and his family is dependent on his daughter's work. Therefore sending her to school is not an option for him. Learning on this level involves contextualizing the content (Level 0) to the context of a specific game. On this level, the players will also realize errors in the game design or illogical elements in the game. Players may question why they can only talk to certain characters and not others, why they can only choose from two or three alternative answers during conversations, and why the characters' accents are not Bangladeshi? Players may also explore what the outcome would be if they randomly choose answers during conversations. To frame the learning challenges in the game, the players also have to explore the game world. Different frames, patterns, and perspectives are confronted and a variety of values and anticipations are redefined and explored. The players learn *through* playing the game how to use different strategies, concepts and patterns to succeed in the game. The learning through playing involves learning about the context of the game and developing strategies to master and use the acquired information. Most games that are developed for entertainment purposes are not designed to foster learning beyond the game. As Christoph Klimmt argues: "Playful action, however, is intentionally limited to a situational frame that blocks out further consequences of action results." (Klimmt, 2009, p. 253). Serious games aim at a further learning level that reaches beyond learning *in* and *through* playing – they want to have an impact on real life context.[5]

[5] Like professional educators and teachers designers of serious game designer should openly discuss their understanding of learning, the goals of their game design, and the instructional methods in use. So far only a few serious games offer a deeper insight in what their educational approach is.

4.3.3 Learning Beyond Serious Games

By exploring the third level of learning we are not only examining one of the most crucial aspects of *serious* learning, but we also reach the learning level, of which serious game designers have marginal control over. The question on a third level of learning can be summarized as "What does this mean to me?" On this learning level, the perceived and achieved learning *in* the game and the contextualized and framed learning experiences made *through* playing the game are transferred. Thereby – in theory – the player's concept of themselves, of others, and of the world is transforming. At this stage, the learning process is expanded to real life contexts and the game fosters a *transformation* of the player's self- and worldview. This transformative learning process is often labeled "meaningful learning" (Novak and Gowin, 1984; Mitgutsch, 2011a), "value-laden deep learning" (Gee, 2008), and "meta- or double loop-learning" (Argyris and Schön, 1974; Mitgutsch, 2011b). Gregory Bateson herby talks of "deutero-learning" (Bateson, 1972). Through transformational learning experiences the players' approach to a problem changes fundamentally:

> Players experience the subject domain or situation in new ways, form new affiliations and thereby prepare for future learning and problem solving in the domain or transfer of learning to related domains. (Mitchell and Savill-Smith, 2004, p. 21)

The transfer does not occur in a linear or direct manner, but indirect as a process of transferring contextualized frames of reference from the virtual setting to real life (cf. Mayer and Wittrock, 1996; Schwartz et al., 2007). The experience simulated by the digital game is not transported at a ratio of 1:1, but is changed by the player's perception, his/her prior experiences and judgments, his/her way of *framing,* and by the form of adaptation to real life. In the cognitive sciences, transfer and learning is researched widely (cf. Barnett and Ceci, 2002) and even in the area of game studies some investigations focus on its exploration (Steinkuehler, 2007; Peng et al., 2010; Mitgutsch, 2011a). Nevertheless Bateson's understanding of transformative learning offers us a novel view on meta-learning, that focuses on the recontextualization of the game play experience in real life settings. While most studies in the area of education game studies focus on the measurable transfer of knowledge, literacies or skills from the virtual learning space to real life (Squire, 2006; Steinkuehler, 2007; Barab et al., 2010), Bateson's concept of transformational learning focuses on a different aspect: *Serious* learning *beyond* playing video games involves a fundamental transfer of frames of reference patterns that structure the players' body of experiences. Hereby not only the players' knowledge about *something* is improved, but their way of approaching and interpreting a problem is restructured in a meaningful way. In short: The players concept of themselves, others, and the world changes fundamentally.

In educational research, this form of learning is defined as *transformative learning* (Mezirow, 1996; Buck, 1989; Mitgutsch, 2009). Transformative learning is the process of expanding the learner's body of experience through a change in the frames of reference patterns that structure the expectations and interpretations:

> Frames of reference are structures of culture and language through which we construe meaning by attributing coherence and significance to our experience. They selectively shape and delimit our perception, cognition and feelings by predisposing our intentions, beliefs, expectations and purposes. (Mezirow, 2010, p. 92)

If humans learn on a transformative level they develop new perspectives on the world, others and themselves (cf. O'Sullivan et al., 2002, p. 18). Thereby prior beliefs and judgments form an expectation that is confronted, which challenges the learner to restructure his/her expectations and his/her body of experience. The transfer of meaningful learning patterns can be understood as a transformative learning process confronting prior interpretation to construe new or revised interpretations of something (cf. Mitgutsch, 2011b). As Jack Mezirow states:

> We very commonly check our prior learning to confirm that we have correctly proceeded to solve problems, but becoming critically aware of our own presuppositions involves challenging our established and habitual patterns of expectation, the meaning perspectives with which we have made sense out of our encounters with the world, others and ourselves. (Mezirow, 2003, p. 207)

In different research settings on transformative learning it became evident that these challenging trigger moments differ: One might develop a different perspective on something by a singular dramatic event, or by a chain of different experiences or surprising confrontations. Some of these "disorienting dilemmas" or "catalytic events" (Kovan and Dirkx, 2003, p. 114) can occur in a gradual or over an extended period of time rather than in a single trigger moment. In the research on transformative learning it became evident, "that being on the edge is a variable experience" (Berger, 2004, p. 344) to foster transformative learning. If serious games are designed to change the player's perspective on *something*, they aim at *serious* and *transformative* learning processes. When we ask what the motivation and learning benefits of serious games are, we need to research, *if* and *how serious* games foster transformative learning. For the process of learning through games, it remains essential that these transfers induce a change in the player's concept of "real life". As Wei Peng, Mira Lee, and Carrie Heeter state "games for change focus on persuasion, such as forming or changing attitudes about political or religious agendas, or simply increasing awareness of social issues" (2010, p. 723). However, it remains to be seen whether the playing of games such as *Darfur is Dying* (mtvU, 2006), *Ayiti: the Cost of Life* (Gamelab/Global Kids 4 Keeps), or Global Conflicts: Sweatshops (Serious Game Interactive/Global Conflicts, 2009) and others leads to a *transformation* of the players.

In our example, *Global Conflicts: Sweatshops,* this serious level of learning would include a change of the player's thinking about child labor, poverty, oppression, journalism, violence and pollution through experiences fostered in the game. Without investigating the impact the game has on the players' thinking, on their values and beliefs on an empirical level (beyond short-term effects), this claim can not be verified. Thus, it can be identified on which levels the game provokes the development of novel frames of reference patterns and where the players find possibilities to connect their prior experiences to these novel patterns. For example, the game confronts the players with a problematic concept (child labor, poverty, violence), but the impact players have on child labor in real life in countries such as Bangladesh remains unexpressed in this game. The game does not even identify the relationship between the child labor situation and the player's actual circumstances and actions. Furthermore, the game provides only a very limited scope of action and the players cannot explore the situation in depth. In addition, players can only choose from two to three optional answers during conversations with characters, which limits the potential to relate personal views to the game play. From a learning theoretical point of view – based on the concept *serious* learning – the potentials of *Global Conflicts: Sweatshops* appear limited. *Global Conflicts: Sweatshops* offers learning *in* and *through* playing the game, but triggers for learning beyond the context of the game are missing.[6] But beside this case example, what empirical evidence do we have that *serious* learning beyond playing serious games takes place in other games?

4.4 Evidence of Transformative Learning in Serious Games?

There are several theoretical claims that learning in serious games takes place (cf. Gee, 2008; Shaffer, 2006; McGonigal, 2011), but what empirical evidence do we have that serious and transformative learning can take place in serious games? One of the most detailed studies of the impact of a serious game conducted in recent years investigates the game *Re-Mission* (HopeLabe/Realtime Associates, 2004).

In the game, designed for young adults with cancer, the players play the female action hero *Roxxi* (Fig. 4.2), who defeats cancer with a medicine gun. The game was designed in reference to popular action games and uses the mechanics of first-person shooters. But *Roxxi* shoots medicine and what she shoots at are cancer cells. The impact of the game was evaluated between 2004 and 2005 and 375 children in the USA, Canada and Australia took part in the study (cf. Kato et al., 2008; Tate et al., 2009). The study showed that children who played *Re-Mission*, successfully and significantly acquired information about cancer, therapies and medication through learning *in* the game. On a further learning level, they were able to recontextualize their learning and changed their behavior beyond the game. As the researchers conclude, "a video-game-based intervention can have a positive impact on treatment-relevant behaviors and outcomes in a patient population with serious life-threatening illnesses." (Kato et al., 2008, p. 314). The study showed that the medication intake of the players improved 16% and that "blood chemotherapy metabolite levels" increased by 40% (Tate et al., 2009, p. 30). Although the researchers did not identify the core mechanics in the game that lead to the learning

[6] Although the transformational potential of Global Conflicts: Sweatshop appears limited, as the game focuses more on teaching debating skills and delivering information than on connecting to the players perspectives, more empirical data on players' serious learning processes is needed. It should be mentioned that the game is intended to be supported by educators, who can download teaching materials for their pupils (cf. www.globalconflicts.eu).

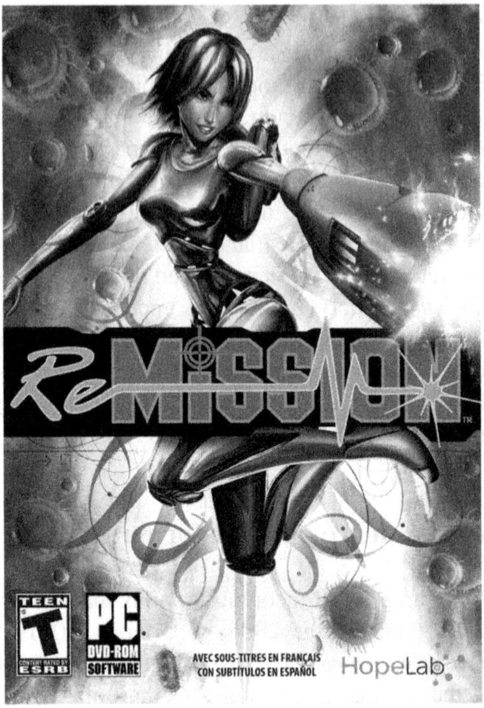

Fig. 4.2 Roxxi fighting cancer in Re-Mission (2004) *Source*: http://www.re-mission.net

transfer, they highlighted the reported feeling of self-efficacy as the key trigger for the learning success. As one of the patients explained: "It feels like you have control over your own destiny" (Tate et al., 2009, p. 30). Thus, the improvement of the feeling of self-efficacy stayed limited to the intake of medicine and the players could not essentially change their frames of reference patterns about their life situation and their illness. The players learned *through Re-Mission* that they can take control over their medication, but their perspective on their illness and life did not change significantly (Kato et al., 2008, p. 312). Although the success of this serious game is indisputable, it gives evidence that serious games can change behavior, but do they foster *serious* and transformative learning?

In a well designed meta-study on serious games by O'Neil, Wainess and Baker (2005) show that from 1990 to 2005 only 19 out of thousands of studies on simulations and educational games fulfilled the standards of providing either quantitative or qualitative data on measured learning outcomes. From these 19 studies only three (Mayer and Wittrock, 1996; Tkacz, 1998; Parchman et al., 2000) evaluated the transfer impact of the outcomes. Their findings demonstrated that the pedagogical effect is insufficient, when not supported by educational instruction: "In other words, outcomes are affected by the instructional strategies employed" (O'Neil et al., 2005, p. 465). To reach *beyond* the learning *in* and *through* the game, support from outside increases the possibility that learning beyond the game takes place. For instance a game like *Re-Mission* could also be used by physicians, therapists, coaches and educators to work with patients on the transfer of frames of reference patterns related to self-efficacy in their personal lives. Thus the question arises if a first-person shooter like *Re-Mission* provides enough possibility space for connection to the prior experiences of the patients. The game does not challenge the players established and habitual patterns of expectation (cf. Mezirow, 1996, 2003), it does not offer a "catalytic event" (Kovan and Dirkx, 2003), it just offers a different perspective in one particular context.

One of the only empirical studies available at this time on how players change their behavior, their attitude and willingness to help is a recent study by Wei Peng, Mira Lee and Carrie Heeter. In their study "The Effects of a Serious Game on Role-Taking and Willingness to Help" (2010) 133 undergraduate students were asked to play the Serious Game "Darfur is Dying" (mtv-u 2005) or read a text on the problematic situation in Darfur. Afterwards, their willingness to take supportive action on the crisis in Darfur was measured and compared. The students were asked to use a 7-point scale to rate how likely it was that they would donate money, sign a petition, discuss the situation with friends and family or forward a website link to others. The results showed that playing the game significantly increased the student's willingness to support people in Darfur in all categories. In a second experiment a further media format, in form of a recorded video of the game play, was added to the experiment. The researchers concluded: "Both studies demonstrated that game playing resulted in greater willingness to help and greater role-taking." (Peng et al., 2010, p. 735). Although these results appear promising, one could argue that the willingness to donate or support shortly after the game play session does not entirely mirror the transformational change and that the comparison to other target groups is missing. In addition, it would have been of interest to compare the game experience with other media forms like critical documentaries or personal reports by victims and test the use of instructional support. Finally, further investigations on a qualitative level could have showed *how* and *if* players changed their frames of reference patterns through playing the game on a long-term scale. Thus, this study is one of the first educational investigating transformational learning in games that reaches beyond transfer of knowledge or skills. To develop a deeper understanding of the potential and limits of serious games, more studies on the transformative impact of serious learning in games is needed. So what conclusions can we draw from these empirical insights and theoretical reflections?

4.5 Conclusion: "Serious" Learning in Serious Games

When we speak of the learning impacts of serious games we have to differ between different levels of learning processes. Based on Bateson's approach, learning can be understood as an experience-based and situated process of change. In serious games, we can differentiate between basic learning *in* games, as acquiring information, collecting data and reacting to stimulus. On a second level, players learn *through* playing in the context of the game. They relate the collected data to the framing of the game and choose between different actions and possibilities. On a third level, the players' learning processes reaches *beyond* the game space and the frames of reference patterns are restructured and recontextualised in real life contexts. Hereby a transformative learning process is set in motion, in which the players explore new perspectives and develop new concepts of themselves, others and the world that they connect to real life circumstances. This form of learning is *serious* and has a deep and meaningful impact on the player's life. If games aim at changing the players' perspectives, as many serious games do, they are trying to foster learning on this *serious* level. While most studies research the transfer of behavior, of knowledge, literacies and skills, little is known about deep and meaningful transformative learning processes through playing serious games. Previous studies show that games offer a possibility space for transformative and serious learning and that games as a media form might have more potential to encourage players to change their perspectives and attitudes than other media. Thus, little is understood about *how* players process learning *beyond* the game space and transform their self- and worldview. Furthermore, it could be shown that the connection to the players expectations, values and beliefs appear relevant, and that *serious* learning can only be processed if the frames of reference patterns developed in the game can be transferred to real life settings. How games provoke the transfer of frames of reference patterns is the pivotal question that designers, teachers and educators have to relate to. Until today we still lack knowledge on *how* players learn on serious levels. If serious games are to encourage players to change their ways of thinking and acting, their designers and facilitators need to consider how the transformation can be inspired. Thereby, the enrichment by trainers and educators appears crucial, as many studies show (O'Neil et al., 2005; Clark, 2007; Ritterfeld et al., 2009).

Serious learning as an outcome of playing serious games cannot be guaranteed, and presently there is not enough evidence to prove that serious games are useful tools for fostering *serious* and transformative learning. Although the potential of serious games for serious learning is promising, there is a lack of quantitative data, and further qualitative research on players' experiences is needed to determine if and how players change their self- and worldview through playing serious games. As promising as the spoonful of sugar of serious games might seem for curing problems in a 'delightful way', the patient is not yet cured for sure. What is clear however is that it will take experienced and open minded educators and designers to foster *serious* learning through serious games.

References

Abt, C.A.: Serious Games. Viking, New York (1970)

Argyris, C., Schön, D.: Theory in Practice. Increasing Professional Effectiveness. Jossey-Bass, San Francisco, CA (1974)

Barab, S.A., Gresalfi, M.S., Ingram-Goble, A.: Transformational Play: Using Games to Position Person, Content, and Context. Educ. Res. **39**(7), 525–536 (2010)

Barnett, S.M., Ceci, S.J.: When and where do we apply what we learn?: A taxonomy for far transfer. Psychol. Bull. **128**(4), 612–637 (2002)

Bateson, G.: Steps to An Ecology of Mind. The University of Chicago Press, Chicago (1972)

Berger, J.G.: Dancing on the threshold of meaning: Recognizing and understanding the growing edge. J. Transformative Educ. **2**(4), 336–351 (2004)

Bloom B.S.: Taxonomy of Educational Objectives, Handbook I: The Cognitive Domain. David McKay Co Inc, New York (1956)

Buck, G.: Lernen und Erfahrung – Epagogik. Zum Begriff der didaktischen Induktion. Wissenschaftliche Buchgesellschaft, Darmstadt (1989)

Clark, R.E.: Learning from serious games? Arguments, evidence, and research suggestions. Educ. Technol. **7**, 56–59 (2007)

Egenfeldt-Nielsen, S., Smith, J.H., Tosca, S.: Thoughts on learning in games and designing educational computer games. http://game-research.com/index.php/articles/thoughts-on-learning-in-games-and-designing-educational-computer-games (2006). Accessed 01 June 2011

Fröbel, F.: Die Menschenerziehung, die Erziehungs-, Unterrichts- und Lehrkunst, angestrebt in der allgemeinen deutschen Erziehungsanstalt zu Keilhau. Verlag Erziehungsanstalt zu Keilhau, Keilhau (1826)

Gagné, R.M.: Instructional Technologies: Foundations. Lawrence Erlbaum, Hillsdale (1987)

Gee, J.P.: What Video Games Have to Teach Us About Learning and Literacy. Palgrave/Macmillan, New York (2003)

Gee, J.P.: Learning and games. In: Salen, K. (ed.) The Ecology of Games: Connecting Youth, Games, and Learning, pp. 21–40. MIT Press, Cambridge, MA (2008)

Gee, J.P., Hayes, E.R.: Women and Gaming: The Sims and 21st Century Learning. Palgrave Macmillan, New York (2010)

Kato, P.M., Cole, S.W., Bradlyn A.S., Pollock B.H.: A video game improves behavioral outcomes in adolescents and young adults with cancer: A randomized trial. Pediatrics **122**(2), e305–e317 (2008)

Klimmt, C.: Serious games and social change. Why they (should) work. In: Ritterfeld, U., Cody, M., Vorderer, P. (eds.) Serious Games. Mechanism and Effects, pp. 248–270. Routledge, New York (2009)

Kovan, J., Dirkx, J.M.: "Being called awake": The role of transformative learning in the lives of environmental activists. Adult Educ. Q. **53**(2), 99–118 (2003)

Locke, J.: An Essay Concerning Human Understanding. William Tegg, London (1689)

Mayer, R.E., Wittrock, M.C.: Problem-solving transfer. In: Berliner, D.C., Calfee, R.C. (eds.) Handbook of Educational Psychology, pp. 47–62. Simon & Schuster Macmillan, New York (1996)

McGonigal, J.: Reality is Broken. Why Games Make Us Better and How They Can Change the World. The Penguin Press, New York (2011)

Mezirow, J.: Contemporary paradigms of learning. Adult Educ. Q. **46**(3), 158–172 (1996)

Mezirow, J.: How critical reflection triggers transformative learning. In: Jarvis, P. (ed.) Adult and Continuing Education: Teaching, Learning and Research, pp. 199–214. Taylor & Francis, London (2003)

Mezirow, J.: An overview of transformative learning. In: Illeris, K. (ed.) Contemporary Theories of Learning, pp. 90–105. Routledge, London (2010)

Mitchell, A., Savill-Smith, C.: The use of computer and video games for learning. http://www.lsda.org.uk/files/PDF/1529.pdf (2004). Accessed 01 June 2011

Mitgutsch, K.: Lernen durch Enttäuschung. Eine pädagogische Skizze. Braumüller Verlag, Vienna (eng.: Learning through resistant experiences) (2009)

Mitgutsch, K.: Playful learning experiences. Meaningful learning patterns in players' biographies. Int. J. Games Comput. Mediated Simulat. **3**(3), 54–68 (2011a)

Mitgutsch, K.: Learning through play – a delicate matter. Experience-based recursive learning in computer games. In: Fromme, J., Unger, A. (eds.) Computer Games and New Media Cultures: A Handbook of Digital Games Studies. (2011b, in print)

Montessori, M.: Il Metodo della Pedagogia Scientifica Applicato all'Educatione Infantile nelle Casa dei Bambini. Città di Castello, Perugia (1909)
Novak, D., Gowin, D.B.: Learning How to Learn. Cambridge University Press, Cambridge (1984)
O'Neil, H.F., Wainess, R., Baker, E.L.: Classification of learning outcomes: Evidence from the computer games literature. Curriculum J. **16**(4), 455–474 (2005)
O'Sullivan, E., Morrell, A., O'Connor, M.A. (eds.): Expanding the Boundaries of Transformative Learning. Palgrave, New York (2002)
Parchman, S.W., Ellis, J.A., Christinaz, D., Vogel, M.: An evaluation of three computerbased instructional strategies in basic electricity and electronics training. Mil. Psychol. **12**(1), 73–87 (2000)
Pavlov, I.P.: Lectures on Conditioned Reflexes. International Publishers, New York (1928)
Peng, W., Lee, M., Heeter, C.: The effects of a serious game on role-taking and willingness to help. J. Commun. **60**(4), 723–742 (2010)
Piaget, J.: Der Aufbau der Wirklichkeit beim Kinde. Klett, Stuttgart (1974)
Ritterfeld, U., Cody, M., Vorderer, P. (eds.): Serious Games. Mechanism and Effects. Routledge, New York (2009)
Rousseau, J.-J.: Émile. Dent, London (1762)
Salen, K.: Gaming literacies: A game design study in action. J. Educ. Multimedia Hypermedia **16**(3), 301–322 (2007)
Schwartz, D.L., Blair, K.P., Biswas, G., Leelawong, K., Davis, J.: Animations of thought: Interactivity in the teachable agent paradigm. In: Lowe, R., Schnotz, W. (eds.) Learning with Animation: Research and Implications for Design, pp. 114–140. University Press, Cambridge (2007)
Shaffer, D.: How Computer Games Help Children Learn. Palgrave Macmillan, New York (2006)
Shaffer, D., Squire, K.D., Halverson, R., Gee, J.P.: Video games and the future of learning. Phi Delta Kappan **87**(2), 104–111 (2005)
Skinner, B.F.: About Behaviourism. Alfred Knopf, New York (1974)
Squire, K.D.: From content to context: Video games as designed experiences. Educ. Res. **35**(8), 19–29 (2006)
Steinkuehler, C.: Massively multiplayer online gaming as a constellation of literacy practices. eLearning **4**(3), 297–318 (2007)
Suits, B.: The Grasshopper. Game, Life and Utopia. Broadview Press, Ontario (2005)
Tate, R., Haritatos, J., Cole, S.: HopeLab's approach to re-mission. Int. J. Learn. Media **1**(1), 29–35 (2009)
Thorndike, E.L.: The Fundamentals of Learning. Teachers College Press, New York (1932)
Tkacz, S.: Learning map interpretation: Skill acquisition and underlying abilities. J. Environ. Psychol. **18**(3), 237–249 (1998)
Wolf, M.J.P., Perron, B. (eds.): The Video Game Theory Reader. Routledge, London (2003)
Wu, S.: Reducing unproductive learning activities in serious games for second language acquisition. Dissertation. University of Southern California (2008)

Games

Global Conflicts: Sweatshops (Serious Game Interactive/Global Conflicts, 2009)
Darfur is dying (mtvU, 2006)
Ayiti: the Cost of Life (Gamelab/Global Kids 4 Keeps)
Re-Mission (HopeLabe/Realtime Associates, 2004)

Part II
Theories and Reviews

Chapter 5
Social Flow and Learning in Digital Games: A Conceptual Model and Research Agenda

Christine M. Bachen and Chad Raphael

5.1 Introduction

The psychological account of enjoyment known as flow theory (Csikszentmihalyi, 1990) has been highly influential on the design and research of game-based learning. When people achieve flow they enter into states of intense concentration, exhibit a strong sense of control, and experience an activity as intrinsically rewarding. Games that foster a sense of flow are assumed to be more enjoyable, increasing players' engagement and motivation, and thereby leading to increased learning (Kiili, 2005; Shute et al., 2009). The focus on inducing flow has shaped thinking about game-based learning at each stage of its development, from early educational games (Bowman, 1982), to commercial edutainment (Chen, 2007; Jones, 1998), to today's "serious games" (Egenfeldt-Nielsen, 2007; Garzotto, 2007; Inal and Cagiltay, 2007).

While most versions of gameflow theory focus exclusively on the relationship of the individual to the game, some scholars have begun to incorporate social interaction into their models of gameflow (Choi and Kim, 2004; Choi et al., 2007; Fu et al., 2009; Garzotto, 2007; Jegers, 2007; Jerome et al., 2006; Sweetser and Wyeth, 2005). This is a response both to longstanding observations of how even single-player games are often played in a social context and to the rise of genres in which social play is central to the game, such as networked multiplayer games and pervasive games (which integrate play in the virtual and physical worlds, often among groups). Conceptualizing the social dimension of game play is also of growing importance to address the current aims of game-based learning theory, which prioritizes cooperative learning methods and outcomes (e.g., Gee, 2003; Jenkins, 2006; Steinkuehler, 2004).

In this chapter, we synthesize the literature on games, flow, and cooperative learning to conceptualize social gameflow and propose a model of the role it can play in the learning process. This model aims to capture the distinct opportunities for

C.M. Bachen (✉)
Communication Department, Santa Clara University, Santa Clara, CA 95053-0277, USA
e-mail: cbachen@scu.edu

M. Ma et al. (eds.), *Serious Games and Edutainment Applications*,
DOI 10.1007/978-1-4471-2161-9_5, © Springer-Verlag London Limited 2011

collective flow in games and the contexts in which they are played, and what flow might mean for game-based learning. We conclude by suggesting a research agenda that can test this model in ways that can guide future inquiry and inform game design.

5.2 Flow Theory and Game-Based Learning

The concept of flow stems from the psychologist Mihaly Csikszentmihalyi's theory of happiness. In his early formulation, the flow state was described as an optimal experience that is "so gratifying that people are willing to do it for its own sake, with little concern for what they will get out of it, even when it is difficult or dangerous" (1990, p. 71). These experiences can be found across a wide variety of activities, such as reading novels, composing music, engaging in sports, or playing games. Above all, "[t]he defining feature of flow is intense experiential involvement in moment-to-moment activity" (Csikszentmihalyi et al., 2005, p. 600). Csikszentmihalyi has identified eight elements that often characterize the flow state of consciousness:

> (a) a clear sense of what has to be done moment by moment; (b) immediate feedback as to how well one is doing; (c) an intense concentration of attention; (d) a balance between opportunities for action (challenges) and capacity to act (skills); (e) exclusion of irrelevant content from consciousness; (f) a sense of control over the activity; (g) a distortion of sense of time – usually hours pass by in minutes; and (h) a feeling that the activity is intrinsically rewarding, or worth doing for its own sake (2000, p. 381).

More recently, Csikszentmihalyi et al. (2005) have suggested that three of these elements (clear goals, feedback, and balance between challenges and skills) are best understood as *conditions* for achieving flow, while the other elements comprise the *experience* of flow. Although most of the flow research has focused on individual activities, the theory is compatible with social experience. Csikszentmihalyi has observed that "interactions have many of the characteristics of flow" (1997, p. 42) and that if we recognize that we share common goals with others and invest our attention in their goals, "it is possible to experience the flow that comes from optimal interaction" (p. 81). Other scholars have added to this conceptualization, identifying the antecedents (or conditions) for flow, the experience of flow, and expected outcomes such as learning and changes in attitude and behavior (e.g., Kiili, 2005).

Most efforts to integrate flow with other theories of mediated enjoyment have been focused squarely on the relationship of the individual to the medium. Examples include efforts to meld flow with game design theory (Chen, 2007; Jones, 1998), uses and gratifications theory (Sherry, 2004), information processing (or schema) theory (Cowley et al., 2008; Douglas and Hargadon, 2000), psychophysiological theory (Jerome et al., 2006; Mandryk et al., 2006) and neurophysiological theory (Weber et al., 2009). Adaptations of flow theory to games also tend to focus exclusively on how the flow state emerges from the individual player-game relationship rather than addressing how flow might be shaped as well by the social dynamics of play. In part, this individualistic focus is a legacy of the dominant single-player game design model of the 1970s–1990s, but it also involves an assumption that game play and learning are inherently solitary activities. This assumption is less tenable than ever before. For example, a recent national survey of American adolescents found that just 24 percent of teen gamers *only* play games alone, while the remaining 76 percent play games with others in the same room or online at least some of the time (Lenhart et al., 2008).

The rise of online multi-player games and pervasive games means that newer forms of game play are inherently social. While traditional digital games have always been played in small groups, contemporary games make social engagement central to their goals, rules, and roles. Scholars of game-based learning have especially remarked on the sociability of networked games. For example, Garzotto contends that, in games such as these, "social interaction represents both a vehicle to learn collaboration attitudes and skills, and a powerful *motivator* to engage in educational content" (2007, p. 3). Choi et al. (2007) observe that players are drawn to online role-playing games by "the shared experience: the collaborative nature of most tasks and the rewards of achieving them collectively" (p. 592). Jegers notes that social interaction is also at the heart of pervasive game design, because " [i]nstead of presenting the players with fixed scenarios, pervasive games make use of the social factors and creativity of the players by giving them some overall goal(s) and tools for interaction and then leaving the field open for the players" (2008, p. 5).

The social turn in gameflow research is also a response to educational theorists' increasing recognition that social knowledge and skills are valuable learning outcomes and that cooperative learning is effective pedagogy. As much of the educational system has shifted to prepare students for careers in today's service and knowledge industries, schools increasingly teach the kinds of social capacities valued in contemporary workplaces, such as teamwork, communication, and management. Sawyer (2006) summarizes the related transition in educational theory. He observes that traditional psychologists have tended to "focus on individual learning and assume that all knowledge is individual knowledge" (p. 574). However, educational research increasingly recognizes "the importance of learning in groups, in part because most knowledge work takes place in complexly organized teams ... [and because a] full understanding of learning requires a combination of individual cognitive analysis and social interactional analysis" (p. 574).

In this context, educational research informed by broad a range of theories – including constructivism, communities of practice, situated learning, and project-based learning – finds that cooperative learning is often more effective and enjoyable than individual learning (for recent summaries of the empirical literature, see Johnson and Johnson, 2008; Stevens, 2008). Cooperative learning involves "students working together to maximize their own and each other's learning (i.e., achieve shared learning goals)" (Johnson and Johnson, 2008, p. 404).[1] This kind

[1] While cooperative learning has sometimes been distinguished from collaborative learning, "the two terms ... are increasingly interchangeable and synonymous" (Johnson and Johnson, 2008, p. 404) and we treat them as such in this chapter.

of learning is often contrasted with competitive learning, which involves "students working against each other to achieve an academic goal such as a grade that only one or a few students can attain" (p. 404), and individualistic learning, which refers to "students working by themselves to accomplish learning goals unrelated to those of the other students" (p. 404). Johnson and Johnson (2008) summarize a robust body of research conducted over the past three decades, which has found that well-designed cooperative learning experiences effectively foster higher-order thinking and social competency skills. This seems especially to be true of learning with, and about, computer technologies. For example, many studies indicate that students have more positive attitudes toward computer-based learning when they collaborate than when they work individually and that students experience more enjoyment when using computers to collaborate than when they collaborate without computers. Students seem to learn to use computer hardware and software better when they do so cooperatively. In addition, recent research on flow and education (not involving games) has found that group learning is one contextual factor that may predict flow (e.g., Shernoff and Csikszentmihalyi, 2009). This is not surprising because several elements of successful cooperative learning experiences overlap with flow theory, including the articulation of clear goals, the presence of ample and useful feedback to the learner, and the learner's experience of intrinsic motivation to engage in an activity.

Much recent theorizing about the value of digital game-based learning also recognizes the value of cooperative learning techniques and social learning goals. For example, games theorists influenced by communities of practice theory have emphasized that successful networked educational games teach by creating learning communities: "Designing learning environments is not merely a matter of getting the curricular material right but is crucially also a matter of getting the situated, emergent community structures and practices 'right'" (Steinkuehler, 2004, p. 527). Articulations of necessary skills and knowledge in a digital culture are highly social, including the ability to engage in collective or distributed learning, negotiate diverse communities and perspectives, solve problems collaboratively, and communicate in multiple media (e.g., Gee, 2003; Jenkins, 2006).

Several clarifications are in order. First, our conceptual model of social gameflow aims to account for how game designs and contexts of play (face-to-face or networked) that foster social interaction can induce the flow state in individuals. The unit of analysis remains the individual (in a social context), not the group. While there is growing interest in researching "group flow" in contexts such as musical performances, business work teams, and the like (e.g., Sawyer, 2007), conceptualizing and measuring group flow is a distinct project that presents challenges warranting longer treatment than can be given here. Second, we are not claiming that *all* games must foster social flow in order to lead to learning. Third, we are not claiming that *all* games must be played cooperatively in order to be effective educationally, nor that competition cannot induce flow and learning. It is important to note that within our model of social gameflow, group members may cooperate with each other, while competing with other groups.

5.3 Social Play and Flow

Games scholars have begun to add social interaction variables to the empirical research on flow and learning. This emerging area of interest suggests a number of promises and pitfalls for the design and educational application of games. This work also points to a need for a richer conceptual model of how social interaction in games might promote the flow state in ways that lead to learning.

Studies of game play using a variety of game genres played in a range of contexts suggest that social gaming and flow are, at the very least, not incompatible. Surveys of players' motivations and experiences have found significant positive relationships between social interaction and the flow state in several genres of online games, including multi-user dungeons (MUDs), massively multiplayer online role-playing games (MMORPGs), and real-time strategy (RTS) games (Choi and Kim, 2004; Kim et al., 2005; Voiskounsky et al., 2004). A similar relationship, although not uniform for all players, has been found in small-scale classroom and experimental studies of game play that employ a mix of observational and survey methods (Choi et al., 2007; Garzotto, 2007; Inal and Cagiltay, 2007; Jerome et al., 2006; Weibel et al., 2007).

However, some scholars have raised a concern that social interaction may be a potential barrier to the flow state. Sweetser and Wyeth (2005) hypothesized that social engagement, especially through live chat features, may interrupt individuals' immersion in play, which is a cardinal element of flow. In an observational classroom study of children who played single-player games in groups, Inal and Cagiltay (2007) found that when children entered the flow state they stopped helping their friends play the game because they "were only thinking of passing to the next level of the game or achieving the given task at these times, and they were less aware of both themselves and their friends" (p. 459). However, this finding may be an artifact of the study conditions, especially that the games were not designed to require interaction in order to achieve the game goal, the games involved time limits on a player's ability to pass a level (which is less conducive to discussing strategy with others), and the participants were children aged 7 to 9 years (who may be less adept than teens and adults at expanding their attention to include both the game and the group). In many online games played in teams, such as *World of Warcraft*, social interaction is more necessary to achieving players' collective goals. Concerns about social engagement obstructing learning are also based on the assumption that flow is a mental state in which enjoyment is dependent on *uninterrupted* immersion. It may be that immersion punctuated by social reflection on game play is helpful for players to learn a game and strengthen ties with co-players, and therefore increases individual enjoyment and motivation to play, heightening the flow state when players return to the game. For example, several game scholars suggest that informal face-to-face discussion of games during breaks from play and online meta-gaming (information-sharing and debate about games on related web sites) provide enjoyable insider knowledge about how games work and create community among players (Jenkins, 2006; Barab et al., 2005). There is also the possibility that players experience immersion *in social reflection* on the game through engaging in discussion about it.

Other studies have begun to illuminate how social interaction may be an asset for flow rather than a liability. Garzotto's (2007) classroom study of an educational game played in online and face-to-face groups found that elementary school students rated their experience highly across all measures of flow, including three social interaction measures: connection (co-presence and shared identity with other group members), cooperation (with online and co-present partners), and competition (with other groups). A study by Choi et al. (2007) suggests the importance of the type of social interaction structured by a game. This research also offers a promising example of how the literature on cooperative learning can inform gameflow research. In an experimental study, the authors varied a game's level of task interdependency (which requires players to cooperate to complete tasks successfully) and reward interdependency (which distributes rewards to players equally based on the group's success, rather than to individuals based on individual success). They found that when the game involved high task-interdependency, players experienced greater flow and perceived themselves as having learned to play the game better when reward-interdependency was also high. Conversely, in the low task-interdependency condition players reported greater flow and learning to play the game when reward-interdependency was also low. However, objective measures of the players' performance in the game did not confirm the player's self-perceptions. The lessons of the study were that matching levels of task and reward interdependency may be necessary for inducing flow, but may not be sufficient to guarantee that players will learn more.

This research still leaves much to explain about *how* social interaction in games promotes flow for educational ends. With few exceptions, these studies do not identify specifically the social game features and play contexts that are most effective at generating flow that leads to learning. Most of the research designs incorporate social interaction as a single variable or dimension among many others that may explain the individual player's experience and performance.

5.3.1 The Gameflow Model

Sweetser and Wyeth's (2005) Gameflow model, a heuristic scale for game designers that provides a checklist of optimal design elements for inducing flow, has been cited widely. Social interaction is present but fairly peripheral to this model, appearing as just one of eight dimensions. The social dimension includes several criteria, from which five variables can be derived: games should support competition, cooperation, social interaction between players (such as chat functions), social communities within the game, and social communities outside the game. While the authors offer a very useful translation of each dimension of flow theory to game design, the Gameflow model has not yet been used to distinguish whether social interaction variables are more or less important than each other, or than non-social game features, for inducing flow. Because the model does not aim to link the flow state to larger educational outcomes, the authors do not include measures of learning beyond the dimension of "player skills," which indicate how well the game teaches players to succeed at playing the game, not whether players achieve other learning outcomes. The model also does not allow researchers to draw clear connections between even this limited realm of learning and the social aspects of a game.

5.3.2 The EGameFlow Scale

Fu et al. (2009) adapted Sweetser and Wyeth's model to create an "EGameFlow" scale that can measure users' experience of educational games. This scale is the most developed attempt to measure gameflow, social interaction, and learning in a single instrument. Fu et al. validated the scale by administering it to college students who had played four educational games. The social interaction dimension contains six items, adapted from Sweetser and Wyeth:

I feel cooperative toward other classmates.
I strongly collaborate with other classmates.
The cooperation in the game is helpful to the learning.
The game supports social interaction between players (chat, etc).
The game supports communities within the game.
The game supports communities outside the game.

The authors also transform Sweetser and Wyeth's dimension of "player skill" into "knowledge improvement," which contains five items that focus more on the educational subject matter of the game:

The game increases my knowledge.
I catch the basic ideas of the knowledge taught.
I try to apply the knowledge in the game.
The game motivates the player to integrate the knowledge taught.
I want to know more about the knowledge taught.

The EGameFlow model is a welcome step toward connecting social interaction, flow, and learning for user studies. However, the choice of items in the social interaction and educational dimensions do not appear to be motivated by any particular theory of social learning. Many of the educational theories that prize cooperative learning mentioned above involve more active and expansive notions of learning than simply the acquisition and application of knowledge (including the mutual co-construction and practice of knowledge, skills, dispositions, and learning communities). These theories also suggest more specific conditions for social learning, such as task and reward interdependency, which are not measured in the EGameFlow scale. In fact, only one of the EGameFlow items ("the cooperation in the game is helpful to the learning") links social interplay with learning outcomes. Thus, a game might score well on both the social and learning dimensions, but the EGameFlow instrument cannot tell us much about whether and how the opportunities for social play contributed to the users' learning. For example, participants in the Fu et al. study gave low ratings to the social interactivity of the games they played, probably because some of the games appeared to offer few opportunities for social play and were played individually. While the social interaction items cohered into a scale, it is not clear that players found the social dimension of the games affected their learning either positively or negatively.

If we wish to inform the design and usage of multi-player and pervasive educational games, we need more refined concepts of flow that emerges in social play, motivated by theory and research on cooperative learning. Thus, we aim to develop a richer conceptualization of the users' experience of social gameflow that builds upon the nascent research into the relationship of flow, social interaction, and learning in games. This conceptualization can be used to learn more about how different kinds of social interaction in today's games and play contexts may contribute to flow and learning.

5.4 Conceptualizing Social Gameflow

Table 5.1 presents a comparison of the dimensions of Sweetser and Wyeth's (2005) original concept of GameFlow for traditional computer games, Fu et al.'s (2009) EGameFlow for e-learning games, and our Social GameFlow. (We have reordered some of the dimensions of the other two models, but the wording of each is taken verbatim from the originals.) Our aim here is not to conceptualize all aspects of flow in games, but the dimensions most relevant to *social* flow so that research can evaluate its particular contribution to learning. Our conceptualization draws from the literature on games and flow, as well as on cooperative learning, and would be applicable to the kinds of e-learning games that interested Fu and colleagues. However, it also applies to games developed for broader, not just educational, purposes – we see learning as an outcome across games, not just a property of some games. As we will argue in more detail later, we see the achievement of social flow as dependent not only upon game design but also upon the context in which games are played. We aim to account for the elements of social game play as experienced by the user, which is the product of both the internal properties of games and the external setting in which they are played. Because our focus is on clarifying the nature of the user's *experience*, we do not specify in great detail what game features we think are likely to provoke flow. However, a clearer model of the experience will allow future research to draw stronger connections between the flow state and particular game elements and play contexts.

5.4.1 Interdependent Goals and Rewards

Elaborating upon the importance of clear goals in the original theory of flow, we suggest that players who experience social gameflow are likely to perceive clear and authentic game goals for the group over and above that which can be achieved by

Table 5.1 Dimensions of flow in games

GameFlow (Sweetser and Wyeth, 2005)	*EGameFlow* (Fu et al., 2009)	*Social GameFlow*
Clear Goals: Provide the player with clear goals at appropriate times.	*Goal Clarity:* Tasks in the game should be clearly explained at the beginning.	*Interdependent Goals and Rewards:* Players recognize clear and authentic goals that can only be achieved by a group; players sense that goal interdependence is matched with reward interdependence.
Feedback: Players must receive appropriate feedback at appropriate times.	*Feedback:* Feedback allows a player to determine the gap between the current stage of knowledge and the knowledge required for ultimate completion of the game's task.	*Feedback:* Players feel that they receive clear feedback at appropriate times to the group about its actions in the game and about individual members' contributions.
Challenge: Be sufficiently challenging and match the player's skill level.	*Challenge:* Offer challenges that fit the player's level of skills; the difficulty of these challenges should change in accordance with the increase in the player's skill level.	*Challenge:* Players perceive challenges of different levels that match the group members' collective knowledge and skills, including their collaborative abilities.
Control: Players should feel a sense of control over their actions in the game.	*Autonomy:* the learner should enjoy taking the initiative in game-playing and asserting total control over his or her choices in the game.	*Control:* Players have a sense of control over their individual decisions, their groups' strategies and actions within the game, and their group's influence on the gameworld.
Concentration: Games should require concentration and the player should be able to concentrate on the game.	*Concentration:* Provide activities that encourage the player's concentration while minimizing stress from learning overload, which may lower the player's concentration on the game.	*Concentration:* Players are able to focus sustained attention and reflection on the group's interaction.
Immersion: Players should experience deep but effortless involvement in the game.	*Immersion:* The game should lead the player into a state of immersion.	*Immersion:* Players experience periods of deep involvement in group play.
Social Interaction: Games should support and create opportunities for social interaction.	*Social Interaction:* Tasks in the game should become a means for players to interact socially.	*Intrinsic Reward:* Players value social play and learning as worth doing for their own sakes.
Player Skills: Games must support player skill development and mastery.	*Knowledge Improvement:* the game should increase the player's level of knowledge and skills while meeting the goal of the curriculum.	*Achievement of Learning Goals:* Players sense that they can achieve the game's learning goals.

any player alone. This is also a response to educational theories that value cooperative learning, which find that "it is important for well-structured cooperative learning to have a group goal and individual accountability" (Stevens, 2008, p. 187). Players are more likely to contribute fully to the group's pursuit of its goals, rather than acting as free riders, if each player's contributions are transparent to other players and players experience consequences based on their individual contributions. If they are to matter to players, group goals must be authentic – integral, not peripheral, to succeeding in the game and mastering its subject. This view is grounded in theories of constructivist learning (Jonassen, 1991) and situated learning in communities of practice (Lave and Wenger, 1991), which posit that authentic tasks set in meaningful contexts increase motivation to learn. This approach has inspired social game designers to emphasize that shared learning goals must be central to the gameplay and educational aims (Barab et al., 2005) and that individual contributions should be identifiable (even as the game offers supports to students who struggle) (Padilla Zea et al., 2009).

Social interdependence theory is especially relevant for this dimension of social gameflow. The theory suggests that "the way in which goals are structured determines how participants interact, and those interactions pattern the outcomes of the situation" (Johnson and Johnson, 2008, p. 406). Interdependence may be negative in a state of competition, where individuals perceive that they achieve their ends only if their competitors fail to reach their ends. Positive interdependence arises in a state of cooperation, in which "individuals perceive that they can reach their goals if and only if the other individuals with whom they are cooperatively linked also reach their goals" (p. 406). In some single-player games, no interdependence exists. But in games that involve groups (such as guilds or teams) working together against other groups, both positive interdependence (within one's group) and negative interdependence (against other groups) exist.

Games that provoke the flow state through social play are likely to foster positive interdependence. In other educational contexts, research indicates that this interdependence may include evidence of "mutual help and assistance, exchange of needed resources, effective communication, mutual influence, trust, and constructive management of conflict" (p. 406). The research indicates that positive interdependence tends to promote three results: "*substitutability* (i.e., the degree to which the actions of one person substitute for the actions of another person), *inducibility* (i.e., the openness to being influenced and to influencing others), and *positive cathexis* (i.e., the investment of positive psychological energy in objects outside of oneself)" (p. 406). The last result especially dovetails with the flow state.

The research on social interaction in the classroom cited above finds that student learning in groups is higher than it is in individual work only when positive interdependence is clearly structured, especially by making goals and rewards highly interdependent. Similarly, Choi et al. (2007), as discussed above, found that alignment of common goals and rewards may be necessary (but not sufficient) for improved learning in social gameplay. In addition, Padilla Zea et al. (2009) suggest that groups are more likely to experience interdependence in games if they share a common lifespan (rather than changing membership during the game) and evaluation (such as a group score).

5.4.2 Feedback

Expanding upon flow theory's requirement that individuals can obtain clear feedback on their activities, we suggest that social gameflow likely depends on players' sense that they are receiving clear feedback at appropriate times to the group about its actions in the game and about individual members' contributions. In addition, cooperative learning research finds that feedback on individual performance is crucial for maintaining each member's accountability to the group, which is associated with higher learning gains (Johnson and Johnson, 2008, pp. 407, 409). The literature on flow in face-to-face learning groups also suggests that mutual feedback among group members is important for successful group action (Sawyer, 2007).

5.4.3 Challenge

Achieving social gameflow likely depends also on players perceiving challenges of different levels that match the group's knowledge and skills, including their collaborative skills. One of the hallmarks of flow theory is its sensitivity to the importance of the right fit between challenges and individual skills. If an activity is too easy for the player she grows bored, while if it is too hard she grows frustrated. This insight has led designers to create adaptive games that continually adjust difficulty levels to individual players' skills. In social gameplay, flow is likely to depend upon a good fit not only between challenges and individuals' abilities, but also with the group's collective knowledge and skills, including its members' capacity to cooperate. Social gameplay that scaffolds learning, including learning about collaboration, is likely to be more successful at inducing enjoyment.

Indeed, adding a social dimension to gameplay raises the level of challenge, compared to individual play. "Cooperative learning is inherently more complex than competitive or individualistic learning because students have to simultaneously engage in taskwork and teamwork," yet classroom studies suggest that more teamwork skills lead to more quality and quantity of learning (Johnson and Johnson, 2008, p. 407). An encouraging body of research finds that learning is equally likely among cooperative groups made up of people with heterogeneous abilities and groups with homogeneous abilities (Johnson and Johnson, 2008). This is because in heterogeneous groups advanced students learn in part by teaching their less advanced partners, who benefit from cognitive apprenticeship to more expert learners.

Once again, several educational theories lead us in this direction. Sociocultural learning theory emphasizes the need to introduce new material and skills that are within learners' zone of proximal development, or the range of achievement they can reach with curricular and social support (Vygotsky, 1978). Alternatively, Piagetian theory emphasizes the construction of knowledge from constructive conflict, which spurs the development of cognitive flexibility, problem-solving, and conflict-resolution skills (Piaget, 1962). Similarly, game designers such as Padilla Zea and her colleagues (2009) have called for games to foster online and face-to-face interaction that develop group skills, such as leadership, consensus-building, negotiation, debate, and meta-cognitive abilities to reflect on and evaluate the group's process.

5.4.4 Control

In response to flow theory's concern that individuals have a sense of control over their activities, we posit that social gameflow includes players having a sense of control over their individual decisions, their groups' strategies and actions within the game, and the group's ability to influence the world of the game. The most basic aspect of control is a sense of command over the interface and input devices (Sweetser and Wyeth, 2005). Social play should also enable each player to feel that she can influence the pace of the game, rather than forcing some players to wait until others have finished an activity (Garzotto, 2007). In addition, we posit that individuals cannot feel a necessary sense of agency in social gameplay unless they feel they can influence their own decisions (such as their choice of role) and their group's strategies and actions. Group members who participate against their will or who feel little efficacy within the group are unlikely to enjoy the game. In addition, players need to sense that their actions can influence the gameworld if they are to play it fully, perhaps multiple times, in order to enjoy discovering the consequences of their decisions and the construction of their own knowledge (Gee, 2003).

5.4.5 Concentration

While the original theory of flow includes the dimension of intense concentration, social gameflow likely depends upon players' ability to concentrate and reflect on group interaction, not simply on their own individual actions in the game or distractions posed by the game or play context. Gameflow theory posits that "the more concentration a task requires in terms of attention and workload, the more absorbing it will be" (Sweetser and Wyeth, 2005, p. 4). Social games and play contexts make group interaction in pursuit of group goals the focal point. Under such conditions, enjoyment and learning are likely derived primarily from the social elements of the game. Social gameflow is more likely if the game interface, roles, rules, and goals, as well as the social and physical setting in which the game is played, focus attention on the group activity. Non-game classroom research suggests that group learning, as compared with individual learning, presents both drawbacks and advantages for maintaining focused effort. While group members may distract each other with social-oriented rather than task-oriented activity, the group can also act to keep easily distracted members more on task than they would be if left alone (Corno, 2001).

Social gameflow also involves players' ability to reflect on the group's interaction. Several theories of cooperative learning emphasize the importance of reflective communication within groups, for somewhat different reasons. Social interaction theory emphasizes the value of group processing for improving members' contributions to the task, teaching teamwork skills, and maintaining group cohesion (Johnson and Johnson, 2008, p. 408). Stevens (2008) identifies similar rationales in Bandura's (1977) social learning theory, which also stresses the importance of reciprocal role modeling by group members, and in sociocultural learning theory's emphasis on how less advanced learners benefit from cognitive apprenticeship to more advanced peers (Vygotsky, 1978). Stevens also notes that generative learning theory suggests the importance of learners explaining knowledge to others to solidify their grasp of it, which helps to explain why more advanced students gain as much or more than less-advanced students in cooperative learning groups. These theories have motivated greater attention to designing opportunities for group reflection on learning through exposure to mentors and membership in learning guilds in innovative networked educational games, such as *Quest Atlantis* (Barab et al., 2006).

5.4.6 Immersion

Whereas initial gameflow studies focused on whether the player was continually immersed in individual play, social gameflow involves periods of immersion in group play. Gameflow studies have observed group members in this state of reduced awareness of self, of surroundings, and of time passing (e.g., Inal and Cagiltay, 2007). Some research on computer-based learning (navigational and map-reading problem-solving and writing) suggests cooperative learners (compared to learners in individualistic and competitive conditions) exhibited greater signs of social flow: they talked less with the teacher and more to each other, and they made more task-oriented and fewer social-oriented statements (Johnson and Johnson, 2008, p. 409). However, immersion may not need to be continuous, as is often assumed in individualistic versions of gameflow theory. In social play aimed at cooperative learning, immersion probably needs to be punctuated by critical reflection on the group process and individual contributions to it, in order to improve members' learning and the group's performance. Because survey items in prior gameflow research tend to focus on individual absorption in the game, new measures are needed to capture immersion in social interaction, for example, by studying the group interactions in multiplayer games. In pervasive games, in which players use mobile computing devices to engage in social learning in the virtual and physical worlds simultaneously, immersion should not be thought of as including loss of awareness of surroundings, but as the ability to switch focus seamlessly between the virtual and physical worlds (Jegers, 2007).

5.4.7 Intrinsic Reward

Flow theory indicates that individuals feel a sense of intrinsic reward from engaging in peak experiences. Social gameflow fosters a sense among players that *group* play and learning are worth doing for their own sakes, regardless of other rewards offered by the game. Cooperative learning research increasingly finds that this kind of learning inspires more intrinsic motivation to learn, compared with competitive or individualistic learning (Johnson and Johnson, 2008, p. 408). Educational theorists, like contemporary employers, increasingly prioritize the ability to "play well with others" as an end in itself. In particular, communities of practice theory elevates learning goals that are less focused on products that demonstrate mastery and more on processes: the ability to work intentionally, actively, and communally (Lave and Wenger, 1991). Scholars of social games suggest that players are drawn to them primarily by the lure of connection, cooperation, and competition with others (Choi et al., 2007; Garzotto, 2007; Jegers, 2007; Lazzaro, 2004). Therefore, intrinsic enjoyment of group play seems to be an important prerequisite for learning from social games.

5.4.8 Achievement of Learning Goals

Social gameflow also depends upon players' sense that they can achieve the game's learning goals. We are not aware of any version of flow theory that posits that people enjoy an activity in which they feel they can never succeed, nor of any cooperative learning theory that claims that people learn well in a group setting if they feel they cannot meet evident learning objectives. All games present players with goals, including the goal of learning how to play the game itself. Some games have single pre-defined goals, such as amassing the highest point total or moving one's character, society, or team to an endpoint in time or space. Other games offer a menu of goals, allowing players to choose among a closed-ended number of options. For example, many geopolitical games allow players to choose to prioritize military, diplomatic, or economic success. Multiplayer games that favor social interaction, including role-playing and fantasy games, may expand the range of goals further. Yet even these games encourage players to pursue increasing levels of power, resources, or honors for their group, or to try to explore advanced narrative elements that can only be experienced by playing longer and more skillfully.

5.5 A Model of Social GameFlow and Learning

Grounded in this conceptualization of social gameflow, we offer a theoretical model for testing how social gameflow relates to learning. The previous research cited in this chapter on computer games and flow has tended to focus on whether game design features match well with individual user skills to induce flow. Only a handful of studies have tested whether flow contributes to in-game learning about how to play the game successfully. In the rare cases in which scholars have examined whether flow fosters learning that can be transferred outside the game (e.g., Fu et al., 2009), researchers have relied on limited self-reports about learning gains rather than direct measures. Figure 5.1 represents the gameflow and learning model

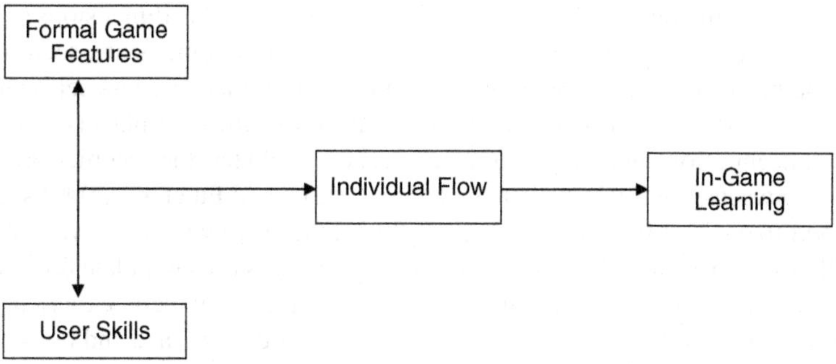

Fig. 5.1 Prior model of gameflow and learning

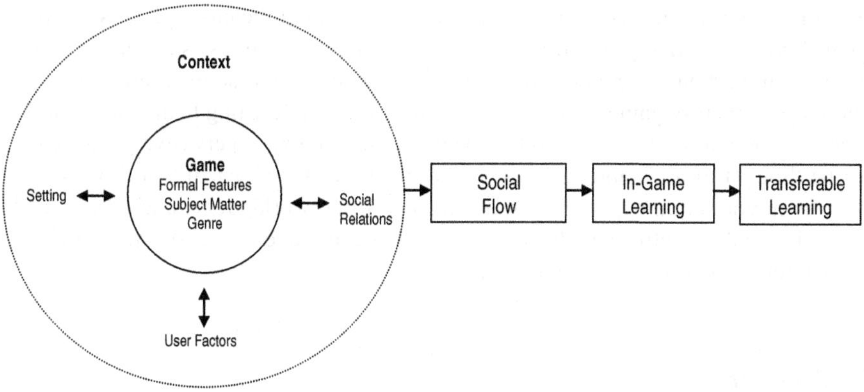

Fig. 5.2 Proposed model of social gameflow and learning

that has been assumed in the existing literature, while Fig. 5.2 presents our model of social gameflow and learning. The major differences we propose include a focus on gameflow in *social* play, greater attention to contextual factors that can influence social flow, and the need to test whether social flow contributes both to in-game learning and learning that transfers outside the gameworld. We suggest that social flow is shaped not only by the elements of the game itself, but also by context (such as the setting of play), social relations among players, and individual user factors. Within each of these factors, we provide examples of variables that previous research indicates will be especially relevant.

5.5.1 Game Elements

Most of the gameflow research and theorizing has focused on identifying which formal elements of games – especially the interface, goals and rewards – influence whether players experience flow. Which formal features of games are the most significant determinants of social gameflow and its particular dimensions? Some relationships between game features and social gameflow dimensions seem clear, such as the need for interdependent goals and rewards. Others are less self-evident. For example, what elements of social gameplay most influence players' sense of control, concentration, and immersion? Researchers could test the specific game elements that Sweetser and Wyeth (2005), Jegers (2007), and Fu et al. (2009) suggest correspond to each of these dimensions of flow. Future studies in this vein should especially use experimental or quasi-experimental designs to manipulate formal features while controlling for contextual factors that influence players' experience, as Choi et al. (2007) did by varying the levels of goal interdependence and reward in a single game.

Some elements of gameflow may be more and less salient to enjoyment and learning in particular game genres. For example, in role-playing games, control (at least of one's role and the gameworld) may be more significant to players' enjoyment (Sweetser and Wyeth, 2005), while clear goals may be less so. Because goal clarity is important for cooperative learning, it is likely that some genres, such as role-playing fantasy games, are less well-suited to group learning than other genres, such as simulations. To offer another example, immersion in pervasive games cannot be thought of as including a loss of awareness of the physical world, which is often as important an exploratory space as the virtual world (Jegers, 2007). Future research should identify which dimensions of social gameflow best predict player enjoyment and learning in different game genres.[2]

5.5.2 Context

Research on game-based learning in general, and the role of social flow within it, needs to control more rigorously for many other factors that can influence flow and learning or we risk making unwarranted universal claims about the elements of game design and the flow experience. Egenfeldt-Nielsen's (2007) review of the empirical research on game-based learning concludes that the setting of play, players' social relationships, and individual user factors can all shape whether players experience enjoyment in game play that leads to learning. If we want to understand *game design features* that influence flow, we have to control more rigorously for these contextual variables. If we want to understand *social flow*, we need to examine the contribution of context to this experience.

[2] Some prior research involving games and other activities has measured flow as a unidimensional concept by simply describing the flow state and asking research participants a few questions about whether they experienced it. However, the importance of examining relationships between each dimension of flow and particular formal features and genres (as well as how each dimension might contribute to learning) underscores the importance of measuring flow as a multidimensional concept, as we have proposed here (see also Hoffman and Novak, 2009).

5.5.2.1 Setting

Gameflow research should address the influence of setting on play, including in formal and informal educational situations, as well as online, in the same physical space, or in a mix of two (as in pervasive games). In formal education, the effectiveness of a game owes a great deal to the surrounding instructional context, especially the role of teachers as "assistants in the discovery of knowledge, guides to the exploration, reflection, and restructuring of the student's understanding" (Norman, 1993, p. 40; see also Andersen, 2004; Egenfeldt-Nielsen, 2007; Squire, 2005, 2006). Research in formal educational milieus needs to identify which elements of the larger instructional setting influence social flow, or need to be controlled. Research in informal social settings, such as online game worlds, after-school clubs, and homes, needs to take stock of the potential effects of how surrounding expectations, norms, and physical locales structure social interaction. Experimental research could shed light on whether and how social play is best facilitated in online, face-to-face, and mixed game platforms. For example, a number of scholars and designers have found that social presence in games (the capacity for making players fully aware of others through a naturalistic game interface) is related to flow (e.g., Franceschi and Lee, 2008; Weibel et al., 2007). Further research on this topic can illuminate the most effective ways of representing social exchange online for learning.

5.5.2.2 Social Relations

Social gameflow research must also be attentive to the influence of social relations in learning groups. This research could try to replicate the findings of cooperative learning studies conducted in the classroom, especially involving other kinds of computer-based instruction (summarized in Johnson and Johnson, 2008). For example, we should expect social flow to be more likely when task and reward interdependency are well-matched (as found by Choi et al., 2007) and among established groups rather than ad hoc groups (as found by Jerome et al., 2006). Classroom studies also give us a basis to hypothesize that social flow and learning are equally likely among cooperative learning groups made up of people with heterogeneous abilities and groups with homogeneous abilities (Johnson and Johnson, 2008). Can this finding be replicated with game-based learning, or does the potential mismatch between each group member's ability to play games and her knowledge of the subject matter complicate the picture?

5.5.2.3 Individual User Factors

Research must also be more attentive to the potential influence of individual factors. Previous studies suggest that flow is more likely among those with greater prior game playing experience, interest in games, familiarity with the genre of the game one is playing, interest in the subject matter, and confidence in one's gaming abilities (Cowley et al., 2008; Egenfeldt-Nielsen, 2007; Gackenbach, 2007; Squire,

2005). Future research needs to control for these factors in order to determine whether flow is simply a function of higher expertise or has independent explanatory power (Engeser and Rheinberg, 2008). Historic differences in gender preferences for game genres and features (Cassell and Jenkins, 1998; Graner Ray, 2004) continue to pose important questions for social flow research. For example, Inal and Cagiltay's (2007) observational study of elementary school children who played games socially in the classroom found that when boys entered a flow experience they were less aware of both themselves and their friends. Girls playing in groups rarely experienced flow at all, perhaps because of the games available to them. Do males and females tend to experience the dimensions of social flow differently? Are females more likely than males to experience social flow and learning in highly social games because females tend to prefer social gameplay, or less likely to do so in strongly competitive and goal-oriented games because they tend to favor narrative and cooperation?

5.5.3 Learning

Studies of gameflow need to test directly whether it enhances learning, what kinds of learning, and whether that learning extends beyond how to play the game itself. From an educational standpoint, psychological states such as flow are important to the extent that they support learning outcomes. Surprisingly, few studies have tested whether flow contributes to game-based learning using objective measures of learning outcomes (rather than self-reports). Of the few such studies conducted to date, some find that experiencing flow enhances in-game learning as reflected in players' performance (Engeser and Rheinberg, 2008; Keller and Bless, 2008), others have failed to find such a link (Choi et al., 2007), and still others have found no link between flow and learning that transfers outside the game (Li-Chun and Ming-Puu, 2010). However, research on non-game educational contexts offers more support for flow's potential contribution to learning (Nakamura and Csikszentmihalyi, 2009), including other forms of computer-based learning (e.g., Skadberg et al., 2005; Ho and Kuo, 2010). Therefore, our model proposes that social gameflow can have an effect on in-game learning of knowledge, skills, or dispositions and on players' ability to transfer that learning by applying it outside the game.

Research designs will need to distinguish between players' engagement with the game and with its educational subject matter and goals. Pearce (2005) differentiated *task flow* and *artifact flow*, based on his findings that learners may report experiencing flow because they are absorbed by the game elements of a simulation, rather than the task (learning objective), especially if the challenge overmatches players' skills. Barab et al. (2006) detected a similar difference between immersion in *narrative flow* and *task flow* that leads to learning. The authors found that some students were deeply engaged with the narrative of water pollution in a local park in *Quest Atlantis*, but not fully with the underlying scientific concepts (about principles of erosion) that were embedded in the story; students especially had difficulty applying these concepts outside the virtual story on follow-up assessments. Effective games would foster task, artifact, and narrative flow, but good research should employ measures that distinguish these kinds of flow rather than assuming that global reports of being in the flow state will always enhance learning. In addition, for social gameflow studies it is important to distinguish between immersion in social-oriented and task-oriented activity.

The balance of immersion in and reflection on group play may be the most complex dimension of flow for learning in greatest need of further study. Ermi and Mäyrä (2005) have proposed unpacking immersion into three elements: sensory immersion (in the perceptual world of the game), challenge-based immersion (in the cognitive and motor aspects), and imaginative immersion (in the narrative of the game). To what extent does immersion in game-based social learning depend upon each of these three elements? Furthermore, is immersion best suited to all kinds of learning? Garris et al. (2002) have expressed concerns that learners may have difficulties deriving and applying general principles from the intensely concrete experiences found in simulations. Habgood et al. (2005) have suggested that the immersive state of flow may inhibit metacognition and therefore may be better suited to practicing and proceduralizing knowledge than acquiring or reflecting on it. Some kinds of learning, such as moral and civic reasoning, likely require both empathetic identification with others and critical distance from them (Raphael et al., 2010). Does social gameplay exacerbate the difficulty of reflection in the flow state by adding social-oriented diversions to the learning experience or does the social element help keep learners on task, as found in some classroom studies cited above?

Reflective opportunities may be designed to exist within gameworlds or to accompany them. Few studies have tested whether in-game reflective techniques disrupt flow and even fewer examine the learning consequences – good or ill – of such game elements. One study, albeit preliminary in nature, suggests that the assumption that invitations to metacognition will kill players' immersion is unfounded. The game, *Immune Attack*, designed to teach about the immune system, risked interrupting flow by allowing the player to stop play and access a generic inquiry management tool to seek help in answering a question that would allow the player to advance in the game (Kelly et al., 2007). In testing the prototype, researchers found a positive, even 'enthusiastic' response to the inquiry management tool, thus allaying some of the concerns that privilege immersion over reflection. Can opportunities to consult, debate, and negotiate with other players during social play, such as those proposed by Padilla Zea et al. (2009), be reconciled with immersion?

Research also needs to address more directly whether achieving flow aids the transference of learning from the game to the world beyond. Some of the early research on math games suggests that those who most immersed themselves in playing these games showed less awareness of the games' learning objectives and less ability to apply that knowledge outside the game world (Klawe, 1998; Klawe and Phillips, 1995). Knowledge transfer may depend upon games making their learning objectives explicit and players practicing intentional learning by reflecting upon those objectives. To assess transference of learning, we need a range of measures of within-game learning and application beyond the game in different contexts. Wherever possible, researchers need to use objective measures of learning, not simply self-reports. In their assessment of learning in *Quest Atlantis*, Barab et al. (2006) provide one model, which includes immediate-level analysis of player discourse relevant to the curriculum in the game (such as responses to quizzes), close-level assessment of player artifacts (such as resources or objects players create in the game), proximal-level measures of whether players can adapt concepts and skills learned in one in-game context to another in-game context, and a distal-level test of players' ability to apply concepts and methods to entirely new contexts and content beyond what players had experienced in the game.

While we believe the social gameflow concept holds promise in understanding learning outcomes from gameplay, research should also test alternate conceptions of the ideal psychological state for educational gameplay. Comparative research could assess whether some educational goals can be met by learners in less intense and demanding psychological states than flow, such as simple engagement, defined as "willingness to invest time, effort and attention in the game" (Brown and Cairns, 2004, p. 1298). Like flow, social flow is a complex construct with many dimensions. In the interest of parsimony, if simpler measures predict learning, they should be used. However, flow theory's staying power offers some evidence of its fascination for researchers who want to offer a rich explanation of the enjoyment we take from games and of the theory's usefulness for informing game design. The conceptual model and research agenda we have laid out here can help focus attention on understanding flow in social gameplay contexts more clearly.

5.6 Summary and Conclusion

This chapter has laid out a model of social gameflow and learning. Our conceptualization of social gameflow builds on the work of Sweetser and Wyeth (2005) and Fu et al. (2009), which outlined the individual and social dimensions of the flow experience of game players. We have suggested that social gameflow includes the perception of interdependent goals and rewards, as well as uniquely social forms of feedback, challenge, control, concentration, immersion, intrinsic reward, and ways of achieving learning goals. This conceptualization is grounded especially in cooperative learning theory and research, although it is compatible with elements of broad a range of learning theories – including constructivism, communities of practice, situated learning, and project-based learning. Our model of social gameflow and learning broadens the scope of gameflow research to examine contextual antecedents of flow, such as setting, the social relations of play, and characteristics of individual users. This model also draws attention to studying flow as a moderating or mediating variable variable that may influence in-game learning and transferable learning. The model can inform educational game design as well as future studies of social gameflow and learning in both formal and informal settings.

References

Andersen, F.O.: Optimal Learning Environments at Danish Primary Schools. Lego Learning Institute, Billund, DK (2004)

Bandura, A.: Social Learning Theory. General Learning Press, New York (1977)

Barab, S.A., Thomas, M., Dodge, T., Carteaux, R., Tuzun, H.: Making learning fun: Quest Atlantis, a game without guns. Educ. Technol. Res. Dev. **53**(1), 86–108 (2005)

Barab, S.A., Sadler, T., Heiselt, C., Hickey, D., Zuiker, S.: Relating narrative, inquiry, and inscriptions: A framework for socio-scientific inquiry. J. Sci. Educ. Technol. **16**(1), 59–82 (2006)

Bowman, R.F.: A "Pac-Man" theory of motivation: Tactile implications for classroom instruction. Educ. Technol. **22**(9), 14–17 (1982)

Brown, E., Cairns, P.: A grounded investigation of game immersion. In: Proceedings of the SIGCHI Conference on Human Factors in Computing Systems (CHI '04), pp. 1297–1300. ACM Press, New York (2004)

Cassell, J., Jenkins, H. (eds.): From Barbie to Mortal Kombat: Gender and Computer Games. MIT Press, Cambridge, MA (1998)

Chen, J.: Flow in games (and everything else). Commun. ACM **50**(4), 31–34 (2007)

Choi, D., Kim, J.: Why people continue to play online games: In search of critical design factors to increase customer loyalty to online contents. Cyberpsychol. Behav. **7**(1), 11–24 (2004)

Choi, B., Lee, I., Choi, D., Kim, J.: Collaborate and share: An experimental study of the effects of task and reward interdependencies in online games. Cyberpsychol. Behav. **10**(4), 591–595 (2007)

Corno, L.: Volitional aspects of self-regulated learning. In: Zimmerman, B.J., Schunk, D.H. (eds.) Self-Regulated Learning and Academic Achievement: Theoretical Perspectives, 2nd ed., pp. 191–226. Lawrence Erlbaum Associates, Mahwah, NJ (2001)

Cowley, B., Charles, D., Black, M., Hickey, R.: Toward an understanding of flow in video games. ACM Comput. Entertain. (2008). doi: 10.1145/1371216.1371223

Csikszentmihalyi, M.: Flow: The Psychology of Optimal Experience. Harper & Row, New York (1990)

Csikszentmihalyi, M.: Finding Flow. Harpercollins, New York (1997)

Csikszentmihalyi, M.: Flow. In: Kazdin, A. (ed.) The Encyclopedia of Psychology, Vol. 3, pp. 381–382. American Psychological Association and Oxford University Press, Washington, DC (2000)

Csikszentmihalyi, M., Abuhamdeh, S., Nakamura, J.: Flow. In: Elliot, A.J., Dweck, C.S. (eds.) Handbook of Competence and Motivation, pp. 598–608. Guilford Press, New York (2005)

Douglas, Y., Hargadon, A.: The pleasure principle: Immersion, engagement, flow. In: Proceedings of the Eleventh ACM Conference on Hypertext and Hypermedia, pp. 153–160). San Antonio, TX (2000)

Egenfeldt-Nielsen, S.: Educational Potential of Computer Games. Continuum, New York (2007)

Engeser, S., Rheinberg, F.: Flow, performance and moderators of challenge-skill balance. Motiv. Emotion **32**(3), 158–172 (2008)

Ermi, L., Mäyrä, F.: Fundamental components of the gameplay experience: Analysing immersion. In: de Castell, S., Jenson, J. (eds.) Changing Views: Worlds in Play (DIGRA '05), pp. 17–25. DIGRA, Vancouver, BC (2005)

Franceschi, K.G., Lee, R.M.: Virtual social presence for effective collaborative e-learning. In: Spagnolli, A., Gamberini, L. (eds.) Presence 2008: Proceedings of the 11th Annual International Workshop on Presence, pp. 254–257. International Society for Presence Research, Padova, Italy (2008)

Fu, F.L., Su, R.S., Yu, S.C.: EGameFlow: A scale to measure learners' enjoyment of e-learning games. Comput. Educ. **52**(1), 101–112 (2009)

Gackenbach, J.: The relationship between video game flow and structure. Paper presented at the International Communication Association conference, San Francisco, CA (2007, May)

Garris, R., Ahlers, R., Driskell, J.E.: Games, motivation, and learning: A research and practice model. Simulation Gaming **33**(4), 441–467 (2002)
Garzotto, F.: Investigating the educational effectiveness of multiplayer online games for children. In: IDC '07: Proceedings of the 6th International Conference on Interaction Design and Children, pp. 29–36. ACM, Aalborg, DK (2007)
Gee, J.P.: What Video Games can Teach Us About Literacy and Learning. Palgrave-McMillan, New York (2003)
Graner Ray, S.: Gender Inclusive Game Design: Expanding the Market. Charles River Media, Hingham, MA (2004)
Habgood, M.P.J., Ainsworth, S.E., Benford, S.: Endogenous fantasy and learning in digital games. Simulation Gaming **36**(4), 483–498 (2005)
Ho, L.-A., Kuo, T.-H.: How can one amplify the effect of e-learning? An examination of high-tech employees' computer attitude and flow experience. Comput. Human Behav. **26**(1), 23–31 (2010)
Hoffman, D.L., Novak, T.P.: Flow online: Lessons learned and future prospects. J. Interact. Market. **23**(1), 23–34 (2009)
Inal, Y., Cagiltay, K.: Flow expeiences of children in an interactive social game environment. Br. J. Educ. Technol. **38**(3), 455–464 (2007)
Jegers, K.: Pervasive game flow: Understanding player enjoyment in pervasive gaming. ACM Comput. Entertain. (2007). doi: 10.1145/1236224.1236238
Jenkins, H.: Confronting the challenges of participatory culture: Media education for the 21st century. MacArthur Foundation white paper. http://digitallearning.macfound.org/atf/cf/%7B7E45C7E0-A3E0-4B89-AC9C-E807E1B0AE4E%7D/JENKINS_WHITE_PAPER.PDF (2006). Accessed 24 Aug 2009
Jerome, L.W., Jordan, P.J., Faraj, N.: Evaluation of group performance in a mediated environment. Ann. Rev. Cyberther. Telemed. **4**(1), 117–126 (2006)
Johnson, D.W., Johnson, R.T.: Cooperation and the use of technology. In: Spector, J.M., Merrill, M.D., van Merrienboer, J., Driscoll, M.P. (eds.) Handbook of Research on Educational Communications and Technology, 3rd edn., pp. 401–424. Routledge, London (2008)
Jonassen, D.H.: Objectivism versus constructivism: Do we need a new philosophical paradigm? J. Educ. Res. **39**(3), 5–14 (1991)
Jones, M.G.: Creating electronic learning environments: Games, flow, and the user interface. In: Proceedings of Selected Research and Development Presentations at the National Convention of the Association for Educational Communications and Technology, pp. 205–214. AECT, Bloomington, IN (1998)
Keller, J., Bless, H.: Flow and regulatory compatibility: An experimental approach to the flow model of intrinsic motivation. Pers. Soc. Psychol. Bull. **34**(2), 196–209 (2008)
Kelly, H.K., Howell, E., Glinert, E., Holding, L., Swain, C., Burrowbridge, A., et al.: How to build serious games. Commun. ACM. **50**(7), 44–49 (2007)
Kim, Y.Y., Oh, S., Lee, H.: What makes people experience flow? Social characteristics of online games. Int. J. Adv. Media Commun. **1**(1), 76–91 (2005)
Klawe, M.M.: When does the use of computer games and other interactive multimedia software help students learn mathematics? http://mathforum.org/technology/papers/papers/klawe.html (1998). Accessed 20 Aug 2009
Klawe, M.M., Phillips, E.: A classroom study: Electronic games engage children as researchers. In: Proceedings of the Computer Support for Collaborative Learning Conference, pp. 209–213. Lawrence Erlbaum, Bloomington, IN (1995)
Kiili, K.: Digital game-based learning: Towards an experiential game model. Internet Higher Educ. **8**(1), 13–24 (2005)
Lave, J., Wenger, E.: Situated Learning: Legitimate Peripheral Participation. Cambridge University Press, Cambridge (1991)
Lazzaro, N.: Why we play games: Four keys to more emotion without story. http://www.xeodesign.com/xeodesign_whyweplaygames.pdf (2004). Accessed 20 Jul 2009

Lenhart, A., Kahne, J., Middaugh, E., Macgill, A., Evans, C., Vitak, J.: Teens, video games, and civics. Pew Internet and American Life Project. http://www.pewinternet.org/Reports/2008/Teens-Video-Games-and-Civics.aspx?r=1 (2008). Accessed 15 Jun 2009

Li-Chun, W., Ming-Puu, C.: The effects of game strategy and preference-matching on flow experience and programming performance in game-based learning. Innov. Educ. Teach. Int. **47**(1), 39–52 (2010)

Mandryk, R.L., Inkpen, K.M., Calvert, T.W.: Using psychophysiological techniques to measure user experience with entertainment technologies. Behav. Inf. Technol. **25**(2), 141–158 (2006)

Nakamura, J., Csikszentmihalyi, M.: Flow theory and research. In: Snyder, C.R., Lopez, S.J. (eds.) Oxford Handbook of Positive Psychology, 2nd edn., pp. 195–206. Oxford University Press: Oxford (2009)

Norman, D.A.: Things that Make Us Smart: Defending Human Attributes in the Age of the Machine. Addison-Wesley, Reading, MA (1993)

Padilla Zea, N., González Sánchez, J.L., Gutiérrez, F.L., Cabrera, M.J., Paderewski, P.: Design of educational multiplayer videogames: A vision from collaborative learning. Adv. Eng. Softw. **40**(12), 1251–1260 (2009)

Pearce, J.: Engaging the learner: How can the flow experience support E-learning? In Proceedings of World Conference on E-Learning in Corporate, Government, Healthcare, and Higher Education 2005, pp. 2288–2295. AACE, Chesapeake, VA (2005)

Piaget, J.: The Psychology of Intelligence. Routledge & Kegan Paul, London (1962)

Raphael, C., Bachen, C., Lynn, K.-M., Mckee, K., Baldwin-Philippi, J.: Games for civic learning: A conceptual framework and agenda for research and design. Games Cult. **5**(2), 199–235 (2010)

Sawyer, R.K.: Conclusion: The schools of the future. In: Sawyer, R.K. (ed.) Cambridge Handbook of the Learning Sciences, pp. 567–580. Cambridge: Cambridge University Press (2006)

Sawyer, R.K.: Group Genius: The Creative Power of Collaboration. Basic Books, New York (2007)

Shernoff, D.J., Csikszentmihalyi, M.: Flow in schools: Cultivating engaged learners and optimal learning environments. In: Gilman, R., Huebner, E.S., Furlong, M. (eds.) Handbook of Positive Psychology in Schools, pp. 131–145. Routledge, New York (2009)

Sherry, J.L.: Flow and media enjoyment. Commun. Theory **14**(4), 328–347 (2004)

Shute, V.J., Ventura, M., Bauer, M.I., Zapata-Rivera, D.: Melding the power of serious games and embedded assessment to monitor and foster learning: Flow and grow. In: Ritterfeld, U., Cody, M., Vorderer, P. (eds.) Serious Games: Mechanisms and Effects, pp. 295–321. Routledge, Taylor & Francis, Mahwah, NJ (2009)

Skadberg, Y.X., Skadberg, A.N., Kimmel, J.R.: Flow experience and its impact on the effectiveness of a tourism website. Inf. Technol. Tourism **7**(3–4), 147–156 (2005)

Squire, K.: Changing the game: What happens when video games enter the classroom? Innovate J. Online Educ. **1**(6). http://www.innovate.info/index.php?view=article&id=82 (2005). Accessed 7 Sep 2009

Squire, K.: From content to context: Videogames as designed experience. Educ. Res. **35**(8), 19–29 (2006)

Steinkuehler, C.A.: Learning in massively multiplayer online games. In: Proceedings of the 6th International Conference on Learning Sciences, pp. 521–528. International Society of the Learning Sciences, Santa Monica, CA (2004)

Stevens, R.J.: Cooperative learning. In: Salkind, N. (ed.) Encyclopedia of Educational Psychology, pp. 187–193. Sage, Thousand Oaks, CA (2008)

Sweetser, P., Wyeth, P.: GameFlow: A model for evaluating player enjoyment in games. ACM Comput. Entertain. (2005). doi:10.1145/1077246.1077253

Voiskounsky, A.E., Mitina, O.V., Avetisova, A.A.: Playing online games: Flow experience. Psychol. J. **2**(3), 259–281 (2004)

Vygotsky, L.S.: Mind in Society: The Development of Higher Psychological Processes. (Trans. Cole, M.). Harvard University Press, Cambridge, MA (1978)

Weber, R., Tamborini, R., Westcott-Baker, A., Kantor, B.: Theorizing flow and media enjoyment as cognitive synchronization of attentional and reward networks. Commun. Theory **19**(4), 397–422 (2009)

Weibel, D., Wissmath, B., Habegger, B., Steiner, Y., Groner, R.: Playing online games against computer- vs. human-controlled opponents: Effects on presence, flow, and enjoyment. Comput. Hum. Behav. **24**(5), 2274–2291 (2007)

Resources

Choi, B., Lee, I., Choi, D., Kim, J.: Collaborate and share: An experimental study of the effects of task and reward interdependencies in online games. Cyberpsychol. Behav. **10**(4), 591–595 (2007)

Csikszentmihalyi, M.: Flow: The Psychology of Optimal Experience. Harper & Row, New York (1990)

Fu, F.L., Su, R.S., Yu, S.C.: EGameFlow: A scale to measure learners' enjoyment of e-learning games. Comput. Educ. **52**(1), 101–112 (2009)

Johnson, D.W., Johnson, R.T.: Cooperation and the use of technology. In: Spector, J.M., Merrill, M.D., van Merrienboer, J., Driscoll, M.P. (eds.) Handbook of Research on Educational Communications and Technology, 3rd edn., pp. 401–424. Routledge, London (2008)

Padilla Zea, N., González Sánchez, J.L., Gutiérrez, F.L., Cabrera, M.J., Paderewski, P.: Design of educational multiplayer videogames: A vision from collaborative learning. Adv. Eng. Softw. **40**(12), 1251–1260 (2009)

Sweetser, P., Wyeth, P.: GameFlow: A model for evaluating player enjoyment in games. ACM Comput. Entertain. (2005). doi:10.1145/1077246.1077253

Chapter 6
A Formalism to Define, Assess and Evaluate Player Behaviour in Mobile Device Based Serious Games

Hanno Hildmann and Jule Hildmann

6.1 Introduction

One of the noted shortcomings for serious games is the lack of guidelines or means to assess and evaluate the performance of the player (Connolly et al., 2007a, b); one of the obvious drawbacks of using questionnaires when investigating human behaviour in psychology is the subjective nature of introspective statements (Ajzen, 2002). This chapter proposes the use of a formal language which can be used to unambiguously represent and automatically evaluate players' behaviour; and can do so according to established guidelines for attitudinal research in the field of psychology.

This formalism proposed in this chapter is of course not restricted to mobile devices. Mobile devices, while by now rather powerful computation devices, are still (and probably always will) trailing the power available in static computers like PCs, servers and clusters. By demonstrating (Hildmann, 2012) the feasibility of implementing the formalism on mobile devices we demonstrate the overall applicability of the approach and justify our claim that this can already be implemented and used. Chapter 8 elaborates on the use of mobile devices in more detail (Section 8.5).

6.2 Background

In this chapter the authors propose the use of logics as a formal language to describe the actions and choices taken by players of a game. Using established guidelines for attitudinal research in the field of psychology a sort of grammar is suggested. The so constructed behavioural statements allow for an unambiguous and automatic observation, recording and evaluation of the players' behaviour, leaving only the interpretation open for dispute amongst psychology researchers.

H. Hildmann (✉)
Etisalat BT Innocation Centre (EBTIC), Khalifa University, Abu Dhabi, UAE

University of the West of Scotland (UWS), Scotland, UK
e-mail: hanno@cypherpunx.org

M. Ma et al. (eds.), *Serious Games and Edutainment Applications*,
DOI 10.1007/978-1-4471-2161-9_6, © Springer-Verlag London Limited 2011

The platform chosen for the implementation of such games are mobile devices. This is due to the pervasive nature of this technology as well as to show that the approach is feasible and can be implemented for less than state of the art platforms and devices.

With this in mind the authors fist provide a brief background on the concepts of games based learning, mobile devices, electronic learning and entertainment and briefly on the field of behavioural and attitudinal psychology.

6.2.1 Games Based Learning

Many of the educational benefits of games were highlighted in the literature even before the time when computer games became ubiquitous. Today games-based learning can be considered a field of its own, spanning a variety of subfields ranging from simulations (e.g. military maneuvers) over serious games (e.g. role playing games in job interviews) and simple kindergarten exercises to complex games on electronic devices equipped with state of the art artificial intelligence.

Games can promote complex problem solving in training applications, promote practical reasoning skills improvement and reduce time for training and instructor load. Games can result in high sustained motivation levels and promote automaticity training where rehearsal becomes second nature. In a survey performed as early as 1987, it was noted that already 4,600 large firms used business or cooperative initiative games in development and training.

What are the main benefits of game-based learning; which skills are developed, which abilities are promoted? The following is a (not exhaustive) list of key benefits of skills likely to be developed through play with properly designed games, (Hildmann et al., 2010):

Problem solving	Analytical thinking
Effective	Communication
Negotiating	Team work
Logical thinking	Discovery
Critical thinking	Visualisation
Social & cultural sensitivity	

The extent to which those skills are exercised in any particular game depends on various factors such as rules, number of players, age range, design of the material or procedures for turn-taking.

6.2.2 Mobile Devices

The concept of *mobility* and the idea of *mobile devices* has become a buzzword, not unlike the words *multimedia* and *interactive* in the 90s. However, what the term mobile device refers to is ill defined. At best we can include all types of devices that are not stationary. This can cover anything ranging from the average laptop to million dollar medical equipment in hospitals, as long as that equipment can be moved from one location to another. In the context of this chapter, the term refers to mobile phones, i.e. to *small, pocket size hand-held computing devices with a small battery and memory supply* (Hildmann et al., 2010). The ideas and results presented do not in any way restrict this to mobile phones, however as cell-phones have become a pervasive technology they can be assumed to be available to everyone and, in addition, they can be obtained at an affordable price.

6.2.2.1 Mobile Devices in Today's Society

As mentioned above, mobile technologies have started to become an integral part of everyday life. To back this claim up we simply ask the reader to look around the next time she or he is waiting for a bus at a bus stop. In today's world you are guaranteed to have a few youngsters around playing with their phones, typing text messages or phoning their friends.

Recently, the numbers reported by the industry have exceeded dimension we can visualise, with (Stenbacka, 2007) (e.g.) quoting figures by the Gartner Research Institute that estimate the global sales of mobile phones in excess of 0.9 billion units in 2006. Reports on the web (from May 2007) compare 800 million cars 1.4 billion credit cards to 2.7 billion mobile phones *in use* halfway through 2007. More recent estimates (by the ITU, the International Telecommunication Union, etc.) expected the volume of active mobile phone subscriptions to exceed 4.5 billion before the end of 2009. And these figures merely regard *subscriptions*, not all actual devices! Finally, (Want, 2007) mentions projected sales for 2010 to be in excess of 1.3 billion cell phones and predicts the smart phone market to expand to 700 million units by 2015.

With these numbers, it is easy to argue that the mobile phone has by now become a pervasive technology which has started to shape our society like few other product families have. For many – and especially the younger – members of our society, a cell phone has become an integral part of their life just as their ability to connect and communicate from *anywhere* and with *anyone* has grown to be one of the main constructs of their social and professional lives.

The above should suffice as justification and motivation to propose the use of mobile phones as a medium to deliver educational contents as well as serious games. We are of course not the first to make a case for the use of mobile devices in the field of games based learning and indeed there are already a large number of implementations for the educational use of games and simulations in different fields covering knowledge management, medicine and computer architecture, to name but a few.

6.2.2.2 Mobile Device Based Applications

The intention of this section is to support the claim that mobile devices in general, and mobile phones in specific, can be used as the platform for computationally demanding applications. To this end two different types of serious games as well as one optimisation tool are mentioned; all three have been created in collaboration with the authors, and the content of the following sections can be understood as a summary of the respective projects. For a more detailed account of these projects the interested reader is referred to the individual project related publications, as indicated where appropriate. All three are ongoing research projects focusing on serious games for mobile devices as well as computationally expensive applications that are ported to (or even designed for) hand-held devices.

These applications are showcased in this book to show that there is currently a trend towards using mobile devices for serious applications in general and serious games in specific, and that the field of games-based learning can benefit from further investigating the use of mobile devices as platforms. The two games are given in Sections 8.5.1.1 and 8.5.1.2. The application presented below which is not a game but an optimisation tool is mentioned to show that computationally expensive applications, which only a decade ago required dedicated and bulky computers, can now be designed for mobile devices. The state of the art features sufficient memory as well as the required computational resources.

MAST This example is not a game but a structural optimum design application for mobile devices. This application is mentioned here because it showcases the implementation of a multi agent system running efficiently on various mobile devices. It is a tool for experts out in the field that want to get advise on efficient design of steel structures (see Fig. 6.1). Just a few years ago an application like this one would have had computational requirements that exceeded not only the mobile phones of the time but also the standard PCs available to the general public.

6.2.2.3 Technical Specifications

A recent article, (Vaughan-Nichols, 2008), titled "The mobile web comes of age", argues that the web as well as web applications for mobile devices have reached a

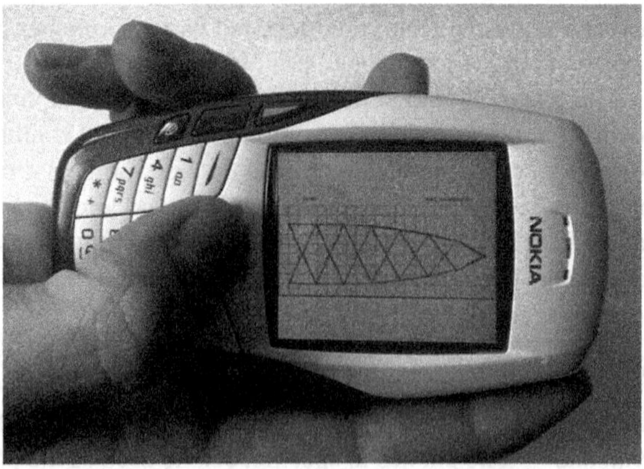

Fig. 6.1 A structural optimum design application (Bitterberg et al., 2009, 2011; Branki et al., 2008) for mobile phones. Recent results have shown that it can now be ported to run efficiently on the latest generation of mobile phones

stage where they are to be treated as fully functional and feasibly usable. The article further claimes that *already 40% of the US mobile customers surf the internet with their phones*. The iPhone, admittedly once a device on the forefront of the state of the art product lines, runs Mac OS X and sports a 620-MHz ARM processor as well as 128 MB RAM, which for the authors and probably most of the readers will make it a phone more powerful than the computers on which they wrote their first code. Some of today's phones can display and execute most materials available on the internet in such a manner that there is no real loss of functionality over using a PC any more.

Mobile technologies can serve both as platform for content applications in general as well as terminals to interact with server-based applications that require more computational power than a mobile device can currently provide. In recent work (Meissner et al., 2001, 2003; Bitterberg et al., 2008) and (Hildmann et al., 2008) the respective authors argue for the use of mobile technologies and point out that, due to the computational power of contemporary mobile phones, complex applications can now feasibly be implemented on such devices.

In recent years mobile phones have received an increasing attention from the scientific community, both as devices of notable computational power (Bitterberg et al., 2008) as well as in their capacity as nodes in distributed computing applications (Kurkovsky et al., 2004; O'Sullivan and Studdert, 2005) argues that the multi-agent paradigm found in the MAST application mentioned above is an ideal middleware for the management of mobile devices.

6.2.3 Mobile Device Based Education

As previously pointed out in (Hildmann et al., 2008; Connolly et al., 2007c) noted that at least some learners seem to have a cognitive preference with regard to the media used in education facilities, i.e. there are learners that have a preference of one medium over the other. Universities across the UK have started years ago enrolling students that are in fact younger than the internet (even if we use the arguably late birth date claimed by Al Gore). Consequently, learning institutions of all levels are today facing (or will soon face) type of students and learners that differs greatly from the ones of only 20 years ago. This next generation of students has grown up in a multimedia culture; they have assimilated the multitude stimuli of the environment to which our increasingly technocratic society subjects them. The traditional, linear approach to teaching is very likely to leave them bored and, subsequently, cognitively under-challenged. This is confirmed by surveys which state that the conventional approach of forcing the students to focus on one physical location and source is frustrating and contra productive. The overwhelmingly stated preferences of this new generation are for mobile video and audio applications and for interactive media.

Mobile devices, in particular mobile phones, are a good example for this trend in teenagers and young adults. This young group of people prefers constant cognitive interaction, a trend that has led to a generation of children for whom the mobile aspect of their gadgets is an integral aspect. While the IT facilities at universities, schools and even kindergartens are constantly upgraded to meet today's standards students started a few years ago to move away from the static terminals and the whole physical aspect of information. The existence of open universities and distance learning institutions is but one indicator for this and one that is in its original form already starting to become outdated again.

This paradigm shift, however, is not necessarily a disadvantage: (Steinfield, 2003) sees the ability to apply eLearning at any time and at any place as one of its stated advantages. Yet the static nature of a PC, and indeed, that of most university facilities, does restrict this *anytime-anywhere* aspect to the times when a student is physically near a terminal. Once the learner leaves the immediate vicinity of that access point for the eLearning infrastructure, all information becomes static. No information can be exchanged or altered, no updates can be received.

There is of course another aspect to the use of mobile phones. The original aim of these devices is to provide a service that is not required in, and very often interfering with, the regular classroom teaching. The idea to provide learners with powerful computers while restricting the use of e.g. pocket calculators to prevent fraud and cheating is actually paradoxical; and it is important to the authors to point out that by no means do they want to make a case for the broad introduction of mobile devices to schools and classrooms. But on the other hand, while it is understood that the practical issues of mobile devices do not make them the platform of choice for the normal school teacher the authors emphasise the potential of the approach and suggest further research into specialised applications. In addition, the authors call for long term experiments to support the suggested approach and to verify the theories from behavioural psychology.

6.2.4 Behavioural Psychology

When talking about *behaviour theory*, the image of a salivating dog is commonly the first association of persons with only a marginal insight into learning theories. This is especially so when the notion of *conditioning* is mentioned (Bandura, 1974). Owing to this, the idea to use theories and models from behavioural psychology as the basis for research on serious games aiming to assess and profile behaviour mainly evokes negative associations in laymen. However, there is a lot of ground work done in that field and specialist with an extensive psychological or therapeutical training are well aware that behavioural therapy is the most effective treatment strategy for a number of phenomena and syndromes. The notion that human decisions with respect to actions and behaviour are partly controlled by their anticipated result is generally accepted. Independent of our values, moral stance or orientation, we model and reinforce our values and our actions reflecting these values (Bandura, 1977).

In 1985 Ajzen proposed the *Theory of Planned Behavior* (ToPB) as extension to his *Theory of Reasoned Action*. This theory stipulates that human decision-making (with respect to actions and behaviour) is guided by three conceptually different considerations and beliefs (Ajzen, 1985):

- *Behavioural beliefs*: The expectations about the likely outcome of one's actions, paired with one's subjective view on these outcomes.
- *Normative beliefs*: The opinion of others regarding the outcomes of one's actions, combined with the intention to adhere to the standards of others and to live up to the expectations of one's peers.
- *Control beliefs*: One's confidence towards all factors relevant to bringing about an outcome and the subjective belief of control over these factors.

6.3 A Formalism to Express Statements About Games

By providing a formalism (adhering to guidelines for questionnaires set out by experts in behavioural psychology) for the description and representation of behaviour (within the context of a serious game) this approach facilitates the profiling, evaluation or assessment of the players' behaviour that lives up to standards set out in the field of psychology.

6.3.1 Background

We first introduce a formal language, which we will call $\mathscr{L}^*$. By formal language we mean a formally defined language that has both syntax (clearly defined structure) as well as a semantic (meaning). That language is, unlike most natural languages, unambiguous; a quality we require for our application in order to provide us with data which can be processed automatically.

As the domain of the language is going to be behaviour in learning and games, it can be rather restricted in the sense that we do not need to include anything that is not required to express this. On the other hand this means that already at this stage we have to have a consensus between the computer scientist (designing the game) and the teacher (using the game), because everything that follows will be constructed around, or on the basis of, this language. Including too many things will make the resulting program or system unnecessarily complex while omitting essential aspect will result in partial or complete lack of functionality.

The language $\mathscr{L}^*$ is constituted by collecting a vocabulary for it. These *'words'* of the language are its smallest building blocks, from which we will construct all sentences (using the syntax rules of the language). In order to provide a meaning to these sentences we relate every word to something in the real world such that at any moment this one word is either true or false (e.g. something either *is* a house or it *is not*). From this we can then deconstruct any however complex sentence, and, using the semantic rules, propagate the truth values of the vocabulary upwards until we can determine for any complete sentence whether it is true or false.

In order to make this language understandable to any non-technically inclined person involved in the project, we make use of the fact that we can (mechanically) translate any sentence of this language into a natural language, for example into English. This gives us a language at our disposal that is both formal (and thus unambiguous) as well as intuitively understandable (Hildmann et al., 2007).

Before we introduce syntax and semantic of our formal language of choice we provide a brief motivation for the use of a formal language: It is out aim to provide the reader with a straight forward means to represent, implement and eventually assess behavioural statements. The main benefits of using a formal language (as opposed to a natural language, e.g. English) are:

- It gives us a well defined and unambiguous way to make statements regarding behaviour. Since the language is semi-natural a teacher can intuitively understand and verify the validity of statements in the context of the specific application, and, therefore, make use of our game.
- Implementing a rigid evaluation method for any aspect expressed in the language allows the game designer or the teacher to amend certain behavioural aspects of the game or the tool without having to change the whole system.
- There are algorithms that allow us to automatically create new behavioural statements which are consistent with existing ones. Furthermore, application specific modules can be implemented that use artificial intelligence to suggest useful and meaningful statements to the user during the game or the project and while the programme is running.

6.3.2 Propositional Logic – Syntax and Semantic

As described by (Hildmann et al., 2007), the language described in the following sections is standard classical propositional logic (PL) as introduced in (van Benthem et al., 1991, pp. 11–23); for advanced reading into logic and modal logics, the interested reader is referred to (Blackburn et al., 2001). It is explained here only to the extent required to understand the approach.

6.3.2.1 Syntax

In this section we provide the rules that allow the construction of arbitrarily long sentences from a chosen vocabulary. As mentioned above, we first need to accumulate a vocabulary. When it comes to computer games, this is relatively safe as a computer can at any moment only represent a finite number of concepts, due to its finite memory. At worst, our vocabulary in this case will be the complete (finite) set of all concepts. When applying this to the non-discrete real world we immediately run into trouble. It is important to understand that the teacher (the user) is the person making the decision what the vocabulary should be, the programmer is only tasked with the construction of the system. For example a moderator in a team building exercise can decide to see the world in 1 min intervals and to allow statements like *"the player has not communicated in the last minute"*. This is going to be either true or false in any given minute, subject to the discussion of what constitutes communication of course.

We define $\mathscr{L}$ as a collection of all statements needed to describe anything of interest in the game. We say that individual statements in this collection are atomic, i.e. that they are not the combination of smaller statements. E.g.: "the player has not moved in the last minute or communicated in the last minute" is the combination of "the player has not communicated in the last minute" and "the player has not moved in the last minute", and is thus not included in $\mathscr{L}$.

Such complex statements are constructed over the statements (words) in $\mathscr{L}$ through the use of the syntax rules which will be explained below. In what follows, we will denote such statements by $\mathtt{p}$ and $\mathtt{q}$ and introduce the means to combine them into complex natural language sentences. We then provide a formal translation into a symbolic representation and define a normal form to asses (on the basis of a simple true-false view of the world) whether a statement is true.

Assume that we already have a set of words, $\mathscr{L}$. From this we want to construct complex sentences. The set of complex sentences constructed $\mathscr{L}$ over will be called the language $\mathscr{L}^*$.

In natural language we have connectives like *and*, *not*, *if ... then* and so on, and we are now going to introduce their formal equivalents. We define our language as follows: If $\mathtt{p}$ and $\mathtt{q}$ are atomic statements in $\mathscr{L}^*$, then the following sentences are part of language $\mathscr{L}^*$:

(1)	"p"	means:	*"it is raining"*
(2)	"*[it is] not [true that]* p"	means:	*"it is NOT raining"*
(3)	"p *and* q"	means:	*"it is raining AND it is Sunday"*
(4)	"p *or* q"	means:	*"it is raining OR it is Sunday"*
(5)	"if p *then* q"	means:	*"IF it is raining THEN it is Sunday"*

For brevity we abbreviate the not connective as indicated by the brackets. The table below lists the symbols used in PL to represent the above given connectors:

(1)	$\mathtt{p})$	stands for:	*"it is raining"*
(2)	$\neg\ \mathtt{p})$	stands for:	*"it is NOT raining"*
(3)	$(\mathtt{p} \wedge \mathtt{q})$	stands for:	*"it is raining AND it is Sunday"*
(4)	$(\mathtt{p} \vee \mathtt{q})$	stands for:	*"it is raining OR it is Sunday"*
(5)	$(\mathtt{p} \rightarrow \mathtt{q})$	stands for:	*"IF it is raining THEN it is Sunday"*

As the above definition covers only atomic statements, we extend this and allow these connectives to be applied to all sentences of $\mathscr{L}^*$, i.e. we include more complex sentences like e.g.: "It is raining and it is Sunday or it is Monday". These connectives and operators are all related to another and can be defined through each other.

These connectives and operators are all related to another and can be defined through each other: only the $\neg$ (*not*) and either the $\wedge$ (*and*) or the $\vee$ (*or*) are needed. This syntactical equivalence is called DeMorgan's Law (van Benthem et al., 1991).

connector	operator	usage		rewritten
not	$\neg$	$\neg\phi$		
or	$\vee$	$\phi \vee \phi$		
and	$\wedge$	$\phi \wedge \psi$	$\equiv$	$\neg(\neg\phi \vee \psi)$
if... then	$\rightarrow$	$\phi \rightarrow \psi$	$\equiv$	$\neg\phi \vee \phi$

6.3.2.2 Semantic

We now have syntax, but that does not suffice to give us a language, insofar as that until now we have not provided a meaning for our statements. Clearly we have an intuitive understanding of the meaning of the connectives as we use them in our daily lives, but they are nevertheless not yet formally defined. Recall that we started our construction of sentences from atomic statements. In what follows we will define the semantics, i.e. the meaning of all sentences on the basis of the truth of the individual statements.

Consider that at any moment we can infer for any statement in $\mathscr{L}$ whether that statement is true or false at that moment. In addition we say that in any moment one of the two has to hold, i.e. that everything we can say at any moment is, from an omniscient point of view, either objectively true or false. Furthermore, to avoid confusing nestings of quotes we use brackets to construct complex sentences. What follows will be common knowledge to the logicians among the readers as it is directly taken from classical propositional logic. We briefly give the semantics for $\mathscr{L}^*$ through the following definitions:

1. "*not* (`statement1`)"
   Since everything is either true or false this is true if sentence 1 is false.
2. "`statement1` *and* `statement2`"
   This is only true if both sentence 1 and sentence 2 are true.
3. "`statement1` *or* `statement 2`"
   This is true if at least one of the two sentences is true.
4. "*if* `statement1` *then* `statement2`"
   This last one is tricky. Clearly if both sentences are true, then the whole statement is true; furthermore, if the first sentence is true and the second sentence is false then the whole statement is false. But what if the first sentence is false? Then, by convention, we say that the whole statement is true. This has to be that way for reasons of consistency (consider the division by zero in math, which is forbidden by convention to protect and ensure the consistency of the system in question). For example, consider the sentence "if (it is raining or it is Sunday) then not (I am going to work)" and let's say that at the moment we evaluate this it really *is Monday*, it *is raining* and I *am going to work*. Then, the part "it is raining or it is Sunday" is true because it is raining, but the whole sentence is false because the *if*-part (the condition) is true while the *then*-part (the conclusion) is false.

The tables below give the truth values for the operators *not* and *and*. Each table covers all possible circumstances under which an operator could be encountered and then defines the truth value of the operator in this case. The left table defines the *not* operator, which is always applied to a single statement, in this case `p`. There are only two possible cases we have to consider since `p` can only be true ($\top$) or false ($\perp$). The second defines the *and* operator which is applied to two statements and thus 4 separate cases have to be considered: both `p` and `q` are false, both are true, and the cases where exactly one is true. The definition of the *and*-operator is intuitive:

p	¬p
$\top$	$\bot$
$\bot$	$\top$

p	q	(p ∧ q)
$\top$	$\top$	$\top$
$\top$	$\bot$	$\bot$
$\bot$	$\top$	$\bot$
$\bot$	$\bot$	$\bot$

Above we mentioned DeMorgan's Law and said that due to these semantic equivalences the operators *or* and *if . . . then* are nothing more than abbreviations, so called *syntactic sugar* to enhance readability of formulae. The table below defined them:

p	q	(p ∨ q)	(p → q)
$\top$	$\top$	$\top$	$\top$
$\top$	$\bot$	$\top$	$\bot$
$\bot$	$\top$	$\top$	$\top$
$\bot$	$\bot$	$\bot$	$\top$

These abbreviations will come back below when we describe how to translate the statements into a form that allows us to check them for validity and satisfiability.

6.3.2.3 Complexity

Above we mentioned consistency in a side note only, and a few brief statements regarding the properties of propositional logic should be made: For one thing, propositional logic is a formal system that allows a logician to take a number of statements which are considered to be true and to construct new statements from them that are then necessarily true as well. More technically, PL is sound and complete. That means that whatever one can prove with PL is indeed true (soundness) and if something is really true then it can be proven by PL (completeness).

Another aspect of a formal system that is of large interest to us is the verification of statements, meaning that given either a new statement of unknown truth value or a description of what is known to be true and false, we want to be able to investigate the truth of statements. There are two sides to this: We can either investigate whether a given statement is true under a specific condition (validity) or whether a given statement could ever be true (satisfiability). The following two statements illustrate these two (respectively): "Today is Sunday" and "Christmas falls on a Sunday". Both, validity and satisfiability are of interest to us in the context of this chapter as we will verify statements as well as at times might care to know whether a statement could be true at all (after all, if a statement can never be true we can ignore it).

The complexity of PL then is as follows: The time it takes to *verify* whether a given statement is true or false under specific circumstances is linear in the length of the statements. That means that the longer the statement is the longer it takes to verify whether the statement is true, but that the additional time it does take increases linearly (if statement B is twice as long as statement A it will take twice as long to verify whether B is true than it will take to verify the truth of A).

Testing for the *satisfiability* of a statement on the other hand is exponential in the length of the statement. To understand this we have to point out that the careful researcher will always assume the worst case scenario, which in this setting means that one will have to compare all possible circumstances and that it will be only the very last possible circumstance, if any, that will make a statement true and by that enable us to decide whether a statement is satisfiable or not. While it is not very likely that we will always be that unfortunate, such a pessimistic view is necessary to provide us with a reliable estimate of how long it could take to investigate the satisfiablity of a statement. And, as stated above, testing a PL statement for satisfiability is exponential in the length of the statement (If statement `B` is but one word longer than statement `A` then it will take twice as long to verify satisfiability for B as it will take to check the satisfiability of `A`).

Practically this means that determining whether a given statement is true is computationally feasible for all statements that the authors consider useful, given an up to date computer and within the context of the applications at hand. Generating random statements and testing whether these statements could ever be true, however, will quickly become unfeasible. Previously published results from benchmark test using mobile phones from 2005 and 2006 have shown this (Hildmann et al., 2010), and, while the computational power of mobile phones is increasing rapidly, the exponential factor will prevent the above stated results from becoming outdated.

6.3.2.4 Algorithms

Translation into a normal form Above we have given the truth values for the operators we are using. We have furthermore mentioned DeMorgan's Law and provided a table illustrating how the *and*-operator and the *if* ... *then*-operator are nothing but practical abbreviations to replace the otherwise much longer formulae using only the *not*- and the *or*-operator.

Therefore any statement can be rewritten as a semantically equivalent statement containing only the operators $\vee$ (*or*) and $\neg$ (*not*) or the operators $\wedge$ (*and*) and $\neg$. Such statements will be a long list of propositions and negated propositions connected by one type of operator. From the truth tables above we can see that as soon as one proposition in a conjunction (`p` *and* `q` *and* `r` *and* ...) is false the whole conjunction is false, and, conversely, that as soon as a single proposition in a disjunction (`p` *or* `q` *or* `r` *or* ...) is true the whole disjunction is true. This means that by predicting what outcome we are expecting we can choose to rewrite a statement to a form that will enable us to verify it faster, thereby saving computation time and enhancing the performance of our game or application. Due to this we give two algorithms for two normal forms:

1. The *and*-normal from
   Do the following steps until all operators but the *not*-operator and the *and*-operator are removed:

   Consider any remaining sub-statement (that is a statement in a set of brackets) containing an unwanted operator and rewrite it as follows:

i. (*if* p *then* q) is rewritten as (*not* p or q)
ii. (p *or* q) is rewritten as not (*not* p *and not* q)
(thus eventually (*if* p *then* q) is rewritten as (*not (not* p) *and not* q))
(thus eventually (*if* p then q) is rewritten as (p *and not* q))

2. The *or*-normal from
Do the following steps until all operators but the *not*-operator and the *or*-operator are removed:

Consider any remaining sub-statement (that is a statement in a set of brackets) containing an unwanted operator and rewrite it as follows:
i. (*if* p *then* q) is rewritten as (*not* p *or* q)
ii. (p *and* q) is rewritten as not (*not* p *or not* q)

Validity When testing a statement for validity we are investigating whether the statement is true or false *given a certain state of the world.* That means that we already know for each relevant proposition whether that proposition is true or false. Using the above rewriting method we either have a conjunction (p *and* q *and* r *and* ...) or a disjunction (p *or* q or r *or* ...) to work with. Now we compare each occurrence of the (possibly negated) proposition to that proposition's truth value and decide the truth value of the whole statement.

Satisfiability In order to determine the satisfiability of a statement we must find *a single state of the world* (i.e. distribution of truth values for the relevant propositions). The most straight forward manner to do so it so enumerate all possible combination of truth values for the propositions and then to test the validity of the statement for each of them until one is found that makes the statement true.

Clearly this is a *brute force* approach and a specific application will most likely allow a computer scientist with insight into the code and/or the intended use of the application to provide some sort of heuristic to speed up the process. The previously stated fact that "the time it takes to test for the satisfiability of a statement is increasing exponentially with the length of the statement" is an upper bound and a well designed application will have elements/modules that aim to reduce that time.

6.4 A Formalism to Define Behaviour in the Context of Games

6.4.1 The TACT Paradigm from Behavioural Psychology

With respect to observable aspects of behaviour we continue to use the works of Ajzen as reference point, specifically the TACT (*Target*, *Action*, *Context* and *Time*) paradigm that was suggested for the design and the evaluation of questionnaires (within the context of ToPB related research). In this work, (Ajzen, 2002) argues that in order to define behaviour sufficiently the above mentioned four aspects have to be distinguished and identified in (introspective) statements regarding behaviour. His running example is "walking on a treadmill in a physical fitness center for at least 30 min each day in the forthcoming month". It is not always clear how to distinguish between the four aspects, a matter to which we will return further below. The labeling of behaviour as well as the distinction of which of the four aspects to assign to a part of a statement describing behaviour is subjective and therefore has to be decided upon by the trainer or the researcher. This opens the door for ambiguity. However, since we are not making any claims towards providing an objective way to assess behaviour this is not of much impact. We merely provide well-defined and consistent means to the assess behaviour. The classification, like the interpretation of the collected data, will remain the task of the person investigating the behaviour.

Ajzen himself points out that there is this ambiguity and that there are many possible additions to the basic TACT paradigm as proposed by him originally (e.g. "within next month" can include "next Tuesday"). The aim of this chapter is to illustrate our suggested approach and owing to this it is bound to be of a rather general nature. The specifics of the project for which it is used will determine the extent to which a finer grained distinction is required; one of the first tasks in the design stage of a project is for the programmer and the trainer to liaise on that matter and to reach a consensus. Furthermore, complicated extensions will complicate the matter without adding value to the conceptual approach and are therefore omitted here. The scope and the intended audience of this chapter do not warrant a more lengthy discourse on this matter.

6.4.2 High Level Versus Low Level Statements

Above we introduced the conceptual approach of TACT proposed by (Ajzen, 2002). In this section we will illustrate how this is incorporated into games. As a running example we will use the game *"Glasgow SoxWars"* (Hildmann and Boyle, 2009) designed to investigate cooperative and competitive behaviour (Fig. 6.2). The interested reader is referred to (Hildmann, 2012).

We start by designing the game around the vocabulary of our formal language, which (as described in the sections above) is a collection of statements which at any

Fig. 6.2 Board game version of "Glasgow SoxWars", tested and played by students at UWS

given moment can be evaluated to be either true or false. What we intend to do is to construct statements regarding the players' behaviour such that:

- The four concepts *Time*, *Action*, *Context* and *Target* are unambiguously defined.
- Given a state of the game we can evaluate any statement about this state to either true ($\top$) or false ($\bot$).
- Each statement is assigned a behavioural label (e.g. *cooperative*, *competitive*).

The last point is quite vague as it will be based on the opinion of the researcher alone. This however cannot be avoided; furthermore it is a problem that is present when constructing a questionnaire as well. In what follows we will use some insight into the example game to decide subjectively whether a stated behaviour should be seen as *cooperative* or *competitive*. It is important to remember that these labels are used to illustrate the approach, not as definitions of either of the two behaviours. In the next few sections we will express behaviour of a player, which we will call *Subject* and use the abbreviation B and B' which stand for either *cooperative* or *competitive* behaviour. Since we, as the researchers, define for any behaviour whether it equates to one of these two we can investigate at any moment whether a player is playing (in our opinion) cooperatively or competitively. Using the complex statements further down, this allows us to investigate the behaviour of the player in *response* to the opponent's actions.

In our game the players have the option to offer their resources to other players. When doing so, the price they can ask for this is fixed (This is to keep things simple: if the price varied, the number of statements as well as their complexity would increase drastically). The player can choose from offering resources to: a single player, all players, all but one player, all players of lower rank and all players of higher rank.

Cooperative

1. Subject offers trading to a single player P who is ranked lower than Subject.
2. Subject offers trading to a single player who plays B against Subject.
3. Subject offers trading to all players that are ranked lower than Subject.

Competitive

1. Subject offers trading to a single player P who is ranked higher than Subject
2. Subject offers trading to all players ranked higher than subject.
3. Subject offers trading to all players but player P who is ranked higher than Subject.

The TACT labels are (omitting *Time* for now, see below):

Action:	Subject offers to trade resources ...
Target:	... with player P/all players/all players but player P...
Context:	... of higher/lower rank than the subject.

Let's consider another action: bidding on resources: At the start of each round the players are receiving resources. Each player is guaranteed a certain amount of the available resources at the current rate for the product. The remaining amount of resources is offered to the players in a sort of auction. To keep this somewhat fair each player is offered an equal portion of the remaining resources at the fixed price. If nobody else is bidding on these resources they will be sold to the respective player at that price. If, however, any other player decides to bid on the resources auctioned to this player the player bidding the highest amount will be granted the resources (at the price of the second highest bid). At this stage the player is advised on the current sales price for the resource, i.e. the player is told what the expected profit will be but will still be allowed to bid a higher price.

Cooperative

1. Subject is not bidding on resources of player `P`.

Competitive

1. Subject is bidding on resources of player `P` for a price higher than the expected profit.
2. Subject is bidding on own resources for a price higher than the expected profit.
3. Subject is bidding on own resources for a price equal to the expected profit.

The TACT labels are (omitting *Time* for now, see below):

Action: Subject is bidding on resources ...
Target: ... of player `P`/Subject ...
Context: ... for a price which is equal to/less than/more than the resulting profit.

In the above statements we have ignored the temporal aspect. We now add three operators to the game: *for n rounds*, *until* and *while*. In the following sentences, provide to illustrate the usage of these temporal operators, cooperative and competitive statements like the ones given above are abbreviated `B` and `A`:

Simple temporal statements

1. Subject plays `A` for *n* rounds.

Until statements

1. Subject plays `B`/`A` until player `P` plays B'/A' against Subject.
2. Subject plays `B`/`A` until all other player plays B'/A' against Subject.
3. Subject plays `B`/`A` until some other player plays B'/A' against Subject.

While statements

1. Subject plays B/A while player P plays B'/A' against Subject.
2. Subject plays B/A while n other player play B'/A' against Subject.
3. Subject plays B/A while at least n other players play B'/A' against Subject.
4. Subject plays B/A while at most n other players play B'/A' against Subject.

Now the latter two statement types *until* and *while* are more complex than the first one. For all three types of statements we are deriving the *Target*, *Action* and *Context* from the behaviour B but the *until* and *while* statements allow us to use time not only in relation to the number of turns but to measure behaviour in relation to the behaviour of others as well. The Repeated Prisoners Dilemma (Binmore, 2007; Poundstone, 1992) is a good example of a setup where exactly this type of behaviour is investigated.

The above listed are merely examples. Many more combinations are possible. We argue that the above suffices to illustrate the complexity and expressiveness of $\mathscr{L}^*$. One can imagine that there are, in theory, statements of almost infinite length possible (restricted only by the number of temporal connectives like *until* and *while* and the upper bound of semantically different statements). Longer statements are of little use for psychological experiments or our games, we are content with statements given above as examples to illustrate the approach.

6.5 Considerations and Conclusion

6.5.1 Considerations and a Critical View

Both, (Hildmann and Hildmann, 2009a) and (Hildmann and Hildmann 2009b) list a number of potential advantages for the use of electronic devices in general and mobile phones in particular. Before we provide a critical view we first briefly reiterate those positive aspects here:

- *Data integrity*: Electronic devices allow the individual monitoring of players or students. The gathered data can then be used to create a user specific profile that is based on the observed actions and not on introspective statements (which are subjective and unreliable).
- *Data authenticity*: There is a variety of mechanisms to ensure the authenticity of the data, ranging from using devices that the users will not likely share, over automatic cross-checking and comparing of answers and answering behaviour to authentication mechanisms as key cards or biometric scanners.
- *Data protection laws and data security*: Electronic data collection allows for a variety of levels of data security that can be controlled centrally and in manners that require a number of people to give their consent for the release of data before it can be accessed. In addition the data can be analysed automatically and the results can remain undisclosed and protected by the same mechanisms.

- *Unobtrusive recording devices*: High-performance recording devices are already embedded in standard mobile technologies (e.g. mobile phones or laptops). Using e.g. a 6 megapixel camera in an up to date mobile phone to record the eye movement or facial expressions is already possible given the latest technologies.
- *Individual recording devices*: Being able to give the recording device into the hands of the subject has the psychological effect that the subject feels more in control and less observed. The surrendering of the physical ownership over the device to the subject is the key issue here.

As stated in (Hildmann et al., 2010), the shortcomings of serious games are not unknown to the field; one of the dominant noted drawbacks for serious games is the lack of guidelines or means to assess and evaluate the performance of the player; therefore efforts have been made to use the aforementioned formalism and mobile devices to assess the progress of the player, both during game play as well as after the game is finished. Previous/recent work has showcased the work done on the game *"Glasgow SoxWars"*. The approach suggested here adheres to earlier work.

Both authors have been active in their fields long enough to be aware of bias found in educationalists against new technologies when these are introduced in their field of practice. The approach of digital games based learning is still suffering from this bias as innovations are often immediately rejected by educational practitioners. This reluctance can be traced to a number of (valid) core problems:

- These new techniques are developed by technicians without practical experience in educational settings. Therefore, their tools work in theory but fail to engage the students or are loaded with negative side effects that outweigh the benefits.
- Educationalists, by nature of their trade, will tend to reject technical devices advertising to achieve pedagogic goals. Their professional training and practical experience has taught them the vital role of personal interaction, which – so far – no computer can truly replace.
- Furthermore, when it come to approaching and handling difficult or demanding situations and issues in their classroom or respective context, practitioners are far more likely to follow their experience based intuition than the instructions of a technical device.
- Children and teenagers nowadays have a far superior understanding of new technologies than most adults, which forces the latter to give up the traditional position of authority that they have held in the past; and loss of authority often results directly in loss of respect, and subsequently, subordinance. (Thus at least is their fear; modern educationalists hopefully have come to know these assumptions to be old fashioned and faulty).
- Additionally, any device can be used as well as misused. And unfortunately, many youngsters are incredibly eager to tamper with new hard- and software in legal as well as illegal ways.
- Finally, some of the technologies which are used are often financially unattainable in the required numbers, hard to maintain, not sturdy enough or too difficult to protect against theft.

The authors believe that on many occasions a good idea is rejected or failing simply because it is applied too directly or without considerations for the environment in which it is supposed to perform. Any digital or electronic device and programme which is intended to aid in the instruction and/or assessment of social skills – as in the example presented above – requires the expertise of a computer scientist and many cycles of design and implementation. This has to be undertaken in close collaboration with the end user, namely teachers, social workers, educationalists and the like to ensure the required functionality, usability and applicability.

6.5.2 Conclusion

We have outlined how the TACT approach can be used to extend the language (propositional logic) used to formally state behaviour within a bounded context. Due to this extension we can make statements regarding behaviour (within the well defined terms of the game or exercise) that live up to the standards suggested by experts in the field of psychology. These statements can be assembled and deconstructed in an unambiguous manner, allowing for an interface within the game to enable the social practitioner or researcher to define the behaviour of interest for the game or the experiment; as well as being evaluated and assessed automatically. Due to this we can claim that we have presented an outline of how to implement a digital device based tool for educationalists to enrich their exercises and game scenarios. We took a critical view on the applicability and usefulness of employing digital devices in education and identified a number of issues and problems.

We agree that the design and implementation of digital or electronic tools has to be undertaken in cooperation with the intended users. The technology has to be a tool and as such one that is hand carved to meet the exact needs of the experts expected to use them. The providers of these tools are not equals to the educationalists in this decision process as their competence lies purely in the creation of the tools. Computer scientists are experts when it comes to building and implementing the tools, however, the educationalists are the ones with the know-how to decide on which tools are needed, what they should do and exactly how they should work.

More research will be necessary on the practical applicability of such programmed devices. Field experiments with children and teen-agers in school-related as well as in out of school settings – such as social clubs, trainings for troubled youth or delinquents, and others – are equally possible as an evaluation of team trainings or other educational programmes designed for adults. Assessment might focus on which activities are most prone to profit from such devices and which same or others are best feasible to be adopted for assessment of participant behaviour.

Independent of contents of a study, all research endeavours should be conducted in cooperation of both fields of expertise, educationalists doing the 'real life base work' and computer scientists capable of designing and programming electronic devices such as mobile phones or GPS-computers used in outdoor activities for orienteering. Both groups of experts would have to be willing to cooperate in such a joint venture and adapt their professional language to achieve successful communication amongst each other – thus proving themselves worthy of assessing other people's will and skill to cooperate.

6.5.3 Resources

It was suggested to provide the interested reader with some recommended references. The task of picking a few select books from the vast numbers that are available is not a simple one and the following list should be understood as a mere suggestion. The field of computer games and games design has grown so fast and become so big that there are special books on almost all aspects of game design. The interested reader would be well advised to consider a few books and consult online versions first in order to identify the special area of interest. The reader is cautioned that reading up on everything is impossible, a claim that is easily backed up by the fact that there are full time MSc courses available for a variety of specialisations *within* the field of computer game design.

An overview might be found in (Hartnell et al., 1985; McIntire, 1979), while the reader interested in serious games could consult (Michael and Chen, 2005), but any of the following is popular for one reason or the other (Bates, 2001, 2004; Crawford, 2003; Pedersen, 2009; Rollings and Adams, 2003; Rouse and Ogden, 2005; Saltzman, 2000). For those amongst the reader that are interested in the artificial intelligence aspect of games, the lead author (who has himself a considerable stake in this area, cf. (Hildmann, 2012) is happy to suggest the following books: (Ahlquist and Novak, 2007; Bourg and Seemann, 2004; Charles, 2008; Floreano and Mattiussi, 2008; Funge, 2004; Rabin, 2008; Schwab, 2004) (without claiming to have read all of them cover to cover).

References

Ahlquist, J., Novak, J.: Game Development Essentials: Game Artificial Intelligence. Game Development Essentials Series. Thomson/Delmar Learning (2007). ISBN 1418038571, 9781418038571. See http://books.google.com/books?id=6HcfAQAAIAAJ

Ajzen, I.: From Intentions to Actions: A Theory of Planned Behavior. In: Action Control: From Cognition to Behavior (eds. Kuhl Julius, Beckmann Jurgen), pp. 11–39. Springer-Verlag, Berlin, New York (1985)

Ajzen, I.: Constructing a Topb Questionnaire: Conceptual and Methodological Considerations. (2002)

Bandura, A.: Behaviour theory and the models of man. Am. Psychol. **29**, 859–869 (1974)

Bandura, A.: Self-efficacy: toward a unifying theory of behavioural change. Psychol. Rev. **84**, 191–215 (1977)

Bates, B.: The Game Design: The Art and Business of Creating Games. Premier Press (2001). ISBN 0761531653, 9780761531654

Bates, B., Bates, R.A.: Game Design, 2nd edn. Course Technology Press, Boston, MA, United States (2004)

Binmore, K.: Game Theory. A Very Short Introduction. Oxford University Press, New York (2007)

Bitterberg, T., Hildmann, H., Branki, C.: Using resource management games for mobile phones to teach social behaviour. In: Proceedings of Techniques and Applications for Mobile Commerce (TAMoCo08), Glasgow, Scotland, pp. 77–84. IOS Press, Amsterdam, Netherlands (2008)

Bitterberg, T., Hildmann, H., Branki, C.: On multi-agent driven structural design applications: a mobile device based implementation of the mast project. In: Proceedings of TAMoCo09: Techniques and Applications for Mobile Commerce. IOS Press, Amsterdam, Netherlands (2009)

Bitterberg, T., Hildmann, H., Branki, C.: A mobile device based, and multi-agent driven structural design solution. Multiagent Grid Syst. (MAGS) 1574–1702 (2011)

Blackburn, P., de Rijke, M., Venema, Y.: Modal Logic. Cambridge University Press, Cambridge (2001)

Bourg, D., Seemann, G.: AI for Game Developers. O'Reilly Series. O'Reilly, Sebastopol, CA, USA (2004). ISBN 0596005555, 9780596005559

Branki, C., Bitterberg, T., Hildmann, H.: A mobile device based multi-agent system for structural optimum design applications. In: Proceedings of 4th International Workshop On Agents and Web Services Merging in Distributed Environments (AWeSoMe '08), LNCS, pp. 118–127. Springer, Berlin/Heidelberg (2008)

Charles, D., Fyfe, C., Livingstone, D., McGlinchey, S. Biologically Inspired Artificial Intelligence for Computer Games. Medical Information Science Reference, 278pp. ISBN 978-1-59140-646-4 (2008)

Connolly, T., , Stansfield, M., Hainey, T.: An application of games-based learning within software engineering. Br. J. Educ. Technol. **38**(3), 416–428 (2007a)

Connolly, T., Boyle, E., Hainey, T.: A survey of students' motivations for playing computer games: A comparative analysis. In: Proceedings. 1st European Conference on Games-based Learning (ECGBL), Scotland (2007b)

Connolly, T., MacArthur, E., Stansfield, M., McLellen, E.: A quasi-experimental study of three online learning courses in computing. J. Comput. Educ. **49**(2), 345–359 (2007c)

Crawford, C.: Chris Crawford on Game Design. New Riders Games Series. New Riders (2003). ISBN-10: 0131460994, ISBN-13: 978-0131460997

Floreano, D., Mattiussi, C.: Bio-inspired Artificial Intelligence: Theories, Methods, and Technologies. Intelligent Robotics and Autonomous Agents. MIT Press, Cambridge, MA, USA (2008). ISBN-10: 0262062712, ISBN-13: 978-0262062718

Funge, J.: Artificial Intelligence for Computer Games: An Introduction. Ak Peters Series. Peters, Natick, MA, USA (2004). ISBN-10: 1568812086, ISBN-13: 978-1568812083

Hartnell, T., Cook, R.: Hartnell's Second Giant Book of Computer Games, 43rd edn. Ballantine Books, New York (1985)

Hildmann, H.: Formalising human and AI behaviour in the context of games [title tbc]. Ph.D. thesis, University of the West of Scotland (2012, forthcoming)

Hildmann, H., Boyle, L.: Evaluating player's attitudes and behaviour through mobile device based serious games. In: International Conference on Mobile Learning. IADIS, Barcelona, Spain (2009)

Hildmann, H., Hainey, T., Livingstone, D.: Psychology and logic: design considerations for a customisable educational resource management game. In: The Fifth Annual International Conference in Computer Game Design and Technology, Liverpool, England (2007)

Hildmann, H., Hildmann, J.: A critical reflection on the potential of mobile device based tools to assist in the professional evaluation and assessment of observable aspects of learning or (game) playing. In: 3rd European Conference on Games Based Learning. API, Academic Publishing International, Graz, Austria (2009a)

Hildmann, H., Uhlemann, A., Livingstone, D.: A mobile phone based virtual pet to teach social norms and behaviour to children. In: The 2nd IEEE International Conference on Digital Game and Intelligent Toy Enhanced Learning (Digitel 2008), Banff, Canada (2008)

Hildmann, H., Uhlemann, A., Livingstone, D.: Simple mobile phone based games to adjust the player's behaviour and social norms. Int. J. Mobile Learn. Organ. (IJMLO), Special Issue on Emerging Mobile Learning Environments for Industries and Pedagogies **3**(3), 289–305 (2010)

Hildmann, J., Hildmann, H.: Promoting social skills through initiative games in the classroom and assessing their success. In: 3rd European Conference on Games Based Learning. API, Academic Publishing International, Graz, Austria (2009b)

Kurkovsky, S., Bhagyavati, Ray, A.: A collaborative problem-solving framework for mobile devices. In: ACM-SE 42: Proceedings of the 42nd annual Southeast regional conference, pp. 5–10. ACM, New York (2004). doi http://doi.acm.org/10.1145/986537.986540

McIntire, T.C.: A to Z Book of Computer Games. McGraw-Hill Professional, Blue Ridge Summit, PA, USA (1979). ISBN-10: 0830698094, ISBN-13: 978-0830698097

Meissner, A., Baxevanaki, L., Mathes, I., Branki, C., Schönfeld, W., Crowe, M., Steinmetz, R.: Integrated mobile operations support for the construction industry: the cosmos solution. In: Proceedings of of the 5th World Multi-Conference on Systemics, Cybernetics and Informatics, SCI 2001, pp. 248–255. International Institute of Informatics and Systemics, IIIS, Orlando, FL, USA (2001). doi http://doi.acm.org/10.1145/986537.986540

Meissner, A., Mathes, I., Baxevanaki, L., Dore, G., Branki, C.: The cosmos integrated it solution at railway and motorway construction sites – two case studies. ITcon, Special Issue eWork and eBusiness **8**, 283–291 (2003). URL http://www.itcon.org/2003/21

Michael, D.R., Chen, S.L.: Serious Games: Games That Educate, Train, and Inform. Muska & Lipman/Premier-Trade (2005). ISBN-10: 1592006221, ISBN-13: 978-1592006229

O'Sullivan, T., Studdert, R.: Agent technology and reconfigurable computing for mobile devices. In: SAC '05: Proceedings of the 2005 ACM symposium on Applied computing, pp. 963–969. ACM, New York, NY, USA (2005). doi http://doi.acm.org/10.1145/1066677.1066901

Pedersen, R.: Game Design Foundations. Wordware Game and Graphics Library. Wordware Pub., Plano, Tex, USA (2009)

Poundstone, W.: Prisoner's Dilemma. Anchor Books, New York, USA (1992)

Rabin, S.: AI Game Programming Wisdom 4. AI Game Programming Wisdom. Course Technology, Cengage Learning, Florence, KY, USA (2008). ISBN-10: 1584505230, ISBN-13: 978-1584505235

Rollings, A., Adams, E.: Andrew Rollings and Ernest Adams on Game Design. New Riders Games (2003)

Rouse, R., Ogden, S.: Game Design: Theory & Practice. Wordware Game Developer's Library. Wordware Pub., Plano, Tex, USA (2005)

Saltzman, M.: Game design: Secrets of the Sages. Brady Games, Indianapolis, Indiana, USA (2000). ISBN-10: 1566869048, ISBN-13: 978-1566869041

Schwab, B.: AI Game Engine Programming. Game Develoment Series. Charles River Media, Florence, KY, USA (2004). ISBN-10: 1584503440, ISBN-13: 978-1584503446

Steinfield, C.: The development of location based services in mobile commerce. Tech. rep., Michigan State University (2003). url http://www.msu.edu/steinfie/elifelbschap.pdf

Stenbacka, B.: The impact of the brand in the success of a mobile game: comparative analysis of three mobile j2me racing games. Comput. Entertain. **5**(4), 1–15 (2007). doi http://doi.acm.org/10.1145/1324198.1324204

van Benthem, J., van Ditmarsch, H., Ketting, J., Meyer-Viol, W.: Logica voor Informatici. Addison-Wesley, Nederland (1991)

Vaughan-Nichols, S.J.: The mobile web comes of age. IEEE Comput. Mag. **41**(11), 15–17 (2008)

Want, R.: iphone: smarter than the average phone. Pervasive Comput. IEEE **9**(3), 6–9 (2010). doi 10.1109/MPRV.2010.62

Chapter 7
Serious Games for Health and Safety Training

Rafael J. Martínez-Durá, Miguel Arevalillo-Herráez, Ignacio García-Fernández, Miguel A. Gamón-Giménez, and Angel Rodríguez-Cerro

7.1 Introduction

Children do not learn to walk, talk or play football from a series of lectures. Instead, they learn by getting immerse in the activity. Although current technology allows the construction of immersive instructional environments for skill training, there are cost reasons that, in many occasions, make them impracticable. Fortunately, this cost can be ameliorated by using simulation technology to produce computer-based products at a reasonable cost. One such product is serious games. Serious games offer an engaging and innovative medium for delivering training to students who are more comfortable with hands-on learning (Dickinson et al., 2011).

Serious games have been applied in a broad spectrum of application areas, e.g. military, government, educational, corporate, and healthcare (Backlund et al., 2007a). Another possible area of application of this kind of techniques is safety training. According to the European Agency for Safety and Health at Work, "every year, 5,720 people die in the European Union as a consequence of work-related accidents, according to EUROSTAT figures. Besides that, the International Labor Organization estimates that an additional 159,500 workers in the EU die every year from occupational diseases. Taking both figures into consideration, it is estimated that every three-and-a-half minutes somebody in the EU dies from work-related causes". Serious games constitute and alternative for safety training, and they are becoming popular mainly because of their potential to allow learners to get involved in scenarios that would not be feasible in a real world context because of cost, time or safety reasons. Either on their own or as a supplement to other existing more formal ways of safety training, serious games provide an opportunity to emphasize safe behaviors in the workplace.

In this chapter, we focus on the application of serious games in safety training. First, previous work on this topic is reviewed, and some existing serious games for health and safety training are described. Then, we give a series of guidelines for

R.J. Martínez-Durá (✉)
Instituto IRTIC, Universidad de Valencia, Paterna, Spain
e-mail: Rafael.Martinez@uv.es

M. Ma et al. (eds.), *Serious Games and Edutainment Applications*,
DOI 10.1007/978-1-4471-2161-9_7, © Springer-Verlag London Limited 2011

the design and evaluation of this type of computer applications. Next, technological aspects are described. Finally, future trends are analyzed and conclusions from the chapter are drawn.

7.2 Serious Games in Safety Training

Several applications of serious games for safety training have been reported. Although space limitations do not make it possible to provide a complete review of all these games, some relevant examples are presented in this section. These have been organized around three major application areas: construction, public safety and pedestrian safety. Some serious games outside these major areas are also presented.

7.2.1 Health and Safety in Construction

Fatal injury rates in the construction industry are higher than in most other industries. Falls from heights, trench collapses, scaffold accidents and electric shocks are common hazards, some of which can be avoided by wearing adequate personal protective equipment or by following proper safety procedures. Construction safety training is thus an essential issue as a prevention mechanism, to assure the safety of all people working in this industry. Serious games provide an alternative to traditional training in this context and some efforts have already been made in this direction.

As an initial investigation into applying edutainment in the construction trades, Dickinson et al. (2011) have reported on a positive experience using a serious game focused on teaching trench health and safety lessons. In this work, authors made a significant effort to provide a realistic looking environment and a rich interactive content to allow the student to establish intuitive relations between the contents of the lesson and the situations where the knowledge can be applied. In this game, students can freely move around a 3D environment as if they were walking; they use the mouse to control their view point; and they can interact with objects in the environment by clicking on them. To this end, a visible cursor provides information on possible actions that the user can perform with each object. The training material is structured around three scenarios that take place on a common simplified construction site. Each of these scenarios has a different goal, and uses a storyline to favor student engagement. In the first scenario the user must safely retrieve a toolbox from the bottom of a trench, locating required tools and avoiding unsafe entry points. In the second scenario, the student has to investigate the possible cause of a trench collapse, considering inadequate storage of equipment, improper trenching for soil conditions, weather conditions and surcharge. In the last scenario, the student has to play the role of a supervisor and plan five trenches on the job site, each with its soil type, obstacles and shoring requirements. An increasing level of difficulty is associated with each scenario. In the first one, an avatar plays the role of a supervisor and warns the student when unsafe actions are carried out. In the last scenario, students are not warned and serious injuries to an avatar that represents a co-worker are possible. The game was implemented using Microsoft XNA Game Studio 3.1 in the Microsoft Visual C# 2008 integrated development environment.

Another serious game which is worth mentioning in the construction area is Safety Inspector, that was been presented by Lin et al. (2011). In this game, the student assumes the role of a safety inspector, and has to explore the jobsite to identify potential dangers in a limited amount of time. Successfully identified hazards are awarded and illustrated with extended explanations on best practices, applicable safety rules, and corrective actions. This game was programmed by using the rendering, physics and animation features provided by the commercial game engine Torque 3D. The assessment of the results revealed that students enjoyed the learning process and showed a positive attitude towards using the game scoring as a way to reflect their safety knowledge.

In this sector, it is quite common to display visible danger warnings or symbols to warn the user about unsafe actions. Figure 7.1 shows an example of this type of procedure.

7.2.2 Public Safety

"Games with serious purposes are establishing a presence in the training of those responsible for public safety. Police and fire departments, hospitals, state and local emergency management agencies, and local decision makers are using serious games increasingly, focusing on situations that require strategy, tactics, coordination, and communication" (McGowan and Pecheux, 2008).

Fig. 7.1 A sample scene of a simulation tool with a focus on safety

As a first example, Hazmat: Hotzone (Carless, 2005; McGowan and Pecheux, 2008) is a serious game that aims at training firemen to respond to the release of chlorine gas in a shopping mall. In this game, players may take the role of either a hazardous material technician or the incident commander and must decide how they rescue and decontaminate as many civilians as possible by using limited equipment. This includes the execution of a number of actions, namely: set up a security perimeter, neutralize the gas source, and evacuate and decontaminate civilians and themselves. The game allows trainers to vary some parameters to adjust the level of difficulty, such as the number of civilians or the amount of equipment.

Another good example of this type of serious game is Sidth (Backlund et al., 2007a), a game-based firefighter training simulator developed in cooperation between the University of Skövde and the Swedish Rescue Services Agency. Rescues of victims from buildings on fire require the use of a breathing apparatus, and the heat and smoke from the fire usually force the firefighters to crawl on the floor. Training firefighters for this type of situations is traditionally performed in areas which have been specially designed for this purpose. Victims are replaced by dummies and firefighters have to rescue them from inside the buildings. When a dummy is found, it is dragged to a safe environment and the search continues. This approach requires both trained instructors and the availability of different set-ups to simulate different environments, such as hospitals, hotels or gas stations. The game Sidth is based on cave technology (Cruz-Neira et al., 1992), and allows the user to move freely in an empty room surrounded by screens, using sensors to read user movements. The main goal of the game is to get the players to develop systematic and thorough search behavior in the presence of physical tension and other stress factors. To this end, the player has to scan various locations and evacuate any victims found. The health status of the player and the score are continuously presented in the game. The health status is decreased by time and distance moved, and also depends on the player position, causing that the mission fails if it reaches zero. The score system assigns the player a basic score that depends on the percentage of the location which has been covered, and this is multiplied by a factor related to the time remaining and the number of previous attempts at completing the level. A scan is considered successful if all rooms have been visited and all victims have been evacuated within the time limit. The game contains 13 levels that model typical rescue scenarios. When a location is successfully scanned, the game advances to the next level. After a mission, the player obtains feedback about the areas which were scanned, by means of a map of the premises.

7.2.3 Pedestrian Safety

Virtual reality has also been used to train children in pedestrian safety. In McComas et al. (2002), a desktop virtual reality application to teach children to safely cross intersections is evaluated. The objective of this study was to determine whether virtual environments are appropriate for this purpose and to what extent the safety learning transfers to real world. An experiment involving children from two schools (urban and suburban) was run. The results showed that, although improved street-crossing behavior transferred to real world behavior in the suburban school children, this was not the case in the urban school.

In this same direction, Liu (2006) presented a cartoon game design to educate Chinese children on traffic safety. The game uses non player characters to guide the game and explain the meaning of different traffic signs and safety regulations, by using text and sound.

Yet another simulation game designed to transfer knowledge about safe pedestrian behavior to school children has recently been reported in Ariffin et al. (2010). The game presents users with a range of very commonly-encountered situations and pedestrian environments. In particular, three different scenarios were developed, using color and realistic traffic sounds to help game engagement and facilitate the acquisition of knowledge. At each scenario, the score is increased each time the player accomplishes a task. When a player fails at completing the task, she is re-directed to a tutorial that instructs the player on specific road safety measures.

7.2.4 Other Example Applications

The use of serious games in safety training is not limited to the three previous areas of application. On the contrary, there exist many other cases in which serious games have been used for a wide range of purposes. This includes Serious Gordon (Namee et al., 2006), a serious game to teach the basics of food safety to workers in the food industry. This game aims at developing a set of nine competencies, namely: (a) wear and maintain uniform/protective clothing hygienically; (b) maintain a high standard of hand-washing; (c) maintain a high standard of personal hygiene; (d) demonstrate correct hygiene practice if suffering from ailments/illnesses that may affect the safety of food; (e) avoid unhygienic practices in a food operation; (f) demonstrate safe food handling practices; (g) maintain staff facilities in a hygienic condition; (h) obey food safety signs; and (i) keep work areas clean. Both technical and pedagogical evaluations of the game were carried out. Technically, users found the game easy to navigate and control. From a pedagogical perspective, the game proved successful at teaching learners induction skills required as part of food safety training.

A similar approach to that used in Backlund et al. (2007a) in the firefighter training simulator Sidth described above, was employed by the same authors in Backlund et al. (2007b), this time with a focus on driving. In this particular set-up, a car is surrounded by seven screens, each showing the output from a LCD projector controlled by a standard PC, and the car movement is simulated by using sound, vibrations and controlling the car's fan so that its force is linear with the speed. Authors used the game to collect data over different traffic safety variables, such as speed, headway distance and lane change behavior, from 70 subjects, and concluded that game based simulations can be used to enhance learning in driving education.

In Chittaro and Ranon (2009), a serious game aiming at developing personal fire safety skills is also presented. The game focuses on building evaluation procedures, and aims at citizens, rather than first responders such as firefighters. The game is organized in levels of increasing difficulty. In each level, the player is presented with a different fire emergency, and has to evacuate the building. To this end, the player has to make use of the most appropriate procedures and avoid other inappropriate actions (e.g. taking the elevator). Scores are calculated according to the time taken to evacuate and the actions performed in the game.

7.3 Design and Evaluation

A common mistake in the design of serious games is to assume that learners will be motivated to learn just because the learning contents have been wrapped with a game. It is not sufficient that the player enjoys the game. She must also meet the intended instructional objectives. For this reason, the design of a serious game should be supported by well-accepted instructional theories and the use of appropriate game design principles.

As in any software development methodology, an analysis stage should precede any implementation efforts. This step should aim at identifying the organization needs in terms of health and safety. This may include a review of previous data on injuries, near misses or cases of ill health; and a series of discussions with the workers. Then, we shall decide on the most appropriate style of game for our particular training priorities. In general, two major approaches can be adopted in the implementation of serious games for safety training:

(a) Mission-oriented interactive games in which the player has to undertake a number of previously designed tasks applying safety procedures.
(b) Observation-based games in which the user has to observe the behavior of avatars in a scene to detect situations which do not conform to safety regulations.

A set of heuristics that can be used to carry out usability inspections of video games has been presented by Pinell et al. (2008). These can also be used as design guidelines:

- Provide consistent responses to the user's actions.
- Allow users to customize video and audio settings, difficulty and game speed.
- Provide predictable and reasonable behavior for computer controlled unit.
- Provide unobstructed views that are appropriate for the user's current action.
- Allow users to skip non-playable and frequently repeated content
- Provide intuitive and customizable input mapping.
- Provide controls that are easy to manage, and that have an appropriate level of sensitivity and responsiveness.
- Provide users with information on game status.
- Provide instructions, training, and help.

- Provide visual representations that are easy to interpret and that minimize the need for micromanagement.

Validation of traditional games focused on entertainment does not require scientific evidence about their quality. In fact, although there exist common guidelines and recommendations to favor game engagement, the parameters that define a "good" game are ill-defined. From an industry perspective, a good game is one that sells well. This is different when a game has a purpose other than entertainment. In the particular case of educational games, it is necessary to validate the contribution of the game to the consecution of the learning objectives.

Although many other newer approaches exist, Kirkpatrick framework (1959) is still being used as a reference model to evaluate training; and the model proposed can be also be applied to assess serious games which have a focus on learning. According to this model, evaluation of training effectiveness is organized in four levels. The information gathered at one level is used for the evaluation of the next, and each successive level is used to obtain more precise details on the effectiveness of the program. The four levels described by Kirkpatrick are as follows:

- Level 1. Reactions. This level measures the reaction of participants to the training program, mainly in terms of learner's satisfaction. Positive reactions are not a guarantee for learning, but negative reactions usually impede learning and should be considered to improve the learning program. Feedback questionnaires and informal comments from participants are common ways to extract the information required at this stage.
- Level 2. Learning. In this level, the learner's progress in skills, knowledge or attitude is measured. Indeed, these are variables which are far more difficult and laborious to measure that those at level 1. Possible approaches to evaluate these aspects in the context of serious games are comparing knowledge before and after playing the game (e.g. Bellotti et al., 2009), or using an experimental group that plays the game and a control group that is taught by traditional methods (e.g. Eagle and Barnes, 2009; Froschauer et al., 2010).
- Level 3. Transfer. At this level, we try to evaluate to what extent the knowledge and skills acquired through the training program are used in the learner's everyday activities. This information can be obtained by e.g. on-the-job observations or reports from peers, customers or the participant's manager. This level is especially relevant at serious games for safety training.
- Level 4. Results. In this level, assessment focuses on business results. Financial reports or quality inspections may be used to analyze the impact of training in the business' objectives. In the case of serious games for safety training, an objective measure of success is usually a reduction in the number of work related accidents.

Although level 4 results are perhaps the most relevant ones, these are sustained by all three other inferior levels. This implies that to achieve the desired results at this level it is necessary to ensure that the other levels have been appropriately covered. A boring game may cause negative reactions and not engage the player, making her adopt a passive attitude that hinders learning. On the other side, an attractive and enjoyable game may encourage a positive player's attitude towards learning. In a similar way, a game design which focuses on providing large amounts of information may fail at level 3 and not have the desired effects. On the contrary, a game design that includes typical scenarios at the workplace may reinforce learning by association and benefit knowledge transfer at this level.

In some sense, serious games for safety training need to focus not only on the contents that should be taught but also on raising the worker's awareness about safety rules and regulations.

7.4 Technological Issues

In this section we describe different technologies for development of serious games aiming at risk prevention. These technologies are not used strictly for that purpose, but they are aimed for building virtual reality environments with a high degree of accuracy. As for today, the most powerful applications use local rendering engines. However, it is worth mentioning that a new trend that deals with 3D applications that execute on Web browsers is emerging. This section has been structured around four subsections. They deal with the representation of virtual environments, the simulation of the physical behavior of the virtual world, the use of virtual actor or *avatars* in the virtual world and the evaluation and the generation of feedback.

Indeed, simulation is an essential part of training games, and a close relation exists between these two fields of research. For this reason, most of the technological issues discussed here are equally applicable to the development of simulation tools.

7.4.1 The Virtual Environment

Nowadays, gaming goes through providing the user with graphical representation of the gaming scenario. Current technologies allow the creation of a virtual environment which is a 3D geometrical description of such a scenario, which can be navigated and modified in some ways.

7.4.1.1 Geometrical Modeling

A virtual environment has to be populated with elements that reproduce the objects that appear in the real or imaginary world of the game. These elements have to be created by means of geometric modeling software and have to be loaded into the game application.

An important issue when developing a simulator is the possibility of building components that can be used in several projects. From this point of view, we can classify the elements of a scenario in three major categories:

- Generic elements. There exist some elements which are common to many virtual environments across various application areas, such as the terrain or the sky.
- Typical components in a certain area. These are elements which commonly appear in certain types of applications, such as scaffolding elements in safety training applications for the construction sector.
- Other application-specific components. Elements which are present in a single application or a reduced set of applications.

The re-usability is very high for generic elements and hence important research efforts have been made to produce both efficient and realistic modeling approaches. Techniques such as the so called *skybox* consist of enclosing the scene within a cube, and using cube mapping to project the sky and other unreachable objects onto the faces of the cube. Various methods for terrain representation have also been developed (e.g., Pla-Castells et al., 2006).

These models can be built either procedurally (by means of algorithms) during the rendering of the scene (Ebert, 2003) or using modeling, rendering and/or compositing software, such as Autodesk® 3D Studio Max®. Models created by such software can easily be exported to different formats which can be loaded by the 3D programming libraries that are used for the development of the game. For example, models created with Autodesk® 3D Studio Max® can be saved in the format used by the scene-graph library OSG, which will be discussed later, using the osgExp (Jensen, 2002) plugin. However, as digital assets have to be easily transported through the content pipeline, from whatever digital content creation tool to whatever runtime engine, the use of a intermediate format, like COLLADA is recommended.

7.4.1.2 Real Time Rendering Engines

Rendering of a complex 3D scene can be a time consuming task. For this reason Real-time rendering is usually achieved by using libraries or engines which have been specially built for this purpose. These software tools also make it easier the tasks related to organizing the element in a hierarchy both for rendering and for updating the state of the scene. In addition, they provide tools for applying the most recent techniques on illumination, shading and rendering of different effects.

Within the open source category, one of the most spread engines is OpenSceneGraph (Wang and Qian, 2010) and Java3D, in between many others. OpenSceneGraph (OSG) is an open source library for high performance real-time rendering which is widely used in a number of computer graphics related fields. Its functioning is based on the concept of a Scene Graph, a data structure that defines the spatial and logical relationship between the components of a graphical scene. This data structure takes the form of a directed acyclic graph (DAG), which contains nodes that represent components or operations that generally propagate to children. Java3D uses a scene structure which is very similar to that used by OSG, and also allows an easy construction of complex scenes which can be manipulated by using high-level constructs. An example of a game scene produced by using OSG is provided in Fig. 7.2.

Fig. 7.2 A scene produced by using the OSG engine

Other common scene graph management libraries include:

- OGRE (http://www.ogre3d.org): The Object-Oriented Graphics Rendering Engine is a scene-oriented, flexible 3D engine written in C++ designed to make it easier and more intuitive for developers to produce applications utilizing hardware-accelerated 3D graphics. The class library abstracts all the details of using the underlying system libraries like Direct3D and OpenGL and provides an interface based on world objects and other intuitive classes.
- Irrlicht Engine (http://irrlicht.sourceforge.net): It is a cross-platform high performance real-time 3D engine written in C++. It is a powerful high level API for creating complete 3D and 2D applications like games or scientific visualizations. It integrates all the state-of-the-art features for visual representation like dynamic shadows, particle systems, character animation, indoor and outdoor technology, and collision detection.
- Delta3D: http://www.delta3d.org: It is a widely used and well-supported open source game and simulation engine. Delta3D is a game engine which is specially aimed to modeling and simulation in military and defense applications, covering many common standards such as High Level Architecture (HLA), After Action Review (AAR). However, it is also appropriate for general purpose applications, such as civil training, education, visualization, and entertainment. Among its features, it includes large scale terrain support, and SCORM Learning Management System (LMS) integration.
- Unreal Engine 3 http://unrealtechnology.com: It is under the hood of the most visually intensive computer and video games on the market. It is available under

license for PC, PlayStation3, and Wii. Its main features are: multi-threaded rendering, 64-bit high dynamic range rendering pipeline with gamma correction, dynamic composition and compilation of shaders, post-processing effects (ambient occlusion, motion blur, bloom, depth of field, tone mapping), artist-defined materials, dynamic fluid surfaces, soft body physics, deformable geometries, texture streaming system for maintaining constant memory usage, particle physics and skeletal animation. A development kit, named UDK (http://www.udk.com), is available which covers the complete workflow of application development, including scene edition, animation, and lighting preview.

- Cry Engine 3 (http://www.crytek.com/): It gives developers full control over their multi-platform creations in real-time. It features many improved efficiency tools to enable the fastest development of game environments and game-play available on PC, PlayStation® 3 and Xbox 360™. Its main characteristics are: road and river tools, vehicle creation, multi-core support, and multithreaded physics, deferred lighting, facial animation editor, dynamic path finding, rope physics, parametric skeletal animation and soft particle system.
- OpenSG is a scene graph system to create real time graphics programs, e.g. for virtual reality applications. It is developed following Open Source principles, it is LGPL licensed, and can be used freely. It runs on Microsoft Windows, Linux, Solaris and Mac OS X and is based on OpenGL. Its main features are advanced multithreading and clustering support (with sort-first and sort-last rendering, amongst other techniques), although it is perfectly usable in a single threaded single-system application as well.

Regarding the web-browser based rendering engines, new technologies have emerged since the establishment of the HTML5 standard. The key concept for having high performance graphics was the ability for using shaders inside the browser, taking shape data and turning it into pixels on the screen by means of using the power of the local graphic processor. Mostly them are OpenGL based, with the additional advantage that also exists a port for the OpenGL ES standard, used in the mobile platforms. The most relevant technologies are WebGL, X3D, Java OpenGL (JOGL), Lightweight Java Game Library, Stage 3D (the Molehill Adobe 3D API) and the many scenegraph management engines and frameworks based on them. Here you have only a few examples just for the shake of completeness: C3DL, CopperLicht, O3D, X3DOM, J3D, jME, Xith3D, JAGaToo, Alternativa3D and Away3d.

7.4.1.3 Performance and Image Quality Improvement

As it has been stated before, there exist different computer graphics techniques that can be used to either provide more realistic effects or to reduce the processing required to render the scenes e.g. bump mapping and texture baking. *Bump mapping* (Max and Becker, 1994) is a computer graphics technique that aims at providing a more realistic view of an object's surface by modeling the interaction of a bumpy surface texture with the lights in the environment. The technique is used to simulate bumps, wrinkles or other effects on the object, and it does this by changing the brightness of the pixels according to a height map for the surface that needs to be specified. *Render to texture*, also called *texture baking*, can be used to avoid the application of shaders in real time and thus speed up the application. This technique consists of recording one or more views of a same surface and using it/them at a later stage during program execution. This approach allows the programmer to pre-compute (offline) textures with illumination or other complex effects which require heavy processing. Although the technique is very useful to model static scenarios that will not change with time, it cannot be combined with dynamic lighting techniques for changing objects in the scene.

At present, hardware solutions to achieve real time processing are also been used. In particular specialized Graphics Processing Units (GPU) are commonly present in most common video cards, and allow high speed processing of graphics data by means of programming the five programmable stages (Vertex, Tessellation Control, Tessellation Evaluation, Geometry, and Fragment). Beside the texture techniques, many other effects can be also combined to get realistic graphics (Refractions, animated textures, realtime shadows), but they are out of the scope of the chapter. For a reference, see the OpenGL specification. The last one, OpenGL 4.1 was announced on 26 July 2010.

7.4.2 Physical Simulation of the Environment

Another important technological aspect is the simulation of the game's physics. Traditional physics engines were mainly based on solid-rigid simulations coupled with joints. This approach does not allow simulating the behavior of objects that can deform elastically and, in many cases, it is limited to produce a realistic effect of only part of the objects in the scene. Nowadays, more complex models are being supported by moving calculations to the GPU and specialized hardware. This allows developers to simulate in real-time and with high accuracy visual effects and the behavior of complex systems with a large amount of interactions, such as plants movements, trees, atmospheric effects, particle systems, fire, fluids, deformable objects, etc.

7.4.2.1 Main Issues in Physics Modeling

Building the physical model for a virtual world consists on defining the main entities that are involved in the simulation in a dynamic manner. But it is also very important to identify the most important behaviors that have to be reproduced according to goals of the project. This will determine the modeling methodologies for the different entities. As an example, for a certain project the elastic behavior of an object can be irrelevant while, for another project, it can be one of the most important elements of the simulation. The properties of the physics models can affect in different ways the success of the game and of the learning process.

One of the key issues is the fidelity of the models. The use of a serious game to make the workers aware of risks at work has a particularity: in most cases the player is familiar with the real environment which is reproduced in the game. From that experience, she already has a set of well-established skills and habits that she will try to apply to the game. If the environment does not give responses very similar to real ones this causes frustration and rejection in the user and provokes a feeling that the experience is not true, thus reducing the degree of acceptance of the new experiences. For this reason it is very important that the environment behaves in a way that is realistic enough to make the user feel comfortable and familiar.

However, the deformation of reality is a tool that can also be exploited in order to increase the quality of the experience and of learning. A very common technique in animation and game development is the exaggeration of the deformation of objects, to obtain a more dramatic effect. In the context of serious games for risk prevention, the exaggeration of the effects of certain actions (in the form of accidents or damage to objects) can be very beneficial to the goal of the game. Although this premise can seem contradictory with the previous statement about realism, it is not; the key is in using this technique in a selected set of situations. During the situations that are less relevant for the goals of the game, realism is important, to make the user confident and to create a believable situation. It is during the situations that cause risk, or when the user performs an action that can have consequences to her health, that these exaggerated dynamics are most adequate. As it is unlike that the user has a large experience in such situations, a lack of realism will not be perceived as a mistake of the game. In addition, an over-actuated behavior will help to make the user aware of the consequences of her actions, and will reinforce learning.

Previous issues are directly related with the dynamic properties of the virtual environment. There is an additional factor that, although it does not relate directly to these properties, can affect the quality of the application. This factor is the efficiency of the implementation of the physics and dynamic models in the game. The reason is that models that take a long time to compute the evolution of the dynamics of the environment can slow down the execution of the application, affecting the frame rate of the graphics application. However, in many cases accurate models, coming from specialized fields of engineering or physics, are computationally intensive. Thus, the election of a model has to reach a trade-off between efficiency and realism or accuracy.

7.4.2.2 Physics Engine Selection

Taking into account the previous considerations, we give next some remarks on the most relevant physics engines, to guide the selection when developing a serious game:

- ODE (http://www.ode.org): ODE is an open source, library for simulating rigid body dynamics. It has advanced joint types and integrated collision detection with friction. Its accuracy is not very high.

- Bullet physics (http://www.bulletphysics.com): It is a professional open source collision detection, rigid body and soft body dynamics library. It is also integrated in MAYA and Blender3D.
- Newton Dynamics (http://newtondynamics.com): It is an integrated solution for real time simulation of physics environments. The API provides scene management, collision detection and dynamic behavior.
- Vortex (http://www.vxsim.com): It simulates the behavior of vehicles, robotics, and heavy equipment in real-time synthetic environments for operator training and test. It is integrated in OSG and VEGA
- PhysX (http://nvidia.com/object/physx_new.html): It delivers real-time, hyper-realistic physical and environmental gaming effects: explosions, reactive debris, realistic water, and lifelike character motion. Everything is computed in the NVidia® GPU.
- Havok FX (http://www.havok.com): It is a physic engine that runs entirely on GPU and provides failure-free physic simulation using proprietary techniques for ensuring robustness, collision detection, dynamics and constraint solving. It provides integrated vehicle solutions and other tools available for simulating clothes, skeletons physics and rigid body destruction.

7.4.3 Use of Avatars

Virtual actors, or *Avatars*, are a major element in most safety training applications, and are especially relevant in observation-based games (see Fig. 7.3). Pre-recorded animations of avatars, using techniques such as motion capture, are able to reproduce detailed and natural human movements (Van Welbergen et al., 2010).

Although avatars are usually represented by polyhedral models or meshes, real-time animation requires a small number of polygons and specific data structures to

Fig. 7.3 An avatar waiting for user interaction

accelerate the computing process (Kalra et al., 1998). Hence, a skeleton approach is generally used to control its movement. A skeleton is defined as an articulated structure and it is composed of a hierarchy of segments which are connected through joins. Different poses can be achieved by rotating the joins of the skeleton.

However, in interactive applications the use of pre-recorded animations alone is not always sufficient. When the player gets in physical contact with other actors in the virtual environment, it is very important that they behave in a feasible way. For this reason the combination of physics based animations with pre-recorded animations is an active research field (Ye et al., 2008; Van Welbergen et al., 2010).

Currently, most game engines include support for avatars e.g. cry engine, unreal engine, havoc. They usually allow the programmer to control different parts of the body, using either a muscle- or a bone-based model. Some of these also include support for facial expressions, and even provide library functions to control the free movement of hair and clothes. A good example of this is NaturalMotion (http://www.naturalmotion.com), which includes an avatar control library called Euphoria.

7.4.4 Game Scoring and Feedback

In an instructional game, it is important to design a scoring system that (a) encourages the player (b) motivates improvement and (c) accurately reflects the user's progress. Although scoring already provides a useful tool from an evaluation perspective, instructional games for safety training should also provide feedback in this direction. In addition, this feedback shall not be limited to the player, but also serve to instructional designers as a means for game improvement as part of the maintenance tasks.

One common form to provide feedback is the creation of game reports that summarize the player's performance and record her progress. Data recorded on these reports are application specific, but common variables are detailed below:

- Date and time of the game
- The score achieved
- The time needed to complete the activity
- Level of achievement of the objectives
- Annotations on potentially dangerous actions

From a player's perspective, this feedback contributes to avoiding the same mistakes in future games. From a designer's perspective, the reports can also be used to determine the educational effectiveness of each task. For example, activities which repeatedly produced empty reports may be removed from the game, or others which do not achieve their instructional objective may be scheduled for improvement.

Hence, evaluation modules and automatic report generators are essential components in instructional games. The former calculate relevant statistics from the user activity in the session. The latter aims at producing a final document that summarizes the results achieved. To this end, a number of parameters and performance information are stored during the simulation process e.g. the time required to complete the activities, the number of collision hits, and the objectives achieved. At the end of the session, all these data are summarized under a number of appropriate variables, and processed to obtain predefined metrics. A popular technique is to use XML files to store the data generated by the evaluation module, and a Stylesheet Transformation Language (XSLT) to convert the XML data into a final report. Chart libraries or command-line plotting programs can also be used to include graphs that facilitate the evaluation of the operator's skills e.g. ChartDirector (http://www.advsofteng.com), Gnuplot (http://www.gnuplot.info).

7.5 Conclusions and Future Trends

Recognizing the important of feedback in learning, there is a current trend towards the development of adaptive training systems. This can be described as "serious game-based systems whose goal is to engender communication opportunities for players to learn about their strengths and weaknesses, receive real-time in-game assessment feedback on their performance, and share diverse solutions and strategies during, between, and after game play in order to update and adapt their understanding" (Raybourn, 2007).

Another trend consists of the use of affective computing, including the use of affective behaviors on game avatars to improve realism; and the recognition of player's emotions to tailor the game and increase the player's engagement.

With regard to the technology used, the use of tools (e.g. the NVIDIA® CUDA toolkit) to program algorithms on GPUs and increase the processing capability are becoming widespread. This type of tools attempt to exploit the parallelism offered by the multiple kernels in the GPUs, allowing for more realistic simulations.

If serious games are already a means to provide health and safety training, these new trends and other technological developments will increase their advantages over other more traditional training methods in the near future. Nevertheless, perhaps the most challenging issues are not at the technology side. Although the achievement of more realistic simulations may also benefit the learning process, further research is still needed on instructional methods that maximize the effectiveness of the training.

References

Ariffin, M.M.; Downe, A.G.; Aziz, I.A.A.: Developing a simulation game to facilitate the acquisition and transfer of road safety knowledge. Information Technology (ITSim), 2010 international symposium, vol. 2, pp. 924–929, 15–17 June 2010

Backlund, P., Engstrom, H., Hammar, C., Johannesson, M., Lebram, M.:. Sidh – a game based firefighter training simulation. In: Proceedings of the 11th International Conference Information Visualization (IV '07), pp. 899–907. IEEE Computer Society, Washington, DC, USA (2007a)

Backlund, P., Engstrom, H., Johannesson, M., Lebram, M.: Games and traffic safety – an experimental study in a game-based simulation environment. In: Proceedings of the 11th

International Conference Information Visualization (IV '07), pp. 908–916. IEEE Computer Society, Washington, DC, USA (2007b)

Bellotti, F., Berta, R., Gloria, A.D., Primavera, L.: Enhancing the educational value of video games. Comput. Entertain. **7**(2), 1–18 (2009)

Carless, S.: Postcard From SGS 2005: Hazmat: first responder gaming, Gamasutra (2005)

Chittaro, L., Ranon, R.: Serious games for training occupants of a building in personal fire safety skills. Games and virtual worlds for serious applications, 2009. VS-GAMES'09. Conference, pp. 23–24, 76–83, March 2009

Cruz-Neira, C., Sandin, D.J., DeFanti, T.A., Kenyon, R.V., Hart, J.C.: The cave: Audio visual experience automatic virtual environment. Commun. ACM 35(6), 64–72 (1992)

Dickinson, J.K., Woodard, P., Canas, R., Ahamed, S., Lockston, D. (2011) Game-based trench safety education: Development and lessons learned, ITcon Vol. 16, Special Issue Use of Gaming Technology in Architecture, Engineering and Construction , pp. 119–134

Eagle, M., Barnes, T.: Experimental evaluation of an educational game for improved learning in introductory computing. ACM SIGCSE Bull. **41**(1), 321–325 (2009)

Ebert, D.S.: Texturing & Modeling: A Procedural Approach. Morgan Kauffmann, San Fransisco, CA (2003)

European Agency for Safety and Health at Work: http://osha.europa.eu/en/statistics/index.stm

Froschauer, J., Seidel, I., Gärtner, M., Berger, H., Merkl, D.: Design and evaluation of a Serious Game for immersive cultural training. In: 2010 16th International Conference on Virtual Systems and Multimedia (VSMM), pp. 253–260, 20–23 Oct (2010)

Jensen, R.S.: OpenSceneGraph Max Exporter (OsgExp), http://osgmaxexp.wiki.sourceforge.net (2002)

Kalra, P., Magnenat-Thalmann, N., Moccozet, L., Sannier, G., Aubel, A., Thalmann, D.: Real-time animation of realistic virtual humans. IEEE Comput. Graph. Appl. **18**(5), 42–56 (1998)

Kirkpatrick, D.L.: Techniques for evaluating training programs. J. Am. Soc. Training Dev. **13**, 3–9 (1959)

Lin, K.Y., Son, J.W., Rojas, E.M.: A pilot study of a 3D game environment for construction safety education. In: ITcon Vol. 16, Special Issue Use of Gaming Technology in Architecture, Engineering and Construction, pp. 69–84 (2011)

Liu, Z.: Design of a cartoon game for traffic safety education of children in China, Technologies for e-Learning and Digital Entertainment. Lecture Notes in Computer Science, Vol. 3942, pp. 589–559. Springer, Berlin, Heidelberg (2006)

Max, N.L., Becker, B.G.: Bump shading for volume textures. IEEE Comput. Graph. Appl. **14**(4), 18–20 (1994)

McComas, J., MacKay, M., Pivik, J.: Effectiveness of virtual reality for teaching pedestrian safety. CyberPsychol. Behav. **5**(3), 185–190 (2002)

McGowan, C., Pecheux, B.: Serious Games that improve performance. Sigma: Information Technology – June, 22–26 (2008)

Namee, B.M., Rooney, P., Lindstrom, P., Ritchie, A., Boylan, F., Burke, G.: Serious Gordon: Using serious games to teach food safety in the kitchen. In: 9th International Conference on Computer Games: AI, Animation, Mobile, Educational and Serious Games CGAMES06. Dublin, Ireland (2006)

Pinell, D., Wong, N., Stach, T.: Heuristic evaluation for games: Usability principles for video game design. In: Proceeding of the Twenty-Sixth Annual SIGCHI Conference on Human Factors in Computing Systems, pp. 1453–1462. Florence, Italy (2008)

Pla-Castells, M., Garcia-Fernandez, I., Martínez-Durá, R.J.: Interactive terrain simulation and force distribution models in sand piles. Lecture Notes on Computer Science, vol. 4173, pp. 392–401 (2006)

Raybourn, E.M.: Applying simulation experience design methods to creating serious game-based adaptive training systems. Interacting Comput. **19**(2), HCI Issues in Computer Games, 206–214 (2007)

Van Welbergen, H., Van Basten, B.J.H., Egges, A., Ruttkay, Zs.M., Overmars, M.H.: Real time animation of virtual humans: A trade-off between naturalness and control. Comput. Graph. Forum **29**(8), 2530–2554 (2010)

Wang, R., Qian, X.: OpenSceneGraph 3.0. Packt Publishing (2010)

Ye, Y., Liu, C.K.: Animating responsive characters with dynamic constraints in near-unactuated coordinates. In: Proceedings of ACM SIGGRAPH Asia. Los Angeles, California, USA (2008). ISBN: 1849512825, ISBN 13: 978-1-84951-282-4

Chapter 8
Augmenting Initiative Game Worlds with Mobile Digital Devices

Jule Hildmann and Hanno Hildmann

8.1 Introduction

In a book dedicated to electronic device based games, this chapter might at first glance appear exotic or even out of place. For the games described on these pages traditionally decline the use of electronic equipment and are on the contrary based on purely real life experiences and interactions. Upon closer inspection, however, they do make use of a form of virtual reality and there are great chances for augmenting these game worlds by means of mobile digital devices in order to intensify and personalise the learning experience as well as to monitor and evaluate the players' progress. A number of parameters are discussed that need to be addressed by a programme designed for this kind of blended learning. Furthermore, a procedure is presented to evaluate its degree of effectiveness.

8.2 Experiential Education and Adventure Initiative Games

Experiential Education is an educational approach not primarily concerned with knowledge acquisition but focusing on the training of behavioural skills in order to increase social and personal competences in its participants. While the roots of this approach can be traced back as far as the philosophers of ancient Greece (Fischer and Ziegenspeck, 2000; Heckmair et al., 2004), it is currently experiencing a wave of mainstream popularity, due to its proven success (Rehm, 1999; Bieligk, 2005; Gass, 1993; Hildmann, 2010) and a high fun factor in many of the "tools" employed in experiential education programmes. Among these tools are outdoor sports, trust activities, expeditions, various "soft" methods such as exercises on awareness or nature perception and adventure initiative games.

The latter is a large field of group challenges ranging from simple and short tasks to complex rallies or treasure hunts of several days duration. Also in terms of means,

J. Hildmann (✉)
Centrum für Erlebnispädagogik Volkersberg, Volkersberg, Germany
e-mail: jule.hildmann@gmx.de

M. Ma et al. (eds.), *Serious Games and Edutainment Applications*,
DOI 10.1007/978-1-4471-2161-9_8, © Springer-Verlag London Limited 2011

Fig. 8.1 Totally different from rock climbing: group challenges in a high ropes cours

the variety is rich: Some initiative problems require complex arrays of material and pre-built structures (up to entire high ropes courses). Others are no less intricate but make do with merely everyday material and common locations. The first author, being a trainer and train-the-trainer in this field, specialises on such *SimpleThings* (Hildmann, 2008) – in order to make initiative games implementable to a wide range of facilitators, not all of which can be expected to have access to large constructions (logs, a 3 m high "escalation wall") and other special equipment often used in the field (Fig. 8.1).

In the last paragraph, we have used the term *initiative game* as well as *task* or *problem*. These activities certainly do fulfill all aspects generally associated with games and playing (e.g. (Hoppe, 2006)). However, in some contexts – for example in a leadership skill workshop for high ranking managers – "playing" would be an instruction strongly frowned upon. The same may be possible with a group of teenagers who would deem it childish to "play games". So, without any change to the content or objectives of the activity, we have a subtle choice of labels to make our players, participants or clients feel more at ease with what they are about to do.

8.2.1 General Structure and Key Aspects

In the most abstract sense, an initiative game is a challenge given to a group of players that can only be completed successfully through cooperative interaction. In addition, depending in the goals of the event, a number of other behavioural or communicative skills can be required (see the section on educational goals below).

Ideally, the games follow the same principles of engagement and effective learning that Clark Quinn (Quinn, 2007, pp. 142/143) suggests for computer-based simulations:

- *Theme*: an integrating world to serve as context for the learning
- *Goal*: a clear goal to achieve
- *Challenge*: the right level of difficulty in achieving the goal

- *Action/domain link*: the learner's actions must meaningfully affect the learner's ability to achieve the goal in the world
- *Problem/learner link*: the goal and world need to be of interest to the learner
- *Active*: the learner will have to make choices and explore the entailments of the world
- *Direct*: the learner must act directly in the world
- *Feedback*: the world must react to the learner's actions
- *Affect*: the world will address the learner's emotional engagement through novelty and humor.

The interested reader who wishes to get more information or examples of these features is kindly referred to the classical literature on adventure initiative games (Rohnke, 1989; Rohnke and Butler, 1995; Sonntag, 2002; Reiners, 2003; Gilsdorf and Kistner, 2003).

Another essential principle of experiential education in general and initiative games in particular is *challenge by choice*. Meant by this is the right of every person which is involved in the exercise or game to decide to what degree he[1] wants to engage and face a challenge. On the one hand, this rule guarantees a sense of safety and self control ("I don't have to do anything here that I don't wish to do"), while at the same time it builds the training ground for self responsibility ("If you want something to happen here and want to make some kind of progress, it is your own responsibility to contribute as much as necessary to reach that goal").

In teenagers, it can sometimes be observed that someone is trying to misuse this right of self determination simply to avoid a potentially unpleasant situation (e.g. outings in bad weather, carrying out conflicts, activities that might cause fear or a felt loss of face and social status, being grouped up with 'uncool' class mates, etc.). In order to prevent this, the alternative to participating must be as dull and *uncool* as possible without appearing as a punishment. Sitting on a chair facing the group, but not being allowed to make comments – helpful or not – or engage in any other activity is a good example: in our experience few *too-cool-for-this-childish-stuff-teenagers* will endure such treatment for longer than two minutes before asking the trainer to be allowed to rejoin the game. And for all legitimate reasons to not participate, some supporting function can easily be created for this person to be of equal value and engagement level as the rest of their team.

Two examples:

1. A Muslim girl rigorously refuses to participate in an activity where all players are tightly bound together with a rope and have to pass through an obstacles parcours. The trainer assumes, that the reason for her objection might be cultural and linked to the close physical contact. So without making this hypothesis a public issue and thereby a possible stage for embarrassment for the girl, he

[1] The authors feel that the politically correct "he/she" will only impact the readability of the chapter and have chosen to use the male version only.

adds the requirement to have a few group members blindfolded. Through this he spontaneously created the new role of a 'safety guard', i.e. someone who has to watch carefully that everybody is aware of all obstacles and nobody gets hurt. This way, the girl can participate meaningfully in the group activity and is not singled out.

2. An office team arrives for a team training at a high ropes course with one gentleman declining to go anywhere above waist hight because of extreme fear of height. In this case, the trainer can explain to the entire group, that the climbing part of the challenge is no more important than the belay partner on the ground (as well as other functioners helping in solving the task set for the team). So by offering a new perspective on the equal value of different roles, the timid person can turn his individual strengths and resources into a valuable asset for the team effort instead of being reduced to one particular weakness.

8.2.2 Function and Role of the Trainer

Since the social dynamics within the group of players present a vital part in the learning process, it is essential that the instructor draws as little attention upon himself as possible. Therefore, his interaction with the group and involvement in the exercise should be strictly confined to the beginning, end and emergencies:

- *Start of the game*: The instructor gives all necessary information and safety rules and provides answers to questions as they arise. Where applicable, he will introduce the players into the frame story.
- *During the game*: He will be as invisible and unobtrusive as possible, merely present to observe the process, guard safety rules and intervene in cases of (physical or socio-emotional) emergency.
- *After the game*: The instructor resumes a central role by conducting the reflexion and evaluation procedure of the learning outcome. Depending on the programme, he will also initiate the transfer of the outcome and/or lead on to a new game or other activity.

From the above, the eager computer scientist will be able to draw a lot of arguments for the potential of using mobile devices. Especially the observation of the players and the maintaining of safety measurements can be greatly supported by such devices. Before we make that case we will first have a closer look at the design and creation of the game scenarios and exercise settings.

8.2.3 Creating Virtual Worlds in Adventure Initiative Games

The 'worlds' or game settings created in an adventure initiative game are not virtual in terms of existing only as a digital construct, but because they are an imaginary setting and scenario. Traditionally, such framing stories are supported by a number

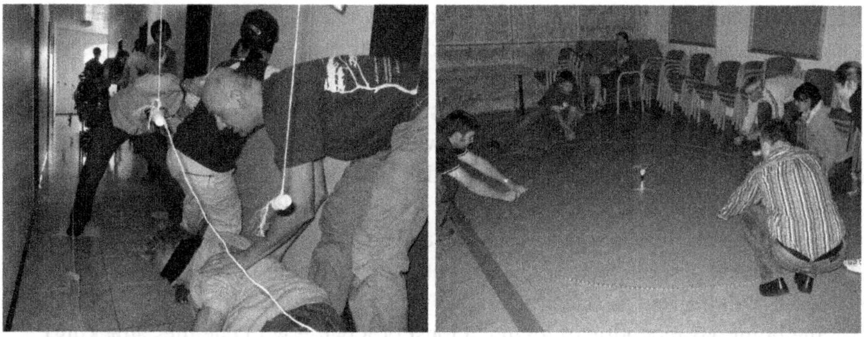

Fig. 8.2 Crossing a jungle and stealing a guarded diamond – two of countless virtual worlds in adventure initiative games

of props. These props by themselves are not the important part of the exercise and their use is normally kept to a minimum (due to cost and effort required to put these real 3-d object into place).

It is also not uncommon for the instructor to assume a certain role in the game world, within which he addresses the participants accordingly. This inclusion of an autonomous intelligent agent into the scenario and story automatically engages the players from the very beginning and often renders meta-instructions obsolete (Fig. 8.2).

8.3 Reaching Educational Goals with Initiative Games

8.3.1 Personality Growth

The main objective of experiential education and therefore also of initiative games is the nursing and training of social as well as personal competencies in the players. Among the large number of *personal skills* are frustration tolerance, problem solving strategies and dealing constructively with one's strengths and weaknesses. Likewise, *social competence* covers a plethora of skills and abilities such as effective communication, helping and motivating others or showing positive conflict behaviour. Since both areas show great overlaps, they usually go hand in hand as one major field of personality growth.

The challenges presented in form of initiative games are designed and chosen to focus on specific social and personal skills – depending to the goals set out by the programme participants and – if applicable – their employer.

8.3.2 Delivering Academic Curriculum Contents

It has recently been shown that even the academic curriculum can be transported via initiative games when they are adapted for regular school lessons (Hildmann,

2010; Hildmann and Hildmann, 2009b). To achieve this, the lesson content is used to create the frame story to an initiative problem that has to be solved by the group of students cooperatively.

For example, in a history lesson on castles, the students might be instructed in groups to build desk size fortress from whatever material they find in the class room. Afterwards, they have to give a "guided tour" around their castle for the other groups, pointing out characteristic features such as crenelations or a keep. For fun's sake, an imaginary history on the building and its famous rulers may be added.

Alternatively, a room size fortress might be jointly built in the gym. In a second phase, this will be used as stage for various role play scenarios illustrating castle life (e.g. the pompous reception of a king, a joust or a battle with enemies attacking).

Also, standard initiative games can be connected to academic contents with a similar effect. In this case, the choice, which game is selected is driven by the attempt to provide *interactive metaphors* (Bacon, 1983; fur Erlebnispädagogik Volkersberg, 2010). This means that the virtual game world and the problem it presents to the players should be structurally as close as possible to the real world situation the learning effect is intended for. This phenomenon is called *isomorphism* (Bacon, 1983; fur Erlebnispädagogik Volkersberg, 2010) compare also (Reiners, 1995, 2003; Sonntag, 2002).

The study mentioned was conducted with eighth graders and covered the subject's history, work life skills, art and physical education, but any age group and school subject appears feasible in the authors' view and experience (Fig. 8.3).

8.3.3 Empirical Findings and Support

The effectiveness of complex adventure trainings following the approach of experiential education has been well proven in a variety of languages and countries (for an

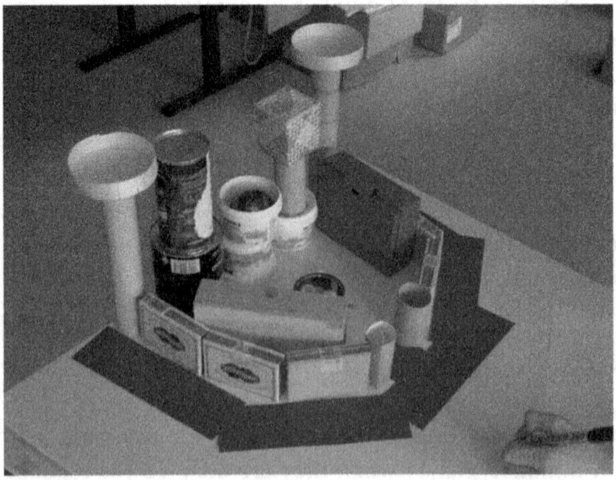

Fig. 8.3 School lessons (here on castles) can be transformed into initiative games by obliging some basic rules of experiential education

overview see (Rehm, 1999; Bieligk, 2005; Gass, 1993). However, the programmes evaluated in these studies consist of a combination of outdoor activities, expeditions, initiative games and other activities.

Regarding the effectiveness purely of adventure initiative games, the only empirical findings known to the authors derive from the study mentioned above on the combination with academic contents. The simple reason for this being that initiative games are one tool among many from which the team trainer chooses to guide the participants in reaching their goals, i.e. increasing and refining their social and personal skills. Therefore, a study evaluating general programmes in experiential education would be ill advised to explore only initiative games.

In the case of the school study, the author focused on initiative games in order to provide concise parameters for the intervention and to present a tool that can easily be adopted by teachers who do not have special qualifications in outdoor sports or other complex activities, which most programmes require from the facilitator.

8.4 Games Based Learning (GBL)

The literature lists many positive aspects of games and playing for general child development and teaching. For example (Spencer and Hafer, 1998, p. 141),

> Play is thought to be a particularly conducive context for promoting further development in cognitive and linguistic skills. Even when a child is playing alone, the freedom and positive affective characteristics of a play context encourage experimentation, flexible application of known behaviors to new objects, and practice and reinforcement of emerging skills

Games have been used to great success to train complex problem solving abilities and practical reasoning skills. When used appropriately, they can significantly reduce the training time as well as the demands put on the instructor. Since games are generally an enjoyable past time, they have the advantage of maintaining high motivation levels in the learners. The act of rehearsing is something inherent to many games and as such is experienced as a pleasant repetition and not a boring drill or automaticity training. Due to this, it has been widely used for decades now by large firms and companies to train their employees (für Erlebnispädagogik Volkersberg, 2010; Hildmann, 2010; Heckmair, 2008).

When investigating the aspects that are credited with making a gaming experience fun, many parallels are found with what researchers think makes for a good learning experience (Gee, 2003; Tiotuico et al., 2008; Quinn, 2007). Findings from the field of psychology indicate that the playing of games is an important factor in the early development of children and young adults. The suggestion to use games in the education sector is neither surprising nor new (Gilsdorf and Kistner, 2003; Reiners, 2003; Hildmann, 2008; Sonntag, 2002).

It should be noted that the intuitive connection to educational institutions is misleading as games based learning is heavily used in the industry both for training and for selection purposes (Hildmann et al., 2010; Hildmann, 2010; für Erlebnispädagogik Volkersberg, 2010; Heckmair, 2008).

8.4.1 Etymology

The young field of games based learning is still struggling to come to terms with itself, with many researchers either being indifferent to a variety of labels slapped on their work or, increasingly insisting on preferring one term over the other. In the early years of (computer) games based learning, games, especially computer games designed for the education sector (or at least containing educational content), were called *edutainment*: a merger of the words *edu*cation and enter*tainment*. While this term fit the intended meaning, it quickly lost its appeal to researchers because the associations it invokes are not balanced between the two words it is derived from. The aspect of entertainment, especially for negative connotations associated with gaming, is seen by some as the antithesis of learning (Connolly et al., 2008), was perceived as the dominant association. Due to this, the two terms *games-based learning* (with or without hyphen) and *serious games* are preferred in the academic literature today.

8.4.2 History of Games Based Learning

The idea of games based learning, or more traditionally: the *educational aspects of games*, is not new. Every military maneuver or every play-acting of household situations (e.g.) can be seen as a game with educational content. Regarding the acceptance of games based learning by educationalists, it should be mentioned that market analysts expect games based learning to become the fastest growing division in the already booming eLearning market (cf. (Connolly et al., 2008)).

8.4.3 Key Concepts of Games Based Learning Intrinsic Motivation

We refer to (Malone and Lepper, 1987) for a detailed account of the important aspects of intrinsic motivation for the designer of educational (computer) games. According to this, there are four individual as well as three interpersonal factors that are the key aspects responsible for creating intrinsic motivation:

Individual factors	Interpersonal factors
Challenge	Cooperation
Fantasy	Competition
Curiosity	Recognition
Control	

Incidentally, these factors also embody the cornerstones a good (i.e. popular) game, irrespective of its educational qualities. For example, two comparative studies, conducted in the years 2005 and 2007 have shown that challenge, curiosity and cooperation consistently emerged as the most important motivations for playing computer games, making games suitable for use in higher education. For the full report on these findings we refer the reader to (Connolly et al., 2007a, b). Generally it is safe to say that the effect of (computer) games based learning has been analysed from many different perspectives, both negative (aggression, violence or gender stereotyping, e.g.) and positive (skills development, engagement, learning or motivation, e.g.) (Connolly et al., 2008).

8.4.4 Fundamental Principles of Good Games

Besides aiming for important aspects of intrinsic motivation identified in the previous section, the game should strive to include as many as possible of the fundamental principles of good games. There is an extensive body of literature that tries to identify those principles; (Gee, 2003, 2004, 2005) singles out the following:

Identity	Agency	Challenge
Consolidation	Interaction	Well-orderd-problems
Pleasantly frustrating	Production	Risk taking
System thinking	Customisation	

Due to limited space, these principles are explained only briefly below:

- *Identity*: Providing a fictional identity (jungle researchers, a rescue squad, plane crash survivors, etc.) automatically puts the players in a, albeit imaginary, situation which imposes all responsibilities and requires all competences associated with the role.
- *Agency*: Giving the participants a sense of self-determination over their decisions (*locus of control*, see (Weber and Rammsayer, 2005)).
- *Challenge and Consolidation*: Mastery of skills is consolidated through repetition in the game, with sufficient challenge and different variations.
- *Interaction*: Offering responses or feedback for the actions of a player.
- *Well-orderd-problems*: Well structured problems lead the participants to logical thinking and to draw on previous experience to solve future problems.
- *Pleasantly frustrating*: Realistically attainable goals at the outer edge of the players *regime of competence* (diSessa, 2000) entice them to develop and employ new skills (compare also (Luckner and Nadler, 1997; Hildmann, 2010; "Centrum" für Erlebnispädagogik Volkersberg, 2010)).
- *Production*: Players are – consciously or unconsciously – steering the game through their decisions.
- *Risk taking*: No or few real world consequences result from actions taken in the game. This allows players to experiment and to take risks.
- *System thinking*: Good games encourage players to think about the effect of their decisions on the game world as a whole. Thereby, the actors reflect on abstract relationships, not just isolated events, facts and skills.

- *Customisation*: By providing a game customized to the specific interests of a group of persons, one can directly challenge and interest them.

Further details and examples can be found in (Gee, 2003, 2004, 2005). Covering these principles should be a mandatory exercise for every game designer with educational intentions.

8.4.5 Key Skills Supported by Games Based Learning

Having identified the fundamental principles of "good" serious games, we now turn to the benefits of playing them. The skills and abilities these games promote are given in Section 6.2.1. For a detailed discourse on these, the reader is referred to (Healy, 2006). All of the listed key skills – and quite a few more – can also be found in the range of classical objectives in initiative games and all of experiential education, as explained above and in Hildmann (2010), the CEP seminars ("Centrum" für Erlebnispädagogik Volkerberg, 2010; Reiners, 2003) or (Gilsdorf and Kistner, 2003). Obviously, the extent to which these skills and abilities are exercised depends on the game's parameters (main goal, rules, player constellations, etc.) and its implementation.

Therefore, it is an early task of the designer of serious games to formalise some sort of preference over these skills as it is unlikely that all can be trained maximally in a single game. This being said, the prototype games presented as illustration and proof of concept in this chapter are primarily challenging the problem solving and social skills of the player. In addition, analytical, logical and critical thinking are required for best performance.

8.5 Mobile Devices

The concept of *mobility* and the idea of *mobile devices* has become a buzzword, not unlike the words *multimedia* and *interactive* in the 90 s. However, what the term mobile device refers to is ill defined. At best we can include all types of devices that are not stationary. This can cover anything ranging from the average laptop to million dollar medical equipment in hospitals, as long as that equipment can be moved from one location to another. In the context of this book, and more specifically of this chapter, the term refers to mobile phones, i.e. to *small, pocket size hand-held computing devices with a small battery and memory supply* (Hildmann et al., 2010). The ideas and results presented do not in any way restrict this to mobile phones, however as cell-phones have become a pervasive technology they can be assumed to be available to everyone and, in addition, they can be obtained at an affordable price.

It is easy to argue that the mobile phone has by now become a pervasive technology which has started to shape our society like few other product families have. For many – and especially the younger – members of our society, a cell phone has become an integral part of their life just as their ability to connect and communicate from *anywhere* and with *anyone* has grown to be one of the main constructs of their social and professional lives.

8.5.1 Mobile Device Based Serious Games

Mobile devices, in particular mobile phones, are a good example for a trend in teenagers and young adults. This young group of people prefers constant cognitive interaction, a trend that has led to a generation of children for whom the mobile aspect of their gadgets is an integral aspect. While the IT facilities at universities, schools and even kindergartens are continuously upgraded to meet today's standards, students started a few years ago to move away from the stationary terminals and the entire physical aspect of information. The existence of open universities and distant learning institutions is but one indicator for this development – and one that in its original form is already starting to become outdated again.

We support the claim that mobile devices in general and mobile phones in specific can be used as the platform for computationally demanding applications. Two games are presented, both of which have been created in collaboration with the authors, and the content of the following sections can be understood as a summary of the respective projects. The interested reader is referred to the individual project related publications, as indicated where appropriate. All three are ongoing research projects focusing on serious games for mobile devices as well as computationally expensive applications that are ported to (or even designed for) hand-held devices.

These examples are given here to show that there is currently a trend towards using mobile devices for serious games and that the field of initiative games and experiential paedagogics can benefit from a framework that focuses using mobile devices to augment the scenarios of these exercises as well as for evaluation, assessment and of course to ensure the necessary safety protocols are in place. The application that is not a game but an optimisation tool is included to show that computationally expensive applications, which only a decade ago required dedicated and bulky computers, can now be designed for mobile devices since the state of the art features sufficient memory as well as computational resources.

8.5.1.1 Utility Tycoon

The first screenshot in Fig. 8.4 shows a screen form the resource management game Utility Tycoon which was previously presented in (Hildmann et al., 2008a, 2010; Hildmann and Hirsch, 2008; Bitterberg et al., 2008) and (Hildmann et al., 2007). This game has been specifically designed to raise awareness for environmental issues and to influence the player's attitudes accordingly.

Figure 8.5 shows three more screens: The module to design new learning targets, the one to amend or combine such targets and the one that allows the tutor or teacher to influence the regular and bonus events in the games for individual players (left to right). The elements concerned with the formal declaration and manipulation

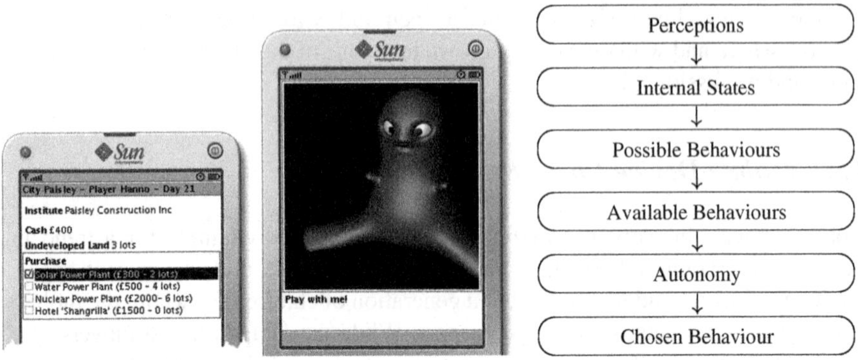

Fig. 8.4 Two Examples: Utility Tycoon and Tama, with an outline of the complex internal behavioural model implemented for TAMA

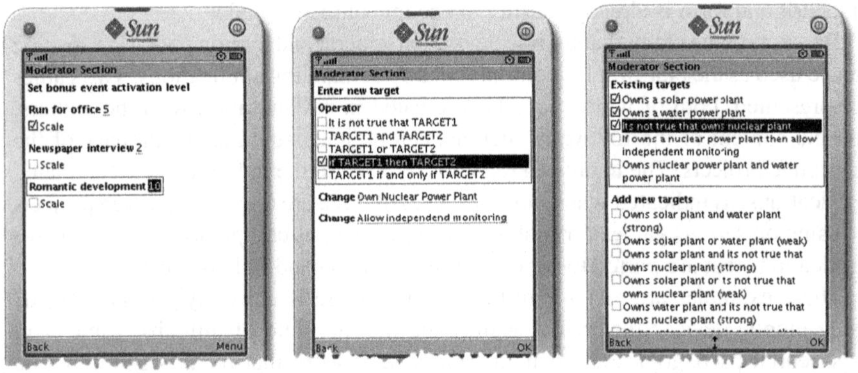

Fig. 8.5 Learning target design, amendment and dynamics (*left* to *right*) of Utility Tycoon

of learning targets have been tested extensively and have been found to be computationally feasible. It has been tested with large test sets on older mobile phones.

8.5.1.2 Tama

The second image in Fig. 8.4 and all in Fig. 8.4 depict a virtual pet called *Tama* which is not unlike the popular tamagotchies that were a hype in the 90 s. This artificial creature was implemented as part of a project on the design of a virtual pet to teach children positive moral values as well as ethics. Tama has a complex behavioural model requiring non trivial amounts of computational power (Hildmann et al., 2008b).

This application showcases the running of this neural network like behavioural model. This computationally expensive application was simulated running multiple incarnations of the model at the same time while performing well within the upper bounds. For more detailed information the reader is referred to (Hildmann et al., 2008b, 2009, 2010) and (Hildmann et al., 2008a).

8.5.2 Mobile Entertainment

Members of the young generation that attends schools and universities today are used to carrying a mobile device with them at all times; and for many, their mobile phone is no longer the only such "toy" they own. In addition to this pervasive nature of the technology, today's students have access to devices that are powerful enough to run computationally expensive applications on them. Most contemporary mobile phones can easily outperform any *computer* on which the 70 s generation played their first games (e.g. Commodore64, Amiga, and Atari). Due to this, we agree with (Motiwalla, 2007) and argue that mobile phones are the ideal platform for the games we have in mind, i.e. for games designed to deliver educational contents.

Like major operating systems, almost all phones come with some simple games pre-installed (e.g. Solitaire, Minesweeper, Snakes) which have become very popular amongst the users. One reason for this fascination is the fact that they are easily understood and designed such that they can be played and paused at any time. Over the last few decades, computer games have steadily replaced more traditional games in the leisure activities sector. In 2007, the Entertainment Software Association reported that "US computer and video game software sales grew six percent in 2006 to $7.4 billion – almost tripling industry software sales since 1996" (Hildmann and Hirsch, 2008).

These numbers are supported by the fact that major console producers (e.g. Nintendo) as well as mobile phone producers (e.g. Nokia) have started to produce mobile gaming devices. There is certainly a trend in the industry to create a market for games specifically conceived and designed to be run on mobile devices.

8.6 Augmenting Game Scenarios in Initiative Games Through Mobile Digital Devices

Much has been said recently regarding the use of "new" technologies in social contexts. As the terms used are often ambiguous or at least used with different references in mind there are a variety of opinions and contradicting stances on the use of immersive technologies and so called "augmented" reality. Some believe that, as part of our natural (for the lack of a better word) evolution/progress, and in order to "to overcome our senses' temporal limitations, we must be able to store and preserve what we perceive as well as access it later" (Schmidt et al., 2011) and go as far as predicting that "by the middle of this century, the boundaries between direct and remote perception will become blurred" more traditional views caution against the use of technology in general and emphasise the importance of low tech approaches. While advocates of the high tech approach concede the point that "[...]

VR applications require expensive hardware and customized software [...]" – but are quick to argue that "[t]he ability to make users believe that they are 'actually there' has made VR a tool of choice for [...] extreme-condition training applications" (Sherstyuk et al., 2010) – we have previously argued for the moderate and well informed use of technologies to supplement the (mainly nature based) training application of experiential exercises (Hildmann and Hildmann, 2009).

On the other hand, adventure initiative games are quite popular and successful without the aid of any digital support or versions. But in the same respect, so were chess and checkers and their popularity or appearance has not changed much when they became digitally implemented. We therefore argue that the field of initiative games can profit greatly from this technological progress.

8.6.1 Enhancing the Gaming and Learning Experience

We see a number of advantages a well considered implementation of programmes run on mobile digital devices could bring to the experiential education trainer as well as programme participants: The primary goal will be to enhance the experience for the players, thereby making the pursuit of their educational goals (see above) more efficient. This enhancement can be achieved by means of increasing the fun and level of engagement within the game, maybe through the use of humorous images and good graphics. Another idea is to spatially separate the players, thus forcing them into telecommunication, while running all opposing teams over one single (e.g. walkie talkie) channel.

Another way of intensifying the experience would be to programme twists and turns into the succession of game moves, such that they can be included into the exercise by the trainer in order to personalise the game parameters and challenges to the specific needs and goals of the players. For example, certain functions on the device (e.g. the transmission of images) have to be used in fixed intervals or the phone will automatically switch off. This would create considerable time pressure and stress on the team of players, since their communication channels are increasingly hindered and diminished. Through options like this, the game would become more versatile and goal-oriented.

Also, the role and degree of the trainer's appearance could be reduced to an attentive observer during the game if a digital scenario master is programmed into the game. This master will nevertheless be run by the trainer, but the players will not be told so. (Ketamo and Kiili, 2009) have shown that this has the effect of the players feeling less observed by the instructor and being more likely to act naturally, ask for help freely and the like.

This thought already leads on to a few crucial pedagogical considerations.

8.6.2 Pedagogical Considerations

Initiative games being one form of games based learning, it must not – despite all enthusiasm for modern technology – be forgotten what the goal of this blended learning is: to support the learning experience and outcome. During the entire process of designing, testing and finally applying such a digitally enhanced initiative game, each step and new adaptation must be scrutinised in respect to whether it actually speeds up, channels or intensifies the pursuit of the educational goals or whether the introduction of a new feature or even the technical device in general is starting to distract energy and attention from the goals, thereby acting counter productive.

This could be the case in an overly complex navigation or if simple add-ons such as a title melody or intro video is so entertaining, that the players procrastinate or even interrupt the actual game progression in order to enjoy this – from an educational point of view unnecessary – feature again and again. It will be the main objective of the evaluation process for such a game (see below) to filter out such distractions.

From the lead author's background in experiential education settings, we encourage that such a new type of initiative game should be designed in a way that it can serve a variety of application fields, for example:

- Professional trainings aiming for team development or leadership skills.
- School groups working to improve social behaviour and team spirit among the students.
- Family events, e.g. families as teams competing against each other.
- Incentive events for companies and other adult groups.

To be able to serve this wide range of applications, the programme will need to include a number of options the facilitator can chose from to customise the game.

- A number of frame stories can be selected to suit the participants age and background. Some examples: a pirate treasure hunt, cracking a secret code to stop a time bomb, creating a medical potion to prevent a virus pandemic, or a fantasy or science fiction setting that might even include costumes and make-up.
- Experience in team work and the level of reflective thinking vary greatly between, say, a class of eighth grade students versus an established team of professionals in a business firm. Therefore, the game needs to be able to run on different levels of complexity (e.g. total number of points gathered, jokers or help desk functions, introduction of stress factors such as time pressure or communication gaps). These might be pre-selected by the facilitator but also need to be influenced process-oriented during the game by the scenario master.
- Although competition is not generally encouraged in experiential education, there are activities that deliberately instruct teams to compete in order to intensify the need for effective cooperation *within* those teams. This option should also be given in the game design by being able to choose either a number of teams for a competitive setting or one single team with a non-competitive task.
- A feature not yet decided upon is the high score, which is a classical part of digital games. While the high score is an incentive for players to play the game and compete against total strangers, neither of which is an objective in this project.

The facilitators will need to know the programme and its features in all details to be able to

- pre-select the framework parameters best suited for the group at hand.
- use all adjustable parameters available during the game (e.g. regarding level of difficulty).
- conduct the game or scenario master's interventions stringently and goal-oriented.
- monitor closely the progress of the players – information valuable for the following reflection and transfer of the learning outcome.

One further aspect is that the general navigation and the use of applications must be simple enough that even persons with a less than average talent for technical devices are not hindered but intrigued by it.

8.6.3 Technical Considerations

Recent roll-outs of new models of mobile devices (specifically phones) have increased the already pervasive nature of respectable computational power carried around by the average person. As e.g. pointed out by Roy Want in his editorial opening Intro for an edition of IEEE's Pervasive Computing (for a issue on Smart Phones), "[a]n important development for smart phone technologies is how they integrate key aspects of what has traditionally been pervasive computing research, including location-based services, context-aware applications, and sensor-driven computing, [. . .]" (Want, 2010).

There are a number of technical issues that needs to be dealt with to ensure an implementation of the programme without interferences. Table 8.1 lists a few cell phone applications that might be used or adapted for the programme. If not readily available on the cell phone chosen by the facilitators, the functions should be adapted to run on the device. Obviously, the only limits to using applications are the limits of computing and creativity. Examples of existing applications that illustrate the use of some of the functionalities mentioned in Table 8.1 below are YELP (Want, 2010), GoogleLatitude, Loopt and Whrrl (Brooker et al., 2010) (GPS), BUMP (Want, 2010) (device recognition/motion sensing).

These requirements evoke further questions, for example which brand and model of mobile phones can be used. The programme must be able to be downloaded from a central server prior to the start of the game. The advantage of this procedure would be that costumers could simply bring along their own cell phone with which they are familiar in terms of handling and menu navigation. Additionally, the need – and therefore cost – for the facilitator to provide one device per participant would become obsolete. Consequently, costs for maintenance and repair could also be minimised to a legal liability level.

However, having costumers use their own cell phones might lead to another set of problems. For example, some older devices might turn out to not or not sufficiently

Table 8.1 Examples for cell phone functions and their possible uses in an initiative game

Cell phone function	Examples for possible uses
GPS	Orienteering tasks, locating players, triggering applications or game moves
Telephone/walkie talkie	Communication among players
Text messages	Communication among players, transmitting clues
Camera	Record results, transmitting images of locations, transmitting visual impressions to team members
Voice recorder	Record sounds in the surrounding as well as spoken messages
Video recorder	Record actions and results of tasks
Internet access	Secured platform for sharing data among team members, home base for frame story, game master and the like
Image display (still and moving images)	Maps, clues, images, interactions with the game master

run all applications of the programme, thereby creating a disadvantage and disturbance factor for this player. It must also be expected that persons attend the session which do not possess an apt device or have forgotten to bring it along. Therefore, there must be a back-up plan, also in case a device displays malfunctions, breaks, runs low on energy, or is too fragile for the owner to be willing to use it in an outdoor setting with possibly wet weather conditions.

We therefore encourage the facilitator to acquire a set of identical mobile phones to ensure that all devices used in the session are

- equal in handling, reception, display quality and transmission speed.
- capable of, and prepared to, perform well for all aspects of the required functionality, i.e. to execute the the programme at optimal speed and quality.
- fully charged.
- durable enough for an outdoor setting and rough handling.

The authors regard this as the only way to guarantee that the pre-phase of the real game session is kept as short as possible and can be cut into a routine, with handing out the devices and a quick run through of the navigation and all necessary functions of the programme, before the participants get started into the actual game. It is even conceivable that the user instructions are integrated into the frame story, say my means of a power point demo, a dressed up role play intro of the game master, e.g.

A note of caution: While there is increasing evidence in the literature for the availability of the required functionalities (across the board) through claims in the tone of "[. . .] smart phones often have extra hardware, like cameras, GPS and compass, built in" (Brooker et al., 2010) and through statements like "Currently-developed prototype systems present unusual, fascinating aspects, enabling real-world screen shots to identified by name or providing relevant information by

Fig. 8.6 The wise manitou and her bison. Dress-up intros by the game master(s) are highly engaging and fun for kids as well as adults

directing a mobile device towards a target." (Lee et al., 2009), the critical investigator will find that optimistic claims like e.g. "With their GPS speed and accelerometer motion sensor, they can be used to monitor activity levels for health applications." (Longstaff et al., 2010) are discredited by the critics stating that e.g. "The GPS in your smartphone can tell you in the best case where you are within 1 – 10 m, but in a city with tall buildings, the accuracy can drop to 40 m because the device can't 'see' enough GPS satellites for a reasonably accurate position fix" (Bogdanowicz, 2011). This highlights the importance of verifying whether the application considered for purchase can actually provide the required functionality *in the location* where it is going to be used and *under all conditions* it will be subjected to during an exercise.

8.6.4 Evaluation and Assessment

The authors are currently designing an outdoor initiative game augmented by mobile digital devices as described above. No empirical data on its success can be provided at this point of time, but a thorough evaluation procedure is included in the project design in a manner we generally recommend for assessing this kind of blended learning project.

A first test run will be carried out with a group of experienced trainers in outdoor and experiential education, in our case recruited from the staff of the *CEP Centrum für Erlebnispädagogik Volkersberg* (*Centre for Experiential Education*, Bavaria, Germany). They will take the roll of regular participants in a professional team training and not have any prior insight into the programme or game. They will receive the device navigation and general playing instructions just like a real client group would. After the face to face game session and an in role evaluation of the learning outcome and transfer value for the "clients", they will be asked to switch roles and make use of their professional expertise to offer critical feedback on technical, practical and educational aspects of the digital construct and the entire game. After incorporating this feedback and adjusting the original programme and game design, a second test run will be conducted. This time, a real client group will be asked to take part in a newly developed intervention method of blended learning. Great consideration will be given to the choice of group, since it should represent well the field of future implementation (see above). After the team related evaluation and transfer activities, the participants will be asked for their opinion and feedback on the game in regard to usability, effectiveness, and measure of enjoyability.

8.7 Conclusion

8.7.1 Main Findings and Issues

Initiative games come in various shapes and sizes but are not traditionally associated with digital devices. However, we see great chances in blended learning, using programmed cell phones – or for that matter other mobile digital devices – to:

- enrich the gaming experience for the players.
- monitor and evaluate the learning progress of the participants more accurately.
- run a series of game versions and adjustable parameters to optimally suit the client group's constellation and goals.
- allow the trainer to become near to invisible during the game through the introduction of a digital scenario master.

In the designing as well as the application process, a number of technical and educational considerations have to be made. Most crucially, it must not be forgotten that such a blended learning project is not intended to please the technology crazed youth and their appetite for new gadgets or to impress with special effects and applications, but purely to augment the learning and training effect for the participants. Therefore, the devices must at all times be regarded merely as a means to serve an end, the handling has to be kept as simple as possible and each function needs to be scrutinised whether it serves the purpose or instead adds unnecessary complexity and distracts attention rather than channel it.

8.7.2 Further Steps and Research

The programme as we have suggested it is currently in the designing phase, but test runs are already scheduled with experts and real clients to assess and optimise the project. This assessment phase should bring forth which elements of the game prove most effective and which will need to be redesigned or deleted. Also, a critical look will have to be given to the question of client groups the game scenarios are deemed appropriate for and which additional adaptations will have to be made. The gathered results will have to be evaluated before further steps towards dissemination, variation or – beware – discarding the project as unsuccessful can be taken.

8.7.3 Summary and Outlook

We argue that mobile digital devices can and should be implemented to augment initiative games in order to intensify the training effect on social and personal skills in the players. A fine balance between computational and educational aspects will have to be reached to not allow the technical devices to become a distraction factor rather than a means to the end of enhancing the interaction and training process.

References

Bacon, S.: The Conscious Use of Metaphor. Outward Bound, Denver, CO (1983)

Bieligk, M.: Erlebnispädagogische Ansätze im Sportunterricht. Zeitschrift für Erlebnispädagogik **7/8/9** (2005)

Bitterberg, T., Hildmann, H., Branki, C.: Using resource management games for mobile phones to teach social behaviour. In: Proceedings of Techniques and Applications for Mobile Commerce (TAMoCo08), Glasgow, Scotland, pp. 77–84. IOS Press, Amsterdam, Netherlands (2008)

Bogdanowicz, A.: Augementing your reality – ieee members are changing the way we look at the world. The Insitute – IEEE.org pp. 6–7 (2011)

Brooker, D., Carey, T., Warren, I.: Middleware for social networking on mobile devices. In: Software Engineering Conference (ASWEC), 2010 21st Australian, pp. 202–211 (2010). doi 10.1109/ASWEC.2010.13

Centrum für Erlebnispädagogik Volkersberg: Erlebnispädagogisches Denken und Handeln I und II - Skript zum gleichnamigen Modul der Weiterbildung zum erlebnispädagogischen Kompetenztrainer. CEP, Bad Brückenau, Germany (2010)

Connolly, T., Boyle, E., Hainey, T.: A survey of students' motivations for playing computer games: A comparative analysis. In: Proceedings of 1st European Conference on Games-based Learning (ECGBL), Paisley, Scotland (2007a)

Connolly, T., Boyle, E., Stansfield, M., Hainey, T.: A survey of students' computer game playing habits. J. Adv. Technol. Learn. **4**(4) (2007b)

Connolly, T., Stansfield, M., Josephson, J., Lzaro, N., Rubio, G., Ortiz, C., Tsvetkova, N., Tsvetanova, S.: Using alternate reality games to support language learning. In: Proceedings. Web-Based Education WBE 2008, Innsbruck, Austria (2008)

diSessa, A.: Changing Minds: Computers, Learning and Literacy. MIT Press, Cambridge, MA (2000)

Fischer, T., Ziegenspeck, J.: Handbuch Erlebnispädagogik. Von den Ursprüngen bis zur Gegenwart. Klinkhardt, Bad Heilbrunn/Obb, Germany (2000)

Gass, M.: Adventure Therapy: Therapeutic Implications of Adventure Programming. Kendall & Hunt, Dubuque, IA (1993)

Gee, J.: What Video Games Have to Teach Us About Learning and Literacy. Palgrave Macmillan, New York, NY, USA (2003)

Gee, J.: Situated Language and Learning: A Critique of Traditional Schooling. Routledge, New York, NY, USA (2004)

Gee, J.: Why Video Games are Good For Your Soul: Pleasure and Learning. Common Ground (2005)

Gilsdorf, R., Kistner, G.: Kooperative Abenteuerspiele 1 & 2. In: *Praxishilfe für Schule, Jugendarbeit und Erwachsenenbildung*, vol. 12. Kallmeyer, Germany, Seelze-Velber (2003)

Healy, A.: Does game based learning, based on constructivist pedagogy, enhance the learning experience and outcomes for the student compared to a traditional didactic pedagogy? Master's thesis, University of Paisley, Paisley, Scotland (2006)

Heckmair, B.: Erlebnisorientierte Lernprojekte. Szenarien für Trainings, Seminare und Workshops, vol. 3. Beltz, Weinheim, Germany and Basel, Switzerland (2008)

Heckmair, B., Michl, W.: Erleben und Lernen. Einführung in die Erlebnispädagogik. Reinhardt, München, Germany (2004)

Hildmann, H., Hildmann, J.: A critical reflection on the potential of mobile device based tools to assist in the professional evaluation and assessment of observable aspects of learning or (game) playing. In: 3rd European Conference on Games Based Learning. API, Academic Publishing International, Graz, Austria (2009a)

Hildmann, H., Hirsch, B.: Raising awareness for environmental issues through mobile device based serious games. In: 4th Microsoft Academic Days, Berlin, Germany (2008)

Hildmann, H., Branki, C., Pardavila, C., Livingstone, D.: A framework for the development, design and deployment of customisable mobile and hand held device based serious games. In: Proceedings of 2nd European Conference on Games Based Learning (ECGBL08), Barcelona, Spain. API, Academic Publishing International (2008a)

Hildmann, H., Hainey, T., Livingstone, D.: Psychology and logic: design considerations for a customisable educational resource management game. In: The Fifth Annual International Conference in Computer Game Design and Technology, Liverpool, England (2007)

Hildmann, H., Uhlemann, A., Livingstone, D.: A mobile phone based virtual pet to teach social norms and behaviour to children. In: The 2nd IEEE International Conference on Digital Game and Intelligent Toy Enhanced Learning (Digitel 2008), Banff, Canada (2008b)

Hildmann, H., Uhlemann, A., Livingstone, D.: An (artificial) neural network driven behavioural model for virtual pets on mobile phones. Comput. Inform. Syst. **13**(2) (2009). School of Computing Journal, University of the West of Scotland.

Hildmann, H., Uhlemann, A., Livingstone, D.: Simple mobile phone based games to adjust the player's behaviour and social norms. Int. J. Mobile Learn. Organ. (IJMLO), Special Issue on Emerging Mobile Learning Environments for Industries and Pedagogies **3**(3), 289–305 (2010)

Hildmann, J.: SimpleThings. Erlebnispädagogik mit Alltagsgegenständen. erleben & lernen **3/4**, 45–47 (2008)

Hildmann, J.: Problems are chances in disguise – promoting social and personal skills through experiential education in the classroom. Ph.D. thesis, Ludwig-Maximilians-Universität, Munich, Germany (2010)

Hildmann, J., Hildmann, H.: Promoting social skills through initiative games in the classroom and assessing their success. In: 3rd European Conference on Games Based Learning. API, Academic Publishing International, Graz, Austria (2009b)

Hoppe, H.: Spiele finden und erfinden. Ein Leitfaden für die Spielpraxis. No. 3 in Forum SpielTheaterPädagogik. LIT, Berlin, Germany (2006)

Ketamo, H., Kiili, K.: New teachership in game worlds. In: 3rd European Conference on Games Based Learning. API, Academic Publishing International, Graz, Austria (2009)

Lee, R., Kwon, Y.J., Sumiya, K.: Layer-based media integration for mobile mixed-reality applications. In: Next Generation Mobile Applications, Services and Technologies, 2009. NGMAST '09. Third International Conference on, pp. 58–63 (2009). doi 10.1109/NGMAST.2009.90

Longstaff, B., Reddy, S., Estrin, D.: Improving activity classification for health applications on mobile devices using active and semi-supervised learning. In: Pervasive Computing Technologies for Healthcare (PervasiveHealth), 2010 4th International Conference, pp. 1–7, Munich, Germany (2010)

Luckner, J., Nadler, R.: Processing the Experience. Strategies to Enhance and Generalize Learning. Kendall & Hunt., Dubuque, IA (1997)

Malone, T., Lepper, M.R.: Making learning fun: a taxonomy of intrinsic motivations for learning. In: Aptitude, Learning and Instruction, vol. 3: Conative and Affective Process Analysis, pp. 223–235. Routledge, New York, NY, USA. ISBN 0898597218, 9780898597219 (1987)

Motiwalla, L.F.: Mobile learning: a framework and evaluation. J. Comput. Educ. **49**(3), 581–596 (2007)

Quinn, C.: Computer-Based Simulations: Principles of Engagement, The Handbook of Experiential Learning. Pfeiffer, San Francisco, CA (2007)

Rehm, M.: Evaluationen erlebnispädagogischer Programme im englischsprachigen Raum. Eine Übersicht über 65 Studien. Wissenschaftliche Forschung in der Erlebnispädagogik. Tagung Hochschulforum Erlebnispädagogik. Ziel, Augsburg, Germany (1999)

Reiners, A.: Erlebnis und Pädagogik. Sandmann, München, Germany (1995)

Reiners, A.: Praktische Erlebnispädagogik. Neue Sammlung motivierender Interaktionsspiele, Vol. 6. Ziel, Augsburg, Germany (2003)

Rohnke, K.: Cowstails and Cobras II. A Guide to Games, Initiatives, Ropes Courses, & Adventure Curriculum. Kendall & Hunt, Dubuque, IA (1989)

Rohnke, K., Butler, S.: Quicksilver. Adventure Games, Initiative Problems, Trust Activities and a Guide to Effective Leadership. Kendall & Hunt/MIT Press, Dubuque, IA (1995)

Schmidt, A., Langheinrich, M., Kersting, K.: Perception beyond the here and now. Computer **44**(2), 86–88 (2011). doi 10.1109/MC.2011.54

Sherstyuk, A., Vincent, D., Treskunov, A.: Toward natural selection in virtual reality. Comput. Graph. Appl. IEEE **30**(2), 93–96,C3 (2010). doi 10.1109/MCG.2010.34

Sonntag, C.: Abenteuer Spiel – Handbuch zur Anleitung kooperativer Abenteuerspiele. Ziel, Augsburg, Germany (2002)

Spencer, P., Hafer, J.: Play as "window" and "room": assessing and supporting the cognitive and linguistic development of deaf infants and young children. In: Psychological Perspectives on Deafness (eds. M. Marschark and D. Clark), vol. 2, pp. 131–152. Lawrence Erlbaum Associates, Hillsdale, NJ (1998)

Tiotuico, N., Kroll-Peters, O., Stelter, T., Odry, D.: Game design: motivation for mobile gaming created by new technologies. In: Hegering, H.-G., Lehmann, A. (eds.) GI Jahrestagung, Vol. 133, pp. 505–506. Lecture Notes in Informatics, BI Bonn, Germany (2008)

Want, R.: iphone: Smarter than the average phone. Pervasive Comput. IEEE **9**(3), 6–9 (2010). doi 10.1109/MPRV.2010.62

Weber, H., Rammsayer, T.: Handbuch der Persönlichkeitspsychologie und Differentiellen Psychologie. In: *Schriftenreihe Handbuch der Psychologie* (eds. H. Weber and T. Rammsayer), Vol. 2. Hogrefe, Göttingen, Bern, Wien, Toronto, Seattle, Oxford, Prag (2005)

Part III
Custom-Made Games and Case Studies

Chapter 9
Enhancing Learning in Distributed Virtual Worlds through Touch: A Browser-based Architecture for Haptic Interaction

Sylvester Arnab, Panagiotis Petridis, Ian Dunwell, and Sara de Freitas

9.1 Introduction

With advances in technology enhanced learning in education and learners' expectations of high fidelity and engaging game-based experiences, innovations in teaching and learning have become a focus of research and development activities. This is increasingly relevant in a time when teachers run the risk of alienating their students via traditional means of education that do not capitalize on the fact that students are becoming a part of the rapid emergence of "digital natives" or "net generation" (Prensky, 2001; Bialeschki, 2007). In support of these needs, virtual learning environments have already been integrated into conventional teaching methods, which include the use of web-based tools and mobile devices, social networking environments and computer games to support formal and informal learning experiences.

However, experiences in a virtual learning environment ultimately represent abstract subsets of their real-world counterparts: regardless of how immersive the environment is, learners are still clearly able to distinguish between artificial and real, and this extends to their perceptions of action, reaction, and consequence, resulting in gaps that may emerge in the experiential learning model between action, experience and reflection (Kolb, 1984; Arnab et al., 2010). These are often evident as unfulfilled learning outcomes due to inadequate fidelity or reports of cognitive overload as learners struggle to address the additional demands required to reflect on virtual experiences in the context of real-world events (Warburton and Garcia, 2008; Warburton, 2009; Parker and Myrick, 2009). Hence, it is fundamental to constrict the fissures between virtual and real spaces, and thus allow experiential learning (Kolb, 1984) techniques to be successfully applied (Arnab et al., 2010).

Multisensory teaching approaches mirror more closely evolved learning processes and promote experiential learning pedagogy, suggesting unisensory approaches are sub-optimal and that their selection is mostly based in practicality

S. Arnab (✉)
Serious Games Institute, Coventry University, Coventry, UK
e-mail: s.arnab@coventry.ac.uk

M. Ma et al. (eds.), *Serious Games and Edutainment Applications*,
DOI 10.1007/978-1-4471-2161-9_9, © Springer-Verlag London Limited 2011

rather than pedagogy (Shams and Seitz, 2008). Multimodal interfaces can create more immersive experience by stimulating various perceptions in a virtual environment (Chalmer et al., 2009).

In support for such pedagogic perspectives, this chapter aims to explore a multimodal approach to learning paying close scrutiny to the deployment of tactile capability in a virtual learning environment towards narrowing the gap between virtual and real spaces.

This chapter reviews the pedagogy and learning styles that influence the need for tactile stimuli in a multisensory learning environment. The use of haptic technology is explored to provide insights into the current trends and future work within this domain. This chapter also reports on the deployment of tactile capability as a part of the Roma Nova project at the Serious Games Institute, UK.

9.2 Exploratory Learning Model

Under an experiential model of learning, individuals are encouraged to reflect on their actions and consequences to foster understanding and reapplying this understanding to future actions. In proposing the experiential model, Kolb (1984) put forth a refined definition of learning as "the process whereby knowledge is created through the transformation of experience". There are four possible learning styles according to Kolb: (i) Diverging (feeling and watching), (ii) Assimilating (watching and thinking), (iii) Converging (doing and thinking) and (iv) Accommodating (doing and feeling).

From these learning styles, the possible outcomes are Concrete Experience (feeling), Reflective Observation (watching), Abstract Conceptualization (thinking) and Active Experimentation (doing). These four parameters of Kolb's learning styles are interrelated, which depend on each individual preference and result in different outcomes (Fig. 9.1).

Reflective observation paired with abstract conceptualization is not uncommon in a typical classroom setting, encyclopaedic learning approach and e-learning environment. As an attempt to address the need to emphasise the importance of concrete experience via active experimentation, stimulating tactile perception may enhance not only engagement with the learning process but also the understanding of experiment subjects/samples.

This approach complements or perhaps enhances conceptualization and observation by placing a high emphasis on transforming the lesson-learned to real applications, implementations and implications as well as analysis-oriented and hands-on skills. Therefore, "physically" examining a virtual object to substantiate understanding of a subject matter may narrow the gap between what we perceive as a virtual and real object in a virtual learning environment.

In their model of exploratory learning, de Freitas and Neumann (2009) expand the experiential learning model to include virtual environments (VEs). Exploratory learning opens up the capability for learning through exploration of virtual environments, and using virtuality as an active training dimension. Tied deeply to social

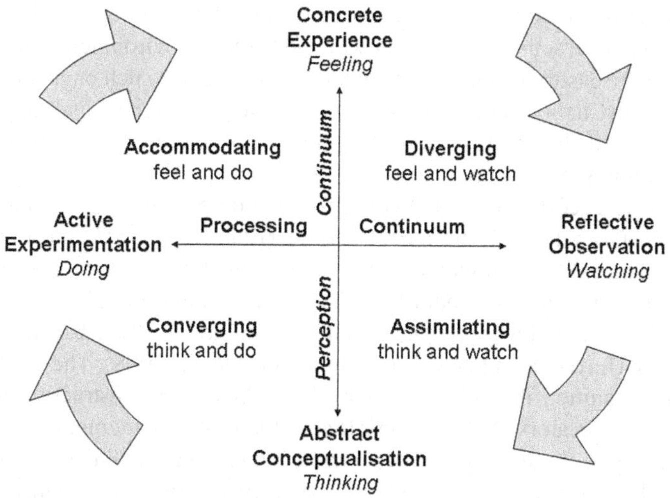

Fig. 9.1 Experiential learning based on Kolb (1984)

interactive learning, the exploratory model aims to provide learning designers with better tools for exploiting three-dimensional VEs. Of particular relevance in this case is the merging of tactile interactions into a broader pedagogic toolkit for tutors. Learning in the exploratory model is choreographed, rather than designed, with the potential to include a myriad of sensory components from touch to smell, taste to vision and hearing. Game design and experience design therefore are not simply aspects of the reflective cycle of experience, but active design tools and components of experience design, leading to wider possibilities about how virtual spaces can be designed and interacted with, towards a seamless transition between physical and virtual spaces. Exploration in this sense then is a design component that facilitates learning in different ways. Here we consider the role of tactile interfaces within the multisensory approach, and in particular the use of haptics to reinforce learning outcomes that are derived, rather than posited.

9.3 Tactile Stimuli

Real value exists in designing learning experiences to support an exploratory and open-ended model of learning to encourage learners to make their own reflections and summations and to come to an understanding in their own way. Schiphorst (2007) stated that technology should be designed "as experience" and not only for experience. A more engaging and involved learning environment may somehow promote concrete experience via active experimentation as a complement to abstract conceptualization and reflective observation, thereby allowing through exploration with virtual and physical elements a unique set of learning outcomes that reinforces reflection and learning.

These desired outcomes can be supported by a multisensory approach towards a more active and interactive engagement with the learning environment. There is evidence that multisensory or multimodal interfaces can create such engagement with a virtual world (Chalmer et al., 2009). Other studies (see Shams and Seitz, 2008) also demonstrated that multisensory training can be more effective than similar unisensory training paradigms.

The pressing need for a "virtual" experience and "presence" to be authentic is critical to experiential (and exploratory) learning (Bialeschki, 2007), one of the most difficult challenges in VE research and development (Brown, 2006). The immersive experience of a learner could be enhanced by adding the ability to not just perceive objects (visually and/or auditorially as in current VEs), but through tactile perception (Laycock and Day, 2003; Butler and Neave, 2008). The implications of touch for cognition that advocates the use of "hands-on" instruction is recognized by many educators (Minogue and Jones, 2006). As an attempt to address the need to emphasise the importance of concrete experience via active experimentation on a multimodal platform, stimulating tactile perception may enhance not only engagement with the learning process but also the understanding of experiment subjects/samples.

This approach complements or perhaps enhances conceptualization and observation by placing a high emphasis on transforming the lesson-learned to real applications and implications as well as analysis-oriented and hands-on skills. Therefore, "physically" touching a virtual artefact may narrow the gap between what we perceive as a virtual and real object.

Tactile feedback can be achieved by haptic technology, designed to communicate through the subtle and sensitive channels of touch. The word "haptic" originated from a Greek word "haptikos", meaning "able to touch," and "haptesthai", meaning "able to lay hold of" (Katz, 1989 as cited by Minogue and Jones, 2006). The term has evolved, in its broadest sense, to encompass "the study of touch and the human interaction with the external environment through touch" (Minogue and Jones, 2006). The use of such technology has been reported to augment the feeling of "presence" in VE (Van Schaik et al., 2004). The "feel and do" approach of learning is highly encouraged by this form of interactivity that promotes "first-hand" experience.

Haptic devices are becoming more cost effective, which opens up exciting possibilities for the inclusion of tactile perception in VE. Technological advancements in haptics have extended its applications in a numerous of disciplines ranging from military to medicine (see Stone, 1992; Srinivasan and Basdogan, 1997; Lieu et al., 2003; Minogue and Jones, 2006). The benefits of using haptics in learning are demonstrated by its increasing deployment in flight training as well as medical training. For instance, military and commercial pilots carry out training using flight simulators, which require the application of force or pressure on the controls corresponding to real experience during an actual flight (Minogue and Jones, 2006). Similarly, haptic interfaces are also widely used for medical simulation, particularly for laparoscopic and endoscopic surgery. Morris et al. (2007) suggested that in conjunction with visual feedback, tactile perception in a virtual training environment may enhance the teaching of sensorimotor skills essential in surgery. The potential of such devices has been reported in literatures on training demonstrating a wide range of virtual applications from surgical simulators to train surgeons in performing surgeries in virtual environments (Dawson et al., 2000; Satava, 2001; Lieu et al., 2003; Laycock and Day, 2003) to breast simulator towards raising awareness of the importance of breast assessment (Arnab and Raja, 2008; Arnab et al., 2008; Solanki and Raja, 2010).

Furthermore, haptic devices have the potential to replicate real experiences. For instance, studies carried out by Chial et al. (2002) and Greenish et al. (2002) demonstrated that the performance in real and virtual experiment, such as the cutting of tissues was similar. When haptic feedback is available during the exploration of three-dimensional objects, studies have shown that individuals develop more three-dimensional understandings similar to real experiences compared to when only visual feedback is available (Jones et al., 2003, 2005). Newell et al. (2001) reported that tactile interaction may increase understanding of the physical characteristic of objects in a virtual world, where there was a preference for tactile/haptic exploration of every single side of three dimensional objects including surfaces hidden from view whereas visually there is a preference for exploring only the visible parts of objects. Minogue and Jones (2006) conclude from existing literature that haptic interaction and feedback is superior to visual responses towards the perception of properties such as texture and microspatial properties of pattern, compliance, elasticity and viscosity.

There is indeed a great potential for tactile stimuli to be introduced in a virtual learning environment. Bialeschki (2007) discussed a potential framework for the use of haptic devices in a classroom setting in support for research and development that promotes experiential education. This framework encompasses the concepts of relevance, relationships, and real (authenticity). In conjunction with the concept of "presence" in a virtual context, this theoretical framework serves as a motivation to explore the implementation of haptics (Bialeschki, 2007; Gillenwater et al., 2007) to support the teaching and learning of a subject matter that requires a "hands-on" approach within a classroom setting.

9.4 Learning Ancient History as a Case Study

Learning concepts about a subject matter that lies beyond immediate reach and understanding is a challenging task, requiring increasing scaffolding and guidance as subject matter becomes increasingly abstracted from everyday experience. As a particular example, learning ancient history within the context of cultural heritage is traditionally dependent upon intangible and text-based narratives, often accompanied by illustrations and historical facts. To promote better engagement with the learning process and absorption of information, complete involvement of learners in their learning environment is essential to narrow the gap between these abstract concepts and real experiences, towards substantiating reflection, conceptualization and application without the need for extensive learner scaffolding.

A selection of reconstructed/replica artefacts may be purchased for teaching purposes, though this imposes a huge cost in obtaining every single artefact and scales poorly to large groups of learners. Driven by the advances in technology, ancient artefacts that are physically unavailable in a classroom setting may be made tangible in a virtual environment (VE). Using virtual technologies, various artefacts can be visualised in a three dimensional space. However, learning via observation without any real interaction with these artefacts may not be as engaging as physically touching a virtual artefact. Stimulating both visual and tactile perceptions in a virtual learning environment may narrow the gap between what we perceive as a virtual and real object.

Existing works exploring such an approach commonly employ specialist technologies, which can be expensive and are not easily available to a general audience. Hence, to promote engagement, the deployed technologies have to support accessibility to a wider demographic. The means of transfer thus require optimisation- simple, familiar, cost effective and easily available for mass consumption. Furthermore, they are mostly driven by technology rather than pedagogy.

The existing learning model based on reflective observation (watching) and abstract conceptualization (thinking) has to be enhanced by emphasizing on concrete experience via experimentation towards a more involving process of learning. As a proof-of-concept, tactile interaction via a haptic device was implemented to promote "feeling and doing" that may substantiate the observation of behaviours of ancient objects upon interaction. The behaviour – solid, deformable, texture impressions may enhance the conceptualization of the subject matter. Hence, with regards to the experiential model, concrete experience via active experimentation may potentially substantiate the outcome and process of observation and conceptualization.

This case study describes a part of the development project (the Roma Nova project) built around the Rome Reborn Model (Guidi et al., 2007; Petridis et al., 2010; Panzoli et al., 2010) towards a multisensory learning platform within the domain of cultural heritage. The proof-of-concept advocates exploratory learning by incorporating tactile interfaces in a VE and accessibility to a wider demographic by capitalising on the fact that internet access, coupled with graphical user interfaces and web browsers, is common in education and at home (Kaklanis et al., 2009), and an abstraction layer provided through middleware allows a wide range of haptic devices to be supported.

9.4.1 Related Development

There have been developments in the domain of a virtual space, where multimodal interfaces were explored towards providing a more engaging learning experience. The research in human-computer interfaces aims to correlate the natural interfaces between human subjects with their surrounding and to constitute their characteristics in a VE.

VEs have also been employed within the domain of cultural heritage. Applications, such as Virtual Egyptian Temple (Troche and Jacobson, 2010) and

Virtual Gettysburg (Recker, 2007), present users with virtual recreation of ancient artefacts as well as events such as a battle in a computer-generated scene, which allow users to move around and observe from any angle or location. First-hand interaction with artefacts is however not advocated by these environments.

In conjunction with the multimodal approach, the stimulation of tactile perception is very useful in cultural applications, where ancient artefacts are mostly beyond reach in a physical world (Bergamasco et al., 2002; Dettori et al., 2003; Brewster, 2005). There is a collection of cultural heritage institutions that have already embraced haptic technology. For instance, The Museum of Pure Form (Frisoli, 2004) allows visitors to interact with 3D art forms and explore the museum via stereo vision and tactile stimuli when interacting with virtual sculptures. Figueroa et al. (2009) demonstrated a similar multimodal platform based on the Gold Museum in Bogota, where commercial devices were integrated in order to allow visitors to see in stereo, hear, and touch replicas of small objects. Rare art pieces can be "touched" in the Interactive Art Museum (Brewster, 2001). The visually impaired may also be empowered, where sight is no longer the only necessary sensory means to appreciate artwork or a virtual space in general (Kaklanis et al., 2009).

However, the deployed technologies are restricted to specific audience and location due to their sophistication, complexity and cost. Some evaluation tasks such as for the Gold Museum (Figueroa et al., 2009) confirmed the interest of using this technology in real-world setups, although there are deployment and usability issues with regards to the general public. To reach a wide demographic, a more accessible media is crucial. Web and mobile platforms are common assets of most households in Britain and may allow beneficiaries in dispersed locations to be supported. For instance, some 73 per cent of UK households have Internet access in 2010 (OFNS, 2010).

Modern cultural heritage exhibitions have evolved from static exhibitions to dynamic and challenging multimedia explorations (White et al., 2008). The main factor for this has been the domination of the web technologies, which allows cultural heritage institutions and other heritage exhibitions to be presented and promoted online. VEs for cultural heritage can offer much more than what many current cultural heritage institution web sites offer, i.e. a catalogue of pictures and text in a web browser. White et al. (2008) introduced a new level of multimodal experience by implementing an augmented-reality platform for cultural heritage on a web. This platform allows users to not only view and interact with web-based cultural artefacts but to also experience a mixed reality visualisation of the artefacts. By using special markers, a webcam and possibly a mixed-reality eyewear, virtual artefacts can be viewed in a real-environment.

To support tactile perception on a web platform, the network architectures needed to add haptic capability to the human computer interface have to be explored. Applications, such as The Hanoi Game and Pool Game implemented a simple haptic interface over the web, which demonstrate a possibility of encouraging a first-hand learning experience over the web compared to a more encyclopaedic approach (Ruffaldi et al., 2006). However, the development of these applications is more technology-led rather than pedagogically-driven.

9.4.2 Roma Nova

The Roma Nova project is based upon the Rome Reborn model (Guidi and Frischer, 2005) of ancient Rome 340AD, the most high-fidelity model of Ancient Rome currently in existence, providing three-dimensional digital model which may be explored in real-time. Rome Reborn includes hundreds of buildings which are procedurally generated based on accurate historical knowledge, 32 of which are highly detailed monuments reconstructed based on accurate archaeological data (Fig. 9.2).

The aim of the project is to provide a distributed tutoring environment for children 11–14 year olds to support cross-disciplinary study, as part of an exploration and social interactive learning model. The model has been integrated with various modules including a serious game based upon the history curriculum in the UK, and current work is integrating text to voice software, virtual agents and haptics. The first critical aspect of the Roma Nova project considers the design of an intelligent tutoring system using gaming paradigms to explore issues related to pedagogic design, such as how desired learning outcomes may be broken down into different scenarios, and how different classes of characters or personality may help the learner to explore different perspectives on events and ultimately how to assess the knowledge effectively learnt.

In order to integrate the interactions between the player and the Non-Player Characters (NPCs) as well as artefacts within the scene, we propose a novel framework called the Levels of Interaction (LoI). The LoI model is a theoretical framework, wherein interactions between a human user/player and background characters are simplified to three levels, each offering different interaction possibilities and playing a well-defined role in the game.

Graphically, the LoI can be represented as auras (Panzoli et al., 2010) of increasing complexity centred on the player's avatar (Fig. 9.3) and based on a simple social space metric. As an illustration, the LoI is divided into three levels. The

Fig. 9.2 Three-dimensional reconstruction of the forum

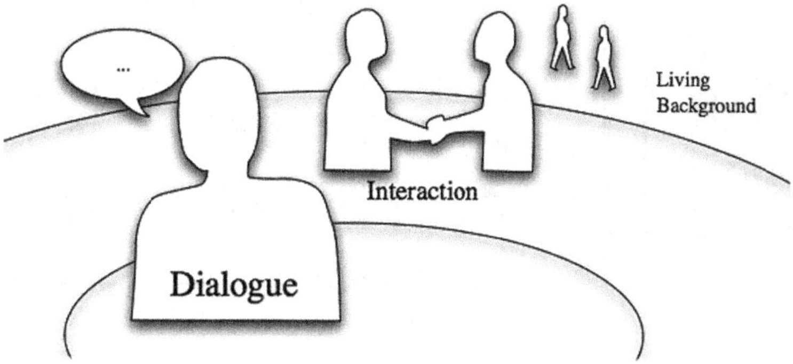

Fig. 9.3 Level of interaction framework (Panzoli et al., 2010)

first level aims to populate the characters with authentic crowd in order to increase the immersion of the player. Characters located in closer surrounding of the player belong to the interaction level. Finally, a character inside the dialogue level interacts with the player in a natural way, ultimately using speech recognition and synthesis. All the NPCs by default belong to the background level, but as the player moves in the environment and they happen to get closer or away from the player and thus enter or exit the interaction or dialogue levels.

This approach can be extended to define the relationship between the players and the artefacts. Tactile interaction can be allowed within the dialogue level, indicating the potential to reduce processes required to support both visual and tactile feedbacks. A diagram that illustrates interaction and visualization technologies employed in the multimodal mixed reality system is shown in Fig. 9.4. The system comprises of:

- The Interaction layer to support various interaction modes that can be grouped in three categories: Brain-Computer Interaction (BCI), Natural Speech Interaction and interaction with haptic devices.
- The Middleware Communication layer (MCL), an interactive framework, to support data sharing between distinct sets of devices
- The Visualization layer to support different game and visualization engines such as Unity, X3D and TV3D

9.4.3 Tactile Interaction with an Ancient Artefact

The existing role-play game prototype for ancient Rome allows users/learners/players to explore the virtual space and interact with the virtual agent in order to learn about history, politics and geography. Incorporating tactile interaction with the surrounding artefacts will essentially enrich learning experience and enhance understanding of ancient artefacts.

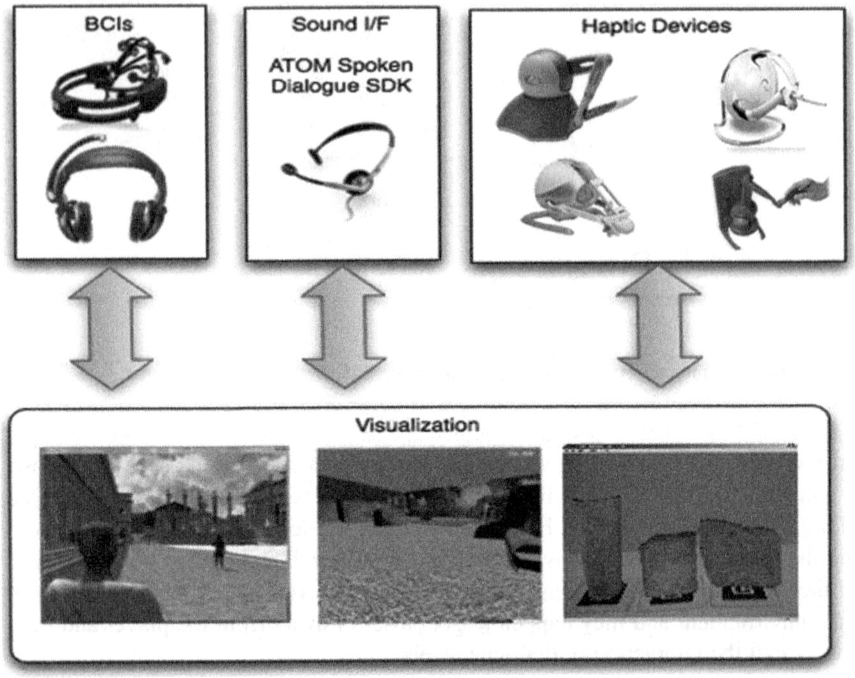

Fig. 9.4 Multisensory framework to support various modes of interaction

To support the inclusion of haptic functionalities within a VE, H3D by SenseGraphics provides an open source software development platform (H3D API). To support real-time interactivity and behaviours, there are three levels of programming for H3D – using C++, X3D or Python. X3D and Python are high level interfaces to the API, which allows the definition of visual and haptic properties as well as the dynamic behaviour upon interaction. For instance, the deformable behaviour of a non-solid surface can be rendered as a response to tactile interaction. For more advance programming, C++ provides an access to the API, where new nodes and fields can be created dependent upon the requirement for new behaviours, objects and interaction. Unlike most other scene graph APIs, H3D API is designed chiefly to support a rapid development process.

H3D essentially is cross platform and haptic-device independent. This implies that existing web-based games and e-learning platform can be extended with haptic capability. Currently, H3D supports haptic devices such as Phantom Desktop, Phantom Omni and Novint Falcon.

The following section describes the scene development that was built on top of the H3D API and web deployment enabled by a plug-in for tactile interaction on a web browser.

9.4.3.1 Scene Development Using H3D

H3D scene graph is based on X3D, which employs a structural division in the scene-graph concept – the use of Nodes and Fields. Nodes and field are used to define geometries, physical attributes and behaviours that make up the artefacts and the surrounding environment within a virtual space. These nodes and fields are used to define the visual and haptic properties of the scene and artefacts.

Models from the Rome Reborn, mainly in 3D Studio Max format, were repurposed and translated into X3D to provide the visual scene-graph, extended with haptic functionality and embedded in an html script to be rendered on a web-browser. Figure 9.5 illustrates the general development process from the original model to the equivalent X3D scene-graph with haptic definition- rendered on a web-browser.

The virtual scene and artefacts were based on the Rome Reborn model, where a complete collection consists of a digital terrain map of the city, 7000 buildings and various ancient artefacts within the late-antique Aurelian Walls. Such digital assets complement the resources required to teach ancient history and cultural heritage within this era. Figure 9.6 displays a screen shot of a scene in ancient Rome.

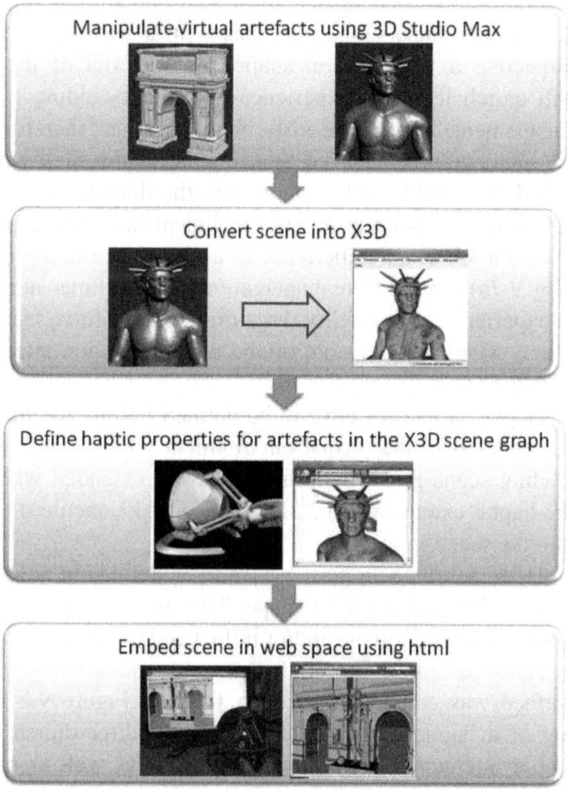

Fig. 9.5 An overview of the scene development stages

Fig. 9.6 A player's view in the Roma Nova game prototype

Towards enhancing experience in a virtual environment, tactile feedback respective of the texture, shape and material of the artefacts upon interaction will enrich learners' experience and understanding through such an exploratory engagement. To promote cost-effectiveness and therefore increase accessibility, tactile interaction is achieved by using an off-the-shelf Novint Falcon, which is more affordable, usable and stable within the domain of games. It is also supported by H3D and does not require prior technical skills and experience.

To enrich users' experience in a virtual world, not only does the Novint Falcon (Fig. 9.7a) support virtual navigation in three dimensional space, it also allows users to experience high-fidelity three-dimensional force feedback that represent texture, shape, weight, dimension, or/and dynamics upon interaction with virtual artefacts (Fig. 9.7b).

Haptic properties have to be defined before any interactions with artefacts can be rendered in the virtual environment. H3D comes with a full XML parser for loading scene-graph definitions of X3D extended with haptic functionality. With the haptic extensions to X3D via H3D API, tactile definition can be incorporated into the scene-graph.

Hence, surface properties have to be defined in order to be able to touch an artefact, in this case an X3D shape. The surface can be smooth, with friction, have a magnetic characteristic and/or influenced by the texture specified for the shape

As an example, the artefact (marble statue) was assumed to be solid and the surface was considered as with friction. Figure 9.8 illustrates real-time rendering of a haptic cursor (in a shape of a three-dimensional hand) that represents tactile interaction with the solid artefact as well as navigation within the virtual scene.

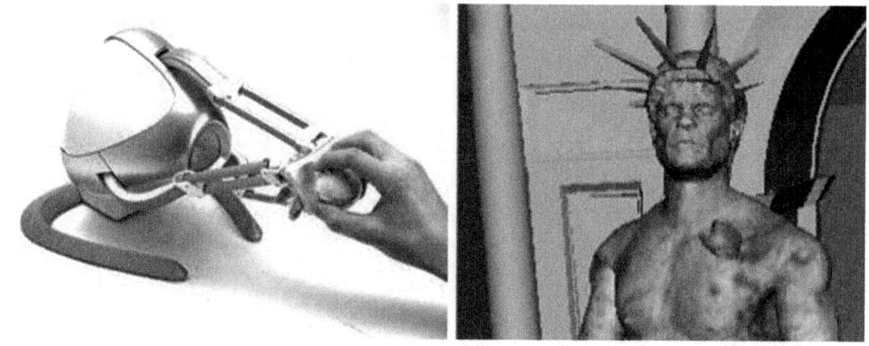

(a) (b)

Fig. 9.7 (**a**) The Novint Falcon and the (**b**) interaction with an artefact

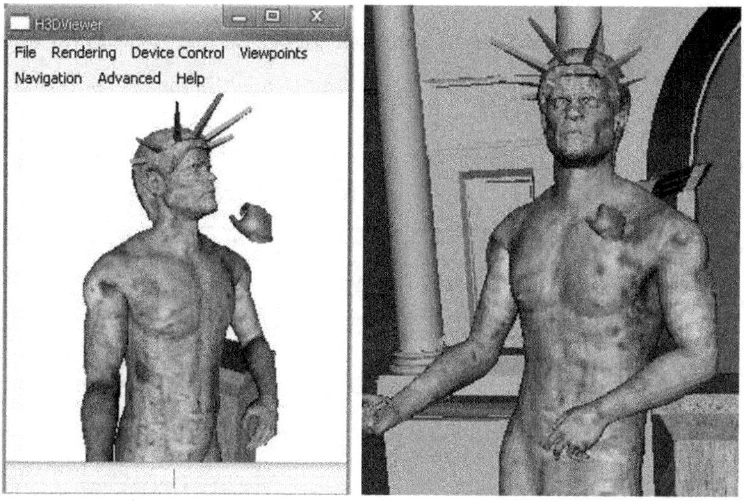

(a) (b)

Fig. 9.8 (**a**) Navigating the scene and (**b**) touching an artefact with a haptic cursor

In H3D, a pre-defined Python scripting can be used to express more behaviour in the scene, such as a deformable behaviour upon interaction. Figure 9.9 demonstrates haptic interaction with a non-solid surface, further exhibiting a great potential to support behaviours and properties of various artefacts in existence within the era.

The scene-graph definition of the virtual environment was embedded in an HTML script, which can now be rendered on a web browser via the H3D-Web plug-in. Figure 9.10 illustrates the proposed architecture for the deployment of a haptic-enabled scene on a web-browser.

By embedding the X3D scene graph within the HTML, a web page can be extended with haptic capability. Figure 9.11 illustrates a haptic-enabled browser,

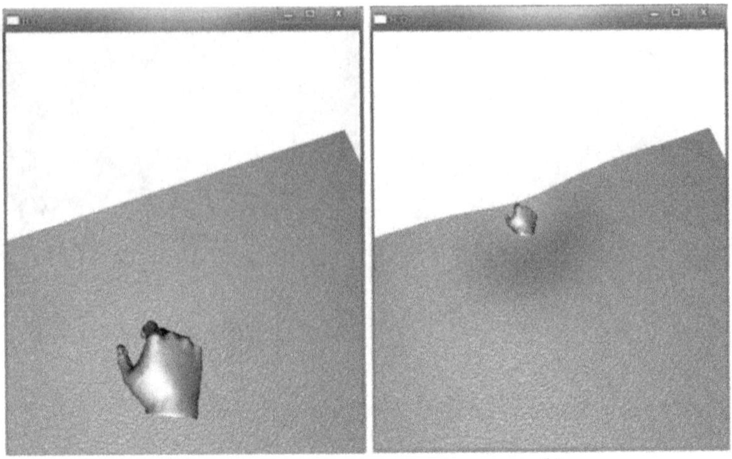

(a) (b)

Fig. 9.9 Haptic interaction (hand cursor) with a soft artefact: (**a**) ready to touch (**b**) visual and haptic feedback upon interaction

Fig. 9.10 A scene built on top of the architecture of a haptic-enabled browser (Arnab et al., 2010)

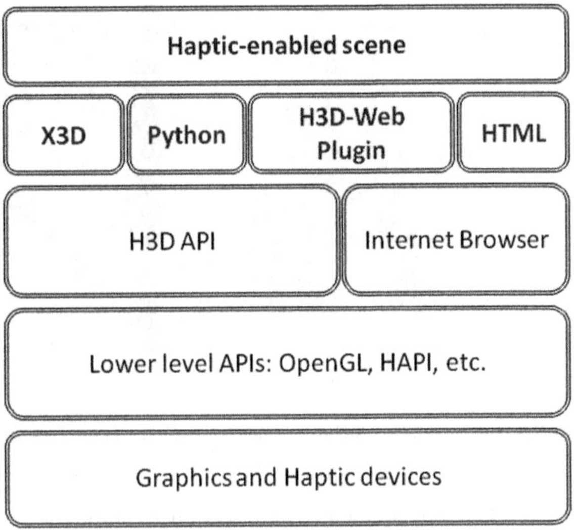

where learners can experience tactile feedback from real-time interactions with ancient artefacts over the web using a Novint Falcon device. To optimise the learning environment, the platform architecture has to be set up on the client's machine as a downloadable installer that encapsulates the required components. The runtime processing, such as rendering, is thus delegated to the client. The web content including the haptic-enabled visualisation may reside at the server side.

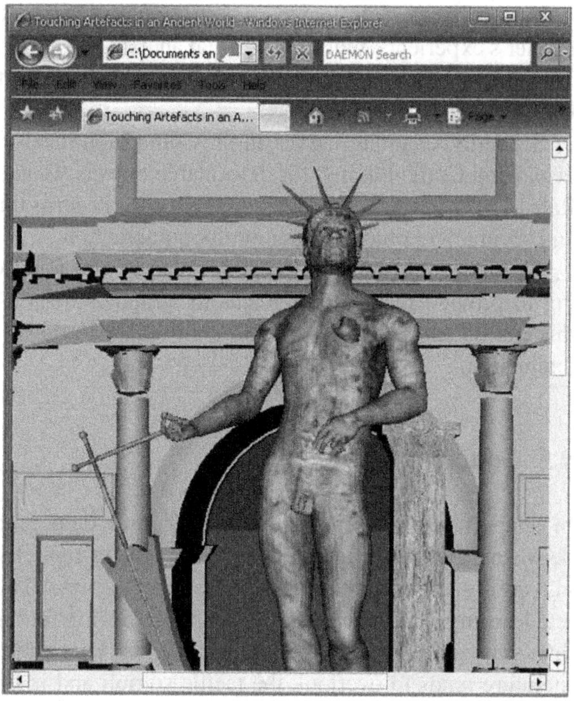

Fig. 9.11 The ancient world rendered on a haptic-enabled web browser

9.4.4 Further Work

The prototype has demonstrated the feasibility of stimulating tactile interaction and perception within a virtual environment, and the potential of promoting experiential and exploratory learning to complement existing class-room, encyclopaedic and e-learning approaches. The haptic-enabled web-browser can be used to extend the level of engagement in learning from observation and conceptualization to a more concrete experience via active experimentation.

However, several limitations exist with the current development, which will prove import`ant areas for further research and development. Firstly, the scene development is dictated by the complexity of the Rome Reborn model, which requires high conversion time into equivalent X3D scene graphs.

Even though the levels of detail of the geometries have been reduced, particularly for background artefacts to simplify the conversion process, the huge number of artefacts dictates an extensive amount of time be required to define haptic properties for the artefacts within the scene. In tandem with the aims of experiential learning, it is more practical to assume that a user/player/learner will only closely examine a selected number of artefacts relevant to the learning objectives, though such limitations and preconceptions of learner behaviour limit the capacity for exploratory learning.

Further work will include identifying the relevant artefacts that will enrich learner's experience within the virtual ancient world through evaluations in schools. This implies that only a selected number of artefacts will provide any tactile feedbacks upon interaction.

Secondly, challenges exist in providing high levels of realism, in terms of both visual and tactile fidelity, for deformable objects. Existing work such as Arnab and Raja (2008) can be adopted to address these concerns through an increase in realism and accuracy in object behaviour upon interaction.

Thirdly, there are also possible latency and bandwidth issues when attempting to provide real-time high quality graphics to non-broadband users; however, this can be addressed by providing an option to download virtual scenes for local interaction.

9.5 Conclusions

In support for the emergence of a learner demographic who migrates rapidly between different technologies, it is essential to capitalise on the use of technologies in learning to engage and to increase receptiveness. Therefore, in order to replicate real learning experiences, a multisensory platform for learning can be more effective than similar unisensory training paradigms. However, much of the multimodality literature tends to overlook the tactile stimuli and is instead subjected by research and development using stimuli in the auditory and visual modalities. However, the underpinnings of this existing research may provide a framework for investigating the impact of haptics in teaching and learning. Some indirect evidence of how haptics may improve learning can be seen in various domains such as in medical education and military training. Moreover, the study of haptics has grown significantly with the advances in the experimentation and implementation of touch in computing, as many researchers are involved in the development, testing, refinement and application of tactile and force feedback devices in other domains.

This chapter has described an innovative approach in introducing tactile perception in learning over the web, seeking to reach a wider demography in a cost-effective way. By employing both visual and tactile perceptions in a virtual learning environment, a "first-hand" learning experience may be advocated. This development complements the existing Roma Nova project on cultural heritage, which has demonstrated the potential of stimulating tactile perception to complement the visual representation of the subject matter. Future research and development work has been discussed. Other further work will include extending the existing multimodal game-based learning framework with the haptic-enabled web environment. The evaluation of the level of engagement, motivation and cognitive benefit of the proposed learning platform will also be explored.

By making available a whole new category of sensations on a web platform, haptic technology will open up various possibilities for developers and researchers of pedagogy and technology driven intervention in learning, including game-based learning approaches and pedagogies.

References

Arnab, S., Raja, V.: Chapter 4: Simulating a deformable object using a surface mass spring system. In: Proceedings of the 3rd International Conference on Geometric Modeling and Imaging. GMAI, IEEE Computer Society, London, pp. 21–26 (2008). doi: 10.1109/GMAI.2008.24

Arnab, S., Solanki, M., Raja, V.: A deformable surface model for breast simulation. In: 20th International Conference of the Society for Medical Innovation and Technology, Vienna, Austria, 28–30 Aug 2008

Arnab, S., Petridis, P., Dunwell, I., de Freitas, S.: Touching artefacts in an ancient world on a browser-based platform. In: IADIS International Conference: Web Virtual Reality and Three-Dimensional Worlds 2010, Freiburg, Germany (2010)

Bergamasco, M., Frisoli, A., Barbagli, F.: Haptics technologies and cultural heritage applications. In: Proceedings of Computer Animation, IEEE Computer Society, Geneva, Switzerland (2002). doi: 10.1109/CA.2002.1017503

Bialeschki, M.: The three Rs for experiential education researchers. J. Experiential Educ.. **29**(3), 366–368 (2007)

Brewster, S.A: The impact of haptic 'touching' technology on cultural applications. In: Proceedings of EVA 2001, Vasari UK, s28, pp. 1–14 (2001)

Brewster, S.A.: The impact of haptic 'touching' technology on cultural applications. In: Hemsley, J., Cappellini, V., Stanke, G. (eds.) Digital Applications for Cultural Heritage Institutions, pp. 273–284. Ashgate Press, Surrey, UK (2005)

Brown, J.: New learning environments for the 21st century: Exploring the edge. Change. September/October, 18–24 (2006)

Butler, M., Neave, P.: Object appreciation through haptic interaction. In: Proceedings of Ascilite, Melbourne (2008)

Chalmer, A., Debattista, K., Ramic-Brkic, B.: Towards high-fidelity multi-sensory virtual environments. Visual Comput. Springer Berlin/Heidelberg **25**(12), 1101–1108 (2009). doi: 10.1007/s00371-009-0389-2

Chial, V.B., Greenish, S., Okamura, A.: On the display of haptic recordings for cutting biological tissues. In: 10th International Symposium on Haptic Interfaces for Virtual Environment and Tele-operator Systems, IEEE Virtual Reality Conference, pp. 80–87. Orlando, FL, USA (2002)

Dawson, S., Cotin, S., Meglan, D., Shaffer, D.W., Ferrell, M.: Designing a computer based simulator for interventional cardiology training. Catheter. Cardiovas. Interv. **51**, 522–527 (2000)

de Freitas, S., Neumann, T.: The use of 'exploratory learning' for supporting immersive learning in virtual environments. Comput. Educ. **52**(2), 343–352 (2009)

Dettori, A., Avizzano, C.A., Marcheschi, S., Angerilli, M., Bergamasco, M., Loscos, C., Guerraz, A.: Art Touch with CREATE haptic interface. In: Proceedings of the 11th International Conference on Advanced Robotics, University of Coimbra, Portugal, June 30–July 3, 2003. doi = 10.1145/ 1180495.1180523

Figueroa, P., Coral, M., Boulanger, P., Borda, J., Londono, P., Vega, F., Prieto, F., Restrepo, D.: Multi-modal exploration of small artefacts: An exhibition at the Gold Museum in Bogota. In: Spencer, S.N. (ed.) Proceedings of the 16th ACM Symposium on Virtual Reality Software and Technology (VRST '09). ACM, New York, pp. 67–74 (2009). doi: 10.1145/1643928.1643945

Frisoli, A.: The Museum of Pure Form. PERCRO. http://www.pureform.org/ (2004). Accessed 10 Feb 2011

Gillenwater, C., Kumar, A., Moynihan, B., Van Drimmelen. J.: Use of haptics to augment presence in an experiential HCI environment. Haptics, presence, & experiential HCI environments, University of North Carolina at Chapel Hill. White paper. http://vandfam.net/haptic/files/Use_of_Haptics_to_Augment_Presence_in_an_Experiential_HCI_Environment.pdf (2007). Accessed 10 Feb 2011

Greenish, S., Hayward, V., Chial, V., Okamura, A.: Measurement, analysis, and display of haptic signals during surgical cutting. Presence **6**(12), 626–651 (2002)

Guidi, G., Frischer, B.: Virtualizing ancient Rome: 3d acquisition and modeling of a large plaster-of-paris model of imperial Rome. In: Videometrics VIII, San Jose, CA, USA, pp. 119–133 (2005)

Guidi, G., Frischer, B., Lucenti, I.: Rome reborn – virtualizing the ancient imperial Rome. In: Workshop on 3D Virtual Reconstruction and Visualization of Complex Architectures, ETH Zurich, Switzerland, 12–13 July 2007

Jones, G., Andre, T., Negishi, A., Tretter, T., Kubasko, D., Bokinsky, A., Taylor, R., Superfine, R.: Hands-on science: The impact of haptic experiences on attitudes and concepts. National Association of Research in Science Teaching Annual Meeting, Philadelphia, PA (2003)

Jones, M., Bokinsky, A., Tretter, T., Negishi, A. A comparision of learning with haptic and visual modalities. Haptics-e Electronic J. Haptics Res. **4**(0). http://albion.ee.washington.edu/he/ojs/viewarticle.php?id=44 (2005). Accessed 21 Feb 2011

Kaklanis, N., Tzovaras, D., Moustakas, K.: Haptic navigation in the world wide web. Universal Access in Human-Computer Interaction. Applications and Services. Lecture Notes in Computer Science, Vol. 5616, 707–715. Springer-Verlag, Berlin (2009)

Katz, D.: The world of touch (Trans., Krueger, L.). Lawrence Erlbaum, Hillsdale, NJ (1989)

Kolb, D.: Experiential Learning. Prentice Hall, New Jersey (1984)

Laycock, S., Day, A.: Recent developments and applications of haptic devices. Comput. Graph. Forum **22**(2), 117–132 (2003)

Lieu, A., Tendick, F., Cleary, K., Kaufmann, C.: A survey of surgical simulation: Applications, technology, and education. Presence **12**(6), 599–614 (2003)

Minogue, J., Jones, M.G.: Haptics in education: Exploring an untapped sensory modality. Rev. Educ. Res. **76**(3), 317–348 (2006)

Morris, D., Tan, H., Barbagli, F., Chang, T., Salisbury, K.: Haptic feedback enhances force skill learning. In: EuroHaptics Conference, 2007 and Symposium on Haptic Interfaces for Virtual Environment and Teleoperator Systems. World Haptics 2007. Second Joint, pp. 21–26, 22–24 (2007). doi: 10.1109/WHC.2007.65

Newell, F.N., Ernst, M.O., Tjan, B.S., Bülthoff, H.H.: Viewpoint dependence in visual and haptic object recognition. Psychol. Sci. **12**(1), 37–42 (2001)

OFNS: Internet access: Households and individuals. Office for National Statistics. http://www.statistics.gov.uk/pdfdir/iahi0810.pdf (2010). Accessed 10 Feb 2011

Panzoli, D., Peters, C., Dunwell, I., Sanchez, S., Petridis, P., Protopsaltis, A., Scesa, V., de Freitas, S.: Levels of interaction: A user-guided experience in large-scale virtual environments. In: IEEE 2nd International Conference in Games and Virtual Worlds for Serious Applications (VS GAMES10), IEEE, Braga, Portugal, pp. 87–90, 26–27 Mar 2010. ISBN: 978-0-7695-3986-7

Parker, B., Myrick, F.: A critical examination of high-fidelity human patient simulation within the context of nursing pedagogy. Nurse Educ. Today **29**(3), 322–329 (2009)

Petridis, P., Dunwell, I., de Freitas, S., Panzoli, D.: An engine selection framework for high fidelity serious games. In: The 2nd International Conference on Games and Virtual Worlds for-Serious-Applications (VSgames'10), Braga, Portugal, 25–26 Mar (2010)

Prensky, M.: Digital natives, digital immigrants. On the Horizon. MCB Univ. Press **9**(5) (2001)

Recker, S.: Virtual Gettysburg: Bringing the battlefield to life. http://www.virtualgettysburg.com/ (2007). Accessed 21 Feb 2011

Ruffaldi, E., Frisoli, A., Gottlieb, C., Tecchia, F., Bergamasco, M.: A haptic toolkit for the development of immersive and web enabled games. In: Symposium on Virtual Reality Software and Technology (VRST), ACM, New York, Cyprus, pp. 320–323, 1–3 Nov 2006. doi: 10.1145/1180495.1180559

Satava, R.M.: Surgical education and surgical simulation. World J. Surg. **25**, 1484–1489 (2001)

Schiphorst, T.: Really, really small: The palpability of the invisible. In: Creativity and Cognition, pp. 7–16 (2007)

Shams, L., Seitz, A.: Benefits of multisensory learning. Trends Cogn. Sci. **12**(11), 411–417 (2008)

Solanki, M., Raja, V.: Modelling palpable masses for a virtual breast examination. In: 9th International Conference on Virtual-Reality Continuum and Its Applications in Industry, Seoul, South Korea, 12–13 Dec 2010. doi: 10.1109/BIYOMUT.2010.5479779

Srinivasan, M.A., Basdogan, C.: Haptics in virtual environments: Taxonomy, research status and challenges. Comput. Graph. **21**(4), 393–404 (1997)

Stone, R.J.: Haptic feedback: A potted history from telepresence to virtual reality. Robotica **10**, 461–467 (1992)

Troche, J., Jacobson, J.: An exemplar of Ptolemaic Egyptian temples. Computer Applications in Archaeology (CAA), Granada, Spain, April (2010)

Van Schaik, P., Turnbull, T., Van Wersch, A., Drummond, S.: Presence within a mixed reality environment. CyberPsychol Behav. **7**(5), 540–552 (2004)

Warburton, S.: Second life in higher education: Assessing the potential for and the barriers to deploying virtual words in learning and teaching. Br. J. Educ. Technol. **40**(3), 414–426 (2009)

Warburton, S., Garcia, M.P.: Defining a framework for teaching practices inside virtual immersive environments: The tension between control and pedagogical approach. In: Proceedings of RELive '08 Conference, United Kingdom (2008)

White, M., Petridis, P., Liarokapis, F., Plecinckx, D.: Multimodal mixed reality interfaces for visualizing digital heritage. Int. J. Archit. Comput. (IJAC) **5**(2), 322–337, Special Issue on Cultural Heritage, Multi-Science (2008)

Chapter 10
Operation ARIES!: A Serious Game for Teaching Scientific Inquiry

Keith Millis, Carol Forsyth, Heather Butler, Patty Wallace, Arthur Graesser, and Diane Halpern

Operation ARIES! is a serious game that teaches critical thinking about scientific inquiry. The player must help to identify aliens on Earth who are intentionally publishing bad research. The game combines aspects of video games and intelligent tutors in which the player holds conversations with animated agents using natural language. The player first takes a training course with a virtual trainee, followed by a module in which the player identifies flaws in research cases. In the third and final module, the player interviews suspected alien scientists on their research. *Operation ARIES!* is designed for high school seniors and adults. This chapter describes the game, learning principles in which it was based, and evidence that it increases learning.

10.1 Operation ARIES!

There is a long history of science fiction novels and movies that feature aliens from other worlds conquering our planet, either overtly as in *The War of the Worlds*, or covertly as in *The Arrival*. Aliens have also infiltrated video games, starting with *Space Invaders*, and more recently with *Aliens vs. Predator*. Extraterrestrials have also appeared in educational games and related learning experiences. For example, in *Alien Games*, girls and boys create a video game within an alien theme teaching principles of outer space (Heeter et al., 2007). Indeed, the idea of aliens taking over Earth is hardly a new idea.

Aliens have recently made their appearance in a serious game called *Operation ARIES!* In this game, players learn how to critically evaluate research that they encounter in various media, such as the Web, TV, magazines and newspapers. ARIES is an acronym for Acquiring Research Investigative and Evaluative Skills. The game focuses on teaching critical thinking and scientific reasoning within scientific inquiry (the "how" of science). In particular, it teaches how to critically evaluate

K. Millis (✉)
Department of Psychology, Northern Illinois University, DeKalb, IL 60115, USA
e-mail: kmillis@niu.edu

M. Ma et al. (eds.), *Serious Games and Edutainment Applications*,
DOI 10.1007/978-1-4471-2161-9_10, © Springer-Verlag London Limited 2011

aspects of scientific investigations (e.g., the need for control groups, adequate samples of observations, operational definitions, etc.) and how to ask appropriate questions in order to uncover problems with design or interpretation. Scientific inquiry is crucial because it comprises the necessary steps of "science as process," the steps that scientists follow in establishing and critiquing causal claims (NSES, 1996).

Scientific inquiry is a crucial aspect of being an informed citizen living in the "information age". The public is constantly being exposed to causal claims made by scientists, advertisers, coworkers, friends, and the press via a variety of media (blogs, TV, Web, print, word of mouth). Of course, some of the claims have relatively solid scientific evidence for support, whereas others do not. In some cases, the research is well executed, but the interpretation or conclusion drawn by the press is inappropriate, as in the case of a headline that makes a causal claim that "wine lowers heart attack risk in women," based on a correlational design which does not support a cause-effect interpretation ("Wine Lowers Heart Attack Risk in Women," 2007).

In other cases, a claim is unfounded because the design of the study itself is flawed. For example, in one "experiment" aired on American TV, reporters secretly recorded a carload of teenage drivers. The footage shows them carelessly driving through stop signs while laughing and joking with each other. The conclusion made by the newscaster is that teenagers are too immature to drive, and the legal age limit for awarding driving licenses should be increased. To the trained eye, however, this was a poor experiment – in fact, it was not an experiment at all. There was no comparison group of older drivers, no mention of confounds (driving errors could solely decrease with the amount of driving experience rather than the age of the driver), and there was a small sample size. Undoubtedly, this "experiment" led to many scared parents lecturing their kids into deeper teenage angst. Unfortunately, more serious consequences than unhappy teenagers can arise from careless thinking about science. According to the U.S. National Institute of Health (NIH), around four million U.S. adults and one million U.S. children used homeopathy and other alternative medicines in 2006, despite research showing little or no effectiveness beyond placebo effects (National Center for Comtemporary and Alternative Medicine, undated). In some instances, people suffer or die from relying on treatments that they believe to be valid despite evidence that they are not. Knowing and applying scientific inquiry skills can literally save lives.

So, how can aliens help learners acquire scientific inquiry skills? *Operation ARIES!* is an adventure game in which intelligent tutoring technology is combined with video game attributes. In the game, alien creatures called "Fuaths" from the Aries constellation are secretly publishing flawed research in various media outlets. By extensively publishing flawed research, they hope to confuse Earth's inhabitants about the proper use of the scientific method. By doing so, humans would not be able achieve inter-galactic space travel, which would seriously hurt their economy. They are also surreptitiously stealing Earth's valuable resources of water, plants, and oil to help rebuild their home world Thoth. Unfortunately for humans, Fuaths have the ability to look and act human, so catching them is not an easy task.

This is the player's primary objective *of Operation ARIES!*: the Federal Bureau of Science (FBS) has recruited the player to become a secret agent in the battle against the Fuaths. The player's mission is to be able to spot flawed research that would then lead the FBS to be able to find and arrest the alien authors. Its target audience includes high school seniors, college students, and members of the military and the interested public.

This chapter describes *Operation ARIES!,* with a primary focus on how the game's design incorporates various principles of learning found in cognitive psychology and the learning sciences. The game contains three modules (or levels): Training, Case Studies, and Interrogation. In the training module, players read an eBook accompanied by multiple choice questions and tutorial conversations. In the case studies module, players apply what they learned in the training module to realistic examples of flawed research. Lastly, in the interrogation module, players learn to ask scientists pointed questions about their research and learn how to evaluate their answers. The storyline is advanced by emails, dialogs, and videos which are interspersed among the learning activities according to a set script. It begins with the player joining the FBS as an agent-in-training and concludes with the player helping to save the world.

Operation ARIES! is unique in its attempt to help students learn how to critically evaluate research descriptions in the world of digital games and learning environments Most digital environments teach scientific literacy or scientific concepts in only one discipline (e.g., environmental science) and typically with didactic content to be read rather than to be applied to solve problems. Some explicitly target scientific inquiry, such as WISE (web-based inquiry science environment) at the University of California, Berkeley (Linn et al., 2004), but very few have a feel of a game. One is River City, a multi-user virtual environment in which players go back to an authentic nineteenth century U.S. town near a river (Ketelhut, 2007). Players work in teams trying to understand why the residents are becoming ill. Players pose hypotheses, perform controlled experiments, interview residents, and make recommendations based on their experiments. River City has a feel of a serious game because the interface allows the user to be represented as avatars in a 3D world, interact with digital artifacts and virtual agents, and communicate with each other. And no digital environment that we know of teaches students how to critically evaluate published scientific reports.

10.1.1 Learning Principles/Design Features

Below we list and describe several learning principles, design features, and gaming characteristics that have been implemented into *Operation ARIES!* Most of these principles are related to one another, and other principles have been implemented but are beyond the scope of this chapter (e.g., reflection, spacing effects, authentic learning, active learning). These learning principles have been compiled by researchers who have shown them to increase learning gains, engagement, interest, or motivation.

1. *Zone of proximal development.* Vygotsky's (1978) "zone of proximal development" refers to the distance between learning that occurs by an individual working alone on a problem and the learning that results when given proper instruction and guidance. When placed outside of the zone, the learning activities are too difficult for the individual, and consequently, students experience frustration or disengagement rather than learning (Rieber, 1996). Indeed, researchers and game designers have argued that optimal learning occurs when the match between the skills acquired by the learner and the requirements of the activities is neither too easy nor too hard (Van Eck, 2007). It is in this "zone" that learners experience "flow" (Csikszenthimhalyi, 2002) and "cognitive disequilibrium" with moderate confusion in the face of temporary impasses during learning (D'Mello and Graesser, 2010; Graesser, Lu, Olde, Cooper-Pye, & Whitten, 2005b). Flow experiences occur frequently while playing digital games (Benyon et al., 2005), whereas both flow and cognitive disequilibrium are positively correlated with learning (Graesser et al., 2008).
2. *Self-explanation.* People do not learn much when they are bored or passive. One strategy that promotes learning is self-explanation, in which the learner (reader, player) *explains* the material to one's self. A form of self-explanation occurs when the individual explains the material to another student, constituting "learning by teaching" (Biswas et al., 2005). Self-explanations include identifying the causes and consequences of states and/or actions, retrieving and incorporating relevant prior knowledge, and reasoning about the information. Self-explaining increases comprehension and has been the hallmark of several learning environments (McNamara et al., 2007; Meyer and Wijekumar, 2007; Palincsar and Brown, 1984). Besides comprehension, self-explanation appears to increase the ability of readers to accurately judge their understanding as assessed by a later comprehension test ("metacomprehension," Griffin et al., 2008), which is notoriously poor under normal reading conditions (Maki, 1998).
3. *Feedback.* Feedback can be given in many forms, such as corrective ("correct" "incorrect") or elaborative/formative (providing hints to help the learner provide a clearer or more complete answer), and may be expressed by points, explanations, achievements, actions in the story world, and skillometers (Oxland, 2004; Shute, 2008). Informative feedback enhances learning, motivation, engagement, and self-efficacy (Anderson et al., 1995; Harackiewicz, 1979; Kulik and Kulik, 1988).
4. *Narrative, fantasy, adventure.* Games often immerse the player in a virtual fantasy world in which the player solves problems and interacts with other real or virtual characters. Often the game play is embedded in a narrative that may contain elaborate settings, characters, goals, subgoals, obstacles, and various other plot devices. Narratives in games are often nonlinear and interactive when the player's actions determine future story states (Whitton, 2010), allowing for a high degree of replay value (Gee, 2003).
5. *Player control.* Games have various design features that allow the player to have control over the learning environment. Allowing player control can be

accomplished by giving the player several options at a given time, and by providing actions that are perceived to be influential and logical to their consequences (Malone and Lepper, 1987). Customization of the display (e.g., avatars, sounds) and the ability of the player to choose levels or difficulties of play also increase player's perceptions of control (Whitton, 2010). Although adopting user control into games is seen positively by game designers, the implementation should be clear and obvious to the user (Salen and Zimmermann, 2004; Van Eck, 2010; Whitton, 2010).

6. *Dialogue.* People often learn by conversations and tutorial dialogs (Chi et al., 2001; VanLehn et al., 2007). Engaging in a conversation entails a number of processes that engender deep learning, such as generating questions and answers, retrieving information from memory, reasoning, active processing and self-explaining. Because of the tremendous challenges posed by computers understanding natural language, there are relatively few games and computerized learning environments that enable the player or learner to converse with a virtual agent or avatar in natural language.
7. *Encoding variability.* It is important that the skills and knowledge that players practice and learn in a learning environment transfer to other situations and contexts. Although achieving transfer is notoriously difficult, providing variability in examples helps the learner to discriminate relevant from irrelevant features (Bransford et al., 1990), which increases transfer to novel problems (Halpern, 2002).

Below we discuss the three modules in *Operation ARIES!*, and also how the various principles relate to each module. In some cases, we present relevant research on the modules.

10.2 Module 1: Training

In this module, the player reads and is tested on various aspects of scientific inquiry. The content is provided by an eBook titled "The Big Book of Science." In many respects, the book is conventional because much of its content is covered by research methods texts published in the social sciences. However, it is unique in a couple of ways. First, it was written by Zlotsky Amapolis, a Fuath scientist who authored the book to teach the scientific method to other Fuath operatives working on Earth. Therefore, the book is a captured alien's spy manual. Second, because it was written for the Fuath spies, it incorporates aspects of Fuath culture in elaborations and examples. For instance, the Fuaths call Human Beings "Beans" and "nose breathers" (the Fuaths do not have noses), and the concept of sample size is illustrated with Blupblops that are plants found on Thoth.

Each chapter is dedicated to one or two important concepts in scientific inquiry. The 20 primary concepts covered by Operation ARIES! are listed below.

Theories and the Experimental Method
Hypothesis
Science and Pseudoscience
Operational Definitions
Independent Variables and Participant Variables
The Dependent Variable
Dependent Variables: Reliability, Accuracy, and Precision
Dependent Variables: Validity
The Dependent Variable: Objective Scoring
Replication of Results
Control Groups
Random Assignment to Groups
Subject Bias
Attrition and Mortality
Representative Samples
Sample Size
Experimenter Bias
Conflict of Interest
Causality vs. Correlation
Drawing Conclusions: Generalizability

We chose the topics by surveying college and university professors who teach psychology, sociology, biology, chemistry, earth science and physics classes on what they considered critical concepts for students in their field to learn.

A screen shot of the training module is presented in Fig. 10.1. There are two animated pedagogical agents, Dr. Quinn and Glass Tealman. Dr. Quinn is the teacher whereas Glass is a fellow student. Both of them speak and show facial expressions, and what they say is presented in a textbox so that the player can have a written record. We chose to use animated agents for several reasons. One is that they are (virtual) humans which players can relate to on a very intuitive and personal fashion. Consequently, animated agents are very engaging. A second reason is that they have been shown to increase learning and motivation in learning environments (Atkinson, 2002; Baylor and Kim, 2005). Another function is that the story line involves the agents as protagonists. Finally, some of the interactions between the agents instantiate important pedagogical roles (Baylor and Kim, 2005). As will be described below, Glass's responses serve as a model to the low knowledge player, yet Glass also serves as a teachable student for the more-knowledgeable player.

Before each chapter, Dr. Quinn and Glass hold a brief conversation, similar to an informal chat between student and teacher before a lecture. For example, early in the game Glass mentions that his new roommate was "chanting and doing Tarot cards last night. Said he was writing a paper saying that there is scientific evidence that Tarot cards can read the cosmic time space continuum. I thought it might be a hypothesis because of connecting two variables. But I also thought it sounded wacko." Dr. Quinn explains that this is most likely pseudoscience, which turns out

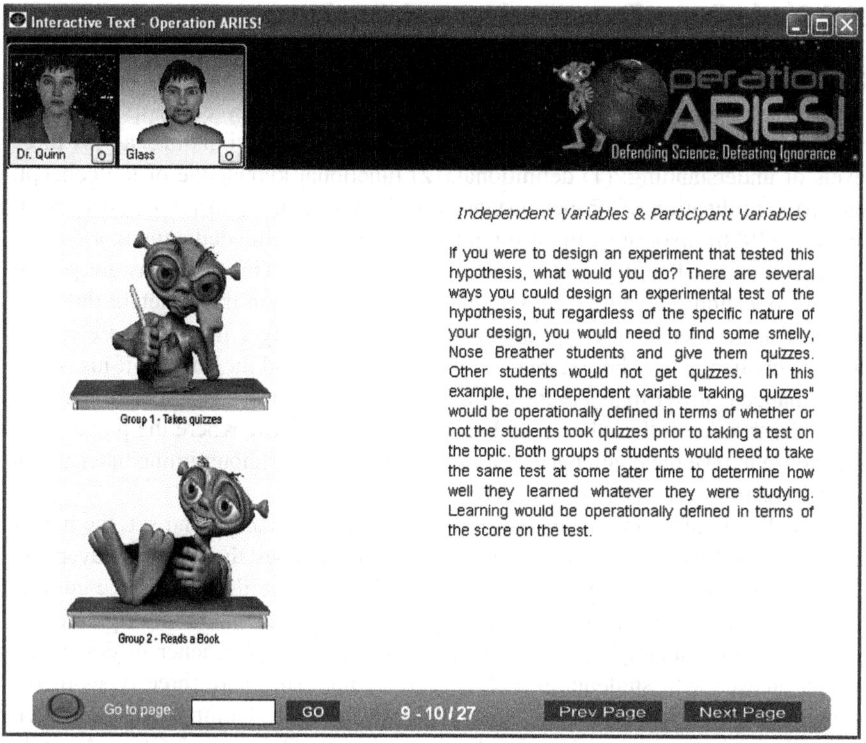

Fig. 10.1 Training module

to be the topic of the next chapter. The content of the dialog achieves two functions. One is that it advances the story line, with depictions of new events. For example, Glass's new roommates turn out to be alien spies. Another is that they introduce the topic of the chapter which is related to the dialog and the story line. This is important because after the dialog, the players are asked whether they would like to take a "challenge test." A high score on this test allows the player to skip reading the chapter. The dialog gives the student enough context of the chapter allowing the player to make an informed decision.

We should note here that *Operation ARIES!* contains different forms of internal assessments of the player's knowledge. In the Training module alone, there are multiple types of assessments. One type occurs within each chapter. These are interactive learning activities which were created by the author of "The Big Book of Science." Readers of the book are periodically given brief problems that require constructed answers (e.g., "write down the hypothesis") or selected responses (multiple choice, matching). These are included to promote reader engagement, activity and reflection with the material. As will be elaborated below, another type of assessment is more dynamic with the player being tested, given instruction, and assessed again (Yeomans, 2008).

10.2.1 Challenge Tests, Trialogs and AutoTutor

The player can test out of reading a chapter by doing well on a "challenge test" that evaluates the player's knowledge of the one or two key concepts addressed by the chapter. It is comprised of multiple choice test questions that assess three levels of understanding: (1) definitional, (2) functional knowledge of the concept, and (3) identification of proper instances of the concept. From the perspective of Bloom's (1956) taxonomy, these roughly correspond to knowledge/memory, comprehension/understanding, and application, respectively. The questions are placed into two question sets, with each set containing one question from each of the three levels. The first set of three questions is given to the player if he or she elects to take the challenge test, but the player will be asked to read the chapter if his or her performance is lower than a predetermined threshold. If the player's performance is above the threshold, then the second set is given. In the case where the player does not choose to take the challenge test and elects to read the chapter immediately, both sets of questions are given after the chapter is read.

Immediately after answering each of the questions in the second set, the player engages in a three-way tutorial conversation that includes the human player, Dr. Quinn, and Glass. We refer to these as "trialogs" because there are three conversational partners. The topic of the trialogs is the material in the multiple choice questions. Consequently, the trialogs are similar to when a teacher discusses the correct answer with students in a classroom setting. There are three types of trialogs. A *standard* trialog occurs when Glass observes Dr. Quinn teach the player. A *vicarious* trialog occurs when the player watches Dr. Quinn teach Glass. A *teaching* trialog occurs when the player teaches Glass as Dr. Quinn observes. The type of trialog that occurs for a particular question is based on the level of knowledge exhibited by the player. Low, intermediate, and high knowledge triggers vicarious, standard and teaching trialogs, respectively. The level of knowledge is defined by the number of questions that the player answers correctly.

Table 10.1 presents examples of the different types of trialogs. The examples were drawn from a study that is summarized below. (We should note that the participants in this study did not read the eBook beforehand, and therefore their answers might be a little sparse compared to students who had read the book.) The examples are presented for illustrative purposes. The point of the trialogs is to get the player to articulate a particular idea regarding the topic of the multiple choice question. The trialogs generally have the following order of presented information: question → hint → prompt → summary. The question is the main question to be answered by one of the agents, and is compared to an "ideal answer" which is also serves as the summary. If the answer to the question is acceptable, then the summary is given and the trialog ends. Otherwise a general hint is given. The hint tries to nudge the tutee into articulating the correct answer by providing retrieval cues. If the answer to the hint is acceptable, then the summary is given. Otherwise a prompt is given. Prompts narrow down the problem space to a particular word or phrase. After the prompt is answered, the summary is presented. The animated agents also provide feedback that can be positive, negative, or neutral ("yes", "no", "OK"). Dr. Quinn

Table 10.1 Examples of teaching, standard, and vicarious trialog tutorial sessions

Teaching Trialog (importance/function question for "operational definition")	Glass: Okay, I know operational definitions are important in research, but I'm not sure why. Let's just go over the importance of these things one more time. Why do we need to have operational definitions? (question)
	Laura: so that they can be reliably measured and used by other researchers
	Glass: OK. (neutral feedback)
	Dr. Quinn: Um, can you add to that? (pump)
	Laura: it is important to create operational definitions because they provide a basis for measuring variables and so that they can be reliably measured and used by other researchers in other studies.
	Glass: That is not clear to me. I thought operational definitions had something to do with telling others about your study. What could that be? (Hint)
	Laura: how to measure a variable.
	Glass: I still don't understand. Wow, it seems like operational definitions have something to do with being able to reliably do something. What is that something? (prompt)
	Laura: measure a variable
	Dr. Quinn: Okay. Reliably recognize variables (neutral feedback, prompt completion)
	Glass: I'm remembering something about how operational definitions make it so that a variable means the same thing to all researchers. That means that when other researchers use the same variable, it is what? (prompt)
	Laura: reliable
	Dr. Quinn: Great! It is reliable (positive feedback, prompt completion)
	Glass: Yeah, I understand. Operational definitions are important to consider because they allow a particular variable to be reliably recognized, measured, and understood by all researchers. (summary)
Standard Trialog ("example" question for "subject variable")	Dr. Quinn: I just want to make sure that everyone really knows this. Why don't you explain why the answer about socioeconomic status is an example of a subject variable?
	Lauren: so that they are getting a generalization for their experiment
	Glass: I do not understand.
	Dr. Quinn: Think about this. As you're considering why the socioeconomic status option is the correct answer, think about how it mentions classifying the participants. Now try to explain why socioeconomic status provides a good example of a subject variable. (hint)
	Lauren: so that they can have the same socioeconomic status

Table 10.1 (continued)

	Glass: still don't understand.
	Dr. Quinn: Okay. Let's try this. In this example, the researcher is using a characteristic about the subjects to put them into what? (prompt)
	Lauren: a specific category
	Dr. Quinn: Okay, into groups. I bet you know the answer to this. In this example, the researcher is using socioeconomic status to group the subjects, and for the subjects, socioeconomic status is a what? (prompt)
	Lauren: specific group
	Dr. Quinn: Alright. Subject variables are characteristics of the subjects, such as socioeconomic status, that are used to categorize them into groups. They are a type of independent variable that is not manipulated. (summary)
Vicarious Trialog (importance/function question for "theory")	Glass: You know, I thought the correct answer was the methodologies. I guess I need some help here.
	Dr. Quinn: Explain why you think theories are important.
	Glass: A theory provides an understanding.
	Dr. Quinn: Okay. Here is a little hint. As you consider why theories are important, think about how theories might relate to how research is conducted and what the research findings are. (hint)
	Glass: They provide predictions for future research projects.
	Dr. Quinn: Tyler (human player), what is your opinion? Does it seem like Glass now understands why theories are important? Please answer "Yes" or "No".
	Tyler: No.
	Dr. Quinn: You are wrong, Tyler. Theories are important in research because by providing explanations for findings, they are able to organize many research findings and make predictions for future research projects. (corrective feedback, summary)

sometimes asks for more information, called "pumps" ("what else?"), or corrects misconceptions given by Glass or the human player.

The agent who delivers the different types of information is dictated by the agent's conversational role: teacher, student, and bystander. In the teaching trialog, the human player serves as the teacher, Glass as the student, and Dr. Quinn as a knowledgeable bystander. Consequently, Glass (as the student), asks the player (who presumable is the expert on this topic) the primary question. Because Glass is the one who is seeking clarification, he poses hints and prompts that are phrased as believably sounding bits of partial knowledge. Also because Glass is being taught by the player, he is the one who gives the summary (this also provides "proof" that he now understands having been taught by the player). In the standard trialog format, the question, hints, prompts and summary are all given by Dr. Quinn directed toward the player, and some feedback is given by Glass, when he asserts that "he doesn't understand." In the vicarious trialogs, the player fulfills the bystander role who listens to Dr. Quinn tutor Glass. To maintain engagement with the material, the player is always asked whether he or she thinks Glass understands the concept based on his answers.

The conversational management, feedback and natural language understanding that the trialogs require is based on AutoTutor (Graesser et al., 2004, 2005c, 2001, 1999). AutoTutor is an Intelligent Tutoring Sytem (ITS) that helps students learn a domain by holding conversational dialogs between the student and an animated pedagogical agent. AutoTutor has brought about considerable learning gains comparable to one-on-one human tutoring (Graesser et al., 2005a, 2001; VanLehn et al., 2007).

Versions of AutoTutor have been built to teach computer literacy (Graesser et al., 2004) and physics (VanLehn et al., 2007). The program simulates human tutorial dialogs in natural language. It was constructed from extensive research on human tutorial dialogs (Graesser et al., 1995), constructivist theories of learning (Aleven and Koedinger, 2002), and other intelligent tutors that adapt to the learner at a fine-grained level (VanLehn et al., 2007).

Conversations in AutoTutor are largely governed by a curriculum script, which provides for each scenario (e.g., a question) an ideal answer, a set of expectations (content that the tutor would like to be expressed by the learner), a set of hints and prompts for each expectation, misconceptions and corrections, and a summary. AutoTutor poses a scenario (e.g., a question) and the learner's answer is assessed against the ideal answer and the expectations to indicate which of the expectations have been adequately answered or "covered". This assessment usually involves a combination of latent semantic analysis (a statistical method for representing semantic similarity between two sets of words, Landauer and Dumais, 1997) and semantic matching algorithms that consider words, word stems, and combinations of these linguistic units in regular expressions. These techniques output a numeric value indicating the semantic overlap between the student's input and the ideal answer or expectation. If the value exceeds a predetermined threshold, then AutoTutor declares that the expectation is covered by the student. If not, it will give hints to the student in order for him or her to express the content of the full expectation.

10.2.2 Learning Principles and the Training Module

Table 10.2 summarizes the links between the learning principles and features of the Training module (as well as the other two modules). The learning activities are based on the eBook and the trialogs. One important feature of the trialogs is that they are adaptive to the knowledge exhibited by the player: low, medium, and high levels of knowledge are linked with vicarious, standard, and teaching trialogs. The

Table 10.2 Learning principles and the three modules

Modules Learning principle	Training	Case studies	Interrogation
Zone of proximal development	Type of trialog is based on prior knowledge.	N/A	Scaffolding of "score card", progressively more difficult
Self-explanation	Reflection questions are posed in eBook; trialogs require player to explain concepts and answers.	Quinn periodically asks player to justify the selection of a flaw.	N/A
Feedback	Agents give corrective and elaborative feedback in the trialogs.	Points are awarded for correct answers; points are correlated with less scaffolding (no hint → hint → prompt); summary of case is presented.	Points, corrective feedback, summary of case is presented.
Narrative, fantasy, adventure	The eBook is an alien spy book and the player is training to be a special agent of the FBS.	E-mails, dialogs, and deciphered flaws advance story line. Nemotoads threaten world.	Story is advanced through news updates, and emails. World is saved.
Player control	Player can opt out of reading by taking "challenge test"	Player chooses case to evaluate, can buy "flaw list" or access the eBook.	Player selects cases and difficulty level.
Dialogue	Player engages in tutorial dialogs called trialogs.	Dr. Quinn gives hints and prompts, similar to the "standard" trialogs.	N/A
Encoding variability	Novel examples and illustrations are presented in the eBook	Research is written in a number of formats; topics in psychology, biology and chemistry.	Research is written in a number of formats; topics in psychology, biology and chemistry.

theoretical foundation for this linking was guided by Vygotsky's zone of proximal development in addition to the general tenet of constructionism that knowledge is actively constructed by the learner.

When prior knowledge is low, it is difficult for the learner to ask, understand, and answer questions using the desired vocabulary, so standard and teaching trialogs would be out of their "zone." Although observational learning of tutorial sessions does enhance learning (Craig et al., 2009), there is some evidence that low prior knowledge participants show greatest learning gains when they watch a tutorial conversation, occasionally commenting on what is being learned, rather than participating directly (Craig et al., 2006). When players show a high level of knowledge, watching a tutorial dialog might be relatively boring and would result in few learning gains. Their level of knowledge enables them to be successful *active* participants. In fact, "playing teacher" is particularly effective in both engagement and learning, as noted earlier in the context of self-explanation as a learning principle. Some learning environments contain "teachable agents" that require the human student to teach a computerized agent (Biswas et al., 2005). One called "Betty's Brain" substantially increased learning gains, transfer and self-regulated learning compared to control conditions (Biswas et al., 2010). The "teaching trialog" encompasses some of the features associated with teachable agents, namely that the students believe that they are contributing to the knowledge of another agent, and the students receive feedback on the imparted knowledge.

There are two other reasons for engaging the player with trialogs. First, they provide an avenue to identify and fix misconceptions held by the player. People often hold misconceptions in science that might be difficult to change (Hynd and Alverman, 1989). The program stores a log of common misconceptions for each topic. If the player (or Glass) mentions any of these, the program will identify it and Dr. Quinn will correct the misconception. Second, the trialogs provide retrieval practice in that the player must identify and use particular words in answers to questions. Roediger and Karpicke (2006) have shown that retrieval practice in testing increases learning ("testing effects").

10.2.3 Preliminary Research on the Training Module

Because it takes several hours to progress through the entire training modules, we have only been able to do some alpha testing on the training module to see how well students learn. Twelve students attending California universities participated across 7 week, one-hour sessions. One-third of the students attended a state university, another third a community college, and the remaining third an elite private university. A pre-post test was created to measure understanding of the concepts covered by the interactive text. The same test was used before and after students went through the interactive text. The questions were a mixture of open-ended and multiple choice. The overall test scores suggested that students learned from the training module. The post scores ($M = 25.04$, $SD = 7.06$), were significantly higher than overall pretest scores ($M = 15.29$, SD $= 8.07$), $t(11) = 7.38$, $p < 0.01$, effect size $= 1.3$, and this improvement occurred for students from each of three institutions.

10.2.3.1 Trialogs

Do the different types of trialogs affect learning? We addressed this question by having students read and answer the sets of questions to five chapters. Immediately, and after 2 days, they answered an open-ended comprehension test of the concepts that were addressed by the questions. Because we were interested in examining the effect of the trialogs, we did not have the participants read the chapter. Instead, they only read and answered the multiple choice questions, and either received a vicarious trialog, a teaching trialog, or a mixture of the three based on their performance (adaptive). Hence, we were interested whether animated agents delivering formative feedback would lead to differential "testing effects" (Roediger and Karpicke, 2006).

We found that the trialogs had little impact on immediate testing but did have an impact after a 2 day delay. The means (the percentage correct) for the vicarious, adaptive and teaching conditions on the immediate test were 0.45 ($SD = 0.19$), 0.48 ($SD = 0.19$), and 0.47 ($SD = 0.18$), respectively. The corresponding means in the delay condition were 0.34 ($SD = 0.16$), 0.44 ($SD = 0.19$) and 0.45 ($SD = 0.21$), respectively. The drop in scores due to the delay was significant in the vicarious condition [$t\ (27) = 4.23$, $p < 0.01$] but not in the other two trialog conditions (p's < 0.40). In addition, the adaptive and teaching scores in the delayed condition were significantly greater than the vicarious condition ($p < 0.05$). The pattern of means indicate greater learning in the adaptive and teaching conditions compared to the vicarious conditions. We had hypothesized that the adaptive condition would outperform the teaching condition, but it did not. Rather, there was no difference between the adaptive and teaching conditions. We kept the adaptive trialogs in *Operation ARIES!* instead of only using teaching trialogs for two reasons. First, they contain a variety of interchanges that we hope players will value. Second, participants in this study only responded to 5 chapters worth of multiple choice items without having read the eBook. Perhaps other patterns of results would be found when participants read the entire eBook.

10.3 Module 2: Case Studies

In this module, the player reads and evaluates a number of brief research reports. Each report describes a study in one of the following domains: psychology, biology, or chemistry. Each is written and formatted in such a way that it resembles newspaper or magazine article, a blog, a web page, or an advertisement. What they have in common is that virtually all contain one or more flaws pertaining to the concepts taught in the Training module. For example, a research report might not include a control group, not have a valid dependent variable, or might suffer from experimental bias. The purpose of the module is to teach the player how to evaluate research reports (called case studies) by having them identify flaws contained in them.

We adopted a case-based learning environment for flaw identification because cases (problems, instances, scenerios) allow learners to encode and discover the rich source of constraints and interdependencies underlying the target elements (flaws) within the cases. The memory of prior cases provides a knowledge base for assessing new cases, in that they help guide reasoning, problem solving, interpretation and other cognitive processes. That is, players implicitly learn the various ways in which the flaws are instantiated in different contexts, and how they are causally and conceptually connected. For example, if a study suffers from biased sample selection, then it would likely suffer from poor generalizability since its finding was

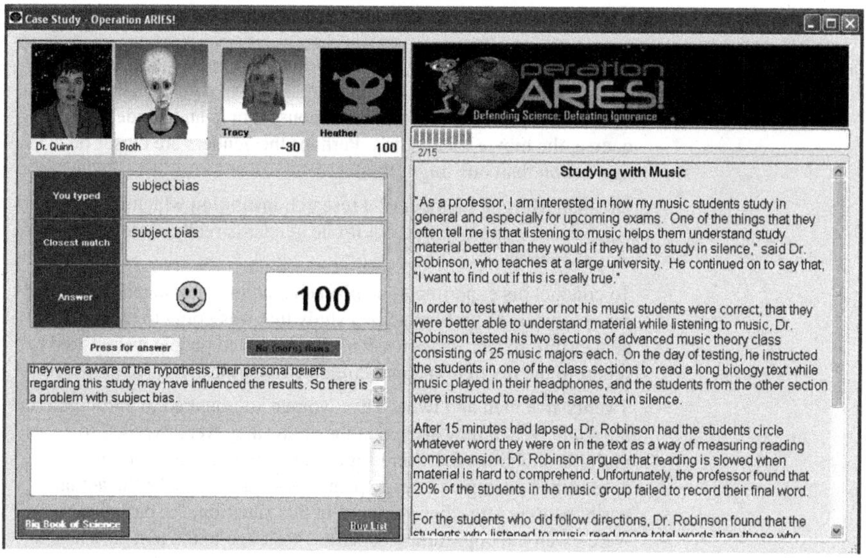

Fig. 10.2 Case studies module

based on a sample with particular characteristics that may not occur in the larger population.

Table 10.3 presents a sample "case" along with the flaws that it contains, whereas Fig. 10.2 presents a screen shot of the case studies interface. There is a picture representing the human player (e.g., "Heather"), as well as two new agents joining Dr. Quinn: Tracy and Broth. Tracy, like the player, is a fellow student agent at the FBS. The human player and Tracy compete against each other for the honor of going forward to the next module where they will interrogate aliens. Broth is an alien defector who wants peace with Human "Beans" and who is observing the sessions. (Glass Tealman, who was the fellow student during the Training module, left at the end of that module to find his older brother who is being held captive by the Fuaths.) As in the training module, Dr. Quinn provides instructional support by giving guidance and feedback to each player (the human player and Tracy). Broth gives feedback to the players as well, but also advances the story line by providing knowledge regarding the Fuath's perspective on their spying mission. During the course of the case evaluations, Broth announces that the Fuath spies communicate with each other by placing specific flaws in the research that they publish. By deciphering the flaws, Broth reports several developments pertinent to the story line, the most distressing being that the very deadly aliens called Nemotoads are en route to Earth. This news is met with some disbelief within the FBS, creating uncertainty and tension.

The human player and Tracy take turns evaluating cases. The current player (human or Tracy) first chooses a case to evaluate from a list, reads it, and then types in flaws into an input box. For support, the player can buy a list of flaws or

Table 10.3 Sample case study, hints and prompts

Case title: The Battle of the Sexes	Who are more aggressive, men or women? Popular media and news reports often portray men as the more aggressive gender. But think again: there was Bonnie in the infamous Bonnie and Clyde, and of course, the movie Mean Girls. Perhaps the genders are closer on aggression than one might think. Dr. Alan Maye, a member of a research institution which focuses on aggression, wanted to find out if one gender is really more aggressive than the other. To conduct his experiment, he placed an ad in a newspaper and asked for volunteers to participate in a study that was going to explore gender differences in aggression. All interested people were asked to report to the institution conducting the research. Twenty-five men and twenty-five women volunteered to participate in the study. When they arrived at the study, they were exposed to multiple situations that were supposed to elicit aggression (an accomplice posing as a participant was used to provoke the actual participants). After they were put in this situation, the participants were given the opportunity to write a message to the person who provoked them. The messages that participants wrote were coded by two independent researchers who were not aware of the participant's gender. The messages were coded on a 7-point scale for the degree of verbal aggressiveness that was used. The results showed that women provided more aggressive messages than men. In a follow-up study, the researchers found the same results – women were found to be more aggressive than men. Based on these results, the researchers concluded, contrary to popular belief, women are actually more aggressive than men.
Flaws	Flaw: dependent variable is not valid Hint: Considering that verbal aggressiveness is simply one type of aggressive behavior, what can you say about the dependent measure used here? Prompt: A dependent variable that measures something other than what it is claimed to measure is called what? Flaw: poor sample selection Hint: What flaw is associated with how Dr. Maye chose participants for this study? Prompt: Because this study only included participants who were interested in answering the advertisement, the study involved a poor selection of the what? Flaw: subject bias Hint: What can you say about the fact that the newspaper ad informed possible participants of the intent of the study? Prompt: If participants can influence results based on their own expectations regarding the experiment, this is what type of bias?

read the "Big Book of Science." After the flaw is entered, the program matches the input to the list of flaws using semantic matching algorithms. The algorithm involves computing a match score between the input and each flaw. If the score falls below a threshold, Dr. Quinn will ask the player to rephrase the flaw; otherwise the flaw with the highest match score will be presented in the "closest match" box. When the player is satisfied with the match, the player requests the answer. Dr. Quinn then gives elaborative feedback as to why the answer was correct or incorrect, and points are either added to or subtracted from the player's current score. If correct, the player retains his or her turn, and is asked to identify another flaw. The player can also push the "No (more) Flaws" button if he or she believes all flaws have been identified (or if there were no flaws in the case in the first place.) If the player is incorrect, then the turn passes to the other player. Periodically, Dr. Quinn asks the player to justify his or her answer by asking "Why did you choose that flaw?" in order to encourage self-explanation and to discourage random answers.

If there are any unidentified flaws left by the time that both players press the "No (more) Flaws" button, then Dr. Quinn provides a brief tutoring session with the current player. The dialog uses a curriculum script similar to the ones used for the "standard" trialogs described earlier. The program selects a hint associated with a flaw that has not been covered, and it is delivered by Dr. Quinn. If the hint is unsuccessful in eliciting the desired response (e.g., there is no control/comparison group), then Dr. Quinn gives an appropriate prompt. Table 10.3 shows some of the hints and prompts. If the player fails to answer this question, then the opponent has the opportunity to answer for maximum points. In regard to points, points are awarded on the basis of the presence and type of question: without hint → hint → prompt.

10.3.1 Learning Principles and the Case Studies Module

One prominent feature of the case studies is that the cases describe a variety of content (psychology, biology, and chemistry) written and formatted in a number of ways. They read and look like blogs, advertisements, and newspaper and magazine articles. The variation in content and format was designed to promote transfer – to use scientific inquiry skills in other contexts. In addition, there are many types of feedback given to the player. When a player types in a flaw, he or she receives immediate feedback as to whether that flaw is present in the case. The feedback is presented verbally by Dr. Quinn and by the addition or subtraction of points.

One important feature not listed in Table 10.2 is competition. The player is competing against Tracy. Competition is often listed as a characteristic of games, both digital and nondigital (Yee, 2006). A survey conducted by the Annenberg School for Communication Games Group at the University of Southern California indicated that competition was the primary reason why players chose certain games (as cited in Bryant and Fondren, 2009). However, some designers caution against competition in favor of cooperation because it may focus on the act of winning rather than on the learning domain (Whitton, 2010). One limitation of the use of competition in Operation ARIES! is that it may not benefit all groups in the same way. For example, boys tend to choose more competitive games than girls (Hartmann, 2003), so competing against Tracy might not be attractive to all players.

10.3.2 Research on the Case Studies

The research that we have conducted using a precursor to the case studies module suggests that having students engage in tutorial dialogs about case studies is an effective strategy in learning how to identify flaws. In a study conducted by Kopp et al. (in press), undergraduate psychology students listened to an animated teacher agent read several research descriptions used in the module, and immediately after each, the participates were assigned to one of three activities: (1) listen to a conversation between the teacher and an animated student in which the participant had to write down the flaws that were identified and summarized by the teacher, (2) write down flaws that the participant noticed before the teacher provided a summary of the flaws, or (3) participate in a tutorial dialog with the teacher agent. The tutorial dialogs were similar to the standard trialogs but without a third agent. Learning gains were assessed by comparing pre- and post-test scores on task that required the participants to critique other flawed studies. When the post-test scores were adjusted for the pre-test scores, Kopp et al. (in press) reported significantly greater learning when participants had participated in full dialogs than when they listened to and wrote down the flaws (Experiment 2). Interestingly, they found that engaging in tutorial dialogs was not necessary for all cases to maintain the advantage. The highest rates of learning occurred when one-half of the cases required full dialogs (condition 3 above) and the other half required an initial answer (condition 2 above). This outcome is somewhat counterintuitive, but makes sense after some reflection. Although dialogs increase learning, it appears that it is most efficient to only have the participants engage in dialogs for one-half of the cases. The extra dialogs might incur fatigue. We used this finding to inform the design of Case Studies in which the human player directly evaluates only one-half of the cases whereas Tracy evaluates the other half.

In another study, we compared learning and reactions to the Case Studies module (game condition) with a version that lacked points, competition, and animated agents (non-game condition). Otherwise, the same materials and feedback were administered in the two conditions. As in Kopp et al. (in press), participants were undergraduate psychology students, and were given a pre- and post-test that required them to correctly identify flaws in research cases. There were four one-hour sessions that occurred across two weeks. Immediately after the first and last sessions, we asked participants about their level of engagement, motivation, interest, challenge, and frustration using a 6-point Likert-type scale. As a measure of the ability to detect flaws, we computed a "flaw identification score" by subtracting the participant's "false alarm" rate (i.e., the percentage of occurrences when the participant said a flaw was present in the research but it was not) from their "hit" rate (i.e., the percentage of occurrences when a participant correctly identified the presence of a flaw). A score of zero on the "flaw identification score" would indicate no ability for a person to discriminate between the presence and absence of a flaw, whereas a score of 1.0 would indicate perfect discrimination. The pre-test means for the game ($M = 0.09$) and no game ($M = 0.07$) conditions were low and nearly identical. The increase on the post-test scores was significantly higher in the game ($M = 0.43$) than in the no game ($M = 0.32$) condition, as indicated by a significant interaction, $F(1, 27) = 3.01$, $p < .05$, $MSe = 0.012$ (one-tailed). Interestingly, few differences emerged on the questions about their experiences. Participants in the game conditions gave significantly higher ratings on interest ($p < 0.05$, one-tailed) and frustration ($p < 0.01$), but there was no significant difference on the other measures. The finding for frustration was unexpected, but holding an informal focus group afterwards was revealing. The participants in the game condition expressed some frustration from having to use the desired vocabulary (e.g., no control group, small sample size) required for a successful match between the user input and the flaw categories. However, they expressed even more frustration by the time taken up by Tracy's responses which appeared as text being typed in real time. Since then, Tracy's text responses on the screen have been dramatically sped up.

10.4 Module 3: Interrogation

The story line heats up in this last third of the game. Thousands of Nemotoad spacecrafts have left the Mother ship and have settled into geocentric Earth orbits. An intercepted message reveals their horrific plans: the Grand Nemotoad will order humans to be subjugated as slaves and they will scorch the Earth. In an attempt to capture the Grand Nemotoad and other aliens, the FBS has conducted a large-scale raid, arresting dozens of scientists suspected of being aliens. However, some of those who were arrested are human. Only through interrogating each suspect on their research can the FBS know for sure the species of each suspect. The aliens are those publishing flawed research, the humans are not. Meanwhile, the clock is ticking toward global disaster.

The Interrogation module teaches the player how to evaluate research by asking questions. The player first reads a summary of research conducted by one of the suspected alien spies. Similar to case studies, the research is presented in different types media (newspapers, blogs, etc.), but unlike the case studies the research is abbreviated and critical information is missing. The description of the research might be the length of an abstract (roughly 150 words), an advertisement, and in some cases, it might be only a headline (e.g., "Study shows music helps plants to grow"). The descriptions do not explicitly signal any flaw. Hence, in order to uncover a flaw, the player must ask the suspect questions about the research, and classify each answer on whether it revealed a flaw or not. If the study is flawed, then the suspect should be judged an alien. If there is no major flaw, or if the suspect acknowledges a flaw found in the study, the suspect should be judged human.

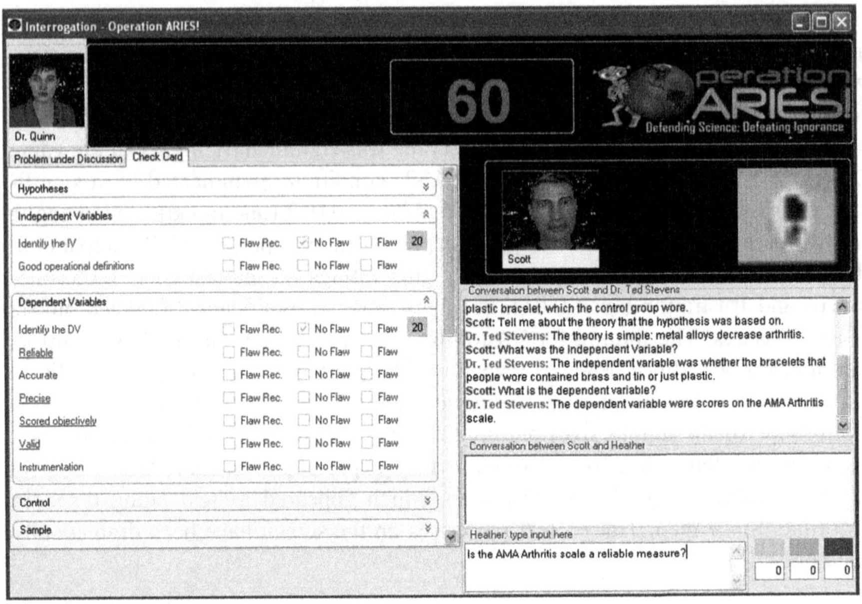

Fig. 10.3 Interrogation module

Figure 10.3 shows a screen shot of the Interrogation module after the research description has been read. In addition to Dr. Quinn, there are two other agents: Scott, serving as the interrogator, and the suspect who is hidden behind a screen. Scott and the suspect are located in the same room, apart from the player, and the player is responsible for sending Scott questions to ask the suspect. The player sends a question by typing it into an input box. Having the player send questions to the suspect via Scott solved a technical problem that could arise if the player and suspect communicated directly. In that circumstance, the program might misclassify a question typed in by the player. If this were to happen, the suspect would answer a question not posed by the player, leading the player to be confused. However, we had the player send questions to Scott, and Scott hedges when there is a low match score between the question typed in by the player and a stored question (e.g., "I think I know what you are getting at." "Your input is coming in fuzzy – I think I heard you"). The hedge allows Scott to ask any question (regardless of the input match) and receive an answer that does not sacrifice the buy-in that Scott truly understands the player's questions.

After the player receives an answer, the player evaluates the answer by checking off options (flaw, flaw recognized, no flaw) on relevant subcategories on a "score card." There is a total of 25 subcategories, arranged under the following superordinate categories: hypothesis, independent variable, dependent variable, control, sample, experimenter, conclusions. For example, the subcategories of "control" are possible confounds, subject bias, control groups, random assignment, mortality and attrition. The player might be able to correctly identify the answers to more than one subcategory from a single answer. For example, consider the following question and answer about the dependent variable (outcome variable) in the context of study that was conducted to test whether an advertised video decreases shyness:

Question: "Tell me about how you defined shyness."
Answer: "I used a shyness scale that I came up with. What you do is count the number of times a person blinks as they talk to you. It is quite reliable. People tend to be consistent in the number of times they blink per minute."

A correct classification of this answer would be "flaw" on the subcategory "validity" because eye blinks are not valid indicators of shyness, and "no flaw" on "reliability" because counting eye blinks is likely to be reliable. Both "valid" and "reliable" are subcategories under dependent variable.

The answer category "flaw recognized" is relevant when the suspect recognizes that there is a flaw or limitation. For example, consider the following question and answer about how the researcher selected participants (sample selection):

Question: "How did you get your participants?"
Answer: "The participants were attendees for a seminar designed to reduce shyness. We had advertised on radio and local television. Oh, wait, this is called selection bias, right? I guess this was a problem."

A sample selection flaw occurs in psychological research when the participants select themselves for the study. When this occurs, the participants might be biased in any number of ways, decreasing the likelihood that the results would generalize to other participants. Therefore, a correct classification would be "flaw recognized" under the subcategory "sample selection" because the researcher acknowledged the problem. The player is also instructed that because of their training, aliens never lie.

The "scorecard" contains a number of design elements that provide for instructional support. These include "clickable" subcategories, which when clicked, Scott asks a question based on that subcategory. The scorecard highlights categories and subcategories that could be addressed by the answer. These features are systematically taken away as the player advances through the module, resulting in four difficulty levels. At the end of the module, the scorecard itself is taken away, and the player is asked to make the "alien/human" judgment as soon as a flaw is revealed. Points are awarded for correct responses and taken away for incorrect responses. The point values vary based on the difficultly level of the game. At the end of the question-answer pairs for a given case, the player is asked to judge whether the suspect is human or alien. If there is at least one flaw, the correct judgment is alien. Otherwise, the correct judgment is human.

10.4.1 Learning Principles and the Interrogation Module

The primary learning principle that this module incorporates is question-asking, a learning principle not covered in Table 10.2. Prior research has indicated that learning is increased by formulating questions, and that students can learn how to ask good questions (Beck et al., 1997; Graesser et al., 2009b; King, 1994; Palincsar and Brown, 1984; Taboada and Guthrie, 2006). Asking questions increases learning not only by receiving answers to the posed questions, but in order to ask a question, the learner must actively read the material, encoding it deeply, and regulate their own learning in the process (Wisher and Graesser, 2007). Rosenshine et al. (1996) reviewed the literature on teaching question-asking strategies while reading and report mean effect sizes of 0.36 and 0.86 (in standard deviation units) when standardized and experimenter-generated tests of comprehension were used. Increasingly, learning environments are incorporating question facilities that encourage users to ask open ended questions (Linn et al., 2004; Palincsar and Brown, 1984).

10.5 Conclusions

Serious games lay at the intersection among content (e.g., research methods), game design (e.g., dialogs, agents, story), and pedagogical theory (e.g., principles of learning and motivation). Ideally, a serious game should be fun to play and educational. This sweet spot is notoriously difficult to achieve. One reason for this difficulty is that a game's enjoyableness and fun depend on a number of factors whose interactions are not clearly understood. Some commonly cited dimensions of enjoyable gaming experiences are overall game design, aesthetic (visual and auditory) presentation, the ease and effectiveness of control, complexity/challenge, social interaction/community, and storyline/narrative (Wang et al., 2009; Whitton, 2010). Ensuring that a game contains these characteristics is monetarily expensive, but also varies based on a player's individual tastes. Second, enjoyable game play experiences may not translate into deep learning (Graesser et al., 2009a). Deep learning of a complicated content or skills will probably require deep cognitive and emotional investments that span many hours of practice which not be considered fun by the player. Like many educational and serious games, *Operation ARIES!* tries to initiate and maintain interest by immersing the player into a larger narrative (Ratan and Ritterfeld, 2009). We have had many positive responses to the storyline of *Operation ARIES!* when presented alone, but it is currently unknown whether it can overcome negative reactions (e.g., boredom, frustration) that might arise from practice and repetition required to learn critical thinking skills in science. One high school student gamer who is skeptical regarding the value of educational games put it this way: "Educational games are homework, and I can smell homework!"

Operation ARIES! is in its final stages of empirical testing and these concerns are currently being explored. We are hopeful that the program will be valued by both students and educators. Pearson Education plans to host the game on a website where students can login and play, and where instructors can monitor their students' progress. Students can play at their leisure, and instructors can incorporate the game into their course in a number of ways. Some instructors might assign it as homework and only care whether the students complete the game, whereas others might incorporate the assessments which are internal to the game into the student's course grade. Still other instructors might only assign some modules and not others. It is anticipated that this level of flexibility will make *Operation ARIES!* a desirable addition to scientific learning in traditional classrooms as well as in distance learning. We hope that you have enjoyed getting to know the science behind *Operation ARIES!* as much as we have enjoyed sharing it with you.

Acknowledgments The research reported here was supported by the Institute of Education Sciences, U.S. Department of Education, through Grant R305B070349 to Northern Illinois University. The opinions expressed are those of the authors and do not represent views of the Institute or the U.S. Department of Education.

References

Aleven, V., Koedinger, K.R.: An effective metacognitive strategy: Learning by doing and explaining with a computer-based cognitive tutor. Cogn. Sci. **26**, 147–179 (2002)

Anderson, J.R., Corbett, A.T., Koedinger, K.R., Pelletier, R.: Cognitive tutors: Lessons learned. J Learn. Sci. **4**, 167–207 (1995)

Atkinson, R.K.: Optimizing learning from examples using animated pedagogical agents. J. Educ. Psychol. **94**, 416–427 (2002)

Baylor, A.L., Kim, Y.: Simulating instructional roles through pedagogical agents. Int. J. Artif. Intell. Educ. **15**, 95–115 (2005)

Beck, I.L., McKeown, M.G., Hamilton, R.L., Kucan, L.: Questioning the Author: An Approach for Enhancing Student Engagement with Text. International Reading Association, Delaware (1997)

Benyon, D., Turner, P., Turner, S.: Designing Interactive Systems. Addison-Wesley, Harlow (2005)

Biswas, G., Leelawong, K., Schwartz, D., Vye, N., The Teachable Agents Group at Vanderbilt.: Learning by teaching: A new agent paradigm for educational software. Appl. Artif. Intell. **19**, 363–392 (2005)

Biswas, G., Jeong, H., Kinnebrew, J., Sulcer, B., & Roscoe, R.: Measuring self-regulated learning skills through social interactions in a Teachable Agent environment. Res. Pract. Technol.-Enhanced Learn. **5**, 123–152 (2010)

Bloom, B.S.: Taxonomy of Educational Objectives, the Classification of Educational Goals – Handbook I: Cognitive Domain. McKay, New York (1956)

Bransford, J.D., Sherwood, R.S., Hasselbring, T.S., Kinzer, C.K., Williams, S.M.: Anchored instruction: Why we need it and how technology can help. In: Nix, D., Spiro, R. (eds.) Cognition, Education, and Multimedia: Exploring Ideas in High Technology, pp. 115–141. Lawrence Erlbaum Associates, Hillsdale, NJ (1990)

Bryant, J., Fondren, W.: Psychological and communicological theories of learning and emotion underlying serious games. In: Ritterfeld, U., Cody, M., Vorderer, P. (eds.) Serious Games: Mechanisms and Effects, pp. 103–116. Routledge, Taylor & Francis, New York and London (2009)

Chi, M.T.H., Siler, S.A., Jeong, H., Yamauchi, T., Hausmann, R.G.: Learning from human tutoring. Cogn. Sci. **25**, 471–553 (2001)

Craig, S.D., Sullins, J., Witherspoon, A., Gholson, B.: Deep level reasoning questions effect: The role of dialog and deep-level reasoning questions during vicarious learning. Cogn. Instruct. **24**, 563–589 (2006)

Craig, S.D., Chi, M.T.H., VanLehn, K.: Improving classroom learning by collaboratively observing human tutoring videos while problem solving. J. Educ. Psychol. 101, 779–789 (2009)

Csikszenthimhalyi, M.: Flow: The Psychology of Happiness. Random House, London (2002)

D'Mello, S., Graesser, A.C.: Multimodal semi-automated affect detection from conversational cues, gross body language, and facial features. User Model.User-adapted Interact. **20**, 147–187 (2010)

Gee, J.P.: What Video Games Teach Us About Language and Literacy. Palgrave/Macmillan, New York (2003)

Graesser, A.C., Person, N.K., & Magliano, J.P.: Collaborative dialogue patterns in naturalistic one-to-one tutoring. Appl. Cogn. Psychol. **9**, 359.1–359.28 (1995)

Graesser, A.C., Wiemer-Hastings, K., Wiemer-Hastings, P., Kreuz, R., the TRG: Auto Tutor: A simulation of a human tutor. J. Cogn. Syst. Res. **1**, 35–51 (1999)

Graesser, A.C., Person, N., Harter, D., the Tutoring Research Group: Teaching tactics and dialog in AutoTutor. Int. J. Artif. Intell. Educ. **12**, 257–279 (2001)

Graesser, A.C., Lu, S., Jackson, G.T., Mitchell, H., Ventura, M., Olney, A., Louwerse, M.M.: AutoTutor: A tutor with dialogue in natural language. Behav. Res. Meth. Instrum. Comput. **36**, 180–193 (2004)

Graesser, A.C., Chipman, P., Haynes, B.C., Olney, A.: AutoTutor: An intelligent tutoring system with mixed-initiative dialogue. IEEE Trans. Educ. **48**, 612–618 (2005a)

Graesser, A.C., Lu, S., Olde, B.A., Cooper-Pye, E., Whitten, S.: Question asking and eye tracking during cognitive disequilibrium: comprehending illustrated texts on devices when the devices break down. Mem. Cognit. **33**, 1235–1247 (2005b)

Graesser, A.C., McNamara, D.S., VanLehn, K.: Scaffolding deep comprehension strategies through Point&Query, AutoTutor, and iSTART. Educ. Psychol. **40**, 225–234 (2005c)

Graesser, A.C., D'Mello, S.K., Craig, S.D., Witherspoon, A., Sullins, J., McDaniel, B., Gholson, B.: The relationship between affective states and dialog patterns during interactions with AutoTutor. J. Interact. Learn. Res. **19**, 293–312 (2008)

Graesser, A.C., Chipman, P., Leeming, F., Biedenbach, S.: Deep learning and emotion in serious games. In: Ritterfeld, U., Cody, M., Vorderer, P. (eds.) Serious Games: Mechanisms and Effects, pp. 83–102. Routledge, Taylor & Francis, New York and London (2009a)

Graesser, A., Ozuru, Y., Sullins, J.: What is a good question? In: McKeown, M.G., Kucan, L. (eds.) Threads of Coherence in Research on the Development of Reading Ability, pp. 112–141. Guilford, New York (2009b)

Griffin, T.D., Wiley, J., Thiede, K.W.: Individual differences, rereading, and self-explanation: Concurrent processing and cue validity as constraints on metacomprehension accuracy. Mem. Cogn. **36**, 93–103 (2008)

Halpern, D.F.: Teaching for critical thinking: A four-part model to enhance thinking skills. In: Davis, S., Buskist, W. (eds.) The Teaching of Psychology: Essays in Honor of Wilbert J. McKeachie and Charles L. Brewer, pp. 91–105. Lawrence Erlbaum, Mahwah, NJ (2002)

Harackiewicz, J.: The effects of reward contingency and performance feedback on intrinsic motivation. J. Pers. Soc. Psychol. **37**, 1352–1363 (1979)

Hartmann, T.: Gender differences in the use of computer-games as competitive leisure activities. Paper presented at *Digital Games Research Association* (DIGRA), November 4–6, 2003, Utrecht, The Netherlands (2003)

Heeter, C., Egidio, R., Punya, M., Winn, B., Caywood, J.: Alien games: Do girls prefer games designed by girls? Games Cult. **4**(1), 74–100 (2007). doi: 10.1177/1555412008325481

Hynd, C., Alverman, D.E.: Overcoming misconceptions in science: An on-line study of prior knowledge activation. Reading Res. Instr. **84**, 12–26 (1989)

Indian Wine Academy: Study finds wine lowers heart attack risk in women. http://www.indianwineacademy.com/dm_145_item_4.asp (2007)

Ketelhut, D.J.: The impact of student self-efficacy on scientific inquiry skills: An exploratory investigation in River City, a multi-user virtual environment. J. Sci. Educ. Technol. **16**, 99–111 (2007)

King, A.: Guiding knowledge construction in the classroom: Effects of teaching children how to question and how to explain. Am. Educ. Res. J. **31**, 338–368 (1994)

Kopp, K., Britt, A., Millis, K., Graesser, A.: Improving the efficiency of dialogue in tutoring. J. Learn. Instr. (in press)

Kulik, J.A., Kulik, C-L.C.: Timing of feedback and verbal learning. Rev. Educ. Res. **58**, 79–97 (1988)

Landauer, T.K., & Dumais, S.T.: A solution to Plato's problem: The latent semantic analysis theory of acquisition, induction, and representation of knowledge. Psychol. Rev. **104**, 211–240 (1997)

Linn, M.C., Davis, E.A., & Bell, P.: Internet Environments for Science Education. Erlbaum, Hillsdale, New Jersey (2004)

Maki, R.H.: Test predictions over text material. In: Hacker, D.J., Dunlosky, J., Graesser, A.C. (eds.) Metacognition in Educational Theory and Practice, pp. 117–144. Erlbaum, Mahwah, NJ (1998)

Malone, T.W., Lepper, M.R.: Making learning fun: A taxonomy of intrinsic motivations for learning. In: Snow, R.E., Farr, M.J. (eds.) Aptitude Learning and Instruction, Vol. 3, pp. 223–253. Erlbaum, Hillsdale, NJ (1987)

McNamara, D.S., O'Reilly, T., Rowe, M., Boonthum, C., Levinstein, I.: iSTART: A web-based tutor that teaches self-explanation and metacognitive reading strategies. In: McNamara, D.S. (ed.) Reading Comprehension Strategies: Theories, Interventions, and Technologies, pp. 397–420. Erlbaum, New York (2007)

Meyer, B.J.F., Wijekumar, K.: A web-based tutoring system for the structure strategy: Theoretical background, design, and findings. In: McNamara, D.S. (ed.) Reading Comprehension Strategies: Theories, Interventions, and Technologies, pp. 347–374. Erlbaum, New York (2007)

National Center for Complementary and Alternative Medicine: Homeopathy: An introduction. Retrieved from the National Institutes of Health website http://nccam.nih.gov/health/homeopathy/ (undated)

National Science Education Standards (NSES): The National Academies Press, Washington, DC (1996)

Oxland, K.: Gameplay and Design. Addison-Wesley, Harlow (2004)

Palincsar, A.S., Brown, A.L.: Reciprocal teaching of comprehension-fostering and comprehension-monitoring Activities. Cogn. Instr. 1, 117–175 (1984)

Ratan, R., Ritterfeld, U.: Classifying serious games. In: Ritterfeld, U., Cody, M., Vorderer, P. (eds.) Serious Games: Mechanisms and Effects, pp. 10–24. Routledge, New York (2009)

Rieber, L.: Seriously considering play: Designing interactive learning environments based on the blending of microworlds, simulations, and games. Educ. Technol. Res. Dev. **44**, 42–58 (1996)

Roediger, H.L., Karpicke, J.D.: Test-enhanced learning: Taking memory tests improves long-term retention. Psychol. Sci., **17**, 249–255 (2006)

Rosenshine, B., Meister, C., Chapman, S.: Teaching students to generate questions: A review of the intervention studies. Rev. Educ. Res., **66**, 181–221 (1996)

Salen, K., Zimmerman, E.: Rules of Play: Game Design and Fundamentals. The MIT Press, Cambridge, MA (2004)

Shute, V.J.: Focus on formative feedback. Rev. Educ. Res. **78**, 153–189 (2008)

Taboada, A., Guthrie, J.T.: Contributions of student questioning and prior knowledge to construction of knowledge from reading information text. J. Literacy Res. **38**, 1–35 (2006)

Van Eck, R.: Building artificially intelligent learning games. In: Gibson, D., Aldrich, C., Prensky, M. (eds.) Games and Simulations in Online Learning Research & Development Frameworks, pp. 271–307. Idea Group, Hershey, PA (2007)

VanLehn, K., Graesser, A.C., Jackson, G.T., Jordan, P., Olney, A., Rose, C.P.: When are tutorial dialogues more effective than reading? Cogn. Sci. **31**, 3–62 (2007)

Vygotsky, L.: Mind in Society: The Development of Higher Psychological Functions. Harvard University Press, Cambridge, MA (1978)

Wang, H., Shen, C., & Ritterfeld, U.: Enjoyment of digital games: What makes them "seriously" fun? In: Ritterfeld, U., Cody, M., Vorderer, P. (eds.) Serious Games: Mechanisms And Effects, pp. 25–47. Routledge, Taylor & Francis, New York and London (2009)

Whitton, N.: Learning with Digital Games: A Practical Guide to Engaging Students in Higher Education. Routledge, New York (2010)

Wisher, R.A., Graesser, A.C.: Question asking in advanced distributed learning environments. In: Fiore, S.M., Salas, E. (eds.) Toward a Science of Distributed Learning and Training, pp. 209–234. American Psychological Association, Washington, DC (2007)

Yee, N.: Motivations of play in online games. CyberPsychol. Behav. **9**, 772–775 (2006)

Yeomans, J.: Dynamic assessment practice: Some suggestions for ensuring follow up. Educ. Psychol. Pract. **24**, 105–114 (2008)

Resources

Key Books

Gee, J. (ed.): Games, Learning, Assessment. MIT Press, Boston, MA (in press)

Gibson, D., Aldrich, C., Prensky, M. (eds.): Games and Simulations in Online Learning: Research and Development Frameworks. Information Science Publishing, Hershey, PA (2006)

Halpern, D.F. (ed.): Undergraduate Education in Psychology: A Blueprint for the Future of the Discipline. American Psychological Association Books, Washington, DC (2010)

Mayer, R.E., Alexander, P.A. (eds.): Handbook of Research on Learning and Instruction. Routledge Press, New York, NY (2011)

Mayrath, M., Robisnon, D., Clarke-Midura, J. (eds.): Technology-Based Assessments for 21st Century Skills: Theoretical and Practical Implications from Modern Research. Information Age Publications, Charlotte, NC (2011)

Ritterfeld, U., Cody, M., Vorderer, P. (eds.): Serious Games: Mechanisms and Effects. Routledge, Taylor and Francis, Mahwah, NJ (2009)

Shaffer, D.W.: How Computer Games Help Children Learn. Palgrave Macmillan, New York (2006)

Spector, J.M., Merrill, M.D., van Merriënboer, J.J.G., Driscoll, M.P. (eds.): Handbook of Research on Educational Communications and Technology. Taylor & Francis, London (2008)

Van Eck, R.: Interdisciplinary Models and Tools for Serious Games: Emerging Concepts and Future Directions. Information Science Reference, Hershey, NY (2010)

Key Survey/Review Articles

Aleven, V.: An intelligent learning environment for case-based argumentation. Technol. Inst. Cogn. Lear. **4**(2), 191–241 (2006)

Bagley, E., Shaffer, D.W.: When people get in the way: Promoting civic thinking through epistemic gameplay. Int. J. Gaming Comput. -Mediated Simul. **1**, 36–52 (2009)

Bråten, I., Strømsø, H.I., Britt, M.A.: Trust matters: Examining the role of source evaluation in students' construction of meaning within and across multiple texts. Reading Res. Q. **44**, 6–28 (2009)

Gee, J.P.: Why game studies now? E-video games: a new art form. Games Cult. **1**, 1–4 (2006)

Graesser, A.C., Jeon, M., Dufty, D.: Agent technologies designed to facilitate interactive knowledge construction. Discourse Process. **45**, 298–322 (2008)

Millis, K., Magliano, J., Todaro, S.: Measuring discourse-level processes with verbal protocols and latent semantic analysis. Sci. Stud. Reading **10**, 225–240 (2006)

Nash, P., Shaffer, D.W.: Mentor modeling: The internalization of modeled professional thinking in an epistemic game. J. Comput. Assis. Lear. **27**, 173–189. (2011)
Shute, V.J.: Focus on formative feedback. Rev. Educ. Res. **78**, 153–189 (2008)
VanLehn, K., Graesser, A.C., Jackson, G.T., Jordan, P., Olney, A.M., Rose, C.: When are tutorial dialogues more effective than reading? Cogn. Sci. **31**, 3–62 (2007)
Wiley, J., Goldman, S.R., Graesser, A.C., Sanchez, C.A., Ash, I.K., Hemmerich, J.A.: Source evaluation, comprehension, and learning in internet science inquiry tasks. Am. Educ. Res. J. **46**, 1060–1106 (2009)

Organisations, Societies, Special Interest Groups

Games for Change http://www.gamesforchange.org/

Research Groups

River City Research Team http://muve.gse.harvard.edu/rivercityproject/index.html
The Discourse and Technology Group at Northern Illinois University http://www.niu.edu/psyc/graduate/cognitive/index.shtml
The Institute for Intelligent Systems at The University of Memphis https://sites.google.com/a/iis.memphis.edu/main/

Key International Conferences/Workshops

AIED: 15th International Conference on Artificial Intelligence in Education http://www.aied2011.canterbury.ac.nz/ (2011)
ITS: Tenth International Conference on Intelligent Tutoring Systems: Bridges to Learning http://sites.google.com/site/its2010home/ (2010)
ST&D: Twenty-first Annual Meeting of the Society for Text and Discourse http://www.societyfortextanddiscourse.org/conferences/index.html (2011)

Chapter 11
From Global Games to Re-contextualized Games: The Design Process of TekMyst

Carolina Islas Sedano, Jan Pawlowski, Erkki Sutinen, Mikko Vinni, and Teemu H. Laine

11.1 Introduction

Come closer, a little bit closer, so I can tell you a secret....
(Clark and Glazer, 2004)

Virtually everyone agrees that the above catch phrase is a powerful invitation to players which motivates them to get involved in certain games where they will discover and learn something new. Games, which invite players to voluntarily immerse themselves in the game world and thereby gain knowledge, deserve our special attention.

The historian, Johan Huizinga, dedicates one chapter of his book, Homo Ludens, to investigating "play and knowing". He states that "[f]or archaic man, doing and daring are power, but knowing is magical power" (1955, p. 105). This phenomenon is found throughout the history of humanity and Huizinga later comments that even "[t]he Greeks of the later period were well aware of the connection between riddle-solving and the origins of philosophy" (1955, p. 115). However, it is the *play function* that interests us and, independently of whether games make use of chance, physical strength, skill or knowledge, all of them possess inherent *persuasive power* (Bogost, 2010).

In recent years, designers, developers, researchers and the public in general have been paying special attention to digital games. There are numerous reasons why digital games are so attractive to the general public including their use of innovative hardware, utilization of outstanding graphics and immersive audio accompanied by dazzling special effects. Digital games can be played anywhere, at any time and with friends around the globe. In short – digital games dazzle us with their many diverse and attractive features.

If we carefully examine digital games we will, however, notice that in spite of their positive features and the substantial involvement of human capital and economic resources that go into their production, their success among the general public

C. Islas Sedano (✉)
University of Eastern Finland, FI-80101 Joensuu, Finland
e-mail: carolina.islas@uef.fi

M. Ma et al. (eds.), *Serious Games and Edutainment Applications*,
DOI 10.1007/978-1-4471-2161-9_11, © Springer-Verlag London Limited 2011

is not guaranteed. Some games fail because the basic gameplay is poor despite outstanding graphics, and others fail because they are nothing more than clones of other successful games. We believe that a possible reason for the vast number of unsuccessful digital games is that designers focus mainly on the *technology* while neglecting the game design aspects which in turn support the player's *game experience.*

The games industry is in need of innovative games and fledgling designers will do well to heed the advice of professional and successful game designers: before attempting to create a game in the new digital world, first understand the dynamics of old non-digital games and stories (Schell, 2008). We should remember that digital games "are simply new mixtures of well-known elements" (Fullerton et al., 2004, p. 99). This fact should be fundamental to the game design.

When viewing digital games for learning, called serious games, we notice that many of these games pay attention to the technical features that dazzle the players into solving teaching-learning engagement challenges. As an illustration, Prensky (2003) states that digital games motivate "digital native" children and teaches them different skills such as multitasking and problem solving. Miloš et al. (2009) analyze the potential of educational games played on mobile devices to promote learning any time and anywhere. Corradini et al. (2005) analyze 3D game characters while keeping an educational goal in mind and Marco et al. (2009) explore younger children's interaction with tabletop technology by using games and then ascertaining their educational potential. Consequently, it is not surprising that the topic of *digital games and their use in education* is often vigorously discussed in educational circles. For example, Gee (2003) argues that knowledge gained by playing video games is transferable to other domains, while Ravenscroft and McAlister (2006) explicitly state that today's digital games are weak in linking the "game-playing activity to transferable social or conceptual processes and skills that constitute, or are related to, learning" (2006, p. 37).

We concur with Ravenscroft's and McAlister's (2006) view that serious games do not pay enough attention to the interplay between the *game* and the *specific learning context* and the *learning content.* Instead some educators, designers and developers focus primarily on the *technology* encapsulated in the game to involve and motivate learners. When one follows this approach one loses the immemorial "magical power" that games for learning possess namely *the knowing.* This connection between the *learning content* and the *learning context* and its consequent presentation is that which makes a learning game successful. The real life experience of one of the authors serves to elucidate this point. The author's father, who was passionate about science, would explain scientific concepts to his children while playing with them. Once, in the middle of a pillow fight, he explained Newton's third law: "for every action there is an equal and opposite reaction." This allowed the author to measure his strength in the battle. Everyone has played the game in which you calculate the sum of the numbers of the car's registration plate in front of you while sitting in the traffic. It is clear then that the elements needed to create games, which in turn support learning, are to be found all around us in our everyday life. Technology offers, as Alessi and Trollip (2001) mention, the ability to add special features which facilitate experiences which otherwise would have been impossible e.g. a real-time conversation with someone on the other side of the world. The real challenge for designers of *digital games for learning* or *serious games* is to join efforts with content experts and technologists to achieve a common aim.

The objective of this chapter is to invite the reader to join us in the design process of a digital game for a specific learning context. SciMyst is a game which was designed for the Joensuu Science Festival and it aims to support the players in discovering the rich content of the festival. The player accesses and navigates SciMyst using a mobile phone. After designing SciMyst for the festival, we deployed it in a different learning context namely the Museum of Technology in Helsinki. However, we first needed to decide whether we wanted to clone, enhance or re-contextualize the game. *Re-contextualization* refers to the process in which all the circumstances involved in the game to support the specific learning aim are reconsidered. In re-contextualizing the game, we should explore *the principles that a game designer should consider when re-contextualizing a game.* At the end of the chapter we attempt summarize our own experiences in this exploration, with the hope that it will help others when they set out to design their own games.

11.2 Creating a Common Ground: Basic Terms and Concepts

Before analyzing any complex topic, like the design process of games, it is necessary to achieve a common understanding of the terms and concepts used. This chapter uses eight main concepts which are explained in this section and aims to build our *common vocabulary*.

11.2.1 Game

We consider a game to be a system that consists of game components, mechanics and dynamics. A game component is any unit essential to the functioning of the game. For example the game components in the game of Chess are the board and its pieces e.g. king, queen, rooks, bishops, knights and pawns. The game mechanics consist of game states and rules that define the allowed transitions. Continuing to use Chess as an example, there are clear rules on how the pieces should be organized, moved and how the game can be lost or won. The *game dynamics* refers to all the possible ways in which the game mechanics are updated. For example, in Chess, when the players are actually playing we can see how, after each move, the state of the game is updated.

An important characteristic of a game according to Islas Sedano et al. (2011b) is that it resides in a play-space. Thus, to access the game an individual, who inhabits her or his *own real life,* can decide at any given time to access the *play-space* and play a *game* while in this space. Other scholars in game research interpret the play-space as the "magic circle" (Castronova, 2005; Woodford, 2007).

11.2.2 Game Designer

According to Cross (2006) anyone has the ability to design. We are constantly designing our clothing outfits and the interior of our home, to mention but two examples. Designing, according to Cross, should be added as one of our diverse intelligences as defined by Gardner (2004): linguistic, logical-mathematical, bodily-kinaesthetically, spatial, musical, interpersonal and intrapersonal.

A game designer defines the game elements and combines them to create game mechanics. The game mechanics draw the players in, support them in creating experiences during the game dynamics and making meaningful decisions to achieve the game's goal (Schell, 2008). Brathwaite and Schreiber (2009) clarify that a digital game designer is not a *game artist* or a *pure programmer* although both of these fields, art and programming, are relevant and helpful in designing a digital game. However, a game designer should be able to create games independently of the technology and artistic sketches, by focusing on the game mechanics.

11.2.3 Riddle-Solving Games

We consider a riddle-solving game to be a system that perplexes its players by offering them challenges that involves words, sentences or objects. Quests, puzzles and treasure hunts are different representations of riddle-solving games. By their very nature riddle-solving games support the players' cognitive skills that are used for learning. These cognitive skills include synthesis and deduction (Clark and Glazer, 2004). Most of these games are based on the use of clues, which "are seductive, and along with them arises the impulse to discover" (Clark and Glazer, 2004, p. 34). Additionally, "[e]very proper riddle must fulfil two conditions, the first is its social function as competition between the riddler and riddlees; the second is its literary form which must be difficult and enigmatic, yet containing the clues necessary to decipher" (Pagis, 1996, p. 81). Consequently, each riddle is the result of a careful analysis by the designers, who want to seduce their players by tempting them to solve apparently unsolvable problems using the available tools. Schell (2008) introduces two varieties of puzzles or riddle-solving games: *explicit* and *implicit*. Explicit riddle-solving games are isolated incongruous problems that a player has to solve like Rubik's cube [URL: Rubik]. Implicit riddle-solving games are well-knitted challenges within other types of games, and they are "anything that makes you stop and think, mental challenges" (Schell, 2008, p. 210). Schell (2008) explains that implicit riddle-solving games are commonly used in digital games as they inject a variety of activities needed to support the players' immersion in digital games. Consequently the solution of different riddles, either in the form of puzzles or treasure hunts, is taken into consideration when determining the player's game mastering skills (Björk and Holopainen, 2004).

There are different strategies and suggestions for the design of riddle-solving games. Schell (2008), for example, offers the design principles of puzzles while

Clark and Glazer (2004) suggest on how to capture the essence of the milieu in the design of quests. Björk and Holopainen (2004) focus on balancing puzzle patterns that are relevant to mastering a game. However, the common aim of game designers is to design experiences (Fullerton et al., 2004; Salen and Zimmerman, 2004) in the player's mind (Schell, 2008).

11.2.4 Aha Moments in Riddle-Solving Game

Game designers are aware that the human brain seeks to make relationships, create patterns and organize things (Brathwaite and Schreiber, 2009; Schell, 2008). Havens (cited in Brathwaite and Schreiber, 2009, p. 50) mentions that when we are facing a challenge and we are working towards its solution, we are trying to connect the new information to previous known relationships that we have already formed in our mind. The steps and decisions we take lead us towards the solution and then finally an "aha moment" is triggered, described by Havens (ibid) as "when something locks into place adding, a layer of sense and understanding to something that previously was chaotic or meaningless". According to Havens these are the most important elements to take into consideration when designing a riddle-solving game. Designers of riddle-solving games bring together elements that are apparently unrelated. These elements include the clues that support the players in building relationships needed to succeed in the game (Brathwaite and Schreiber, 2009).

11.2.5 Clone and Enhance

A strategy of the game industry, which is done in order to lessen financial risks in digital games production, is to "clone" games as Letouneux explains (cited in Arsenault, 2009). *Cloning* means that the game mechanics of successful games are replicated, and *enhancing* games refers to improving them by addressing their weaknesses. Arsenault (2009) clarifies this by stating that games can be *cloned* or *enhanced* in their aesthetics (e.g. the narrative or plot) or in their functionality (for instance button-mapping) or new interactions (e.g. Radio-Frequency Identification – RFID – instead of 2D bar-codes).

11.2.6 Co-production of Knowledge

We consider that learning is a constant and on-going activity, which can be seen as the social construction of knowledge, and which is determined by the social, cultural and historical setting in which it takes place, or is "situated". Brown et al. (1989) state that (situated) learning is promoted when educators harness the learners' physical and social environment to help them co-create knowledge through activities. Our research follows this social-constructivist paradigm. The co-production of knowledge can be supported by extracting the deep structure of a subject from experts and transforming it into a guiding resource that, in turn, aids the learner who is performing an activity on-site (Willingham, 2008).

11.2.7 Learning Context

We view the *learning context* as all those circumstances that are involved when a learner performs an activity on-site in order to co-create knowledge. Consequently, a learning context acknowledges that the learners and the context are in flux, meaning "neither learners nor contexts are homogenous or static entities" (Volet, 1999, p. 639). Each specific learning context presents multidimensional affordances. When one aims to design digital games *in* and *for* a specific location, three multidimensional aspects of context need to be kept in mind namely *environmental*, *intersubjective* and *subjective* aspects (Islas Sedano et al., 2011a).

The *environmental aspect of context* covers those aspects related to the physical environment that we observe and understand by making use of our senses, for instance that which we see around us (e.g. houses, trees, water). This aspect can also be perceived through technological instruments such as sensors that measure levels of illumination.

The *intersubjective aspect of context* refers to all the circumstances that relate to the communication and interaction of an individual with other individuals or with systems, including computers. All possible relationships within this context are relevant, including symbols, behaviors and language. We acknowledge that all interaction involves social aspects (collaboration, cooperation) and cultural phenomena (sets of beliefs, values, assumptions, social expectations) with explicit and tacit rules that are affected by the personal interpretation of a specific moment. Taking into account the intersubjective context allows outsiders to have insight into an individual's reactions or to anticipate specific events or activities.

The *subjective aspect of context* is only be accessed by oneself as it refers to the mental and emotional elements inherent to each person. These elements include skills, cognitive and meta-cognitive aspects, motives, and attitudes.

11.2.8 Congruence Between the Student and the Learning Context

It is difficult to understand the relationship between a student and the learning context. We support our thinking with a framework developed by Volet (1999, 2001). The framework analyzes the appropriateness of learning transfer across different educational learning contexts. Volet considers the existing compatibility between a student's motivation, cognition and behaviour as related to a specific activity within the affordances of the learning context. The relationship is evaluated according to its level of congruence. *Congruence* is defined as the product of mutual dynamic interactions between an individual's capability to produce an effect (subjective aspect of context such as cognition and emotions) and the affordances of the learning context (environmental and inter-subjective aspects of context). According to the level of congruence, Volet recognizes four types of knowledge transfer in reference to experimental interface between the learner and the learning context, namely *appropriate*, *ambivalent*, *difficult* and *inappropriate* transfer (Volet, 1999, 2001). Because our focus is on *transferring* a game designed for a specific learning context to a new context, rather than utilizing four types of knowledge transfer, we refer to four levels of tolerance.

Appropriate transfer (or high tolerance) supposes that the student and the learning context present high levels of congruence. In this case an agreement exists between the student and the learning context. There is also a clear awareness of the tacit and explicit rules that govern the learning context. The student is attuned to the affordances of the learning context. An example is playing a memory game related to today's lecture on the student's mobile phone during the school's recess.

Ambivalent transfer (or low tolerance) refers to a situation where a student and the learning context do not reach general consensus as to what is appropriate or not, mostly as a result of subjective interpretations. Thus, the level of congruence is low. For example, after finishing an assignment in a lecture, a student plays a memory game on his mobile phone unrelated to the subject matter. In this case, the teacher would prefer that the student plays a game related to the subject matter of the lecture.

Difficult transfer *(or almost no tolerance)* refers to a situation where the student's expectations are congruent to a previous learning context but requires re-assessment in the current learning context. For example, playing memory games at home allows the player to use physical clues, but when playing memory games at school the clues are no longer present. Thus the player should re-assess his strategy when playing at school.

Inappropriate transfer (or no tolerance) refers to activities that were congruent in a previous learning context, but become unacceptable in the current learning context. For example a player, supported by his parents, utilizes games to intimidate the neighbors, but at school bullying in any form is unacceptable.

Ideally a student and the specific learning context in which s/he is embedded should present a high level of congruence. In other words, the game should support a high tolerance between the student and the learning context. If this is the case, a common and shared understanding exists and the learner utilizes the affordances of the on-site learning context. On the other hand, a divergence between learning context and learner implies a cognitive, behavioral or social deficit (Volet, 1999, 2001).

We have now established our common vocabulary and we know what we mean when we refer to games, game designer, riddle solving games, aha moments, cloning and enhancing, co-production of knowledge, learning context and the congruence between a learner and a learning context. We now continue *to design* a game for a specific learning context and later we *re-contextualize* it to fit a new context. In both cases the game aims to support a rapport between the players and the learning context. The Hypercontextualized Game design model assists us in analyzing the games presented in this book chapter.

11.3 Hypercontextualized Game (HCG) Design Model

We define an HCG as "a locally designed game system, which helps its players to gain information about different subjects by using specific elements of the continuously changing context in the game" (Islas Sedano et al., 2011b). In other words, an HCG unites different on-site expertise (local game designers, local developers and local content experts) with the common aim of supporting the HCG's players in their topic specific learning activity. The prefix "hyper" supposes that, once the game is designed in and for the specific learning context, other players than those who helped with the original design process will be able to play it. The game thus has a certain level of tolerance for it to be used outside its original design.

Each HCG is designed with a specific purpose in mind and it is further intentionally rooted in the player's learning context. The game thus makes use of the available resources. As a result, the game carries location-specific knowledge, which can be unlocked and experienced by each player. The HCG designers seek to interweave three different perspectives: specific context elements (SCEs), subject matter information (SMI) and game system (GS). Each of these perspectives is described below.

- *Game System* (GS) refers to the conceptualization of the core idea of the game, its game mechanics. It takes advantage of the learning context to facilitate the player's immersion in the game. Thus, GS creates a situation to support a player's experience by utilizing affective elements on-site.
- *Subject Matter Information* (SMI) determines the meaningful activities that the player can perform to co-create knowledge in the learning context, according to a clear aim. SMI supports the player's building of knowledge in a specific learning context by using the intellectual and pedagogical resources on-site.
- *Specific Context Elements* (SCEs) identify the potential game components in the specific context for which the game is designed and in which it is being played. This perspective classifies the components according to the environmental and the intersubjective aspects of context. Additionally, SCEs take into account *the subjective aspects* of context such as thoughts, ideas, reflections and meanings.

Following the HCG design model we will explain how we designed a game, SciMyst, for a specific learning context. Later, the same HCG design model aided us in re-contextualizing the game for a new learning context. Before describing this process, we also aim to clarify the methods used in this chapter.

11.4 Methods

It is relevant that we explicitly document, analyze and evaluate our game design approach. We present two case studies, each of which shows the game design process for a specific learning context. We use case studies, which support the analysis of a phenomenon within a real life setting, with the added possibility of using multiple sources of evidence (Robson, 2002). Furthermore, according to Cross (2006), the common methods for researching design thinking include: interviews with designers, observations and case studies, protocol studies, reflections and theorizing and simulations trials. In this case, we are both the designers and researchers of the games presented in the case studies. We therefore possess valuable material in the form of emails, notes from informal and formal meetings, considerable numbers of sketches and different prototypes. By means of retrospective analysis (Nuutinen, 2009) we analyzed this data focusing on *requirements* and *design decisions*. The relevant patterns which we found allowed us to write this chapter.

To complement each case study we briefly present some player feedback. Although the main focus of the chapter is the *design process*, our participants' views are relevant when interpreting the results of the designed game. In each case study we used more than one mode of data collection from the players. We recorded the players' behavior, collected their feedback via questionnaires (before and after playing), conducted interviews and recorded observations. We use mixed methods (Saunders et al., 2009) because diverse aspects of our research called for different analysis strategies. We should mention that our research is cross sectional as it takes place over specific periods of time. The reason for selecting case studies is because it supports *the study of a phenomenon within a real life setting*, relevant for us in order to analyze an HCG and its re-contextualization. To establish trustworthiness (that our patterns and interpretations are correct) we employed two techniques, namely *prolonged engagement* and the *triangulation of methods,* as recommended by Lincoln and Guba (1985).

11.5 First Case Study: SciMyst for SciFest

Finally, it is time to discuss a specific game designed for a particular learning context. The reader has probably visited a science festival or a festival in general where several exhibitors gather together to eagerly share information with the festival's visitors. The exhibitors come to the festival armed with models, objects of interest and informative reading material. Our aim was to aid visitors and exhibitors, by sharing relevant information pertaining to the content of every booth or stand, in the form of a game. With this aim in mind, we designed and developed SciMyst, a riddle-solving game especially for the Science Festival (SciFest) in Joensuu, Finland.

11.5.1 Description of SciFest Learning Context

SciFest is an annual science festival, which has been held in Joensuu, Finland, since 2007. The festival aims to introduce science, technology and environmental issues to the younger generation (Jormanainen and Korhonen, 2010). To achieve this aim, SciFest invites pupils, educators and the community in general to experience science outside the conventional classroom through a range of workshops and talks. The instructors hail from a wide variety of backgrounds – from academia to industry – and they all voluntarily join the festival to share their knowledge, passion and experience of different topics with the visitors. As a result of the wide diversity of role players, the workshops on offer also vary considerably as far as topics, group sizes and schedules are concerned. There are visitors who attend the workshop activities but a considerable number of people choose to explore the festival on their own.

SciFest is presented in the largest wooden building in Finland. It boasts a floor space of 14,600 m^2. The structure was especially designed to house sports and temporary events and the floor plan is shown in Fig. 11.1. The facilities include a WLAN connection with free Internet access.

Most of the stalls are set up one day ahead of the official opening of the Festival. Each booth decides when and how it will be organized and then the individual exhibitor or instructor coordinates with SciFest's main organizational team. The instructors relay their needs (including booth location, number of students for their workshops and schedules, number of tables and chairs required) to the main committee well ahead of the Festival. They are responsible for providing their own work material that includes posters, paper and pencils, research equipment, building bricks such as legos and computers. The booths, in general, are not weighted down by objects although relevant information is easily attainable in most cases. Some informative material or objects might only be available when the booths are manned and some stands are disassembled before SciFest officially ends.

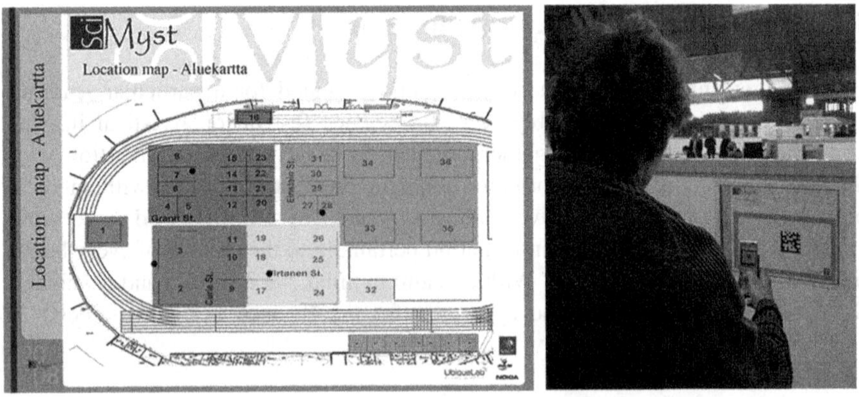

Fig. 11.1 *Left*: game-map based on the layout of SciFest's floor plan. *Right*: player subscribing to one of the game areas

11.5.2 Game Design Decisions for SciMyst

We now have an idea as to the SciFest learning context. Our next step towards designing SciMyst was to create a set of design requirements. Those requirements are the result of analyzing our understanding of SciFest, in concordance with a clear aim. In this case our aim is *to raise players' interest in the festival while promoting a learning experience.* We were particularly interested in those visitors who are not committed to individual workshops but rather see SciFest as a traditional exhibition. We had to find the required design solutions whilst keeping in mind that each decision affects the final product. We acknowledged that design solution is a process that entails several iterations. In the case of SciMyst, we employed the HCG design model to clarify our requirement definition and design solution process by defining each one of its perspectives:

- *Game system (GS)* aims to enhance the visitors' experience by stimulating them to discover through capturing their interest about material which can be viewed at the Festival. This process is especially aimed at those visitors who do not have specific plans.
- *Subject Matter Information (SMI)* aims to use the visitors' skills to uncover that which is not easily seen when merely walking around the festival. Consequently it offers the opportunity for visitors to gather information on diverse themes and also gain deeper insight into those topics which interests them.
- *Specific Context Element (SCE)* uses the objects and information that each instructor brings to the festival. One needs to be aware that the instructors arrive and leave at different times, diverse topics exist, workshops are not homogenous, the materials used and the infrastructure employed is temporary.

We acknowledge an existing intimate interconnection between the three HCG's perspectives and we also acknowledge that it is impossible to isolate specific requirements by perspective (Table 11.1). Instead a consensus between the perspectives should prevail if one wishes to achieve the common aim.

The first SciMyst design decision was to create a riddle-solving game as it is suited to this learning context. We know that riddle-solving games prompt players to search and focus their attention on finding solutions. We wanted players to pay attention to discovering SciFest and therefore we aligned the game to the specific learning context of the festival, by giving solutions to different requirements (Table 11.1). We consider SciMyst 2008 an HCG because it is a locally designed GS that helps SciFest visitors to gain insight into what is being presented at the festival (SMI) by utilizing on-site resources (SCE).

SciMyst was designed and developed especially *for* the festival and it was consequently improved by making use of the experiences of players and designers who attended the festival in 2007 (Islas Sedano et al., 2007).

Table 11.1 Game requirements

Requirement	Description	Design solution
To be inclusive (GS, SMI, SCE)	Supports visitors from different ages and backgrounds.	Uses a mobile phone as a game tool. As most visitors know how to use a phone, their ability to access new applications increases (Botha et al., 2008). It is also possible to develop applications with multilingual features for mobile phones.
To discover what is physically present (SMI, SCE)	To trigger the interest of the players in the festival's exposition and stimulate them to observe things that they might not have seen had they just been walking around without paying attention.	Launch queries by taking a picture and thus the player is standing where the requested object is being displayed. To find a specific object, the player must investigate a location and so they start to pay attention to their surroundings (Clark and Glazer, 2004).
To challenge personal knowledge of the exhibitions' content (SMI, SCE)	Provokes players to rethink their personal understanding of the content of the festival.	Multiple-choice questions challenge the player's understanding of the festival's content.
To respect the visitor's pace (GS, SCE)	Visitors examine and navigate a festival at their own pace. They stop when and where something interests them. When they have seen enough, they resume their exploration.	The *casual* style of the game should encourage the players to stop at any booth which arrests their interest and to spend as much time exploring as they wish without worrying about the game. If and when the player wants to resume the game, this too is possible.
To encourage low school performers to succeed (GS, SMI, SCE)	Competition between players is a strong motivational force in games but may discourage individuals with insufficient skills and knowledge or low self-esteem to participate. However we want to include the weaker performers to take part in the game.	The competitive element of the game should be personal; the game should not encourage rivalry between players. The points earned in the game, besides adding to the player's own personal score, are added to a common score of all the players. Having the luxury to progress at their own pace, supports weaker performers and also gives them the opportunity to use their own strengths to succeed in a game based on equal conditions for all players.

Table 11.1 (continued)

Requirement	Description	Design solution
To persuade introverts to play (GS, SMI, SCE)	To play with others is one of the most evident social characteristics of games and also one of its higher aims. However, not everybody has someone to play with all the time.	One should be able to play the game alone (as all the game resources are available) but at the same time the player should also feel part of a community of players. The players know that their score is added to a common goal. Team play is also possible but the players must organize themselves.
To encourage visitors' interpretations of the festival (GS, SMI, SCE)	One specific event may be perceived differently and by expressing oneself, others have an opportunity to glimpse at your personal impressions.	Allows and encourages players to take photos and to comment on what they thought of the festival.
To recall the experience of the festival (GS, SCE)	After finishing the game, it is useful if the player can retire to a place to recall what s/he did during the game.	A real-time website interaction allows players, and other audience members, to share glimpses of one another's impressions of the festival.

11.5.3 SciMyst

The ignorance is taking over the world. As a result, the world as we know it will be destroyed. The battle against the ignorance is upon us and we need your help. As a SciMyst hero, you can save the world by beating the ignorance through knowledge acquisition. Prepare yourself and show your heroism in SciMyst at the SciFest 2008 festival. The world is counting on you! [URL: SciMyst]

The lines above introduce the SciMyst 2008 website. This is also the video clip message which potential players listen to before they start playing. In this section we present six elements (Table 11.2) that allow us to better understand SciMyst.

Table 11.2 SciMyst components

HCG perspective	SciMyst components
GS, SCE	Pre-requisite for playing
GS, SCE	Storyline and user interface
GS, SCE	Website
GS, SMI, SCE	Playing SciMyst
GS, SMI, SCE	Question format
SMI, SCE	Content creation

Pre-requisites for playing SciMyst. The game is ideally suited to players who are capable of using a mobile phone and who can read English or Finnish (SciFest's target group). The game makes use of the Myst platform, which is based on the client-server architecture (Laine et al., 2010). Therefore, to access the game, the player should have a phone with the correct client software installed. For the duration of the festival we had a booth where we presented the game. We also had 11 phones, with client software already installed, which we could lend to players (eight Nokia N80 mobile phones and three Nokia N95 phones). If a player owned an equivalent Nokia smart phone, it was possible to install the client application on the personal mobile phone. The game uses two-dimensional bar codes that are attached to specific locations and objects. The players are given a game map, which is a colour-coded map of the festival, to aid them in navigating the festival area during the game (Fig. 11.1).

Storyline and user interface. We created a story harmonious with the aim of the festival. The user interface (UI) is simple, consistent and intuitive with the aim of keeping the players focused on the game's content (Fig. 11.2).

Website. The game progress is displayed on the game's website. It shows the players' personal scores. These scores are also logged as contributions to win the epic battle against the ignorance. The current status of the battle against the ignorance is also presented. A gallery of photos, taken by players, and an introduction to the game and the development team is also included.

Playing SciMyst. Once a player has the mobile phone running the game client software and a game-map, s/he should subscribe to a specific game-colour-area by taking a picture of a two-dimensional bar code (Fig. 11.1). The game-map signals the location of the two-dimensional bar codes which in turn provide access to the different game-colour-areas. Once a player subscribes to an area, s/he starts receiving random questions on their mobile phone that are related to the specific area.

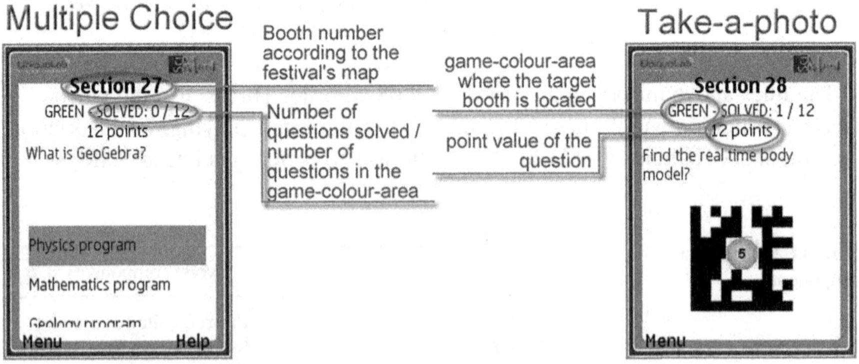

Fig. 11.2 A screenshot of SciMyst shows the hints given to solve the question on the screen. These hints include information such as the booth number and the game-colour-area where the answer can be located

Each question received by the player has a point value and the player must answer the question in order to receive the next. If the answer is correct, the player is awarded full points and if the answer is incorrect, the player has two options: retry or skip the question. However, if the player decides to skip the question, it will show up again later in the game. The point value of the question diminishes with each repetition for the specific player.

After successfully answering a question, the player has the option to "record an impression" meaning that the player can earn points by expressing him or herself. The player can "record an impression" by taking a photo of the area and attaching a comment to it. The player can also change the game-colour-area at will. The only restriction is that one question, pertaining to the area that the player is present in, must be solved before moving to another area.

SciMyst includes three game modes:

1. *Casual mode* consists of the player answering randomly selected questions (multiple choice or take-a-photo) related to different areas of SciFest. This mode does not have any time limitations and therefore players are encouraged to find the correct answers to augment their score. The points collected in *casual mode* are presented on the website under the relevant heading. After correctly answering a certain number of questions in *casual mode*, the player is given the possibility to access *battle mode*.
2. In *battle mode* the player must solve as many random multiple-choice questions as possible in a limited time. In this mode points are awarded for correct answers and subtracted for wrong answers. Once the *battle mode* has been successfully completed, the game ends. The points earned in the *battle mode* are shown on the website under this heading.
3. *Record of impressions* is a game mode wherein players can take pictures of the festival and add personal comments. Additionally, after each question an option to record impressions is offered. The player earns points for each picture s/he uploads. The points awarded in the *recording of impressions* mode are presented on the website under this mode in the player's personal score page.

Question format. Each question is related to an on-site object or piece of information and is then posed in the form of a riddle. The clues required by the player to solve the riddle are given on the UI. These clues include the name and number of the booth where the information can be found (Fig. 11.2). Two types of questions are accessible namely *multiple choice* and *take-a-picture* questions. Through the use of the clues, the player can search for the correct solution in the multiple-choice question or locate the object and take a photo of the two-dimensional bar code attached to it.

Content creation. We contacted the exhibitors via email and requested that the game content be sent to us before the launch of the festival. We designed a website which contained instructions on how to create the questions so that exhibitors could formulate and then mail us their questions. Unfortunately the amount of queries via internet was limited. This was mainly as a result of organizers and exhibitors' busy agendas. We visited each booth in search of content the day before SciFest opened and the first morning of the festival. We explained the purpose of the game and the kind of questions we required. The instructors aided us in finding and formulating proper questions.

It is critical for the success of the game that all the active questions are supported with physical materials found at SciFest. If the exhibitors change the material, or quit the festival, questions pertaining to their particular booth should immediately be eliminated.

11.5.4 Learning Experiences

The HCG concept of SciMyst has a clear objective and that is to support SciFest's visitors to discover elements of the festival by using the artefacts available in this learning context. In 2007 we ascertained that the main driving force urging players to finish this game was *curiosity* followed by *meeting a challenge* (Islas Sedano et al., 2007). Because *curiosity* is a driving motivator in playing the game, we infer that our players are open to learning things on their own and are more likely to retain their learning experience since they entered into it willingly (Schell, 2008).

From the information that we collected from 17 players in 2008, evidence exists that the game fulfilled its design aim. We present two evidence indicators. The first indication is to be found in the post-questionnaire where we asked: *Did SciMyst (the game) help you to discover something interesting about SciFest (the festival)?* Three of the respondents did not answer the question and ten players reported that they did learn something playing SciMyst. Some of their discoveries included the workings of an eye tracking system, how to make your one's 3D photos and the chemical program. The last four players responded that they did not learn anything with SciMyst, however one of them commented later in the same questionnaire:

> It was interesting to view new things, even if I have already been here – Female, 23 years from Russia.

The second indication is found in the players' personal impressions of the game, which are compatible with SciMyst's design aim:

> Very nice way to familiarize oneself with the festival and what it has to offer – Female, 38 years from Finland.

Some Taiwanese visitors submitted essays a few weeks after the festival to the SciFest organizers in which they discussed their experiences in Finland. One of the students referred to SciMyst in his composition:

> Our group played the cell phone game in which you use a cell phone to answer question and find answers in SciFest. We could spend the whole afternoon playing the cell phone game without doing anything else. That's kind of interesting memory I have – Male, 15 years old.

The players' feedback provides evidence that SciMyst is *appropriate* for SciFest and that the players and the learning context experience is congruent. SciMyst supports visitors, who are not committed to individual workshops, to learn by discovering SciFest as the organizers had envisioned. The players search for information in the casual mode of the game, they pay attention to their environs by recording their impressions and they challenge their own understanding of the festival through the battle mode. The question remains: is SciMyst still appropriate when we play it in a similar learning context other than the one it was originally designed for?

There is space for improvement as far as SciMyst is concerned. The content creation, for example, requires a considerable amount of time and effort. It is not advisable to create questions for the game only a few hours in advance. We need to find a better way in which to involve SciFest's exhibitors so that they contribute questions earlier. We should also aim to understand SciMyst cycles better so that we can identify when and how to refresh them to ultimately avoid repetition in the game. Last, but not least, we should analyze how an explicit riddle-solving game like SciMyst relates to different ages and genders.

11.6 Second Case Study: TekMyst for The Museum of Technology

While SciMyst was in the developmental stages, we searched for an opportunity to test the game in a similar but not quite the same learning context. The technical infrastructure supporting SciMyst is portable and extendable (Laine et al., 2010) and this allowed us to test the game in other learning contexts as well. In 2008, The Museum of Technology situated in Helsinki, granted us the opportunity to test SciMyst at their facility. Hence, SciMyst's learning context changed from a festival (SciFest), where diverse exhibitions are gathered together in a building for temporary events, to a facility which houses permanent exhibitions.

In order to assure the success of the game in the new learning context, we had to analyze the level of congruence between the players' capability to produce an effect and the affordances of The Museum of Technology as learning context. To begin with we acknowledged the distinctive difference between specific learning objectives in a museum and the explorative nature of a festival. Curators and researchers together agreed on the new game's aim: *to test the Hyper-contextualized potentialities of a game for The Museum of Technology by utilizing the topic of simple machines*. Before we explain the re-contextualization process of *SciMyst* into *TekMyst*, we should aim to better understand the Museum of Technology as a learning context.

11.6.1 Museum of Technology Learning Context

The Museum of Technology was founded in 1969 by a group of various industrial and engineering organizations, cities in the Metropolitan area and the Ministry of Education. The purpose of the newly established foundation was – and by and large still is – to preserve, study and exhibit Finland's industrial and technological heritage and its impact on society. The Museum of Technology, which is still a privately

Fig. 11.3 *Left*: game-map based on the floor plan of the museum. *Middle*: view of the museum. *Right*: access to the game level of a game-colour-area

owned foundation supported by the founding members, held its first exhibition in 1972 and has been open to the public ever since.

The Museum of Technology is located in the Old City of Helsinki, in the historical buildings of the first Water Utility Company. The Museum's collection includes objects, books, photographs and other archive materials. The permanent exhibitions ($\sim$2500 m^2) representing chemistry, mining, metal and forestry are located primarily in the round exhibition building that originally housed the first water treatment facility in Finland. This circular and open exhibition space offers interesting possibilities but also navigational challenges to visitors as it lacks normal navigational landmarks (Fig. 11.3).

The museum is constantly searching for better ways in which to convey the value and significance of the collections and exhibitions to the public. An example of this is the InnoApaja-project (funded partly by the Ministry of Education) which has facilitated innovative learning methods by introducing the museum to school groups as a learning environment (Juurola, 2007). Avara Museo is an EU-funded project with a similar goal to that of InnoApaja but its target group is working professionals.

11.6.2 Re-contextualize, Clone or Enhance

We acknowledge that *The Museum of Technology* and *SciFest* are two different learning contexts which expect different outcomes from SciMyst. Consequently, we expect a certain amount of *ambivalent transfer (or low tolerance)* as a general and governing consensus about the content and activities of the game are missing. The curators (part of The Museum of Technology learning context) expect the players to reflect upon simple machines and SciMyst to support its player to find information that is displayed on-site. We could "dump" the game (Bada et al., 2009) onto the new learning context, but this action would assure an unsuccessful test, as it will not reach The Museum of Technology's aims due to the ambivalence. It is not possible to build a new HCG as we do not have the economic resources. We

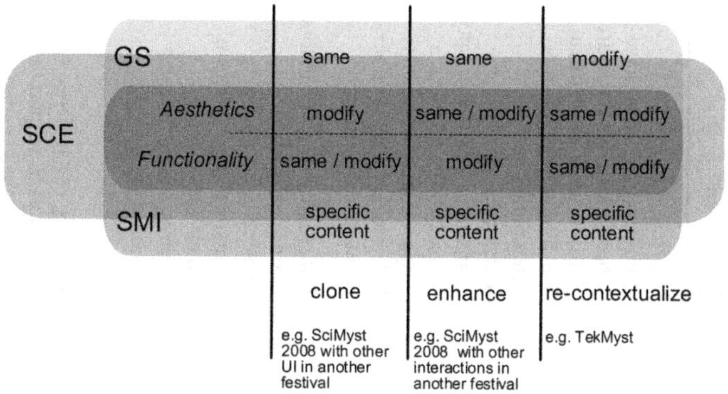

Fig. 11.4 Possibilities of modifying a HCG in order to maintain congruence in new learning contexts other than the original for which it was designed

could clone or enhance the game but previous game interventions have shown that one needs to re-contextualize the game in order to improve its success (Laine et al., 2011).

Figure 11.4 illustrates our analysis of the possibility to clone, enhance and re-contextualize an HCG with the aim of adding congruence to the players utilizing the game in a new learning context. We should recall that an HCG is a locally designed game for a specific learning context with a clear aim. GS and SMI share the aesthetics and functionality of an HCG game based on the SCE. We *clone* an HCG when the GS is the same as in the original game, but we primarily modify the aesthetics to match the new learning context. For example, if we modified the aesthetics (story and UI) we could use the game at another festival. We *enhance* an HCG when the GS is the same as in the original game, but we primarily modify its functionality to match a new learning context. A possible form of enhancement is to use SciMyst 2008 at another festival but with RFID technology instead of 2D bar-codes. We *re-contextualize* an HCG when we modify the GS so that it improves its congruence of the players' experience as promoted by the game within the new learning context. It means we reconsider the circumstances involved in the design of the game. TekMyst, the game designed for The Museum of Technology, is a re-contextualized version of the HCG SciMyst.

To re-contextualize an HCG game, we follow four steps:

I. Immerse ourselves in the new learning context.
II. Collaborate with locals to balance the efforts towards a common aim.
III. Reconsider the design solutions to achieve the common aim and
IV. Be constructive and critical in our contribution.

The *first step* is to immerse ourselves in the new learning context which allows us to note the explicit and evident contextual learning differences between SciFest and The Museum of Technology. Table 11.3 presents the implications of these contextual differences.

Table 11.3 Learning contexts differences of SciFest and The Museum of Technology

Context aspect	SciFest	MoT	Implications
Environmental aspect	Temporary	Permanent	Different layers of information, which have been added over time, are displayed in a permanent exhibition rather than a temporal one
	Relatively empty space	Full	Individuals' perceive and analyze a relatively empty space differently than a space filled with objects
	Booths are spread in a quadrilateral distribution	Exposition scattered in a circular construction	Individuals navigate these two spaces differently
Inter-subjective aspect	Diversity of exhibitors	Defined group of curators	Involve expertise of curators since early phase
	Exhibitors share their experiences of what is possible with science with visitors	Curators want to support their visitors in gaining knowledge of the process of technical progress and industrial activities in Finland	The exhibitors' and the curators' expectations of their visitors in the corresponding learning context are different
Subjective aspect	Personal motives to be in the specific location	Personal motives to be in the specific location	Knowing our audience will allow us to support them in their game experience

In the *second step* we join efforts with local role players to identify and then achieve a common aim. We clearly established that we wanted to transform SciMyst to *test the Hyper-contextualized potentialities of a game for The Museum of Technology by utilizing the topic of simple machines.* Curators and designers accepted that the new game would not be a perfect HCG for The Museum of Technology. However the re-contextualized version of SciMyst shows that it could be in line with The Museum of Technology's goals.

We agreed that the curators were responsible for the game's content creation on the topic of *simple machines.* The questions would follow SciMyst's question format namely *multiple-choice* and *take-a-picture*. Furthermore the players should be able to answer the queries by utilizing the things (information and objects) available in the Museum. The designers made the modifications (e.g. aesthetic, technical) needed to suit the content developed by the curators.

The *third step* is to reconsider the design solutions in order to achieve the common aim. Once the curators and designers understood the needs of the new learning context and brainstormed how to best re-contextualize the game, we reviewed SciMyst's requirement list. Table 11.4 highlights the requirements modified to achieve the actual common aim.

All requirements, but two, use the same solution as SciMyst. The first modification is that instead of the players *discovering what is physically present,* they will *follow the path of simple machines.* Thus, as opposed to adding questions about arbitrary objects in the game system, the questions pertain to carefully selected items that are connected to the *simple machines* topic. The second modification is that instead of *challenging the player's personal knowledge of the exhibitions' content,* we now want *to challenge the players as regards their understanding of simple machines.* Hence the multiple-choice questions designed to challenge the players' knowledge of the exhibition's content must be transformed to evaluate the players' understanding of the topic of simple machines. Therefore, different off-line activities are involved and the game only evaluates the outcome of the

Table 11.4 Requirements for SciMyst

Requirement	Re-contextualize decision
To be inclusive (GS, SMI, SCE)	SciMyst's solution
To discover what is physically present (SMI, SCE)	Modify
To challenge personal knowledge of the exhibitions' content (~Museum's content in simple machines) (SMI, SCE)	Modify
To respect festival's visitors pace (~Museum's visitors) (GS, SCE)	SciMyst's solution
To encourage under performers to succeed (GS, SMI, SCE)	SciMyst's solution
To persuade introverted individuals to play (GS, SMI, SCE)	SciMyst's solution
To encourage visitors to interpret the festival (~Museum's content) (GS, SMI, SCE)	SciMyst's solution
To recall the experience of the festival (~Museum) (GS, SCE)	SciMyst's solution

off-line activity e.g. pulling different pulleys to see which one is the lighter one. Furthermore, curators and designers agreed that there should be different difficulty levels for the questions, and thus the game should have different levels.

The *fourth step* is to be constructive and critical in our contribution. Both parties worked together to re-contextualized SciMyst to TekMyst. A preliminary trial a couple of weeks before the official test allowed us to constructively evaluate our work and identify the improvements which we needed to make to TekMyst.

11.6.3 TekMyst as a Re-contextualized SciMyst

Two of the solutions to SciMyst's requirements were modified to attain TekMyst (Table 11.4). Consequently, TekMyst elements were modified accordingly (Table 11.5). Figure 11.5 offers a glimpse of TekMyst by sketching the game's possibilities using the game's main menu.

11.6.4 Results

There is evidence that TekMyst's aim, which was to test the Hyper-contextualized potentialities of a game for The Museum of Technology by utilizing the topic of simple machines, has been achieved. The first indicator is that The Museum of Technology sought financial resources to enable them to develop their own Hypercontextualized Game, which currently has the working title TekMyst 2.

Table 11.5 Description of the modified elements for TekMyst

SciMyst components	TekMyst	Description of modification
Storyline and user interface	Modified	We modified the storyline and the User Interface accordingly. We use the character in the story to highlight certain areas and to also represent a narrative element
Prerequisite for playing	Same as in SciMyst	–
Website	Modified	A more comprehensive website [URL: TekMyst]
Playing SciMyst	Modified	The game includes levels and the player should subscribe to the game-coloured-area level I first. Once the player has played this level, it is possible to subscribe to level II of the same area. Some questions are paired. Thus, one specific question must be solved first in order to solve the next
Question's format	Same as in SciMyst	–
Content creation	Modified	Was done completely by the curators

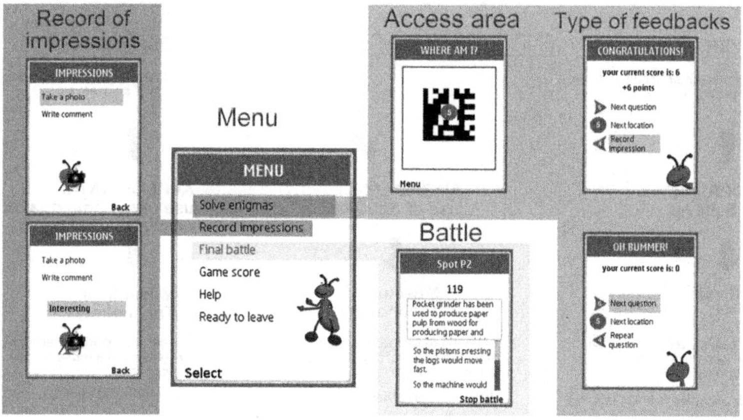

Fig. 11.5 Overview of TekMyst's screens

Another indicator is the responses from the players. The preliminary analysis of 129 questionnaires filled in by TekMyst players indicates that the motivators that drive the players to finish the game are *curiosity* and *challenge*. If curiosity is one of the main motivators we can assume that they were open to the content that the game presented to them. The players search for answers to the different questions on *simple machines* in the *casual mode* of the game. To give proper answer to some of the questions, the players need to perform different activities. The *game mode* records impressions and allows curators and researchers insight into what the players found interesting and note worthy. The *final battle mode* challenges the players' understanding of simple machines.

The final indicator we used is a short interview conducted by one of the curators with two pupils who played TekMyst while their school was visiting the museum. This interview can be found in a press release (Juurola, 2008). The pupils mentioned that they quickly familiarized themselves with the technology and that the tasks were suitable and challenging and that they recall specific content. The pupils expressed their desire to return with their parents to test the game. This feedback in itself is evidence of the level of congruence achieved in TekMyst between the players producing an effect and the affordances of the learning context. The players' experience is attuned to the expectations of the learning context.

11.7 Analysis

SciMyst is a HCG developed *for* SciFest (its original learning context). Thus, the experience that the game promotes is appropriate *or highly tolerant* (highly congruent) to the learning context of the festival as expected (Fig. 11.6). However, if we transfer SciMyst to a similar context our assumption is that it would continue to promote congruence between the players' experience and the affordances

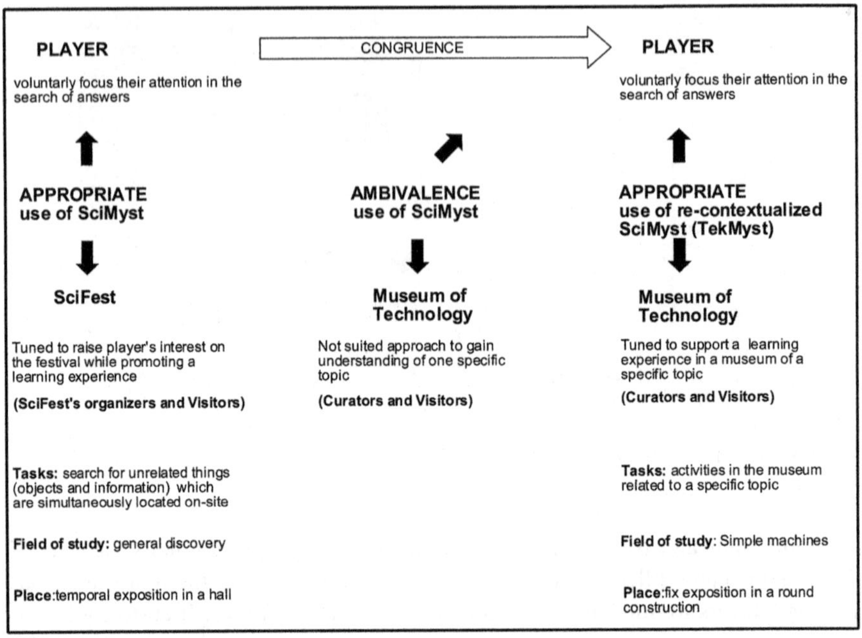

Fig. 11.6 Analysis of the congruence of SciMyst with the different learning contexts using Volet's framework (Volet, 1999, 2001)

of the learning context. We explored this possibility by testing SciMyst in a similar learning context namely The Museum of Technology in Helsinki.

Once we had analyzed the characteristics of SciFest and The Museum of Technology, their differences became evident starting with the difference in expectations between the two learning contexts. Without re-contextualizing SciMyst, we foresaw that the use of the game in The Museum of Technology would result in an *ambivalent* experience. The curators' expectations of the game were not the same as in SciMyst. The congruence between them is low.

In order to change an *ambivalent situation* to an *appropriate* one (increasing the congruence) we decided to re-contextualize SciMyst as TekMyst. Now, TekMyst supports an appropriate player experience as it matches the affordances of the learning context, including its expectations, with the player's effectiveness in the game (Fig. 11.6).

11.8 Conclusions

As an answer to our question "What are the principles that a game designer should consider when re-contextualizing a game?" we should start by clarifying that in our view there are not enough contextualized games and even fewer hypercontextualized ones. Today most digital games do not anchor their system in specific learning contexts; instead they focus on global accessibility.

If one wants to alter a game to fit a new learning context (in our case we decided to re-contextualize it), we suggest that the following principles be taken into consideration:

I. Immerse oneself in the new learning context.
II. Collaborate with locals to balance the efforts towards a common aim.
III. Reconsider the design solutions to achieve the common and
IV. Be constructive and critical in your contribution.

The four principles, as in any design, should be kept iterative. Additionally, we notice that the four principles are useful as operational guidelines in creating an HCG.

The process of re-contextualizing has taught us that all stakeholders need to work together. We also discovered that the modification of small design decisions support core changes. For example, instead of only searching for an object as was the case in SciMyst, TekMyst also supports the player in locating the physical spot where the question is set, perform an activity and evaluate the activity's result using the game. Additionally, the preliminary analysis of TekMyst helps us to understand the basic requirements and areas of improvement to take into account while conceptualizing the HCG for The Museum of Technology today.

Finally, two pre-conditions were fundamental to the success of TekMyst and we affirm that they should be considered for any other re-contextualization processes. Firstly, it is relevant to have a portable and expandable technology (Laine et al., 2010) that smoothes out the transition between learning contexts. Secondly, it is important to collaborate with content experts who know the essence of their subject and the on-site resources well and are able to transform them into playful riddle-solving problems. One should also keep the important pre-condition for promoting the magic of the learning games in mind: *the knowing*.

Acknowledgement The authors would like to express their appreciation to the SciFest organizational team for their trust and support, and the festival's exhibitors who allowed us to use their subject content in SciMyst. In addition we would like to express our gratitude to the personnel of The Museum of Technology in Helsinki and to Marjo Mikkola who allowed us to test TekMyst. We especially want to express our gratitude to Leenu Juurola and Riina Linna who created the content for TekMyst and who have supported us unconditionally.

References

Alessi, S.M., Trollip, S.R.: Multimedia for Learning – Methods and Development, 3rd edn. Allyn and Bacon, Needham Heights, MA (2001)

Arsenault, D.: Video game genre, evolution and innovation. Eludamos. J. Comput. Game Cul. **3**(2), 149–176 (2009)

Bada, J.K., Duveskog, M., Suhonen, J., Sutinen, E.:. Towards viable technology for HIV/AIDS education. In: Conference Proceedings/IIMC. Presented at the IST Africa, Kampala, Uganda (2009)

Björk, S., Holopainen, J.: Patterns in Game Design, 1st edn. Charles River Media, Hinghman, MA (2004)

Bogost, I.: Persuasive Games: The Expressive Power of Videogames. The MIT Press, Cambridge, MA (2010)

Botha, A., van der Berg, M., Batchelor, J., Islas Sedano, C.: Ability Through Mobility. In: Remenyi, D. (ed.) Proceedings of the 3rd International Conference on e-Learning, pp. 43–48. Presented at the 3rd International Conference on e-Learning, Cape Town, South Africa (2008)

Brathwaite, B., Brenda B., Schreiber, I.: Challenges for Game Designers, 1st edn. Charles River Media a Part of Course Technology, Cengage Learning, Boston, MA (2009)

Brown, J.S., Collins, A., Duguid, P.: Situated cognition and the culture of learning. Educ. Res. **18**(1), 32–42 (1989)

Castronova, E.: Synthetic Worlds: The Business and Culture of Online Games. University of Chicago Press, Chicago (2005)

Clark, D., Glazer, S.: Questing: A Guide to Creating Community Treasure Hunts. University Press of New England, NH (2004)

Corradini, A., Mehta, M., Bernsen, N.-O., Charfuelan, M.: Animating an interactive conversational character for an educational game system. In: Proceedings of the 10th International Conference on Intelligent User Interfaces, IUI '05, pp. 183–190 (2005)

Cross, N.: Designerly Ways of Knowing, 1st edn. Springer, Germany (2006)

Fullerton, T., Swain, C., Hoffman, S.: Game Design Workshop. CMP Books, San Francisco, CA (2004)

Gardner, H.: Frames of Mind: The Theory of Multiple Intelligences, 3rd edn. Basic Books, New York (2004)

Gee, J.P.: What Video Games Have To Teach Us About Learning and Literacy, 1st edn. Palgrave Macmillan, New York (2003)

Huizinga, J.: Homo Ludens. A Study of Play-Element in Culture. Beacon Press, Boston, USA (1955)

Islas Sedano, C.I., Laine, T.H., Vinni, M., Sutinen, E.: Where is the answer?: the importance of curiosity in pervasive mobile games. In: Proceedings of the 2007 Conference on Future Play, pp. 46–53. Toronto, Canada (2007)

Islas Sedano, C., Harteveld, C., Sutinen, E.: Role of context in digital game design. Under review (2011a)

Islas Sedano, C., Sutinen, E., Vinni, M., Laine, T.: Designing hypercontextualized games: a case study with LieksaMyst. Educ. Technol. Soc. (accepted) (2011b)

Jormanainen, I., Korhonen, P.: Science festivals on computer science recruitment. In: Proceedings of the 10th Koli Calling International Conference on Computing Education Research, pp. 72–73 (2010)

Juurola, L.: InnoApaja: innovative learning at the museum of technology. In: Kräutler, H. (ed.) HERITAGE LEARNING MATTERS Museums and Universal Heritage, p. 356. Presented at the ICOM/CECA '07 (Committee for Education and Cultural Action within the International Council of Museums), Vienna, Austria: Schlebrügge. http://www.schlebruegge.com/icom_e.htm (2007)

Juurola, L.: Tekniikan museossa pelataan mobiilipeliä. *Luova-verkkolehti. Luma-keskus, Helsingin yliopisto.* http://www.eluova.fi/index.php?id=392 (2008, August 30)

Laine, T., Vinni, M., Islas Sedano, C., Joy, M.: On designing a pervasive mobile learning platform. ALT-J **18**(1), 3–17 (2010)

Laine, T.H., Nygren, E., Sutinen, E., Islas Sedano, C., Joy, M., Blignaut, S.: Ubiquitous mathematics from South Africa to Finland: does reverse transfer work? In: Chen, I., Kidd, T. (eds.) Ubiquitous Learning: Strategies for Pedagogy, Course Design and Technology, pp. 249–282. Information Age Publishing Charlotte, NC (2011)

Lincoln, D.Y., Guba, D.E.G.: Naturalistic Inquiry, 1st edn. Sage, Thousand Oaks, CA (1985)

Marco, J., Cerezo, E., Baldassarri, S., Mazzone, E., Read, J.C.: Bringing tabletop technologies to kindergarten children. In: Proceedings of the 23rd British HCI Group Annual Conference on People and Computers: Celebrating People and Technology, BCS-HCI '09, pp. 103–111. British Computer Society, Swinton, UK. http://portal.acm.org/citation.cfm?id=1671011.1671023 (2009)

Miloš, M., Miroslav, M., Miroslav, L., Dušan, S.: Mobile educational game: adventure anywhere. In: Proceedings of the 11th International Conference on Human-Computer Interaction with Mobile Devices and Services, MobileHCI '09, pp. 66:1–66:2 (2009)

Nuutinen, J.: Nucleus model for designing social mindtools: woven stories (Doctoral dissertation, publication in department of computer science and statistics No. 25). University of Joensuu, Joensuu, Finland. http://joypub.joensuu.fi/publications/dissertations/nuutinen_nucleus/index_en.html (2009, September 18)

Pagis, D.: Toward a theory of the literary riddle. In: Hasan-Rokem, G., Shulman, D. (eds.) Untying the Knot: On Riddles and Other Enigmatic Modes, pp. 81–108. University of Oxford Press, New York (1996)

Prensky, M.: Digital game-based learning. Comput. Entertain. **1**, 21–21 (2003)

Ravenscroft, A., McAlister, S.: Digital games and learning in cybespace: a dialogical approach. E-Learning **3**(1), 38–51 (2006). doi:10.2304/elea.2006.3.1.37

Robson, C.: Real World Research: A Resource for Social Scientists and Practitioner-Researchers, 2nd edn. Wiley-Blackwell, Oxford (2002)

Salen, K., Zimmerman, E.: Rules of Play. Game Design Fundamentals. MIT Press, Cambridge, MA (2004)

Saunders, M.N.K., Thornhill, A., Lewis, P.: Research Methods for Business Students, 5th edn. Prentice Hall, Harlow (2009)

Schell, J.: The Art of Game Design: A Book of Lenses, 1st ed. Morgan Kaufmann, San Francisco, CA (2008)

Rubik: http://www.rubiks.com/ (2010). Accepted 16 Mar 2011

SciMyst: http://cs.joensuu.fi/SciMyst/2008/index.htm. Accepted 17 Mar 2011

TekMyst. http://cs.joensuu.fi/scimyst/tekmyst/index.php. Accepted 15 Oct 2010

Volet, S.: Learning across cultures: appropriateness of knowledge transfer. Int. J. Educ. Res. **31**(7), 625–643 (1999)

Volet, S.: Understanding learning and motivation in context: a multi-dimensional and multi-level cognitive-situative perspective. In: Volet, S., Jäverlä, S. (eds.) Motivation in Learning Contexts: Theoretical Advances and Methodological Implications, Advances in Learning and Instruction, 1st edn. pp. 57–82. Elsevier, London/New-York (2001)

Willingham, D.T.: Critical thinking: why is it so hard to teach? Arts Educ. Policy Rev. **109**(4), 21–29 (2008)

Woodford, D.: Abandoning the Magic Circle. Presented at the Breaking the Magic Circle seminar, Tampere, Finland. http://www.dpwoodford.net/Papers/MCSeminar.pdf (2007, April)

Chapter 12
Using Serious Games for Assessment

Aidan Sliney and Dave Murphy

12.1 Introduction

Assessment in education is the process of gathering, interpreting, recording, and using information about pupils' responses to an educational tasNk (Gibbs, 2007, pp. 215–230). There are many common methods of assessment in use today; essay examination, multiple choice testing, written assignments, oral assessments, presentations, group projects, portfolios to name but a few. How do we know if one method would return a higher standard of assessment over another? How should we decide which method suits our assessment needs best? The main reason and function of assessment is to provide a balanced picture of the user's strengths and weaknesses. Each of the methods mentioned have their own list of advantages and disadvantages. The decision to use one method over another is dependent on many factors including cost, speed, value, importance, location. Adding computer assisted methods into the mix extends the list of options even further. Again each of these methods contains many advantages and disadvantages. Computer assisted methods of assessment will not replace traditional methods. They can be complimentary to a traditional method or act as an alternative form of assessment. With more options come more decisions.

One computer assisted assessment method that is beginning to assert itself within the assessment domain is serious games (Waldmann et al., 2008, pp. 17–24). With the cost of production continuously dropping, speed, value, familiarity and the variety of accessible locations increasing, serious games have become a viable option for assessment in many situations (Hays et al., 2010, pp. 1–5). Medicine is one of the key domains at the forefront of adopting serious games for assessment. Validated and accepted examples are being used throughout the medical curriculum (Gesundheit et al., 2009, pp. 759–768; Round et al., 2009, pp. 739–742).

The objective of this chapter is to establish the case for using serious games as a viable form of assessment procedure. We will explain some serious game design methods that can be utilised to optimise the assessment process within a

A. Sliney (✉)
University College Cork, Cork, Ireland
e-mail: aidansliney@gmail.com

M. Ma et al. (eds.), *Serious Games and Edutainment Applications*,
DOI 10.1007/978-1-4471-2161-9_12, © Springer-Verlag London Limited 2011

serious game. We give examples that show how relevant (primary and secondary) information can be chosen, obtained and returned from within serious games. This information can then be utilised for assessment.

Primary information, direct answers to questions, alone do not fully utilise all the benefits of serious games. This information is returned to the assessor by most assessment methods. Without concrete rules, determining the degree of a user's abilities, strengths and weaknesses cannot be accomplished exclusively by checking multiple-choice responses. Multiple measures are needed to get a complete understanding of trainees' comprehension and competence (Hays et al., 2010).

Serious games have the potential to look deeper into this and other information to provide the assessor with all the sufficient information needed to return a clearer understanding of the user (Froschauer et al., submitted). We will discuss this secondary data and how it can be used for assessment.

The chapter further explains this background information on assessment within serious games by providing examples within a number of serious games already in use (Sliney and Murphy, 2008, pp. 131–136). User action assessment and evaluation are an integral and fundamental part of many serious games. These actions can be assessed and evaluated by the user (known as self or, novice) or by an instructor (known as senior or expert). Irrespective of who assesses the actions, much of the same information is extracted and reported to the assessor. The difference and advantage that serious games have over structured formal testing is the potential for retrieving secondary information to extend and advance the assessment procedure. We discuss how this information can be used to enhance the primary information gathered. One of the key issues with all forms of assessment is choosing what to assess. How do you assess a user concisely and accurately? In a task oriented setting, assessments are made on how the user performed at a specific task. If the assessment goal is to assess knowledge then these tasks need to be specifically designed for this purpose. This in turn raises a number of questions, namely which tasks can be used for assessing knowledge? Are all tasks equal or should different tasks be weighted differently? These questions need to be given serious thought by the assessor and the assessment method chosen needs to be flexible enough to cater for the assessor's decisions.

For an assessment method to truly report the standard of a user it needs to recognise their level of overall knowledge and understanding. This again shows how important it is to understand the goal of the assessment. Each task within the assessment process needs to be carefully chosen. These assessment criteria are then evaluated and compared to other assessments, be it the user's past assessments or other users' assessments.

Serious games can potentially gather vast amounts of data. Some of this data can be derived from the user's interaction within and with the game itself, and other forms of data can be gathered from the user's performance with the tasks at hand. This wide spectrum of information can make it difficult to assess a user correctly. Within a serious medical game, should a doctor lose credit for being overly cautious? An example of this might include a simulated patient with the flu; how does the assessor compare a student who immediately diagnoses the patient with the flu, with another student who first takes the patient's bloods, then an electrocardiogram (ECG) and then diagnoses the patient with the flu. In simple outcomes based assessment both students would be equivalent, however the first demonstrates an intuitive understanding and performed the task quicker. However, in a systems approach to error and error avoidance, this would be viewed as non-systematic, error prone, and possibly cavalier. This dilemma is one of the many reasons assessment within serious games can prove difficult, however it highlights potential advantages a serious game with a good assessment procedure can have over regular training and testing methods.

12.2 Assessment

To understand how we intend to use serious games for assessment we will first discuss the assessment process in general. Before we can setup an assessment process we need to have an understanding and answer to three questions. Why are we assessing? Who is the assessor? What should we measure?

> It is sufficient to recognise here that the process exists and involves three major decisions. The first is a decision on what information is relevant, the second a decision on how to gather the information, and the third a decision on how to do the reporting, and to whom (Hols-Elders et al., 2008).

The development of a serious game for assessment should be informed first by the learning objectives of the exercise. This, in turn, is used by the game designers to determine the tools and techniques required to achieve those learning objectives.

The easiest but most important of these questions is the reasoning behind the assessment. Why are we assessing? Are we assessing to gather user information, course information, to group? to teach? Although formative and summative assessments are interconnected they have very different primary reasons for assessment. These differences can result in very different assessment procedures. Summative assessment is assessment that is used to signify competence. Formative assessment, on the other hand, is assessment strictly used to provide feedback to the student on their learning (O'Farrell, 2002). Knowing who is going to assess is also a very important factor when creating your assessment process. The differences between self assessment and peer assessment dictate compellingly what needs to be recorded and how it is returned. Knowing what to measure is very much dependant on why the assessment is taking place and who is the assessor (R. Anderson, n.d., pp. 141–170). To know what to record you need to know and understand all the different variables that can be used to differentiate one user over another towards the aim of the assessment. If the task is speed critical then time is a variable that needs to be recorded and returned to the assessor. Not only could you return the overall time the user took to complete the task you could also return the time taken at each section of the task. Small optimisations like these can pinpoint exactly what or where the student is having difficulty. This gives the assessor a lot more firm information with which an advanced assessment may be undertaken. The possible data that could be returned to the assessor is endless. It is therefore important this information is filtered down. This may be done by the designer if they know exactly what information is beneficial to the assessor or it can be left so the assessor themselves can decide what data is returned. Either way the prevention of oversaturation is important.

To explain these processes further we have created two prototype serious games, JDoc (Sliney and Murphy, 2008) and SiteSafety. These prototypes will validate different methods of assessment by recording different sets of data for different assessors. Although these differences were chosen to demonstrate some of the many different techniques both serious games could have used any combination of these methods.

12.2.1 Why Assess?

If questioned lecturers would say that we assess for the following reasons (O'Farrell, 2002):

- To determine that the intended learning outcomes of the course are being achieved
- To provide feedback to students on their learning, enabling them to improve their performance
- To motivate students to undertake appropriate work
- To support and guide learning
- To describe student attainment, informing decisions on progression and awards
- To demonstrate that appropriate standards are being maintained
- To evaluate the effectiveness of teaching

In the early 1990s the two primary reasons for assessment were to find out how well are students learning and how effectively are teachers teaching (Hays et al., 2010, pp. 1–5; Angelo, 1993). Two decades later this still remains true. One advance to this statement is the addition of "what" to the who is doing the teaching. The updated 2011 version could read; the two primary reasons for assessment are how well are students learning and how effectively are they being taught (Spragins, 1966, pp. 223–230). A teacher being involved in learning is becoming a less common situation (T. Anderson, 2004, chapter 5). Online teaching has a much a place in the teaching domain as the classroom.

In order to assess correctly you need to know the goals of the assessment. Why assess? Knowing why we are assessing gives us clarity in what to look for when within the assessment (Shepard, 2000, pp. 4–14). Do we want to know the standard of the student? Do we want to group the students? Do we want to know how effectively they are being taught? Do we want to know the standard of the teacher or the method used to teach? Each of the many reasons for assessment alters what you are looking for within the assessment.

When a teacher wants to know if the class has learned their eight times tables he can simply give the class a written test. Once corrected, he knows if each student is up to scratch. He also gets information on the quality of his teaching. If so they can move forward to their nine times tables but if not they will have to spend more time on their eights. Knowing why we are assessing lays the foundation for the assessment.

Grading is the primary and most widely used reason behind assessment. Without the facility to grade and label we lose the consistency and focus assessment brings to training. A patient would not use a doctor that is self proclaimed competent but has never been assessed. His abilities may be at a high standard but without clarification his skills will always come into question. Proof beyond the skill learned is an essential necessity. This proof is acquired by some form of assessment. With the progression of computers new methods of assessment are being created, validated and used daily. From the familiar computer-based multiple choice questions (MCQs) (Ramesh et al., 2005, pp. 1–15) to the use of video conferencing (Jill Winters and Jack Winters, 2007, pp. 51–57), computers have extended the possibilities of assessment. Not all methods of assessment are comparable nor should they be. Assessment will always be driven by the situation its needs grew from. Some situations call for a form of computer based assessment where for others a basic pen-and-paper test would suffice.

12.2.2 Who Is the Assessor?

The assessor is for obvious reasons essential to any assessment. The assessor may be a master of the subject. It may be computerised results. It also may be the student. No matter who assesses these actions, be it in a serious game or a structured formal test, much of the same information is extracted and returned to this assessor.

There are many differences between self assessment and master assessment (Anon, n.d., pp. 287–322; Pandey et al., 2008, pp. 286–290). Self-assessment helps students build self-reflection skills and identify areas of improvement (Sandars, 2009, pp. 685–695). Once mastered, in addition to judging one's own work, the concept of self-assessment develops skills in self awareness and critical reflection. Many of the benefits of peer assessment apply to self-assessment. When students self-assess they have a clear understanding of how and why they made each decision (Falchikov and Goldfinch, 2000, pp. 287–322). When someone, other than the person being assessed, is the assessor they only have the data that is returned to them to try and understand the students' reasoning. This returned data is the only information the assessor has to make an evaluation of the student's performance. For the assessor to evaluate correctly this information needs to be a true representation of the user's actions. If the user makes any relevant action or decision this needs to be portrayed in the returned information.

The assessor is the key to any assessment. They need to decide what assessment method to use, what information they need returned and how they will interpret this information.

12.2.3 Computer Based Assessment

Computer based assessment is a broad term for the use of computers in the assessment of student learning. Various other forms exist, such as Computer-Aided Assessment, Computerised Assessment, Computer Assisted Assessment and Computer-Based Testing. Online Computer Based Assessment has existed for a long time in the form of Multiple Choice Questions (MCQ's). Computer Based Assessment is commonly directly made via a computer, whereas Computer Assisted Assessment is used to manage or support the assessment process (O'Farrell, 2002).

Using computers for assessment is a familiar and universal practice. Time efficiency of computer based assessments compared with standard paper based tests was the primary incentive to move assessment procedures towards computer based versions. Computer based assessment has progressed from basic problem solving assessment and bulk marking to being an acceptable means of assessment in significant enterprise examinations. As computers advance so do their benefits for assessment. Cost, consistency and security have, for the majority of situations, assisted time efficiency in promoting the advantages using computers for assessment. The real progression in assessment when using computers comes from their ability to simulate real world tasks and scenarios. Having safer, faster, cheaper assessment are all positives that come with using computers assisted methods. As well as matching the standard of other methods it is now becoming possible to advance assessment procedures with computers. The advancement comes from computers being able to do things other assessment methods cannot; simulation, data acquisition, data filtering, data analysis and scenario adaption (Kneebone et al., 2003, pp. 19–23). Although many assessment methods can also utilise these techniques it is the ability to combine these techniques that will move computers to the forefront of assessment.

The main obstacle preventing a more expansive use of computers for assessment is the lack of knowledge and basic understanding of the advantages available. The initial and most widely known advantage of computer based assessment is the facility to spend less time marking. With computer based assessment results are returned faster so assessors are alerted earlier. This makes it possible for the assessor to adapt their teaching methods earlier. This advantage is generally counteracted by the length of set up time required for computer based assessments. To sway the balance towards computer based assessment we need to look beyond time and cost saved. Students can self assess in their own time, in their own place, at their own speed and when they are ready (Weiss et al., 2005). Feedback can be given during or after the test. The test can incorporate images, audio and video.

12.3 Computer Simulation

Simulation is one technique that adds context to an assessment method (Issenberg et al., 2001, pp. 16–23). It is commonly used to assess likely competency in hostile and critical environments (Ziv et al., 2000, pp. 16–23; Debra Nestel et al.,

2009, pp. e18–e23). Simulation takes advantage of the benefits from learning by experience or experiential learning (Kolb, 1984, pp. 19–38). Conventional training methods comprised of texts and images provide restricted possibilities to describe a difficult context, whereas three dimensional views of complex situations can sometimes increase understanding giving simulated training.

A person's competency in a test environment is not always equal to contextual competency. Simulation goes some way to removing this issue by making the test environment as similar to the end environment as possible. The two main forms of simulation are recreational acting and computer simulation. Recreational acting has many advantages over computer simulation and therefore used where feasible (Collins and Harden, 1998, pp. 508–520). Simulated environments, as advanced as they have become, cannot yet compete with reality. The cost and time associated with recreational acting is a major barrier when it comes to using it for assessment. Assessors and actors are needed for each run of the simulation. Continuity also comes into question when using actors. Taking this into account computer simulation becomes the primary choice for many assessment circumstances.

12.3.1 Serious Games for Assessment

Assessment within serious games has always been challenging (Nielborg, 2004). How do you assess a user concisely and accurately? Assessments need to be made on how the user performed a variety of tasks. These assessments are then evaluated and compared to other assessments, be it users past assessments or other users' assessments.

Many articles and books have been published on the benefits of serious games for learning (Amoia and Gardent, 2011; Michale and Chen, 2010; Hargreaves, 2009; Smothers et al., 2008). This list continues to grow as the standard of serious games progress. Many of the current serious games available have methods of assessment built within as a resultant to learning but very few are built primarily for assessment. Just as many learning platforms contain methods of assessment many assessment methods have the extra capacity of being used as a learning environment. Although serious games being built primarily as an assessment tool are still rare many serious games built for learning are embedding assessment practices within (Stone, 2008, pp. 1–22; Amoia and Gardent, 2011).

K. Corti believes that assessment is a key area that can be advanced by serious games. He believes that immersive simulations and complex serious games offer the opportunity to address some of the major weakness of traditional eLearning and classroom instruction. Assessment is one of the most obvious of these (Hays et al., 2010; Sliney and Murphy, 2008; Corti, 2008).

There are many companies that are experts in e-learning and virtual reality simulation. One such company is Skills2Learn. They develop e-learning, virtual reality, serious-games and creative multimedia solutions. Using virtual reality as an assessment solution allows learners to be left to their own devices in a controlled environment and provides a different method of evaluation. Learners are empowered with freedom and choice to carry out actions and decisions in order to resolve the task or problem at hand. Their actions and progress are marked against certain criteria which gives an overall outcome at the end of the assessment. By developing thought provoking scenarios you can specifically test users on certain aspects of underpinning knowledge. This constructive and detailed breakdown of actions taken during the assessment provides learners and teachers with a clear indication on not only the results of the scenarios but the thought process and underpinning knowledge of how that result was achieved.

The benefits of serious games for learning over more common learning platforms have been well documented (Froschauer et al., submitted; Stone, 2008, pp. 1–2). Utilising as many of these benefits as possible is a key factor in the development process of any serious game. The same can be said for the benefits serious games can bring to assessment.

Implementing an assessment process into any serious game is fundamental procedure. At any stage the user's knowledge can be assessed with an MCQ. As this method is probably the easiest to implement, closest to "what people know and understand" and can be easily use to categorise (pass, fail, good, bad) it is used and will continue to be used most often. Using a MCQ within a serious game can affect the fidelity of the scenario by removing the user from the scenario.

The question needs to be asked when choosing to use a MCQ to assess; does it utilise all the benefits the serious game can make available for the assessment process? Can this assessment be done in a less invasive and more intuitive manner towards the scenario? Keeping the user within the scenario and not making them fill out an MCQ would go a long way for the fidelity of the scenario. So how do we assess without intervening. The aim is to enable an assessment of competencies and learning progress during the game, which does not compromise the game flow and therefore does not negatively impact intrinsic motivation.

12.4 What Information Is Relevant?

Measuring and returning the correct information is a key factor in any tests validity. To work out what information is needed for a correct assessment firstly the goal of the assessment needs to be understood. If the assessment goal is to purely certification then the only information that needs to be returned is pass or fail. Conversely if the assessor wants to know a student's strengths and weaknesses the amount of information that could be returned is endless. The assessor should be able to be able to answer the below four questions on each section of work or task assessed (O'Farrell, 2002).

1. What aspects of the assessment was successful, and why
2. What aspects of the assessment work was less successful, and why
3. How the student could improve this particular piece of work or task
4. How the student could do more successful work in future.

Serious games and other computer based assessments have the potential to return countless amount of information. For this reason more time needs to be given to making sure the correct data is returned to the assessor. 3D environments surround the users with vast amounts of information. Knowing what information is relevant and beneficial for the goals of the assessment helps utilise the benefits a serious game can give as an assessment tool. Only relevant data should be returned to the assessor. Returning excess data can saturate the data the assessor needs to look through whereas by not returning all potentially relevant data you may miss an important piece of diagnostic information. Giving the assessor the ability to choose what will be returned to them gives the assessment process the flexibility to fit the assessment needs.

In JDoc, one of our example serious games, an important element of the assessment process is "time spent". To exploit the benefits of this element choosing the correct amount of information to return to the assessor is essential. If we were to return the minimum amount of information captured by time spent we would simply return the overall time taken for the scenario. Although this is does tell us how long someone took to complete the scenario it does not let the assessor know why it took them that length of time. If we were to return all the information acquired by time spent we would be returning where the user was every second within the scenario. This is information overload. Although the assessor could trawl though these figures and get a good understanding of exactly why the user took a length of time completing the scenario this is not practicable and may cause the assessor to miss other important information. The key to returning the relevant information is knowing what stages of the scenario are significant. Do we need to know how long it took the user to get to the hospital? In some assessments this is significant information in others it is irrelevant. The assessor needs to be able to decide the relevance of different situations within the scenario before the assessment takes place. Therefore it is the assessor's decision on what information they will leave out and what information they want to include in the assessment report.

When I am deciding what information is to be included in the assessment report I split it into two collections; primary assessment information and secondary assessment information. Primary information is any essential information that the assessment process would not be valid or reliable without. All the answers in a MCQ would be primary assessment information. The assessment may still be valid without returning one of the MCQ's answers but as a group they are clearly essential to the assessment process. Secondary assessment information is data captured within a scenario that helps advance the assessors understanding of the users' actions. Without this information the assessment would still be valid and reliable. Capturing and returning this data helps assessors get a deeper understanding of the user. This deeper understanding is just one of the reasons we believe serious games have the potential to advance assessment. Incorporating secondary information within the assessment process gives serious games another advantage over traditional formative testing.

12.4.1 Primary Assessment Information

Primary assessment information is the backbone of all assessment procedures. When a student undertakes a pencil and paper assessment the only results that can be returned to them are the results of the questions asked, primary assessment data, and if relevant the time it took for them to complete the assessment.

Returning valid and relevant primary assessment information is fundamental to a correct assessment. When a user completes a scenario within a Serious Game, not only do they return the relevant primary information there is also the possibility of returning masses of secondary information. Returning what is relevant of this information can give the assessor a better understanding of the user's journey.

12.4.2 Secondary Assessment Information

One difference and advantage serious games have over structured formal testing is their potential for retrieving secondary information. They can advance assessment by obtaining and utilising more information. This information can be used to add greater depth and scope to the primary information gathered. Secondary data is any data that can be collected throughout the user's use of the simulator. This data has many uses that can sometimes be overlooked. The key attribute of secondary data is its reliability. Users spend different times undertaking different tasks. Some become stressed, some don't. It is this variability combined with its reliability that makes secondary data excellent for assessment.

12.4.3 Using Triggers to Gather Secondary Information

12.4.3.1 Data Triggers

Serious games have the ability to copy real world triggers. Triggers are used in both, real life scenarios and within virtual scenarios to alert at a point where important change occurs. A simple example would be the speed limit. An assessor would have a trigger set on the speed limit. If the student goes over the speed limit the trigger is fired and the mistake is noted. This is a data trigger. These can be placed in any location and on any variable. These triggers can give us a structured overview of a situation.

12.4.3.2 Trigger Boxes

Another trigger that can be used for assessment is the trigger box. Trigger boxes can be used to return very beneficial information to the assessor. Trigger boxes contain three main functions; onEnter, whileInside and onExit. The two main uses for trigger boxes are around game assets (non player characters, items,) and locations (buildings, rooms). For example, has the student talked to a non player character? For how long did they talk? Did the student look at the correct records? Did the student enter the radiography lab (Fig. 12.1)?

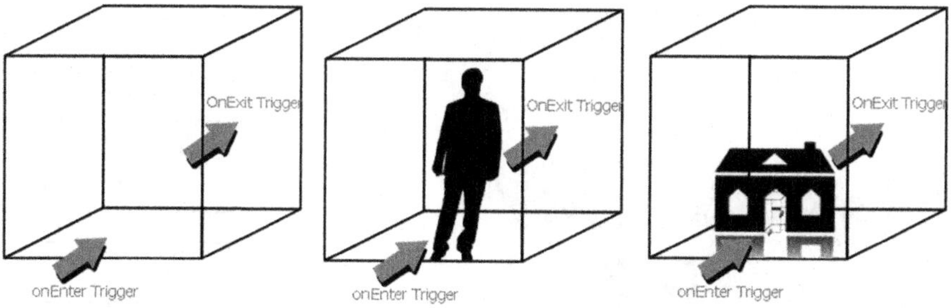

Fig. 12.1 Three different uses of trigger boxes

There are many different programming methods to capture the above information. Trigger Boxes have advantages over other methods as they bring an ease of understanding and visualisation to the creator of a serious game scenario. The assessor can use these techniques to capture any information they believe may be relevant to the assessment process.

12.5 Examples – JDoc and SiteSafety

12.5.1 JDoc

JDoc is an interactive, computer-based cognitive 1st and 3rd person junior doctor simulator. It is used to train and teach junior doctors (Sliney and Murphy, 2008). It is a simple, cheap and easy-to-use development model, where people are assisted by information technology. It can be installed on any home computer that meets the minimal required specification. The users' actions are continuously logged for reviews and revision by either the user or by a senior doctor dependent on which situation is preferred. Interactive prototypes of specific fidelity enable a better understanding of end-users and their tasks, lead to a better collaboration and make it possible to produce better software faster. Realistic prototypes help resolve detailed design decisions in layout, visual presentation, and component selection, as well as finding points in interaction design and interface behaviour (Fig. 12.2).

The purpose of the JDoc is to familiarise junior doctors with the day-to-day stress of a hectic hospital. By simulating patients and creating scenarios using basic parameters provided by senior doctors, JDoc supplies junior doctors with valuable (virtual) experience, which otherwise may be difficult to obtain due to many constraints such as cost or time.

It both immerses the player in the believable world of a busy hospital at night and educates them as to the diagnostic procedures and medical criteria required while working on-call in a hospital ward. When the simulator is fully loaded, the user has to proceed from waiting on call to assessing the patient. When the user has finished using the simulator, all actions can be reviewed and assessed either by themselves or their supervisor in an individual txt file. Once a junior doctor logs onto JDoc they

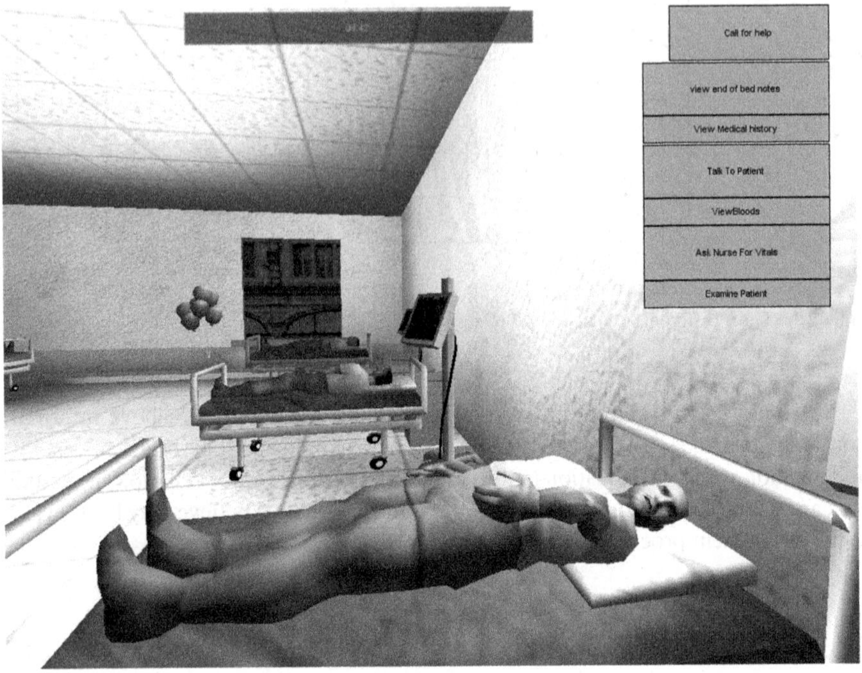

Fig. 12.2 A typical scene in JDoc

take control of a doctor model (an on call junior doctor). JDoc creates a file under the doctor's name in which all their actions are documented. The user must make his way to the hospital and then find and assess the patient. To accomplish this they must talk to other doctors and nurses (Non-Player Characters (NPCs)) ask questions and follow the correct protocol in assessing the patient. Each assessment and every reaction from the in-game doctors and nurses, and factors like ECGs, blood test results and patient history can differ as the senior doctors create a new scenario.

When we began to design the assessment procedure within JDoc we had to make important decisions that would dictate how JDoc's users would be assessed. Who was going to assess the actions of the user? Was JDoc intended as a testing facility or a training facility? The difference being, if JDoc was set up as a testing program a senior doctor would have to extract and assess the users' actions whereas if JDoc was set up simply as a training tool then the user would have to assess his own actions. If a senior doctor was to assess a users' action then they would need a lot more information than simply the actions taken and answers given. They would need many other factors such as time taken at each action, what order the actions were taken, how many times the user repeated an action, what information did the user ask for and what information was given for each answer etc.

JDoc set out as both a testing and training program. In order for a senior doctor to correctly assess a user of JDoc they would need to know everything about the users' experience within the simulator. JDoc is set around a 3D environment which leads to difficulties capturing all the user actions. Trigger boxes are used to overcome this problem. By placing trigger boxes at all significant points of the simulator we can capture relevant secondary information. Examples of such, did the user enter a room? What path did the user take? Three functions are connected to each trigger box, onEnter, onExit and whileInside. With these three functions it is possible to record all the users' input actions. By knowing exactly how efficient a user is at a task we are able to select test items according to the ability of the student.

How many trigger boxes used is decided by the creator of the scenario. The number depends on the quantity and quality of the secondary information required. In Fig. 12.3 we only use two trigger boxes we can still acquire a lot for information. For example; did the user go to reception? How many times he went to reception? How long he stayed at reception? Did he listen to all the receptionist had to say or did he leave mid sentence? Did he ask for directions? How many times did he ask for directions? How long before he made his way upstairs? Did he come down stairs again? Other trigger boxes could have been added in one of the rooms downstairs but the extra secondary data acquired by this trigger box (in this scenario) would be irrelevant to the assessment.

It is from these triggers boxes that the sample report below is generated (Fig. 12.4). The creator of this scenario decided what data retrieved should be printed out in the report. This method is elastic and easily extendable to add more or less data dependant on the requirements of the report. The creator could print all data captured to the report or simply just a few important lines. Each scenario will differ. With one scenario you could have many different assessment setups, again dependant on who is looking at the report and what information they are looking for. If the user himself is reading his own report, the creator can add redefined correction lines (below). If the user does something incorrect it will appear on the report so he can see and learn from his mistakes making self assessment and reflection possible.

- *(6.25)He spent 12 minutes at a peripheral nervous exam*

NO PERIPHRAL NERVOUS EXAM SHOULD HAVE DONE. TIME WASTED

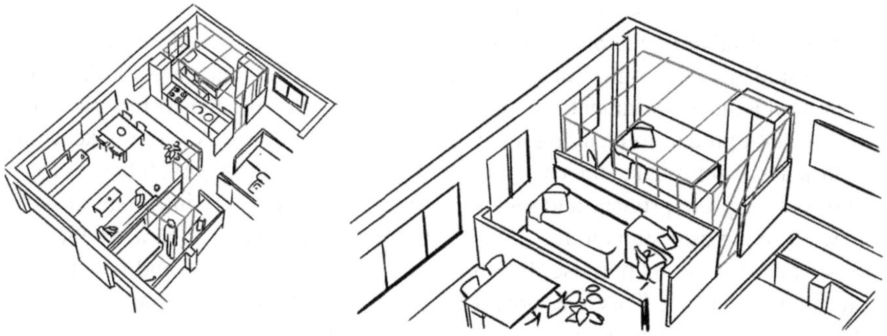

Fig. 12.3 Trigger boxes around the JDoc hospital

Student: J. T Smith
Scenario: ST Elevation
Date: 23/11/10

Dr Murphy started the Simulator. He then went on to call the hospital
(1.12)After ringing the hospital Dr. Murphy thought the patient could have been suffering from peptic ulcer disease
(2.15)He talked to Dr Smith but Dr. Murphy left before the doctor finished talking
(4.43)He talked to Nurse Carla
(5.02)He walked into the patient's room
(5.30)He asked him did he have shortness of breath.
(5.55)He asked his patient was he feeling sick He asked for the bloods He looked at the end of bed notes
+++ He began to examine the patient +++

When the Medicial reg asked What's wrong with the patient and what's your reasoning behind your answer? Dr. Murphy replied: "ST Elevation, ECG showed it."
When asked "What treatment would you like to start while the medical Reg is on his way?" Dr. Murphy replied: "Give him Panadol"

Fig. 12.4 Example report

Assessment is defined upon designing a new scenario by its creator but can be easily adapted many times to suite the reports needs.

With the addition of a "timer" as well as trigger boxes, we advance the assessment process. Examples of this include the ability to pinpoint students' strengths and weaknesses' using selections and trigger boxes, where as the incorporation of time spent on a task can be used to infer "proof of rising" benefits.

Figure 12.4 is a shortened version of a report given to an assessor. It contains example secondary information captured by the timer and trigger boxes.

12.5.2 SiteSafety

The main objective of SiteSafety is to teach students how to be safe in a building site. The students take control of a character and have to complete tasks for the foreman around a 3D environment. The tasks range from selecting the correct personal protective equipment, to cleaning up sheds to putting out fires. A score is kept for each task and is returned to the user at the end of the simulation. SiteSafety uses trigger boxes to capture primary and secondary information. Primary information such as how close the user stood to the fire or if they entered a restricted area. SiteSafety differs from JDoc in its purpose. It is primarily an assessment tool and is not used for formative learning. This does not take from the importance of secondary data. It is still used and needed to help the assessor understand the users level of competence (Fig. 12.5).

Fig. 12.5 Two scenes from SiteSafety

12.6 Adaptive Assessment

Diagnostically assessing a group with varied abilities can be problematic. Setting the level of measurement to cater for all capabilities is a difficult task. Setting the assessment too easy could end up returning very little information on the higher standard students whereas setting it too hard would return the same problem for the lower standard students. Setting the assessment to an average difficulty could give little information about both sets of students. Computer based assessment, in particular serious games, can be set up to resolve this problem. A high performer can be provided with fewer but more complex situations than an underachiever. Moreover, based on the presence or absence of certain skills, specific objects can be presented and tasks can be adjusted to the learner's needs. This is another benefit serious games have when being used for assessment.

Adaptive games are simply games that adapt to users input (Gilleade and Dix, 2004, p. 232). Adaptive games are dependent on variables. When these variables change the game adapts. In fact most games are adaptive. An example in adaptive assessment's simplest form would be a user selecting the level of difficulty in an options screen. The game would then adapt to the users chosen level of difficulty. The games that progress adaptive gaming are games that change dynamically midgame unbeknown the user. These games, like the example above, still only adapt to changing variables but this process is hidden to the user. This is an important factor for immersion. Adaptive games can take in hundreds of variables to dictate how the game should change. This technique can be used in assessment. The scenario and assessment process can adapt dependent on the secondary data created by the user undertaking the previous or current tasks.

By using adaptive assessment methods the students can be filtered into their appropriate level. The basic principal behind adaptive testing is within the assessment there is a level to assess all competencies. Each student can progress through the assessment until they find their own level of competency. Serious games can also be setup to give students second attempts and hints to help them move to a more advanced group. For adaptive assessment to work as a method of diagnostics the correct information would need to be returned to the assessor. The progression of the assessment may not always be towards a harder task. It may be something

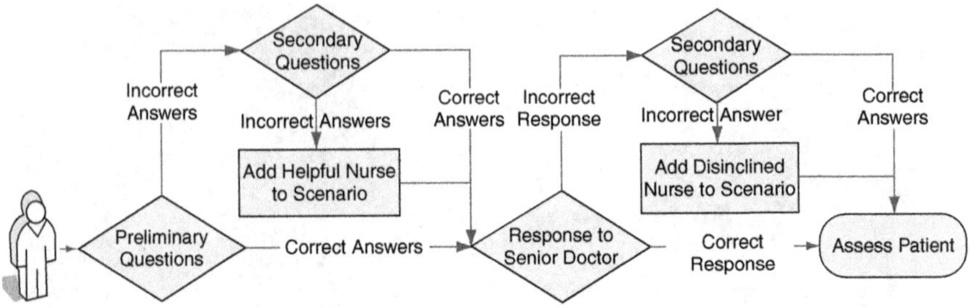

Fig. 12.6 A simple adaptive scenario example

as simple supplying a student with the required information to help them progress in the assessment. Having this information available to the student helps them to move forward and be assessed on other sections of the assessment. This "supplying of help" needs to always be returned to the assessor. Returning to the assessor that the student needed this information to move any further gives them diagnostic information to help advance their assessment process. In paper based tests if a student did not understand one section of a question they may not be able to continue to sections they do understand.

Scenarios within a serious game have the advantage of being dynamic throughout the assessment process. They can be built to adapt towards the users' skill level. Dependant on how well a user does on one section can dictate what help is available in the next section. This method stops users from falling at the first hurdle (Fig. 12.6).

JDoc and SiteSafety are both setup as adaptive diagnostic assessment tools. They both contain techniques to move advanced users onto advanced topics but also contain means for a student struggling on a section to obtain help to progress. If a student does move forward to an advanced topic or requires help on particular topic then this is recorded and returned to the assessor as vital diagnostic information.

12.6.1 Adaptive Assessment Within JDoc

The scenarios within JDoc have a start and ending but unlike most assessment procedures are not linear. The methods used to return information to the user allows JDoc to be used as a adaptive diagnostic tool. Returning what information and where the user required this information can then be returned to the assessor. The main assessment section within JDoc is diagnosing a patient. Throughout each simulation the user undertakes multiple tasks. They talk to Doctors, Nurses, and Receptionists. How well they do on these tasks dictates variables within the next task. If they give bad advice to the doctor then the next nurse will give them extra information on the patient. The assessor sees all this going on in a report. If the user should not have needed this help then the assessor will not look kindly on them receiving it. The assessment becomes more real. If a student was stuck in a real situation they would be given help. If it was something they should not have needed help with then it would be frowned upon. Within JDoc all the student's actions before assessing the patient dictates the diagnosis difficulty. The students who return all the correct information in the run up to the patient assessment are given a difficult patient. Secondary assessment data can also be used to dictate the direction a scenario can go. Within JDoc "time" is one measurement used for secondary assessment data. If a student takes too long assessing a patient or wastes time with incorrect assessment actions then the patient may turn critical. If the assessor sets up the scenario correctly each user should find their own correct level. Every student should be pushed to their limit. At the end of the assessment the assessor should know exactly what issues the student has and where they need to improve.

12.6.2 Adaptive Assessment Within SiteSafety

SiteSafety is also adaptive assessment procedure but in a very different way to JDoc. JDoc's main assessment goal is to find each student's weakness. SiteSafety's main assessment goal is to certify the user. These different goals dictate which adaptive methods can and cannot be used. As SiteSafety needs to be consistent across users, the game adapts has to kept within limits. Giving users help that would mean they could not get certified would be pointless. SiteSafety's assessment process is task orientated. It is made up of four scenarios. For a user to become certified they need to complete each scenario. Unlike JDoc these scenarios are independent of each other and how the user does in one will not affect another.

12.7 The Future of Serious Games for Assessment

Information is essential to any assessment process. Having additional relevant information available gives the assessor a better understanding and picture of the user's journey within the assessment process. As the benefits of using computers for assessment becomes widely recognised the use of simulations to assess will increase. With the added advantage of adaptive scenarios serious games for assessment will someday become widespread and ordinary.

References

Amoia, A., Gardent, A.: A serious game for second language acquisition. In Proceedings of the 3rd International Conference on Computer Supported Education Noordwijkerhout, The Netherlands (2011)

Anderson, R.: How to construct achievement tests to assess comprehension. Rev. Educ. Res. **42**(2), 145–170 (n.d.)

Anderson, T.: Theory and Practice of Online Learning. Athabasca University, Athabasca (2004)

Angelo, T.: Classroom Assessment Techniques: A Handbook for College Teachers, 2nd edn. Jossey-Bass Publishers, San Francisco, CA (1993)

Anon: Student peer assessment in higher education: a meta-analysis comparing peer and teacher marks. Rev. Educ. Res. http://rer.sagepub.com/content/70/3/287.abstract (n.d.). Accessed 7 Dec 2010

Collins, J.P., Harden, R.M.: AMEE – Medical Education Guide No. 13: real patients, simulated patients and simulators in clinical examinations. Med. Teach. **20**(6), 508 (1998)

Corti, K.: Using immersive simulations as assessment tools – the untapped potential of the medium. Serious Games, Immersive Simulations and eLearning 2.0. http://theevilnumber27.wordpress.com/2008/01/05/using-immersive-simulations-as-assessment-tools---the-untapped-potential-of-the-medium/ (2008). Accessed 21 Mar 2011

Falchikov, N., Goldfinch, J.: Student peer assessment in higher education: a meta-analysis comparing peer and teacher marks. Rev. Educ. Res. **70**(3), 287–322 (2000)

Froschauer, J., Seidel, I., Gartner. M., Berger, H., Merkl, D.: Design and evaluation of a serious game or immersive cultural training. In: 16th International Conference on Virtual Systems and Multimedia, VSMM '10. Submitted for publication

Gesundheit, N. et al.: The use of virtual patients to assess the clinical skills and reasoning of medical students: initial insights on student acceptance. Med. Teach. **31**(8), 739 (2009)

Gibbs, T.: Advancing Medical Education: the new series of AMEE guides in medical education. Med. Teach. **29**(6), 525–526 (2007)

Gilleade, K.M., Dix, A.: Using frustration in the design of adaptive videogames. In: Proceedings of the 2004 ACM SIGCHI International Conference on Advances in Computer Entertainment Technology. Salzburg, Austria, p. 232 (2004)

Hargreaves, D.H.: Serious game son the move. Sch. Organ. **15**(3), 215–228 (2009)

Hays, M.J., Ogan, A., Lane, H.C.: The evolution of assessment: Learning about culture from a serious game. In: Proceedings of the 4th International Workshop on Intelligent Tutoring Systems and Ill-Defined Domains Held at the 10th International Conference on Intelligent Tutoring Systems, ITS '10. Pittsburgh, PA, p. 37 (2010)

Hols-Elders, W., et al.: Twelve tips for computer-based assessment in medical education. Med. Teach. **30**(7), 673 (2008)

Issenberg, S.B., et al.: Simulation and new learning technologies. Med. Teach. **23**(1), 16 (2001)

Kneebone, R., et al.: The use of handheld computers in scenario-based procedural assessments. Med. Teach. **25**(6), 632 (2003)

Kolb, D.A.: Experiential Learning: Experience as the Source of Learning and Development, pp. 21–38. Prentice- Hall, Englewood Cliffs, NJ (1984)

Michale, D., Chen, S.: Serious Games; Games that Educate, Train, and Inform, 3rd ed. Thomson Course Technology, London (2010)

Nestel, D., et al.: Evaluating training for a simulated team in complex whole procedure simulations in the endovascular suite. Med. Teach. **31**(1), 18 (2009)

Nielborg, D.: America's Army: more than a game? In: International Simulation and Gaming Association. Ludwig, Maximilians Munich, Germany (2004)

O'Farrell, C.: Enhancing student learning through assessment. http://learningandteaching.dit.ie/documents/assessment_toolkit_v41f.pdf (2002). Accessed 24 Mar 2010

Pandey, V. et al.: Self-assessment of technical skill in surgery: the need for expert feedback. Ann. R. Coll. Surg. Engl. **90**(4), 286–290 (2008)

Ramesh, S., Sidhu, S.M., Watugala, G.K.: (2005) Exploring the potential of multiple choice questions in computer-based assessment of student learning. Malays. Online J. Instr. Technol. **2**(1), 1–15 (2008)

Round, J., Conradi, E., Poulton, T.: Improving assessment with virtual patients. Med. Teach. **31**(8), 759 (2009)

Sandars, J.: The use of reflection in medical education: AMEE – Guide No. 44. Med. Teach. **31**(8), 685 (2009)

Shepard, L.A.: (2000) The role of assessment in a learning culture. Educ. Res., **29**(7), 4–14 (2009)

Sliney, A., Murphy, D.: JDoc: a serious game for medical learning. In: First International Conference on Advances in Computer-Human Interaction. Sainte Luce, Martinique, pp. 131–136. http://ieeexplore.ieee.org/lpdocs/epic03/wrapper.htm?arnumber=4455971 (2008)

Smothers, V., Ellaway, R., Greene, P.: The e-learning evolution–leveraging new technology approaches to advance healthcare education. Med. Teach. **30**(2), 117 (2008)

Spragins, J.: (1966) Learning without a teacher. IEEE Trans. Inform. Theory **12**(2), 223–230 (2008)

Stone, R.: Serious games: Virtual reality's second coming? Virtual Real. **13**(1), 1–2 (2008)

Waldmann, U.-M., Gulich, M.S., Zeitler, H.-P.: Virtual patients for assessing medical students–important aspects when considering the introduction of a new assessment format. Med. Teach. **30**(1), 17 (2008)

Weiss, P.M., et al.: How do medical student self-assessments compare with their final clerkship grades? Med. Teach. **27**(5), 445 (2005)

Winters, J., Winters, J.: Videoconferencing and telehealth technologies can provide a reliable approach to remote assessment and teaching without compromising quality. J. Cardiovasc. Nurs. **22**(1), 51–57 (2007)

Ziv, A., Small, S.D., Wolpe, P.R.: Patient safety and simulation-based medical education. Med. Teach. **22**(5), 489 (2000)

Chapter 13
Designing and Evaluating Emotional Student Models for Game-Based Learning

Karla Muñoz, Paul Mc Kevitt, Tom Lunney, Julieta Noguez, and Luis Neri

13.1 Introduction

Computer tutoring has developed over time in order to adapt to students' expectations (Oblinger, 2004) and has proven more effective than traditional classroom instruction (Regian et al., 1996). Intelligent Tutoring Systems (ITSs) offer advantages, such as following students' performance over time, generalising pedagogical actions to different problems and domains and understanding and responding suitably to students' needs (Clancey and Buchanan, 1982).

On the other hand, serious games have emerged as a field that combines serious aspects, e.g. teaching, learning, communicating or informing, with playful characteristics of entertainment activities (Alvarez, 2007). Serious games employ attractive features that can achieve and hold students' attention and are also used for the delivery of learning content. As a result, the term 'edutainment' was created to define a specific application of serious games. Edutainment is an approach that combines education and entertainment (Qianping et al., 2007).

Edutainment enhances the significance of games by incorporating pedagogical techniques to deliver educational content, present education in a less stressful way than traditional methods and enable students to enjoy the learning process and increase their interest in content. In addition, edutainment environments take advantage of students' technological skills to incorporate attractive features that support the learning process. Similarly, the characteristics of edutainment environments can be aligned to students' varied learning styles to achieve learning objectives (Cela, 2008).

Cognitive and affective mechanisms have proven deeply interrelated (Norman et al., 2003). Emotion influences learning, performance, motivation, interactions and personal growth (Pekrun et al., 2007). The research field of Affective Computing (Picard, 1995) merged with ITSs and edutainment. As a result, researchers have

K. Muñoz (✉)
Faculty of Computing and Engineering, School of Computing and Intelligent Systems, Intelligent Systems Research Centre, University of Ulster, Derry/Londonderry, UK
e-mail: Munoz_Esquivel-K@email.ulster.ac.uk

M. Ma et al. (eds.), *Serious Games and Edutainment Applications*,
DOI 10.1007/978-1-4471-2161-9_13, © Springer-Verlag London Limited 2011

focused on the creation of a new generation of ITSs and educational games, which are capable of recognising and showing emotion (Picard et al., 2004; Sykes, 2006). The ultimate goal is to encourage students' learning and understanding whilst achieving and maintaining students' motivation and interest. Our research is mainly focused on this endeavour.

The challenges involved when reasoning about students' emotions are to know how and when emotion arises, to understand which factors determine an emotion or an affective state and determine what emotions are relevant to the learning experience. In addition, it is important to know that personal preferences and differences influence the presence and communication of an emotional state (Conati and Maclaren, 2009). Therefore, it is important to deal with the inherent uncertainty of the emotional domain. Also, in education, the effects of positive and negative emotions are not totally understood. It is also not always clear what should be the appropriate response to a student's emotion (Alexander and Sarrafzadeh, 2008; Lepper et al., 1993; Schutz and Pekrun, 2007). Additionally, the creation and acceptance of educational games involves creative design and academic concerns, such as the difference between game content and curriculum content and resistance to the idea that games can be an effective method of teaching (McFarlane et al., 2001).

In this chapter, we focus mainly on how to develop an emotional student model that can reason about students' emotions using observable behaviour, i.e. interaction data, and questions answered during game dialogue. Our emotional student model is focused on reasoning about achievement emotions, which are experienced in academic settings and arise in response to activities and their outcomes when the quality of achievement is judged according to established standards (Pekrun et al., 2007). Therefore, our emotional student model uses Control-Value theory from Pekrun et al. (2007) as a basis for representing emotion. The theory is an integrative framework that assumes that control and value appraisals are the most significant factors when determining an emotion. Control-Value Theory has not previously been employed to create a computational and emotional student model. Our approach employs Probabilistic Relational Models (PRMs) to facilitate the derivation of Dynamic Bayesian Networks (DBNs), which enable us to handle uncertainty effectively. In addition, we discuss what features an emotional game-based learning environment of this nature must have in order to achieve this goal.

This work is summarised in six sections. In Section 13.1, we provide a succinct overview of the challenges involved and we discuss the state of the art of educational game-design, evaluation of affective applications and emotional game-based learning environments and the different research approaches employed by the new generation of ITSs to recognise and respond to emotion. Section 13.2 focuses on our research approach, emotional student model and the description of an affective enhancement of the Olympia architecture (Muñoz et al., 2009). In Section 13.3, we discuss the application of our research to a specific case study – the design and implementation of PlayPhysics, an emotional game-based learning environment for teaching Physics at undergraduate level. PlayPhysics was developed using Java, the Unity Game Engine, 3D Studio Max and Hugin Lite. Section 13.4 discusses the results of the evaluation of our emotional student model. Tests were conducted on 79 students enrolled in an undergraduate engineering course at Tecnólogico de Monterrey, Mexico City campus (ITESM-CCM). In Section 13.5, we discuss our findings in the context of related work. Finally, we conclude by outlining the advantages of our research approach and discussing future enhancements.

13.2 Background and Related Work

Our research focuses on recognising and responding to emotions effectively in a game-based learning environment, which will ensure students' learning and understanding and hold students' interest and motivation. To achieve this endeavour, it is necessary to be aware of existing approaches and the challenges involved.

13.2.1 Challenges of Emotional Game-Based Learning Environments

Advances in psychology, cognitive science, multimodal applications, neuroscience, cinematography and artificial intelligence (AI) have promised dramatic changes in computer tutoring. Research efforts have focused mainly on two main challenges: achieving the most accurate perception of students' needs and responding in the most suitable manner to these needs in order to nurture and grasp students' knowledge, understanding, motivation, attention and interest (Du Boulay and Luckin, 2001). When ITSs were incorporated into game-based learning environments to offer adaptable instruction and ensure the achievement of specific learning goals (Blanchard and Frasson, 2006; Conati and Maclaren, 2009), the learning environments inherited these challenges.

Student modelling is an area focused on achieving an abstract knowledge representation of the student (Woolf, 2009). Research focused first on the representation of students' cognitive state. Clancey and Buchanan (1982) noted that students' errors were related to students' misconceptions about domain knowledge and endeavoured to represent teaching and problem solving knowledge in the GUIDON ITS. Research has also attempted to characterize students' learning styles (Jungclaus et al., 2003) and more recently, students' personality traits, attitudes (Arroyo and Woolf, 2005), motivation (Del Soldato and Du Boulay, 1995; Rebolledo-Mendez et al., 2006), self-efficacy (McQuiggan et al., 2008) and affect and emotion (Conati and Maclaren, 2009; D'Mello et al., 2008; Sarrafzadeh et al., 2008). AI techniques, such as semantic nets, rules, constraints, plan recognition and machine learning, are applied to make computers capable of reasoning about knowledge (Woolf, 2009).

The interest in researching the influence of emotion in education has been relatively recent and still not completely known (Pekrun et al., 2007; Picard et al., 2004). It is noted that diverse factors influence the presence and communication of people's emotion, e.g. personality traits, attitudes, preferences, goals and cultural and social conventions. Hence, an expert human identifies affect or emotion with approximately 70% accuracy (Robson, 1993). In an attempt to identify the relevant factors that determine relevant affective and emotional states, researchers computing have focused on observing, annotating, recording and analysing students and lecturers' interactions (Alexander and Sarrafzadeh, 2008; D'Mello et al., 2008) or reviewing research in education and cognitive psychology (Conati and Maclaren, 2009; Del Soldato and Du Boulay, 1995). It is important to emphasise that there is not a universal classification of emotion (Ortony et al., 1990). Additionally, the context where emotion arises influences the type of emotions that are frequently observed (Pekrun et al., 2007). Therefore, determining the emotions relevant to the specific learning experience also constitutes a challenge.

Two key features that must be accomplished by computer tutoring, in order to effectively adapt to students, are: (1) effectiveness of representing and handling domain knowledge to achieve flexibility in different teaching situations and (2) believability of the communication of pedagogical responses (Lester et al., 1997). Therefore, research has focused on implementing Embodied Pedagogical Agents (EPAs) (Lester et al., 1999) and synthetic characters (Dias et al., 2006). Their common challenges are adapting to changes in the environment, incorporating planning and execution mechanisms and performing collaborative activities (Johnson et al., 2000; Mateas, 1997). Since emotion modelling is a relatively new and unknown field, it is not clear how computers should respond effectively to students' emotions (Pekrun et al., 2007). As a result, research has focused on observing teaching-learning interactions to identify suitable responses (Lepper et al., 1993; Porayska-Pomsta et al., 2008).

13.2.2 Game Design Principles, Frameworks and Models

In addition to the challenges faced when creating a game-based learning environment capable of recognising and showing emotion, there is the challenge of ensuring that the environment is also capable of delivering effective learning and understanding that it is aligned with the academic curriculum. The Games-to-teach research team, created by the Massachusetts Institute of Technology (MIT) and Microsoft, outlined some design principles that should be considered whilst creating educational games (Squire, 2003). From these principles, we selected what we consider the most important:

- Originate the educational game's creation from a standard simulation
- Enhance the basic attributes and abilities of game features and characters through the incorporation of learning objects as intrinsic motivators
- Identify real-world applications of the concept that is going to be taught
- Design goal-based scenarios, decisions, consequences and join goals

Game-based learning environments should have as features challenge and fantasy, must be capable of offering a sense of control and evoke curiosity (Malone, 1981). In addition, it is important to spend time on designing the *gameplay*, since this comprises the core of the game. *Gameplay* does not have a single definition. It is a mixture of diverse entities and the resultant interaction between them (Rollings and Adams, 2003). A way of creating *gameplay* is setting challenges, which can be of different types. Types of challenge highly related with the educational domain are: (1) *logic and inference challenges*, which confront players' skills to take the best course of action by grasping and using information; (2) *knowledge-based challenges*, which depend on the player's knowledge, which can or cannot be acquired through the game world; (3) *moral challenges*, which rely on meta-ethics and the player's view, develop from general aspects to more specific ones and may be of universal, cultural, tribal and personal character, and (4) *applied challenges*, which are comprised by a combination of pure challenges, e.g. races, puzzles, exploration, conflict, economies, concepts, applied to a specific situation.

On the other hand, there are design paradigms, which describe how to incorporate games into learning environments. As an example, the Fuzzified Instructional Design Development of Game-like Environments (FIDGE) model is an instructional design development model (IDDM) for designing, developing and implementing game-based learning environments. It is comprised of phases, e.g. pre-analysis, analysis, design, development and evaluation. The progression between phases is not linear and is without clear established boundaries (Akilli and Cagiltay, 2006). Its key characteristic is an awareness of real-world uncertainty, since it was created using real life scenarios for reference. The strategies proposed by the FIDGE model offer time management efficiency, early decision making about the technology to use, continuous evaluation and flexibility and modularity of the final product.

In addition, it is important to remember that the adoption and acceptance of the final product depends on understanding correctly the learners' and lecturers' needs. As an example, the Demographic Game Design 1 (DGD1) is a design model used to take into account the player's styles or preferences during the design process.

13.2.3 Approaches to Recognising Emotion

As mentioned earlier, our work is focused mainly on reasoning about student's emotions, i.e. creating an emotional student model. ITSs are beginning to incorporate emotional aspects in their architectures. There are three discernable approaches: (1) identifying the physical effects of emotion, (2) reasoning about emotion from its origin and (3) a hybrid approach, which comprises the first two approaches.

To identify the physical effects of emotion, it has been necessary to enhance computer perception through the incorporation of cameras, microphones and sensors, which are capable of capturing a variety of interaction data, e.g. facial gestures, eye movement, voice prosody and inflection, galvanic skin response, heart rate and body posture (D'Mello et al., 2008; Sarrafzadeh et al., 2008; Pasch et al., 2009). However, to be capable of reasoning about this information it is necessary to employ AI techniques, such as artificial neural networks. In addition, it is necessary to associate distinguishable patterns of interaction with specific emotional states. To attain this goal, expert judges and students' self-reports are employed. A challenge of this approach is its general unavailability online, since sometimes the hardware employed is expensive and difficult to find. Therefore, students typically have to travel to a lab where they can interact with an application of this nature (Burleson and Picard, 2007).

For reasoning about emotion, researchers often use a cognitive theory of emotion as a basis (Jaques and Vicari, 2007). The most common theory employed in the literature is the Ortony, Clore and Collins (OCC) model, which reasons about attitudes, standards and goals (Ortony et al., 1990). Jaques and Vicari (2007) adapted the theory to learning context. However, there is no evidence of the effectiveness of the approach. Its main challenge is how to be aware of students' attitudes, goals and social standards. The OCC model has been employed more effectively to reason about emotions in text (Li et al., 2007), since Ortony et al. (1990) based the rationale of their theory on a specific case of study of experiences registered in personal diaries. Existing student models that reason at a cognitive level about observable behaviour, motivation (Arroyo and Woolf, 2005; Del Soldato and Du Boulay, 1995; Rebolledo-Mendez et al., 2006) and self-efficacy (McQuiggan et al., 2008) have proved the most effective.

A hybrid approach reasons about the variables that determine an emotional state at a cognitive level and employs analysis and classification of interaction data to ensure that the emotion inferred has occurred (Conati and Maclaren, 2009). This approach inherits the challenges of previous approaches.

Recently in the field of cognitive psychology and emotion in education, emotion has proven to be interrelated with motivational and cognitive factors (Pekrun et al., 2007). In the context of achievement, where activities are performed in the light of their possible outcomes, students experience *achievement emotions*, which are mainly determined by control and value appraisals. This is known as the Control-Value Theory of achievement emotions (Pekrun et al., 2007). Control is related to students' beliefs about being capable of initiating and performing an activity, whilst value is related to the attainment of success and the prevention of failure. At present there is no computational and emotional student model based on this theory.

13.2.4 Affective Evaluation of Game-Based Learning Environments

The evaluation of affective applications focuses on two key goals: (1) knowing whether the emotion demonstrated by the computer application was genuine, i.e. naturally expressed (Höök, 2005) or (2) ensuring that the emotion experienced by the student was accurately identified (Conati and Maclaren, 2009; Conati, 2002). Context and cultural differences have to be considered when attempting to achieve effective emotion modelling employing EPAs or synthetic characters. The aims are to understand how end users react to applications that show emotion or affect and to achieve design that ensures effectiveness and facilitates the application's acceptance. Methods employed to evaluate these systems are quantitative-scientific and open-ended interpretation (Höök, 2005). Quantitative-scientific methods encounter difficulty trying to capture a more detailed view of end-users' interaction experience.

Open-ended interpretation offers results that are temporary and culturally dependent. However, it provides results that are user-specific instead of results that can be generalised to a particular population.

Höök (2005) proposes an evaluation method at two different levels of interpretation about cases where the system was unsuccessful at attempting to communicate its intention. The first level is related to knowing if the student understands the expressed emotion, and the second level is about determining if the system can understand students' emotions accurately. The most frequent problems experienced in the design and implementation of these kinds of emotional applications are synchronization, contextualisation, users' interaction control, timing and realism. The latter is related to users' beliefs and expectations about the response that avatars which look like humans should be capable of offering.

Wizard-Of-Oz is a method employed to design and evaluate emotional applications and involves making users believe that they are interacting with the computational system when they are actually interacting with a human (Andersson et al., 2002) . Its main advantage is that the possible answers to users' interactions are unlimited.

On the other hand, focusing on the problem of evaluating the accuracy of an emotional system recognising or reasoning about emotions, research has included interfaces to register students' self reports at anytime or to interrogate students about their emotional state over time (Conati, 2002). Statistical methods are then employed to search for a significant correlation between the interaction data and the reported emotion. This method may be perceived as intrusive. Another method employed is to use expert judges for observing, annotating and reviewing interaction videos or other type of material. The judges determine the emotions experienced over time by users (D'Mello et al., 2008). As was stated earlier, an expert human can recognise emotion with approximately 70% accuracy, which represents a limitation for this approach.

In the next section we focus on describing in detail our proposed emotional student model taking the reviewed state of the art into account, the research methodology involved and the affective enhancements proposed for the Olympia architecture. Olympia (Muñoz et al., 2009) combines ITSs and game-based learning environments. It is applied to the specific case study of teaching Physics at undergraduate level, since a key challenge is to encourage learning to assist students understand the underlying theory.

13.3 Formalisation of Emotional Student Model

Our aim is to create an emotional student model capable of reasoning about students' emotions using answers to questions posed during game dialogues, observable interaction data and Control-Value Theory. Once the model is defined, it has to be evaluated. Accordingly, we created a research methodology, which uses students' self-reports and Multinomial Logistic Regression. The latter was chosen since control and value appraisals are categorical variables. In addition, Olympia was enhanced by incorporating this emotional student model and a motivational modulator, which comprises affective and motivational strategies.

Achievement emotions are dependent on the teaching domain, since the factors that determine an emotion also depend on it (Pekrun et al., 2007). As an example, a student learning History experiences different types of *achievement emotions* than a student who is learning Physics. In addition, types of *achievement emotions* are defined according to the focus and time frame. For example, when the student is focused on the future outcome of an activity or task, the student may experience *outcome-prospective* emotions, such as anxiety and hope. On the other hand, if the student is focused on the activity at present, the student may experience *activity* emotions, such as enjoyment and frustration. Finally, according to this theory the student may be focused on the latest outcome after performing a task or activity. Hence, the student might experience *outcome-retrospective* emotions, such as shame or pride. It is important to signal that if an appraisal of control or value is lacking, it is assumed that an achievement emotion is not present. Pekrun et al. (2007) created the Achievement Emotions Questionnaire (AEQ) (Pekrun et al., 2005) through Structural Equation Modelling (SEM) to determine through students' self-report whether *achievement emotions*, were present in classroom instruction, independent learning or tests.

Emotional student modelling involves handling the uncertainty of the emotional domain, in order to reason about the possible causes of emotions and infer whether emotions are present or not (Woolf, 2009). Dynamic Bayesian Networks (DBNs) are an AI technique used to model dependencies when prior domain knowledge is available (Jensen and Nielsen, 2007). Random variables comprise the nodes of each DBN. They are two steps involved in creating a DBN: (1) defining the causal dependencies, i.e. structure and (2) defining the probabilities on the Conditional Probability Tables (CPTs). To facilitate the derivation of DBNs structure, Probabilistic Relational Models (PRMs) are employed (Sucar and Noguez, 2008), the key advantage of which is to enable the handling of information and random variables simultaneously. PRMs are an object oriented representation of the domain.

Using these ideas as a basis, first we focused on creating a general PRM of control-value theory, which is shown in Fig. 13.1. This PRM schema was then used to derive three specific PRMs, each one corresponding to one of the types of *achievement emotions* defined by Pekrun et al. (2007). Control-value theory is a framework that uses motivational, cognitive, physiological and affective factors to ensure that students experience an *achievement emotion*. The PRMs corresponding to the *outcome-prospective*, *activity* and *outcome-retrospective* emotions are shown in Figs. 13.2, 13.3 and 13.4 respectively. It is important to note that the random variables used are not always available and come from different sources. The random variables for the *outcome-prospective* emotions (Fig. 13.2) were selected from the AEQ, e.g. attitude beliefs towards Physics and confidence towards the possible level of performance. For this time frame, the variables involved comprise students' beliefs and expectations. Therefore, to enquire about these, we created questions that were incorporated into the game dialogue.

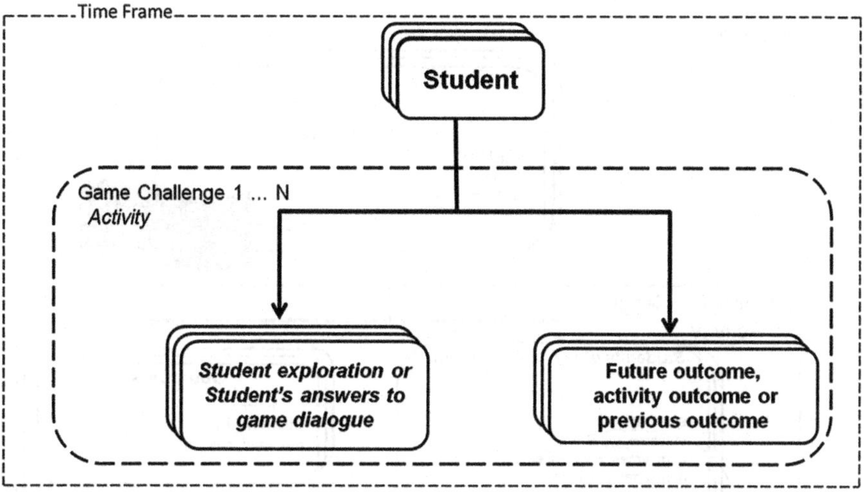

Fig. 13.1 General PRM of control-value theory

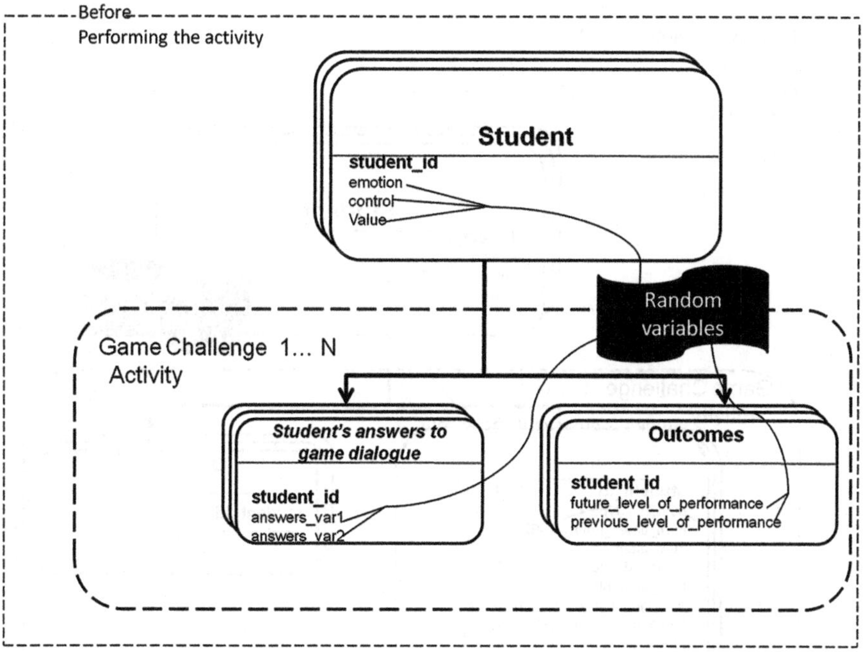

Fig. 13.2 Outcome-prospective emotions PRM

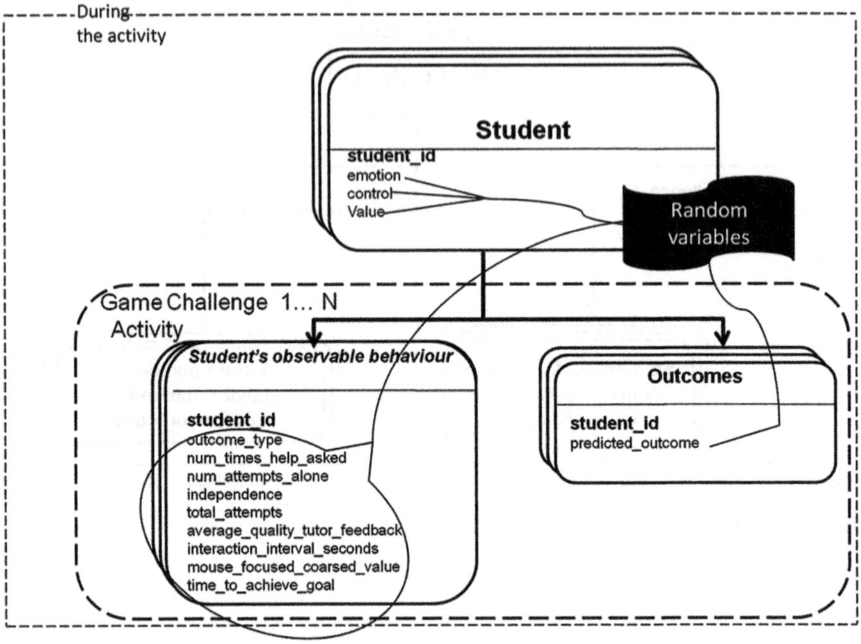

Fig. 13.3 Activity emotions PRM

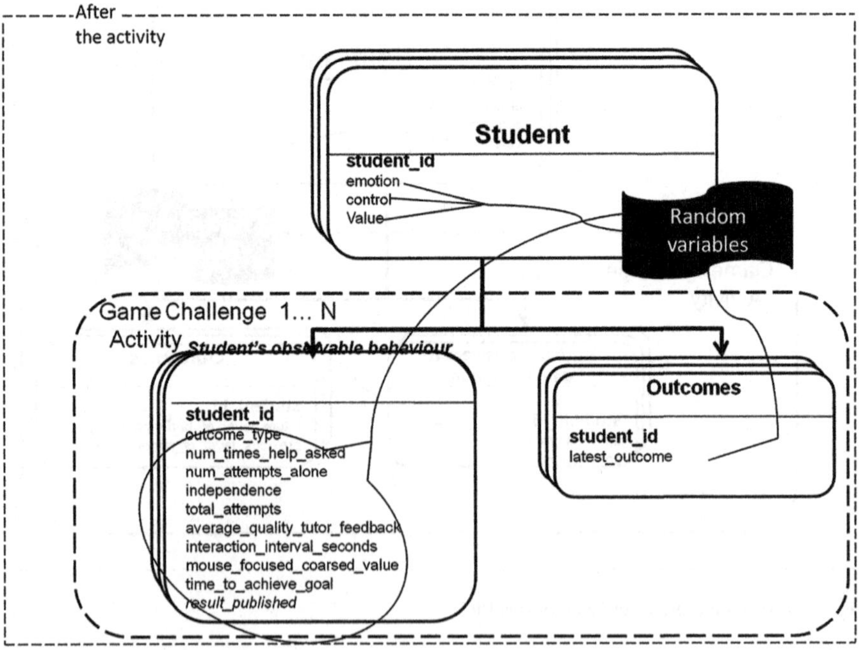

Fig. 13.4 Outcome-retrospective emotions PRM

To select the interaction random variables that we assume related to students' control and value appraisals during or after the student interaction with the game challenge, we considered the observable variables employed by models of motivation (Del Soldato and Du Boulay, 1995) and self-efficacy (McQuiggan et al., 2008) that have proven effective and that are highly related to the factors incorporated into the AEQ and the type of game challenges that we want to implement. For the *activity* emotions (Fig. 13.3), we selected the following random variables:

- Type of outcome, i.e. *outcome_type*, corresponds to the end condition of the challenge. It represents the kind of domain misconception identified. As an example, if the student sets the acceleration with a positive direction in order to stop, it is noted that the student may not understand that acceleration is a vector quantity, and fail as a result.
- Outcome, i.e. *predicted outcome* or *latest_outcome*, is the quantitative percentage of completion of the task. A percentage below 70% indicates a failed mission.
- Number of times that the student asked for help, i.e. *num_times_help_asked*, is related to the number of times the student requested a hint or consulted the learning assistant.
- Number of attempts that the student takes to solve the challenge alone, without the learning companion's help, i.e. *num_attempts_alone.*
- Independence is calculated by comparing the number of times the student asked for help and the number of times the student tries to solve the challenge alone. At the beginning it is zero, which does not provide any information about the student's level of independence. If the student asks for a hint, the level of independence is decremented by one. However, if the student tries to solve the challenge alone a one is added to the student's level of independence per attempt. Therefore, a positive index above zero is an indicator of an independent student, while a negative index indicates that the student's independence is lacking.
- Total attempts, i.e. *total_attempts*, is the total number of attempts by the student with or without the learning companion's help.
- Average quality of tutoring feedback, i.e. *average_quality_tutor_feedback*, is related to students' perception about the effectiveness of the hints provided to achieve the learning goals during a session by the learning companion. A session begins when the student starts to interact with the game and finishes when the student ends his or her interaction. The student evaluates the hints provided and classifies them into one of three possible categories of helpfulness: (1) low, (2) medium and (3) high.
- Interval of interaction, i.e. *interaction_interval_seconds*, is the total time that the student has interacted during a session.
- Students' focus level, i.e. *mouse_focused_coarsed_value*, is an average value corresponding to the position of the mouse on the screen while the student is interacting with the game during a session. The position of the mouse was selected, since users usually move the mouse where their sight is located.
- Time to achieve the learning goal, i.e. *time_to_achieve_goal*, is the time that the student has taken to achieve the learning goal for the first time.

For the *outcome-retrospective* emotions (Fig. 13.4), we employed the same random variables selected for the *activity emotions* (Fig. 13.3) and we added the random variable related to the student's decision to publish the achieved result, i.e. *result published*, which allows all the students to view each other's progress. At the end of each challenge a list with the ten best scores is displayed to give the students the possibility of competing for the best result.

From PRMs in Figs. 13.2, 13.3, and 13.4, three DBNs were derived employing random variables. The *outcome-prospective* emotions DBN derived from the PRM in Fig. 13.2, is shown in Fig. 13.5. As a first approach, it is assumed that all these variables are related to appraisals of control and value. However, we need to know which variables are actually relevant when identifying category membership. Multinomial Logistic Regression is employed for this purpose, since control and value appraisals are qualitative regressors, i.e. categorical variables. This approach does not hold assumptions of multivariate normality or homogeneity of variance-covariance matrices (Kinnear and Colin, 2010). As an example of the possible categories, Table 13.1 shows the corresponding appraisals of control and value for the *activity emotions* according to control-value theory. Once the interaction data is analysed through Multinomial Logistic Regression and we change the structure of the DBN according to these results, we can employ probabilistic methods based on the data of our population to calculate the probabilities on the CPTs.

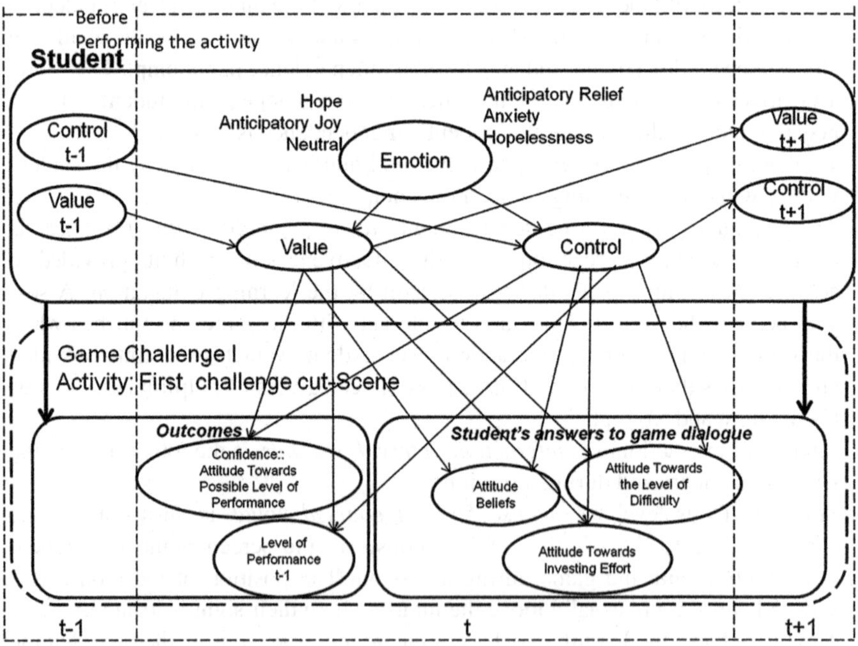

Fig. 13.5 Outcome-prospective emotions DBN

Table 13.1 Control and value appraisals for *activity* emotions by Pekrun et al. (2007)

Focus/time frame	Value appraisal	Control appraisal	Emotion
Activity/present	Positive	High	Enjoyment
	Negative	High	Anger
	Positive/negative	Low	Frustration
	None	High/low	Boredom

The interface of the game-based learning environment is designed to enable students to report their emotional state at any time. Hence, the emotional student model is validated by comparing the number of cases that were accurately classified against the number of cases, where the reported emotion was not correctly identified.

13.3.1 Olympia Architecture

The Olympia architecture combines game-based learning environments and ITSs (Muñoz et al., 2009). It has previously been applied to the specific case study of teaching Physics at undergraduate level, since we noted that undergraduate students usually find it difficult to understand underlying principles of Physics. Here, Olympia (Fig. 13.6) has been modified to reason about students' emotions and to

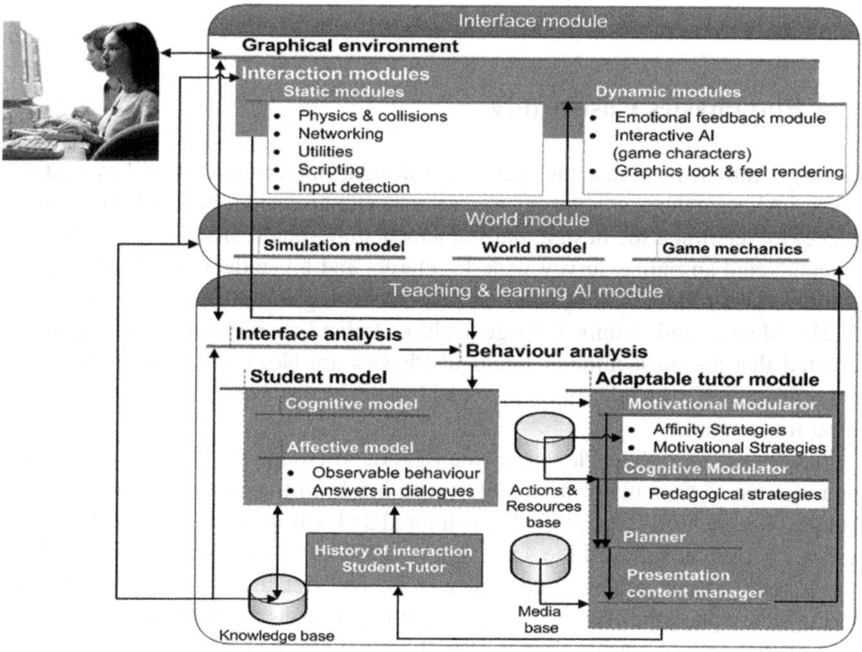

Fig. 13.6 Olympia architecture comprising emotional aspects

show emotion. It comprises an *affective student model* and a *motivational modulator*. The former uses observable behaviour and answers to questions during game dialogues. The latter is comprised of a learning companion, which is focused on mirroring students' behaviour, encouraging the student over animated expressions and offering help. As stated earlier, it is still not clear what the emotional response to students' emotions should be.

Olympia is a semi-open environment (Bunt and Conati, 2003), where the student explores the game guided by the achievement of specific learning goals or outcomes. The interface analysis module filters the events that provide information about students' cognitive and motivational states. The selected events are sent to the behaviour analysis module to be appraised. The evidence is forwarded to the student model, where cognitive and motivational needs are identified. The results are communicated to the tutor model. The planner of the tutor module selects a suitable response. Cognitive and motivational modulators choose the media and information to communicate the message. The presentation content manager modifies the game-mechanics, i.e. action-challenge relation, and the world model, which is related to the dynamic modules. The dynamic modules are adapted according to the message that is to be communicated and may comprise music, colours and game characters.

Olympia, extended with the described emotional enhancements and our formalised emotional student model, was applied to the specific case study of *PlayPhysics*, an emotional game-based learning environment for teaching Physics at undergraduate level. The next section is focused on *PlayPhysics*' design and implementation.

13.4 PlayPhysics Case Study

As stated earlier, involving the user in the design, implementation and evaluation loop is important when attempting to achieve an effective and functional application. Hence, to determine the design and implementation requirements of *PlayPhysics*, we conducted an online survey with 4 lecturers and 53 students at undergraduate level in an introductory Physics course at Tecnológico de Monterrey (ITESM-CCM), Mexico and Trinity College Dublin, Ireland. It was noted that students reported that the most difficult topics of Physics are Newton's laws for particles and rigid bodies, principles of circular and linear kinematics, vectors, collisions and linear momentum.

PlayPhysics is a Role Playing Game (RPG), where the student is an astronaut on a mission to save his or her mentor, who has been trapped on a space station, Athena. The mentor, Captain Foster, is injured and was unable to escape when the rest of his crew abandoned the space station, after the station's computer, VNUS, was attacked as the result of a computer virus. The first level of the game is about docking the spaceship, Alpha Centauri, with Athena using the student's knowledge of Physics. To ensure alignment with curriculum requirements, an expert in Astrophysics assisted us in modelling the domain knowledge, the marking scheme and the pedagogical feedback of *PlayPhysics*. *PlayPhysics* was implemented using Java, the Unity Game Engine, 3D Studio Max and Hugin Lite.

To ascertain students' expectations and beliefs involved in determining if the student experiences an *outcome-prospective* emotion, we enquire about them during the game dialogue. Figure 13.7 shows a fragment of the game dialogue enquiring about the student's self-efficacy expectancy. This game dialogue introduces the first level and the mission. To accomplish the first level the student has to perform four challenges: (1) after being launched from Earth, Alpha Centauri acquires a relative velocity with respect to Athena and the lieutenant has to activate its front engines to stop at some distance from the station on its rotational axis, (2) the student has to use upper and lower engine trust to align the Alpha Centauri's longitudinal axis with the station's longitudinal axis, (3) the student has to achieve the same frame of inertia of Athena station by activating Alpha Centauri's lateral engines, i.e. achieving the same rotational velocity, and finally, (4) the student has to enter to the docking bay, where the Alpha Centauri has to acquire a very slow movement around its rotational axis.

Focusing only on the first challenge, the spaceship, Alpha Centauri, is initially travelling at speed v_i at a Distance D from Athena and moving towards it along a linear path, see Fig. 13.8. The restriction variables set randomly by *PlayPhysics*, are the distance D and the maximum limit Time, T, to not exhaust the spaceship fuel. The ranges are: $D \in [15, 70]$ km and $T \in [180, 120]$ s.

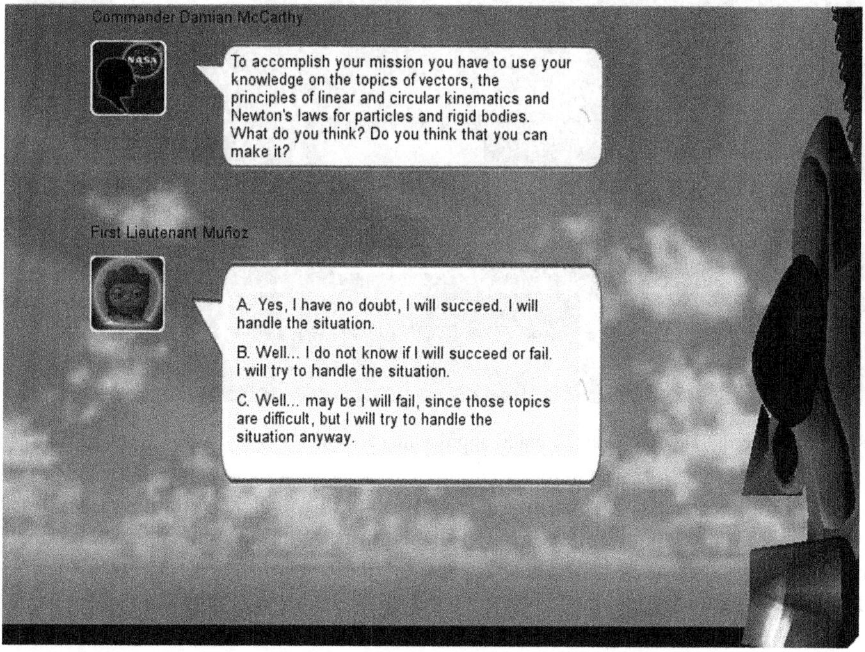

Fig. 13.7 *PlayPhysics* game dialogue enquiring about students' self-efficacy

Fig. 13.8 External view of Alpha Centauri approaching lineally Athena station

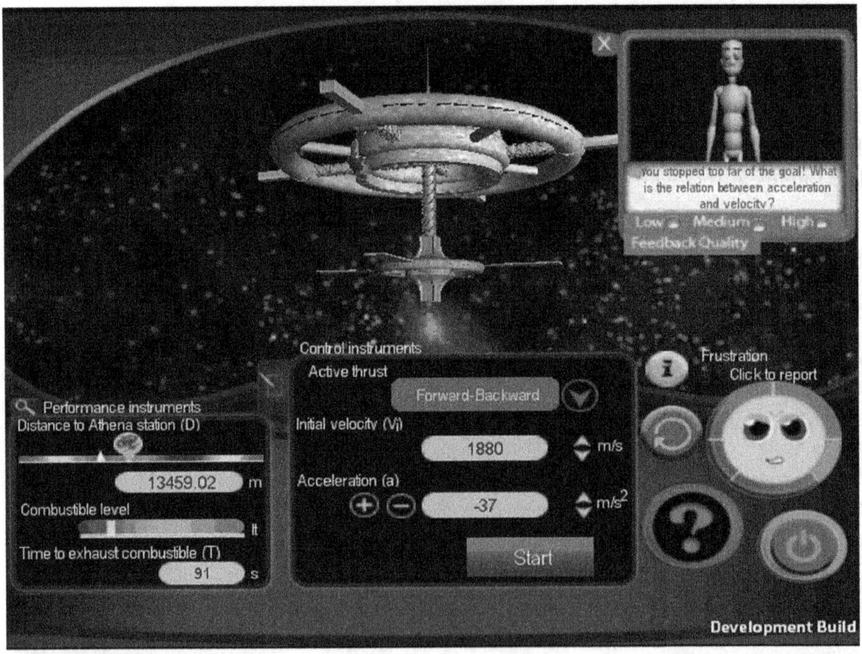

Fig. 13.9 Internal view of Alpha Centauri approaching Athena

To complete this first goal, the user is prompted to select suitable values for: (i) the direction of the acceleration, (ii) its magnitude, and (iii) the spaceship's initial speed, v_i (see Fig. 13.9). These are the exploration variables for this scenario. The possible choices for the direction of the acceleration are towards or away from Athena's position. The available range values for the spaceship's acceleration and initial speed, which the student has to choose from, are respectively: $a \in [0,100]$ m/s^2 and $v_i = [1000, 2000]$ m/s.

Note that, first of all, the student should choose the acceleration direction away from Athena, in other words, the opposite direction to Alpha Centauri's initial velocity, in order that the Alpha Centauri decelerates and stops just below Athena's rotational axis. If the student chooses the acceleration towards Athena, which is in the same direction of the Alpha Centauri's velocity, the spaceship will accelerate forever and so will never stop and hence it will be lost in space.

Once the student chooses the correct deceleration direction, he or she has to select the appropriate values for a and v_i, from the given value ranges, which make the Alpha Centauri decelerate and stop just below Athena's rotational axis. The student has to realise that the Alpha Centauri's motion has to be rectilinear with constant deceleration. To calculate both, the distance travelled by the Alpha Centauri, d, and the required time to stop, t, Equations (13.1) and (13.2) are applied.

$$\text{From kinematics we know that } d = \frac{v_i^2}{2a} \tag{13.1}$$

$$\text{and } t = \frac{v_i}{a} \tag{13.2}$$

Additionally, there are some constraints that should be taken into account:

- The acceleration magnitude, a, should not be greater than 40 m/s^2. This value is nearly four times the gravity acceleration on Earth's surface, i.e. approximately $4g$. Otherwise, the student feels sick, dizzy and blacks out. When this occurs and the student asks for a hint. *PlayPhysics*' learning companion, *M8* robot, tells the student what the error is, enabling the student to select a smaller value than this limit.
- The calculated distance d has to closely match the distance, D, which is randomly assigned within a predefined range by PlayPhysics. From the selected values for a and v_i. *PlayPhysics* calculates d using Equation (13.1) and compares it with the value of D. PlayPhysics also calculates the relative error of the distance, which is defined by:

$$e_d = \frac{|d - D|}{D} \tag{13.3}$$

We assume that the maximum allowed relative error is 0.10, or 10%. If the error is equal to or less than 2%, the student achieves the best performance. When the relative error e_d is less than or equal to 0.10, we assume that the spaceship did stop at the right position just below Athena. Otherwise, the distance travelled by the spaceship was too short ($d<D$) or too far ($d>D$) from Athena's rotational axis. In this case, the *M8* robot explains to the student the error, if the student asks for a hint after committing this mistake. The relative error can be modified, if the lecturer wishes to make it more challenging.

- The required time to stop Athena, t, should not exceed the allowed time T for this mission. From the selected values for a and v_i, *PlayPhysics* calculates t according to Equation (13.2) and compares it with the value for T, which is generated randomly. If $t > T$, the *M8* robot explains to the student that the fuel was exhausted so has to start the challenge again.

In order to succeed at this first challenge, the three constraints previously discussed must be satisfied. If the student succeeds he or she is congratulated (see Fig. 13.10) and allowed to continue with the next stage and choose to publish their score, making it available for viewing by other students.

The values corresponding to the restricted variables D and T, and the interaction variables, a and v_i, were selected so that the problem solution is non-trivial. The difficulty level of the problem depends on the initial values set for T and D. If T and D are large quantities, there is a wider range of values to choose for both a and v_i, so that a and t do not exceed their limit values ($a < 40$ m/s^2 and $t < T$). On the other hand, if T or/and D are small quantities, the range of values that can be chosen for the values a and t is smaller. Therefore, there is a larger probability of exceeding the respective limits of these variables. As an example, if *PlayPhysics* initialises $D = 60$ km and $T = 90$ s, a successful selection of values may be $a = -25$ m/s^2 and $v_i = 1732$ m/s. As a result, $a < 40$ m/s^2, 1000 m/s $< v_i < 2000$ m/s and $t = 69.3$ s $< T$. Finally, it is important to mention that for a successful set of selected values

Fig. 13.10 *M8* robot congratulating the student for the level of performance achieved

corresponding to the interaction or exploration variables, a and v_i, *PlayPhysics* assigns a grade depending on the resultant t value. The student is assigned higher grades for lower t values and lower grades if it is close to the T limit. There is still fuel remaining for future motions if low t values are achieved. Therefore, if the t value achieved is closer to T, it is inferred that the available fuel has been exhausted.

During the interaction with the game challenge, the student's emotion can be reported at anytime, using the *EmoReport* wheel. In addition, the emotion relating to the outcome at the end of the challenge is always enquired, whether the challenge finishes due to an error or misunderstanding or due a successful end. *M8* provides an emotional response every time the student reports his or her emotional state. For example, if the student reports that he or she is frustrated, *M8* smiles, offers help and reminds the student that they can ask for a hint.

13.5 Results and Evaluation

PlayPhysics' first challenge and emotional student model, specifically the *outcome-prospective* emotions DBN, were evaluated through a test with students of Engineering at ITESM-CCM. The evaluation was conducted as follows: first, we asked students to solve an online pre-test, making them aware of their actual knowledge of the topics taught by *PlayPhysics*. Then students started their interaction with *PlayPhysics*' first dialogue and reported their emotional state before performing PlayPhysics' first challenge. While performing the first challenge, students could report their emotion anytime, and the *M8* robot would remind them to do so periodically. Every time that the outcome percentage was displayed to the student, the student reported their emotion towards the outcome achieved.

In previous research (Muñoz et al., 2011), the *outcome-prospective* emotions DBN was designed, calibrated and evaluated to the point of achieving 70% accuracy. We noted that *confidence towards the possible level of performance* and the *attitude beliefs towards Physics* were the relevant random variables for the prediction of category membership of control and value appraisals. Here, we assessed again the accuracy of classification of this DBN with the data obtained from 79 students (54 men and 25 women) aged 18–23, when they interacted with PlayPhysics' game dialogue. Results are shown Fig. 13.11. Table 13.2 shows the contingency table corresponding to these results. Negative and neutral emotions were again classified with more accuracy than positive ones (77.42%). However, positive emotions were reported more frequently.

These results validated our previous findings. The final outcome-prospective emotions DBN is shown in Fig. 13.12. To determine the significance of our findings and their generalisation to this specific population of students, we employed a Binomial test or Bernoulli trials, since our population and amount of data collected is small and Chi-square test (χ^2) can be effectively applied on and interpreted using large populations and quantities of data.

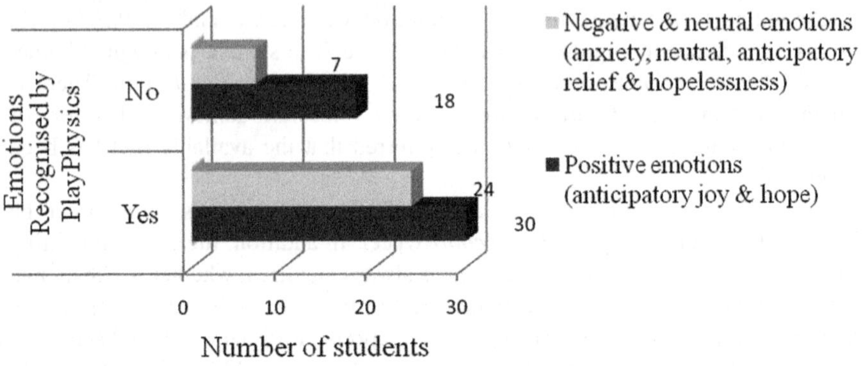

Fig. 13.11 Reported emotion vs. inferred emotion for the outcome-prospective emotions DBN

Table 13.2 Contingency table corresponding to outcome-prospective emotions DBN

	Recognised			
Emotion set	yes	No	Total	%Classification
Positive emotions (anticipatory joy and hope)	30	18	48	62.5
Negative and neutral emotions (anxiety, anticipatory relief, hopelessness and neutral)	24	7	31	77.42

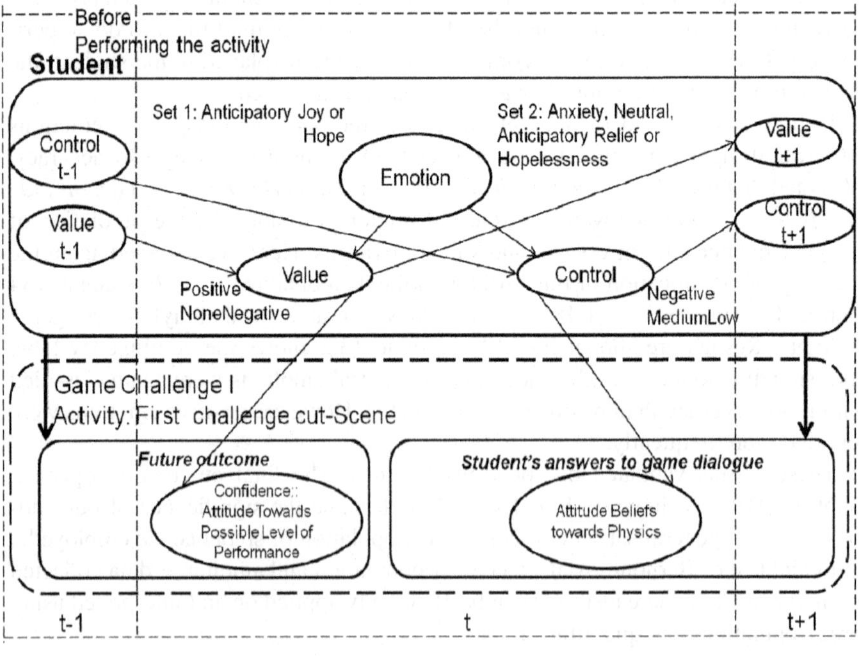

Fig. 13.12 Final outcome-prospective emotions DBN

The Binomial test is a non parametric test that it is employed in experiments that have the following characteristics: (1) there is a fixed number of indistinguishable experiments or trials, (2) the outcome of each experiment can be divided into two dichotomous categories, e.g. *success* or *failure*, (3) the experiments' outcomes are independent and (4) the probability of a successful outcome is the same in all experiments. The binomial probability model enables us to set a probability to a specific number of observations related to the happening of an event over n Bernoulli trials (Kinnear and Colin, 2010). To ensure that the statistical test has the sufficient power to reject the null hypothesis we employ the *statistic* g, an index of effect size, which states the difference between two populations. The *statistic* g, Equation (13.4), is the difference of the proportion of the outcomes in the category (P) and the probability of an outcome supporting the null hypothesis (p).

$$g = |P - p| \tag{13.4}$$

The first step for applying Binomial test is to define the null and alternative hypotheses. In our case, we want to validate that the accuracy of classification of our emotional model, e.g. *outcome-prospective emotions* DBN, is at least of 70%, which corresponds to a probability of 0.7. From Table 13.2, we can signal that 31 cases correspond to negative and neutral emotions reported by students. If our emotional student model has an accuracy of 50%, it is not considered an accurate classifier. Hence, the null and alternative hypotheses are defined as follows:

H_0. p = 0.5
H_A. p $\neq$ 0.5 (At least 0.7)

The observed probability (p), corresponding to the accurate classification of 24 cases of negative or neutral emotions, was calculated as P = 0.77[1]. Accordingly, the probability of classifying 7 cases incorrectly is p = 0.23. The p-value is 0.003. To know the effect size, we calculated the *statistic* g, $g = 0.27$. Using these results, we can reject the null hypothesis and affirm that our emotional student model identifies the emotions in the negative and neutral set, with an accuracy equal to or above 70%. In addition, the effect size of this test is *large*.

If we conduct the same analysis for the total number of cases correctly classified in the positive and negative-neutral sets, which corresponds to 54 cases out of 79, (see Table 13.2), we achieved an observed probability of $0.68 \approx 0.7$ and a p-value of .001. The *statistic* g was also calculated for this case, $g = 0.18$. Using these results, we can conclude that there is sufficient evidence to reject the null hypothesis (H_0) and the statistical analysis shows the model permits an accurate inference in c.70 of all cases. Also, the value of the *statistic* g suggests a *medium* effect size.

From the interaction with the first challenge, we obtained a log of interaction with 1640 entries corresponding to 79 students. 1321 entries corresponded to the time during which the student was interacting with *PlayPhysics*' first challenge and

[1] SPSS (Statistical Package for the Social Sciences) was employed to conduct statistical analysis.

319 entries correspond to the number of times that the student was presented with the final outcome. We analysed this data in two ways: (1) obtaining the descriptive statistics of our data, e.g. frequencies, minimum value, maximum value, mean and standard deviation, and (2) analysing the data using Multinomial Logistic Regression using SPSS to understand which variables are the most relevant for inferring students' control and value appraisals towards the challenge and its outcome. As part of this analysis, we observed that emotions were reported as follows: *neutral* emotion was reported 990 times (74.9% of our population), *enjoyment* was reported 155 times (11.7% of our population), *boredom* was reported 89 times (6.7%) and *anger* and *frustration* were reported 42 (3.2%) and 45 (3.4%) times respectively. We also analysed lecturers and students' comments to improve *PlayPhysics*' first challenge and user interaction.

13.6 Comparison with Related Work

Computational models of self-efficacy, which employ students' observable behaviour, e.g. time in current location and progression, have attained 70% accuracy (McQuiggan et al., 2008). This accuracy increases by 10% when using physiological data, e.g. average heart rate and galvanic skin response. On the other hand, computational models of motivation have also proved effective when using students' observable behaviour, e.g. times that the student asked help and time invested (Del Soldato and Du Boulay, 1995; Rebolledo-Mendez et al., 2006). Control-value theory is a framework of assumptions corresponding to other emotional theories. It employs cognitive, motivational, physiological and affective factors to determine the presence of an achievement emotion (Pekrun et al., 2007). It is assumed that these factors are related to control and value appraisals. The AEQ has been employed effectively to assess students' emotions in Physics, Mathematics, German and English language domains (Goetz et al., 2007). Results showed that similar emotions are experienced in comparable domains, e.g. Mathematics and Physics. The AEQ was validated conducting tests with 389 students of Psychology.

Some of the motivational and cognitive factors employed in the control-value theory are comprised in the computational models of self-efficacy (McQuiggan et al., 2008) and motivation (Del Soldato and Du Boulay, 1995). Therefore, we decided to employ these two models as a basis for our model. Our results show promise, since negative and neutral emotions are classified with accuracy above 70%, which is comparable to the accuracy obtained by McQuiggan et al. (2008). In addition, it is interesting to observe that positive emotions are more frequently reported than negative ones, 48 times out of 79. Statistically, using Binomial test, our model, specifically the *outcome-prospective* emotions DBN, proved that our findings can be generalised to this population of students.

In addition, it was observed that students reported that they experienced neutral emotions more frequently (74.9% of the cases), which is not very different from the results obtained by Alexander and Sarrafzadeh (2008) when they were observing one-to-one human tutoring while teaching Mathematics. They noted that students and lecturers showed a neutral face expression 86% of the time. This may also be due to social and cultural standards and personal preferences, which may bias the study. It was observed that incorporating physiological signals in our model may assist us in reducing this uncertainty. However, if the student does not want to reveal the emotion that he or she is feeling, it is not useful, since physiological data cannot be taken as evidence of emotion and students' self report is still needed. Pekrun et al. (2007) focuses specifically on heart rate. However, Pekrun et al. (2007) only asked students about their physiological sensations, e.g. whether they feel their heart beating very quickly, or whether they feel any stomach pain. Research in physiology and computing has shown more promise when using galvanic skin response signals, and studies demonstrate that these are more sensitive to emotion changes (Rajae-Joordens, 2008). This research is based on findings that suggest that skin conductance changes according to the emotions and thoughts that we are experiencing.

13.7 Conclusion and Future Work

We described the main challenges faced when designing and implementing an emotional-game based learning environment for teaching Physics, i.e. one that recognises and shows emotion. We focused mainly on two aspects: (1) creating an emotional student model using observable behaviour and questions posed during game dialogue, and (2) designing and implementing *PlayPhysics*, an emotional game-based learning environment for teaching Physics. Our model uses Control-Value Theory as a basis and a research methodology comprising the creation of PRMs to facilitate the derivation of DBNs to handle the uncertainty of the emotional domain. PlayPhysics' challenges, pedagogical feedback and marking scheme were designed with the help of an Astrophysics domain expert. The calibration and structure of the *outcome-prospective* emotions DBN was validated through testing with 79 students of Engineering at ITESM-CCM. Results showed that negative and neutral emotions are classified with above 70% accuracy, which is comparable to the accuracy of a human expert. Neutral emotions are the most frequently reported, though this may be due to social and cultural standards or personal preferences. Future work will focus on analysing the interaction data of PlayPhysics' first challenge to complete and validate the design corresponding to the *outcome-retrospective* and *activity* emotions DBNs. Additionally, students' and lecturers' comments will be taken into account in order to improve *PlayPhysics*' user interaction. Finally, other challenges will be incorporated into *PlayPhysics*' first level and the incorporation of physiological signals to enhance the accuracy of our model will be assessed.

Acknowledgments We would like to convey our thanks to the anonymous reviewers of this paper and the editors of this book, Dr. Eunice Ma, Dr. Andreas Oikonomou and Prof. Lakhmi Jain. We thank the University of Ulster for its support with a Vice Chancellor's Research Studentship (VCRS) and acknowledge recommendations from Prof. Mark Shevlin from the Psychology Research Institute and Dr. Girijesh Prasad and Dr. Abdul Satti from the Intelligent Systems

Research Centre. Also, we would like to thank Dr. Deaglan Page and Dr. Donncha Hanna from the School of Psychology, Queen's University Belfast for their advice in statistical methods. We recognise the technical support provided during the design, implementation and deployment of PlayPhysics by Dennis Heaney from Beep Blip Games and Gabriel Deak from the Intelligent Systems Research Centre. Additionally, we would like to express our gratitude to Richard Walsh from ZooCreative for modelling the player characters in PlayPhysics. We want to thank Peter Starostin for creating *LowMax*, the free rig for 3D Studio Max, which was adapted to be the learning companion *M8* in PlayPhysics. Finally, we wish to acknowledge the assistance of the members of the E-learning Research Group at Tecnológico de Monterrey, Mexico City campus (ITESM-CCM), Víctor Robledo, Dr. Moises Alancastre, Dr. Lourdes Muñoz, M.Sc. Gerardo Aguilar, Gilberto Huesca and Benjamín Hernández in the evaluation of PlayPhysics.

References

Akilli, G.K., Cagiltay, K.: An instructional design/development model for the creation of game-like learning environments: the FIDGE model. In: Pivec, M. (ed.) Affective and Emotional Aspects of Human-Computer Interaction, pp. 93–111. IOS Press, Netherlands, Amsterdam (2006)

Alexander, S., Sarrafzadeh, A.: Foundation of an affective tutoring system: learning how human tutors adapt to student emotion. Int. J. Intell. Syst. Technol. Appl. **4**(3/4), 355–367 (2008)

Alvarez, J.: Du Jeu Vidéo au Serious Game: Approches culturelle, pragmatique et formelle. Université Toulouse, Toulouse, France (2007)

Andersson, G., Höök, K., Mourão, D., Paiva, A., Costa, M.: Using a wizard of Oz study to inform the design of SenToy. In: Proceedings of the 4th International Conference on Designing Interactive Systems (DIS-02): Processes, Practices, Methods and Techniques, London, ACM Press, New York, pp. 349–355, 25–28 June 2002

Arroyo, I., Woolf, B.P.: Inferring learning and attitudes from a Bayesian network of log file data. In: Looi, C.K., McCalla, G., Bredeweg, B., Breuker, J. (eds.) Proceedings of the 12th International Conference on Artificial Intelligence in Education, Frontiers in Artificial Intelligence and Applications, Vol. 125, pp. 33–40. IOS Press, Amsterdam (2005)

Blanchard, E., Frasson, C.: Easy creation of game-like virtual learning environments. In: Workshop on Teaching with Agents, Robots, and NLP International Conference on Intelligent Tutoring System (ITS). Jhongli, Taiwan, June 26–30 (2006)

Bunt, A., Conati, C.: Probabilistic student modeling to improve exploratory behavior. User Model. User-Adapted Interact. **13**(3), 269–309 (2003)

Burleson, W., Picard, R.W.: Evidence for gender specific approaches to the development of emotionally intelligent learning companions. IEEE Intell. Syst. **22**(4), 62–69 (2007)

Cela, K.: Web 2.0, Estilos de Aprendizaje y sus Implicaciones en la Educación. Université de Poitiers & Universidad Nacional de Educación a Distancia de Madrid, Poitiers, France & Madrid, Spain (2008)

Clancey, G.L., Buchanan, B.: Exploration of Teaching and Problem Solving Strategies '1979–1982'. Stanford University, Stanford, CA (1982)

Conati, C.: Probabilistic assessment of user's emotions in educational games. Appl. Artif. Intell. **16**, 555–575 (2002)

Conati, C., Maclaren, H.: Empirically building and evaluating a probabilistic model of user affect. User Model. User-Adapted Interact. **19**(3), 267–303 (2009)

Del Soldato, T., Du Boulay, B.: Implementation of motivational tactics in tutoring systems. J. Artif. Intell. Educ. **6**(4), 337–378 (1995)

Dias, J., Paiva, A., Vala, M., Aylett, R., Woods, S., Zoll, C., Hall, L.: Empathic characters in computer-based personal and social education. In: Pivec, M. (ed.) Affective and Emotional Aspects of Human-Computer Interaction, pp. 246–254. IOS Press, Netherlands, Amsterdam (2006)

D'Mello, S.K., Craig, S.D., Witherspoon, A., McDaniel, B.T., Graesser, A.C.: Automatic detection of learner's affect from conversational cues. User Model. User-Adapted Interact. **8**(1–2), 45–80 (2008)

Du Boulay, B., Luckin, R.: Modelling human teaching tactics and strategies for tutoring systems. Int. J. Artif. Intell. Educ. **12**, 235–256 (2001)

Goetz, T., Frenzel, A.C., Pekrun, R., Hall, N.C., Lüdtke, O.: Between- and within- domain relations of student's academic emotions. Educ. Psychol. **99**(4), 715–733 (2007)

Höök, K.: User-centred design and evaluation of affective interfaces. In: Ruttkoy, Z., Pelachaud, C. (eds.) From Brows to Trust: Evaluating Embodied Conversational Agents, Vol. 7, pp. 127–160. Springer, Netherlands (2005)

Jaques, P.A., Vicari. R.M.: A BDI approach to infer student's emotions in an intelligent learning environment. J. Comput. Educ. **49**(2), 360–384 (2007)

Jensen, F.V., Nielsen, T.D.: Bayesian Networks and Decision Graphs. Information, Science and Statistics, 2nd edn. Springer, Berlin (2007)

Johnson, W.L., Rickel, J.W., Lester, J.C.: Animated pedagogical agents: face to face interaction in interactive learning environments. Int. J. Artif. Intell. Educ. **11**(1), 47–78 (2000)

Jungclaus, J., Stephenson, P., Schmitz, D., Encarnacao, M.: The virtual study desk: towards learning based user modeling for content adaptation in online learning environments. In: Rossett, A. (ed.) Proceedings of the World Conference on E-learning in Corporate, Governement, Healthcare, and Higher Education 2003, Chesapeake, pp. 1636–1639. AACE, VA (2003)

Kinnear, P.R., Colin, D.G.: PASW Statistics 17 Made Simple. Psychology Press, East Sussex (2010)

Lepper, M.R., Woolverton, M., Mumme, D.L.: Motivational techniques of expert human tutors: lessons for the design of computer based tutors. In: Lajoie, S.P., Derry, S.J. (eds.) Computers as Cognitive Tools, pp. 75–105. Lawrence Erlbaum Associates, Mahwah, NJ (1993)

Lester, J.C., Converse, S.A., Kahler, S.E., Barlow, S.T., Stone, B.A., Bhogal, R.S.: The persona effect: affective impact of Animated Pedagogical Agents. In: CHI '97: Proceedings of the SIGCHI Conference on Human Factors in Computing Systems, Vol. 359–366. ACM Press, New York. (1997)

Lester, J.C., Voerman, J.L., Towns, S.G., Callaway, C.B.: Diectic believability: coordinating gesture, locomotion and speech in life-like pedagogical agents. Appl. Artif. Intell. **13**, 383–414 (1999)

Li, H., Pang, N., Guo, S., Wang, H.: Research in textual emotion recognition incorporating personality factor. In: Proceedings of the IEEE International Conference on Robotics and Biomimetics (ROBIO 2007), Sanya, 15–18 December 2007, pp. 2222–2227. IEEE Press, USA (2007)

Malone, T.W.: Toward a theory of intrinsically motivating instruction. Cogn. Sci. **6**(4), 333–369 (1981)

Mateas, M.: An Oz-Centric Review of Interactive Drama and Believable Agents. School of Computer Science, Carnegie Mellon University, Pittsburgh, PA (1997)

McFarlane, A., Sparrowhawk, A., Heald, Y.: Report on the educational use of games. http://www.teem.org.uk/publications/teem_gamesined_full.pdf (2001). Accessed 11 Mar 2011

McQuiggan, S.W., Mott, B.W., Lester, J.C.: Modeling self-efficacy in intelligent tutoring systems: an inductive approach. User Model. User-Adapted Interact. **18**(1–2), 81–123 (2008)

Muñoz, K., Kevitt, P.M., Lunney, T., Noguez, J., Neri, L.: An emotional student model for game-play adaptation. Entertainment Computing **2**(2), 133–141 (2011)

Muñoz, K., Noguez, J., McKevitt, P., Neri, L., Robledo-Rella, V., Lunney, T.: Adding features of educational games for teaching Physics. In: Proceedings of the 39th IEEE International Conference Frontiers in Education, Hotel Hilton Palacio del Rio, San Antonio, TXas, 18–21 Oct 2009, pp. M2E-1–M2E-6. IEEE Press, USA (2009)

Norman, D.A., Ortony, A., Russell, D.M.: Affect and machine design: lessons for the development of autonomous machines. IBM Syst. J. **42**(1), 38–44 (2003)

Oblinger, D.G.: The next generation of educational engagement. Interactive Media Educ. (8), 1–18 (2004)

Ortony, A., Clore, G.L., Collins, A.: The Cognitive Structure of Emotions. University Press, New York (1990)

Pasch, M., Bianchi-Berthouze, N., Van Dijk, B., Nijholt, A.: Movement-based sports video games: Investigating motivation and gaming experience. Entertain. Comput. **9**(2), 169–180 (2009)

Pekrun, R., Frenzel, A.C., Goetz, T., Perry, R.P.: The control value theory of achievement emotions. An integrative approach to emotions in education. In: Schutz, P.A., Pekrun, R. (eds.) Emotion in Education, pp. 13–36. Elsevier, London (2007)

Pekrun, R., Goetz, T., Perry, R.P.: Achievement Emotions Questionnaire (AEQ). User's Manual. University of Munich, Munich (2005)

Picard, R.W.: Affective Computing. Vision and Modeling. Massachusetts Institute of Technology (MIT), Massachussetts, USA (1995)

Picard, R.W., Papert, S., Bender, W., Blumberg, B., Breazeal, C., Cavallo, D., Machover, T., Resnick, M., Roy, D., Strohecker, C.: Affective learning – a Manifesto. BT Technol. J. **22**(4), 253–269 (2004)

Porayska-Pomsta, K., Mavrikis, M., Pain, H.: Diagnosing and acting on student affect: the tutor's perspective. User Model. User-Adapted Interact. **18**, 125–173 (2008)

Qianping, W., Wei, T., Bo, S.: Research and design of edutainment. In: First IEEE International Symposium on Information Technologies and Applications in Education (ISITAE '07), Kunming, 23–25 November 2007, pp. 502–505. IEEE (2007). doi:10.1109/ISITAE.2007.4409335

Rajae-Joordens, R.J.E.: Measuring experiences in gaming and TV applications: investigating the added value of a multi-view auto-stereoscopic 3D display. In: Westerinck, J.H.D.M., Ouwerkerk, M., Overbeek, T.J.M. (eds.) Probing Experience: From Assessment of User Emotions and Behaviour to Development of Products, Vol. 8. Philips Research, pp. 77–90. Springer, Netherlands (2008)

Rebolledo-Mendez, G., Du Boulay, B., Luckin, R.: Motivating the learner: an empirical evaluation. In: Ikeda, M., Ashley, K., Chan, T.W. (eds.) The 8th Intelligent Tutoring Systems International Conference, pp. 545–554. Springer Berlin, Heidelberg (2006)

Regian, J.W., Seidel, R.J., Schuler, J., Radtke, P.: Functional area analysis of intelligent computer-assisted instruction. Training and Personnel Systems Science and Technology Evaluation and Management Committee (TAPSTEM), Washington, DC, USA (1996)

Robson, C.: Real World Research: A Resource for Social Scientist and Practitioner Researchers, 2nd edn. Blackwell, Oxford (1993)

Rollings, A., Adams, E.: On Game Design. Pearson, Old Tappan, NJ (2003)

Sarrafzadeh, A., Alexander, S., Dadgostar, F., Fan, C., Bigdeli, A.:How do you know that I don't understand? A look at the future of intelligent tutoring systems. Comput. Hum. Behav. **24**(4), 1342–1363 (2008)

Schutz, P.A., Pekrun, R. (eds.): Emotion in Education. Educational Psychology Series. Elsevier, San Diego, CA (2007)

Squire, K.: Video games in education. Int. J. Intell. Simul. Gaming **2**(1), 49–62 (2003)

Sucar, L.E., Noguez, J.: Student modeling. In: Pourret, O., Naïm, P., Marcot, B. (eds.) Bayesian Networks: A Practical Guide to Applications, pp. 173–185. Wiley, West Sussex, England (2008)

Sykes, J.: Affective gaming: advancing the argument for game-based learning. In: Pivec, M. (ed.) Affective and Emotional Aspects of Human-Computer Interaction, pp. 3–7. IOS Press, Netherlands, Amsterdam (2006)

Woolf, B.P.: Building Intelligent Interactive Tutors: Student-Centered Strategies for Revolutionizing E-learning. Elsevier, Burlington, NJ (2009)

Additional Resources

Malone, T.W., Lepper, M.R.: Making learning fun: A taxonomy of intrinsic motivations for learning. In: Snow, R.E., Farr, M.J. (eds.) Aptitude, Learning and Instruction III: Conative and Affective Process, pp. 223–253. Analyses Erlbaum, Hillsdale, NJ (1987)

Pourret, O., Naïm, P., Marcot, B., (eds.): Bayesian Networks: A Practical Guide to Applications. Wiley, West Sussex, England (2008)

Westerinck, J.H.D.M., Ouwerkerk, M., Overbeek, T.J.M. (eds.): Probing Experience: From Assessment of User Emotions and Behaviour to Development of Products, Vol. 8. Philips Research. Springer, Netherlands (2008)

Chapter 14
Fun *and* Learning: Blending Design and Development Dimensions in Serious Games through Narrative and Characters

Tim Marsh, Li Zhiqiang Nickole, Eric Klopfer, Chuang Xuejin, Scot Osterweil, and Jason Haas

14.1 Introduction

Too often research on serious games and games for learning are expected to take the form, "Did Game X increase learning about Subject Y." But in fact, the questions that we can and should be investigating are much more nuanced and complex. What we need to investigate is the relationship between learning and particular well-known components of games. The component we have chosen to focus on in our research described in this chapter is one that is typically left out of educational games, much to their detriment. The focus of our research project is on investigating the role of narrative in puzzle-based learning games in engaging students, their learning experience and understanding of displacement and velocity (Marsh et al., 2010a, b, 2011). In this chapter we outline the development of four versions of a game for learning in preparation for the study. In particular, we describe the introduction of an off-screen character in an attempt to reach a synergy of fun *and* learning, through an optimal blend of design and development dimensions, including: constructionist and instructionist learning, and hidden/incidental and direct/explicit learning, as well as creating opportunities for reflection. The off-screen character achieves this through narration of an extended narrative/story intertwined with aspects of the learning topics. In this way the character's purpose is twofold: firstly, as part of the narrative/story and secondly, as learning partner or assistant. Next, we describe the results of a comparative study carried out in a Singapore high school to test the four versions of the game. The work described herein is a collaborative research project between the National University of Singapore (NUS) and Massachusetts Institute of Technology (MIT) as part of the Singapore-MIT GAMBIT Games Lab.

T. Marsh (✉)
James Cook University, QLD, Australia
e-mail: tim.marsh@jcu.edu.au

M. Ma et al. (eds.), *Serious Games and Edutainment Applications*,
DOI 10.1007/978-1-4471-2161-9_14, © Springer-Verlag London Limited 2011

14.2 Test Environment: Puzzle and Narrative Game

The game Waker (2009) was developed as test bed for our research. It is a flash-based puzzle game wrapped in a narrative. The narrative, largely at the beginning, in-between levels and at the end of the game, is told in cutscenes and voiceovers. The narrative tells of a child trapped in a dream and provides the game objective to fix broken pathways and journey through levels of the dream world to awaken the child (see: Fig. 14.1a, b).

The core puzzle gameplay and game mechanic in order to do this, is to figure out how to create or construct appropriately inclined paths/graphs that will enable the player to move up through levels (in the y-axis) by moving a corresponding direction, distance and speed along the x-axis. Path construction is akin to a constructionist learning approach. Path/graph construction also provides the learning goals: to learn about aspects associated with the physics concepts of displacement and velocity. Performing path/graph construction bridges the gap to their learning

Fig. 14.1 (**a** and **b**) Screen shots of Waker 1.0 showing construction of pathway to journey up through levels of the child's dream world

goals. Through observation, it was found that after only short gameplay, path construction became intuitive for players. As the game proceeds gameplay becomes progressively more complex.

As demonstrated through on-line blogs, being voted as Indie Game of the Week on Bytejacker, and nominated as one of six non-professional finalists in the Indie Game Challenge, Waker is fun and engaging. Gameplay has been identified as thought-provoking, stimulating and creating a pleasant level of frustration that encourages the player – from beginner to experienced gamer – to continue playing to figure out how to build pathways and journey through levels to save a child from a broken dream.

In addition, the music and artwork are singled out as being impressive and provide a complementary blend with gameplay. As well as being fun and engaging, Waker is intended to be a game for learning – to help students learn about the physics concepts of displacement and velocity.

14.2.1 Limitations in Test Environment

As identified in pilot studies and demonstrated in on-line blogs, as well as being a fun and engaging game, generally players didn't identify that our game was a game for learning. In this respect, learning from gameplay in Waker can be described as hidden and is intended to be incidental to the fun and entertaining gameplay.

While elegant in design, for some researchers this highlights a widely held belief, that there is an inherent tension between fun and learning in the design and development of games for learning and serious games. From this perspective, putting learning in games has been described as "sucking the fun out" of gameplay, while attempting to make games for learning that are fun and entertaining invariably has meant for many developers forgoing some of the learning. Our view is that we can design and develop games for learning and serious games for *both* fun and learning.

In order to address the potential limitations of hidden or incidental learning, we are planning to run teacher-led instructional sessions after students have finished playing the Waker game in order to build upon students' game learning experience and to help fill-in gaps in learning about displacement and velocity. This is a design dimension that Henriksen (2006) refers to as in-game and off-game learning. While this blended learning approach provides a natural way to complement and introduce game-based learning into the classroom and a link to the curriculum, it is however, expensive in terms of resources and manpower. Further studies intend to provide answers to some of these questions and to shed light on whether the advantages of this blended in-game and off-game learning approach outweighs the cost of increased resources.

Identified in interviews with players in pilot studies, players are left to make sense of some of the gameplay and mechanics. One shortcoming was identified to be the narrative and how it was communicated to players. That is, in the form of cutscenes and narration at the beginning, in-between levels, and at the end of the game with no attempt to explain, direct player's attention to, or reflect on, the connection between gameplay/game mechanics and learning. For example, players know that there is a connection between their movements and the way the path is drawn but there is nothing in the narrative to describe why it is connected. Therefore, for learning to take place, it was necessary to make this connection and to create opportunities for reflection.

Furthermore, in contrast to the original Waker game, another goal has been to make learning more explicit in order to address the potential limitations of hidden or incidental learning as identified previously. To this aim, one approach has been to incorporate instructional design features and in drawing players' attention to the constructionist learning gameplay. However, by making learning more explicit to players we anticipate that we may turn some players off and/or take some of the fun and entertainment out of the game. Therefore, to address these two limitations, we have been involved in redesign and development to create a synergy between fun *and* learning, and to find an optimum way to encourage reflection without, or minimally, disrupting game play.

In order to do this, we explored the amendment and inclusion of various design features to the original version of the game Waker. For example, event triggered text boxes that would appear at appropriate predetermined stages in the game to provide more instruction about the learning and how it links with gameplay; and answering questions before proceeding to the next level, etc. However, these and similar instructional design approaches and features make learning too explicit, and so potentially disrupt the flow of the game and in turn, the fun game experience.

Therefore, our solution to create a closer link between narrative and the gameplay/mechanics, and make learning more explicit without disrupting fun gameplay experience, was to extend the narrative/story throughout the game through an off-screen character, as described in the following sections. We review the related published literature and describe the design considerations and development work in order to do this and to make learning more explicit, while at the same time creating a synergy of learning and fun.

14.3 Fun and Learning: Through Narrative and Character

Using characters as learning partners or assistants has received considerable attention in e-learning, simulation and games for learning. As we build on the published literature in this area, it is reviewed here. Next we describe our design and development solutions and how it addresses the issues, limitations and considerations identified.

14.3.1 Related Work: Characters as Learning Partners

According to Gulz (2004), using characters as learning partners is a fairly complex endeavor. His research findings indicate that, while there is existing research on the short-term effects of using characters in a learning context, there remain uncertain and sometimes contradictory findings as to the true efficacy of these characters as learning partners.

Haake (2009) states that another complexity arising from characters as learning partners is that characters are never socio-affect neutral. For example, humans bring with them biases and preconceptions and so are prone to evaluating, making assumptions or having expectations of characters based on aspects such as visual appearance, accent and gender; and these were sufficiently significant to effect players' experience. So for instance, slight changes in the visual appearance led to notable changes in player perception. However, when the visual component of the character was removed, players' expectations shifted from reliance on visual cues of the character to aspects of the character's verbal communication. Character accent was sufficient to have effect on players' expectations of the character's personality attributes. The cause of this was identified as being because players associated certain personal and social attributes to the accent heard. In this case, the players thought the characters were equal on measures like personal warmth and intelligence irrespective of gender (Haake 2009).

Likewise, Gulz (2004) concurs with the finding that the visual appearance of a character can and will strongly affect the players' engagement with the game, and thereby the game's overall effectiveness in getting information across via the character. In this respect, Gulz and Haake (2006) suggest carefully designing a character's visuals to account for the social cues that are inherent in the character, to create a character that is cohesive, believable and ultimately likeable by the player. Care should be taken, however, to also consider possible differences in cultures and subcultures where the game would be deployed, such that the design is tailored to the audience concerned (e.g. in schools in Singapore and the US).

While the first impression and socio-affect of the character can strongly affect the perception of their competencies and personality, the role of the character in the game is equally important. The character can take on various roles, such as being dominant or equal to the player as a mentor, peer or guide, or even as a dependant who needs the assistance of the player in order to complete the challenges.

Kim (2007) found significant interaction effects between the character and the player. The competence of the character affected the desirability of the character depending on the competence of the players. Academically strong players showed higher self-efficacy when paired with similarly competent characters, while academically weaker players were so with less competent characters. Players not only experienced improvements in self-efficacy when paired correctly; they also experienced improved recall (learning) through the appropriate pairing. An effect attributed by Kim (2007) to Bandura's (1997) concept of "attribute similarity" whereby such pairings were found to be necessary for "effective social modeling in traditional human-to-human instructional settings" (Bandura, 1997). Thus, it can be argued that players may feel more affiliated to the game characters that resemble them. Behrend and Thompson (2011) recently reported similar findings with the use of online virtual agents or "helpers" that appear on-screen to guide learners through training programs. In studies, they found that if the appearance (race and gender) and communication style of the helpers matched learners, then learners reported liking the helper more, and were more engaged and focused on training. In addition, they found that effective helpers could also make the experience more social.

Another major observation by Kim (2007) was that academically strong players had higher self-efficacy perceptions when the character was controlling the influx of information, while weaker players had the opposite experience. In addition to this, Kim (2007) suggests that this can be attributed to the possibility that academically weaker players were overwhelmed by the information coming in a flow beyond their control.

Gulz (2004) also observes that there is room for creating characters that can fulfill the emotional needs of players through the formation of deeper personal relationships in learning. One strong way to achieve this is to have the character react to the player's actions in a meaningful way. This may be an emotive response in the visual sense, or perhaps in a verbal way.

Other concerns regarding the use of characters identified by Gulz (2004) are that players can and do react differently to the presence of characters as learning partners. Thus, it is largely insufficient to implement a single character as a learning partner and expecting all players to react in an identical way. To deal with this, Gulz (2004) recommends the implementation of character and character-free variants for players to select from. Alternatively, multiple characters with different attributes could be implemented, to cater to differing preferences. Realistically, it may not always be possible to have multiple fleshed out characters in a given title due to resource constraints.

In summary, the complexity of the effect of using characters as learning partners serves as a caution for researchers, such that they are aware that subtle cues can have major effects on the research, and controls need to be present to compensate for or perhaps isolate the effects of these subtle social cues. It is important to note that characters are never socio-affect neutral, and care must be taken to account for this. Alternatively, it can be surmised that excluding the visual component of the character may be advisable should there be insufficient resources available to design and create a character that can satisfy all or at least a majority of the social cues required to make a character that's believable and likeable.

The next section describes the creation and development of the narrative and off-screen character and how it subtly interweaves background story with learning to address many of the issues raised above.

14.3.2 Development of Extended Narrative and Off-Screen Character

Within the original version of the game Waker (2009), hereafter referred to as Waker 1.0, the story of a child trapped within a dream is told through voiceovers and cutscenes at the beginning and updates given following completion of each level and completion of the game. To address many of the issues raised above we redesigned Waker 1.0 with an extended narrative throughout the game told from the perspective of an off-screen character representing the child trapped in her dream (Waker, 2011); referred to as Waker 2.0.

The extended narrative provided the opportunity to create a closer link between narrative and the gameplay/mechanics, and make learning more explicit without disrupting the player's fun game playing experience. This was achieved by subtly interweaving the background story, told from the child's perspective, with aspects of the learning topics. In this way the character's purpose is twofold; firstly, as a character in the narrative/story and secondly, as learning partner or assistant. The child's role was both as an equal to the player, such as being a mentor, peer or guide, as well as being dependant on the player and needing their assistance in order to complete the challenges of constructing pathways to help release her from a dream.

As the character wasn't seen on-screen, potential problems associated with visual representations affecting players, as discussed above, were avoided. In addition, the use of an off-screen character meant that cultural and racial issues arising from visual representations could generally be avoided. As we focused on the development of just one non-personalized character, attempts were made to limit issues arising from verbal communication by opting for a neutral accent. To this aim, the child's voice was selected to be a neutral English accent. Due to limited resources, no attempt was made to provide multiple or personalize characters. So issues resulting from personalized pairing are not considered in the reporting of development and study given herein.

However, effects as a result of ill-pairing from culture, gender, academic ability may have been offset because the character is a child and is dependant on the player to released her from her dream. We anticipate that sympathetic and empathetic attachment from the player towards the dependant child who requires the player's help may be a contributing factor in this and is an area that requires further investigation.

Additional advantages of using an off-screen character as partner or assistant include, providing encouragement to the player when figuring out the puzzles, responding to player's actions in a meaningful way (e.g. on successful completion of a task), attempting to strengthen social dimensions, providing an opportunity to introduce technical/scientific terms and a language connected with the topics of learning in simple manner incorporated in the narrative, and encouraging reflection.

The child's narration is given during, or following, the occurrence of triggered events. As shown in Fig. 14.2a, when a player reaches a certain point in the game a voiceover starts. For example, when the player begins to move in level two of the game, the voiceover begins and text displayed: "Have you noticed that the farther you displace the orb from its stand, the higher the path goes".

14.4 Study

A formal study was carried out with 57 male students, aged 13–14, in a High School in Singapore. The purpose of the study was to compare puzzle and narrative learning games in engaging students, their learning experience and their understanding of the

Fig. 14.2 (**a** and **b**) Screen shots of Waker 2.0 with extended narrative interweaved with instruction through event-triggered character voiceovers while at the same time the text of the voiceover is displayed (**a**), and voicelogs and replay functions for recall and reflection (**b**)

physics concepts of displacement and velocity, and in addition, test the effectiveness of an extended narrative and off-screen character as storyteller and learning partner.

All of the students who took part in the study had no prior classroom-based lessons on physics concepts of displacement and velocity, having their first exposure to the topics through the Waker game versions used in the study. The students were divided into four groups and each group played one of the four versions of our game Waker as detailed briefly below.

Group 1: Waker 2.0 – Puzzle and Narrative (voiceover, cutscenes, voice logs & repeat function)

Narrative extended (to original Waker 1.0: see group 3) throughout the game, off-screen child and cutscenes (as described above), and with added features to allow the player to either listen to the last voiceover or sort through all voiceovers to allow for recall and reflection (Fig. 14.2b).

Group 2: Waker 2.0 – Puzzle and Narrative (voiceover, cutscenes)
Identical to group 1's version with extended narrative throughout the game, off-screen child and cutscenes, but without features for voiceover or recall/reflection (Fig. 14.2a).
Group 3: Waker 1.0 – Puzzle and Narrative (voiceovers, cutscenes)
Original waker game as described above (Fig. 14.1a, b). Narrative and cutscenes at the beginning to set-up the story and on completion of levels and game.
Group 4 – Waker 1.0 puzzle-based (voiceovers, cutscenes removed)
This version of the game provides the puzzle-based only or abstract version of the game. This has been achieved by removing all narrative and cutscenes from the game altogether. In this version of the game, the game starts immediately with no introduction, narrative or guidelines and players have to figure out the gameplay and game mechanics.

It must be noted that the gameplay remained consistent between the versions, so any differences between games identified in the study can largely be attributed to the feature set. Data on learning and fun was primarily gathered through questionnaire and observation.

14.4.1 Results

After playing the game, most of the students were able to draw on paper the graphs that resulted when they moved their character left, right or held them stationary, as shown in Figs. 14.3 and 14.4. This shows that nearly all students were familiar with the construction and resulting shape of graphs for both the displacement and velocity stages of the Waker games for both the narrative and puzzle only versions. There were no outstanding trends in inability to draw the graphs, hence suggesting that most of the students became familiar with the Waker game mechanics.

When asked in an open-ended question to identify any difficulties they had experienced when constructing the graphs, students from groups 1 and 2 self-identified that they had primarily experienced difficulty from aspects relating to the game

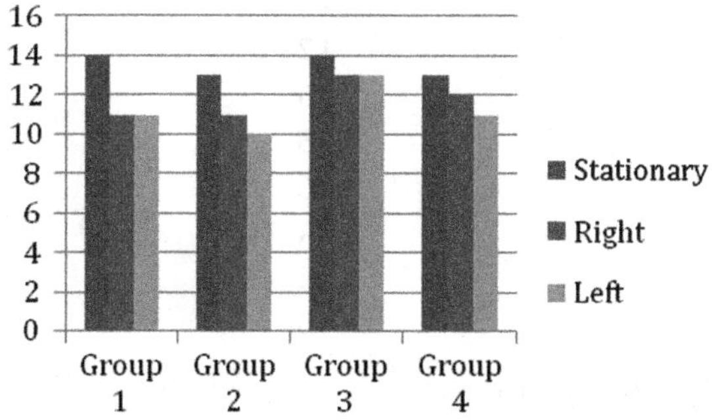

Fig. 14.3 Ability to draw displacement graph

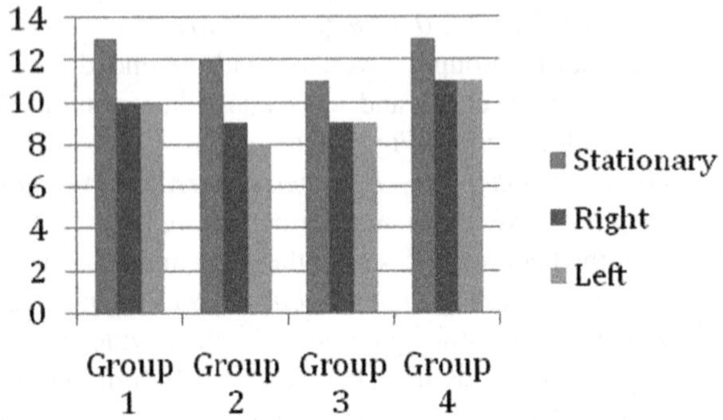

Fig. 14.4 Ability to draw velocity graph

mechanics themselves while students from groups 3 and 4 experienced difficulty in comprehending the concept in addition to aspects relating to the game mechanics.

Figure 14.5 shows that groups 1 and 2 perceived noticeably more in-game assistance compared to groups 3 and 4. Over two thirds of the students from extended narrative and off-screen character groups 1 and 2 felt that they had help in completing the levels, while those from 3 and 4 rarely did.

When asked an open-ended question in the questionnaire regarding what sort of assistance the students felt they received, groups 1 and 2 stated that the primary form of assistance was from the voice of the child providing instructions and hints. One student explicitly stated that the presence of a storyline helped in the completion of the levels.

Figure 14.6 shows the main types of responses that the students provided when asked to explain what displacement meant. As can be seen, only students from groups 1 and 2 understood displacement as a vector measure (as intended in the game), while students from groups 3 and 4 primarily reasoned that displacement to be connected with aspects relating to a volume measure, whereby one volume was being displaced by another volume in the game.

Figure 14.7 shows the types of responses students provided when asked about velocity. The findings show that mostly all the students from all groups consistently

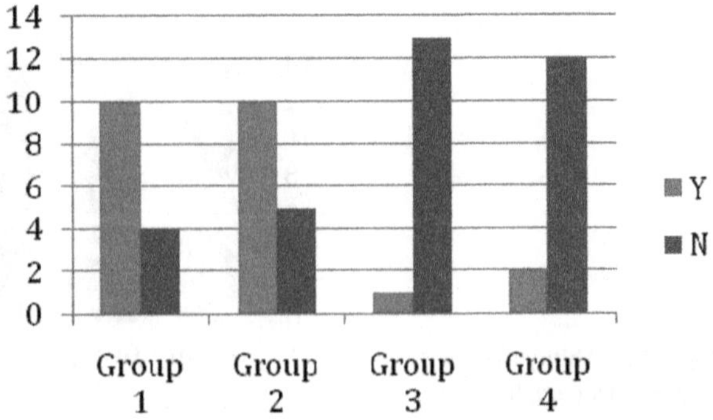

Fig. 14.5 Perceptions of assistance

Fig. 14.6 Understanding displacement

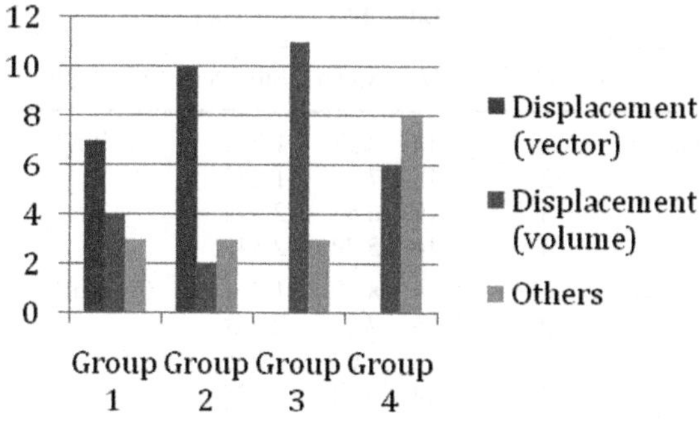

Fig. 14.7 Understanding velocity

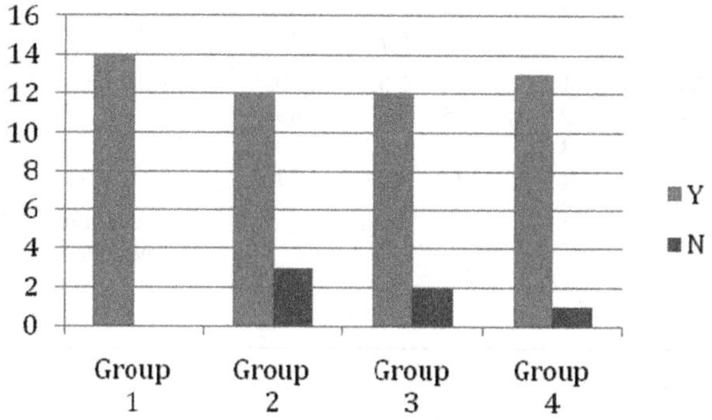

understood velocity in terms of speed, rather than as the rate at which displacement is changing.

In reference to Table 14.1 and described below, students were asked to rate each game version against particular aspects and game features on a scale of 1–10, with 1 being the lowest and 10 the highest.

14.4.1.1 Fun, Excitement and Attention

In reference to Table 14.1, students rated the group 1 version (Waker 2.0 with voicelogs and recall) as most fun (mean: 7.6), exciting (mean: 6.9) and most able to hold their attention (mean: 8.3); this was followed by group 2 version (Waker 2.0) and then group 3 (Waker 1.0). Group 4 rated the puzzle version lowest in these measures. This suggests a positive correlation between narrative (and in particular narrative provided throughout the game) and the perceived fun, excitement and attention holding in the game.

14.4.1.2 Frustration and Distraction

Group 2 game version (Waker 2.0 without voicelogs and recall) was rated the lowest in frustration (mean: 4.2), and lowest in distraction (mean 2.27). Group 3

Table 14.1 Student perceptions of Waker versions

Measures	Groups	*N*	Mean	Std. Dev.	Measures	Groups	*N*	Mean	Std. Dev.
Fun	1	14	7.57	1.284	Exciting	1	14	6.86	1.512
	2	15	7	1.852		2	15	6.47	2.134
	3	14	6.5	2.594		3	14	6.43	2.593
	4	14	5.79	2.547		4	14	5.79	2.424
Attention	1	14	8.29	1.541	Frustrating	1	14	5.07	2.868
	2	15	7.27	2.251		2	15	4.2	2.597
	3	14	7.07	2.759		3	14	6.07	3.43
	4	14	6.93	2.235		4	14	6.29	3.099
Music	1	14	8.07	1.439	Artwork	1	14	8.14	1.46
	2	15	7.27	2.604		2	15	7.47	1.995
	3	14	7	3.038		3	14	8.07	1.639
	4	14	5.71	2.367		4	14	6.57	2.102
Play again	1	14	6.57	2.102	Distraction	1	14	3.43	1.284
	2	15	5.8	2.833		2	15	2.27	1.28
	3	14	7.07	2.702		3	14	2.36	2.023
	4	14	4.57	3.275		4	14	4.36	3.153
					Play again in free time	1	14	6.07	2.336
						2	15	4.07	2.549
						3	14	6.07	2.556
						4	14	3.57	3.106

(Waker 1.0) and 4 (puzzle version) were rated higher for both frustration and distraction. Suggesting that narrative reduces the sense of frustration and distraction. The markedly lower frustration value may be attributed to the narrative providing hints to help players throughout the game.

So group 4 rated the puzzle game less fun, exciting and attention holding and was more frustrating and distracting, in comparison to other groups narrative games versions. In contrast, groups 1 and 2 rated their game versions with narrative throughout the game to be higher on fun, more exciting and attention holding, with lower distraction.

14.4.1.3 Music and Artwork

Interestingly, players in groups 1, 2 and 3 appreciated the artwork and music more in the narrative versions than in the puzzle version even though they were almost identical in all four versions.

14.4.1.4 Playing Again, or in Your Free Time

In reference to Table 14.1, students from groups 1 and 3 felt they were more likely to want to play again and also play the game in their free time. Groups 2 and 4 gave slightly less ratings for wanting to play again (means: 5.8 and 4.6 respectively) and in playing their free time (4.07 and 3.57, respectively).

14.5 Discussion

In summary, although learning about constructing and interpreting graphs for both the narrative and puzzle versions were almost the same, the two extended narrative and character Waker 2.0 versions (groups 1 and 2) also provided an opportunity to introduce technical/scientific terms and a language connected with the topics of learning in simple manner incorporated in the narrative, and link this to game play.

Over two thirds of the students from extended narrative and off-screen character groups 1 and 2 were aware that they had help in completing the levels, while those from 3 and 4 rarely did; identifying the primary form of assistance to be from the voice of the child providing instructions and hints. One student explicitly stated that the presence of a storyline helped in the completion of the levels.

All three narrative versions (groups 1, 2 and 3) were rated higher on every aspect related to gameplay and game features in comparison to the puzzle only based version of the game. For example, the narrative versions were rated as being more fun, more exciting, more engaging, with players less distracted to activities outside of the game, less frustrating, with players preferring to play the narrative versions again and in their free time, and surprisingly, players appreciated the artwork and music more in the narrative versions even though they were almost identical to the puzzle only version.

Of the narrative versions, Waker 2.0 with extended narrative, off-screen character, voicelogs and recall functions, was almost consistently rated the highest. Invariably this was followed by the Waker 2.0 version without voicelogs and recall, and then Waker 1.0 followed this.

Waker 2.0 incorporated a simple narrative extended throughout the game and a character that was positioned off-screen. The character's purpose was twofold; firstly, as a child in the game's narrative/story relating the narrative/story from their perspective and secondly, as learning partner or assistant, interweaving learning with narrative. The child's role was both as an equal to the player, such as being a mentor, peer or guide, as well as being dependant on the player and needing their assistance in order to complete the challenges of the game. Because of this dependent relationship of the child on the player, we anticipate that sympathetic and empathetic attachment or connection from the player towards the dependant child who requires the player's help may be a contributing factor to the results and is an area that requires further investigation.

As the child character and extended narrative appeared easy for players to relate to, this helped set a context to the learning experience that was designed not to seem tacked on to the core gameplay. It is this integration that helps preserve the immersiveness or engagement in the gaming experience, instead of having jarring dialog that is out of context and draws the player's attention to the artificiality of the overall learning experience.

Additional advantages of using an off-screen character as partner or assistant include, providing a way to respond to player's actions in a meaningful way (e.g. on successful completion of a task), providing encouragement to the player when they are figuring out the puzzles and working through the game, providing a way to strengthen social dimensions, encourage reflection on learning, and providing an opportunity to introduce technical/scientific terms and a language connected with the topics of learning in simple manner incorporated in the narrative.

14.6 Future Directions

While it can be argued that much more can be done with the development of dynamic intelligent narratives that adapt to a player's gameplay, such as basic interactive storytelling in the style of dime store choose your adventure books, the approach described herein is a relatively simple and cost-effective approach. Even so, we have already taken steps in this direction to explore and implement dynamic intelligent narratives or interactive storytelling in the next version of Waker. Connected to this, the inclusion of more complex characters is possible, perhaps affording a degree of a player's emotional investment in the character, creating an attachment to a game that is really educational at its core.

While the narrative in Waker was somewhat direct and every effort was made to create a narrative that only mentioned specific physics terms in passing, more can be done to further integrate the narrative into the gameplay. For example, morals can be taught implicitly in a game where non-player characters react emotionally and realistically to a player's actions, thereby learning through doing. Or perhaps learning specific concepts like money management through peripheral game mechanics like a sophisticated trading system embedded in an adventure game, thereby using an embedded narrative that effectively distracts the student from the core educational content. Further study in these areas can do much to improve the state of the art, and thus enabling students to learn while having a gaming experience that is virtually indistinguishable from the entertainment-oriented games on the market.

14.7 Conclusion

This chapter has described the development of four versions of a serious game and study carried out in a Singapore high school to shed light on the effectiveness of puzzle and narrative-based games in engaging students, their learning experience and understanding of the physics concepts of displacement and velocity. In particular, we have described the introduction of an off-screen character to help reach a synergy of fun *and* learning, through an optimal blend of design and development dimensions, including: constructionist and instructionist learning, and hidden/incidental and direct/explicit learning, and so creating opportunities for reflection. The off-screen character achieves this through narration of a carefully crafted narrative intertwined with aspects of the learning topics. In this way the character's purpose is twofold; firstly, as part of the narrative/story and secondly, as learning partner or assistant.

Results from the comparative study show that while some aspects of learning are comparable in both puzzle and narrative versions of the games, the extended narrative and character game versions also provided an opportunity to introduce technical/scientific terms and a language connected with the topics of learning in a simple manner incorporated in the narrative. In addition, all narrative versions were rated higher on every aspect related to gameplay and game features in comparison to the puzzle only based version of the game. For example, the narrative versions were rated as being more fun, more exciting, more engaging, with players less distracted to activities outside of the game, less frustrating, with players preferring to play the narrative versions again and in their free time, and surprisingly, players appreciated the artwork and music more in the narrative versions even though they were almost identical to the puzzle only version. Hence, results demonstrate that seeking creative solutions such as, in the development of a well-crafted narrative, can increase *both* fun and learning; a perspective that differs from the widely held views to find a balance between fun and learning.

The findings described herein are valuable for informing design and development of narrative through character blending game story with learning in serious games. While steps are already in place to explore and implement more intelligence into our games, the relatively simple cost-effective approach described herein provides a way to create fun and learning without going to the complexity and expense in terms of resources, time and cost of using intelligent-based approaches. Hence, making this approach more accessible to academics and teachers in schools by informing the customization of their own virtual environments, games for learning and serious games, or commercially available off the shelf titles (COTS) with topics from the curriculum.

The power of characters and narrative is only just being realized in the area of educational games, and it can be of great service to society should we attain a deeper understanding of the creation of *both* fun and learning. By investigating the relationship between learning and particular well-known components of games, similar to the work described herein on puzzle and narrative, and their effects on engagement, experience and learning, allows us to develop a body of knowledge that can inform design and development for the creation of truly enjoyable games for learning, serious games and simulations for education for all concerned.

Acknowledgements The research described herein is funded through the Singapore-MIT GAMBIT Games Lab and is part of the project "Investigating the role of narrative in puzzle-based games and their relationship to students' engaged learning experience". Thanks to all members of the original Waker 1.0 development team (MIT, Summer 2009): Chuang Xuejin, Brandon Cebenka, Rini Ong Zhi Qian, Steven Setiawan, Anna Loparev, Lin Yuanqin, Eunice Khoo, Wong Chang You, Rich Vreeland, Kevin Driscoll, Sara Verrilli, Geoffrey Long, and product owners: Scot Osterweil, Eric Klopfer, Tim Marsh and Lan Xuan Le. Thanks also to Waker 2.0 development team led by Tim Marsh (NUS, 2010–2011): Lin Yuanqin, Steven Setiawan, Ho Yun, Diana Marsh, Yih-Lun Huang and Audrey Tan who assisted with programming, artwork, audio, character voiceover, study preparation and studies, respectively. Special thanks to teachers, staff and students of Hwa Chong Institution, Singapore.

References

Bandura, A.: Self-Efficacy: The Exercise of Control. W. H. Freeman, New York (1997)

Behrend, T., Thompson, L.F.: Similarity effects in online training: effects with computerized trainer agents. J. Comput. Human Behav. **27**, 1201–1206 (2011)

Gulz, A.: Benefits of virtual characters in computer based learning environments: Claims and evidence. Int. J. Artif. Intell. Educ. **14**, 313–334 (2004)

Gulz, A., Haake, M.: Visual design of virtual pedagogical agents: Naturalism versus stylization in static appearance. In: Proceedings of the 3rd International Design and Engagability Conference, NordiChi 2006, Oslo, Norway (2006)

Haake, M.: Embodied pedagogical agents: From visual impact to pedagogical implications. Doctoral Thesis, Department of Design Sciences, Lund University, Sweden (2009)

Henriksen, T.D.: Dimensions in educational game-design: Perspectives on designing and implementing game-based learning processes in the educational setting. Nordic Playground, Reykjavik (2006)

Kim, Y.: Desirable characteristics of learning companions. Int. J. Artif. Intell. Educ. **17**(4), 371–388 (2007)

Marsh, T., Li Zhiqiang, N., Chuang, X., Klopfer, E., Osterweil, S., Haas, J.: Narrative and puzzle-based serious games and their relationship to students' engaged learning experience. In: CGames 2010, 15th International Conference on Computer Games: AI, Animation, Mobile, Interactive Multimedia, Educational & Serious Games, Louisville (2010a)

Marsh, T., Li Zhiqiang, N., Chuang, X., Klopfer, E., Osterweil, S., Haas, J.: Investigating narrative and puzzle-based serious games and their relationship to students' engaged learning experience. In: 1st International Workshop on Serious Games Development and Applications, Derby, UK (2010b)

Marsh, T., Li Zhiqiang, N., Klopfer, E., Chuang, X., Osterweil, S., Haas, J.: Fun and Learning: The Power of Narrative, Foundations of Digital Games 2011 (FDG2011), Bordeaux, France (2011)

Waker: Versions 1.0 and 2.0. Available from: Singapore-MIT GAMBIT Games Lab, MIT: DOI=http://gambit.mit.edu/loadgame/waker.php (2009, 2011)

Part IV
Use of Commercial-Off-the-Shelf (COTS) Games in Education

Chapter 15
Choosing a Serious Game for the Classroom: An Adoption Model for Educators

Kae Novak and Rurik Nackerud

List of Acronyms

COTS	Commercial-off-the-shelf games
DGBL	Digital gamed based learning
ESRB	Entertainment Software Rating Board
IT	Information technology
LMS	Learning management system
MMORPG	Massively Multi-player Online Role-Playing Game
WoW	World of Warcraft

Model Specific Acronyms

CYTIE	Cause You To Ignore Everything
RCIPR	Research, choose, investigate, pilot and reflect

15.1 Introduction

Educators eager to integrate serious games into the curriculum, but who are not trained or funded for game development, must choose an off-the-shelf or online game. These educators face a special set of questions. What game should I choose? How will I know if it meets the course's learning objectives? What are the technical considerations of integrating it into the classroom? Will students learn from it, or perceive it to be merely an entertaining waste of time? (Rice, 2007).

Current instructional design models do not address how an educator should conduct formative evaluation prior to the integration of online serious games or off

K. Novak (✉)
Front Range Community College, Westminster, CO, USA
e-mail: que.jinn@gmail.com

M. Ma et al. (eds.), *Serious Games and Edutainment Applications*,
DOI 10.1007/978-1-4471-2161-9_15, © Springer-Verlag London Limited 2011

the shelf games that are not specifically designed for their course. Is it possible to develop and implement an evaluative framework that enables educators from multiple disciplines to effectively incorporate serious games into their curriculum? What is needed to know if a game will deeply engage students in learning?

A team comprised of online instructors and an instructional designer developed and tested an approach on evaluation and implementation of commercial-off-the-shelf (COTS) video games. This adoption model for evaluating COTS harnesses the power of player and instructor evaluation to achieve a comprehensive grasp of the deep learning made possible by playing a well-chosen video game. For purposes of this chapter, only commercial games were considered. Games designed as "edutainment" (Egenfeldt-Nielsen, 2007) or for purely educational purposes are beyond our scope.

Members of the team presented papers on Serious Games and Digital Game-Based Learning (DGBL) (Prensky, 2001) at inter-college and system-wide professional development events for faculty. During each of these events, participants were surveyed, and subsequently targeted for focus groups and personal interviews. The data collected showed that participants were interested in DGBL but experienced cognitive dissonance (Festinger, 1957) about the implementation of DGBL in the classroom. The majority of participants indicated their concerns were choice of the game, establishing the games credibility to their students and the amount of technical support that would be required. The team drew from the fields of business, instructional design and education to develop a model that would allow the faculty to reduce their cognitive dissonance. This chapter presents and analyzes this model. The model serves as a catalyst to bridging this chasm between DGBL "early adopters" (Moore, 2006) and the "early majority" (Moore, 2006).

Currently most educators do not have the prerequisite skills to develop interactive, immersive games using a game engine. Game engine software provides for rendering of visual objects, physics within the game, sound, artificial intelligence, scripting and animation. There are virtual world environments such as Second Life and OpenSim where barriers to content creation are lower. But these environments still require the investment of hundreds of hours learning how to build and how to script to achieve the design and integration level of most COTS.

The games discussed in this chapter, fit a video game genre known as MMORPGs or Massively Multi-Player Online Role-Playing Games. MMORPGS for the most part are persistent 3D immersive environments that allow for social interaction, have varying degrees of content creation and have physics that are at the very least consistent with the rules of the game. In World of Warcraft, the largest MMORPG, over 12 million players subscribe monthly (Blizzard Entertainment Inc., 2010). In these games, the player is represented by a 3D character known as an avatar or more colloquially as a "toon." For most of these video games, the perspective of the player is looking over the character's right shoulder. A player in these games can choose to interact with other players or non-player characters (NPCs) that are controlled by the game's artificial intelligence. The ability to play with others or the social aspect has resulted in the formation of associations as guilds in many of these MMORPGs.

15.2 RCIPR Model

Based on 3 years of experience at the community college level with the adoption of virtual worlds, educational video games and COTS and feedback from educators at professional development events in 2010 and 2011, the following model was developed (Fig. 15.1):

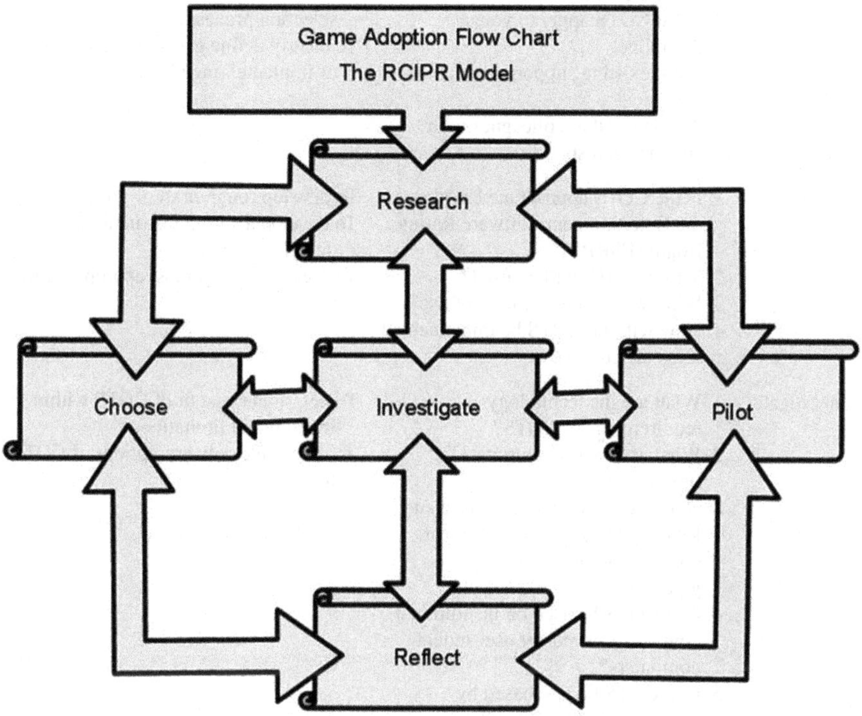

Fig. 15.1 RCIPR model

The five aspects of the RCIPR model are:

1. Research
2. Choose
3. Investigate
4. Pilot
5. Reflect

Using the RCIPR method, COTS were adopted in seven courses at Front Range Community College. The courses represent a variety of disciplines and in a variety of formats. COTS were successfully piloted in accounting, anthropology of folklore, introduction to business and multimedia courses. COTS were offered in both the campus and online section of three accounting courses.

Practically how does this model work? In the following section, a sample adoption plan of the RCIPR model is shown (Table 15.1):

Table 15.1 Sample adoption plan for a COTS game

Aspect	Action step	Purpose
1. Research	1. What are your learning objectives? 2. What COTS apply to your discipline? 3. What existing support communities are there? 4. Are there other colleagues with similar interests?	To develop a point of reference for the selection process. To clearly define goals and objectives of implementing COTS.
2. Choose	1. Is the COTS appropriate based on the Entertainment Software Rating Board (ESRB)? 2. Which COTS will be used? 3. What will be the duration of use? 4. How will the COTS be implemented into curriculum?	To develop rough draft of project. To develop a strong instructional design foundation. To pick the COTS most appropriate for use.
3. Investigate	1. What are the technology requirements of COTS? 2. What are your institutions IT limitations? 3. Does COTS Terms of Service and End User Licensing Agreement comply with institutional guidelines? 4. Can COTS be used on institutional computers or must it use student computers? 5. Can COTS be purchased by institution or by student?	To determine best fit of COTS within institutional limitations. To determine delivery options of COTS to students.
4. Pilot	1. Where does COTS fit in your lesson plan/syllabus? 2. How many points is COTS worth? 3. What are student deliverables? 4. What rubric will be used to assess student performance? 5. Will you use the COTS as an extracurricular activity or co-curricular?	To finalize COTS project and implement. To develop relevant assessment and evaluation tool. To collect student performance data for later analysis.
5. Reflect	1. How will COTS be documented for future reference? 2. How will feedback and outcomes be implemented for next offering? 3. How can additional resources discovered during pilot be incorporated into next offering?	To analyze data collected. To document COTS implementation. To develop strategies for future implementation of COTS.

15.3 Research

To begin, educators should acquaint themselves with the Entertainment Software Rating Board (ESRB). The ESRB is a nonprofit self-regulatory organization where the entertainment software companies can submit their games for age ratings and have their games screened for advertising and privacy factors. The website is located at http://www.esrb.org/index-js.jsp. Familiarization with this rating system will allow educators to see age appropriateness, content descriptors which allow the educator to see why the games received its rating and platforms. For example, LEGO Universe receives a rating of "Everyone 10+" for cartoon violence contrasting with World of Warcraft that receives a teen rating for Blood and Gore. The ESRB allows the teacher not only to research a game for age appropriateness and content but also by software platform.

Educators who may be the early adopters at their institutions should be aware that they are not first adopters. There is actually a community of practice (Lave and Wagner, 1998) that consists of educators who are using video games to include COTS in the classroom. When an educator is conducting their research they should either read the forums and/or consider becoming involved with this community of educators using games in the classroom. This community of practices meets in synchronously and asynchronously for discussions and activities.

Below are some asynchronous discussions forums and resources:

Rezed http://rezedhub.ning.com/ is an online forum that is run by the non-profit organization, Global Kids, Inc. Rezed was established in 2008 by a Digital Media and Learning grant administered through the Humanities, Arts, Science and Technology Advanced Collaboratory (HASTAC) Initiative of the MacArthur Foundation. Several groups on this site use the forum to ask questions and share their investigations and implementation projects. The two most active are:

WoW in Schools http://rezedhub.ning.com/group/wowinschools Lego Universe http://rezedhub.ning.com/group/legouniverse. Another forum was just recently started on Minecraft http://rezedhub.ning.com/group/minecraftinschool

Gamesnetwork is a listserv maintained by the Digital Games Research Association. While the discussion list is meant to focus on digital gaming and games studies, the use of COTS in the classroom and their appropriateness is a frequent topic.
The Second Life Educators (SLED) list https://lists.secondlife.com/cgi-bin/mailman/listinfo/educators while hosted by Linden Labs and nominally only for Second Life discussions includes educators who are using virtual worlds others than Second Life and COTS in their classroom.

WoW in Schools http://wowinschool.pbworks.com/w/page/5268731/FrontPage is a wiki that reports on schools using World of Warcraft and is starting to build a repository of lesson plans and curriculum.

Saving the Universe http://savingtheuniverse.wikispaces.com/ is newly developed wiki that is reporting on a educator who is chronicling her third and fourth graders' after school program that uses Lego Universe.

In addition to asynchronous activities there are several events online and face-to-face where the educators who are using COTS in the classroom have discussions, do presentations, and conduct meetups.

The Games Learning and Society Conference (GLS) http://www.glsconference.org/2011/ held yearly in Madison, Wisconsin provides a face-to-face forum for educators to meet with games and education researchers, game designers and fellow educators using games for teaching in the classroom. This conference has been held since 2004. Past conference webpages also give the educator a resource to see what educators belong to their community of practice and what COTS they use in the classroom.

Virtual Worlds Best Practices in Education Conference (VWBPE) www.vwbpe.org held yearly in the virtual world Second Life has been taking educators on online field trips. World of Warcraft, Runescape and Club Penguin have been visited by educators new to these COTS to show them the affordances of these games. Additionally there have been presentations and discussions of Lego Universe, Aion, WarHammer, Myst, Habbo Hotel and Cesar III.

The International Society for Technology http://www.iste.org has two special interest groups (SIG) that provide for opportunities to connect with this community of practice. At its annual meeting, two special interest groups, Games and Simulations and also Virtual Environments hold discussions, presentations and "birds of a feather" meetings. Additionally SIG Virtual Environments http://sigve.iste.wikispaces.net/ holds weekly and monthly meetings where speakers do presentations about COTS in classroom among other topics.

Rockcliffe Consortium, a Second Life based educational and professional development consortium, offers World of Teachcraft sessions and tours http://www.urockcliffe.com/education/world-of-teachcraft/ during their Sword and Board summer program as well as developing new sessions on the recently released MMORPG Rift.

Jokaydia http://jokaydia.com/ is an educational community of practice that has regular meeting in the virtual worlds of Second Life and Reaction Grid. They also sponsor tours into World of Warcraft that are attended by educators new to the game with mentoring by veteran players.

Cognitive Dissonance is an educator World of Warcraft guild, U.S. server in the Sisters of Elune realm. http://cognitivedissonance.guildportal.com/Guild.aspx?GuildID=228854&TabID=1927706

While the focus is not the development of curriculum or using COTS in the classroom, it is a guild for educators to play and learn about the gaming aspects of World of Warcraft.

Table 15.2 List of educators and COTS used who presented at VWBPE 2011

Educator	COTS	Affiliation	Grade level	Course/Program
Marianne Malmstrom	Lego Universe World of Warcraft	Elisabeth Morrow School	Grade 3 and 4 middle school	extra-curricular clubs
Lucas Gillispie Peggy Sheehy	World of Warcraft	Cape Fear Middle School, Suffern Middle School	Middle school	After school program, language arts elective
Gord Holden	Cesar III	North Island Distance Education School	Grade 7	Face-to-face and online courses
Diane Lewis	World of Warcraft	Sanford Middle School	Middle school	After school program
John Carter McKnight	World of Warcraft	Arizona State University	University	Public policy, English
Elisabeth Hayes	World of Warcraft	Arizona State University	University	English
Don Marguilis	City of Heroes WarHammer World of Warcraft	Middlesex Community College	2 year college	Psychology
Dona Cady	City of Heroes WarHammer World of Warcraft	Middlesex Community College	2 year college	English Composition, Creative Writing
Chris Luchs Kae Novak	Club Penguin Habbo Hotel World of Warcraft	Front Range Community College	2 year college	Fundamentals of Accounting, Principles of Accounting I, Principles of Accounting II, Intro to Business
Cherry Emerson Kae Novak	Club Penguin Habbo Hotel WarHammer World of Warcraft	Front Range Community College	2 year college	Anthropology of Folklore
Kate Hagerty	Runescape, World of Warcraft, Jade Dynasty	Front Range Community College	2 year college	Intro to Multimedia, Intro to Illustrator

Early adopters are members of a community of practice that has been enhanced by media on the Internet to include social media. Asynchronous discussion forums and synchronous events generate a large amount of information concerning COTS in the classroom projects. Twitter is especially useful for following individuals, groups and projects using COTS.

For example here is a listing of educators using COTS who presented at Virtual Worlds Best Practices in Education Conference (Table 15.2).

15.3.1 Research Resources Available at Your Institution

15.3.1.1 Educational Technology Personnel

Many of the early adopters of COTS listed above are educational technologists or instructional designers. Do your research and see if there are any educational technology personnel at your school, district, college or university. If there are, they may be available to assist you starting with your research and then continue as a partner as you go through most if not all the elements of the RCIPR model. At Front Range Community College, the instructional designer assigned to student success, functioned as an embedded instructional designer. The instructional designer developed step-by-step text and screenshot material to be included in the course learning management system (LMS). She was introduced to the class whether face-to-face or online early in semester, maintained office hours to meet with students and also the classes were given her email and office phone to contact her with issues and concerns.

15.3.1.2 In-house Grants

Does your institution offer faculty grants or stipends to support educators who are trying out new pedagogy or emerging technology? Inquire to see if you can receive initial funding for your pilot project. These funds could help pay for or subsidize the initial purchase of COTS software and subscriptions. These pilots may also facilitate cross discipline collaboration. Typically, these types of programs allow multiple educators to request larger amounts than individuals.

15.4 Choose

After evaluating faculty responses and conducting faculty focus groups, it was found that the instructional design process could have the greatest impact relieving cognitive dissonance in the formative evaluation phase. The team developed a model that addresses social learning (Bandura, 1977), metagaming (Gee, 2001; Squire and Jenkins, 2003), content analysis and supplemental material (Van Eck, 2006). Rubrics for selections of games and ensuring learning objectives were tested in a 3 week online faculty professional development course titled *Introduction to Serious*

Games. The educators who took the course self-selected. They decided to be early adopters of serious games in the classroom. They had confidence in their teaching ability and their ability to choose the correct text book and supplemental material. However, they did not have a high comfort level in choosing a game, developing the lesson plan or project, assessing the learning happening in the game and integrating the technology required for the games. Faculty participants wanted to know prior to introducing the game that it could be effectively adopted into the curriculum.

The team developed and tested a formative evaluation rubric for student engagement in online serious games called the CYTIE Rubric. It is based on Csíkszentmihályi's concept of *flow* (Csíkszentmihályi, 1990), Huizinga's concept of the *magic circle* (Huizinga, 1950), Keller's (1984) ARCS motivation model and Malone and Lepper's (1987) intrinsic motivations for learning. We departed from the FIDGE model of instructional design (Akilli and Cagiltay, 2006) by deepening the formative evaluation phase in order to specifically address faculty cognitive dissonance. If serious games, as a form of new educational technology, are to be adopted in an educational setting special care must be taken to address the "cognitive dissonance of the initially enthusiastic adopters" (Bentley, 2006).

15.4.1 CYTIE Rubric

The CYTIE rubric has two parts. It consists of an instructor review (Fig. 15.2) and a student review (Fig. 15.3).

In testing this rubric, educators played the game for 1 hour to test game navigation, audio quality, text quality and tutorials. After the hour of game play the educator were able to evaluate game play quality and ease of use for their students. Upon reflection of the game experience, the educator could rate the COTS game for education value, class use and duration.

To complete this formative evaluation of the game, student volunteers also played the COTS game for 1 hour. While the instructor review asked questions of education value and class use, the student reviews has students rank degrees of immersion, CYTIE and complexity. CYTIE or "Cause You to Ignore Everything" is based off Csíkszentmihályi's factors of flow (1990). CYTIE is most closely related to the optimal flow factors of concentration and distorted sense of time. Students in courses that piloted COTS game did report that they became so involved in playing the game that they continued past the required 1 hour.

Educators who are part of the early majority are more likely to experience cognitive dissonance than the educators who are early adopters. Early adopters are more likely to have integrated a greater number of emerging technologies already in their classrooms. By using this two part evaluation, educators can reduce the cognitive dissonance concerning using COTS games in the classroom. The educator will have tested the game themselves as well as piloted the game with students. They will be able to evaluate the degree of difficulty the students will have in playing the games as well as the level of immersion that may happen. The rubric provides the early adopters with a familiar type of evaluation while introducing specific attributes associated with game play.

INSTRUCTOR REVIEW

Game Title:

Ranking System Description: (One scroll is the low end, most negative, and three scrolls is the high end, most positive.)

	Ranking Continuum		
Questions			
Game Navigation (How easy is it to learn the game controls or game objectives?)	The user interface is not intuitive and the game is difficult to control	The user interface requires some learning and the game is reasonable to control	The user interface is intuitive and the game is easy to control
Educational Value (How applicable is the game to learning objectives?)	Some value in specific instances	Value can be found with careful deliberation	Concepts are easily identified and explored
Duration (How much time do you need to become engaged?)	Very Slow	Decently Engaging	Engrossing
Audio Quality (How effective was the Audio?)	Takes a while to load, monotone, volume fluctuates	Good audio, informative and life like	Clear, clean audio, very specific to activity
Text Quality (How easy was the text to read?)	Hard to see text, user interface is too cluttered, reading level is inappropirate for some students	Legible text, user interface is fairly balanced, reading level is fair for most students	Clear text, user interface is extremely clear, reading level engages all students
Tutorials (How effective are the tutorials/ directions given?)	Took a while to get the hang of it	Challenging at first, but quickly figured it out	Clearly defined game rules

Fig. 15.2 CYTIE rubric for instructors

15.5 Investigate

15.5.1 Develop a Dynamic IT Plan

Planning should revolve around flexible goal oriented objectives; resources, personnel and time investments may change.

STUDENT REVIEW

Game Title:

Ranking System Description: (One scroll is the low end, most negative, and three scrolls is the high end, most positive.)

	Ranking Continuum		
Questions			
Game Navigation (How easy is it to learn the game controls or game objectives?)	Not great, felt too clumsy, too many buttons, etc.	Once I read the directions, I was able to get it	Intuitive controls, I was able to start playing right away.
Game Play (How smoothly does the game flow from one frame to the next?)	Game felt disorganized, slow, with errors and technical distractions	Some errors and minor halting or slow game play	Error free, fast game play with few technical distractions
Graphics (How aesthetcially pleasing are the graphics?)	Hard to see images, screen is too busy	Good graphics, though not the best I have seen	Great graphics, highly detailed and interesting
Degree of Immersion (To what degree, do you feel are part of the game?)	Some, but nothing compelling to make me want to do more	OK storyline, but not much character backstory, history, or society	Great story and lore drew me into the game's plot and setting
CYTIE Index* (To what degree, do you lose track of time when playing the game?)	Very slow	Good way to spend 30 minutes	What time is it?
Complexity (How easy is it to understand the game rules and/or objectives?)	Took a while to get the hang of it	Challenging at first, but quickly figured it out	Clearly defined game rules

* *CYTIE stands for "Causes You to Ignore Everything."*

Comments:
(Strategies, Cheats, Shared Knowledge, Helpful Websites.)

Fig. 15.3 CYTIE rubric for students

1. *Measure Your Infrastructure* – Check the application's basic and recommended requirements. If your equipment meets the basic requirements, be ready to adjust the time investment portion of your plan or look to increase resources.
2. *Discover the IT's Realistic Capabilities* – Be realistic about what IT personnel can and will do. IT personnel may never have been asked to install an application similar to a commercial off the shelf game. Share your research regarding other educational institution's successful implementation of a game.
3. *Follow Protocol* – Use the official channels to make your requests; most educational institutions have standard operating procedures and paperwork that needs to be filled out in order to have software installed. Additionally many institutions have set times of the year where new software installations take place. Make sure you are aware of these procedures and dates. Meeting established procedures ensures your request has the appropriate administrative and technical evaluations and approvals. Check with administrators first as the appropriate channel to develop new curricular adaptations.
4. *Build a Relationship with an IT professional* – You should also develop a positive relationship with a member of the technical staff who can advise you of the current system capabilities and upgrades needed for your implementation. Ask other educators who have worked with your technical department in the past who they would recommend as collaborative and understanding of educational affordance. Approaching the IT personnel most likely to encourage early adopters will assist in removing barriers that are not based on IT capabilities. They can also advise you of adoption hindrances to your specific selection.

15.5.2 When the Technical Staff Cannot Fulfill Your Request

During your first attempts at implementing COTS and other games into your curriculum, you may run into concerns with IT compliance at your institution. Most IT departments will not allow users to download programs onto institutional computers for security reasons. There may also be issues with graphics cards and broadband access at your institution. Many IT directors will request that you provide them with references on what other peer institutions are using COTS and games for learning. The key is to remember that IT personnel will be looking at issues from campus informational security perspectives and will focus on the Terms of Service and End User Licensing Agreement not necessarily the educational value of the COTS game.

The researchers have found that when negotiating with IT staff to have software applications installed, you may have to call upon the educators' community to talk to your institutional IT personnel. The researchers did work with an educator at an outside institution to assist him in having software installed. While the educator did not know the exact requirements, the researchers had two phone conversations with the educator's IT personnel on how to give access without compromising the institution's firewall.

Another strategy is to engage IT staff in the selection of the game to develop departmental buy in. This may also lead to introductions to other games and genres that the educator was not initially aware of or considering. Having an IT member's assistance during selection will ensure that the final COTS game is compatible with campus IT resources.

15.6 Pilot

15.6.1 Low Risk Options (Safe-to-Fail)

For primary and secondary level schools try piloting a game as part of an after school activity or student club. Several World of Warcraft in Schools projects have sprung up around the idea of targeting at-risk students, leveraging the attraction of the game both to teach twenty-first century skills and Internet based literacies as well as encourage homework completion and positive study habits. There are other possibilities as well, the important point is to find a venue where the use of the game allows for experimentation and reveals the learning potential to critics in a non-threatening environment.

At the K-12 level, educators will want to look for pilot programs that are safe-to-fail or low risk. Low risk programs offer educators an optimal test bed to trial possibly contentious educational applications and curriculum. Under the guise of "for fun only" setting educators can comfortably explore the limits of a particular activity's curricular potential. Every school seeks out those on the staff who are willing to engage the hardest to reach students. Schools entertain many traditional and non-traditional extra and co-curricular activities. In a school that runs a games design course it seems natural to have a club called game explorations.

While educators at higher education institutions may have more flexibility on the initial adoption of COTS for the classroom, these same educators based on the 15 week semester in the United States, have less time for successful implementation.

At the community college and university level, there are two low risk options available. The first is the extra credit project and the second is as one of the options in a project assignment. In the accounting courses, World of Warcraft was introduced as an extra credit project. Once the World of Warcraft project was developed further, it was then introduced as a one of two options for the last project of the semester.

15.6.2 Prepping the Students

At Front Range Community College, in courses that have adopted COTS and other emerging technologies, students at the beginning of the semester are given a detailed survey of their use of technology. This survey includes questions on amount of time spent daily using the Internet, their social media activities and their familiarity and usage of MMORPGs. This allows the instructor and instructional designer to see the student's level of involvement with technology outside the classroom.

In the accounting courses, based on these responses, the instructor and instructional designer plan the course project as either an individual effort or a group project. If a group project is assigned, the instructor based on the survey results ensures that there is at least one student that plays MMORPGs outside the classroom. The results of this grouping have been that this allows for additional peer-to-peer learning.

Additionally, the researchers have found that writing statements explaining to traditional age and adult college students the educational value of the gameplay reduces the number of inquiries concerning the game. An example curriculum statement is:

> How does this relate to you as a student in an Accounting class? As an accountant, your job is to conservatively estimate value and ensure GAAP appropriate accounting standards are used. This project puts your current knowledge of accounting to the test. You will draw from the all the chapters you have covered in ACC 121 and ACC 122 so far; Chapters 1–20. These chapters contain all of the accounting background that you will need to complete this project. Both of Projects III's options will call on what you have learned in the class this semester. You will use what you have learned to apply accounting terminology, concepts and principles in accordance with GAAP in a setting new to you. You will also be asked to make recommendations of basic internal control principles to protect assets, of cost accounting aspects, and general accounting/ business strategies. Developing these accounting skills, being able to think critically and adapt to novel business situations will make you a very valuable employee.

15.6.3 Feedback from Students

As a way of receiving feedback, the accounting instructor had students post their results and impressions in the LMS's weekly discussion forum. Besides their results, students were asked to answer the following questions:

1. As far as illustrating business and accounting principles, what did this do well?
2. As far as illustrating business and accounting principles, what did this not do well?
3. Would you recommend this game to friend if they wanted to learn about accounting?

By requesting feedback, the instructor was able to elicit frank feedback and commentary from students regarding COTS game and project instructions and rubric. This feedback was then incorporated into the next rendition of the project to continuously improve the project and hone learning objectives and instruction. By avoiding yes, no responses, the students were required to construct their thoughts regarding successes and shortfalls of the COTS and project.

A secondary benefit was that the students were able to voice their concerns and any issues that they had with the game in a group context. Students were able to see that other's shared their challenges and also share tips and tricks to fellow students to ease future game play. An interesting byproduct of this discussion was the development of student's troubleshooting for other students to resolve issues and encourage collaboration.

During the documentation of the pilot, the instructor will typically become aware of some potential negative aspects of utilizing COTS versus games designed specifically for the curriculum. Some examples would be the student does not immediately comprehend how the COTS assesses a topic or skill, the student becomes distracted by game play or other game mechanic issues and not learning objectives, the student feels that the game is too simple for their grade level, and the student misinterprets the purpose of utilizing the game to achieve the learning outcome. These are all common themes when students are first exposed to pilots. Typically, resolution of these issues occurs when the faculty reviews the curriculum statement with the student focusing on the learning objectives and outcomes.

15.6.4 Examples of Possible Pilots

Course or activity	COTS	Grade level	Course/program
History class	Cesar III	Middle school	Extra credit activity – Roman campaigns
English or literature class	War Hammer	High school, community college, university	Optional project – Joseph Campbell's the Hero's Journey
Before or after school program	Lego Universe	Middle school	At risk students as extra-curricular activity
Business course	World of Warcraft	High school, community college, university	Extra credit activity – auction house
Physical science class	Minecraft	Middle school	Rotating computer lab station

15.7 Reflect

Reflection is an additional means for documenting your project's progress. In teacher training and professional development for the past 20 years has used a model of "teacher as reflective practitioner" (Grushka et al., 2005, p. 239). The last aspect of the RCIPR model is reflection (Luttenberg and Bergen, 2008).

Since there is an active community of practice on the Internet, it is suggested that educators also consider posting their reflections on social media outlets such as twitter, blogs and wikis. It will also allow educators to receive feedback, be asked questions and also share the knowledge they have gained. Presentations at conferences and participation in live discussions events also allow sharing your findings and best practices with your colleagues.

15.7.1 Official Documentation

The first part of the reflection starts during the pilot when the educator is documenting their pilot project. Beyond their pilot project, educators should be tracking student academic performance as a whole. This would be done by also measuring.

Educators should commit serious time and thought to implementing their plan and drafting an explanation for how the game environment supplements the curriculum and expands the general learning environment of the course. The explanation should involve assessable pedagogical benchmarks that can be measured through documentation. Educators, as early adopters, should be willing to commit to documenting the trials, successes and failures of their project. For an implementation to succeed past a single instructor there needs to be an evidential trail for successive implementation for the early majority.

Machinima is another method for documenting your pilot program. Machinima is a portmanteau of Machinima and cinema. It is live screen capture of the 3D animation in MMORPGs. You will need to check with the terms of service in the MMORPG you are using to see if screen capture for educational purposes is allowed. If it is allowed, Machinima is a very effective way of documenting your project. It also acts as a medium to allow other educators who may not necessarily be able to willing to login into the COTS to see what learning is taking place.

15.7.2 Collecting Data

In addition to documenting, there should also be formal and informal data collection instruments built into the pilot program. Formal data collection may take the form of student generated content, responses to surveys or quizzes, screen shots of live events, student journals, class blog or website, or performance on assessments covering the concepts and learning objectives outlined in the research phase of the RCIPR model.

Informal data collection may take the form of student comments in class, chat logs from COTS, discussion overheard in hallways, or simply unsolicited discussion on the COTS from students.

Data collection should not just focus on the COTS, but also seek to measure student performance in other curricular activity. What skills and study tactics are students applying to other areas of the class? How is overall class performance compared to non-pilot classes? COTS and games are not just entertainment simulations; they also address new media literacy (Jenkins et al., 2005).

15.8 Conclusion

The RCIPR model offers educators a framework to effectively implement their COTS pilots at their institutions. As educators continue to consider the adoption of COTS, the need to critically evaluate games, communicate the software and hardware requirements to IT, pilot the games, reflect on implementation, and document the results will become increasingly important. For educational institutions to consider COTS seriously, educators and instructional designers will need to develop dynamic implementation plans, collect data, document their work, and present their results to peers. The RCIPR model addresses how a faculty member or instructional designer should conduct formative evaluation prior to the integration of online serious games or off the shelf games that are not specifically designed for their course. This model is an evaluative framework that enables faculty from multiple disciplines to effectively and conveniently incorporate serious games into their curriculum.

References

Akilli, G.K., Cagiltay, K.: An instructional design/development model for the creation of game like learning environments: the FIDGE model. In: Pivec, M. (ed.) Affective and Emotional Aspects of Human-Computer Interaction Game-Based and Innovative Learning Approaches, Vol. 1, pp. 93–112. IOS Press, Amsterdam, The Netherlands (2006)

Bandura, A.: Social Learning Theory. General Learning Press, New York (1977)

Bentley, J. Implementing technology initiatives: the impact of individual cognitive dissonance on success. In: Pearson, E., Bohman, P. (eds.) Proceedings of World Conference on Educational Multimedia, Hypermedia and Telecommunications 2006, pp. 1344–1349. AACE, Chesapeake, VA (2006)

Blizzard Entertainment Inc.: World of Warcraft® subscriber base reaches 12 million worldwide. http://us.blizzard.com/en-us/company/press/pressreleases.html?101007 (2010)

Csíkszentmihályi, M.: Flow: The Psychology of Optimal Experience. Harper and Row, New York (1990)

Egenfeldt-Nielsen, S.: Third generation educational use of computer games. J. Educ. Multimedia Hypermedia **16**(3), 263–281 (2007)

Festinger, L.A.: Theory of Cognitive Dissonance. Stanford University Press, Stanford, CA (1957)

Gee, J.: What Video Games Have To Tell Us About Learning and Literacy. Palgrave, New York (2001)

Grushka, K., McLeod, J.H., Reynolds, R.: Reflecting upon reflection: Theory and practice in one Australian University teacher education program. Reflective Pract. **6**(2), 239–246 (2005)

Huizinga, J.: Homo ludens. The Beacon Press, Boston, MA (1950)

Jenkins, H., Puroshotma, R., Clinton, K., Weigel, M., Robinson, A.: Confronting the challenges of participatory culture: media education for the 21st century. http://www.newmedialiteracies.org/files/working/NMLWhitePaper.pdf (2005). Accessed 20 Mar 2011

Keller, J.M.: The use of the ARCS model of motivation in teacher training. In: Shaw, K., Trott, A.J. (eds.) Aspects of Educational Technology Volume XVII: Staff Development and Career Updating, pp. 140–145. Kogan Page, London (1984)

Lave, J., Wenger, E.: Communities of Practice: Learning, Meaning, and Identity. Cambridge University Press, Cambridge (1998)

Luttenberg, J., Bergen, T.: Teacher reflection: the development of a typology. Teach. Teach. Theory Pract. **14**(5–6), 543–566 (2008)

Malone, T.W., Lepper, M.R.: Making learning fun: a taxonomy of intrinsic motivations for learning. In: Snow, R.E., Farr, M.J. (eds.) Aptitude, Learning and Instruction: III. Cognitive and Affective Process Analyses, pp. 223–253. Erlbaum, Hillsdale, NJ (1987)

Moore, G.A.: Crossing the Chasm: Marketing and Selling Disruptive Products to Mainstream Customers. First Collins Business Essentials Edition. Harper Collins Publishers, New York (2006)

Prensky, M.: Digital Game-Based Learning, 1st edn. McGraw Hill, New York (2001)

Rice, J.W.: New media resistance: Barriers to implementation of computer video games in the classroom. J. Educ. Multimedia Hypermedia **16**(3), 249–261 (2007)
Squire, K., Jenkins, H.: Harnessing the power of games in education. *InSight* 3. http://www.edvantia.org/products/pdf/InSight_3-1_Vision.pdf (2003). Accessed 28 Dec 2008
Van Eck, R.: Digital game-based learning: It's not just the digital natives who are restless. Educause Rev. **41**(2), 16–30 (2006)

Chapter 16
Learning Narratives with Harry Potter. "Manuel de Fallas's The Prophet Newspaper"

Sara Cortés Gómez, Rut Martínez Borda, and Pilar Lacasa

16.1 Introduction: Bringing Commercial Games into the Classroom

The arrival of video games has brought about a new means of entertainment as well as a new form of art and has been treated as an event separate from cultural history but which is, in fact, part of the way we transform our leisure time, social relations, knowledge development, learning and, of course, education. *Will video games change the way we learn?* These new means are a reality that should not be ignored and which is altering our way of learning and developing knowledge. Therefore, they deserve to be studied and researched to facilitate the natural integration they should have into the formal educational system (Gros, 2008) and education is to play a special role in this process (Buckingham, 2000).

This chapter describes an approach to the design of learning environments that builds on the educational properties of games but deeply grounds them within a theory of learning which is appropriate for an age marked by the power of new technologies. We argue that to understand the future of learning, we have to look beyond schools to the emerging arena of video games. Video games have become one of the most successful technological resources among children and teenagers and they have carved out an important and valuable niche in our society. This perspective helps us to think about why and how cultural objects designed for fun rather than for educational purposes can be used to improve digital literacies at school (Lacasa and GIPI, 2009; Lacasa, 2010, 2011). It is indisputable that there is something about video games which gets people really excited and which makes children, teens and adults play for hours on end: the fantasy, the graphics, the gaming possibilities, the challenges and the complexity, but above all, the continuous decisions the player must make as part of his strategy and to meet goals or get past levels (Prensky, 2005). For this reason, one of our goals will be to help clarify the rich and complex

S.C. Gómez (✉)
Department of Psychology, Education and Physical Education, University of Alcala, Madrid, Spain
e-mail: sara.cortesg@uah.es

M. Ma et al. (eds.), *Serious Games and Edutainment Applications*,
DOI 10.1007/978-1-4471-2161-9_16, © Springer-Verlag London Limited 2011

relation between video games and formal learning. *What and how can we learn from video games at the school? How can we use the power of video games as a constructive force in schools?*

The idea of learning in the school is related only to schoolwork, the content of the curriculum and particularly, those specific materials that have traditionally been present in the classroom: books, paper, pencils, textbooks and so on. All these cultural tools are associated with the academic culture and the school context. Theories of learning and instruction embodied in school systems designed to teach large numbers of students a standardised curriculum are outdated in this new world. These perspectives may change when commercial video games are introduced in the physical context of the classroom. Commercial computer games have great potential as learning tools as many require complex problem solving, theory testing, collaboration and evaluation, all of them components of experiential learning (Gee, 2004). Moreover, this instrument contributes to bringing the day-to-day routine of children closer, overcoming barriers in the learning environment and favouring motivation.

We might also hypothesise that games in the classroom would leverage players' desires to develop new skills, participate in new roles or better understand the world from a new or "professional" perspective (Gee, 2005; Shaffer, 2005). Playing is undeniably a powerful, pervasive method of learning outside of schools; indeed, most psychologists would agree that it is a crucial method through which we test ideas, develop new skills, and participate in new social roles (Piaget, 1962; Vygotsky, 1978). Vygotsky (1978) emphasises this concept when writing about how the imaginary world is a strong space for potential for the child's development.

Likewise, James Paul Gee argues in his book What Video Games Have to Teach Us about Learning (2003) that educators might benefit from studying how game players learn through game play. As he explains, "When kids play video games they experience a much more powerful form of learning than when they're in the classroom... Each level dances around the outer limits of the player's abilities, seeking at every point to be hard enough to be just doable". Digital games play a meaningful and natural role in the everyday life of children and young people, a world of games which provides them with new experiences, interesting stories, social events, fun, challenges, excitement and also many moments of learning. We suggest that video games matter because they present players with simulated worlds: worlds which, if well constructed, are not just about facts or isolated skills, but embody specific social practices. We also argue that video games thus make it possible for players to participate in valued communities of practice and as a result develop the ways of thinking that organise those practices. This new approach allows us to understand the value of video games, as well as to observe and research the first multidisciplinary attempt to analyze this new form of entertainment from diverse perspectives.

But how should we use these new tools? Video games are only a means of entertainment developed in a computer environment which allows the player to play a role by interacting with his surroundings and by using the right commands in a context simulated under a clearly designed structure and a minimum set of rules. They were not designed to be used in the learning/teaching process, just like many films screened in the classroom. For these reasons, the role played by the adult becomes essential, in the transformation process of the video game into an educational resource. One of the most important conditions for a successful experience in terms of motivation and reflective processes is that the teachers should feel comfortable with the materials they are using. Bringing commercial video games into the classrooms, however, remains a challenge as teachers are generally less familiar with games than they are with other entertainment mass media (Lacasa et al., 2008). Taking these premises as our starting point, the need arises to look into the effects digital culture is having on the school's educational mission in order to explore and suggest new strategies to bridge the cultural gap separating what usually motivates and gets students involved and what teachers plan and implement as part of their job (Esnaola, 2001). The teachers' mission will not only be to design the educational sequence of contents, but also to analyze the learning environments. As we can see, the use of video games in the classroom allows us to focus their study on different fields that arise from the link between the gamer and the game in an educational context.

In this research we will focus on one key aspect present at the time of playing any video game: the existence of narratives and the possibilities to create stories with these tools. We see tremendous opportunities for using adventure games to engage students in the narrative world, where they can play, discover and then write about their stories.

16.2 Learning to Tell Stories with Adventure Video Games. Harry Potter a "Transmedia" Phenomenon

When video games are considered as educational tools in formal education (Jenkins and Lacasa, 2010), these elements, originally designed for leisure, are used to work on curriculum contents. It is about supporting teaching and learning with a tool designed for entertainment, and in this case opportunities to consolidate curriculum contents are sought. Teachers have traditionally used different media, for instance, films, comics, literature classics, etc. The results from the study show the contribution of commercial video games to the design of educational scenarios that develop children's narrative thinking while students learn to tell stories with a video games adventure. We try to understand the concept of narrative through this relationship with video games, the possibilities and how to use them in educational contexts.

16.2.1 From Storytelling to Interactive Narrative

We understand narrative as the act of narration; therefore, the narrative consists of content (story/fable), a way to tell (story/sjuzet) and the act of narration. *How do I move this process to the interactivity of the virtual world?* To try to answer this question we draw on theories of Orihuela (1997). This author provides a set of distinctions between traditional linear narrative and interactive narrative and understands that linear narrative is characterised by closed stories, preset stories and the hegemony of a narrator, as in films and novels whereas interactive narrative is made up of open stories with multiples possibilities. In this narrative there is no predetermined beginning and end but several possible beginnings and multiple endings. In any case, the selection of these "roads narrative" and the creation of the story partially in the hands of the user. This new model for understanding the narrative introduces for the first time the active user participation in the construction of history. Thus, since the game features an interaction between player and game, we talk about the narrative function as an interactive narrative.

Narrative genres can be different according the prominence they give to physical action and the interpersonal relations that motivate these actions, but the stories that focus entirely on problem solving through physical actions are extremely rare. To rival the narrative richness of other media, then, a system of interactive storytelling must be able to stage both physical actions that change the fictional world and verbal acts that affect the minds of its inhabitants and motivate them to take action.

This view of interactive narrative provides a balance between the need to give the user some control over the story, make it interactive and, at the same time, maintain some consistency (basically, internal logic and narrative universe identity of the characters) to make some sense (Orihuela, 1997). The player becomes a narrator who chooses paths and the game plot becomes a detached and almost unique experience. Decisions made by each player are different stories. Xavier Berenguer defines the connection between the player and the choice of history as an interactive dilemma between "the author's need to control history and the freedom of the interactor to change" (Berenguer, 1998). Video games, and more specifically the adventure game analyzed in this chapter are built around this dilemma. The game designer sets a storyline and a set of rules that should allow the story to progress but, in turn, offers a certain degree of freedom and motivates the player to act in the game. "*Progression games*" *in which the player must advance through predetermined sequences to complete the game*" (Juul 2001). In fact, the player is solving a story, not creating it actively (Egenfeldt et al., 2008). The game designer determines the steps that the player should be given and shows how to follow the story in the game world. The player becomes the narrator to act in the game and thus reconstructs the stories that define the game.

We will continue with the process of understanding the narrative and its connection to the gaming world by using Bruner's contributions (2001), who understands the narrative as a process that shapes the real world things that often come to prevail over that reality. The narrative constructs the imaginary world of realities that appear to overlap with reality itself. Through the narrative, the child is able to construct theories on how the world should be both preventable and fanciful. Additionally, Murray (1997) states that digital media have brought the narrative to this field, and in this sense this is a dramatic experience for the subject. The game promotes the child's desire to live a fantasy, which is intensified by the participative immersion and the pleasure associated to the possibility of moving to a fictional place where wishes come true. From this perspective we find that these two ways of understanding the narrative offer the player two views: other possibility of creating a story and the subsequent narrative reconstruction of what they experienced there. This is the main goal of the workshop: to analyze the teacher's work proposal.

Some authors, such as Ferraro (1994), believe that "the narrative form constitutes a basic tool for meaning construction and event interpretation. It could be said that, more than language, narrative should be considered the primary modeling system" (Ferraro, 1994). In this case the narrative is a tool that interprets and constructs one process. Based on this idea, we can consider narrative not just as a formal discourse issue but also as "a cognitive construct, or mental image, built by the interpreter in response to the text" (Ryan, 2004). Focusing on our connection between the narrative and the video game world, we can say that the reader (in this case player) moves to the world of the writer (in this case game designer) when living the adventures that take place in the virtual world of the game.

16.2.2 The Possibilities of Video Games: Virtual World and Narrative

If there is one contribution that digital technology has made to game design it is their narrative. This new digital era has brought about a new way to live adventures, ceasing to have a merely recreational and non-participative use to make it possible for the player to recreate circumstances that allow him to anticipate them in non-virtual world. We could say that video games are a new way, a new tool and a new technology that transports the individual to imaginary worlds, thus becoming a context which offers fictional situations in which to reproduce real conducts and behaviours. The virtual world likes a reality in which the individual has the feeling of living in a different and fictional world. In this case, we can say that one of these technologies are video games, which allow us to be transported to other worlds (figured worlds) and live "as if" we were the main character and we could create our own story.

This sort of figured world can inspire new actions or, paradoxically, alternative pleasures for the individual, which may lead him to look for a way to evade reality. This context is the foundation of the development of narrative. The virtual world in which the player acts and identifies himself with the characters also immerses the user in a universe of stories. The space of the video games is computer-generated, three-dimensional simulation of a fictional world, where the player is invited to step into this world, to impersonate a character, and to interact through language (Ryan, 2009). Thus, we can understand that virtual world connects the user with a simulated reality in which he can discover, imagine and therefore create a story, and this is the great power of the video games; interaction between the machine and the user is the process that generates the interactive narrative in the game. No matter what the user says or does, the synthetic agents respond coherently and integrate the user's input into a narrative arc that sustains interest. The fictional world in the video games is a tool with the irresistible chance to actively participate and "being part of the story", reconstructing the narrative which articulates the game. As a result, the child has the opportunity to develop strategies through action, not only to generate narratives, but also to discover procedures in decision-making that take place in a fantasy world where the player must choose and decide against the basic objectives the game proposes.

Therefore, virtual reality offers the user the possibility to move in the world as he wishes and become involved in other environments that come alive through his words and actions. The user enters (active embodiment) an image (a spatial context) which represents a complete environment (diversity detection). Although the world of the image is the product of a digital code, we cannot see the computer/screen/console (transparency of the medium). We can manipulate objects in the virtual world and interact with its inhabitants as in the real world (the dream of a natural language). We become the characters in the virtual world (alternative embodiment and interpretation of a role). In our interaction with the virtual world comes a story (the simulation and narration) and representing this argument is a pleasant and relaxing activity (virtual reality as an art form.) (Ryan, 2004)

Video games make players interact with this "faked" world and face situations which force them to make decisions which will determine the game's plot. With this idea, we mean that the virtual world (or the world of video games) does not have any previous history that defines it; it does not exist in its own and is recreated as a context for the activities that take place in it. The theories of narrative state that games are closely linked to narration and must be analyzed. Murray (1997) states that the positions of narrator, character and reader merge and refers to narrative authorship in digital narratives as the presence of an author who writes the rules determining the text apart from writing the text itself, so that the stages of the game become the scenario in which the plot takes place and the text develops according to the actions or activities of the player. In this regard, the characters or "heroes" in the game become the actors in the "novel", and the player becomes the author or director of the story. Along these lines, we must speak of the shared construction of texts. "One way of describing a computer game is a series of interesting decisions". "If we like computer games is because they allow us to interact with the story, rather than just see it and receive it passively. Therefore, to create a game, see that the player has a huge capacity" (Saltzman, 2001).

When playing, the player discovers the game mechanics while experience a story based on his actions. Henry Jenkins (2003, 2004) understands the relationship between video games and narrative from a space perspective in which space is the key of narrative possibilities. The construction of complex plots and characters is not as crucial as the space to be explored, controlled and mapped. This is how the possibility to invent stories comes up. For this reason, and as we mentioned earlier, video games also have great potential for the narrative development of stories with multiple endings in which the reader-player-narrator is invited to choose the narrative options himself. In computer games, players must interact with the story, which is opposed to the linear structure of narrations (Calquist, 2002). Both the game and the narrative situation move in a world that is only alive as long as there is someone to interpret the signs appearing in those contexts. By inviting the player to become involved in the sequence election process, the narrator opens a transitional space, which allows the reader/player to participate in narrative creation. Space generates narrative in video games (Jenkins, 2004). By taking part in these choices, the reader "moves the focus away" from himself and feels "as if" he was the one creating the story. This way, narratives in video games generate an affective, cognitive involvement that gives way to an immersion process in the plot and we can understand the concentration and interest generated by the game (among other skills) and reject the argument of a lack of concentration of the users.

We have chosen to refer to these ideas because by introducing video games in the classroom as a game element we will offer students moments of interaction and decision-making, turning them into "authors/writers" of their own adventures. As we will see later on, these narratives will truly acquire an educational value as they offer great possibilities to tell stories. Our challenge therefore lies in understanding the codes, learning how to read them and telling consistent stories by using a method as changing as the times we live in.

We must not forget an important element in the game world and that connects directly the player with the game, – the character or hero. Recent studies on the narrative of the games have highlighted the character functions that allow the narrative drive. This way, the character is acting and living the story of the game. This is important, for the player adopts an identity and the possibilities for action, spatial relationships and connecting with other characters multiply (Egenfeldt et al., 2008). From this perspective, the character is considered the necessary link between the player and the narrator, i.e. the junction between interactive options taken by the player and the narrator's response. The player needs the character, but he has the ability to become the author of his own adventures. In this research, moreover, the character's value is twofold as it represents a cultural hero of society. Harry Potter is a world-renowned hero which originated in the literary world, as part of a narrative, and in the game the player is allowed to enter the narrative and live the game. Students took their identity and lived their adventures. This ratio was also the language teacher to select the game and work on narratives based on the reconstruction of the adventures.

16.2.3 The Adventure Video Games: Harry Potter as a Transmedia Phenomenon

We have also reflected on how, by using adventure video games, students have managed to dominate, step by step, narrative thinking and some problem-solving processes hidden behind the plot of the stories. From this point of view, three questions may be asked: *What characteristics define this type of game? What educational possibilities do the challenges hidden behind the screen hold? What kind of work can teachers develop based on their use?*

In addition to the hidden action and resolution of problems the video game has, the game features contents (space, time, actions and characters) that offer the perfect space for the player's action. It is for this reason that adventure games are more related to the ability to create narratives. In this type of games, the player makes a narrative reconstruction of events planned by its creator, in some cases across platforms, testing, achieving goals, etc. The decisions made by the player determine the path that achieves the ultimate goal of the game. The adventure game presents one method that starts from a specific story world and inserts possibilities of user action to make it interactive. This is the approach in games on Harry Potter. Because the plot of these games must be adapted to the possibilities of action offered by game controls, it is usually fairly different from its literary or cinematic source. Many of the games based on a pre-existing story tend to become stereotyped shooters and quests, with weak integration of the player's actions into the storyline. These games attract players much more for the spatial and visual pleasure of finding themselves in a familiar fictional world and of encountering favorite characters than for the temporal pleasure of enacting a specific sequence of events. In this kind of design, the story world takes precedence over the story. Let's see how the game is introduced in the instructions manual that comes with the video game:

HARRY POTTER'S MOST DANGEROUS COURSE

Live through all the thrilling action of Harry Potter's fifth year at Hogwarts *School of Witchcraft and Wizardry, from the attack of the dementors in Little Whinging up to the epic battles at the Ministry of Magic. While the magical world refuses to accept the return of Voldermort, Harry recruits a small group of students and secretly prepares them in defensive magic practices. They call themselves "Dumbledore's Army" (DA). Hold Harry's magic wand and explore the dark corridors, the secret rooms and the extensive grounds at Hogwarts. Compete in mini-games, talk to enchanted portraits and perfect your spell-casting techniques. In summary: sharpen your magical abilities, gather up the courage and prepare to fight Lord Voldemort and his fearful dark forces in Harry's most dangerous and complicated year until now.*

This description shows that, from the beginning, the player faces two essential elements that define the game: On the one hand, the adventures Harry Potter and his friends are going to go through, and on the other, the problems the player will have to solve in order for the story line to advance. This combination of the problems presented and the fictional experience ended up being determining factors for what happened during the workshop. This simple instruction embodies both representational and ludic design, it continues the narrative events, characters, unresolved conflicts and episodic trajectory, while also issuing a ludic imperative which provides the object of the game.

The children play this game because of a passionate commitment to the character and his narrative. There are interesting implications here for how narratives are experienced across literature, film and game, and how they are differently constructed across these media; and this can be exploited in the context of literacy work in English or media studies, as the work of Catherine Beavis (2001) has shown. There are also many questions about the nature of the media industries, and how they organise such franchises, that can be posed in the context of media education.

Due to the educational implications, we have to highlight two characteristics that define these games. As opposed to other genres, the adventure told by the video game may borrow elements from other media, especially from literature and films. This phenomenon, that specialists have called "transmedia", means that a story is presented transversally through different formats. That is to say, it can be expressed and communicated in many ways, using several languages. Each text will introduce a specific and valuable contribution to the entire story line. For example, nowadays, hero adventures like Harry Potter are present in more than one medium and appear in multiple platforms. From and with the aid of video games, new discourses associated to multiples ways of becoming literate are acquired. These video games give us the opportunity to reflect upon how different literacy means are put in practice and interconnect between one another.

The data obtained in the research have allowed us to analyze how students develop their creative skills, especially related to the way in which they build stories on the basis of the contents of the video games. From this point of view, Harry Potter and the Order of the Phoenix was especially useful. It is well known that, in video games, the stories are only possible if the player's activity updates the hero's life, with some independence of who designed the video game. Analyzing the written productions from the children in the Harry Potter stories we can observe the use of space (characters: Harry, Ron, Hermione, the Hogwarts school) as the context where the action is temporary and the predominance of a temporary, as students reconstruct the actions experienced in the game as a narrative.

16.3 Case Study: Hogwarts' World in the Secondary School

The methodology on which our analytical process is based consists of our own case study techniques, combined with the use of some practices of ethnography and an ecological approach which explores what happens in natural situations (Atkinson et al., 2001; Lacasa and Reina, 2004). Its validity is based on a detailed description of the cases in which we can explain how people make sense of their activities in defined socio-cultural contexts. We focus on ethnography because we observe people's activities in a certain environment, the classroom (Atkinson and Hammersley, 1994). In this case, we are exploring how adventure games can be used in the classroom, the possibilities and features they have and how teachers and researchers can work with them; examining the possibilities offered by video games from a research perspective of the internal narratives this possesses, and analyzing the presence of stories in the games which help narrate the plot and allow the construction of new stories generated from their use in language class.

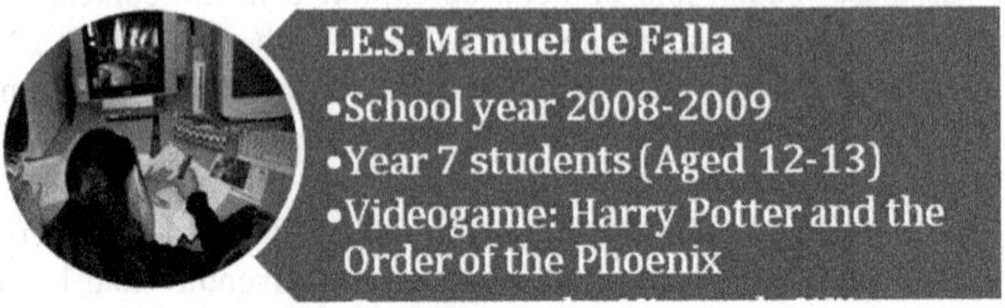

I.E.S. Manuel de Falla
•School year 2008-2009
•Year 7 students (Aged 12-13)
•Videogame: Harry Potter and the Order of the Phoenix

Schools participating in the research

16.3.1 Workshop Around Harry Potter: Participants, Instruments and Process

This paper presents some of the results of a project carried out in collaboration with teachers to explore how commercial video games can be used in elementary classrooms. The data collected and analyzed for this research were gathered at public schools in the Madrid region. During school year 2008–2009, we conducted research in a secondary school where we worked with several grades. 300 students aged between 11 and 16 participated in the general experience. Most of them were secondary school students, although sometimes the workshops also welcomed some secondary high school students, students with special needs and vocational education students. This level of involvement had a huge impact in the centre, which incorporated this project to the school's innovation scheme involving its 7 educational departments.

The teachers' collaboration with the researchers made the development of different workshops possible. These took place during school hours and regular lessons. What is different from a regular lesson is the methodology, not the content, even though this can be extended and adapted, just as in any other educational context. Video games become one more element of a wide multimedia context in which participants combine the use of a number of technologies. For example, besides game consoles and computer games, in the classroom we find books, notebooks, the Internet, cameras, mobile phones and every other device which may be deemed necessary.

We will focus on the workshop carried out with students aged 12–13 (groups A and B) and their language teacher. The teacher was highly experienced, very education-minded and innovative. He had already worked together with the research team in a previous workshop with another game and another group of students. This made him aware of how important it is to play before the video game is introduced and, in fact, he had already "got past" 100% of the game's levels by the time the workshop came to an end. In this case, the work sessions took place for a month at the end of the school year.

The secondary school, the classroom and the tools

The video game was played once a week for the hour corresponding to the language lessons, although some more work was done at a later stage in the classroom whenever curriculum issues came up on the language book related to the aim of the workshop and the use of the video game. This was one of the teacher's objectives, working with the issues related to literary creations and narrative texts. For this reason, the teacher thought it would be interesting to create a newspaper in which the students could show their experiences with the game in the form of articles, interviewing the characters or simply evaluating the educational experience. Its introduction in the workshop also allowed us to explore the construction and development of narrative skills in the classroom by means of task resolution.

The teacher tried to get his students to apply theoretical learning curriculum text types (narrative, description and dialogue) and the literary language they learned in the language class. The game therefore became a tool that offers multiple language text. To achieve this aim, during the duration of the workshop the teacher explained the lesson plans related to the narrative, description and dialogue (Items 11 language book presented here), with abstracts and contributions from the students themselves.

When analyzing the content featured in the language book, we can see that "the narrative is the story of an event occurring to characters in a given time and space (...) these events can be real or imaginary just like the characters, time or space in which they occur". Again, we see the connection we generated in previous theoretical sections between the relationship of game and narrative. In this case, the game will be used as an element leading to the creation of real or imaginary texts based on the argument that includes the game, the characters (Harry, Ron and Hermione) and context (the Hogwarts magic school) and main elements of the narrative text according to the book. The value of play is that allows the creation of interactive narrative in game and the reconstructions of the adventures in writing at a later stage.

We worked with the video game "Harry Potter and the Order of the Phoenix". This adventure video game offered new ways to tell stories in which characters, objects, time and space combine to make the hero's adventure more attractive. During the workshop, the students were deep into the secrets of Hogwarts facing multiple tasks and solving various problems they encountered as they progressed on the game. Later, with the recreation of the newspaper "The Prophet", all their adventures were written, resulting in multiple texts. In this paper we find stories based on the game as well as other fully imagined vivid recreations of scenes in the game to achieve a goal or decide what is the ideal tool to compare the two worlds (real and virtual), interviews with Harry Potter himself, his personal opinions about the workshop, etc. What do all these texts have in common? The role that the students play by becoming writers and conveying a message by telling their stories through both text and image.

This workshop was organised around three main phases:

- *Experienced players*: This first phase was determined by the four sessions that took place in the computer room or "video games room", as the teacher dubbed it. During this time, the students entered the dynamics of the game and discovered the goals set by the teacher and their evolution in a real situation. The students group had to become both explorers and observers, taking notes of everything that happened for their final project. The teachers and researchers became aware of the video game's main feature: problem-solving.
- *Thinking phase*: The thinking phase refers to all the sessions held by the teacher during a regular class with a more "curricular" attitude. We refer to those moments in which the teacher teaches the material in the language book from a different perspective since the video game becomes a work and reflection tool. We can thus talk about applying knowledge after the workshop.
- *Creation phase*: This last phase focuses on the specific analysis of the process which took place until the creation of final products, in this case Manuel de Falla's The Prophet newspaper. The teacher proposes the creation of several documents ("articles") to be gathered in the newspaper. They can choose between creating documents close to the tasks in the video game or else more creative texts. These documents go through three phases: a first phase of creation in paper, its Word scan with images and writing and finally, its posting on the blog (http://www.uah-gipi.org/aventuras/). The documents created by the students for the newspaper become key materials for the workshop. These texts offer information about the perspective of students towards the workshop and, in addition, the links established between the game and the player. The students identify with Harry Potter and his adventures by facing multiple tasks and solving problems and by writing about them later as if they were the authors of the story. The work created by the students and collected for further analysis is incredibly valuable, as it allows us to examine the way they viewed what happened during the workshop, the problems they encountered, the identification with the protagonist of the game, etc. By analyzing some of the articles in the paper, we can see how the students put in practice what they learned in class about how to reconstruct narratives.

16.3.2 Creating a Newspaper: "Manuel de Falla's The Prophet"

One of the goals of this chapter is to explain how an adventure game (Harry Potter) can become a narrative game where the player acts, performs an action, solves problems and creates a story. The game's narrative is presented during the time of play and after the game. This process is even more evident when after playing and from a language classroom the teacher uses the game to create narrative, thus

Students playing in the classroom

reconstructing what happened in the game and putting in practice the educational content of the course. This way, the students become writers during the time of game – narrative reconstruction where the player is resolving a history of action – and during the creation of the newspaper to make written reconstruction of their experiences.

The game, therefore, will be a fictional universe in which through the scenarios, characters, dialogues, etc. the player's actions make sense in a story. This shows that, while all video games are not narratives, the construction of the plot refers to the narrative. The most interesting thing is the virtual world shared, how players create the game's story. The story starts, occurs and ends by the action of the player.

Following the premises of each of these trends, we will try to discover the presence of narratives and their use as generators of new stories. In this process and as shown in previous page, we have resorted to the ideas of Orihuela (1997), Ryan (2004) and Jenkins (2004) about the different styles of narrative structures behind literary texts and video games and educational power in the school. Thanks to these ideas, we find a close relationship between the action possibilities and narrative possibilities generated by a game. The video game narrates how the game develops as it is being played. This is one of the conclusions we drew when analyzing the workshops. We sensed that Harry Potter could be a very appropriate game for the creation of narratives, but during the workshop we found out that this was not the only use, as it became an adventure video game that made students think and make decisions.

Helping our hero to complete tasks. IES Manuel de Falla. Opinion article: The Wii in the classroom. Student of 1st ESO A

During this experience, the teacher gave each group a sheet of paper with several tasks to complete. So, while we had a laugh, we helped our new friend Harry Potter to take a camera from the roof, find talking gargoyles all over Hogwarts, taking a flying book using charms... and not only that, because there were also minigames, such as a game of magic cards.

In this text the student explains that the mission in the game is helping Harry Potter to solve some problems such as "take a camera from the roof, find talking gargoyles all over Hogwarts, taking a flying book using charms". Therefore, the game takes them to other actions in which we can see the hero's superpowers and heroic actions. In video games, identification is more intense because the user leads the hero with a subjective or semi-subjective vision, seeing what he sees and feeling his successes as his own. It is also interesting to see how the first person of the plural is used ("we helped our new friend Harry Potter") to refer to her action in the game. That is, the player helped the character to complete tasks but it was the character the one who acted, not the player.

We will include some of the texts written by the students to show that solving problems and telling stories is not contradictory, but complementary. Let's recall that this type of dichotomy had been continually present in the workshop sessions. The work by these students, published in their online newspaper, shows what Jerome Bruner (2001) had already said some years ago in relation to these two human capabilities, analyzing and telling.

The creation of texts in which they interviewed the game's protagonist and in which they had to compare their real school to Hogwarts School of Wizardry made them think and compare their real world and the virtual one. We can find many interviews in which they actually interview the actor playing Harry in the films, while others interview the wizard in the imaginary world. It is even more interesting to discover in their text on their ideal school how students are able to spot aspects and features of the virtual world in their real-world environment: behaviour rules, the value of learning, etc.

> **Our ideal secondary school. IES Manuel de Falla. Narration product. Student 1st ESO B.**
> **OUR IDEAL SCHOOL**
> We like our school very much, but we also like some things about Hogwarts. They are taught to obey the rules just as we are and to not marginalise others. Disobedience in Hogwarts is punished as it is in our school.
> In both schools you have to study in order to have a future and a reward.
> In Hogwarts there are fair and unfair teachers, and we think the same happens in our school.
> (...)
> Teaching there is much more exciting but also much riskier.
> We would only change that, otherwise we like our school better.

This article by two other students shows aspects in common between Hogwarts and IES Manuel de Falla: "They are taught to obey the rules just as we are (...) Disobedience in Hogwarts is punished as it is in our school". It is remarkable that both examples should refer to how respect to the rules is taught and how disobedience is punished, both attitudes typical of schools, apart from the importance to study in order to have a future and a reward. The students have understood that both worlds teach values and behavioural patterns. Going back to the principles of learning and identity in the world of video games according to Gee (2005), this situation lets students understand cultural models about the world and about learning. Both in Hogwarts and in their school there is a set of rules, values and fairness which is important and valued by the students. Children who learn with video games end up thinking about their cultural models in relation to the world and to themselves as people who learn without denigrating their identities, skills or social affiliations, and they compare them to the new learning models. Now we will see another text written by another student:

Interview with Harry Potter. IES Manuel de Falla. Narration product. Student 1st ESO A.

- Hello everyone, we have a very special guest today. He is someone that has achieved a lot of success among teenagers with his books and films. Without further ado, here is Harry Potter. Hi Harry.
- Hi Pablo, I am delighted to be here with you.
- As you know, you have achieved a lot of success worldwide thanks to the books and films that tell about your adventures. How are you coping with such a luxurious life?
- Well, don't think it's just a matter of luxury and easy life. People think it is very easy to do this, but that is not the case. I wake up at 6:30 every morning. Life at Hogwarts is not just adventures and parties: there are also things like in any other school, there are millions of exams and homework. (...)

The text shows that students are aware of the presence of Harry Potter in different media: "He is someone that has achieved a lot of success among teenagers with his books and films". In addition, we see he adopts the character's perspective, by turning him into a "real" character that can be interviewed. "How are you coping with such a luxurious life?" Well, don't think it's just a matter of luxury and easy life. People think it is very easy to do this, but that is not the case." In the newspaper we can also find opinion articles on how the workshop went and what they discovered. These opinions also include the existing relationship among the different media.

From the point of view of the narrative, both at the time of playing and at the time of telling about the game, the player becomes the author of his actions and texts. The story is created at the time of playing and moves forward according to the design of the game, but given the textual nature of the video game, he narrates and textualises whenever he plays. As for Harry Potter and the creation of literary texts, we would focus on a more temporal vision, meaning that the students' narrations have an introduction, climax and ending typical of literary novels. The stories that the students wrote focused on specific missions of the video game, but were developed as if they had been written by J.K. Rowling herself. This proves that the students created a link between the literary theories explained by the teacher and the creation of their own "works" based on the game. A clear example of the presence of narratives in the classroom stemming from the use of the video game can be found in the Harry Potter workshop and the articles the students created for their final project (the newspaper). Here is one of the many texts written by the students and published in the paper. We can see that the video game provides context for the story and that the text is worthy of a novelist.

Narrating Harry Potter's adventures. IES Manuel de Falla. Narrative product. Student 1st ESO A

The gigantic Great Dining Room at Hogwarts School was full of people. Large window-panes at both sides lit the room in which four rows of tables were situated along the dining room. Teachers had their own tables, in front of all the others. Harry was with Ron and Hermione. Ron Cheevey wanted to enroll in DA, Dumbledore's army, but they had to perform a task for him. They must find an apple that could only be found in the Forbidden Forest, to use it in making a potion.

We could say that this is one of the detailed descriptions by the author of the novel, since this student surely used it for his story: "The enormous Great Hall at

Hogwarts was full of people. Large stained glass Windows on the sides filled the room with light, in which there were four rows of tables along the hall". On the other hand, it should be noted that the episode narrated by this student in this text is not found on the film or the novel, but it is one of the missions they had to carry out in the game: "They had to find an apple which was only to be found in the Forbidden Forest in order to create a potion".

However, as discussed in previous pages, covering curricular contents is a permanent concern among teachers, but the knowledge that should be acquired does not always motivate students. If, traditionally, cinema, television and newspapers were good allies to motivate them, today video games can also play that role. But playing is not enough, the fact of considering them educational instruments requires teachers to use strategies that foster reflection processes. Moreover, if we take into account that this was a Spanish language teacher, we will understand it was necessary to look for resources that allowed them to reflect upon the game and also to put in practice certain linguistic abilities and, why not, within a transmedia experience in which the video game could co-exist with other types of text and other types of discourse. All this drove the teacher to propose the creation of the newspaper "The Prophet" in which, based on the adventures experienced in the game, students could tell the story or describe the characters. They could also tell about their experiences at the workshop and how they learned.

Description about what happened in the workshop. IES Manuel de Falla. Narrative product. Student 1st ESO B

During the third quarter, we used the computer room to play Wii for an hour every Tuesday for four weeks in the language area (Tuesday).

The experience consisted of the following:

- The game we played was "Harry Potter and the Order of the Phoenix"
- When we reached the room, the teacher gave us a series of tasks to complete, for example, recruiting people for Dumbledore's Army, the headmaster of Hogwarts (…)
- After playing, we went to the classroom. In the following language hours, the teacher took advantage of the material used to do dictations, texts and work on the book or the game of Harry Potter.

I found the experience very positive, because on the one hand I could work in groups with some of my peers and share opinions. I also think it's interesting because the game can be used for learning, it is a good way to enhance the pleasure of reading and it also helps us to pay attention to a perfect narrative. (...) Conclusion: Playing can also be a means to learn.

This opinion article created by a student briefly describes many aspects so far discussed in our work, both in the history of the workshop and in this chapter. First, they used the Wii console with the game "Harry Potter and the Order of the Phoenix". Second, how teachers use the game as an instrument for the kids to live many adventures and then work on language issues such as dictation, texts, etc. in class (video games and hidden curriculum). Third, the final product in newspaper format was the key for students to be aware of the value of the word, different forms of narration and the fact that a game can be a lot more than just a game.

16.4 Conclusion and Educational Implications

We are aware that our society is currently facing new technological changes in which the Internet, TV or, like we said, video games, are both tools for entertainment and also new means of communication for the younger generations. These media offer the possibility to receive and transmit information in a quick way and through different channels. In this regard, we can ask the following: Do students have the necessary qualities to face this in a reflective and critical way?

The school must play a very important role in this process, being aware of the new possibilities offered by the media and the qualities that boys and girls acquire through them. If we stop fearing change and understand it as something positive, we will be able to regard these resources as a source of knowledge and not as a hindrance in the path of learning. For this reason, the school should turn its eyes to everyday life to look for new ways of facilitating the learning of cultural practices necessary for people to be able to adapt to the social, cultural and historical reality they live in. In this context, video games become a motivating and interesting tool, so why not work with them?

We must be aware that, for children, they are a tool they know and which is part of their everyday life, and in most cases they even occupy a very high position in their scale of interests. This is the main reason which leads us to study video games and work with them – we are used to see them as something fun and entertaining, but if we analyse them in depth we can see that they can also become powerful learning tools.

We have found that the use of tools such as game guides or the educational guide created by the language teacher became mediators which facilitated the game discovery process. However, they were not the only mediating element between the children and the game: Even though the video game turns out to be a tool which can promote knowledge, it also needs other elements to optimise its use in the classroom from an educational point of view. In this case, the adults also became key to the process by provoking thought through their questions or through classroom activities. The teacher had a clear goal in language arts class, since it used the game as a tool to achieve a goal.

In our analysis we have focused on finding out how children had the chance to enter the protagonist's magical world living his feats through him. In adventure games such as Harry Potter, the game introduces the player to an unreal world created by the author of the novels. We discovered an interactive narrative, in which students reconstructed adventures in the game through their literary texts. The students became authors of "stories" which narrated their experiences in the video game, and in some cases they even seemed to have been taken out of J.K. Rowling's books. During the workshop, the teacher worked on the creation of narrative and literary texts from the video game, which made it easier for the students to make the link between curricular topics explained by the teacher and the creation of their own "works" based on the game. For example, in their texts they used what they had learned about the description of characters, the use of dialogues, introducing the story's plot, explaining how it unfolds and, finally, reach an ending.

References

Atkinson, P., Coffey, A., Delamnont, S., Lofland, J., Lofland, C. (eds.): Handbook of Ethnography. Sage, London (2001)

Atkinson, P., Hammersley, M.: Ethnography and participant observation. In: Denzin, N. (ed.) Handbook of Qualitative Research. Sage, Thousand Oaks, CA (1994)

Beavis, C.: Digital culture, digital literacies: Expanding the notions of text. In: Beavis, C., Durrant, C. (eds.) P(ICT)ures of English: Teachers, Learners and Technology, pp. 145–161. Wakefield Press, Adelaide (2001)

Berenguer, X.: Historias por ordenador, p. 201. http://www.upf.edu/pdi/dcom/xavierberenguer/textos/histor/narrc.htm (1998). Accessed 8 Mar 2011

Bruner, J.: Realidad mental y mundos posibles. Los actos de la imaginación que dan sentido a la experiencia. Gedisa. Barcelona (2001)

Buckingham, D.: Infancias cambiantes, medios cambiantes: nuevos desafíos para la educación mediática. Cultura y educación **20**, 23–38 (2000)

Calquist, J.: Playing the story – computer games as a Narrative Genre. Human IT **6**(3), 7–53 (2002)

Egenfeldt, N., et al.: Understanding Video Games. Routledge, New York (2008)

Esnaola Horacek, G.: El discurso narrativo del relato electrónico: el caso de los videojuegos Investigación inscripta en la Universitat de Valencia, Departamento de Didáctica y Organización escolar (2001)

Gee, J.P.: Learning by design: Games as learning machines. Interact. Educ. Multimedia **8**, 15–23 (2004)

Gee, J.P.: Lo que nos enseñan los videojuegos sobre el aprendizaje y el alfabetismo (Trans., Pomares, J.M.). Ediciones Aljibe, Malaga (2005)

Gros, B.: Videojuegos y aprendizaje. Barcelona Grao (2008)

Ferraro, G.: Percorsi virtuali nella formazione d'immagine. In: Grandi, R. (ed.) Semiotica al Marketing, pp.155–172. FrancoAngeli, Milan (1994)

Jenkins, H.: Transmedia storytelling. Paper presented at the MIT Technology Review (2003). http://www.technologyreview.com/biotech/13052/. Accesed 25 Oct 2011

Jenkins, H.: Game design as narrative architecture. In: Wardrip-Fruin, N., Harrigan, P. (eds.) First Person: New Media as Story, Performance, Game, pp. 118–130. MIT Press, Cambridge, MA (2004)

Jenkins, H., Lacasa, P.: Entrevista a Henry Jenkins. Monográfico de videojuegos. Cuadernos de pedagogía, N° 398. (2010) *Alfabetizaciones múltiples*. Wolters Kluwer España, S.A, Barcelona (2010)

Juul, J.: Games telling stories? A brief note on games and narratives. Game Stud. **1**(1). http://www.gamestudies.org/ (2001)

Lacasa, P., GIPI.: Videojuegos en el Instituto. Ocio digital como estímulo en la enseñanza. Informe de investigación. http://www.aprendeyjuegaconea.com/files/informe_UAH_2009.pdf. Last view 24 Oct 2011. Madrid. *Electronics Arts de España y Universidad de Alcalá* (2009)

Lacasa, P., Reina, A. (coord).: La televisión y el periódico en la escuela primaria: Imágenes, palabras e ideas. Ministerio de Educación, Cultura y Deporte. Centro de Investigación y Documentación Educativa, Madrid (2004)

Lacasa, P., Mendez, L., Martinez-Borda, R.: Bringing commercial games into the classroom. Comput. Compos. **25**, 341–35 (2008)

Lacasa, P.: Entrevista a Henry Jenkins: Cultura participativa y nuevas alfabetizaciones. Cuadernos de Pedagogía **398**, 52–56 (2010)

Lacasa, P.: Videojuegos. Aprendiendo en mundos reales y virtuales. Madrid, Morata (2011)

Murray, J.H.: Hamlet on the Holodeck: The Future of Narrative in Cyberspace. The MIT Press, Cambridge, MA (1997/2001)

Orihuela, J.L.: Narraciones interactivas: el futuro no-lineal de los relatos en la era digital. Palabra-Clave, no 2. Universidad de la Sabana, pp. 37–45 (1997)

Piaget, J.: Play, Dreams and Imitation in Childhood. Norton, New York (1962)
Prensky, M.: "Don't Bother me, mom – I'm learning": How Computer and Video Games Are Preparing Your Kids For Twenty-first Century Success – and How You Can Help!: Paragon House, St. Paul, MN (2005)
Ryan, M.L.: Narrative as Virtual Reality: Immersion and Interactivity in Literature and Electronic Media. Paidos, Barcelona (2004)
Ryan, M.L.: From narrative games to playable stories toward a poetics of interactive narrative. StoryWorlds J. Narrative Stud. **1**, 43–59 (Article) (2009)
Saltzman, M. (Compilador). Cómo diseñar un videojuego, los secretos de los expertos, Norma (2001)
Shaffer, D.W.: Epistemic games. Innovate **1**(6). http://www.innovateonline.info/index.php?view=article&id=79 (2005). Accessed 8 Mar 2011
Vygotsky, L.S.: Mind in Society: The Development of Higher Psychological Functions. Harvard University Press, Cambridge, MA (1978/1986)

Chapter 17
Using *Dungeons and Dragons* to Integrate Curricula in an Elementary Classroom

Alexandra Carter

How can an elementary teacher integrate a set math program with social studies, literature, and writing? In this chapter, I will trace the development of a yearlong project undertaken with my third-grade math students that addresses this challenge. I planned for the students to design and play a game that would reinforce the concepts covered over the course of the year, integrating social studies, writing, and literature curricula with their math lessons. Both skill and content goals across the curriculum informed lessons and activities. While I maintained overall control over the direction of the project, students were intimately involved in planning and executing the design, and we often altered plans to accommodate new, creative ideas and suggestions provided by the students. I will discuss the background and rationale behind this project, goals and learning objectives for the students, lessons and activities created, and learning outcomes and experiences of the students.

17.1 Background and Rationale

The impetus for the *Dungeons and Dragons* project came from my work with a third grade math class in a developmental private elementary school dedicated to the philosophies of John Dewey and Jean Piaget. This school uses the math program *Everyday Mathematics,* a cyclical program that introduces students to a topic that they will delve into more deeply either later in the year or in a later grade. The program can sometimes feel a bit disjointed for students and teachers, as introduces a new concept each day. Creating an ongoing project for the students would help foster conceptual continuity, reinforce the material, and provide students with a record of their work.

The math group with which I worked offered a series of challenges familiar to many educators. Several students were struggling in reading, writing, and math. Other students had difficulty paying attention, completing assignments and

A. Carter (✉)
University of California, Los Angeles, CA, USA
e-mail: alexcarter@ucla.edu

M. Ma et al. (eds.), *Serious Games and Edutainment Applications,*
DOI 10.1007/978-1-4471-2161-9_17, © Springer-Verlag London Limited 2011

tasks, following classroom procedures, and working independently. These issues compounded with the requirements of the math program, which presents a new concept and lesson every day. Because of the wide variety of needs I faced in the classroom, I felt that the students needed a more engaging approach to the material. They greeted the idea of creating and playing a game with great enthusiasm, and the experiences and outcomes that I witnessed testified to the success of this project.

Originally, the project was much more limited in scope. I envisioned creating a game that would allow students to engage meaningfully with the math concepts covered and provide them with a tool for ongoing review and assessment. These original objectives are addressed below. However, when the students expressed an interest in creating a game similar to *Dungeons and Dragons*, I realized that one project could incorporate several different objectives across the curriculum. Pulling from these objectives and developing others that would be met by the game determined my approach.

I have often used games in classes and in tutoring to reinforce concepts taught through traditional methods, including directed instruction, small group work, and written assessments. I have developed games that target the specific needs of students and have used pre-packaged educational games that focus on specific skills. In previous years, I worked with students to adapt games in class. In one history course, I asked college students to modify the word-association game *Apples to Apples*. They were each assigned a series of themes and were asked to create different examples from the class materials for each. After discussing their results, they combined their work and played the game. The students all retained and engaged with the material, and they had a lot of fun. The game served as a review of the course concepts for the students and provided me with a flexible assessment tool for progress. I could evaluate the materials the students had created and the way in which they interacted with the game to gauge their comprehension and application of class themes.

I have also worked with high school students in designing a board game as part of a special studies course in game theory, history, and design. Because of my research interests, the students approached me to ask if they could work with me to design a board game as a student-initiated, teacher-guided independent study. I developed a reading list with the students on game theory and design. After reading, we analyzed the components, rules, and play of various board games and discussed which games we thought were the strongest. The students then designed their own game, incorporating their previous analyses and ideas into their own game. Although the game did not incorporate material from other classes, the students learned to work cooperatively to plan, research, and delegate. They learned to evaluate game design and think critically about their own creative work. This experience demonstrated that student-directed game design could have several positive educational outcomes that were not directly related to the material of the game.

The growing research and experience of others working in education, psychology, anthropology, and game design has inspired my decision to use games and game design to teach. Following such theorists as Lev Vygotsky and Jean

Piaget, several educational specialists have argued that play provides the foundation for later success in school. Fantasy play in particular offers many developmental benefits. These include assimilation and associative thinking, problem solving, interaction with others, and empathetic development (Crawford, 1996; Donaldson, 1984; Driscoll, 1994; Satterly, 1987; Vygotsky, 1978; Wertsch and Sohmer, 1995; Wood, 1998). Fantasy play also presents opportunities to expose students to a wide variety of preparatory educational experiences, such as introduction to and application of literacy, numeracy, and logic (Macintyre, 2001). For older students, researchers have focused on the role that games can play in facilitating retention, engagement, and interest (Randel et al., 1992). Combined with traditional educational methods, such as lecture and assessment, games provide an additional means to support and apply concepts. Students introduced to material through games and simulations report a higher level of retention and enthusiasm for subjects than those who were introduced to a subject through traditional lecture-style courses (Randel et al., 1992).

Other research shows how game design and the use of technology can also have a positive impact on the ways in which students interact with information. This research primarily focuses on the development of video games and the use of technology by students. However, some of the conclusions drawn by researchers and practices used by video game developers have broader application to game design in general. Game designer Lloyd Reiber and his laboratory demonstrated that video game design creates a climate that encourages a love of learning and an interest in the material (Reiber, 2001). Reiber maintains that game design teaches students the "power of interdisciplinary problem finding, problem solving, collaboration, communication, persuasion, [and] argument." (Reiber, 2001). Students are more involved and therefore more mentally engaged with the material during game creation, develop important interpersonal skills and problem-solving strategies, and enhance their chance of retention. While the students in my math class did not design a video game, the experiences they had and the outcomes achieved closely paralleled the findings that Reiber described in his work.

The decision to adapt *Dungeons and Dragons* for math came from the students. At the start of the school year, I suggested to the students that we create a game for our math group that we could play all year, which would integrate what they were learning in other subject areas into math. At the end of the year, they would receive a copy of the game, which would be both a record of their work and a tool for review. We discussed our options: creating a board game, a card game, a jeopardy-style game show, and modifying one of the games that came with the *Everyday Mathematics* program. I then encouraged students to go home and think about the games they enjoyed, and we would come to a decision after discussing everyone's thoughts. Watching the students on the playground throughout the week, I was struck by how many of them enjoyed playing their own interpretation of *Dungeons and Dragons*. Some of the students had older *Dungeons and Dragons* manuals from their parents or older siblings and shared these materials with others on the playground. The game usually followed a loose resemblance to the actual rules: students had a "dungeon master" who would direct the narrative and several players who would participate in the story by asking questions about actions they could take. The dungeon master would answer "yes" or "no" and continue the story accordingly. On the playground, students also played *Dungeons and Dragons* as an on-going chase or fantasy game, frequently involving humans and zombies. The students clearly understood *Dungeons and Dragons* as fantasy-based storytelling game under the direction of a narrator.

I asked students then if they would be interested in developing a version if *Dungeons and Dragons* for our yearlong project. Most of the students were enthusiastic, so I suggested that we would start with a sample game and then see what we could adapt, change, or borrow from the original to create our own *Dungeons and Dragons*. I used an introductory version of the game that would be suitable for young players who were not familiar with it. Wizards of the Coast produces a version of *Dungeons and Dragons* with a recommended age range of six and up entitled "Heroes of Hesiod," available for free on their website (Morris, 2010). Susan Morris, the author, created this game for teachers, librarians, and others who wished to introduce the game to young players. The website emphasizes the educational benefits of the game. Players apply mathematical skills, reading comprehension strategies, creative thinking, and problem solving skills to the game (Morris, 2010). The "Heroes of Hesiod" adventure provides a map and pre-made heroes and monsters, therefore bypassing most of the initial preparation. This made it easier for the students to play quickly and get a sense of the overall structure. The students decided which elements of the game they would like to change after they finished their first game. It became immediately evident that *Dungeons and Dragons* offered wonderful opportunities to integrate math, social studies, literature, and writing curricula into the project. After I developed the project objectives, we began to design our own version of *Dungeons and Dragons*. The assignments and projects evolved organically from the students' ideas and interests during design of the game. I did not create set lesson plans, but developed lessons and activities with the students, directed by the objectives I had set. It seemed natural to use Reggio Emilia approach, which emphasizes the development and implementation of self-guided curricula. In this process, the teacher develops activities based on student interest, asks questions to further understanding, and engages in activities alongside the children (Cadwell, 2002; Lewin-Benham, 2005). The students designed this project, and I provided materials and activities that incorporated student suggestions and the objectives I had outlined before beginning the project.

17.2 Objectives

I created specific learning objectives for each of the content areas the game design would address and attempted to integrate these objectives into every step of the project. I developed these objectives from those in different skill and subject areas across the curriculum, and they correlate to school, state, and national standards. These objectives guided lessons and activities.

17.2.1 Mathematics

- Solve problems as they arose and related to the project
- Create word problems of varying degrees of difficulty that integrate new math concepts for others to solve during game play
- Employ problem-solving strategies and techniques to solve in-game math problems
- Use mathematical concepts to plan elements of design

17.2.2 Social Studies

- Develop characters and settings that are historically appropriate to the class social studies theme, the Middle Ages
- Develop monsters and enemies based on research into myths, mythical creatures, and superstitions, correlating with the social studies theme
- Develop chronological thinking and demonstrate chronological awareness

17.2.3 Research Skills

- Develop research questions to guide development of settings and characters
- Use a variety of sources for research (books, interviews, internet, articles)
- Begin to develop good internet-based research practices
- Analyze sources for reliability
- Maintain a record of research questions, sources, and answers
- Synthesize group research
- Evaluate and apply appropriate information to the creation of characters and settings
- Present findings to class and demonstrate application of research to characters and settings
- Evaluate other students' research and research-based creations

17.2.4 Written and Oral Communication

- Develop a background setting for the story to take place that integrates grammar concepts covered in class (descriptive adjectives, colorful verbs, prepositions, nouns, proper capitalization and punctuation)
- Use colorful and descriptive language to bring characters, settings, and monsters to life
- Write well-constructed paragraphs to describe or explain different aspects of project
- Organize presentations
- Demonstrate and explain historical research in oral presentations

- Develop questions to engage audience after presentation is over
- Answer questions raised by the audience

17.2.5 Artistic and Creative Development

- Use mixed media (paint, colored pencils, markers, clay) to create characters and monsters
- Integrate visual reference materials, including books and outside observation, to create settings, monsters, and characters
- Extend research imaginatively to develop rich details for characters, monsters, and settings, both in written and visual forms
- Create a system of symbols to represent elements in the game
- Thoughtfully analyze others' creative works
- Provide thoughtful feedback about others' works

17.2.6 Social and Emotional Development

- Cooperate to develop maps and characters
- Negotiate decisions with team-mates during game play
- Plan out projects and divide tasks evenly among group members
- Support team members, classmates, and partners during project development and game play through suggestions, hints, praise, and encouragement
- Participate in all projects assigned according to ability and interest
- Compromise and allow other members of the group to share equally
- Provide thoughtful, considerate, and specific feedback to group members and other groups during work and presentations

The project was group-based, including large design teams and partnerships of two or three. Some of the groups were allowed emerge naturally, based on students' interests. Other partnerships were comprised of mixed mathematical and verbal ability. I hoped that the students would be able to work with and benefit from each other's strengths in these partnerships. The partners were equally responsible for developing characters and solving problems, and it was my hope that partners could teach each other, making the game fun and rewarding while minimizing frustration.

17.3 The Project

The *Dungeons and Dragons* design project was broken into six major steps, which were co-developed by the students and me. This included the initial play and discussion of the game, the three major design steps, the play of the game, and post-game debriefing and modifications. This entire process would lead to the creation of a second set of maps, characters, and monsters. The materials created by the students, in-class discussions, presentations, and the game play itself provided numerous occasions to assess the student progress in math, social studies, and language arts.

For each design step, all of which followed the same basic format, students began by discussing the elements they believed were crucial to creating the specific component of the game, and we outlined the necessary steps to complete each task. I then developed a series of worksheets and organizers that integrated students' suggestions and ideas with components that addressed the objectives I had outlined. For the settings, characters, and monsters, students developed their own research questions to facilitate their creation. They then looked for answers independently, in groups, and with my guidance. Students then designed the different game elements, ensuring their research was reflected in their work. After conferring with each other and checking their work with me, they created their final copies and presentations for the class. Students enjoyed showing off and explaining their work. The audience was expected to listen thoughtfully, make note of elements that they thought would be of use to them in their own work, and come up with one specific compliment and suggestion or question that they would like answered by the presenters. Pupils were therefore actively engaged in listening and responding thoughtfully. They also benefited from the work that others had done, making the project more robust overall.

17.3.1 Introducing the Game

I created reference handouts based on the "Heroes of Hesiod" materials that broke the steps of the game down in simple language for the introduction to our game. Students were placed in mixed pairs according to mathematical ability. Before playing, we discussed the rules of the game as a class, pausing to check for comprehension and answer any questions. We also discussed proper behavior while working in pairs and solving math problems during the play of the game. Students then looked over their character and asked the dungeon master (in this instance, me) questions. Characters were not allowed to attack each other, thereby eliminating the possibility of students working against one another. Student pairs could work with others and use the cooperative advantages built into the game, such as working with another hero to perform a special attack. Some students eagerly took advantage of this opportunity.

We began our game by looking at each character and discussing various strategic possibilities. Because the students had already played other strategy games as a part of their social studies curriculum, they had begun to develop some sense of long-term strategic thinking. They applied this experience to their suggestions for possible strategies and tactics they could use in the game. The entire introduction took about two and a half hours.

The pre-game discussion also addressed some of the mathematics objectives. We talked about the different ways we could calculate area and perimeter while considering the game map. Some students were already comfortable with multiplication and quickly found the area after counting the numbers of squares in the rows and columns. I had other students double-check by counting and adding the squares. We also discussed various ways to find the perimeter and ratios for the number of cages and barriers on the map. I also decided to use three 6-sided dice instead of using one 20-sided die to determine the outcome of an action. Students would therefore have to work through addition problems with multiple addends to figure out if their attack hit their target. Each pair was given a small whiteboard and two dry-erase markers. When a math problem came up, such as calculating whether or not an attack hit, all students were expected to solve the problem quietly on their whiteboard. The pair attacking had to check to make sure their answers were in agreement. Once they had solved the problem, they could share their answer with the group. If they were correct and their attack hit, then damage was done. If they were incorrect, other students had a chance to share the correct answer. The pair with the correct answer could then move their character one space. I noticed that several students who typically worked slowly through addition problems eagerly volunteered correct answers, supporting the argument made in the research reviewed above that students who are engaged in a project or game will more actively apply skills towards a goal in which they are invested.

After the game was over, we discussed ways to modify the game for our math lessons. Students quickly agreed that there should be a variety of problems for the heroes to solve, ranging from easy to difficult, and they quickly began creating problems based on the math unit in which they were working. This was an ongoing process. I often asked students to create problems based on a math lesson that had just been taught or on the content of the unit that had just been covered. Students eagerly developed math problems as a warm-up activity or as homework. It helped them reinforce the concepts that had been covered in class and provided me with an ongoing assessment of their understanding and application of mathematical concepts. I also got a sense of their own self-assessment, as they created problems in accordance with their definition of what "easy," "medium," and "hard" were. While some students created straightforward math problems, others created very involved riddles and puzzles that demonstrated a sophisticated understanding and application of concepts. Having the students share their problems in class inspired others to develop and solve more intricate problems.

Students were also excited about designing the settings, maps, monsters, and heroes for our game. They decided that we should create the settings first, and then students could create their own monsters and heroes. Part of each math lesson was dedicated to creating problems for our game, and we had special blocks of instructional time dedicated to developing the other elements of the game.

17.3.2 Where Will Our Story Take Place? Designing the Setting

Our version of *Dungeons and Dragons* had to conform to our social studies theme, the Middle Ages. The first design step was the creation of settings and maps for our adventure. The students had just finished a project in which they created a medieval manor house and village, so they had several ideas ready. They had also had some exposure to different settings in their "Story Starters: The Middle Ages" writing program, which helped students develop characters, settings, and plots that were historically appropriate. Using their suggestions, we created a master list of locations: monastery, village, forest, castle, dungeon, mill, and manor. Students were then asked to vote on the different settings. After the votes were tallied, we discussed a reasonable way to decide which settings would be used. One student suggested using data landmarks (maximum, minimum, median, mode, and range) for the tallied votes, as we had just finished a unit about them. We decided that the main part of the story should take place in the setting that got the maximum number of votes, the beginning of the story would take place in the setting that got the minimum, and the story would end in the setting that received the median number of votes. Students created bar graphs, found the landmarks, and determined that our story would start in a monastery, continue into a forest, and end in a castle with a dungeon. I then asked students which setting interested them the most, and assigned them to groups based on their preference.

The students and I discussed the different elements that made up the setting in the original game before beginning the setting design. We talked about the role of the dungeon master in describing the setting, the elements on the map, including cages and barriers that existed in the "Heroes of Hesiod" village, and the perimeter, area, and ratio of barriers and cages. As we talked, the students recognized the need to do some research into the different settings before they could create maps within those settings. They also decided that the forest map should be bigger than the monastery and castle-dungeon maps, as the story would mainly take place in the forest. After exploring these issues, I developed some handouts for the students to organize the steps they would need to take in designing their settings, and we developed specific area parameters for their maps. The monastery and castle both had areas of 200 square inches, as they were the beginning and the end of the story, whereas the forest had an area of 250 square inches. Students also examined the ratio of barriers to cages in the original game. We decided to modify the ratios of the barriers and cages to the total area; the ratio for all of the maps was 1:25 for cages and 1:10 for barriers. The students felt this would give the heroes enough space to move around and a reasonable number of challenges for the heroes. The students also determined the organization of the groups and developed a list of jobs for the members based on their experience in science class, in which each student played a specific role within a group. The jobs for the groups included: the "organizer," who was responsible for overseeing the direction of the project, keeping everyone on task, and making sure that everyone had a chance to participate; the "secretary," who would be responsible for the group's materials, maintaining neat, clean records, and keeping track of assignments; "getters," who would get or return the materials needed by the group and ask the teacher questions; and the "checker," who would double-check the assignments as they were completed to make sure the work was accurate and correct. I emphasized that all of the students were responsible for the work that the group produced and had to perform each role at different points to produce high quality work efficiently. Students negotiated between themselves which roles they would most like to have in the group. They decided amongst themselves when to switch roles according to preference and perceived skill.

The first step in designing the settings was developing research questions and finding answers. I gave the students some handouts to organize their questions and keep track of the resources they were using. We discussed what sorts of general questions students would need to ask to create settings that were historically appropriate. We also talked about ways to manage their information, including keeping research journals, using note cards, and dividing questions among group members. After the groups were given time to develop their own research questions, we gathered to share the questions with the rest of the class. The other groups had a chance to suggest other ideas to the group and modify the questions presented to fit their own research needs after groups presented. For example, the group designing the forest developed a series of questions about what trees exist and what animals live in European forests. The monastery group asked the students working on the forest if the forests had changed from the Middle Ages to the present. The forest group agreed that this question should be researched, as the trees they wanted to draw may or may not have existed during the medieval period. The castle group praised the forest group for developing questions about the appearance of the forest and added questions to their own research about the appearance of the building materials used to construct a castle. Sharing questions helped students refine their own research questions, and the questions asked demonstrated the students' developing understanding of chronological thinking creating targeted, specific research questions.

To complete the research, students brought in books from our classroom library, the school library, and from their houses and public libraries. We spent some time as a class exploring the different features of these books to guide independent research, including the table of contents and the index. We explored three different resources as a class to find the answer. I also set up my computer for guided Internet research. Students could come and work with me individually or in groups to find questions to their answers using the Internet. We developed guidelines for search terms, examined different websites, and discussed accuracy and reliability by comparing websites to one another and to the information in books. We developed questions to ask when looking at a website to analyze its reliability, including who the author is and what resources he or she used. The web-based research was limited and guided carefully because I was working with a younger group of students, but it provided the opportunity to introduce important questions of reliability and safety. During class, I kept a running list of questions posted on the board to remind students of all the questions the different groups were answering. Students shared their resources with both their own group mates and with the class as a whole, making the research experience richer, more robust, and efficient. This process took approximately two weeks, with about three and a half hours each week given to the project. The students' research prepared them for their subsequent research for their character and monster development, which they conducted independently and with a partner.

Students created their maps based on their research. Using the parameters they developed at the beginning of the design, they figured out how many sheets of 9×6 one-inch grid paper they needed, how many barriers and cages their map needed (based on ratios), and what the perimeter of their map was after they had created it. These activities reinforced the concepts that had already been covered in the math lessons and introduced using and applying ratios, which would be taught formally toward the end of the year. After giving students some time to figure out these issues independently and with their group, we discussed the problem-solving strategies the different groups used. Students had a chance to hear what strategies their classmates were using and worked together to develop shortcuts for solving these problems. The groups then created their rough drafts, designing barriers and cages based on modifications of historically appropriate objects. Students used thick cardstock to create their final draft maps after having their work checked and approved. The entire process reinforced planning strategies and careful attention to detail, as well as using math and research creatively. The final maps were laminated for the game.

Students described their settings and created a style sheet that the dungeon master could use to guide the players through the game. We developed a list of elements all settings should contain. These included the weather and time of day, the appearance of the interior and exterior of the setting, different sounds that the characters might hear in that setting, and objects, people, and monsters that the heroes might run into. Students determined what these elements would be for their setting as a group, wrote short, two-paragraph stories set within their setting, and had their work edited by peers in their groups for content and form. Some of the stories were quite involved. For example, one student in the monastery group was particularly excited about having zombie Templar Knights rise from the grave to attack heroes who had forgotten their homework. His work integrated the writing goals of including descriptive details, such as "dark, smelly tombs," and his research, as the Templar had been buried after being killed in Crusade before coming back to life. After peer editing, students worked with me to edit and produce a final draft. The dual editing process helped foster a greater awareness of grammar rules, proper organization, and well-crafted sentence construction. Groups gave short presentations in which they showed off their maps, shared their stories, and talked about interesting facts that they discovered in their research. The students in the audience took notes and gave feedback, which included thoughtful questions, suggestions, or specific compliments for the members of the group.

The experiences that the students had creating the maps and settings provided a framework for the last two pieces of development, the monsters and the characters. With some modifications, the process the students used to develop the monsters and heroes followed the same steps that were used to develop their settings. Each student was responsible for creating at least one monster and co-creating a playable character for the game. Students were prepared to develop their own research questions, find their own answers, and create their own monsters and heroes based on that research because of their work developing the settings.

17.3.3 What's that Medusa Doing in the Monastary? Creating Our Monsters

Students were responsible for developing one monster that would exist within their settings. They could then create any monsters they wished for the other settings, which only had to follow the same basic parameters developed for the monsters. Students researched medieval myths, mythical creatures, and medieval superstitions and created monsters based on their findings. Some students' monsters were based on different mythical creatures, including those from Greek and Roman mythology. After doing preliminary research, students came up with the following research questions: whether or not they thought medieval Europeans would have believed in the creature, when people believed in the creature, where the creature first originated, what the creature looked like, and what special powers it had. I made up a short worksheet that included these questions and a place to record the titles of books and websites the students consulted. We also discussed the concept of myths as foundation stories or explanations for the way in which the world worked, but the students were not expected to figure out how the creature they researched fit within that worldview. Some visual aids were used to track our research, including a class timeline and a world map of myths. Students put their myth or monster on the timeline and used thumbtacks to mark on a map where the myth originated during their presentations.

The parameters for the monsters were based on those found in the "Heroes of Hesiod." The students decided that the monster attacks would be determined by the roll of a 20-sided die, rather than having the dungeon master solve math problems, and that the attacks would be based on the actual special powers of the creatures and myths they researched. Students also felt that monsters should have more hit points and special attacks as they moved through the game. Monsters in the beginning of the game were therefore weaker and more easily defeated than those at the end. Accordingly, students developed three attacks for the monsters in the monastery, four for those in the forest, and up to six for those in the castle. Monsters in the monastery would also have two-thirds the amount of hit points as those in the forest, and those in the forest would have three-fourths the amount of hit points as those in the castle. We decided that all of the monsters in each setting would have the same amount of hit points, giving us an opportunity to introduce fractions of a whole. The monsters in the castle had between 20-35 hit points, and students used base-10 blocks, money, and other manipulatives to figure out the fractional parts and the appropriate number of hit points for each of the monsters in the other settings based on this. The students shared their problem-solving strategies with the class after working through the problem independently and in small groups. Fractions were later introduced in a formal math lesson, and we revisited the issue of hit point fractions at that time, adjusting the numbers and developing new monsters accordingly.

In presentations, students shared background information about their creature and discussed the modifications they made to make their creature a part of our game.

Although the students were not required to write a back-story for their monsters, they did have to write a one-paragraph summary of the information that they had found on the monster, which would be included in the game. The dungeon master would introduce the monster as it was released from its cage, giving a bit of background information to help the players know what to expect. Students were encouraged to go back and add in interesting and colorful adjectives to make their monsters more exciting during game play. We used the thesaurus in this activity, and the class developed a long list of alternatives for adjectives, such as "scary" and "evil," and this list was referred and added to throughout the rest of the year. This activity helped reinforce the writing objectives for using colorful and descriptive language and using the thesaurus to improve writing.

Some students also developed creatures that had special mathematical abilities, such as the power to slow heroes down according to their ability to solve fraction problems. Should the hero fail to solve the problem, the "fraction ghost" would slow the hero's speed down by the correct fraction for two turns. Although these additional creatures were not based on historical research, they demonstrated the application of mathematical concepts to the game in ways that were creative, innovative, and engaging for the other students.

The monsters and presentations served as an assessment of the research skills introduced during the development. Because of the experience that the students had working in a group to develop questions and using a wide variety of sources to find the answers, students quickly moved through the research process and had monsters ready for the game in a week of four, one-hour lessons, including two nights of homework. The presentations, which were each about five minutes with two or three minutes of questions and feedback, took another hour.

17.3.4 And then I Snuck up from Behind. . .Creating the Heroes

The last step in modifying *Dungeons and Dragons* was creating the heroes. The entire hero production process was the shortest. Students had done a lot of the preparatory work and had given much thought to the characters they wanted to create. Therefore, character development focused less on research skills and more on writing. This step took one week: three one-hour sessions in class and one research and note-taking assignment given as homework. In pairs, students developed their own character, whose specific traits and skills came from the medieval occupation that he or she had. Students reviewed information about their characters' occupations in their social studies materials and reviewed the specification sheets for the heroes to develop general parameters. Students decided that their character sheets should have a picture, the character's occupation, one-paragraph back-story, two weapons (one of which based on a tool that their character would use in their occupation), three types of attack (which would correlate to the easy, medium, and hard math problems heroes had to solve), hit points, armor strength, speed, and a special attack.

Students were required to figure out what the ratio of armor to hit points was for the heroes that already existed in the game to develop ratios for their own characters. They then applied that ratio to their own character using different numbers. Before assigning them this task, I reminded the students of the work we had done to figure out the fractions for the monster hit points and the use of ratios in the number of barriers and cages for the maps. I asked the students to try to recall the various solution strategies we had used as a class to solve these problems. I anticipated that some students would struggle with this activity because it had not been covered formally. We discussed using even numbers, sets of ten, and numbers related to money to make the ratio problem easier. Most students applied the skills they developed in creating the maps and monsters to this assignment, which helped me assess their progress in math and prepared them for formal ratio and fraction lessons. I used the think-pair-share strategy for this activity. Students thought about the problem independently, discussed it with a partner, and then shared their problem-solving strategies with the whole class. The pairs then developed a hit-point-to-armor ratio for their character, using one of the strategies discussed.

In their social studies lessons, students had learned about the different types of medieval armor and weapons and some medieval occupations. Students therefore did not need outside research to complete their character development and began writing. Using the work that they had done with the "Story Starters: The Middle Ages" writing program, which provides a detailed list of all the elements needed to describe a character fully, the students developed rich descriptions of their characters' faces, eyes, hair, clothing, occupation, hopes, and desires. Students created images of their characters based on their descriptions and made tokens that would represent their character on the game board. Students also created one weapon for their character that was a modified version of a tool commonly used in their occupation. For example, one pair created a fearsome woodcutter who wielded a pair of axes to attack his enemies. His other weapon was taken from the work the students had done with medieval arms and armor; in this case, he had a long bow. The stories were edited and transferred to cardstock, and the tokens were laminated. Students then shared their creations with the class and were ready to play!

17.3.5 Solve to Attack! Playing the Game

The game play followed the same instructions as the original "Heroes of Hesiod," with the only modifications being those that the students had created. The game itself was used as a reward for the whole class completing the work assigned during the week. Students therefore had a greater incentive to finish and often worked more cooperatively and quickly through their assignments. They also continued to develop problems as we covered new material.

The tokens the students developed to represent both the monsters and the heroes were attached to the board using a piece of sticky-tack. This made it easier to track progress from week to week. Students also had folders in which they kept their hero's statistic sheet and a sheet of paper for keeping track of hit points, damage to monsters, and the math problems they were asked to solve. One of the students suggested that they also keep a log of the heroes' adventures. Students eagerly created hand-made journals and wrote in the voice of their hero as she or he progressed. They routinely shared these journal entries with the class. These entries were often humorous and integrated the work the students had done creating the game. Students colorfully described settings and monsters and built upon these descriptions to create a rich fantasy world. They employed vibrant, colorful adjectives and verbs to describe near misses, frightful encounters, and heroic victories. For example, the woodcutter ran into the "dreaded" fraction ghost in the forest. The ghost, who was "translucent white and floated about three inches from the ground" attacked the woodcutter, "holding him in the ghost's terrifying math clutches." The student wrote that the ghost "demanded, with a voice that sounded like the Black Death" the answer to a "challenging" fraction problem. It was only by the help of the "ingenious hawker" with her "helpful hawk" that the woodcutter was able to solve the problem and escape. This activity strengthened the students' engagement, helped them develop stronger writing skills, and demonstrated their application of social studies, writing, and math.

17.4 Experience and Outcomes

Because the students were involved in this project as designers and co-creators, they maintained a high level of enthusiasm for math class in general and for the design activities specifically. Frequently, students expressed that they were very excited about the project and disappointed that we could not spend more time working on it each day!

At each stage of development, the students were intimately involved in the direction of the project and were instrumental in determining what actions should be taken to complete the project. They often developed new and innovative suggestions for monster and character elements that I had not anticipated. The experiences I had and lessons I developed will serve as a guideline for future project; I am confident that using this model with other students could yield interesting, unique, and rewarding results.

The particular group of students I worked with offered a series of challenges, as many of them were struggling in math and reading, while others had serious attention and concentration challenges. These issues made following a set math curriculum extremely difficult. When I first suggested that we play a game, the students were very enthusiastic and the students struggling the most received the greatest benefit. Students who normally refused to participate eagerly offered answers when designing, adapting, or playing the game. However, these students enthusiastically applied the knowledge they hesitated to share previously in class or demonstrate on written assessments. They reflected on the project and said it did not even "feel like math." These students felt confident about using their math skills and demonstrated an aptitude for math that they did not show elsewhere. One student, who frequently demonstrated an apprehension towards math that translated into poor performance in class, on assignments, and during assessments, made significant progress as we worked through the project. She eagerly offered answers to questions posed to the whole class that related to the project (for example, easily finding the median, maximum, mode, and range of the votes for the setting) and slowly transferred this confidence in math as it applied to the project into a confidence in regular math. Her assessment performance improved dramatically and her retention and engagement rose significantly. By maintaining records of the problems they created and solved themselves, as well as the progress they showed orally, I was able to assess her mathematical ability more accurately, which I did for the other students as well. During the course of the project, I noticed that the other struggling students were also translating the math skills they developed into their written assessments, homework, and class work.

Students willingly used and further developed their reading and writing skills while creating stories, narratives, and presentations for the project. The students struggling in these areas academically enthusiastically poured through books and took careful notes. They felt invested in what they were doing and were excited about the goal-oriented work they were producing. One student reflected on his progress in reading and said that he "felt like he was actually reading for something," rather than "having to read." The aspects of reading that challenged him were therefore met with more enthusiasm than a "regular" assignment because he felt that his work was purposeful. Working with their own texts and creating written summaries of research also gave students a chance to have several different reading and writing experiences, strengthening their developing language arts skills. I monitored the progress students made in applying formal grammar rules, using spelling strategies, and employing descriptive language in their different writing assignments. Nearly all of the students had made progress in these areas, creating sustained narratives that were grammatically appropriate and used varied, colorful adjectives and verbs to bring the action to life. Editing also helped reinforce phonemic awareness, writing strategies, and application of proper grammar. The struggling students have developed stronger skills and found elements of writing and reading that they can enjoy.

The project also offers several chances to assess the students' progress both formally and informally. Because the students create a great deal of written work, including math problems, back-stories, and summaries of research, I was able to maintain a portfolio of progress in both math and writing. The records that the students keep during the game also track progress. I was able to see progress in all of the students and was especially impressed with the work that those who struggled the most produced. For example, the student whose work regarding the fraction ghost and the woodcutter I quoted above was one of the students struggling with writing. At the beginning of the year, he was unwilling to write anything but the bare minimum for written assignments. He later developed into one of the most prolific journal-entry writers in the class, working both collaboratively and independently on fantastically embellished adventures of the heroes within the settings of the game. For many of the students, the project resulted in longer and more well crafted pieces of writing, better class work and homework, and a greater confidence in their mathematical ability.

The project gave me a chance to assess students' social and emotional progress working in a variety of different configurations, from large groups and partnerships to sustained individual work. I routinely asked students to reflect on their experiences working with different groups. We talked about how students negotiated the division of labor, how they ensured that everyone contributed, and how they managed disputes. Students shared problem-solving strategies and worked through issues in a safe and caring environment. We role-played different scenarios that came up in groups and developed good solutions for managing conflict. While different configurations offered different social challenges, several of the students began to use strategies whole class had developed to cope with conflict. Towards the end of the project, many of the students who had struggled socially developed better social strategies for coping with others who upset them, managing their social issues with greater independence, tact, and success.

17.5 Modifications, Extensions, and Suggestions

I was lucky and grateful to have had the opportunity to undertake a sustained design project like this in an elementary classroom. I think that this project could be used in a wide variety of educational settings, including high school, and could offer more sophisticated opportunities to integrate other subjects, including science. The game could be easily adapted for different social studies themes in different elementary, middle, and high school settings.

One of the biggest challenges teachers may face in using this project is having enough time. There are, however, several possibilities that this project presents to address this issue. In the elementary classroom, students could work on the project in each of the content areas, creating math problems during math class, researching during social studies, and writing during language arts. Students could integrate formal lessons into their specific project design goals during instructional time, rather than carrying these skills into periods devoted only to the project. Teachers can also modify this project according to the time they have. The game itself offers opportunities to use problem solving skills, mathematical concepts, and creative thinking. Teachers could therefore play the game as it is, or with modifications that they develop, as a stand-alone math activity. Students could write reflections and extensions of the adventure after playing the game, applying language arts skills to their experience. Teachers could also decide which elements of the game they would want students to modify, thereby having students work through the research, design, and implementation without using instructional time to discuss and decide on these steps with the students. Teachers could also choose one or two elements to modify and allow students to initiate the process with teacher direction, rather than modifying the entire game.

The project also offers opportunities to integrate other curricula, including science. For example, physics students could calculate the force and distance traveled by different weapons, create ratios of scale, and then apply it to the weapons that the heroes use. Geography students could create scaled-down maps of actual locations for the game and research these areas to add in appropriate details. These students could also direct their heroes using latitude and longitude. Art students could create small statues of their heroes, three-dimensional cages and barriers, and lavishly illustrated maps and drawings of their adventures. The basic elements of the game offer many different opportunities to teachers in all different disciplines, and I hope that my experience demonstrates some of the possibilities it presents.

Lastly, this experience has demonstrated that game design in the classroom offers a plethora of opportunities for students to grow as creative, critical thinkers. My students generated a list of very interesting game design possibilities and were particularly excited about using *Dungeons and Dragons*. Other students may be excited to develop their own versions of *Monopoly* or *Risk* or use elements of many different games to create their own. Older students would definitely benefit from the opportunity to pull apart and critically examine several different types of games before designing their own. It would bolster their critical thinking, analysis, and synthesis abilities and provide the teacher with different opportunities to assess their progress. Student-initiated design projects invest and engage students in meaningful work that requires them to pull upon a diverse array of skills to create something of which they can be proud. I look forward to using game design as a foundation for building other lesson plans and projects for students, and I hope that my experience will encourage others to do the same.

References

Cadwell, L.B.: Bringing Learning to Life: A Reggio Emilia Approach to Early Childhood Education. Teacher's College Press, New York (2002)

Crawford, K.: Vygotskian approaches to human development in the information era. Educ. Stud. Math. **31**, 43–62 (1996)

Donaldson, M.: Children's Minds. Fontana, London (1984)

Driscoll, M. P.: Psychology of Learning for Instruction. Allyn & Bacon, Needham, MA (1994)

Lewin-Benham, A.: Powerful Children: Understanding How to Think and Learn Using the Reggio Emilia Approach. Teacher's College Press, New York (2005)

Macintyre, C.: Enhancing Learning Through Play: A Developmental Perspective for Early Years Settings. David Fulton Publishers, London (2001)

Morris, S.: The heroes of Hesiod: A monster slayer adventure. Wizards of the Coast. http://www.wizards.com/dnd/Article.aspx?x=dnd/4dnd/monsterslayers (2010). Accessed 1 Oct 2010

Randel, J.M., Morris, B.A., Wetzel, C.D., Whitehill, B.V.: The effectiveness of games for educational purposes: A review of recent research. Simul. Gaming **23**, 261–276 (1992)

Reiber, L.: Designing learning environments that excite serious play. In: Paper presented at the annual meeting of the Australasian Society for Computer Learning in Tertiary Education, Melbourne, Australia (2001)

Satterly, D.: Piaget and education. In: Gregory, R.L. (ed.) The Oxford Companion to the Mind. Oxford University Press, Oxford (1987)

Vygotsky, L.S.: Mind and Society: The Development of Higher mental Processes. Harvard University Press, Cambridge, MA (1978)

Wertsch, J.V., Sohmer, R.: Vygotsky on learning and development. Human Dev. **38**, 332–337 (1995)

Wood, D.: How Children Think and Learn, 2nd edn. Blackwell, Oxford (1998)

Chapter 18
Modding in Serious Games: Teaching Structured Query Language (SQL) Using NeverWinter Nights

Mario Soflano

18.1 Introduction

In educational technology, the invention of the E-learning system has been a major breakthrough . And yet, while E-Learning, with its slogan 'Anytime, Anyplace', has proven to be educationally useful, it does have difficulty in keeping students engaged and motivated over the course of a long learning process (Connolly and Stansfield, 2007). These same problems are also found in classroom education.

The learning materials in E-Learning system are usually presented in a less interesting way and provide limited scope for interaction which restricts how engaging they can be. Many E-learning systems have been abandoned by students through boredom.

On the contrary, video games are highly engaging and people of all ages and genders can play games for many hours without realising it. Consequently, over the past 15 years, educationalists have investigated the potential of using video games in teaching and this has given rise to terms such as Games-based learning (GBL) or Serious games (SG).

While SG exploits the benefits of video games, it also shares the same complications in the development process. Compared to E-learning, the development of video games, whether for educational or for commercial purposes, is considerably more complex.

18.2 Serious Games Development Life Cycle

Video games development shares many similarities with software development and some games developers categorise games development as a branch of software engineering. Both developments involve a process which has key elements including the following:

M. Soflano (✉)
School of Computing, University of the West of Scotland, Paisley, Scotland, UK
e-mail: Mario.Soflano@uws.ac.uk

M. Ma et al. (eds.), *Serious Games and Edutainment Applications*,
DOI 10.1007/978-1-4471-2161-9_18, © Springer-Verlag London Limited 2011

- Requirements Identification
- System definition
- Design: System Design, Program Design
- Coding/Implementation
- Testing

Because the key elements are similar, games developers can adopt development life cycles from software engineering. There are certain software engineering life cycles which can be used in games development, such as the Waterfall model, the V-process model, the Incremental model and the Iterative model (Whitten, 1995; Hughes and Cotterell, 2006). To choose which model to use, the developer must refer to the requirements and specifications defined in the early stage of the development.

The Waterfall model is usually used when the requirements and specifications are clearly defined, and this then allows the project to proceed from one stage to another stage in a sequence. Essentially, the Waterfall model only allows one way forward, from the beginning to the end without any back-tracking. While this approach generally requires less development time compared to other models, uncertainties sometimes arise during the development phase which result in the need for a more flexible approach (Fig. 18.1).

The V-process model has a similar structure to the Waterfall model. However, after coding/implementation, each element is tested and modified if required. This can lead to a longer development time but has the advantage of normally producing well-tested results (Fig. 18.2).

While the Incremental model follows a similar structure to the Waterfall model, the result of the design process is broken down into small components. Each component is designed specifically and then developed and tested separately before all the components are integrated and tested together in later stage. This model is also used when requirements and specifications are clearly defined (Fig. 18.3).

Unlike the previous model, the Iterative model is usually used when the requirements and specifications are not clearly defined. In this model, each individual requirement is designed, developed and tested. When a requirement is fulfilled, the next requirement is the next iteration and undergoes the same process as the previous requirement (Fig. 18.4).

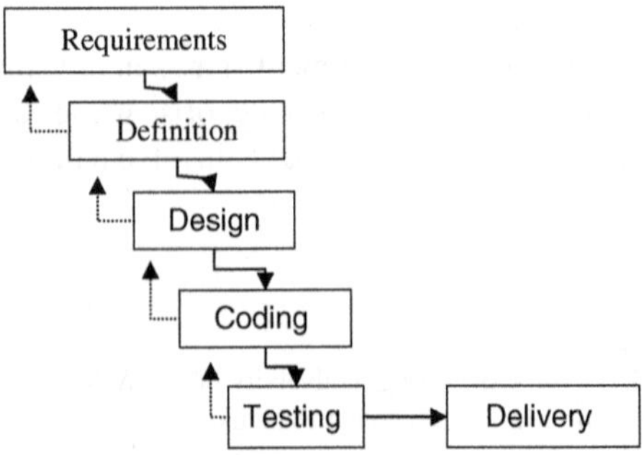

Fig. 18.1 Waterfall model (Whitten, 1995, p. 20)

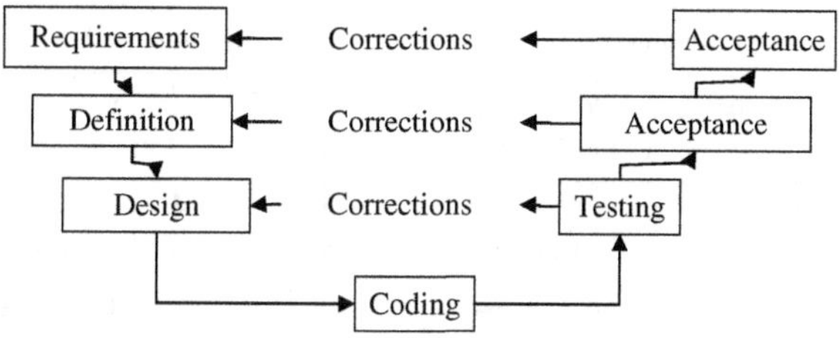

Fig. 18.2 V-process model (Hughes and Cotterell, 2006, p. 77)

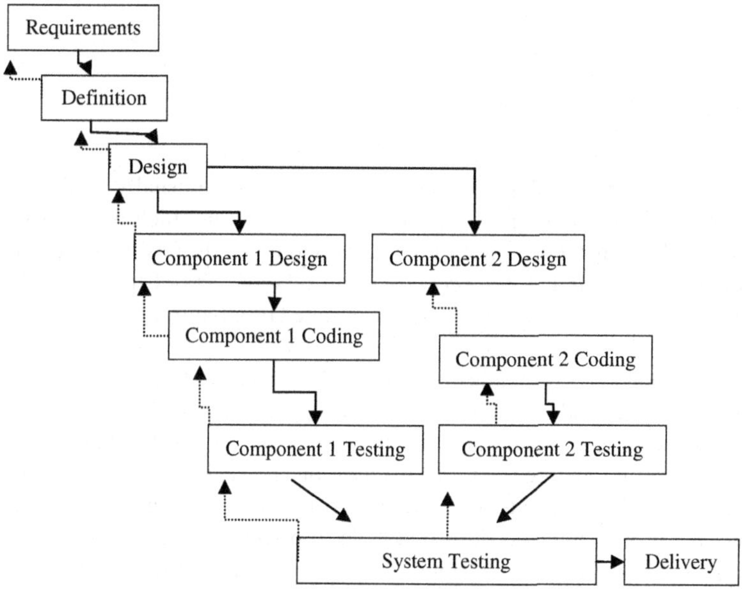

Fig. 18.3 Incremental model (Whitten, 1995, p. 21)

In the early stages of serious games development, user requirements and the purposes of the game are usually identified through brainstorming. Target user identification and the outcome expected from playing the game are examples of elements which need to be identified at this stage. These requirements determine how the game will be designed. For example, if the game is targeted at school children then it should be a simple one with a simple storyline and interface.

Based on requirements, the game concept is specified by identifying certain details such as genre, game mode (single player or multi player), platform on which the game will run, interface style (2D or 3D), gameplay (using mouse or keyboard), engine to be used, etc. As the result, it is possible to identify the essential elements of the game including its properties.

The next stage is the design of the game. In video games design, there are 2 main areas: game design and technical design (Bethke, 2003). Game design is basically an extension of the game concept specified previously. The detail of the gameplay, the

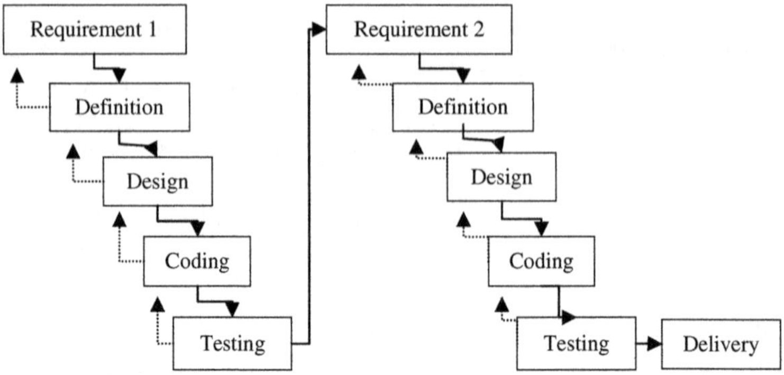

Fig. 18.4 Iterative model (Whitten, 1995, p. 22)

storyline and the relationships between game elements are usually finalised at this stage. The result of this stage is a game design document which provides detailed information about the appearance of the game and how it is played. Then, based on the game design document, the properties and relationships of the game elements are coded into either a procedural or object-oriented programming logic, in technical design stage.

In requirement analysis, game definition, game design and technical design stage, the project manager and the game designer occupy the main roles. In the implementation stage, more roles are required, such as those of graphical designer, animator, programmer, sound engineer, etc. Depending on the scale of the game, each role could require more than one person and each role has its own responsibility. For example, the project manager has to be able to plan the project to meet deadlines and budgets, a designer must design the environment and the story of the game and also produce graphical assets, the programmer will create interactions and backend scripts and also assemble all the game elements, etc. The skills required for each position are also different. For example, a designer needs to be familiar with Adobe Photoshop for 2D objects and 3DMax for 3D objects, a programmer needs to know how to script depending on the game engine used, etc. Thus, in games development, various skills are required.

At the same time, most SG developments are less well-resourced in comparison with commercial game development so there are limitations when it comes to recruitment to the different sections of the SG development team. One solution is to choose a game engine and a game development toolset that fits the game and also accommodates the skills of the members of the SG development team. For example, if the members of the team are less skilled at programming, then it is better to find an engine that provides pre-defined functions. Choosing the right engine is also important as it can help the development process to run smoother and faster.

When designing and developing serious games, the main concern is to design a game that can teach the subject to be learnt effectively while remaining fun and challenging. While it is relatively easy to make a game which is fun and challenging, not all games manage to teach the subject effectively. A further problem is that some students lose interest in the game when the learning process is either too obvious or too demanding. In other words, by fitting the learning materials to the gameplay and the gamestory, the player is expected to see the learning material as part of the game. By doing so, the game can still be fun and manage to challenge the player to master the material in order to complete the game. The learning process must also be gradual so that the beginner does not find the learning curve is too steep and be put off by this.

18.3 Game Modding

As the name suggests, games modification or modding is a process of gameplay modification which includes the modification of the game's storyline, its goals, interaction or environment. Games modification was started when game companies bundled game creation toolsets together with original campaign games. The game creation toolsets were originally targeted at game fans who were creative or who had new ideas about how to improve the game or to create a new game with different characteristics from those of the original game. The new modules/games produced from modding are usually called 'mods'. However, although the mods may have a different gameplay which provides a different gaming experience from that of the original game, the characteristics of the original game are largely maintained. That is because the mods and the original game run on the same game engine and most mods are created by using the assets of the original game.

Although there are no official statistics about number of modders, most game companies nowadays provide their own game creation toolset for their games. Famous game titles like *Half Life, Warcraft 3, NeverWinter Nights, Unreal Tournament, The Sims 3, Command and Conquer, Civilisation, Dragon Age* and many more come with their own game creation toolset. This indicates that the game companies recognise the potential of game modding in boosting the activities of their fan-based communities and also as a means to get feedback to enable them to make improvements to the original game and to help in their next game development. The game companies also support their fans and modders by establishing official online communities. For example, Bioware has official websites and forums for their fans including modders (e.g. http://social.bioware.com). Many mods have been created with various different purposes and some of them are published on websites such as http://www.moddb.com.

18.3.1 Counter Strike

Amongst all the mods created, there are some which gain global success. One such mod is a 3D First-Person-Shooting (FPS) called *Counter Strike* which was developed based on the original title *Half Life* developed by *Valve. Half Life* was released in 1998 and *Counter Strike* was first released about a year later. Since then *Counter Strike* has been a global phenomenon and has featured in international game competitions such as World Cyber Games (http://www.wcg.com). *Counter Strike* is also still being played in many gaming cafes and an online game portal, *Steam*, suggests that over 4 million players have played *Counter Strike* through the portal.

While *Half Life* has a science fiction story which requires the player to use weapons to kill alien monsters, *Counter Strike* has a short story about a war between a counter-terrorist squad and a terrorist squad. Compared to *Half Life*, *Counter Strike* has a significantly shorter gameplay and is usually played in multiplayer mode while *Half Life* is played in single player only mode. In *Counter Strike*, there are only two groups, the terrorist group and the counter terrorist group, fighting each other and the main objective is to defeat the opposition by destroying the opposition's base with a time bomb or to kill all members of the opposing group.

Although the *Counter Strike*'s game story is relatively simple and shorter, it still provides huge fun and challenges and also has potential to be used for teaching and training purposes. When playing *Counter Strike*, the individual player is required to display precision in shooting, reflexes and individual strategy when encountering enemies. Collectively, as part of a squad, each member has to be able to work with others in order to win the game. The teamwork skills include communication, planning and strategy. By playing the game over and over again, both the player's individual skills and his/her teamwork skills can improve. These benefits of playing *Counter Strike* have been recognised and some training programmes already use this game to train their personnel. For example, in one of the main cities in China, Tianjin, the local police use the *Counter Strike* competition for training purposes (http://english.peopledaily.com.cn/90001/90776/6262328.html).

18.3.2 Defense of the Ancients (DotA)

Another successful mod is *Defense of the Ancient (DotA)* which was developed by fans of *Warcraft 3*. While *Warcraft 3* was developed by Blizzard, *DotA was* designed and developed subsequently by 3 fans nicknamed *Eul, Guinsoo* and *IceFrog* in the period since 2003 using *Warcraft 3* W*orld Editor*. Since then changes and improvements are still being made to the game, such as the addition of new skills, new units, new items, new maps and improved computer artificial intelligence (AI). These changes and improvements usually provide new experiences and challenges and that is perhaps why many people still actively play *DotA*.

While *Warcraft 3* is a Real-Time-Strategy (RTS) game, *DotA* shares more characteristics with Action Role-Playing-Games (RPG). *Warcraft 3* has a single-player campaign scenario and a multiplayer game while *DotA* essentially focuses more on a multiplayer game against other players or computer AIs. In *Warcraft 3*, the player needs to micro-manage all the game activities from building a base, managing resources and training armies to controlling units when attacking opponents. The winner in *Warcraft 3* is determined when all opponents' bases are destroyed.

Meanwhile, in *DotA*, the war is between 2 groups: *sentinel* which is located in the south west and *scourge* which is located in the north east of the map. Each group has its own base and a main building located in the middle of the base. The main objective in *DotA* is to destroy the main building of the opponent. Compared to *Warcraft 3,* which requires the player to control whole units, the player in *DotA* only controls one special unique unit/hero. Each side also has armies which automatically regenerate after a certain time and automatically attack enemies on their fixed paths. There are 3 fixed paths which connect both bases and the armies automatically follow these paths to the enemy's base and attack any armies or heroes of their opponent on the way. Each killing of a unit or destruction of an opponent's building wins money as a reward and also gives experience which allows the player to increase their level and upgrade their skills. The money can be used to buy items. The player can also micro-manage the controlled hero to get a last hit at the enemy which brings a bonus of extra money and experience.

Winning at *DotA* relies heavily on the teamwork skills of the team members which makes this game very challenging, interesting and useful for teamwork training. It is very difficult to win this game single-handedly. Each group member has to be able to plan and agree on a strategy in which each member will have different responsibilities and tasks to perform. In forming a strategy, the members need to understand the strengths and weaknesses of their teammates and it is important that they help each other out when a teammate is in trouble. During the game, the players must concentrate and be aware of their surroundings if they are to avoid being ambushed by their opponents or to be able to help teammates when required. Figure 18.5 is the screenshot of *DotA* gameplay.

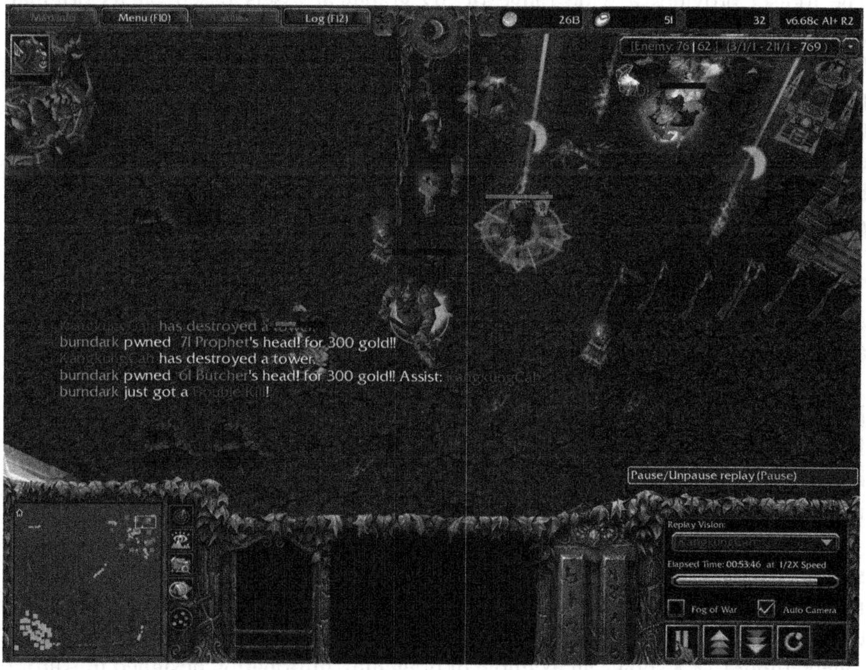

Fig. 18.5 A screenshot of *DotA* game

18.4 Modding Toolset from Commercial Games

As previously mentioned, there are many commercial games bundled with a toolset which allows the player to create *mods*. Amongst these, there are some best-sellers which allow modding and these games will be described in this chapter. These games are *NeverWinter Games 2*, *Unreal* and *Warcraft 3*.

18.4.1 NeverWinter Nights 2

NeverWinter Nights 2 (NWN2) is a three dimensional (3D) Role-playing Game (RPG) developed by *Obsidian* and published by *Atari* in 2006. It is the sequel of *NeverWinter Nights* developed by *Bioware* and, like its predecessor, is also one of the best-selling RPGs. Since its release, NWN2 has established fan-based communities which are still active today.

NWN2 uses an engine called *Aurora Engine* and this engine, along with a toolset based on the engine, is bundled together with the original NWN2 campaign game. Through the toolset, the player can modify the game and also create a new module (mod) for a variety of purposes.

18.4.1.1 Aurora Toolset

The toolset provides a wide range of 3D graphical assets based on its original campaign. The three main categories of assets are static objects/*placeables*, tiles, Non-Playing-Characters (NPCs) and triggers. Trees, houses, tables are the examples of static objects while the tiles provided by the toolset include external tiles (e.g. grass) and internal tiles (e.g. wooden floor). All NPCs available in the original campaign also can be used in the mod. Each asset has its own properties which can be modified to suit different purposes. While there are some special trigger objects, *placeables* and NPCs also can be modified so that they can trigger actions.

The assets can be used by direct drag and drop from the assets panel to the canvas. They can also be rotated, repositioned and resized. Figure 18.6 shows an example of a map created in Aurora Toolset. The map consists of objects, such as houses, trees and tiles, which are available by default in the toolset.

While the toolset provides pre-defined actions such as walking, talking, attacking, dodging, picking up, etc.), the toolset also allows scripting to create new functions according to need. The scripting in NWN2 is called NWN Script and its syntax is similar to C programming language. Figure 18.7 shows a scripting area in Aurora Toolset

One of the most useful features provided in the toolset is branching conversation. The mod created by the toolset can use conditional conversations which allow the player to make choices during a conversation with NPCs. Each choice can be designed to have various different effects on the player and the game elements. Figure 18.8 shows an example of branching information designed in Aurora Toolset.

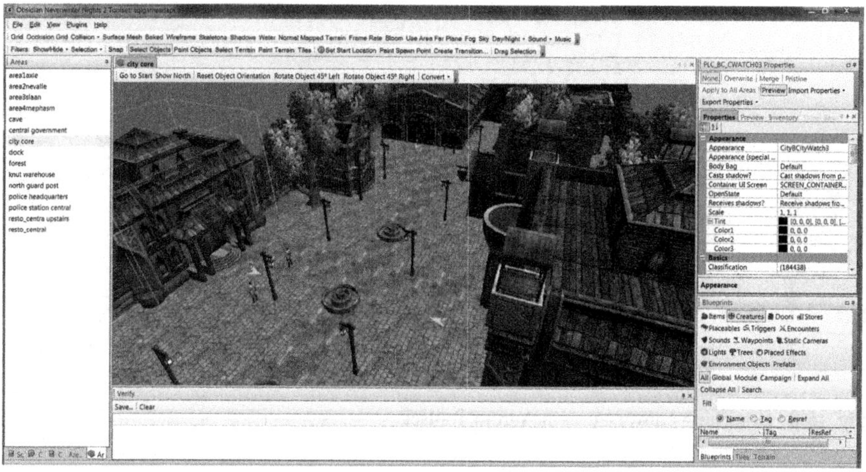

Fig. 18.6 A map created in Aurora Toolset

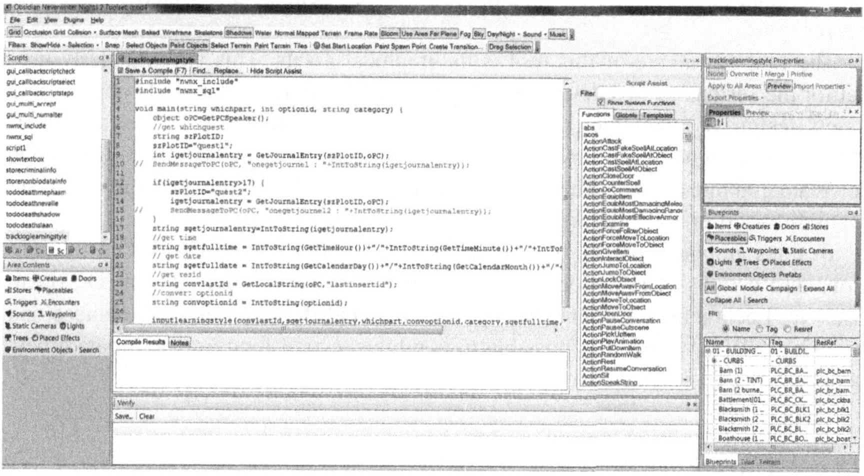

Fig. 18.7 Scripting in Aurora Toolset

By using the branching conversation, the developer can give alternative instructions depending on the player's response and to give the player options to choose between different learning paths.

As NWN2 has been extremely popular since its release, it has established an online community of fans and developers who are usually very responsive when a development problem arises. Some developers have also developed additional functions and plug-ins for different purposes. One of the NWN2 developer communities has developed NeverWinter Nights Extender (NWNX) which can connect the mod to an external database such as MySQL and also host a multiplayer

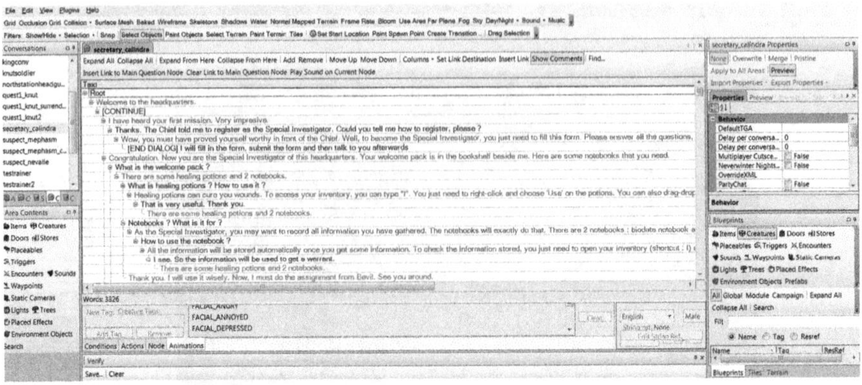

Fig. 18.8 Branching conversation in Aurora Toolset

game. The ability to connect to an external database can be used to record player response such as the learning path and the options chosen by the player. For example, the data recorded can be used to identify the strengths and weaknesses of the player.

The first advantage of this tool is its graphical assets. This is particularly useful for the serious games developer who does not have particular skills in graphical assets design. By using the graphical assets provided by this toolset, the game environment is designed faster and more easily insofar as the developer no longer needs to create graphical assets. The graphical assets are also highly customisable and can be used for different purposes.

Besides graphical assets, the toolset also has a library that provides basic functions and actions. The actions usually used in RPG are walk, talk, attack, open, use, etc. Each action is controlled by functions and the functions can be accessed by using NWN Script. It is possible to combine several functions to create a new action.

18.4.2 Unreal

In first person shooting (FPS) game, one of the famous titles is *Unreal* developed by *Epic Games* in 1998. Prior to its release, *Unreal* was often compared to *Quake* and *Doom* because of the similarity in its gameplay. However, *Unreal* with its *Unreal Engine* has proven to be technically superior to its competitors especially in terms of its graphical display capabilities. For some graphic card companies, *Unreal* has become a benchmark for quality testing. Since then, *Unreal Engine* has undergone further development and, at the present time, the engine is considered to be the best game engine. Especially for 3D games. The engine itself is highly appreciated in the gaming community and this is reflected in the awards it has won since 2005.

Besides the *Unreal* series, *Epic Games* is also developing a *Gears of War* series and both are best-selling games. There are other game companies which use *Unreal*

Engine for their game development and successful game titles released using this engine include the *Tom Clancy Rainbow Six* series developed by *Ubisoft*, the *Mass Effect* series by *Bioware*, the *BioShock* series by *2 K Games*, etc. *Unreal Engine* is also used in animation drama, such as *Lazy Town* and some serious games (http://www.unrealengine.com/showcase).

18.4.2.1 Unreal Engine

Unreal Editor or *UnrealEd* was first bundled with the first release of the *Unreal* game and it was intended for creating 3D FPS game mods and map editing. In further development, *UnrealEd* has been included in Unreal Development Kit (UDK) which can be downloaded and unlike other mods, the games created by UDK can run independently without requiring the original *Unreal* game to be installed. UDK brings more flexibility for game developers to create totally new games with a different gaming experience to the original *Unreal* game. UDK can also create games for any platform, from PC to console (Xbox 360 and PS3) and smartphone (iOS)

Since UDK mainly used for 3D games development, the development interface of UDK consists of four windows which represent different 3D views. Every object created in UDK is always in 3D (X-axis, Y-axis and Z-axis) although it is possible to create 2D objects by using only two axis to work on. As an example, the screenshot below shows a 3D box and the windows show views from different axes.

Unreal also provides some ready-used objects, such as graphical objects, textures, sound objects, etc. These objects can be added directly to the map created. The result can be seen in screenshot below (Fig. 18.9).

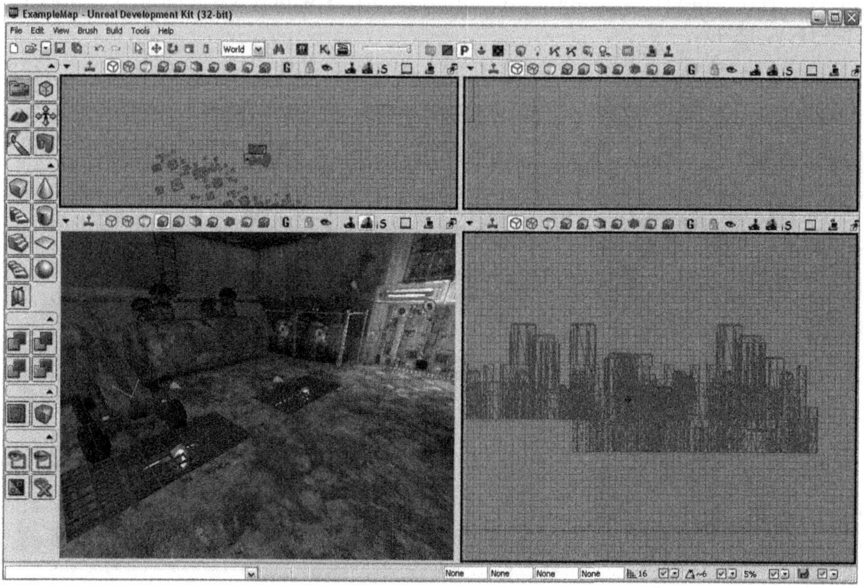

Fig. 18.9 A map created in UDK

18.4.3 Warcraft 3

The *Warcraft* series are developed by *Blizzard Entertainment* and were first released in 1994. The *Warcraft* series were originally real-time strategy games with the exception of the latest one, *World of Warcraft* (WoW) which is a Massively Multiplayer Online Role-Playing Game (MMORPG). Since WoW is in a different genre, the engine used in WoW is not the same as the one used for the other *Warcraft* series and there is no toolset for creating mods provided in WoW.

As for *Warcraft's* real-time games, Blizzard released 3 different titles with the newest version, *Warcraft III: Reign of Chaos*, being released in 2002 also bundled with *Warcraft World Editor*. The world editor allows modders to create custom maps and game scenarios.

18.4.3.1 Warcraft 3 World Editor

The usability and functionality of Warcraft 3 World Editor are similar to those of NWN2's Aurora Toolset and it also has graphical objects which can be used by drag-and-drop to the canvas. The editor also includes other objects, such as camera objects, sound objects and trigger objects. A dialog object for creating conversation is included amongst the trigger objects. Figure 18.10 shows a map created in Warcraft 3 World Editor.

Each object in the game can have a number of conditions and actions. There are pre-defined conditions and actions available in the editor which can be used for objects and for artificial intelligence (AI) of the Non-Player Characters (NPCs). The NPC's AI can be modified in AI editor. It is also possible to create custom functions for Warcraft 3 mods by using a programming JASS which has a similar syntax to C++ (Fig. 18.11).

Fig. 18.10 A map created in Warcraft 3 World Editor

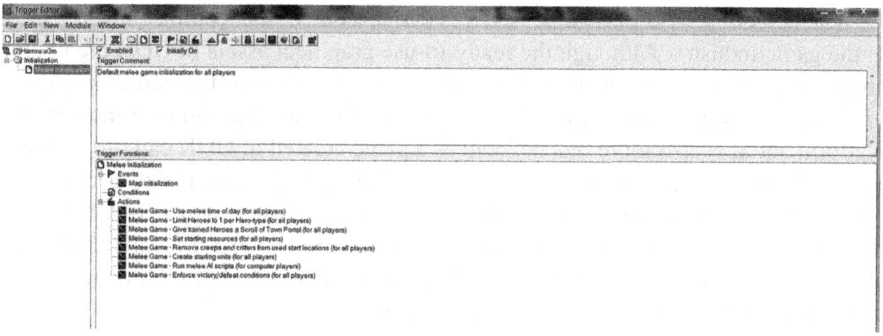

Fig. 18.11 Triggers and events handler in Warcraft 3 World Editor

18.4.4 Overview of Modding Toolset

There are many commercial games that provide toolsets for modding and the toolsets described here represent different game genres. Amongst the genres, RPG is potentially useful for teaching through game because it gives freedom to the player to explore. Furthermore, there are some RPG elements, such as branching conversation, which can be used to deliver instructions by using different conversation paths. However, choosing a toolset for developing SG depends on the requirements and the purposes of the game also on the skills of the SG developer.

Each toolset has its own advantages and disadvantages. The toolsets mentioned here have ready-to-use graphical assets, especially in the cases of NWN2's Aurora toolset and Warcraft 2 World Editor. The toolsets also have pre-defined functions. However, these functions are mostly specific to a certain genre. For example, Aurora Toolset is more appropriate for creating an RPG, although it is possible to create custom functions for different purposes on these toolsets depending on the skill of the SG developer. The mods created on these toolsets support single-player and multi-player games.

Compared to other toolsets, the Aurora Toolset has a feature for creating branching and conditional conversation. The toolset also links to an external database, such as MySQL and SQL Server. Since the Aurora toolset was originally developed for RPG, the mods created also follow the same control system as the original NWN2 game. The control system in NWN2 is mainly by clicking buttons on the interface with some shortcuts available for more experienced players. Another benefit is the fact that the engine and toolset have been bundled together with every purchase of the original NWN2 campaign games and since its release a few years ago, the price has remained relatively low. However, any mod created for commercial purposes has to be licensed by Obsidian.

In terms of functionality and of the usability of the toolset, Warcraft 3 World Editor is similar to the Aurora Toolset. However, Warcraft 3 World Editor provides simple conversation and it does not allow connection to an external database. To create more complex conversation and in the case of custom functions, the game developer needs to create scripts.

When creating a 3D FPS game, UDK is perhaps one of the leading game engines in the game industry. Although the ready-to-use graphical assets in UDK are not as abundant as they are in other toolsets, UDK gives freedom to the game developer to create a 3D game with high-quality graphics. UDK can also run on almost every platform and it is also more independent as a game created in UDK can run without the installation of an original Unreal game. However, the creation of a complex conversation in UDK is not as straightforward as it is with the Aurora Toolset and its default functions do not allow connections to an external database. While UDK can be used freely for non-commercial purposes, any games created with commercial intent must be notified to and licensed by Epic Games.

However, there is also a drawback to modding. While modding allows the SG developer to develop an SG with a similar look to that of commercial games, most commercial game modding toolsets require the original game to be installed. For example, to play a mod created in Aurora Toolset, the original NWN2 game must be installed. In other words, the hardware requirements for playing a mod are the same as those for the original game and most commercial games nowadays require a reasonably high hardware specification. By means of example, for NWN2, released in 2006, the minimum hardware requirements are: 3.0 GHz Intel Pentium 4 or equivalent processor or equivalent, 1024 MB RAM, 6500 MB Hard Drive Space and ATI Radeon X800 series, NVIDIA GeForce 6800 series or higher video card.

18.5 Serious Games for Teaching Structured Query Language

To demonstrate how games can be used to support education, a role-playing game (RPG) has been developed and the subject material chosen is structured query language (SQL). SQL is a basic database language which has similar structure to English and is used by the majority of database systems available nowadays, such as SQL server, Microsoft access, MySQL, Oracle, etc.

18.5.1 Structured Query Language (SQL)

In a decision-making process, it is important to have sufficient data to support the decision to be made; that is why people tend to gather as much data as possible, whether for immediate or later use. Given the growing amount and size of data, it is likely that the data need to be processed before it can be used. SQL is a language used to store data to a database and it is also used to manipulate the data stored in that database so it can be more useful for various purposes.

The skill to be able to make full use of information stored in database is one of the key skills required not only in IT but also in non-IT sectors such as the commercial sector. Database and SQL skills are required not only in jobs related to information technology and information systems but also in many other areas such as administration, biology, medicine, etc. Universities and some secondary schools in the UK regard database and SQL skills as one of the most important subjects on the curriculum.

SQL has two major components (Connolly and Begg, 2009):

- *Data Definition Language (DDL)*: related to the structural design of the database, such as Create table, Alter table, Drop table, etc.
- *Data Manipulation Language (DML):* related to information manipulation such as retrieve, update, delete and insert.

While DDL is important for database design, DML is used more often than DDL because DML allows the user to interact with the data. Through DDL, the user can insert, update and delete information and more importantly the user can specify which data is to be retrieved according to the user's needs.

To be able to retrieve the correct data, the user has to understand the structure of the database in which the data is stored. A database consists of tables and each table has its own columns/field, for example: in table *user_tbl*, there are columns *firstname*, *lastname*, *age* and *address*. The data can be stored in the tables and categorised per column, for example for the following information:

- First Name: John
- Last Name: Doe
- Age: 29
- Address: 3/5 Paisley Street
- City: Glasgow

when it is stored to table *user_tbl,* a new row or record is created and it will look like this (Fig. 18.12):

So when the user wants to retrieve information from the database, the user has to identify which table and column(s) the information is to be retrieved from and then combine this information with keywords to form a SQL query statement. Since the database can store different data, conditional clauses can be set to limit the results so that only the intended results are retrieved.

In this game, some basic forms of SQL retrieval syntax (SQL SELECT) are to be taught, for example:

- **SELECT** * **FROM** *user_tbl*
  This SQL statement means 'retrieve all information from table *user_tbl*'
- **SELECT** firstname, lastname **FROM** user_tbl
  This SQL statement means 'only retrieve *firstname* and *lastname* from table *user_tbl*'
- **SELECT** lastname **FROM** user_tbl **WHERE** city = 'Glasgow'

Firstname	Lastname	Age	Address	City
John	Doe	29	3/5 Paisley Street	Glasgow

Fig. 18.12 The structure of table *user_tbl*

In this example, a condition is included. This SQL statement means 'retrieve the *lastname*(s) of those who lived in Glasgow stored in table *user_tbl*'

- **SELECT** firstname, lastname **FROM** user_tbl **WHERE** age > 27 **AND** city = 'Glasgow'
  As in the third example, a condition is included to filter the result so that only the intended data retrieved. This SQL statement means 'retrieve *firstname* and *lastname* of those who are older than 27 years old and lives in Glasgow'.
- **SELECT COUNT**(*) **FROM** *user_tbl*;
  This SQL statement means 'retrieve the total number of records in table *user_tbl*'
- **SELECT MIN** (age) **FROM** *user_tbl*;
  This SQL statement means 'retrieve the lowest age from column *age* in table *user_tbl*'
- **SELECT MAX** (age) **FROM** *user_tbl*;
  This SQL statement means'retrieve the highest age from column *age* in table *user_tbl*'
- **SELECT AVG** (age) **FROM** *user_tbl*;
  This SQL statement means 'retrieve the average age from column *age* in table *user_tbl*'
- **SELECT DISTINCT** (city) **FROM** *user_tbl*;
  This SQL statement means 'retrieve distinctive city from column *city* in table *user_tbl*'. By using this function, the result is limited to unique data from the column.
- **SELECT** *firstname*, *lastname* **FROM** *user_tbl* **ORDER BY** age **DESC**
  This SQL statement means 'retrieve *firstname* and *lastname* from table *user_tbl* and then sort the result based on age (from older to younger)'.

In database and SQL courses and literatures, a case study is often used to describe a task including its conditions and requirements. Through the case study, the student is expected to learn how to construct SQL statements based on the identification of the task.

18.5.2 Game Story

In the implementation of the game used in this research, a story of a criminal investigator has been selected. As is the case in a real-life crime investigation, the player also needs to collect information and evidence before a warrant to arrest the criminals can be issued. The information and evidence collected will automatically be stored in a database. So, in order to get the warrant, the player must retrieve the information and evidence required and to do so the player must use SQL SELECT. By blending the learning process with a gamestory, it is expected that the game will motivate the player not only to learn about SQL but also to complete the game as the player see the learning process as part of the challenge of the game. Furthermore, the use of a real-life crime investigation process as the gamestory may also help the player to understand the implementation of the learning contents. The level of complexity of the SQL queries which the player must construct increases as the gamestory progresses.

At the beginning of the game, the player can create and personalise their avatar. After the avatar is created, the player will appear in the police headquarters as the new recruit. In the first mission, the player is required to investigate the case of a missing classified document which later connects to further missions investigating cases of corruption and assassination. In order to gather information and evidence, the player will have to travel between areas to talk to NPCs and will also encounter enemies. There are fighting scenes (Fig. 18.13) which require very simple mouse control from the player (in fact the player character can react automatically when attacked by enemies). The story of the game is guided so the player can easily find out what to do and where to go. The game also has a map marked for important elements/characters.

In total, there are 3 main missions with a number of side missions as build-up stories to the main missions. To complete the game, the player has to obtain warrants to arrest key criminals for each mission. Before the player can issue a warrant to arrest a key criminal on the first mission, the player has to answer multiple-choice questions about basic database theory, such as the database structure (tables and columns) which are used in the game. The purpose of these multiple-choice questions is to introduce the database into the game and to give an introduction to

Fig. 18.13 The gameplay: fighting scene

database theory before the player learns SQL. Once the player has answered the multiple-choice questions, the player can learn how to carry out tasks and attempt to complete them in order to obtain the warrants. The tasks relate to translating basic statements into SQL statements.

For each mission, the player learns different forms of SQL SELECT. To help the player to complete the tasks, there are instructions specific to each task. Through the tasks, the player can learn how to create and use SQL SELECT to solve the given tasks.

Figure 18.14 shows the first task to be completed to get the first warrant. The task is to retrieve all the information that has been collected. To complete the task, the player needs to type in an SQL SELECT statement.

If the player needs to know how to translate the task into an SQL statement, they can get explanations through texts and pictures (Fig. 18.15).

Once the player has successfully created SQL queries in response to the task requirements, the warrant will be issued. Having the warrant, the player can now arrest the key criminals (Fig. 18.16).

Besides learning from the tasks, the player also can choose an option which allows them to learn about database and SQL SELECT which includes basic and conditional SQL SELECT. When the player has learnt about SQL SELECT, the player also can test his/her SQL SELECT knowledge by choosing 'freestyle' practice. In 'freestyle' practice, the player can test different variations of SQL SELECT statements and see the results. There are 2 modes of 'freestyle' practice: assisted and non-assisted practice. In assisted practice, the game will provide all the keywords so the player just needs to specify which columns and table are to be used while in non-assisted practice, the player can directly create an SQL statement by typing it to a textbox. After reviewing the SQL statement created, the player can execute the SQL statement and the result of the statement will be displayed (Figs. 18.17 and 18.18).

Fig. 18.14 Screenshot of the textbox in warrant issue

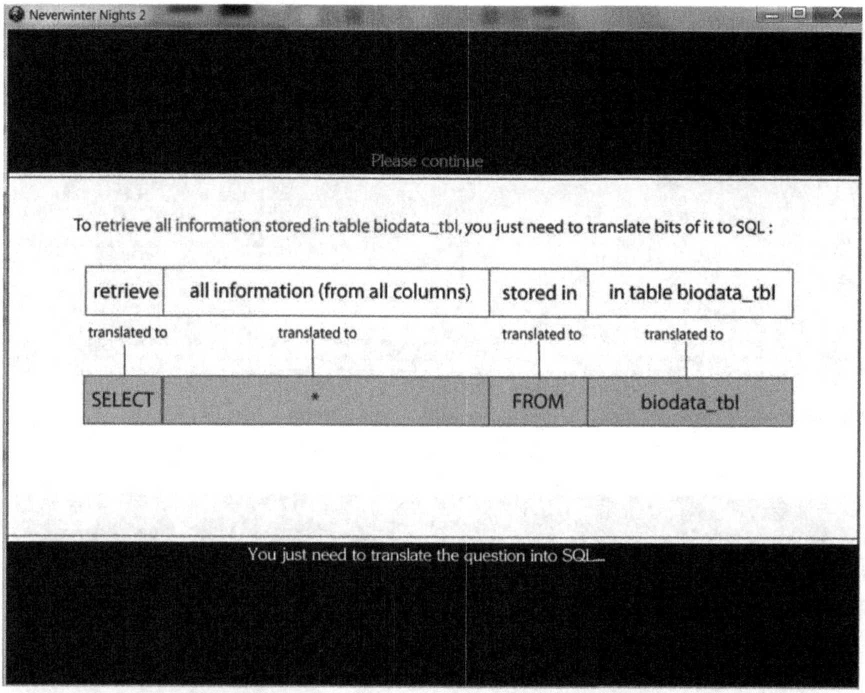

Fig. 18.15 Picture explanation

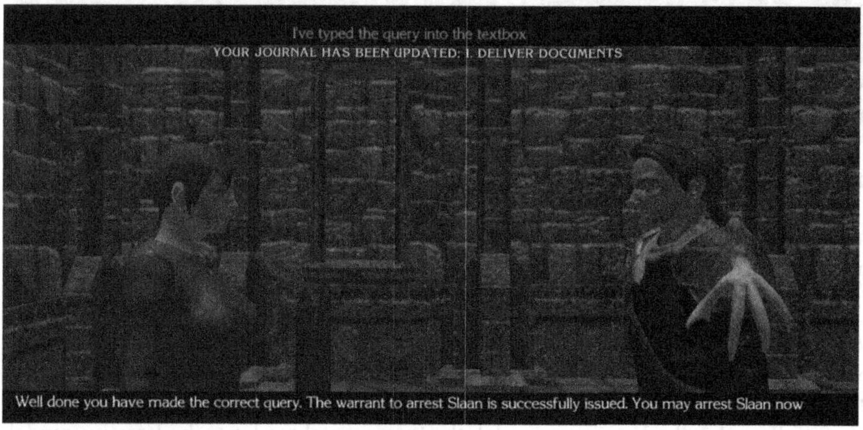

Fig. 18.16 Screenshot of the warrant issued

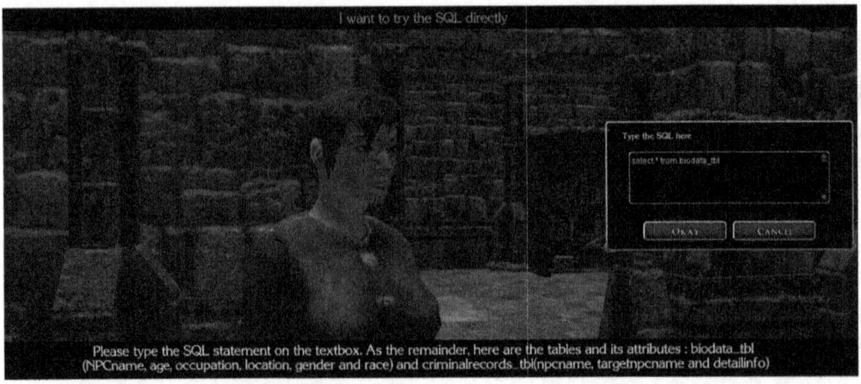

Fig. 18.17 Screenshot of the SQL practice session – type a query

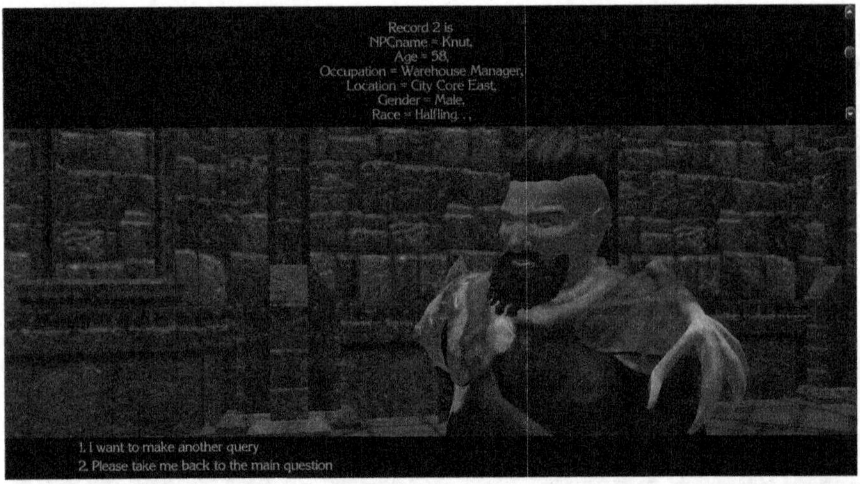

Fig. 18.18 Screenshot of the SQL practice session – the result of the query

18.6 Conclusion and Future Work

As a branch of software engineering, SG development consists of key elements such as requirements identification, system definition, design, implementation and testing. In developing a serious game, the SG developer can choose from the Waterfall model, the V-process model, the Incremental model or the Iterative model as the development life cycle. By choosing a development life cycle model, the SG developer is able monitor the project so that it can finish on time and on budget.

The implementation stage of SG development may require different skills for different areas. For example, a graphical designer is required to create graphical assets, a programmer is required to make scripts for computer AI, etc. However, like other software projects, project cost is an important consideration. To limit development costs, one solution is to choose an engine which suits the purpose of the development and the skills of the developer. For example, if the developer lacks skills in writing programming scripts then it is better to choose a game engine with a toolset that provides ready-made functions.

To acquire an engine of this nature, it is possible to use engines and toolsets bundled together with commercial games such as NeverWinter Nights 2, Unreal, Warcraft 3, etc. Most of these toolsets have functions and graphical assets similar to the original campaign game and these toolsets can be used to create custom game/mod with a different gameplay and gamestory from the original one. Choosing a game engine for SG development depends on the kind of game to be created, the skills of the developer and the subject to be taught in the game. The main purpose of SG development is to deliver learning materials through games in a fun and challenging way

One of the mods created with NWN2's Aurora Toolset is used to teach structured query language (SQL). SQL is a database programming language used to manipulate information in database. This game focuses on teaching SQL statements for retrieving information (SQL SELECT), including conditional clauses and special functions for SQL SELECT such as minimum, maximum, average, etc.

In the game, the player plays the role of a detective who needs to investigate criminal cases. As part of the investigation, the player will collect information by talking to non-player characters (NPCs). The information will be automatically stored in the game's database. To complete the game, the player needs to arrest several key criminal masterminds and, to do so, the player has to obtain a warrant which only issued if the player can present enough evidence. To get the relevant evidence, the player needs to create some SQL SELECT statements based on the task description. The game also provides information about database and SQL SELECT theory and also an option to do 'free-style' SQL SELECT, by which player can test themselves and see the results of their SQL SELECT statements.

The game is expected teach SQL SELECT in more fun and challenging way compared to E-Learning and classroom education. By playing this game, the player is expected to be able to create various SQL SELECT statements based on the tasks given. For example, when the player is asked to 'retrieve all information from table *user_tbl*', the SQL SELECT statement the player has to create is 'SELECT * FROM user_tbl'.

This game is designed and developed as part of the author's research and currently being used for experiment to investigate the learning outcomes when learning SQL through this game.

Resources

DOTA

http://www.getdota.com/: official website of DOTA
http://www.playdota.com/: DOTA community website
http://www.dota-utilities.com/: DOTA community website which provides some DOTA tools

Counter Strike

http://www.valvesoftware.com/: Valve's official website, the developer of Counter Strike engine
http://store.steampowered.com/app/240/: online gateway for online playing

Neverwinter Nights 2

http://www.nwn2.com/: NeverWinter Nights 2 official website
http://social.bioware.com/forum/1/subindex/156: new official forum of NeverWinter Nights 2 http://nwn2forums.bioware.com/forums/: discontinued official forum of NeverWinter Nights 2. Although it is no longer active, it is still accessible and it may contains useful information

Unreal

http://www.unrealengine.com/: official website of Unreal
http://www.udk.com/: official website contains information about unreal development kit
http://www.epicgames.com/: official website of Epic Games, the developer of Unreal engine

Modding

http://www.moddb.com/: online portal for game modding. The portal contains showcaase of mods developed from various different games

References

Bethke, E.: Game Development and Production. Wordware Publishing, Plano, TX (2003)
Connolly, T.M., Begg, C.E.: Database Systems: A Practical Approach to Design, Implementation, and Management, 5th edn. Addison-Wesley, Boston, MA (2009)
Connolly, T.M., Stansfield, M.H.: From eLearning to games-based eLearning: Using interactive technologies in teaching an information system course. Int. J. Inf. Technol. Manage. **6**(2), 188–208 (2007)
Connolly, T.M., Stansfield, M., Hainey, T.: An Application of Games-based Learning Within Software Engineering, vol. 38, pp. 416–428. Blackwell, Malden, MA (2007)
Hughes, B., Cotterell, M.: Software Project Management, 4th edn. McGraw-Hill, London (2006)
Whitten, N.: Managing Software Development Projects: Formula for Success, 2nd edn. Wiley, New York (1995)

Bibliography

Meigs, T.: Ultimate Game Design: Building Game Worlds. McGraw-Hill, London (2003)
Van Eck, R., Gikas, J.: Analyzing & Designing: Instructional Design Guide. Gaming Theory as a Teaching Tool at All Levels. The University of Memphis, Memphis, TN (2004)

Chapter 19
Expanding a VLE-Based Integration Framework Supporting Education in Second Life

Peter R. Bloomfield

19.1 Background

> *3D works for games because the user does not want to accomplish any goals beyond being entertained (Nielsen, 1998)*

Everyday computer use shows that a majority of user interfaces for non-entertainment purposes still use 2D graphics, despite advances in 3D graphics technology. As such, it could appear that the above statement on interfaces remains correct more than 20 years later. However, it suggests the assumption that something is inherently wrong with 3D user interfaces, preventing their use for serious purposes such as learning. This assumption has the potential to curtail valuable avenues of research as the use of 3D virtual worlds for education increases.

The SLOODLE project is involved in this area of research, and in helping to enable the adoption of virtual worlds by educational institutions. However, there are gaps in the literature, and it is surmised that these may be explained by a lack of understanding of effective user interfaces in a 3D virtual world.

This chapter presents work which is being carried out to address these gaps. The methodology used emphasises usability evaluation and refinement, prior to pedagogical evaluation. The aim is to enable research to advance without being skewed by faulty interface design.

19.1.1 Virtual Worlds

One of the technologies which has developed from the field of computer games is virtual worlds. Some such worlds remain focused on entertainment alone, but others have more general or serious purposes (Bartle, 2003).

P.R. Bloomfield (✉)
School of Computing, University of the West of Scotland, Paisley, Scotland, UK
e-mail: peter.bloomfield@uws.ac.uk

M. Ma et al. (eds.), *Serious Games and Edutainment Applications*,
DOI 10.1007/978-1-4471-2161-9_19, © Springer-Verlag London Limited 2011

Data gathered by Kirriemuir (2009) show that virtual worlds have been used at nearly every Higher Education institution in the UK, and that usage has been increasing year-on-year. The "Second Life" virtual world by Linden Lab has been identified as the predominant virtual world for this purpose. This finding is reflected by an increasing body of literature on the topic (e.g. Bowers et al., 2009; Salmon, 2009; Yee and Hargis, 2010).

There are reported benefits of using such virtual worlds in education. These include improved synchronous communication (compared to text-only chat rooms); the ability to illustrate and visualise more rich and interactive content than is possible in the real world; support for collaborative tasks such as design and building in a shared space; rapid and cost-effective prototyping of ideas; and flexible content creation (Chu and Joseph, 2008; EDUCAUSE Learning Initiative, 2008; Falloon, 2010; Gollub, 2007; McVey, 2008).

In contrast, there are those urging caution with the uptake of virtual worlds in education. For example, Dalgarno and Lee (2010) identify a disparity between the comparatively limited pedagogical research supporting the use of virtual worlds, and the large amount of development work being carried out. It is also suggested that better communication and collaboration is needed between developers and educators in future research (de Freitas, 2006).

Other literature shows a general uncertainty over how the use of a virtual world benefits the learning process (Kelton, 2008; Welch, 2008). There are known risks, particularly regarding the temporary novelty and motivation of a new technology which could be mistaken for a genuine improvement (Whitton and Hollins, 2008).

19.1.2 Virtual Learning Environments (VLEs)

A VLE is a software platform which is designed to facilitate e-learning on the web. Examples include "Blackboard" and "Moodle". Flood (2002) stated that there were 169 VLEs commercially available in the UK. This level of interest and activity is reflected by a finding of Browne et al. (2006). They showed that 81% of Higher Education institutions in the UK had adopted VLEs by 2001. They also showed that this increased to 95% by 2005, and that nearly half of the institutions at that time were using more than one type of VLE.

Despite this level of adoption, literature also shows resistance and scepticism regarding the use of VLEs and e-learning in general. Njenga and Fourie (2010) identify and challenge several ideas and arguments in the field, making particular criticism of the "technopositivist" attitude which assumes e-learning is always a good thing. McPherson and Nunes (2008) also urge caution, and suggest several areas for improvement and support.

Studies shows that the primary use for VLEs in Higher Education is to augment or supplement face-to-face classes. However, they are also used for distance learning classes, which may be delivered exclusively online (Browne et al., 2006; Morgan, 2003).

In both contexts, there is literature discussing multiple ways of using a VLE, with an apparent majority pertaining to constructivist and social constructivist pedagogies (Mayes, 2001). For example, communication and collaboration tools, such as wikis, have been shown to help learners work and study together more effectively (Minocha and Thomas, 2007).

19.1.3 Sloodle

The SLOODLE project (Simulation Linked Object Oriented Dynamic Learning Environment) is a research and software development project to integrate web-based VLEs with virtual worlds. The focus of the project is currently the Moodle VLE, and the Second Life and OpenSim virtual worlds (Konstantinidis et al., 2010; Livingstone and Kemp, 2008).

The initial approach adopted by the SLOODLE project was a mapping of the 2-dimensional structure of individual VLE webpages onto 3-dimensional layouts in the virtual world (Kemp and Livingstone, 2006). However, it was found that educators tended to resist this idea, so a metaphor-based data interaction approach was adopted instead (Livingstone and Kemp, 2008).

Support for the SLOODLE integration is not universal. Di Cerbo et al. (2009) infer an inherent flaw in the way SLOODLE operates on two platforms which are otherwise separate. Their suggestion is that a complete integration, which contains the virtual world within the VLE, is more secure and adoptable. It is worth noting that this separation of platforms has been addressed on a general level by some (largely informal) work to create browser-based clients for Second Life and OpenSim (Chenaux, 2010; Meeks-Ferragallo, 2010).

19.1.3.1 Activities Integrated

With the metaphor-based approach, several of the standard features of the Moodle VLE have been integrated into the virtual world by the SLOODLE project. The method has been to create a tool in the virtual world which represents and allows interactions with a particular activity or resource in the VLE. Data to and from the VLE is passed in the background over the web.

For example, the WebIntercom is the in-world representation of a chatroom. It allows text-based synchronous communication to flow between the virtual world and the VLE, so that users on either platform can participate in the same discussion (Maresca and Savino, 2008). Other VLE activities which also have an in-world SLOODLE representation include: quiz, choice (single question survey), glossary, blog, and assignment submission (Livingstone and Kemp, 2008; Yasar and Adiguzel, 2010).

In addition to this, the SLOODLE project has also implemented tools which extend normal VLE and/or virtual world functionality. This includes: the ability to prepare a sequence of presentation slides in the VLE for display in-world; materials (or "inventory") distribution facilities which can be controlled from the VLE; a tool for performing common classroom-related gestures and actions; and mechanisms for associating and identifying a virtual world avatar account with a corresponding VLE user account (Polychronis et al., 2010).

19.1.3.2 Activities Not Integrated

According to a survey conducted by the SLOODLE project in 2007, there are certain activities which educators expressed a strong interest in seeing integrated. The most popular by a notable margin were lesson, discussion board (forum), wiki, quiz, and assignment (SLOODLE Project, 2007).

As was noted above, the quiz and assignment have already had some degree of integration. Elements of functionality similar to that of Moodle's "lesson" have also been explored since then as part of the SLOODLE project in the form of the Presenter, quizHUD, and Browser (Bloomfield and Livingstone, 2009; Crowe and Livingstone, 2009; Yasar and Adiguzel, 2010).

It can also be noted that since SLOODLE changed to a metaphor-based approach, it ceased to give a sense of structure from the VLE. Communicating the structure of a course is identified as being an important part of an e-learning system in other literature (Laurillard, 2002). This was not raised in the SLOODLE survey, nor is it covered in any SLOODLE literature, and as such it can be considered another significant gap.

The gaps in the literature are therefore those concerning the discussion board, the wiki, and the course structure.

19.2 Research Overview

The aim of this research has been to build on the work of the SLOODLE project. In the past, SLOODLE has used a rapid prototyping and somewhat participatory design model (Livingstone and Bloomfield, 2010). However, a different approach was taken for this research in an effort to fill certain key gaps.

Each gap represents an area which is well-established in web-technology. However, it is not something which appears to have received much attention from a virtual worlds integration point-of-view. The premise for this research is therefore that the gaps in the literature exist due to a lack of understanding of user interfaces, and that a more user centred approach would be beneficial.

As such, the outcome of this research is a set of usable prototype tools. The future aim is to inform further pedagogical research into the worth of such virtual world tools in an educational context.

19.2.1 Tools Being Developed

As was noted in the section on "Activities not integrated" above, there are gaps in SLOODLE and related literature concerning the following:

1. Discussion board
2. Course structure
3. Wiki

These were selected as candidates for integration because they are common to many VLEs and are identified as having importance in other literature. There is also evidence in the first and last cases that educators using virtual worlds want the integrations to be made possible.

The discussion board and the course structure activities were both explored from the outset of this research. However, the wiki was not explored until later due to the lack of technological support.

19.2.2 Methodology

This research draws on principles of software design methodology which focus on usability. User Centred Design (UCD) covers several relevant approaches, although many are more common in the software industry than in academic research.

In a well-known article, Gould and Lewis showed that these approaches were popular among developers. However, they also found that the popularity did not tie-in with practice in the field (Gould and Lewis, 1985). More recent literature suggests that adoption of such approaches is now more common (Bygstad et al., 2008; Venturi et al., 2006).

19.2.2.1 Evaluation Methods

A wide range of different Usability Evaluation Methods (UEMs) are available. They can typically be divided into two families: empirical and analytic (Gray and Salzman, 1998).

Empirical evaluation methods are also known as Usability Testing. These rely on the stakeholders being directly involved in the evaluation. This can include focus groups, interviews, thinking-aloud protocol, surveys, observed labs, and field/pilot studies (Dix et al., 1998; Rubin, 1994).

Analytic evaluation methods are sometimes referred to as Usability Inspections, as they involve a practitioner (or group of practitioners) inspecting and evaluating a system, based on a standard practice. Significant methods in the literature include heuristic evaluation, cognitive walkthrough, and pluralistic walkthrough (Nielsen, 1994).

Where possible, this research has made use of empirical evaluations, as they tend to be more useful and robust (Lazar et al., 2010).

19.2.2.2 Research Phases

A common guideline in relevant literature is that the development lifecycle should be iterative. This involves continually evaluating and refining the software in order to improve its design. There is no fixed number of iterations to be carried out, partly because of the unquantifiable differences between projects, and partly because it is not possible to achieve "perfect" usability.

This project was divided into three phases, drawn from literature such as Rubin (1994) and Lazar et al. (2010).

The exploratory phase aimed to establish a starting-point for the investigation, in the form of speculative interface mock-ups, and gather information about users' needs. This included a focus group and a survey. This was followed-up by a refinement phase, which aimed to develop the designs into functional prototypes. This phase included a series of interviews, and a period of development informed by a usability inspection.

The summative phase, which has yet to be conducted, aims to provide a preliminary evaluation of the working prototypes, and identify any significant issues which need to be addressed before moving forward into pedagogical research.

19.3 Exploratory Phase

This section summarises the work carried out to explore a starting point for addressing the gaps in existing research. This involved creating mock-ups of the tools, and evaluating them using a focus group and a survey. Where possible, these mock-ups were partly based on existing research of some kind. However, the lack of existing implementations meant that most of the ideas were speculation on potential solutions.

19.3.1 Interface Mock-Ups

19.3.1.1 Discussion Board

Conventional discussion boards based on the web are primarily text-based, and can take two forms: linear and threaded. A linear discussion board shows all messages on a given topic as part of one sequence. Threaded discussion boards, however, allow the discussion to branch off at any point, creating a tree-like discussion structure.

There are two main usage modes of a discussion board: interacting with a list of discussions, and interacting with the contents of a discussion. The latter is where majority of the user interaction lies, and it is also more complex. This mode was therefore the focus of this research.

A timeline concept was chosen as the main interface metaphor for representing the contents of a discussion, as it has been found useful in another context for reviewing discussion data (DiMicco et al., 2007). It helps emphasise the sequence of messages, which is particularly useful in the case of linear discussion boards. It also highlights periods of heightened activity (in terms of frequency of messages), which could be useful to a user when identifying important parts of a discussion to review.

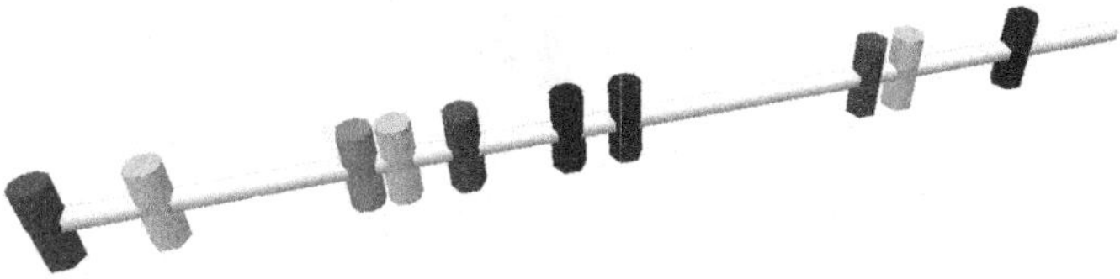

Fig. 19.1 Initial linear timeline mock-up of discussion board tool

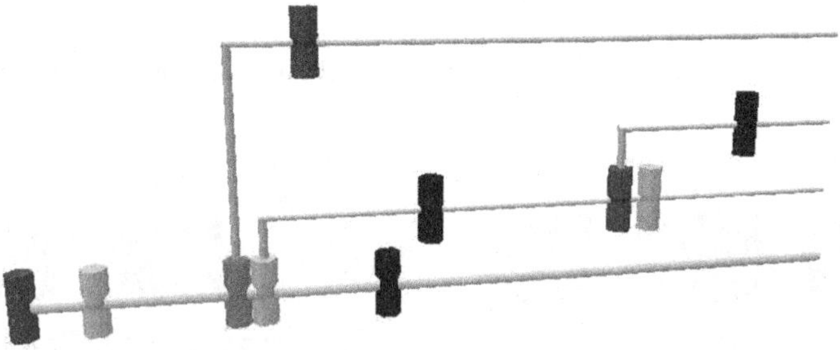

Fig. 19.2 Threaded variant of the initial discussion board timeline mock-up

Figure 19.1 shows the basic concept. A white horizontal line represents the timeline, and each coloured marker represents a single message. The markers are spaced horizontally according to when the message was posted. The colours represent individual users, in order to distinguish between different contributors at a glance.

From an interaction point-of-view, the user would click on an individual marker to read a message. The content of the message would appear on a HUD (Heads Up Display – the term for an extension of the Second Life user interface).

A threaded variant of the same mock-up was also created, and is shown in Fig. 19.2. It maintains the concept of a timeline. However, each time a new reply is added to a given message, it creates a new secondary timeline, parallel to (and above) the first.

In addition to the main mock-ups for the discussion board, an additional concept was designed, shown in Fig. 19.3. It was based on the linear discussion structure. However, the messages from each contributor are separated onto different parallel timelines. The benefit of this is that users do not have to rely on colour to distinguish each contributor. However, the disadvantage is that it could make the sequence less intuitive, since it no longer progresses in a straight line, and could run the risk of implying a threaded structure which is not present.

19.3.1.2 Course Structure

In comparison to the complexity of a discussion board, the structure of a course is fairly simple. Engaging with a course structure can help students identify current

Fig. 19.3 Discussion board timeline with each contributor's messages on a separate row

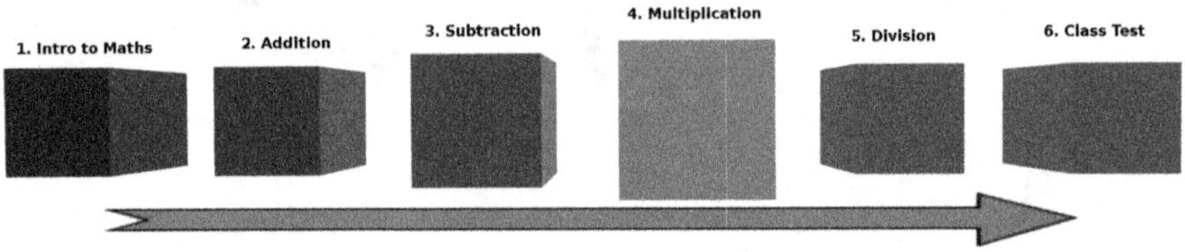

Fig. 19.4 Initial mock-up of the course structure tool

material, look ahead to future material, and revise past material. If a course is well-structured, then it can also help provide a logical flow to facilitate learning.

A VLE such as Moodle can structure webpages into topics (or "weeks"), in the same way that courses are often taught as a sequence of units or modules. Figure 19.4 shows a mock-up of a course structure visualisation for the virtual world. The system would examine the VLE course, and generate one box for each topic. Above each box is a short caption giving the name of the topic. The size and colour emphasises the current topic – it is biggest and brightest. Future topics are shown greyed-out.

A user would click on a topic to see more information about it, or to follow a link to open the VLE topic in a web-browser.

19.3.1.3 Wiki

A wiki is a collaboratively-built collection of linked pages, primarily consisting of text. Wikipedia is a well-known but extremely large example. In classroom settings, wikis tend to be much smaller. Most of the interaction with a wiki takes place at the page level. A user views a page, and can edit it or follow the links to associated pages.

During this phase of the research, text support was very limited in Second Life. Fairly small amounts of static text could be displayed. However, the inability even to scroll a page meant that any prototype wiki was not feasible. As such, none was developed at this point.

19.3.2 Evaluation 1 – Focus Group

A focus group was conducted because the interface possibilities for the discussion board were found to be very wide. The purpose was therefore to gain preliminary insight into users' perceptions of the possibilities, prior to conducting a larger evaluation.

19.3.2.1 Evaluation Design

The target demographic for the focus group was individuals involved in education in Second Life; this included educators and educational technologists, and to a lesser extent, students. This target was focused on those who had experience of using Second Life because of the learning curve for first-time users. It was expected that any individual who was unfamiliar with the technology would have had difficulty providing meaningful contributions in group discussion.

Participants were self-selected in response to open invitations sent to relevant online communities. The group was conducted remotely within the Second Life virtual world, with each participant attending in the form of an avatar. This was done partly for convenience. Given the relative newness of the field, it would have been very difficult to gather a significant number of representative users in a single place by any other means. In addition, it allowed the group to see the interface mock-ups in a realistic context.

Communication occurred using Second Life text chat, as this allowed for an accurate log of discussion to be kept. It also avoided alienating users who might have had technical or other difficulties participating through voice chat.

During the group, the discussion board mock-ups were shown individually. After each one, an explanation of the concept was given, and the participants had the opportunity to ask questions and discuss what they were seeing. Afterwards, the data was coded and investigated using critical incident analysis.

19.3.2.2 Results

The duration of the focus group was approximately 1 h, with 13 individuals actively contributing to the discussion. A few additional individuals watched silently. The discussion was fairly lively, with a variety of views being raised.

Purpose and Value

There was some general debate in the group regarding the justification for accessing a discussion board in the virtual world. The challenge of "3D for the sake of 3D" was raised by one participant. Another suggested that the virtual world and the VLE serve different purposes, and ought to remain separate.

However, other participants showed an appreciation for being able to combine the benefits of the platforms. For example, one indicated that accessing the discussion board from the virtual world could help users to feel "more connected with other people". In addition, it was suggested that the ability to use elements of both platforms in a single application could reduce distraction, as it would avoid the need to switch between the virtual world and the web browser.

One other area of concern shown in the group was the value of the in-world tool compared to the established style of web-based discussion board. A desire for a closer resemblance was expressed.

Structure

The timeline approach in general received mixed responses from the group. The most notable issue was that it needed an explanation. This is not surprising, as the participants were not likely to have seen any similar interfaces. In addition, the mock-ups shown were very simple and not self-explanatory at all.

Following an explanation of the tool, some participants were able to understand it, and appreciated the visual representation of discussion activity. However, the concept of the timeline was not readily understood by all participants. One asked:

> what's the meaning of the diferent spaces between messages? [sic]

In addition to this, some participants also expressed some concern over the scalability of the timeline structure. Members of the group asked whether additional messages would cause the timeline to expand, or whether the message markers would get "scrunched". In either case, it was noted that problems could arise, and a potential preference for a vertical structure was seen. It also appeared that participants might have preferred an interface which more generally resembled a web-based discussion board.

The alternative structure mock-up, which divided each user's messages into a separate timeline (Fig. 19.3), was received with disinterest by the group. The presence of multiple timelines which only represented a single thread of discussion did not appear to be clear to the participants.

The threaded discussion board structure appeared to make more sense and be better understood by the group.

Coloured Markers

The use of colour to distinguish contributors to a discussion was mostly well received by the group. However, it was pointed out that some kind of key or legend would be required to enable a viewer to identify which colour was associated with which user. A scalability concern was also raised, as there are a limited number of easily discernable colours available. As such, if too many users contributed to a single discussion, then the same colour might be used more than once.

19.3.2.3 Discussion

Some resistance to or uncertainty about the value of the discussion board integration was visible in the group. However, the potential of the idea appeared to receive broad acceptance. This was not significant in itself, considering the size of group. However, it was in line with expectations based on existing research.

As a consequence of the group's responses, it seemed that the threaded discussion board mock-up was worth further investigation. In contrast, it appeared that the representation which separated user contributions into parallel timelines did not represent as high a priority, as the potential for confusion appeared to be too great.

No further development work was carried out at this point on the basis of the focus group data. However, the information gathered helped to guide the creation of the second evaluation.

19.3.3 Evaluation 2 – Survey

The aim of the survey was to gather general data on the potential usability of the mock-ups. The focus group had provided some insight, and allowed the number of possible discussion board mock-ups to be reduced. However, it was only on a small scale. A broader sample of stakeholders was required to obtain a reliable basis for moving forward with design decisions, and to identify areas requiring deeper investigation.

The target demographic for the survey remained similar to that of the focus group – individuals involved in education in some capacity, preferably who had used virtual worlds. An online survey was conducted with open invitations posted to several relevant web-based communities. Respondents were self-selected.

The main body of the survey showed images of each mock-up, along with an explanation. Most of the questions were 5-point Likert-style scales, asking the respondents to indicate their agreement with certain statements. These were used to assess general usability, while free-text questions were added to each section to allow respondents to expand on or add any points as they felt necessary. A section of demographic and general background questions was also included.

A pilot of the survey was conducted to identify any major issues. Fourteen individuals took part, drawn from two distinct user groups – the SLOODLE community, and a general computing interest group which had no connection to virtual worlds. The only issue raised by the pilot was that respondents with little or no virtual world experience found it very difficult to answer the questions, and most dropped-out before the end. As a result, it was decided that data would be discarded from any respondents who dropped-out early from the main survey.

19.3.3.1 Results

The survey received 197 responses, of which 125 continued to the end. All data given in the below analysis considers only these 125 responses. However, it should be noted that all questions were optional, resulting in some individuals skipping specific questions. In such cases, the proportion of non-answering respondents is given.

It was found that virtual world experience had no significant impact on the data. This was not due to lack of survey completion, as several respondents with little or no virtual world experience completed all questions. This implies a robustness to the data from a usability standpoint, as it shows similarities between different user groups.

Discussion Board

This section of the survey asked whether or not the respondents had used web-based discussion boards before. 90.4% indicated that they had, and 7.2% indicated that they had not (the remaining 2.4% did not answer this question).

Respondents were then shown the linear discussion board mock-up, along with an explanation, and asked to indicate their agreement with the following statements on a 5-point Likert-style scale:

1. Showing the sequence of posts as a timeline is useful
2. Representing different users as different colours is useful
3. The discussion would be easy to follow like this
4. This representation illustrates the structure of the discussion better than web-based forums

The responses to these statements are given in Table 19.1, and illustrated in Fig. 19.5.

Respondents were later shown the threaded discussion board mock-up, along with an explanation, and asked to indicate their agreement with the following statements:

1. The structure of the discussion is clearly visible
2. This is more useful than the simple linear timeline which shows no threading
3. Interacting with discussions like this could get difficult
4. Threaded discussion forums in general are a waste of time

The resulting data is shown in Table 19.2, and illustrated in Fig. 19.6.

Table 19.1 Exploratory survey results for questions on linear discussion board mock-up

	Agree	–	Neutral	–	Disagree	No answer
1. Timeline is useful	51.2%	20.8%	16.0%	4.0%	6.4%	1.6%
2. Colours are useful	52.8%	25.6%	11.2%	3.2%	5.6%	1.6%
3. Easy to follow	25.6%	22.4%	24.8%	16.0%	9.6%	1.6%
4. Better then web-based	21.6%	17.6%	28.8%	8.8%	18.4%	4.8%

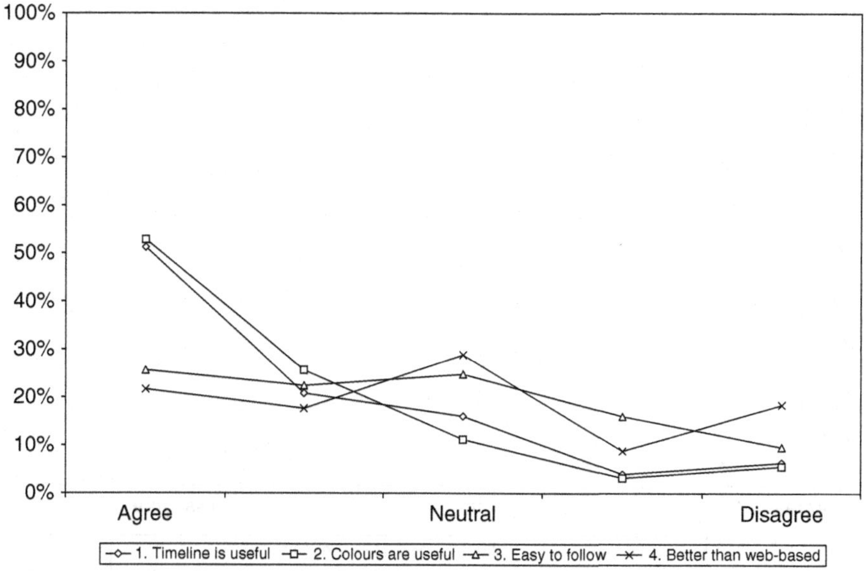

Fig. 19.5 Chart illustrating exploratory survey results for linear discussion board mock-up

Course Structure

Respondents were shown the course structure tool and asked to indicate their agreement with the following statements:

1. It is important for students to be able to see the structure of their course
2. The course structure is clearly visible
3. Students would benefit from seeing course structure illustrated in this way
4. Course structure should be left in the VLE, not brought into the MUVE[1]

Data from these statements are shown in Table 19.3, and illustrated in Fig. 19.7.

Table 19.2 Exploratory survey data for questions on threaded discussion board mock-up

	Agree	–	Neutral	–	Disagree	No answer
1. Structure is clearly visible	48.0%	24.8%	12.0%	3.2%	7.2%	4.8%
2. More useful than linear	44.0%	24.8%	11.2%	7.2%	6.4%	6.4%
3. Could get difficult	29.6%	28.8%	22.4%	7.2%	6.4%	5.6%
4. Threaded discussions a waste of time	4.8%	9.6%	20.8%	13.6%	42.2%	8.8%

[1] MUVE = Multi User Virtual Environment; another term for "virtual world"

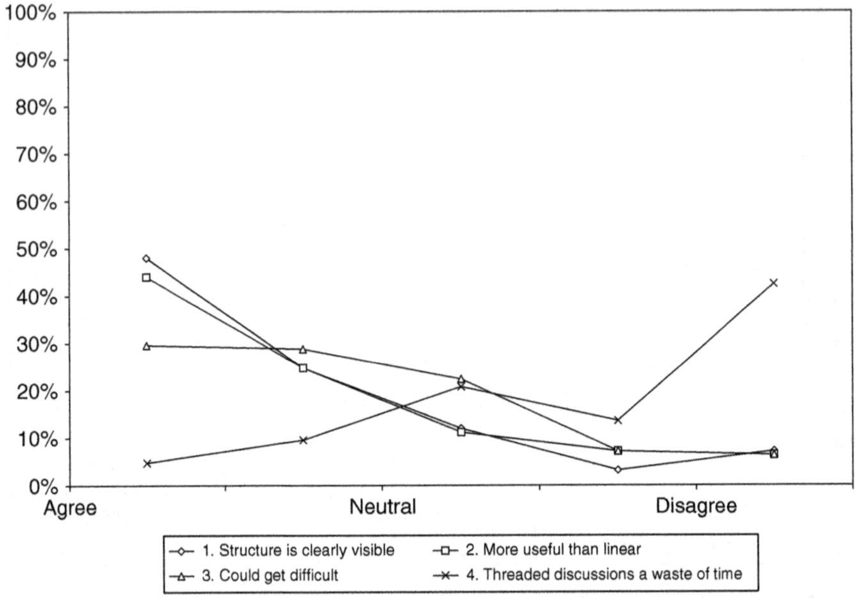

Fig. 19.6 Chart illustrating exploratory survey results for threaded discussion board mock-up

Several additional comments about the course structure tool were also provided. A few respondents raised concerns about the simplicity of the tool, and the fact that it only represents a linear relationship. It was suggested that this is misleading, as in reality, each topic will have much more complex relationships with other topics.

General Feedback

At the end of the survey, respondents were asked to suggest any additional tools which they would like to see included in the VLE/virtual world integration. Approximately half of the respondents gave some kind of feedback to this question. Several ideas were put forward, and the most repeated suggestions are shown in Table 19.4.

Space for any additional comments was also given, resulting in a mixture of feedback. Strong opinions were shown for and against the use of virtual worlds in

Table 19.3 Exploratory survey data for questions about the course structure tool

	Agree	–	Neutral	–	Disagree	No answer
1. Important for students to see structure	81.6%	9.6%	1.6%	1.6%	2.4%	3.2%
2. Course structure is clearly visible	39.2%	36.8%	12.8%	5.6%	4.0%	1.6%
3. Students would benefit from this	28.0%	27.2%	28.0%	8.0%	6.4%	2.4%
4. Should be left in VLE, not MUVE	9.6%	6.4%	40.8%	10.4%	26.4%	6.4%

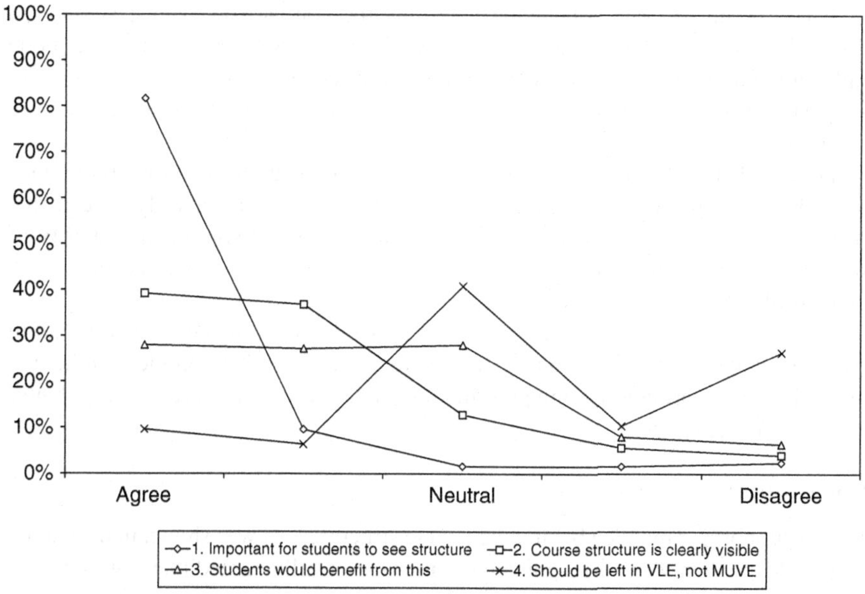

Fig. 19.7 Chart illustrating exploratory survey results for questions on course structure mock-up

education. A few comments suggested that the idea was "gimmicky", too complex, or unhelpful. Others indicated that they felt virtual worlds in education are a good idea, and that it is or could be very helpful. The number of comments for and against were exactly even, but not sufficiently high to draw any general conclusions in the context of this survey.

19.3.3.2 Discussion

Discussion Board

The data show the significant majority of respondents (over 70%) somewhat or fully agreeing that the linear timeline structure was useful. However, the same majority is not visible regarding the apparent ease of following the discussion with such an interface.

This could suggest that respondents found the timeline idea novel, and that the information it provides could be useful. However, it could also suggest that the representation has room for improvement from a usability point-of-view.

Table 19.4 Additional tools suggested in exploratory survey

Tool	Frequency of suggestion
Wiki	18%
Quiz/test	15%
Blog	9%

It is difficult to draw conclusion regarding the comparison against web-based discussion boards. If both categories of agreement are combined, then the mode falls on the agreement side of neutral. The lack of cohesion in the responses could suggest that the question is being asked too early, and that users would need more information to give a clear answer.

Data gathered on the threaded discussion board suggest a strong preference towards the more complex structure. Nearly 70% somewhat or fully agreed that it would be more useful than the linear one. In addition, a significant majority of respondents also appeared to feel that threaded discussions boards in general could be helpful.

However, a significant concern was shown that the mock-up could be difficult to use – more than 68% somewhat or fully agreed with this. The implication here is again that the information being presented is useful. However, there may be a better interface for representing it.

Course Structure

Strong support for the idea behind the course structure tool was shown in the survey results. More than 90% of respondents somewhat or fully agreed that it was important for students to see the structure of their course. This support was not as strong when respondents were asked about whether the course structure should be brought into the virtual world (or "MUVE" in the wording of the survey).

The large number of neutral responses to this issue could suggest that the question was not understood, or could simply mean that respondents would need to know more about the mock-up before giving a more definite answer. However, disregarding the neutral category, other responses were notably weighted in favour of bringing the course structure into the virtual world.

A significant majority of respondents (approx. 77%) agreed that the structure of the course was clearly visible in the mock-up, whereas only a small majority (approx. 56%) agreed that the tool would benefit students. Approximately 29% gave a neutral response, meaning that only a small minority (approx. 15%) actively felt that it would not benefit students. These results suggest that the course structure tool shown in this evaluation has potential. However, they may also suggest that there is room for improvement or expansion.

A few respondents gave additional comments on this section of the survey. Some raised the issue that the course structure tool could be misleading, as it fails to show the interconnections between areas of study. These comments suggest a misunderstanding of the purpose of the tool, as it is only intended to demonstrate the way a course is structured for teaching purposes. A separate mind-map tool to help visualise the subject in the wider knowledge context may be a useful idea for future research.

General Feedback

The general feedback about wikis given by respondents corresponds to data gathered previously by the SLOODLE project. Desire for such a text-based tool in a graphical environment is surprising, although the form respondents expected it to take was not explored in this survey.

The other two tools mentioned by respondents in general feedback (quiz and blog) have already been integrated by SLOODLE.

19.4 Refinement Phase

This section covers the second phase of this research project. The aim was to improve the tool concepts which had already been explored, and to develop them from interface mock-ups into working prototypes. The introduction of "Shared Media" in Second Life occurred at the start of this phase, introducing new possibilities.

In order to ensure the continued focus on users' needs, further data were also gathered from a series of follow-up interviews with the exploratory survey participants. Development work was also carried out, using data from a cognitive walkthrough to help ensure user tasks were addressed.

19.4.1 Impact of Shared Media

Throughout the exploratory phase, there were considerable technical restrictions on the presentation of text within the Second Life virtual world. Notable among these restrictions were the single webpage limit per "parcel" of land, and the lack of interactivity (such as the ability to scroll a long page or enter data into a form).

The introduction of Shared Media lifted these restrictions, allowing multiple webpages to be viewed and interacted-with, at the same time, by any users in the virtual world. These new technical capabilities enabled a wiki tool concept to be included in this research, and allowed for some changes to be made to the discussion board and course structure tool.

19.4.2 Discussion Board Changes

Based on the feedback from the exploratory phase, the focus of research on the discussion board was directed towards the threaded version of the timeline. No structural changes were made at this point. However, two Shared Media screens were added at one side of the timeline.

One of these screens displayed the colour-coded list of contributors to the discussion, as was discussed in the focus group. The other screen displayed the contents of a discussion message – a user could click a message marker to see the content here. The use of Shared Media screens in this way allowed the content of the messages to have a presence in the virtual world, alongside the timeline structure. It was hypothesised that this would be helpful in maintaining a focus of attention in a single place, instead of adding more to the GUI (Graphical User Interface).

A simple arrow was also added beneath the timeline structure to clarify the direction of flow.

19.4.3 Course Structure Changes

The main body of the course structure tool remained unchanged. However, as with the discussion board tool, a Shared Media screen was added to the design. In this case, it was a small drop-down screen which would appear a topic when clicked. The screen would show a brief summary of the activities and resources associated with the topic, and provide links to view or interact with them.

19.4.4 Introduction of Wiki Tool

The exploratory survey highlighted users' desire to see a wiki tool included in the integration framework. The text-heavy nature of wikis made this impractical prior to the availability of Shared Media, as at best some wiki pages would have been truncated.

The primary point of contact a user has with a wiki is at the page level – a single page is being viewed at a time, and links to associated pages can be followed as needed. Some higher-level navigation is sometimes provided, such as the ability to view all articles in a given category. A graphical environment suggests the possibility of mapping and visualising the structural elements of a wiki. For example, the links between pages could be shown as a kind of mind map.

This was considered for the development of a wiki mock-up tool, but it quickly became apparent that scalability would be a major problem. As such, the focus was placed on allowing interactions at a page-level. Figure 19.8 shows the mock-up which was developed.

The proposed mock-up shows the content of the page in the main panel. Boxes down each side represent important links to other pages, divided into three types. The green boxes on the left represent "backlinks", which are pages which link to the current page. At the top-right are cyan boxes, representing links to other existing pages. The red box at the bottom-right represents a link to a page which has not been written yet. The colours of these boxes has no significance at this stage – they were only selected to differentiate the link types.

At this point, the mock-up was designed to be very simple, allowing user input during this phase to guide any further decisions.

19.4.5 Evaluation 3 – Interviews

Data gathered through the focus group and survey had provided insight into potential tool designs. Some aspects of the design were identified as being positive and having

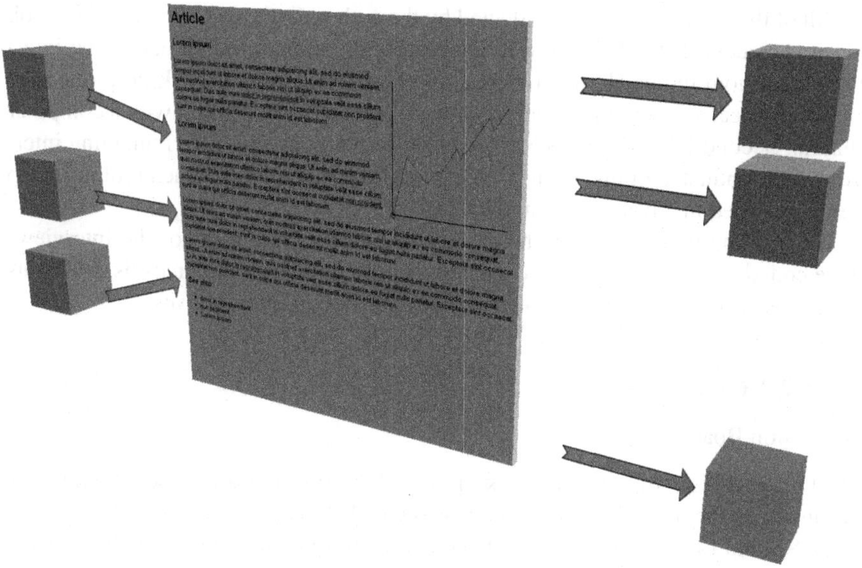

Fig. 19.8 Initial mock-up of a wiki tool

potential. However, areas needing improvement were also suggested. In addition, the subsequent introduction of Shared Media changed the boundaries of design possibility. A series of follow-up one-on-one interviews was therefore conducted, with three main aims:

1. Clarify how refinements/improvements could be made
2. Investigate if and how Shared Media could be incorporated into the tools
3. Explore the initial design ideas in the wiki mock-up

19.4.5.1 Evaluation Design

The final question in the exploratory survey had asked respondents if they would be willing to participate in follow-up research. 46 respondents had indicated positively. Potential interviewees were selected incrementally over a few weeks, allowing selection to adapt depending on who agreed to participate. The aim was to obtain a representative sample of stakeholders based on survey respondents. In total, 27 individuals were selected. 10 agreed to the interview, although only 9 were able to attend. None of the interviewees had participated in the focus group.

Each interview was planned around a similar structure, although tailored somewhat depending on the individual's responses to the survey. This allowed key points to be drawn out and expanded where appropriate. In addition to general background questions, the interview outlines involved questions about each tool mock-up. These covered questions of usability, intuitiveness, and usefulness.

All of the interviews were conducted by the author. In 6 cases, the interview took place in Second Life. This allowed geographically distant individuals to be interviewed without the need for travelling, and it allowed for the mock-up tools to be shown in a realistic setting. 2 interviews were conducted in-person, with a computer running Second Life in the same room to show the mock-ups. The remaining interview was conducted online using Skype, with screen captures of each tool mock-up being provided in advance via email.

As with the focus group in the exploratory phase, transcripts of the interviews were coded, and issues were investigated using critical incident analysis. Incidents were cross-referenced between interviewees to compare perspectives.

19.4.5.2 Results

Discussion Board

The threaded discussion board mock-up was of interest to most of the interviewees, insomuch as the potential of the idea was seen. However, divided attitudes towards using Second Life in education were evident, with some interviewees being notably more positive in general than others.

Difficulties engaging with the timeline-style structure were also visible. For example, one individual noted a problem which had also been raised at the focus group:

> What I don't understand, or don't know, is whether the distance between [the message markers] resembles anything

Questions about the value of such a different interface were raised. It was suggested that following existing conventions might be a better approach:

> it's not clear why re-inventing the wheel would be beneficial

It was also suggested that making more use of Shared Media in the visualisation could be helpful. Interviewees noted that it is much easier to browse the content of a web-based discussion board, because all of the text is visible. It was also suggested that having to move attention from the timeline structure to the separate message display screen could be quite distracting.

Course Structure

In the survey, confusion was mentioned the use of colour and size in the course structure tool was seen. The original design used both to illustrate which was the current topic. These issues were discussed during the interviews and the potential for confusion was confirmed. The use of a colour graduation across topics, leading to the current topic being the brightest, was not obvious. Additionally, size appeared to be more readily associated with either importance or amount of content. It was also noted that progression direction was not obvious to all interviewees, despite an arrow being placed underneath the topic boxes.

Possibilities for user interaction were also discussed; i.e. what happens when a user clicks on a topic box. A wide range of vague possibilities were suggested, but none appeared to be practical or useful.

Wiki

The last item shown was the wiki mock-up. The first issue discussed about it was the different levels of interaction. In general, interviewees agreed that a page-level tool would be more useful than one which mapped the structure at a higher level. For example, it was observed that:

> The whole wiki would probably be too big, so you couldn't really deal with that.

The link representation was also discussed. The idea of labelling each box with the name of the article was suggested. However, there was also enthusiasm regarding the possibility of using Shared Media to show a small version of each page on each box.

19.4.5.3 Discussion

The interviews helped to confirm and clarify some of the identified issues with the mock-ups. It became clear that a timeline structure was not appropriate for the discussion board tool. However, the ability to visualise the structure of the discussion threads was still found to be popular. This suggested that a better representation might find a way to mimic the top-down structure of a forum, but making better use of the visual space where possible.

The need to change certain appearance attributes of the course structure tool was shown by the data. Size and colour were not illustrating the progression in an intuitive way, suggesting that these concepts ought to be dropped. However, there was very little data to draw any conclusions regarding what the tool should do in terms of interaction. The lack of any opposition to the existing function (displaying information about the contents of a topic) suggested that change on this point may not be necessary. It is possible that users would need to use the tool in order to provide further feedback.

Without the benefit of a focus group or survey, the interviews acted as an exploratory evaluation for the wiki tool. There was some opposition to the idea. However, expectations for the suitability of the page-level tool were largely confirmed. Useful ideas were also gathered for further interface possibilities.

19.4.6 Prototype Development

The intended end-product of the refinement phase was a set of functional prototypes. This required a significant development period, in which existing designs were revisited and improved where necessary. This process drew on data gathered in the previous evaluations to inform the changes. A cognitive walkthrough approach was adopted to ensure that the focus remained on realistic user tasks.

19.4.6.1 Discussion Board

A substantial structural change was made to the discussion board tool, moving away from the timeline structure. Research participants had shown or expressed difficulty engaging with this aspect of the interface, despite seeming to find the idea interesting. A desire to see a representation which more closely resembled a web-based discussion board was also observed. As such, the prototype was redesigned to use a vertical orientation, with the first message appearing at the top, in the same manner as a web-based discussion board. The redesigned prototype can be seen in Fig. 19.9. Note that the white lines have been added to clarify the reply structure.

The prototype continues to use colours to distinguish users. However, each block in this case represents a message. The root message in the discussion appears at the top, with replies appearing underneath. Each time a new thread of discussion branches off at a given point, the parent block expands horizontally to accommodate the new child branch.

Based on feedback from interviews, the original prototype had used Shared Media to display each message on the surface of the box representing it. This was intended to address issues of separating the structure from the content, and help make the discussion easier to browse. However, it was found during development that Shared Media could not consistently display more than one or two messages at a time in this way. The prototype therefore had to revert to using a separate user interface extension to display the content of each message. Similar to the original design, the user clicks a message to view its content.

19.4.6.2 Course Structure

One of the significant visual changes made to the course structure tool was that the size and colour gradients were removed. They had been used to show an ordinal progression, leading up to the current topic being the biggest and brightest. However, as these were being misunderstood, all boxes were changed to be the same size. The "current" topic is highlighted, and a label appears underneath to clarify it.

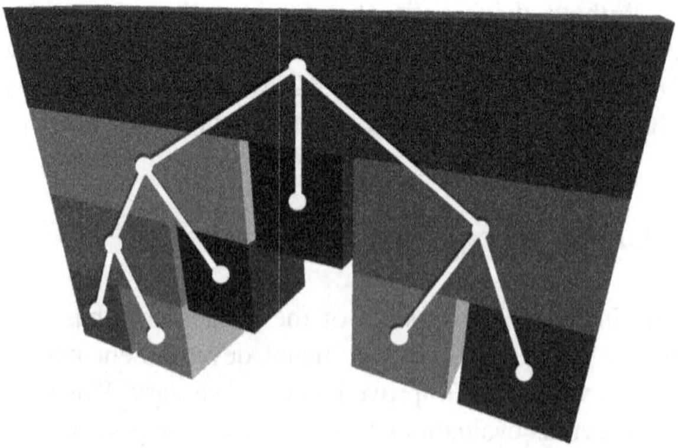

Fig. 19.9 Discussion board prototype, redesigned to use a vertical block-based interface, with tree structure overlaid for clarity

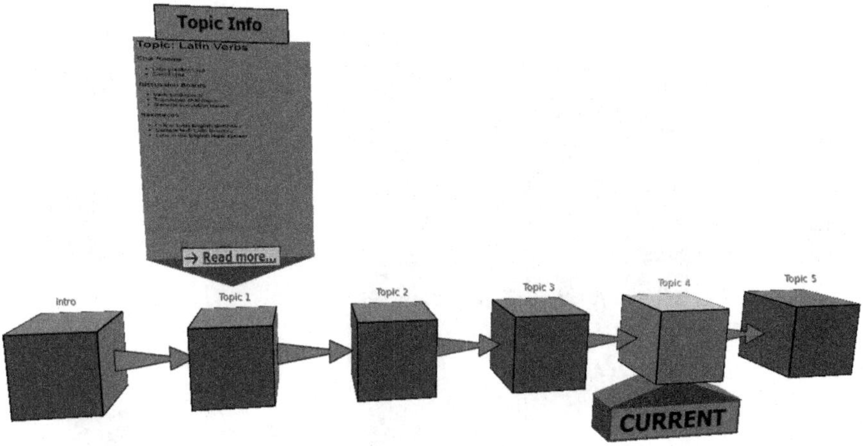

Fig. 19.10 Refined prototype of course structure tool

A minor structural change was made to help make the order of topics more visible. The single arrow underneath did not appear to be as noticeable as expected. As such, it was replaced by a small arrow between each box. This allows the directionality to be seen even when the user's view is very close to the tool. The prototype course structure tool can be seen in Fig. 19.10.

As can be seen in the illustration, another change was to expand the topic information and move it above. It had previously been a fairly limited "drop-down" style information panel. However, this could be easy to miss, and is limited by the available space beneath the tool. More complete and obvious information is now shown by using a large Shared Media panel above the given topic box. The "Read more" link allows the user to visit the course materials in the web-based VLE.

When a user clicks on a different topic box, the information panel moves to give information about that topic. This means that information about only one topic is visible at a time.

19.4.6.3 Wiki Tool

The structure of the wiki tool did not change. However, one of the intended modifications was to alter the way linked pages appear. In the original mock-up, they were represented as plain boxes, with the intention that interviewees would suggest alternatives. Based on the data, a prototype was developed which uses Shared Media to display the content of each linked page on the relevant box. This allows users to preview a page before visiting it. (Shared Media allows users to zoom in for a closer view of small pages.)

Unfortunately, as with the discussion board, it was found that the technology could not support this reliably. As a consequence, the boxes were replaced with a simple static graphic which resembles a page of text. Each graphic has the title of

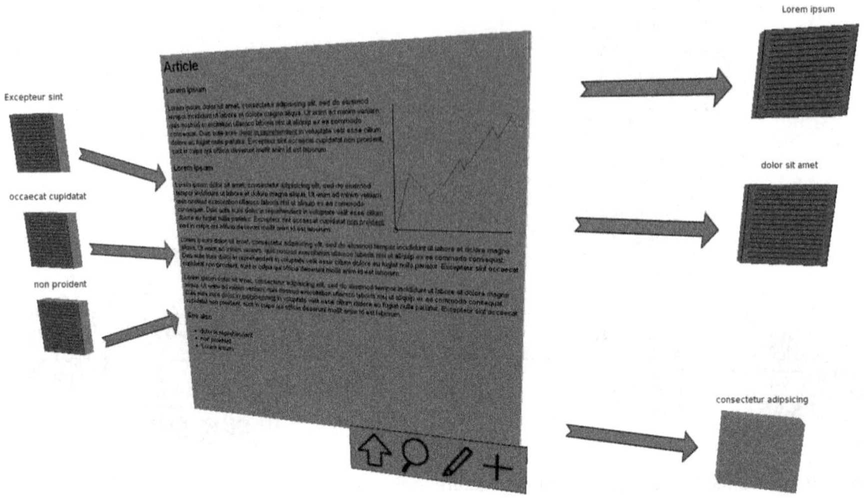

Fig. 19.11 Refined prototype of wiki tool

the page written above it to allow users to see which page each one links to. The refined prototype is shown in Fig. 19.11.

Another change which came from the cognitive walkthrough was the addition of a small toolbar, which is visible at the bottom right of the tool's main page display. It is a series of buttons providing the following functions: "Home" (i.e. return to the root page of the wiki), "Search", "Edit page", and "Add page".

19.5 Conclusion

This chapter has presented work towards filling key gaps in research related to the SLOODLE integration of web-based VLEs with virtual worlds. These gaps concerned three activities/resources: discussion boards, course structures, and wikis. The hypothesis guiding the work has treated it as a software usability issue – existing research had not made progress in the identified areas due to a lack of understanding of usable user interfaces in a 3D virtual world. As such, the approach adopted drew heavily on usability research and design methods, such as User Centred Design.

An iterative methodology was used, which divided the project into three phases. The first phase was exploratory in nature, and began by creating speculative interface mock-ups. These were evaluated using a focus group and survey, which helped narrow the focus of the designs and identify areas requiring improvements.

The second phase aimed to refine the designs already proposed. A technology advancement during this phase prompted design changes. However, it also enabled an avenue of research which had previously been identified as being desirable. Several interviews were conducted during this phase, following-up on the earlier survey. This data helped to clarify some of the areas needing refined, and provide potential routes for improvement.

The third and final phase has yet to be conducted. It aims to be a summative evaluation of the working prototypes developed so far. It is described more fully in the "Future work" section.

19.5.1 Tools Developed

Each of the proposed tools has been developed into a working prototype which is capable of being used to carry out required tasks. Feedback from stakeholders has been involved on the way through, and so it is expected that the interface designs have some merit. At present, the designs are still fairly basic and only carry out the essential tasks. There is also little in the way of aesthetic appeal. However, the main concepts being developed should have a degree of transferability, regardless of cosmetic or additional features.

It should be acknowledged that the initial mock-ups on which this research was started were largely speculative in nature. It is an unfortunate reality of interface research that it is very difficult to start from scratch. If users are faced with a blank page and asked what would work, then they will not tend to provide much useful or consistent information. It is also unfortunate that some of the intended modifications during the refinement phase are not supported by current technology. As such, the findings here are by no means exhaustive, and very different results may be found if different initial mock-ups are used, or if the technology advances to allow the missing features.

Nonetheless, the remaining phase in this project will conduct a practical evaluation on the prototypes in their current functional state. This information will be beneficial in expanding understanding of virtual world interfaces, and may help advance virtual world pedagogies.

19.5.2 Future Work

The next stage of research, which is already underway, will involve a summative usability evaluation of the tools developed so far. Each tool will be lab-tested by a sample of 5–6 students who have previously used Second Life in a learning context. This prior experience is important to help ensure that lack of familiarity with the virtual world platform does not mask usability problems with the tools.

Each lab test will involve a set of common tasks which would be associated with each tool in a realistic usage scenario. Performance metrics will be gathered to assess each participant's success and efficiency in each task. A post-test survey will also be administered, with a focus on gathering qualitative data about each individual's subjective experience. All of the data gathered will be used to identify any remaining usability issues, and to propose improvements.

Subsequent evaluations will need to field test the tools in a class-based setting in order to determine any impact on the learning process. An established survey instrument, such as the CSUQ (Computer System Usability Questionnaire), could be used to validate the tools from a usability standpoint.

As the tools are based on the work of the SLOODLE project (which is open source), any useful software developed by this research will be released back to the SLOODLE community.

Acknowledgments My thanks are due in particular to my supervisor, Daniel Livingstone, as well as to Malcolm Crowe and Ewan MacArthur. They have each provided valuable input and support at various times during this research.

References

Bartle, R.: Designing Virtual Worlds. New Riders Games, Berkeley, CA (2003)

Bloomfield, P.R., Livingstone, D.: Multi-modal learning and assessment in Second Life with quizHUD. In: Proceedings of the 1st IEEE Conference in Games and Virtual Worlds, pp. 217–218. Presented at the VS Games 09, IEEE, Coventry, UK. http://doi.ieeecomputersociety.org/10.1109/VS-GAMES.2009.35 (2009)

Bowers, K.W., Ragas, M.W., Neely, J.C.: Assessing the value of virtual worlds for post-secondary instructors: A survey of innovators, early adopters and the early majority in Second Life, pp. 40–50. Int. J. Human. Soc. Sci. **3**(1) (2009)

Browne, T., Jenkins, M., Walker, R.: A longitudinal perspective regarding the use of VLEs by Higher Education Institutions in the United Kingdom. Interact. Learn. Environ. **14**(2), 177–192 (2006)

Bygstad, B., Ghinea, G., Brevik, E.: Software development methods and usability: Perspectives from a survey in the software industry in Norway. Interact. Comput. **20**(3), 375–385 (2008). doi:10.1016/j.intcom.2007.12.001

Chenaux, A.: In your browser! *Ch'know*. http://aliciachenaux.blogspot.com/2010/11/in-your-browser.htm (2010, November 15). Accepted 8 Mar 2011

Chu, K.-H., Joseph, S.: Using Second Life to demonstrate a concept automobile heads up display (A-HUD). In: Proceedings of the 10th International Conference on Human Computer Interaction with Mobile Devices and Services, pp. 497–498. ACM, Amsterdam, The Netherlands (2008). doi:10.1145/1409240.1409327

Crowe, M., Livingstone, D.: Collaborative web-browsing in a virtual world. In: Proceedings of the 1st IEEE Conference in Games and Virtual Worlds. Presented at the VS Games 09, Coventry, UK. http://doi.ieeecomputersociety.org/10.1109/VS-GAMES.2009.38 (2009)

Dalgarno, B., Lee, M.J.W.: What are the learning affordances of 3-D virtual environments? Br. J. Educ. Technol. **41**(1), 10–32 (2010). doi:10.1111/j.1467-8535.2009.01038.x

de Freitas, S.: Learning in Immersive Worlds: A Review of Game-Based Learning. JISC, Bristol, UK. http://www.jisc.ac.uk/media/documents/programmes/elearninginnovation/gamingreport_v3.pdf (2006)

Di Cerbo, F., Dodero, G., Forcheri, P., Gianuzzi, V., Ierardi, M.G.: Hybrid learning experiences with a collaborative open source environment. In: Wang, F., Fong, J., Zhang, L., Lee, V. (eds.) Hybrid Learning and Education. Lecture Notes in Computer Science, pp. 45–54. doi:10.1007/978-3-642-03697-2_5 (2009)

DiMicco, J.M., Hollenbach, K.J., Pandolfo, A., Bender, W.: The impact of increased awareness while face-to-face. Hum. Comput. Interact. **22**(1), 47–96 (2007). doi:10.1080/07370020701307781

Dix, A.J., Finlay, J., Abowd, G., Beale, R.: Human-Computer Interaction, 2nd edn. Prentice Hall Europe, London (1998)

EDUCAUSE Learning Initiative: 7 things you should know about Second Life. http://net.educause.edu/ir/library/pdf/ELI7038.pdf (2008)

Falloon, G.: Using avatars and virtual environments in learning: What do they have to offer? Br. J. Educ. Technol. **41**(1), 108–122 (2010). doi:10.1111/j.1467-8535.2009.00991.x

Flood, J.: Read all about it: Online learning facing 80% attrition rates. Turk. Online J. Distance Educ. **3**(2). http://tojde.anadolu.edu.tr/tojde6/articles/jim2.htm (2002)

Gollub, R.: Second life and education. Crossroads **14**(1), 1–8 (2007). doi:10.1145/1349332.1349334

Gould, J.D., Lewis, C.: Designing for usability: Key principles and what designers think. Commun. ACM **28**(3), 300–311 (1985). doi:10.1145/3166.3170

Gray, W.D., Salzman, M.C.: Damaged merchandise? A review of experiments that compare usability evaluation methods. Hum. Comput. Interact. **13**(3), 203 (1998)

Kelton, A.J.: Virtual Worlds? "Outlook Good." Educause Rev. **43**(5), 15–22 (2008).

Kemp, J., Livingstone, D.:. Putting a Second Life "Metaverse" skin on learning management systems. In: Livingstone, D., Kemp, J. (eds.) Proceedings of the Second Life Education Workshop at the Second Life Community Convention, pp. 13–18. University of Paisley, Paisley, UK. http://www.sloodle.org/whitepaper.pdf (2006)

Kirriemuir, J.: Virtual world activity in UK universities and colleges: An academic year of expectation? (Snapshot #7: Winter 2009). Virtual Worlds Watch. http://virtualworldwatch.net/snapshots/virtual-world-activity-winter-09/ (2009)

Konstantinidis, A., Tsiatsos, T., Demetriadis, S., Pomportsis, A.: Collaborative learning in OpenSim by utilizing sloodle. Advanced International Conference on Telecommunications, pp. 90–95. IEEE Computer Society, Los Alamitos, CA. doi:http://doi.ieeecomputersociety.org/10.1109/AICT.2010.75 (2010)

Laurillard, D.: Rethinking University Teaching, 2nd edn. Routledge, London (2002)

Lazar, J., Feng, J.H., Hochheiser, H.: *Research Methods in Human-Computer Interaction*, 1st edn. Wiley, Chichester (2010)

Livingstone, D., Bloomfield, P.R.: Mixed-methods and mixed-worlds: Engaging globally distributed user groups for extended evaluation and studies. In: Peachey, A., Gillen, J., Livingstone, D., Smith-Robbins, S. (eds.) Researching Learning in Virtual Worlds, pp. 159–176. Springer, London (2010)

Livingstone, D., Kemp, J.: Integrating web-based and 3D learning environments: Second Life meets moodle. UPGRADE Eur. J. Inf. Prof. **IX**(3), 8–14 (2008)

Maresca, P., Savino, N.: An environment for didactics for first level university courses based on Eclipse technology. J. e-Lear. Knowl. Soci. **4**(3), 141–150 (2008)

Mayes, T.: Learning technology and learning relationships. In: Stephenson, J. (ed.) Teaching and Learning Online: Pedagogies for New Technologies, pp. 16–26. Kogan Page, London (2001)

McPherson, M.A., Nunes, J.M.: Critical issues for e-learning delivery: What may seem obvious is not always put into practice. J. Comput. Assisted Learn. **24**(5), 433–445 (2008). doi:10.1111/j.1365-2729.2008.00281.x

McVey, M.H.: Observations of expert communicators in immersive virtual worlds: Implications for synchronous discussion. ALT-J **16**(3), 173 (2008). doi:10.1080/09687760802526673

Meeks-Ferragallo, C.: Making history with Unity and OpenSim. Unity Technologies Blog. http://blogs.unity3d.com/2010/06/30/making-history-with-unity-and-opensim/ (2010, June 30). Accepted 8 Mar 2011

Minocha, S., Thomas, P.G.: Collaborative Learning in a Wiki environment: Experiences from a software engineering course. New Rev. Hypermedia Multimedia **13**(2), 187 (2007). doi:10.1080/13614560701712667

Morgan, G.: Faculty Use of Course Management Systems. EDUCAUSE Center for Applied Research, Boulder, CO. http://net.educause.edu/ir/library/pdf/ers0302/rs/ers0302w.pdf (2003)

Nielsen, J.: Usability Inspection Methods. Wiley, New York, Chichester (1994)

Nielsen, J.: 2D is better than 3D. http://www.useit.com/alertbox/981115.html (1998, November 15). Accepted 17 Feb 2009

Njenga, J.K., Fourie, L.C.H.: The myths about e-learning in higher education. Br. J. Educ. Technol. **41**(2), 199–212 (2010). doi:10.1111/j.1467-8535.2008.00910.x

Polychronis, N., Patrikakis, C., Voulodimos, A.: Combining immersive virtual worlds and virtual learning environments into an integrated system for hosting and supporting virtual conferences. Next Generation Society. Technological and Legal Issues, pp. 397–407. http://dx.doi.org/10.1007/978-3-642-11631-5_36 (2010)

Rubin, J.: Handbook of Usability Testing. Wiley, New York, NY (1994)

Salmon, G.: The future for (second) life and learning. Br. J. Educ. Technol. **40**(3), 526–538 (2009). doi:10.1111/j.1467-8535.2009.00967.x

SLOODLE Project:. Sloodle survey – Nov. 2007 – summary results. *SLOODLE Project*. http://www.sloodle.org/moodle/mod/resource/view.php?id=523 (2007, November). Accepted 10 February 2009

Venturi, G., Troost, J., Jokela, T.: People, organizations, and processes: An inquiry into the adoption of user-centered design in industry. Int. J. Human-Comput. Interact. **21**(2), 219–238 (2006). doi:10.1207/s15327590ijhc2102_6

Welch, D.J.: Virtual worlds: Moving beyond today. EDUCAUSE Rev. **43**(5), 12–13 (2008)

Whitton, N., Hollins, P.: Collaborative virtual gaming worlds in higher education. ALT-J **16**(3), 221–229 (2008). doi:10.1080/09687760802526749

Yasar, O., Adiguzel, T.: A working successor of learning management systems: SLOODLE. Procedia Soc. Behav. Sci. **2**(2), 5682–5685 (2010). doi:10.1016/j.sbspro.2010.03.928

Yee, K., Hargis, J.:. Jumping head first into second life for higher education. MountainRise **6**(2) (2010)

Part V
Social Aspects and Gamification

Chapter 20
Casual Social Games as Serious Games: The Psychology of Gamification in Undergraduate Education and Employee Training

Richard N. Landers and Rachel C. Callan

20.1 Introduction

The current psychological research literature surrounding serious games tends to focus on immersive environments where parts of the "real world" are recreated. Military videogames, for example, are most typically 3D-rendered environments where teammates perform cooperative tasks, from basic drill exercises to complex collaborative missions (e.g. Orvis et al., 2009). The purpose of immersion in such games is certainly clear; a real in-person environment must be recreated, with all the complexities of the technical and social interactions typically found there. This specific kind of game, called a simulation game, maximizes the fidelity of the learning environment so that it more completely represents the real world, combining elements of both games and simulations (Wilson et al., 2008). This is certainly a valuable application of videogaming. But this use is most appropriate when training and educational objectives *require* this immersion.

In the military example above, videogames offer a safe and high fidelity alternative to live field exercises at a reduced cost. But most education and training does not require this level of fidelity, as skills training is not the most typical instructional outcome. Instead, the most common course objective is transference of knowledge: facts, details, procedures, and other discrete pieces of information. With such goals, serious games as we traditionally think of them are not necessarily best used as representations of the learning material. Instead, for knowledge outcomes, serious games are best used to *support* the learning process. One way to do this is gameification (or gamification), which will be defined here as the addition of elements commonly associated with games (e.g. game mechanics) to an educational or training program in order to make the learning process more engaging.

In the present chapter, we explore the course development process in order to identify when gameification is most appropriate. Next, we explore the conditions under which gameification should be most successful and the psychological theories

R.N. Landers (✉)
Old Dominion University, Norfolk, VA, USA
e-mail: rnlanders@odu.edu

M. Ma et al. (eds.), *Serious Games and Edutainment Applications*,
DOI 10.1007/978-1-4471-2161-9_20, © Springer-Verlag London Limited 2011

supporting this. Finally, we discuss a 600-student mixed methods study of gameification in a major east-coast university in which a learner-focused online social network was deployed with casual social gaming elements to encourage students to complete optional multiple choice quizzes in their free time.

20.2 Select Games from Course Objectives, Not the Reverse

To maximize the impact of any course,[1] objectives must first be specified to meet learning needs. Each objective typically includes one of four specific capabilities that the instructor wants to affect. The first of these is *knowledge*, which is defined as the memorization and understanding of facts, rules, procedures, plans, goals, objectives, and any other discrete pieces of information. In the simulation game above, a course designer might wish to improve knowledge of weapon types or knowledge of approved procedures for interacting with enemy combatants. The second capability type is *observable skills*, which involves the application of knowledge capabilities to accomplish tasks with clear paths from task start to finish. In the game above, a designer might wish to improve use of appropriate radio jargon (e.g., saying "Alpha-Bravo-Charlie" instead of "ABC") when communicating with teammates mid-mission. While the jargon itself is a knowledge capability, the use of it is an observable skill. The third capability type is *problem solving skills*, which involves the application of both knowledge and observable skill capabilities without a clear path from task start to finish. In the game above, a designer might wish to train a squad to investigate bunkers containing unknown enemy forces, which incorporate many other specific, easier-to-train knowledge and observable skill capabilities. The fourth capability type is *attitudes*, which involves changing learners' attitudes and beliefs. In the game above, a trainer might want to improve squadmate relationships through their experiences in the game. Together, these four types are an exhaustive list of what capabilities might be trained or taught in any organizational or educational program (Campbell and Kuncel, 2001).

For each capability to be trained, one or more specific course objectives must be drafted. These objectives should include the capability to be trained, along with a specific description of that capability such that it can be evaluated. For example, to summarize the capabilities above, we might see the course objectives below (although it should be noted that a real set of objectives would need to be longer and more exhaustive):

By the end of this training program, trainees will:

- Visually identify weapons in the standard outfitting and describe the differences between them (*knowledge*)
- Describe all tactical plans involving enemy combatants (*knowledge*)
- Use radio jargon as appropriate during combat exercises (*observable skill*)

[1] In the remainder of this chapter, we will refer to "courses" generally, but the concepts described apply to both organizational training programs and classes in higher education.

- Work with squadmates to assault enemy positions with unknown countermeasures in place (*problem solving skill*)
- Improve their relationships with their squad mates (*attitude*)

After a list of specific objectives has been drafted, specific instructional methods must be chosen that will best address these objectives while simultaneously address the four basic principles of effective instruction (adapted from Kraiger, 2003):

- *Presentation*: The information presented is relevant to course objectives.
- *Demonstration*: The capability to be learned is demonstrated.
- *Practice*: Opportunities to practice are provided.
- *Feedback*: Feedback on learner performance is provided during and after practice.

For example, consider the third sample course objective listed above: "Use radio jargon as appropriate during combat exercises (*observable skill*)." Given this objective, a designer might choose the following lesson plan:

- The instructor lectures on what radio jargon is and how it is used. (*presentation*)
- The instructor provides an example of radio jargon in a simulated field exercise in a 3D simulation game. (*demonstration*)
- Learners participate in exercises in the 3D simulation game and practice the skill. (*practice*)
- The instructor provides feedback on the learner's practice. (*feedback*)

In a complete curriculum plan, the instructor might try to address multiple objectives simultaneously (e.g., using radio jargon while coordinating an assault on an enemy position) but should ensure that all four of these principles are followed for each objective.

A warning commonly cited in psychology is the following: "It is tempting, if the only tool you have is a hammer, to treat everything as if it were a nail" (Maslow, 1966, pp. 15–16). It is important to emphasize that chronologically, the decision to use a simulation game or any other instructional method only comes *after* the needs assessment and objective specification phase. For the course designer, picking a method (e.g. our hammer, the 3D game) and then trying to figure out how it might be used to learn in a particular situation is, quite simply, backwards. Worse still, a course designer might say, "I have a game, and I have course objectives. What objectives need to be sacrificed so that I can use this game?" Decisions about course objectives must be made definitively, and only then can decisions about specific methods be made. Otherwise, learner time is wasted and costs rise unnecessarily. Interactive 3D games may be the best choice for a given set of objectives, but applying such games broadly without specific consideration of those objectives helps neither students nor instructors.

This presents a new question: given a set of course objectives, how does one go about choosing a game? Aside from general advice derived from the four general principles described above (e.g. "if a skill specified in a course objective requires navigation in a 3D space to demonstrate it, a game requiring interaction in 3D space should probably be used"), there is little research to guide answers to this question. At this point in the development of the research literature, the problem must be tackled more broadly.

20.3 Direct and Indirect Determinants of Course Performance

When games are considered for their potential to improve learning, it is not really the games themselves that are being considered. Instead, it is the properties of those games that are important. This might include the mechanics and playability of the game, the accessibility of the game, the learning curve of the game, and any of a number of other game design characteristics, in isolation or in combination. But what about these properties actually affects learning?

For example, the learning curve might be an important piece of this puzzle because learners must spend time learning the game rather than learning the material. This could be time wasted in the learning process, if learning to play the game was not itself linked to course objectives. But it is not simply that a steeper learning curve decreases learning. Instead, a steeper learning curve decreases time spent with the course material, which in turn decreases learning. In more technical terms, time spent with the course material mediates the relationship between learning curve and learning outcomes.

The mediator here is called a *direct determinant* of course performance because it represents a psychological state affected by the game that itself affects learning. The length of the learning curve is thus an *indirect determinant* because it affects learning only through a direct determinant (see Fig. 20.1 for an illustration of this relationship). Ideally, a parsimonious model of course performance should include an exhaustive list of all direct determinants of course performance.

An example of this sort of modeling can be found in industrial/organizational psychology where a comprehensive model of the determinants of job performance is available. This model, proposed by Campbell (1990), specifies three and only three direct determinants of job performance: declarative knowledge, procedural knowledge and skill, and motivation. Any other characteristic of an individual affects job performance through one of these three. For example, if a person is highly conscientious and organized, this character trait is considered an indirect determinant of job performance, because it affects job performance only by affecting motivation to

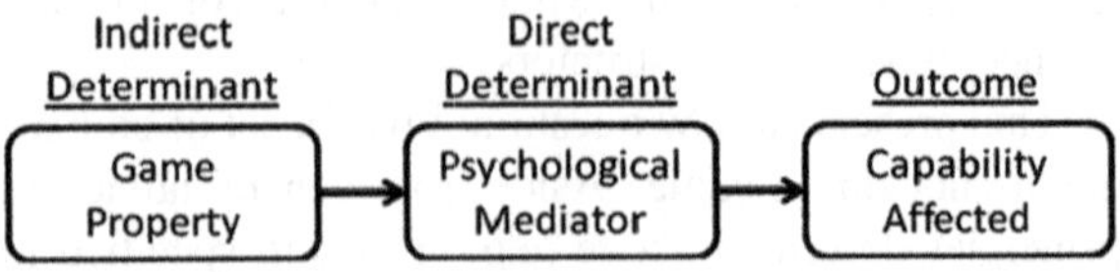

Fig. 20.1 Idealized model of the determinants of course performance in relation to games

be conscientious and organized on the job. Thus the relationship between conscientiousness (indirect determinant) and job performance (outcome) is mediated by motivation (direct determinant).

Models of course performance giving a definitive list of direct determinants are more difficult to find, but two characteristics arise clearly in a model provided by Kraiger (2003) that reflect portions of the Campbell (1990) model: learner trainability (itself consisting of cognitive ability and basic skills) and motivation. Kraiger also includes "work environment" but this will be more broadly defined here as opportunity to learn, while trainability will be broadened to "teachability." To illustrate this model, consider the example in Fig. 20.2.

In this model, course outcomes are driven by three direct determinants and three only: teachability, motivation, and opportunity. Teachability refers to the readiness of the learner to participate in the course. This reflects a wide variety of learner traits, including psychological characteristics like intelligence, studiousness, trait motivation to learn, and so on. Motivation refers to the learner's willingness to participate in the learning process. Opportunity refers to the time and resources allocated to support the learner.

Like Campbell's (1990) model of job performance, this is a multiplicative model: all three must be present for learning to occur. This can be articulated mathematically as Learning = Teachability * Motivation * Opportunity (L = T*M*O). If any of these are zero, learning will also be zero. For example, if the learner is highly prepared to learn and highly motivated but lacks opportunity, learning cannot occur. Consider the employee who wants to take on personal development projects to improve his own skills who works in an organization that does not provide any support for him to do so. This employee cannot learn because there is no opportunity to attempt to learn. Also consider the college student who is highly teachable (e.g. highly intelligent, meta-cognitively prepared) in an organization that clearly supports his learning (college) but is not at all motivated. He too will learn nothing, despite being high in two of the three direct determinants.

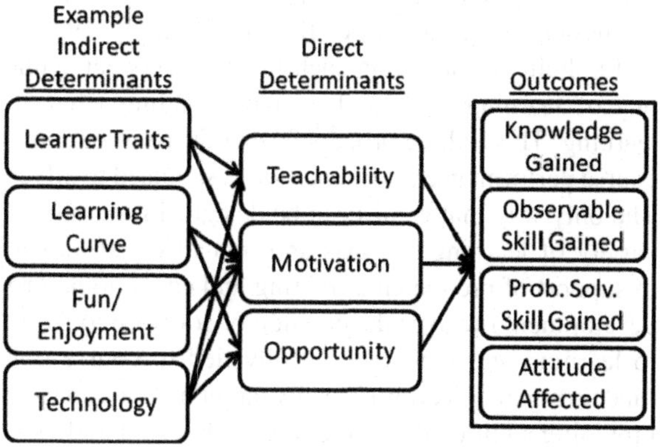

Fig. 20.2 General example of the determinants of course performance

The indirect determinants in Fig. 20.2 are included only illustratively; this list is not exhaustive. Each affects learning through one of the three direct determinants described above. For example, learner traits affect learning through their effect on teachability and motivation. One potential learner trait, intelligence, affects teachability: a more intelligent learner is likely to absorb the information more quickly. This trait also might affect motivation: a more intelligent learner is more likely to recognize the benefit of learning and put in more effort.

The learning curve example described earlier involves effects on motivation and opportunity. If the learning curve is too steep, the learner is more likely to become frustrated and give up (decreased motivation, thus decreased learning). If the learning curve is too shallow, the learner may also never have time to get to the learning material itself (decreased opportunity, thus decreased learning).

Fun and enjoyment affects only motivation. The more enjoyable a learning game is, the more likely the student is to persist playing it, regardless of whether or not that learning game is efficient at teaching the concepts it claims. And yet, if the game is incredibly dull, the student will not persist in playing it (remember the multiplicative model), and will learn nothing.

Technology is included in this figure to illustrate by what mechanisms technology (and by extension, games) can impact learning. Technologies can affect teachability by improving learner skills before training begins. For example, an optional asynchronous online pre-training program might be used to improve meta-cognitive skills; the relationship between completion of the program and learning outcomes is mediated by teachability. A fun game might encourage a learner to engage with the material longer than they otherwise would have; the relationship between the fun level of the game and learning outcomes is mediated by motivation. A game that can be played at home might enable the learner to engage with the material when they otherwise would not have; the relationship between the accessibility of the game and learning outcomes is mediated by opportunity.

Mediation can occur either partially or fully. Full mediation implies that all effect on learning outcomes is through the mediator. Using the example above, assume that the relationship between the "fun" level of a game and learning outcomes is fully mediated by motivation. If so, no matter how fun a game is, if motivation is not affected, learning outcomes will not be affected either (for a more complete discussion of mediation, see Baron and Kenny, 1986).

Explicitly establishing such linkages between game properties and the psychology of learning is critical to understanding why and how games can influence learning. This linking process further draws attention to the specific determinants of course performance that games are best poised to affect: motivation and opportunity. The only way that games can be designed generally enough to apply across a wide variety of learning contexts and domains is to target these determinants broadly, in support of pre-existing training and educational programs. While learning game development involves the creation of software to facilitate cognitive activity related to learning and must be carefully tied to course objectives, casual social games (and thus gameification) broadly target motivation to engage with the material while providing additional opportunities to learners to do so.

20.4 Psychological Research Supporting Gameification

Given that technology most directly affects learning through learner motivation and opportunity, whatever elements of games best increase these two determinants should be targeted to maximize the ultimate effectiveness of a course. The process of gameification, which involves the creation of casual social games to support (but not replace) courses, accomplishes exactly this.

The label of "casual game" reflects the viewpoint of the current videogames industry more than it reflects a psychological exploration of game types and the experiences surrounding them. Casual games are typically contrasted with "hardcore" games. The prototypical hardcore game is targeted at a demographic of teenage and young adult males, and typically involves active competitive play against other persons and/or the game's algorithms and artificial intelligence. First-person shooters, driving games, open world games, action-adventure games, real-time strategy games and platform games are commonly placed in this category. Casual games might be defined as any other game that does not fit that paradigm. Stereotypes of hardcore games typically include multimillion dollar productions with fast action, immersive worlds, graphics as realistic as current technology allows, and navigation of 3D environments, while casual games tend to emphasize rote behaviors, puzzle solving, simplistic graphics, and straightforward play mechanics. But this distinction is simplistic, and many games have characteristics of both.

Few systematic explorations of games and gamer types are available in psychology, but one study by Westwood and Griffiths (2010) identifies six general categories of gamer, each with their own preferences regarding the games they play: (1) story-driven solo gamers, (2) social gamers, (3) solo limited gamers, (4) hardcore online gamers, (5) control/identity solo gamers, and (6) casual gamers. The existence of such diverse preferences for game playing suggests that games themselves are at least as complex. Thus the labels of hardcore and casual are not a definitive breakdown of game types; however, they do serve as a reasonable starting point.

Under the heading of casual games, several subcategories of games are beginning to emerge, one of which is the "social game." As of 2011, the most prominent of these games is FarmVille, by Zynga, Inc., a game that focuses on the planting and harvesting of crops. As players accomplish in-game tasks (e.g. planting crops, building decorations), they are rewarded with a slew of relatively easy-to-attain virtual badges. These badges stay with the player's account as a mark of accomplishment, and in turn unlock more difficult, more time-consuming badges. Each time a badge is earned, players can choose to be socially recognized in an attached online social network (e.g. Facebook, MySpace). Zynga even includes special rewards for sharing these badges socially, which serves the dual purpose blurring the line between FarmVille and the player's social network profile while also gaining free targeted advertising to the player's friends and acquaintances. One potential contributor to FarmVille's success is that at the beginning of play, it does not require a great deal of time commitment; in fact, FarmVille does not even suggest that the full attention of the player would be valuable. The most effective method of growing crops in FarmVille is quite literally not to play the game. Simply leaving and returning to the game a few hours or even days later can be more productive than actively engaging with it – and yet, by engaging casually, player easily earn badges that they can show off to their friends. As the player increases their emotional investment in the game, these badges become increasingly difficult and time-consuming to achieve. By all accounts, this approach is extremely successful, as FarmVille was the most popular videogame in the world in 2010 (AppData, 2011). Zynga properties in general, all of which could be characterized as casual social games, maintain an active player base of at least 215 million monthly users (Zynga, Inc., 2011).

This emphasis on the accomplishment of relatively mundane tasks followed by recognition is well explored in marketing, where reward programs give purchasers points, tiers, or other psychological rewards in exchange for behaviors desired by program creators (Kim et al., 2001). The most common examples of such programs are the major airlines' frequent flier programs and credit card companies' earned-points for goods. These programs effectively maintain both the behavioral and affective loyalty of customers (Gomes et al., 2006).

Gameification takes advantage of this mechanism shared by both casual social games and tiered marketing plans to motivate learners. The term itself is unfortunately as poorly defined a concept as games, which is what led to the somewhat general definition used within this chapter: "the addition of elements commonly associated with games (e.g. game mechanics) to an educational or training program in order to make the learning process more engaging." But again, this is a reasonable starting point.

Videogames in general are highly motivating to college-age students, and recent estimates indicate at least 70% of college students play them (Jones, 2003). Motivations to play games vary, but challenge and competition, within what is often a highly social context (Axellson and Regan, 2006), are among the most commonly reported reasons (Olson, 2010). Videogames can also influence behavior and attitudes: violent games seem to encourage violent behavior while prosocial videogames can encourage empathy in players (Greitemeyer et al., 2010).

Inspired by FarmVille, the present authors investigated which psychological research might explain the success of such casual social games, and how they might be taken advantage of for educational outcomes. These research streams were then integrated and operationalized to produce a casual social game to support undergraduate education and employee training. These areas of research are summarized below:

- Research on *social network sites* suggests an online social network with easy access to current classmates will be attractive to students.
- Research on *test-enhanced learning* suggests low-stakes automated online testing will improve learning for students who take part in such testing.
- Research on *goal-setting theory* suggests that online social rewards connected to completion of automated online tests will motivate students to complete those

automated online tests without being offered any scholastic reward (e.g. points, extra credit).

Each of these areas of research will be described in turn.

20.4.1 Social Network Sites

The use of technology to communicate with peers has become one of the most common leisure activities for college students. In one study of 350 traditional university students, 78.5% of survey respondents reported using technology 7 or more times per day for communicating, while 99.6% of respondents reported doing so at least daily (Gemmill and Peterson, 2006). The fundamental drive for social interaction and the maintenance of interpersonal relationships is unsurprising; this basic human need is well documented as a part of virtually every psychological theory on human motivation (Baumeister and Leary, 1995). Many web-based technologies make such interactions simple and convenient, but social network sites have recently come to dominate this domain.

Social network sites (SNS) can be defined as:

> web-based services that allow individuals to (1) construct a public or semi-public profile within a bounded system, (2) articulate a list of other users with whom they share a connection, and (3) view and traverse their list of connections and those made by others within the system. (Boyd and Ellison, 2008)

Such technologies provide college students opportunities to interact with their classmates and even professors outside of traditional face-to-face interactions. Active integration of social media into the classroom may be an important way for faculty to connect with and motivate students (Hung and Yuen, 2010).

By far, the most popular of such sites is Facebook, with estimates that as high as 94% of college students use the site (Ellison et al., 2007). Reported motivations for use of Facebook vary somewhat, but communicating with friends, looking at photos, procrastination, and planning or researching upcoming events are the most commonly supplied reasons (Pempek et al., 2009). Although the current favorite, Facebook is unlikely to hold that status indefinitely; MySpace is a clear example of a once-dominating social media platform now out of favor. Recently, Facebook has been scrutinized for its controversial profit-driven privacy practices (Wakefield, 2010), and its user interface and data security policies can change at any time. These concerns limit the value of Facebook specifically as a tool to enhance student outcomes in training and higher education. But it is clear that a SNS with specific added value to students should motivate them to participate on it in the context of education.

20.4.2 Test-Enhanced Learning

One of the most problematic issues in the psychology of test scores is understanding the meaning of those scores. Variance in knowledge test scores contains much more information than simply knowledge; it also reflects the effects of individual differences like testing self efficacy (individuals' scores may be biased downwards due to poor attitudes about their ability to do well on tests; Spielberger, 1966) and other cognitive effects like test familiarity (upon retaking a test, individuals' scores may be biased upwards due to familiarity with the test questions rather than an increase in the general knowledge domain measured by the test; Anastasi, 1981). However, recent research has suggested a new, unexpected value for testing: the act of testing itself appears to help people learn, potentially even more efficiently than dedicated studying.

In their seminal paper on the topic, researchers Roediger and Karpickei (2006) picked passages from the reading comprehension portion of the Test of English as a Foreign Language (TOEFL; Rogers, 2001) and tested participants during two sessions. The first session was divided into 7-minute segments. In the first segment, they read a TOEFL passage and in the second, they studied the passage. They were randomly assigned to one of two conditions in the third segment: half studied again, and half were given a free recall test on the passage content. The second, follow-up session occurred at one of three times: 5 min, 2 days, or 1 week later. Students who studied twice scored better on the recall test 5 min after reading it, suggesting studying is better for immediate recall. However, for those completing the follow-up 2 days or 1 week later, the trend reversed; students who took a test remembered more than those who studied. Further, it should be noted that none of the students received feedback about their test performance. Instead, the experience of testing itself improved their long-term recall of the texts.

In their second study on this topic, Roediger and Karpicke split participants into three groups, where S is a study segment and T is a testing segment: SSSS, SSST, and STTT. The same pattern emerged: when students were tested multiple times, their performance on a 5-minute follow-up (remembering; short-term gain) was worse than those who studied multiple times, but their performance on a 1-week follow-up (learning; long-term gain) was better.

Since long-term gains are the real learning objective of higher education (rather than short-term recall), this suggests that the act of testing students could be a key pedagogical tool to improve student learning. Even in subject areas where test results are not commonly interpreted as indicative of learning (e.g. the humanities), the act of testing itself should still benefit students as it activates cognitive processes related to understanding the learning material and applying it. The remaining question is how to motivate students to take optional tests.

20.4.3 Goal Setting Theory

Goal-setting as a theory of human motivation is one of the most well-explored areas of psychology, with a large body of research literature spanning several decades. Humans, generally, have a need to fulfill goals that they have set and have been set for them. People are highly motivated by well-crafted performance goals that are specific, measureable, and difficult but attainable (Fishbein and Ajzen, 1975).

As long as a person is committed to achieving a performance goal (i.e. motivated), has the ability to meet that goal, and does not have conflicting goals, the relationship between goal difficulty and task performance is linear and positive (Locke and Latham, 2006). Goals affect an individual's performance by directing attention and increasing motivation, but this is moderated by the person's ability to complete the task (Locke and Latham, 2002). An example of a performance goal in a learning game might be to reach a specific score by the end of the game.

Learning goals (goals in which learning itself is the goal) have also been investigated, and are effective at improving both learning itself and later performance on tasks related to what was learned (Lepper and Malone, 1987). There is some evidence that goals operate differently during learning tasks. When a performance goal is specific and difficult, rather than simply "do your best," performance decreases, while specific and difficult learning goals have been shown to be superior to do-your-best learning goals in affecting learning (Seijts and Latham, 2001). Further, it has been found that college students who set performance goals in a course improve their grades but do not improve their interest in the course, while those who set learning goals improve their interest without improving their grades, although both produce better outcomes in comparison to no goals at all (Harackiewicz et al., 1997). An example of a general learning goal in a learning game might be to "learn as much about plant biology as you can" while a specific learning goal might be to "learn the difference between oomycetes and viroids." A combination of goal types may be most beneficial.

Casual social game designers employ principles from the goal-setting literature, perhaps not even knowingly, by creating games with multi-tiered goal structures to encourage players to reach higher and higher. By reaching a game objective (i.e. meeting a goal set by the game designer), a player earns a virtual badge that can be displayed on his/her social network site profile which is then visible to other users in the player's social network. Simultaneously, players unlock the ability to earn badges associated with more difficult goals, which creates a cyclical motivational pattern that keeps players playing: players meet game objectives, feel a sense of accomplishment by meeting a goal, display those accomplishments publicly, receive positive feedback from others in their social network, and are motivated to pursue the next, more difficult playing goal to receive more rewards. Because the goals are largely self-motivated (i.e. many goals are available, and the player chooses which ones to pursue), goal commitment is high, and motivation is maximized, regardless of the purpose of those goals.

20.4.4 Integration of Psychological Models

Incorporating these three research areas produces a picture of a casual social gaming embedded within an online social network that should motivate students to engage with the material more often than they otherwise would. An integrative model appears in Fig. 20.3.

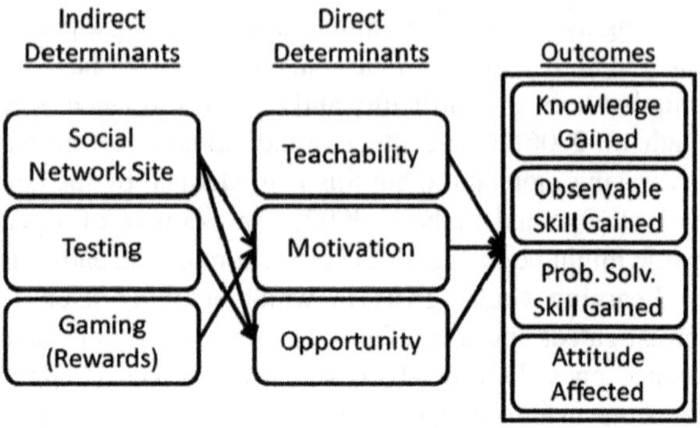

Fig. 20.3 Integrative model of the determinants of course performance in relation to casual social games

First, the ability to communicate more easily with classmates in a SNS increases motivation to engage with those classmates as well as the learning material shared with those classmates, although it is critical to deploy a SNS in such a way that it provides incremental value beyond any SNS already being used (e.g. Facebook, MySpace, Twitter). It furthermore increases opportunity to engage with the material by serving as a resource accessible 24/7 and from home. Second, additional testing gives added opportunity for students to engage with the material that they otherwise would not have, along with additional supporting evidence that testing is more beneficial to students than studying. Third, the provision of social game rewards for testing increases student motivation to complete those tests (i.e. because the SNS makes the social rewards meaningful, students are motivated to take advantage of the opportunity provided to complete tests).

20.5 A Mixed Methods Study of Gameification

To examine the value of this integrative theory, all of these principles were combined to produce a single online social networking platform for undergraduates. All faculty and students completing a course in the Psychology department at a major east-coast university during the Summer 2010 semester were automatically enrolled in this system, which the primary author titled *socialPsych.*

20.5.1 Features of the socialPsych Platform

The *socialPsych* platform integrated features common to most social network sites with new education-focused features developed to implement the theory described above.

Features common to most social network sites follow:

- *Personal profiles.* Each system user (faculty and students alike) could create a personal profile to represent of him/herself. Specific profile features included:

username, profile picture, personality profile, year in school, employment during school, major, favorite class, clubs/organizations, college activities, interests, favorite music, favorite films and television.

- *Profile posts.* Users could post text status updates to their own profile, which were cross-listed in the Classmate Updates Feed.
- *Classmate updates feed.* Profile posts by all current classmates and instructors appeared in the updates feed.
- *Direct messaging system.* Users could privately direct message any other user of the system.
- *Communication options.* Users could specify how the system contacted them by e-mail and how frequently. This was used to notify students when instructors and/or other students posted in the discussion areas associated with their classes.

Features that we felt represented an expansion over traditional SNS follow:

- *Classroom discussion areas.* Each course had its own private discussion area, and students enrolled in those courses were automatically enrolled in those areas. Comments were threaded only one deep (i.e. a comment could only have one level of replies). See Fig. 20.4.
- *Protected discussion environment.* Unlike classes with social elements run in Facebook, all conversations and discussions took place behind a password-protected barrier accessible only to department faculty and students. No one without a valid student or instructor username/password combination could see student or class interactions – the same level of protection available in most learning management systems (LMS; e.g. Moodle, Blackboard).
- *Certification (gameification) system.* This system was designed to motivate students to complete optional multiple-choice tests. More detail is available on this feature further in the next section of this chapter. Also see Fig. 20.5.
- *Mentoring system.* This system used scores from the certification system to qualify students to mentor other students, using a matchmaking procedure.
- *Open community with protection.* All classroom discussion areas were visible to anyone in the department. This was to encourage students to perceive themselves as part of a larger community, and may be an element of the "critical mass" needed for online social media to develop a lasting user base. This increased perception of community should also have contributed to the perceived impact of the social rewards offered by the system. To enable privacy when desired, authors of any particular comment thread could specify that their thread was to be private, i.e. only visible to students currently enrolled in that course and the faculty.
- *Instructor highlighting.* When an instructor or TA posted in a course discussion area or made a profile post, the post was highlighted in both the Classmate Updates Feed and Classroom Discussion Area for the instructor's current students. This was designed to increase the perception that this was an education-focused SNS, and not just a place for students to socialize.

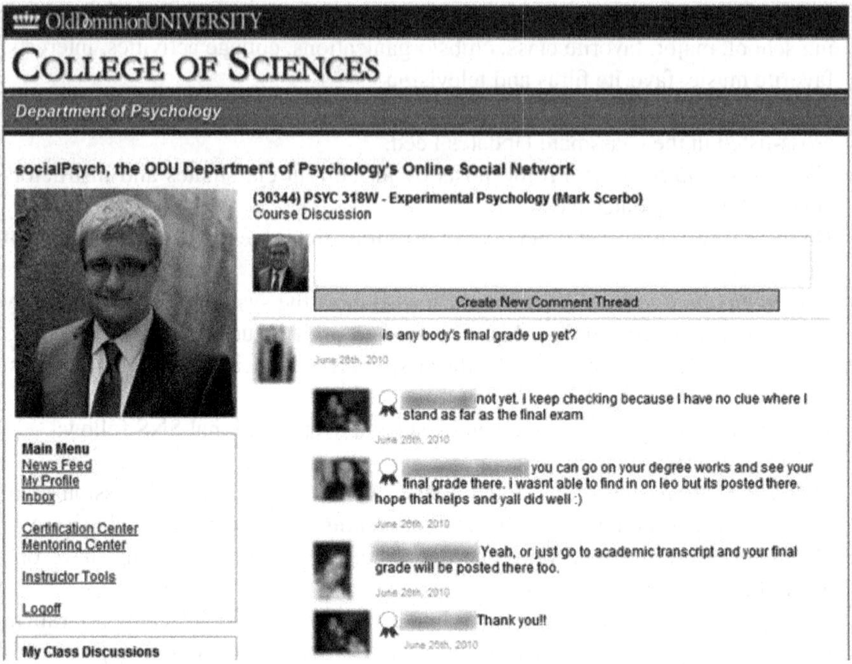

Fig. 20.4 Sample classroom discussion area (student names and photos blurred to protect their identities)

20.5.2 Deploying socialPsych

The *socialPsych* platform was written by the lead author of this chapter to run on a LAMP platform – an acronym representing four open-source, freely available software packages that run together as a web server: Linux as the operating system, Apache as the HTTP provider, MySQL as the underlying database, and PHP as the server-side scripting language that provides dynamic content. This was done to minimize costs of upkeep and to maximize portability to other departments and universities.

Instructors were approached individually about their willingness to allow the *socialPsych* platform to support their classes, and about 80% of instructors gave their permission. Within this group, instructors were given complete freedom to integrate *socialPsych* into their classes however they saw fit. Some instructors chose to post required assignments in *socialPsych*, others chose to place extra credit assignments there, and still others never mentioned *socialPsych* to their students again. It was important to provide this freedom in order to see how a SNS and gameification platform performed in a realistic educational environment. Most research points to general resistance to online education by university faculty (for some discussion of this, see Clark, 1993; Dillon and Walsh, 1992; Gibson et al., 2008), so the present

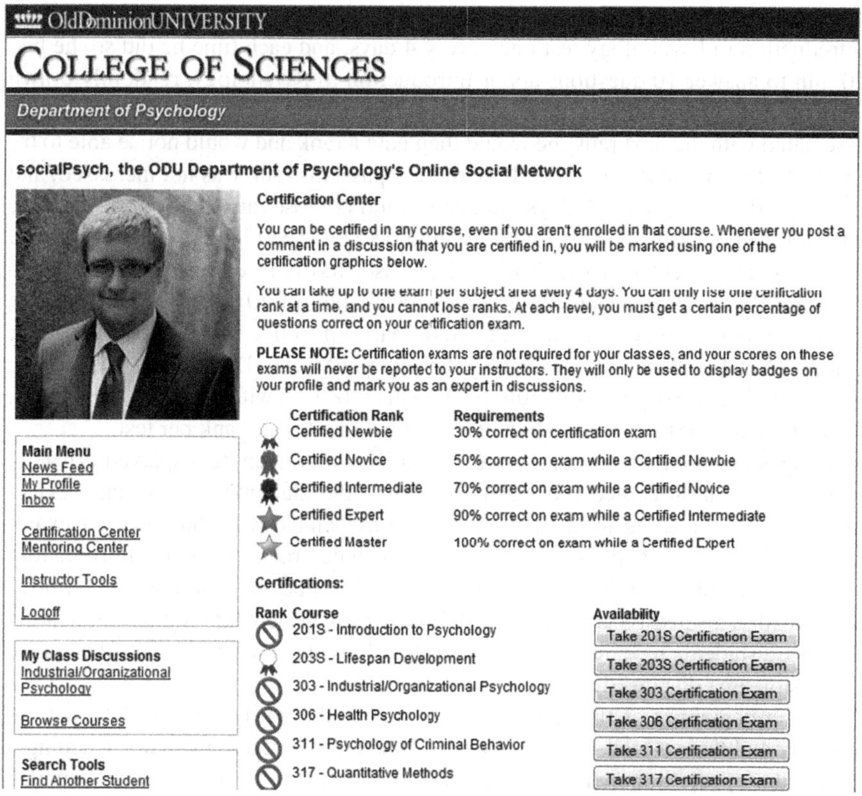

Fig. 20.5 Certification system utilizing gameification (current user has completed one rank in PSYC 203S – Lifespan Development)

authors did not want to assume such support when evaluating the system. A technological intervention of this scale (i.e. deployed across multiple classes and subjects) should not be considered successful unless it still improves outcomes with limited or no faculty support.

After creating the software platform itself and acquiring instructor permissions, the content for the certification (gameification) system was collected. This was the most time-consuming aspect of the project preparation stage. To do this, each instructor was approached and asked to supply practice test questions related to their course. If the instructor did not wish to supply these, the test bank from the textbook associated with their course was used. If the instructor did not want us to use this test bank (for example, if the instructor used test bank questions on their own tests), test banks from other textbooks on the same topic were used. Each of the 17 test banks ultimately used in the overall certification bank consisted of between 101 and 150 questions, with a grand total of 2219 questions. After the system was deployed, students were able to complete up to one 10-minute 10-question quiz per course category per 4 days. These questions were randomly drawn from the test bank associated with that course. For example, a student could complete the 201S Introduction to Psychology test once every 4 days, and each time he did so, he had 10 min to answer 10 questions about Introduction to Psychology, randomly drawn from the 150 questions associated with that course. If he passed the threshold score associated with the next rank, he would then gain a rank and would not be able to try for the following rank for 4 days. If he did not pass, his rank was not increased, and he was told to try again in 4 days. Students could not lose ranks, as this would have a negative motivational effect for attempting quizzes. See Fig. 20.5 for a picture of the certification center in which the current user has reached one rank in 203S – Lifespan Psychology. Seventeen tests were available (of 20 courses in the project, 17 were unique topics), and students could earn up to five ranks in each of those courses: Newbie, Novice, Intermediate, Expert and Master. Directed by goal setting theory, each rank was more difficult to attain than the last, with cutoffs of 30%, 50%, 70%, 90% and 100% correct. Students could gain up to one rank per test.

Badges associated with ranks for each course would then be displayed privately in the certification center and publicly in both the student's profile and next to his name when posting in the discussion area associated with that test. For example, if a student reached the "Certified Intermediate" rank in 201S – Introductory Psychology, a blue ribbon would appear next to that student's name whenever posting in a 201S discussion area. In Fig. 20.4, three posts have white ribbons, indicating that those students have reached the "Certified Newbie" rank in 318 W (the course discussion area displayed).

At the beginning of the semester, after approval from university IRB, lists of students and their e-mail addresses were collected from each instructor teaching a course during the Summer 2010 semester. A total of 592 students were e-mailed an invitation to join *socialPsych*, and the second author of this chapter gave a brief 5-minute presentation to all participating face-to-face classes to explain to students what *socialPsych* was and why they might want to join it. Instructors of online courses were encouraged to post an announcement with the same information presented in person. To encourage initial activity, various monetary prizes were offered for participating.

20.5.3 Project Results

Two major areas of the project were evaluated separately: (1) the motivational value of the overall system and (2) the motivational value of the certification (gameification) center.

20.5.3.1 Overall Motivation to Use socialPsych

Students electing to open the invitation completed an informed consent document and completed setup of their social network profile. Of the 592 students e-mailed invitations, ultimately 385 (65%) created profiles and signed into the service. Students could choose to be a part of *socialPsych* but not supply permission

Table 20.1 socialPsych summary statistics

Count	Event
592	Invitations sent to students
385	Student profiles created
246	Profile pictures set
1106	Conversation threads in course discussion areas
4595	Comments in course discussion threads
546	Total certification ranks reached
113	Unique students gaining ranks

for their data to be used for research purposes, but very few students chose this (14 of 385; 4%), though these students will not be reported in any further statistics. Of these 385, 246 (64%) uploaded profile pictures, suggesting a fairly high level of engagement (or at least, intended engagement) (Table 20.1).

Course discussion areas were used often and enthusiastically, with 2219 total conversation threads and 4595 total comments. 20 summer courses participated with a typical length of 6 weeks, suggesting a great deal of conversation. Content of these conversations varied a great deal. In courses where the instructor required participation or presented extra credit, most (though not all) posts were generally to satisfy these requirements. But in courses where the instructor did not participate at all, students actively engaged with each other more casually. The following represents a common type of exchange:

> Student A: "Can someone who used the study guide on the first test tell me whether it is an effective study method??"
>
> Student B: "i used it all and got a 94, but you should study the study guide, not just fill it out"

Students often discussed studying with others that they ostensibly did not know personally. This sort of interaction would not be likely without a class-focused SNS. Emotional appeals and support regarding coursework and progress were also common:

> Student: oh man this class has been confusing, but we only have the final left and then we're DONE! :) ! i hope everyone does well! Good Luck!

From these comments and others like them, it became clear that students using *socialPsych* generally found it motivating to use, supporting the first of the three theories the platform was based upon. Being connected to all of their classmates virtually in a somewhat informal environment spurred students to interact in ways they otherwise would not have been able. General class-wide requests about study materials and techniques would have been otherwise impossible.

An end-of-semester survey was provided to students to gain feedback on the system, to which 155 students responded. Within this survey, students were asked to respond to four open-ended questions: the best thing about *socialPsych*, the worst thing about *socialPsych*, the most needed change for *socialPsych*, and general comments.

Only two comments were provided that indicated a general dislike of the *socialPsych* platform. One was for a technical reason:

> I didn't like it and would not use it again unless it was easier to use

This emphasizes the importance of user-friendliness and human factors in the creation of SNS, although it should be noted that many more comments were made on the platform's ease of use. The second negative comment was a bit more philosophical in nature, presumably from an older student:

> Why encourage a woefully inadequate way of communication just because it is popular in mainstream America? Younger people, adolescents today have severely disabled abilities to communicate verbally and are even inable [sic] to ask questions when they need to to [sic] understand a particular subject. Rather than supporting and encouraging this deficiency the higher learning institution should be looking for ways to encourage more face-to-face communication among adults and peers rather than a poor attempt to further disable oral communication.

Though this student's perspective is appreciated, these concerns seem to focus on generational differences more so than the platform itself. While *socialPsych* does encourage online communication between faculty and classmates, it certainly does not replace face-to-face communication. Other than these two comments, feedback for the continued use of *socialPsych* was quite positive. A few examples follow:

> SocialPsych is a great way for students and teachers to stay connected with one another. I think this program should be for all class. I am glad I got the opportuniy [sic] to use this programing. [sic]

> It helped make this class one of the best classes I took. . .because it allowed me to interact with other students in the class on a regular basis. If I had any questions, I could ask them on socialPsych and someone always commented or answered my questions. It was wonderful!

> I think its use should be encouraged. It's a great social working network site. It's much safer to use than the internet (meaning, you are speaking with students you have something already in common with- class and school).

20.5.3.2 Motivation to Use Certification (Gameification) Center

The gameification component was enthusiastically adopted. Of the 385 students who created profiles, 113 (29%) completed optional multiple choice tests. At the end of the semester, students had completed 546 total ranks (a mean of 4.8 ranks per student). This only includes tests successfully passed; failed certification exams did not result in ranks gained. One particularly motivated student completed 54 ranks across all content areas; removing her outlying data results in 492 unique ranks (a mean of 4.4 ranks per student).

Comments regarding the certification exams were positive; they were mentioned by several students as the best aspect of the platform, and were not mentioned by any students as the worst aspect about the platform. When asked about the most needed change for *socialPsych*, one student even suggested making the questions more difficult.

Three questions were asked in the end-of-semester survey regarding the certification center. Each question was assessed with a 5-point Likert-type scale from Strongly Disagree (1) to Strongly Agree (5). Fun was assessed with the statement, "The certification exams were fun." Enjoyment was assessed with, "I enjoyed taking certification exams." The extent to which students found it rewarding was assessed with "I felt good gaining ranks through certification exams." Results appear in Fig. 20.6.

Generally, we interpret this as strong support for the motivational value of gameification. Students not only completed extra multiple choice exams for no direct scholastic reward (no instructor required or offered extra credit for completion of certification exams) but also, on average, rated those exams as fun, enjoyable, and rewarding.

Reasons that students did not use the certification exams or did not take many exams were difficult to identify, but a few comments offer a window into this issue:

> The certification exams are a good idea, but I never had any time to do them.

This comment indicates a motivational deficit. While the gameification strategy was clearly motivating to many users, this was not true for all. Further work is needed to identify which users are not motivated by a gameification strategy

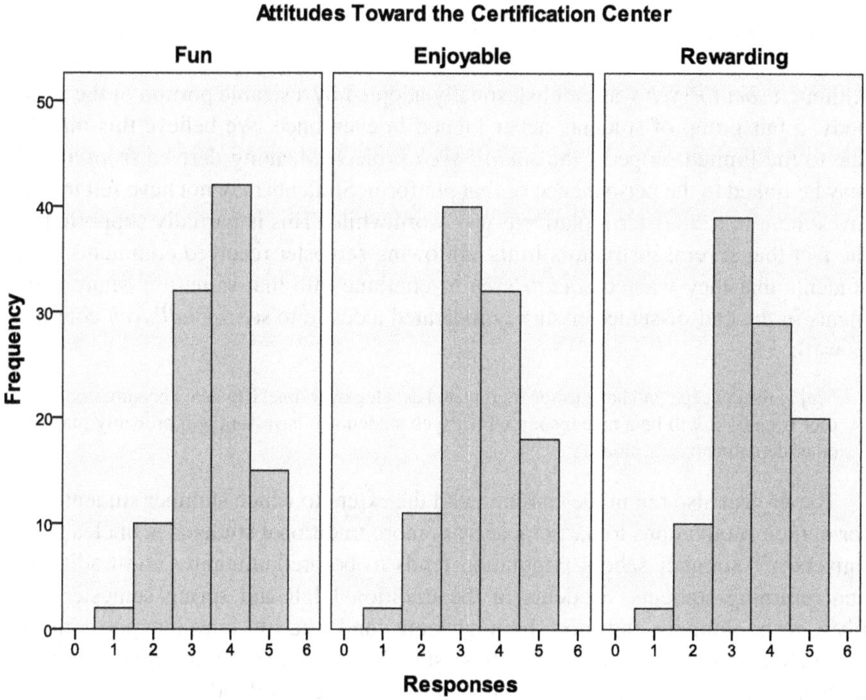

Fig. 20.6 Frequency of responses to attitude items, with 5 = strongly agree and 1 = strongly disagree

and what might be done to increase participation from these users. Even among motivated users, there were other problems:

> I think it is a great features [sic], but I didn't know anything about certification exams was that because I was not qualified to take them? I would have liked to be informed about that.

This comment indicates high motivation to participate but low motivation to understand how to participate. Again, human factors and usability are critical to the creation of a gameification system that learners will actually use. Finally, there were some system design choices that were not universally appreciated:

> I did not like that the certification exams did not tell you which answers u got wrong

Users were not given feedback on correct answers for two reasons. First, test-enhanced learning does not require this for learners to benefit. Simply engaging with the material – thinking through responses – is sufficient to improve later learning outcomes. Second, test security made this impossible regardless. With only 150 questions, a student that completed the test repeatedly would quickly learn which answers were correct without putting in the cognitive learning effort that is the goal of the system. Such a user could gain ranks without actually earning them; withholding correct answers prevents this.

20.5.4 Limitations

Although *socialPsych* was enthusiastically adopted by a sizable portion of the study body, a fair group of students never logged in even once. We believe this may be due to the limited scope of the *socialPsych* project. Meaning derived from a SNS may be linked to the permanence of that platform. Students may not have felt that an investment in a short-term platform was worthwhile. This is partially supported by the fact that several instructors in the following semester received comments from students that they wanted *socialPsych* to continue into that semester. Many comments in the end-of-semester survey indicated a desire to see *socialPsych* continue as well:

> I enjoy the concept, and hope to see it grow and develop over time. If/when it becomes more user friendly it will be a nice resource for Psych students to have, and will probably make other departments. . .jealous.

The project also ran in the summer, and the extent to which summer students differ in their motivations to participate from more traditional students is unclear. The university's summer school population tends to be predominantly non-traditional and returning students. Students in the traditional fall and spring semesters are likely to be younger and more homogeneous, and a result, may interact with the *socialPsych* platform even more enthusiastically. The demographics related to SNS use and game playing in this context need to be studied explicitly.

It is also important not to underestimate the effect of student culture. If a platform like *socialPsych* became part of the social landscape of a university, much as Facebook has, it would be expected that most students would engage with it. Because the value of the certification center is based upon the hypothesis that increased testing leads to increased learning, students would only need to try the platform and then try the certification exams to benefit; simply testing should improve their understanding of the material covered by those exams, regardless of whether or not the students' scores on those tests have meaning.

20.6 General Conclusions, Best Practices, and Discussion

We hope this study to be regarded as a "proof-of-concept." Online social network platforms can be deployed in an educational setting, and students will use them as long as the SNS provides functionality they cannot get elsewhere. The strength of the *socialPsych* platform, the feature that made the game rewards meaningful, was the automatic connection of all students in classes with one another. Without having to introduce themselves, collect e-mail addresses, add Facebook friends, and so on, students were able to communicate online with those experiencing courses with them.

Beyond this general support for SNS in education, the present study supports the use of gameification to motivate undergraduates to participate in optional learning activities in their free time. In this study, students volunteered to complete online exams that they were not required to complete and for which they received no academic rewards. Because the act of testing appears to consolidate long-term memories better than studying does, these exams should improve long-term student understanding of the concepts covered within. Many expansions of this concept are possible; one can imagine a system where viewing of supplementary videos or participating in a variety of external learning activities are rewarded with points and badges in the SNS. With the evidence from this study, the present authors produced this list of current best practices for casual social games used for learning:

- A meaningful social context in which to nest the game is needed. Long term sustainability and privacy concerns suggest a dedicated SNS, but the "SNS of the moment" (e.g. Facebook, MySpace, Twitter) would also likely be sufficient to motivate learners, as long as privacy concerns were respected.
- The social game will be better utilized if more integrated within its social context. For example, the launching of an external application may create a psychological barrier between the two systems, which will inhibit the use of the external system.
- Rewards must be explicitly recognized in the social context to make them meaningful; the more explicit this recognition among the learner's peers, the stronger the motivation to continue will be.
- Immediacy of feedback is an important motivational element. As a result, rewards must be immediate; test grading must therefore also be immediate.
- Game rewards must be matched to difficult but attainable learning tasks. Some research even suggests that the best way to engage students with a game is to confuse them first; the feeling of satisfaction and accomplishment from overcoming

confusion leads to increased engagement (Rodrigo, 2010). Still, designers must be careful not to make the game *too* difficult, or students will simply give up.
- Game performance should never be explicitly required by instructors; this changes the learning goal ("I want to learn more so that I can be recognized for my learning") to a performance goal ("My instructor wants me to get a good score on this test") which will ultimately produce poorer learning outcomes.
- Starting with easy rewards but ramping up quickly to difficult or more time-consuming rewards (i.e. the FarmVille model) may combine the motivational value of satisfaction/accomplishment with the challenge associated with well-designed goals, although the ideal rate of acceleration for maintaining interest and motivation is currently unknown.
- Usability and human factors of both the SNS and the game are critical to ensuring learners actually use the system. If learners become bored or frustrated, they are likely to give up.

Considering evidence found for the general motivational aspects of this system, this study also promotes the idea that gameification could be used to support learning activities in the workplace. The creation of a training-focused SNS may furthermore be able to contribute to a culture of organizational learning, potentially quite valuable at a time when self-directed learning is becoming increasingly critical for organizational success. While the theory discussed above supports such an application, organizational employee demographics and motivation vary to a much greater degree than do undergraduate demographics and motivation, and thus it is unclear to what extent these results would generalize to that setting.

Additional evidence is needed on the learning benefit of this system. Though theory and preliminary evidence supports the tie between test taking and learning outcomes, empirical evidence is needed to verify this. One of the biggest challenges in research on such large system is that randomization is nigh impossible; to truly examine causal differences in learning due to the implementation of such a system, researchers would need to randomly assign many institutions to SNS-enhanced versus non-SNS-enhanced conditions. This is clearly unrealistic; researchers must find a way to investigate these learning benefits without the use of such powerful randomization designs. In lieu of randomization, carefully considered correlational and survey-based studies appear to be a necessity in this research domain, at least in the short-term.

It is also unclear what specific game design principles will lead to the greatest motivation. For example, there is thus far little research to guide whether a point-and-level system (where learners earn points to achieve levels at different plateaus) or a reward-for-action system (where learners earn unique awards for unique accomplishments) would be more effective.

Caution and restraint must also be used in the design of such systems. Abusing or overloading learners with goals can be quite dangerous, as it may lead to unintended side effects, such as increases in unethical behavior and reduced intrinsic motivation (Ordóñez et al., 2009). Overprescribing goals decreases the value of all goals in the reward system. Keeping the reward system relatively easy-to-understand and targeted to learning outcomes desired is critical to maintaining goal commitment. Further research must explore the boundary conditions under which gameification is valuable and at what point learners are overburdened.

Gameification does not involve the creation of a game for learning purposes. Instead, it takes the motivational properties of games and layers them on top of other learning activities, integrating the human desire to communicate and share accomplishment with goal-setting to direct the attention of learners and motivate them to action. With a gameification model, an instructor can offer rewards for virtually any learning activity. Generally, this is more powerful than a learning game because attention can be directed at the instructor's discretion, whereas a learning game is by definition targeted at a single set of learning objectives as chosen by the game designer. The extent of the benefit from a learning game, unless the instructor is the original programmer, can be found in the static list of features included in that game.

In conclusion, gameification offers a great deal of potential for the improvement of learning in both undergraduate education and employee training. Offering rewards within a social context that is meaningful to learners, which are of no physical cost to instructors, can motivate students to complete optional learning tasks that they otherwise would be unlikely to complete. Perhaps even more importantly, they are likely to report these tasks as fun, enjoyable, and rewarding – even if the task is as mundane as a multiple-choice test.

Acknowledgement We offer special thanks to the Old Dominion University Research Foundation for funding a Summer Research Fellowship to support this project.

References

Anastasi, A.: Coaching, test sophistication and developed abilities. Am. Psychol. **36**, 1086–1093 (1981)

AppData: Top applications leaderboard Facebook application metrics. http://www.appdata.com/leaderboard/apps (2011). Accessed 15 Feb 2011

Axellson, A.-S., Regan, T.: Playing online. In: Vorderer, P., Bryant, J. (eds.) Playing Video Games: Motives, Responses, and Consequences, pp. 291–306. Lawrence Erlbaum, Mahway, NJ (2006)

Baron, R.M., Kenny, D.A.: The moderator-mediator distinction in social psychological research: Conceptual, strategic, and statistical considerations. J. Pers. Soc. Psychol. **51**, 1173–1182 (1986)

Baumeister, R.F., Leary, M.R.: The need to belong: Desire for interpersonal attachments as a fundamental human motivation. Psychol. Bull. **117**, 497–529 (1995)

Boyd, D.M., Ellison, N.B.: Social networking sites: Definition, history, and scholarship. J. Comput. Mediated Commun. **13**, 210–230 (2008). doi: 10.1111/j.1083-6101.2007.00393.x

Campbell, J.P.: Modeling the performance prediction problem in industrial and organizational psychology. In: Dunnette, M.D., Hough, L.M. (eds.) Handbook of Industrial and Organizational Psychology, Vol. 1, 2nd edn., pp. 687–732. Consulting Psychologists Press, Palo Alto, CA (1990)

Campbell, J.P., Kuncel, N.R.: Individual and team training. In: Anderson, N., Ones, D.S., Sinangil, H.K., Viswesvaran, C. (eds.) Handbook of Industrial, Work, and Organizational Psychology, Vol. 1: Personnel Psychology, pp. 278–312. Sage, Thousand Oaks, CA (2001)

Clark, T.: Attitudes of American higher education faculty toward distance education: A national survey. Am. J. Distance Educ. **7**(2), 19–33 (1993)

Dillon, C.L., Walsh, S.M.: Faculty: The neglected resource in distance education. Am. J. Distance Educ. **6**(3), 5–21 (1992)

Ellison, N.B., Steinfield, C., Lampe, C.: The benefits of Facebook "Friends:" Social capital and college students' use of online social network sites. J. Comput. Mediated Commun. **12**, 1143–1168 (2007)

Fishbein, M., Ajzen, I.: Belief, Attitude, Intention and Behavior: An Introduction to Theory and Research. Addison-Wesley, Reading, MA (1975)

Gemmill, E., Peterson, M.: Technology use among college students: Implications for student affairs professionals. NASPA J. **43**, 280–300 (2006)

Gibson, S.G., Harris, M.L., Colaric, S.M.: Technology acceptance in an academic context: Faculty acceptance of online education. J. Educ. Bus. **83**, 355–359 (2008)

Gomes, B.G., Arranz, A.G., Cillan, J.G.: The role of loyalty programs in behavioral and affective loyalty. J. Consumer Market. **23**, 387–396 (2006)

Greitemeyer, T., Osswald, S., Brauer, M.: Playing prosocial video games increases empathy and decreases schadenfreude. Emotion **10**, 796–802 (2010)

Harackiewicz, J.M., Barron, K.E., Carter, S.M., Lehto, A.T., Elliot, A.J.: Predictors and consequences of achievement goals in the college classroom: Maintaining interest and making the grade. J. Per. Soc. Psychol. **73**, 1284–1295 (1997). doi: 10.1037/0022-3514.73.6.1284

Hung, H.-T., Yuen, S.C.-Y.: Educational use of social networking technology in higher education. Teach. Higher Educ. **15**, 703–714 (2010)

Jones, S.: Let the games begin: Gaming technology and entertainment among college students. Pew Research Center's Internet & American Life Project. http://www.pewinternet.org/Reports/2003/Let-the-games-begin-Gaming-technology-and-college-students.aspx (2003). Accessed 31 Dec 2010

Kim, B.-D., Shi, M., Srinivasan, K.: Reward programs and tacit collusion. Market. Sci. **20**, 99–120 (2001)

Kraiger, K.: Perspectives on training and development. In: Borman, W.C., Ilgen, D.R., Klimoski, R.J. (eds.) Handbook of Psychology: Industrial and Organizational Psychology, Vol. 12. Wiley, Hoboken, NJ (2003)

Lepper, M.R., Malone, T.W.: Intrinsic motivation and instructional effectiveness in computer-based education. In: Snow, R.E., Farr, M.J. (eds.) Aptitude, Learning, and Instruction, Vol. 3, pp. 107–141. Hillsdale, NJ: Erlbaum (1987)

Locke, E.A., Latham, G.P.: Building a practically useful theory of goal setting and task motivation: A 35-year odyssey. Am. Psychol. **57**, 705–717 (2002). doi: 10.1037/0003-066x.57.9.705

Locke, E.A., Latham, G.P.: New directions in goal-setting theory. Curr Dir. Psychol. Sci. **15**, 265–268 (2006). doi: 10.1111/j.1467-8721.2006.00449.x

Maslow, A.H.: The Psychology of Science: A Reconnaissance. Harper & Row, New York (1966)

Olson, C.: Children's motivations for video game play in the context of normal development. Rev. Gen. Psychol. **14**, 180–187 (2010). doi: 10.1037/a0018984

Ordóñez, L.D., Schweitzer, M.E., Galinsky, A.D., Bazerman, M.H.: Goals gone wild: The systematic side effects of overprescribing goal setting. Acad. Manage. Perspect. **23**, 6–16 (2009)

Orvis, K.A., Horn, D.B., Belanich, J.: An examination of the role individual differences play in videogame-based training. Mil. Psychol. **21**, 461–481 (2009)

Pempek, T.A., Yermolayeva, Y.A., Calvert, S.L.: College students' social networking experiences on Facebook. J. Appl. Dev. Psychol. **30**, 227–238 (2009). doi: 10.1016/j.appdev.2008.12.010

Rodrigo, M.: Dynamics of student cognitive-affective transitions during a mathematics game. Simul. Gaming **42**, 85–99 (2010). doi: 10.1177/1046878110361513

Roediger, H.L., Karpicke, J.D.: Test-enhanced learning: Taking memory tests improves long-term retention. Psychol. Sci. **17**, 249–255 (2006)

Rogers, B.: TOEFL CBT Success. Peterson's, Princeton, NJ (2001)

Seijts, G.H., Latham, G.P.: The effect of distal learning, outcome, and proximal goals on a moderately complex task. J. Organ. Behav. **22**, 291–307 (2001). doi: 10.1002/job.70

Spielberger, C.D.: Theory and research on anxiety. In: Spieldberger, C.D. (ed.) Anxiety and Behavior, pp. 3–20 . Academic, New York (1966)

Wakefield, J.: 2010, the year that privacy died? *BBC News*. http://www.bbc.co.uk/news/technology-12049153 (2010, December 31). Accessed 31 Dec 2010

Westwood, D., Griffiths, M.D.: The role of structural characteristics in video-game play motivation: A Q-methodology study. Cyberpsychol Behav. Soc. Networking **13**, 581–585 (2010)

Wilson, K.A., Bedwell, W.L., Lazzara, E.H., Salas, E., Burke, C.S., Estock, J.L., Orvis, K.L., Conkey, C.: Relationships between game attributes and learning outcomes: Review and research proposals. Simul. Gaming **40**, 217–266 (2008)

Zynga, Inc.: About Zynga Inc. http://www.zynga.com/about/facts.php (2011). Accessed 1 Mar 2011

Chapter 21
Experiences of Promoting Student Engagement Through Game-Enhanced Learning

Therese Charles, David Bustard, and Michaela Black

21.1 Introduction

The teaching experiences described here started with the simple vision of students learning with a level of engagement similar to that of playing digital games. The vision seemed plausible because the inherent rule-bound structure of digital games is essentially a learning process, encouraging players to take on challenges that build up skills and knowledge as they pursue specific goals (Prensky, 2002; Koster, 2004; Gee, 2007; Oblinger, 2008).

In education, engagement is essentially the measure of a student's participation in a learning task. Skinner and Belmont (1993) suggest that those engaged '. . .show sustained behavioural involvement in learning activities accompanied by a positive emotional tone. They select tasks at the border of their competencies, initiate action when given the opportunity, and exert intense effort and concentration in the implementation of learning tasks; they show generally positive emotions during ongoing action, including enthusiasm, optimism, curiosity, and interest.' Studies have consistently highlighted the important relationship between engagement and learning, with students who are highly motivated being more likely to engage in the learning process (Malone and Lepper, 1987; Wishart, 1990; Prensky, 2007; Garris et al., 2002; Greenagel, 2002; Zepke and Leach, 2010).

Games encourage engagement in various ways. For example, the level of game challenge at any point is subtly matched to the player's current ability level so that each challenge is just within their competence to avoid negative feelings from frustration and failure. Also, providing meaningful and timely feedback on performance and progress encourages involvement. The possible link between engagement in games and engagement in education has led, in recent years, to a significant growth of interest in *serious games* (Prensky, 2002; Michael and Chen, 2005; Kelly et al., 2007; Ulicsak and Wright, 2010; Sheldon, 2011), a term used here for any game with an educational purpose.

D. Bustard (✉)
University of Ulster, Coleraine BT52 1SA, UK
e-mail: dw.bustard@ulster.ac.uk

M. Ma et al. (eds.), *Serious Games and Edutainment Applications*,
DOI 10.1007/978-1-4471-2161-9_21, © Springer-Verlag London Limited 2011

One approach to using games techniques in teaching is to create what is effectively an educational game. That is, the student is presented with what seems like a game but which when played has an educational benefit, as a side effect. In practice, this usually means tailoring educational material to whatever game frameworks are available (Mitchell and Savill-Smith, 2004). Another approach, however, is to wrap a game framework around existing teaching material. This has the significant advantage of being usable for any content, in any context. In effect, it means making a game of the teaching process rather than the teaching content. This is the basis of GEL, the Game-Enhanced Learning framework presented here.[1] The approach is an example of what is now known as *gamification*, meaning the use of game-play mechanics in non-game applications (Gamification Encyclopedia, 2011; Lee and Hammer, 2011).

Our first step was to identify the factors in games that promote player engagement. These then had to be brought into a teaching and learning environment in a way that produced a net increase in student achievement. The first section of this chapter explains how the games factors contributing to engagement were identified. The design of GEL and its use in the teaching of first-year programming in Java is then presented. This includes a consideration of the game rules and the use of challenges and rewards to encourage student participation. A final section discusses the lessons learned from this experience, including a consideration of the factors that can influence the level of success achievable with the GEL approach. Practical implementation requirements, benefits and problems encountered by the lecturer concerned are also considered, and the overall cost-benefit assessed. The chapter concludes with an outline of future development plans.

21.2 Game-Enhanced Learning Framework

Student engagement can promote deep and meaningful learning (Quinn, 2005), thereby improving overall academic performance and helping validate a student's beliefs and expectations about their academic ability (Skinner et al., 1998). Engagement with academic activities is a reliable predictor of a student's long term academic achievement, and their immediate chances of successfully completing their chosen course of study (Connell et al., 1994; Zepke and Leach, 2010). Engagement can also be a measure of social involvement, with engaged students spending more time interacting with peers and teachers (Eccles et al., 1998). Additional indicators include intrinsically motivating factors, such as pleasure in work and the willingness to exert effort (Steinberg et al., 1989), and a preference for challenge, mastery, interest and feedback (Harter, 1978; Harter and Connell, 1984; Ginsburg and Bronstein, 1993; O'Brien and Toms, 2008).

Games are intended to provide an experience that intrinsically motivates players to progress in the absence of extrinsic rewards (Malone and Lepper, 1987; Bisson

[1] GEL previously had the mnemonic GOLF: game-oriented learning framework

and Luckner, 1996; Koster, 2004). This can mean that players spend many hours mastering a game that is often difficult, complex and long (Prensky). The motivational qualities of games have led many to argue that games have the potential to engage students and ultimately enhance the way in which they learn (Prensky, 2002; Koster, 2004; Squire and Jenkins, 2004; Shaffer et al., 2005; Oblinger, 2008).

Although their work did not specifically focus on game design, two of the most significant studies relevant to motivation in games are Malone and Lepper's intrinsic motivation taxonomy (1987) and Csikszentmihalyi's flow framework (1991). Malone and Lepper defined intrinsic motivation (player engagement) as having seven individual and interpersonal elements: *challenge, curiosity, fantasy, control, recognition, competition* and *cooperation*. Csikszentmihalyi (1991) considered flow as an experience 'so gratifying that people are willing to do it for its own sake, with little concern for what they will get out of it, even when it is difficult or dangerous'. His framework was adapted for digital games by Sweetser and Wyeth (2005), creating the *GameFlow* model, which identified eight key aspects of player engagement: *control, concentration, challenge, clear goals, feedback, immersion, mechanics* (player skills) and *social interaction* (socialization).

Other authors have developed similar lists and in doing so often tried to base their proposal on an analysis of earlier work. For example, Garris et al. (2002) proposed six broad dimensions of *fantasy, rules/goals, sensory stimuli, challenge, mystery* and *control* in categorizing the earlier published literature. Subsequently, Yee (2006) added *advancement, discovery, relationships, customization* and *escapism* to the growing list of motivational factors.

Most recently, a review by Bostan (2009), of the work of Malone and Lepper (1987), Sweetser and Wyeth (2005) and Yee (2006), noted a lack of consensus on naming, and the complexity resulting from a proliferation of terms, many of which had similar or overlapping meanings. Figure 21.1, for example, illustrates apparent differences in terms cited in the three studies analyzed by Bostan.

Looking across the recent literature, a substantial number of motivational factors can be identified. Forty are listed in Table 21.1. The strategy used to identify a workable set of motivational qualities for use in teaching was to first select those qualities that seemed directly relevant. This reduced the forty characteristics in Table 21.1 to eighteen. These were then grouped to produce six key student engagement factors as identified in Fig. 21.2.

The first and arguably the most important factor is *fun*. Research suggests there is a strong connection between fun and learning (Bisson and Luckner) but it is not routinely identified as an essential educational requirement.

The second factor is *structure*, which covers the provision of clear rules, achievable goals and opportunities for choice and control. *Challenge* and *feedback* are identified as the two main sub-components of structure. The pleasant frustration experienced by game players as they attempt to complete challenges produces a level of engagement that can hold their attention until the task is accomplished. To maintain this level of engagement, however, appropriate and timely feedback is needed to ensure success. Without feedback, relevant to progress and performance levels, the player loses focus and engagement gradually diminishes.

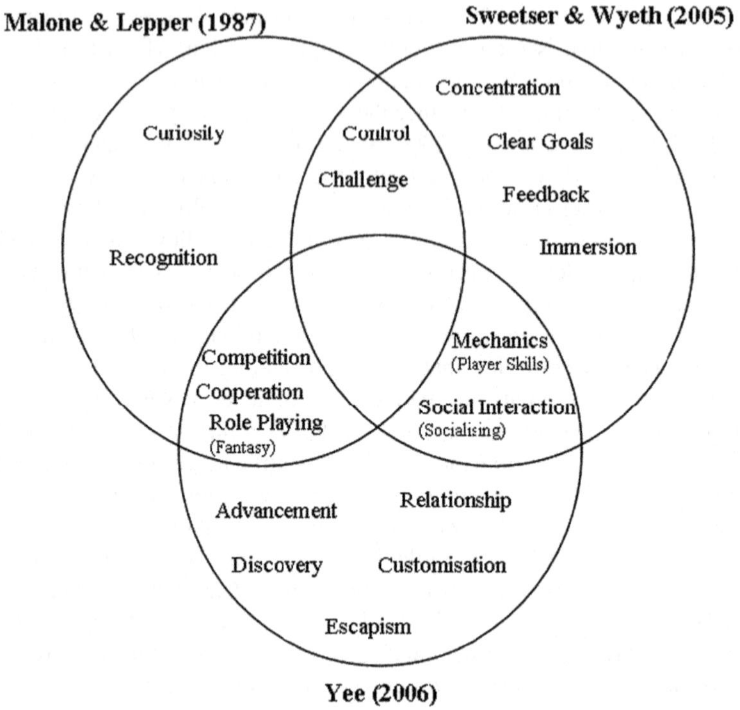

Fig. 21.1 Bostan's comparison of three motivational studies (2009)

Table 21.1 Collection of motivational factors associated with digital games

Advancement	Context	Fun	Recognition
Autonomy	Control	Goals	Relatedness
Challenge	Cooperation	Identity	Relationships
Chance	Curiosity	Immersion	Risk
Choice	Customization	Interaction	Role playing
Collaboration	Discovery	Learning without consequence	Rules
Competency	Dynamic visuals	Mechanics	Sensory stimuli
Competition	Escapism	Mystery	Social interaction
Complexity	Fantasy	Player skills	Strategy
Concentration	Feedback	Presence	Team Work

The final two factors are *social* and *identity*, which although not main factors in gameplay, are important within education and so are included here. The various qualities encompassed by the social factor include team work, cooperation and relationship development. The importance of collaborative learning is well known (Dillenbourg et al., 1996; Dillenbourg, 1999). Also, a visible identity in a learning group can trigger and enhance the benefit of feedback on performance and progression.

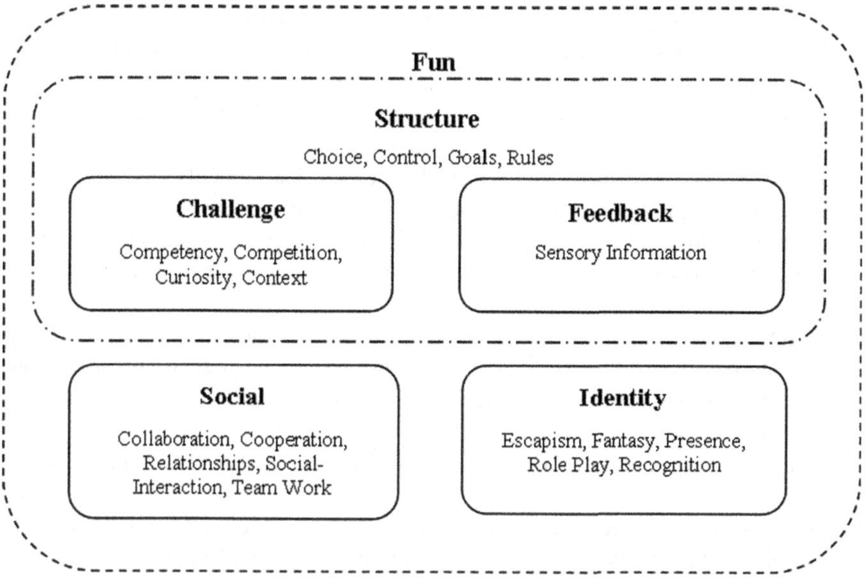

Fig. 21.2 Key student engagement factors

These factors are the basis of GEL, the game-enhanced learning framework. They can be taken into account in both the creation of teaching materials and in their delivery. The current focus of GEL is on delivery, where it is assumed that a game (or games) will be developed around an existing presentation of teaching material in a course. The approach is generic in that it is aimed at a wide variety of teaching situations. More specifically, this means that it is intended to be largely independent of the type of material studied, the level of study involved, and the duration of that study.

The basic game concept is to make students compete for points awarded for desirable behavior in a way that had a positive educational benefit, without any negative side-effects. The framework can be described in terms of the assumptions and requirements associated with each of its six elements, as follows:

1. FUN: As a game, it is assumed that the results are not linked to formal assessment of the course. The game is essentially an additional activity that students undertake voluntarily. It should be fun but it should also have an educational benefit. In addition, it should have no negative impact on the course itself, or on any other course being studied at the same time.
2. SOCIAL: Students are encouraged to collaborate with fellow students to complete challenges. This cooperation helps provide a supportive environment in which students with mixed ability can all enjoy the game. It also implies that it is beneficial to make the game a group activity where that is practical.
3. IDENTITY: A key assumption is that there is technology support for each game developed. This support will maintain details of the game, including the names of

those who are playing and their performance to date. This gives each student and their group (if present) a unique identity. Further, it is assumed that this identity is reinforced by displaying performance publicly.
4. CHALLENGE: To provide a challenge, the game should include a selection of optional activities, with a suitable breadth of difficulty.
5. STRUCTURE: The basic game model assumes that students can earn game points by completing activities, some of which are considered 'core' and others that are 'optional'. For example, points could be awarded for attendance at lectures, which is expected, and for participating in class, by answering questions, which is desirable but optional.
6. FEEDBACK: To maintain enthusiasm, it is assumed that the time gap between students earning game points and seeing the impact on their performance (as individuals or in groups) should be as short as possible.

There are four stages in designing and running a game based on this framework:

1. *Understand the Context*: This means identifying requirements and constraints relevant to the design of the game. In particular, there will be operational constraints on when material is taught, when assessment is performed, and the availability of resources. An awareness of operational constraints helps identify when activities need to be performed to ensure appropriate and timely feedback. Also, a set of core and optional tasks need to be extracted from the existing way that the material is taught and the associated learning outcomes. For example, attendance is likely to be core, and there may be a core range of assessment methods, class and home exercises, tests and formal examinations associated with the course. The level of achievement in meeting learning outcomes is optional. Learning outcomes cover the knowledge and skills that are to be developed, including an understanding of the subject, general intellectual qualities, specific practical skills and general transferrable skills.
2. *Define the Challenge*: Once the context is understood the game can be developed. This creates a set of challenges that emphasize social and collaborative learning. These challenges should be designed hierarchically, using small challenges to build up the skills and abilities required to achieve more demanding tasks later in the course. The tasks should be achievable but with a level of difficulty that ensures a sense of achievement on completion. These challenges should be directly related to the core and optional tasks associated with the course. Once the challenges are known, a reward system is developed. This determines the points to be earned for each task and how positive feedback is to be implemented. Points should be weighted according to the perceived importance and difficulty of each challenge. To maintain a positive feel to the game, points can only be earned and never deducted.
3. *Initiate the Game*: The game starts by establishing identities for the participating students. These may be individual and/or group identities. Such identities are necessary to present the performance of individuals and groups but also promote student engagement.

4. *Run the Game*: The game then runs, with points accumulated for each activity completed successfully. Feedback can take a number of forms, including online graphical summaries, publicly displayed leaderboards and the awarding of achievement prizes.

21.3 Experimental Case Studies

The GEL framework has been developed and evaluated by applying it experimentally to a number of undergraduate modules at the University of Ulster. This section describes that experimental work with respect to the teaching of first year programming.

21.3.1 Case Study 1

The first experimental use of GOLF was in the first semester of the academic year 2007/08. It was applied to Software Development I (COM158C1), a module taken by all first-year computing students. The module was taught by one lecturer supported by postgraduate teaching assistants (demonstrators). All teaching was through lectures with additional resources and information available via WebCT® Vista. Assessment was through regular coursework and an examination.

The first stage in developing the game was to identify the structural elements of module COM158C1 in terms of operational constraints, core tasks and optional tasks, as summarized in Table 21.2.

Next, a set of challenges was created. Points were weighted according to their perceived level of importance. Table 21.3 shows these points for the module in the academic year 2007–2008.

For example, 'outstanding work' was acknowledged by the lecturer by displaying it publicly for others to follow and awarding game points. Note that Table 21.3 shows that there were two parts to the game, with some of the challenges changing after Week 6.

Table 21.2 Structural elements of COM158C1

Operational constraints	Core tasks	Optional tasks
12 week semester. Teaching week has two 1 h lectures, a 1 h tutorial and a 2 h laboratory session.	Attendance Personal development plan (PDP) exercises Lab exercises Class test Tutorial quiz Group assignment Final examination	Class presentations Outstanding work Revision quizzes Contribution to tutorials

Table 21.3 COM158C1 points allocation

Week	Attendance	Input to tutorials	Outstanding work	PDP & reflection	Lab task	Tutorial quiz	Class test	Design document	Revision quizzes	Class presentation
	COM158C1 Challenges									
1	40	10	10	10	5	5				
2	40	10	10	10	5	5				
3	40	10	10	10	5	5				
4	40	10	10	10	5	5				
5	40	10	10	10	5	5				
6							30			
7	40	10								
8	40	10								
9	40	10								
10	40	10						40	210	10
11	40	10								
12										
Total (940)	400	100	50	50	25	25	30	40	210	10

At the beginning of the game, its rules were explained to the students and ethical consent forms completed. The lecturer also divided the class into teams of 6–8 students, with each team choosing its own unique name. The names were then used in displaying performance, as illustrated in Fig. 21.3.

During the game, the points achieved by team members were added to cumulative totals and made available through WebCT. The team performance charts were also presented on a plasma screen in a public area and discussed during a weekly tutorial class. The charts provided teams with a summary of their overall performance in relation to other teams and a breakdown of where points were earned. Most of the challenges encouraged the teams to work collaboratively. For example, to maximize the points earned teams needed to encourage their members to attend classes and to share answers to questions in tutorials. At the end of the first part of the game (Week 6), small prizes were awarded to encourage further participation. All groups were recognized for at least one achievement.

A tool was developed to accumulate and present performance based on Google Spreadsheets (part of the Google Docs Suite of online applications). The spreadsheets were accessed using the Google web interface. Using the Google Docs publishing facility, the URL of the charts was linked to WebCT and the chart updated dynamically from within WebCT when new game data was added.

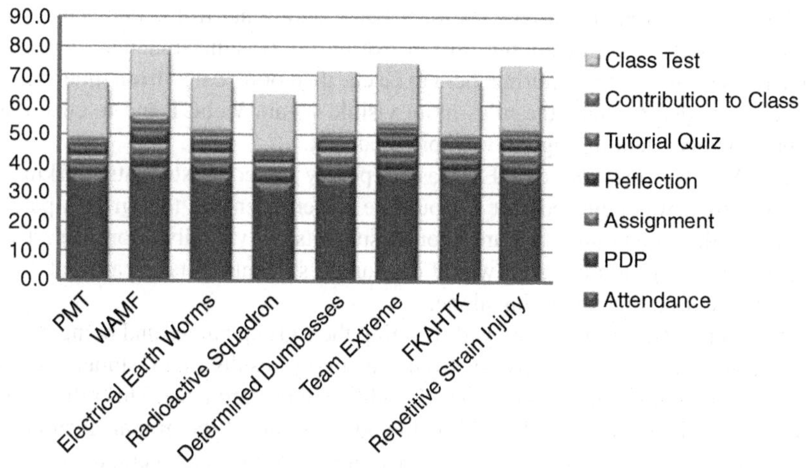

Fig. 21.3 Case study 1 (Weeks 1–6) leaderboard

21.3.1.1 Case Study 1 Evaluation

The effect of the game was assessed in several different ways. The key performance indicator was student performance in the final examination. Encouragingly, the improvement was more substantial than expected, with the pass rate rising from 82 to 95% and the game having no apparent detrimental effect on other modules. Figure 21.4 shows the distribution of marks across the class from one year to the next. The effect of the game had been to tighten the distribution of marks and avoid the long tail of weak performance.

In relation to the student engagement factors, the main points to note were:

1. FUN: In a survey conducted at the end of the game, 88% of 40 participants agreed or strongly agreed that they enjoyed the game and felt their work improved as a result; only one person disagreed, with the others giving a neutral answer. The game, however, was slower to take off than originally anticipated.

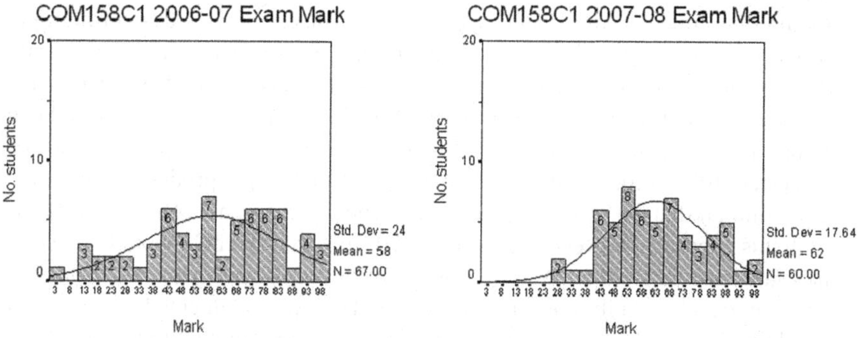

Fig. 21.4 COM158C1 exam marks

This seemed to be a consequence of it being additional to the demands of the module itself. One indication of the lack of uptake was the students 'forgetting' the rules of the game, requiring them to be clarified or repeated from time to time. It was decided to make the rules more visible within WebCT and to encourage better involvement through more rapid feedback.

2. SOCIAL: The first use of GEL was purposely aimed at students working in groups as it was believed that it would be easier to ensure that groups participated in the game rather than monitor all students individually. Moreover, it was expected that group pressure would encourage students to take part that might otherwise drop out if working alone.
3. IDENTITY: The students enjoyed selecting their group names and being closely associated with their groups but from the survey results many students (70%) wanted some form of feedback on their individual performance. This information was certainly available and could be included as part of the graphical summary presented through WebCT. It was decided, however, that such personal information would be unsuitable for public display as it may have a significant negative impact on those who were not performing well.
4. CHALLENGE: The survey results also revealed that over half of the participants would have liked more opportunities to earn points. The difficulty here is that each challenge requires additional resources to gather and enter the associated data. This could delay feedback even further and so have an adverse effect on the game overall. In general, there is a difficult balance to be found between having sufficient challenges to stimulate the students and keeping the administrative costs at an acceptable level.
5. STRUCTURE: In this first experimental use of GEL the structure was adjusted dynamically in an attempt to ensure active student participation. In practice, that meant introducing additional challenges across the semester. Table 21.3 summarizes the final position.
6. FEEDBACK: In general, if there was any significant delay between obtaining points and having them entered, possibly because of other commitments among those administering the game, the students became dissatisfied, reducing the effectiveness of the game. However, gathering and entering data was time-consuming. Automation was desirable and attempts were made to extract data directly from WebCT. Unfortunately the format of the data that emerged required significant adjustment, and a manual check, before it could be input to Google Docs, so it was never used. Instead, data was entered directly into the Google spreadsheets. There was some inherent delay if points were awarded for activities that had to be assessed. This made it important to meet scheduled return dates for coursework—a target that became more difficult to achieve as the semester progressed. The display system, based on Google products, was a low-cost solution that was quick to implement. There were some technical problems with this approach, however. In particular the link from WebCT would occasionally fail, especially when WebCT was in heavy use. It was therefore decided to develop a custom-built tool for performance display, implemented in a way that would make it relatively easy to transfer from one environment to another. With such a tool, the level and form of feedback could be tailored as required.

21.3.2 Case Study 2

The second case study followed immediately after the first, in Semester 2 of the academic year 2007/08. The module was Software Development II, COM164C2, taken by the same cohort of students and presented by the same lecturer, with the same postgraduate demonstrators. Table 21.4 shows that the structural elements were very similar to the first case study, but with some variations to the core and optional tasks. The total number of challenges increased from 10 to 12 and the allocation of points was adjusted to give the same total. As in the first semester there were two parts to the game, with different challenges available in the second half of the semester. In particular, the number of points awarded for attending classes each week was dropped from 40 to 10 to free up points for the additional activities and so effectively award more for tasks that were more difficult to achieve. Although some of these challenges still had a strong emphasis on teamwork and collaboration, points were also awarded for individual effort. As an experiment, it was decided to stop showing group performance and have nothing displayed publicly.

An improved tool was developed for this game. It displayed an individual's performance using a personalized set of web-based gauges and graphs. Figure 21.5 shows the interface presented by the tool.

At the top of the screen is a gauge (1) indicating a student's current satisfaction with the display tool, introduced to help assess student views throughout the game. Below that is a button (2), which when clicked gives that person's rank within the class. Below that again is a gauge (3) displaying the overall game points achieved, with two additional indicators noting the lowest and highest points obtained by fellow students. At the bottom of the screen is a graph (4) identifying the 12 available challenges and the points earned so far for each one. Up to the top right is a gauge (5) displaying percentage attendance in class, with a lower graph (6) indicating attendance week-by-week.

Access to the web-based tool required a unique username and password. On entry, the feedback provided was unique to that student with no access to anyone else's performance. The tool was developed using an ASP.NET front-end connected to an SQL database back-end. The dashboard displayed was constructed using FusionWidgets software.

Table 21.4 Structural elements of COM164C2

Operational constraints	Core tasks	Optional tasks
12 week semester	Attendance	Class presentations
Teaching each week has two 1 h lectures, a 1 h tutorial and a 2 h laboratory session.	Personal development plan (PDP) exercises	High quality performance
	Lab exercises	Revision quizzes
	Class test	Team work
	2 x Mini assignments	Contribution to tutorials
	Group assignment	Contribution to lectures
	Final examination	Completion of a CV

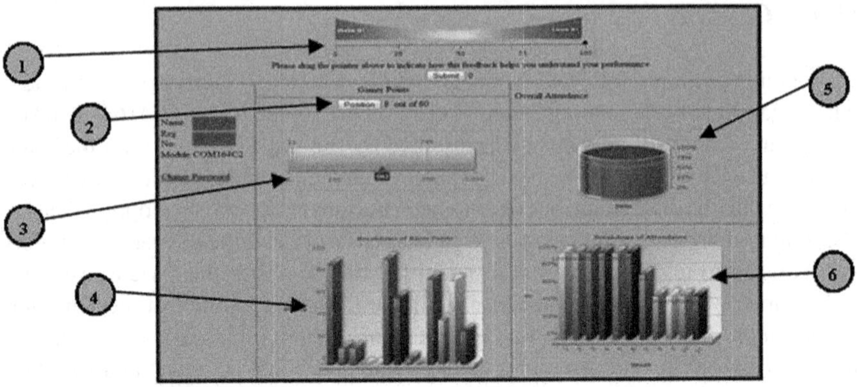

Fig. 21.5 COM158C1 exam marks

21.3.2.1 Case Study 2 Evaluation

As in Case Study 1, the key performance indicator was student performance in the final examination. Comparing the 2007–2008 class with the equivalent cohort in 2006–2007 again showed significant improvements. Attendance was up by 4% and examination performance had also improved significantly as shown in Fig. 21.6.

In this traditionally demanding module, initial failure rates of the order of 25% had been common over many years but dropped to less than 10% in 2007–2008. As in the first semester, there was a clear improvement in performance at the lower end of the class but there was also improvement in general, suggesting that the game approach was bringing benefits to those with a range of abilities. Most significantly, Fig. 21.6 shows a smooth distribution of marks for 2007–2008, whereas the 2006–2007 results suggested that a group at the bottom end had largely given up.

In relation to the six student engagement factors:

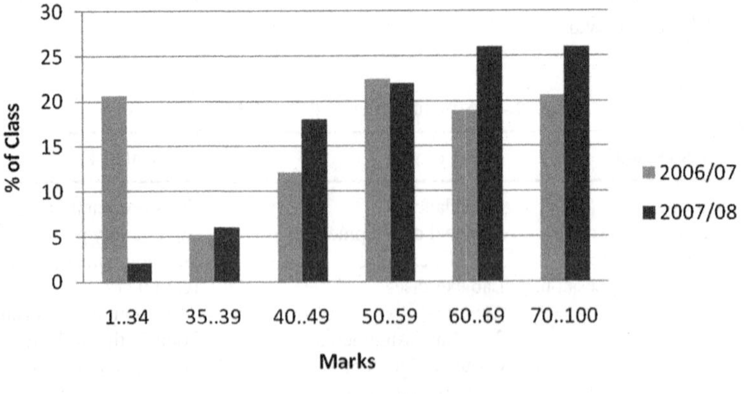

Fig. 21.6 COM158C1 exam marks

1. FUN: As in the first semester, the game was slow to take off, with the students finding it difficult to remember the rules. This was surprising as the game structure was essentially the same and the rules were now more visible. It might be that the students were giving more priority to understanding the main requirements of the module before turning to the game or there was less pressure because of the removal of the group game. The net effect, however, was that the lecturer had to again encourage involvement over the first few weeks. In the survey, 82% agreed or strongly agreed that the game helped them engage with the module.
2. SOCIAL: The individual game produced a significant improvement in performance but the students still preferred the group structure used in the first semester. Overall, most students (89%) indicated a preference for a group game, so it was decided that it should be the main focus. In detail, students felt more encouraged by the group game than the individual game to gain higher marks (85 versus 64%) and study additional material (75 versus 41%). They also felt that their work had improved to a greater extent through the group game (88 versus 53%) and that it was more effective at encouraging interaction in face-to-face sessions (60 versus 41%).
3. IDENTITY: Students could only observe their own performance in this game. They declined an offer to have individual identities assigned.
4. CHALLENGE: The additions and changes to the challenges, with the resulting readjustment of points, increased overall student satisfaction with the game. The uptake of these additional challenges was relatively slow, however, with many students delaying participation in the development of a CV and completion of revision quizzes until late in the game.
5. STRUCTURE: Both the performance results and the evaluative questionnaire results indicated that the game was well received by the participating students, with many commenting that personalized feedback helped identify their strengths and weaknesses. Also the visibility of class position helped build the confidence of some students, who could now see that they were 'keeping up' with their peers.
6. FEEDBACK: Gathering and entering data continued to be demanding, delaying feedback on occasions. This was made worse by the students accelerating their efforts towards the end of the semester at a time when coursework marking was at its peak. The performance display tool was reasonably effective, receiving an overall satisfaction rating of 82%. For future use it would be modified to include the display of group performance. Space was created by reducing the information on attendance, which had been over-emphasized.

21.3.3 Further Experimental Studies

The overall conclusion from the first two case studies was that the game-oriented learning framework was indeed helping to improve student engagement, resulting in improved performance, with no apparent negative side-effects. The evaluative questionnaires also indicated that the students found the games enjoyable, encouraging and motivating. As a result, it was decided to continue with the game across both modules from then on. The main points to note about the game since then were:

- The first named author led the first-year experiment but was also one of the postgraduate demonstrators supporting the teaching process. There was therefore a risk that this dual role could have contributed to the successful outcome. As a result, she withdrew from involvement in demonstrating in subsequent years to reduce the possibility of bias. In practice, the results were unaffected, with the influence of the lecturer appearing to be much more significant.
- There was initial concern that the improved results in 2007–2008 might also be explained by having a more able set of students that year. In running the experiment several times since then, however, each year has shown the same level of improvement.
- TurningPoint© interactive response systems were introduced in 2008–2009. It was hoped that they could be used to monitor attendance and to track students answering questions in class. In practice, however, the underlying software had limited administrative features for the extraction of data, so it could not be sent directly to the game display system. One benefit, however, was that the students enjoyed the interactivity provided by TurningPoint. Its main impact therefore was to increase class engagement and give all students an equal opportunity to contribute to class discussions. TurningPoint also helped encourage a sense of competition among groups as it was possible to provide instant feedback on responses.
- The game display system was redesigned in 2008–2009 to include group performance, with the revised interface shown in Fig. 21.7. The screenshot shows an angular gauge (1) that displays a team's overall game points. Below that, linear gauges indicate the total points achieved for attendance (2), tutorial exercises (3), contribution to tutorial discussions (4), assignment marks (6) (this was a cumulative score containing points earned through PDP exercises, lab tasks and a class test), contribution to lectures (7), and revision quiz completion (8). There was also a drop-down section at the bottom of the screen to report on significant achievements in specific areas. These were displayed as 'badges' for:

  Attendance: awarded when the average weekly attendance of a team was greater than 70%

  Outstanding Work: awarded to the team if a team member received outstanding work in any of the five weekly lab tasks. No points were awarded for this achievement.

  Contribution to Lecture: awarded to the team if a team member contributed to a lecture or tutorial

  Presentation: awarded to a team if it successfully completed a presentation

  CV: awarded to a team when all members have completed a CV

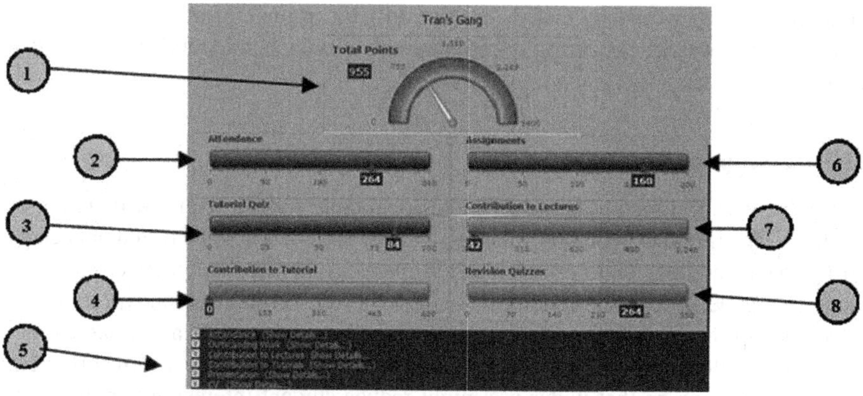

Fig. 21.7 2008–2009 game display

- At the beginning of the academic year 2010–2011 funding was obtained to support the development of a generic tool to facilitate the portability of the GEL approach. This was evaluated experimentally in the second semester of the year and is expected to be released for general use in August 2011 (Bustard et al., 2011).

21.3.4 Lessons Learned

This section summarizes the overall lessons learned from using the GEL framework, highlighting the factors that can affect the success or otherwise of the approach proposed.

21.3.4.1 Overall Benefit

The use of the GEL framework in the delivery of first year programming modules has brought a number of substantial benefits. In particular, the students now enjoy taking these modules to a greater extent, have attended more regularly, have engaged more fully and, most importantly, have completed successfully in greater numbers. Modules that were once considered 'difficult' are now producing results that suggest they are more 'straightforward'. As indicated, the students that seem to have benefitted most are those at the weaker end of the class. In principle, stronger students could well resent the game as they are effectively pressured into helping weaker colleagues. From the survey, however, in which students were happy to identify themselves, those at the top end of the class reported enjoying the game as much as anyone else. The ones who enjoyed the game least seemed to be those who had general problems with group work and in interacting with their peers. No one, however, withdrew from the game, which was allowed at any time. The lecturer and support demonstrators also benefitted from teaching a more engaged set of students who were enthusiastic in class and who actively took on tasks that promoted their skills in areas that they would normally consider difficult or uncomfortable. One significant example was in answering questions in class, which students had previously avoided.

21.3.4.2 Scope of the Game

The game was designed to be generic and so suitable for use with a wide range of modules. The initial expectation was that, if successful, it would be rolled out across all first year modules and possibly carried into second year. In practice, however, using the game in just one module in each semester has had the unexpected side effect of improving student performance across all modules taken at the same time. There is therefore no apparent advantage in extending the game within first year and indeed a concern that wider use might reduce student interest and enthusiasm overall.

21.3.4.3 Role of the Teacher

Each time the game has been run, it has been slow to start. This implies that the teacher has to promote the game enthusiastically until the students take over. In effect, as in many games, the teacher is essentially the Dungeon Master—the organizer responsible for creating the details and challenges of the game, controlling all aspects of play, except for the actions of the player characters. Implementing GEL successfully, therefore, relies on the motivation and enthusiasm of the teacher responsible. This means reminding the class about the existence of the game, its rules (opportunities for earning points), and discussing performance.

21.3.4.4 Operational Effort

The teacher implementing GEL also has to identify the challenges initially, determine how the points are to be collected and ensure that they are entered into the display system promptly and accurately. Ideally, the game should be integrated fully within an existing virtual learning environment (VLE) so that there is an acceptable level of effort in gathering game data. So, for example, recording coursework marks in the VLE would make them available to the students but also update the game display system at the same time. Similarly, in class, the use of TurningPoint or some similar interaction device should record attendance in the VLE and add appropriate points to the game system. In practice, while such integration has been attempted there remain technical problems that give the lecturer additional work in ensuring that all points are recorded as required.

21.3.4.5 Initiating and Sustaining Student Enthusiasm

As indicated, the teacher needs to be enthusiastic about the game, and this will help energize the students. A reliable implementation of the game is also important so that there are no disputes about the points scored and no unnecessary delay in the points being recorded. Feedback, in particular, is crucial in maintaining the students' enthusiasm for the game and encouraging them to look for opportunities for additional points. Computerized games, in general, have led players to expect immediate feedback. This is then a problem, however, for a game that extends over many weeks. Sustaining interest over that period is inherently difficult but further refinement of the timing of the game and its individual challenges has been ongoing and produced improvements. Other factors include:

- Increasing the visibility of the rules has been beneficial
- The game has become more established and many students are now aware of it; some before they join the University
- The public display of photographs of previous winners has further improved the visibility and reputation of the game
- The demonstrators have taken a more involved role and encourage the teams to participate in challenges
- The lecturer has become more skilled in managing the game

21.3.4.6 Tool Support

Tool support is also an important factor in the success of the game. As indicated, this should ultimately be integrated within the Virtual Learning Environment (VLE) of the students. The experimental work within the study produced a series of prototypes that revealed limitations with the current technology available but helped identify the type of facilities and information required to support the game effectively. The game structure is relatively simple, however, so it is possible to run the game with simple spreadsheets and paper summaries of team performances.

As indicated, a generic game support tool has been produced and will shortly be released for general use. It makes no assumptions about the availability of a VLE but does allow for bulk upload of data in CSV format. To generalize the display of performance a separate gauge is used for each challenge and the leaderboard is now a simple ordered list of individuals or groups. It is expected that this tool will continue to be refined through experience gained from its use. Its immediate effect, however, has been to reduce the administrative overhead associated with managing the game significantly and made it possible to introduce spontaneous challenges that have added interest to the game (Bustard et al., 2011).

21.3.4.7 Student Engagement

The research performed so far has convinced the authors that the six engagement factors identified can indeed be brought into teaching and learning to achieve a beneficial effect. In summary:

1. FUN: engagement is easier if the experience is enjoyable. Koster (2004) argues that 'fun is just another word for learning', implying that effective learning is inherently enjoyable. Certainly 'fun' improves engagement but surprisingly isn't

given as much attention in the educational literature as might be expected, perhaps because it can be difficult to align with the basic outcome-driven demands of a typical learning process. The programming case studies examined here were 'fun' and that has been beneficial.

2. SOCIAL: engagement is reinforced by the social support of others going through the same experience. When players interact within a game environment there is social interaction though competition or when the players share their experiences (Salen and Zimmerman, 2003). Educationally, it is recognized that such social interaction is important in any learning process and so ideally should be facilitated explicitly. Having students work in groups isn't essential in the GEL framework but it is what the students strongly prefer, as indicated through the surveys, and certainly benefits weaker students in the class.
3. IDENTITY: engagement can be encouraged if everyone has a visible role in the learning environment. In games, a player usually has a visual representation of themselves within a game system. Gee (2007) suggests that this identity deepens personal investment in the game and encourages players to interact and engage to a greater extent through the projected character. Usually, there is no equivalent explicit mechanism in education, but identities do develop, particularly if group work is involved (e.g., group identity and team leader). This aspect of engagement seems to have been least influential in the experimental worked performed so far. The students enjoy dreaming up team names but in first year seem happier being part of a group than operating individually, and are more effective overall when working in a team.
4. CHALLENGE: engagement can build on human competitive drive, enhanced by social pressure. In practice, 'challenge' means rising to meet demanding but achievable goals. Challenge (or conflict) is an intrinsic element in game systems but isn't always emphasized in education, perhaps because it can be seen as demotivating for students with low expectations. In practice, this has been the most important element of the framework in terms of encouraging personal development among students. Each student, no matter what their current level, has some additional challenge to consider, urged on by peer pressure.
5. STRUCTURE: engagement is more likely if objectives and constraints are clear and acceptable. The rule-bound, goal-oriented structure of games contributes to an engaging experience. So, in education, objectives, required levels of achievement, and rules of acceptable behavior need to be explicit and appropriate. This has helped clarify what individual modules are seeking to achieve and make that information explicit to students. This is much better understood than any bland documented list of learning outcomes.
6. FEEDBACK: engagement is reinforced by making achievement explicit. Feedback in games is important in providing players with timely and relevant information on their progress towards goals and identifying their level of achievement so far. Progress within the game will often be summarized in a map, and achievement indicated though ongoing game statistics, measuring attributes such as player skill, strength and health. Equivalent information is provided in education but tends to be less detailed at university level. The game has helped

bring that information to the surface and its timely return is crucial to GEL's success. Tool support is essential in practice and the wider use of GEL requires a highly parameterized tool that can be tailored to a wide range of different teaching situations. As indicated, the first version of that tool will be released in August 2011.

21.4 Conclusions

This chapter has described a generic game-enhanced learning framework (GEL) intended to improve student engagement and so enhance the process of teaching a wide variety of subject material. The approach was illustrated through discussion of its experimental use in first-year undergraduate programming modules from 2007 to 2008. The results have exceeded expectations in terms of student performance and we are currently encouraging others to experiment with the approach.

A possible first step is to try and take account of the engagement factors in delivering course material. Addressing these factors alone, without using an explicit game can still be beneficial. In summary the factors are:

1. *Fun*: the extent to which learning is an enjoyable experience; engagement is easier if learning is enjoyable.
2. *Social*: the level of social support provided by others going through the same learning experience; colleagues encourage engagement by providing reminders about goals and deadlines, and in giving support during the pursuit of associated learning tasks.
3. *Identity*: the visibility of a student in the learning environment; greater visibility of students in a learning environment and a clear explanation of their role can encourage their engagement.
4. *Challenge*: the level of difficulty associated with a learning task; engagement can build on human competitive drive, enhanced by social pressure.
5. *Structure*: the rules defining a particular learning task; engagement is more likely if objectives and constraints are clear and acceptable.
6. *Feedback*: information on how well a student is progressing through a learning task; engagement is encouraged by making achievement explicit.

For those wishing to try the game, it can be run using the ideas outlined in this chapter, with game data managed through a spreadsheet. This is practical for small classes but for larger numbers the generic GEL tool is recommended. At the time of writing this is scheduled for release in August 2011. Those interested can find details on the associated GEL website or contact the authors directly for details. Further information can also be found in (Bustard et al., 2011; Charles et al., 2009a, b; Charles, 2010).

Research is continuing as there are remaining questions that need to be answered in trying to fully understand the strengths, weaknesses and limitations of the approach. These include the impact of the size of the class, the type of material taught, the link between the game and the formal assessment of a course, and how best to deal with the few remaining students who do not engage. It is likely that this research will draw on the experiences of those now active in the rapidly expanding field of serious games (Prensky, 2007; Michael and Chen, 2005; Kelly et al., 2007; Ulicsak and Wright, 2010; Sheldon, 2011), especially closely related emerging approaches. One example is the work of Sheldon (2011), which has reported similar improved class performance though is different in integrating the game with formal assessment of the course.

In the meantime, the use of the GEL approach is now an established part of teaching programming at the University of Ulster and will continue to provide an excellent test-bed for further experimental studies.

References

Bisson, C., Luckner, J.: Fun in learning: The pedagogical role of fun in adventure education. J. Exp. Educ. **19**(2), 108–112 (1996)

Bostan, B.: Player motivations: A psychological perspective. ACM Comput. Entertain. **7**, 2 (2009)

Bustard, D.W., Black, M.M., Charles, T., Moore, A.A., McKinney, M.E.T., Moffett, P.: GEL: A generic tool for game-enhanced learning. In: Proceedings of International Conference on Engineering Education, Belfast, UK, iNEER (2011)

Charles, D.K., Charles, T., McNeill, M.: Using player and world representation techniques from computer games to improve student engagement. In: Proceedings of 1st IEEE Conference in Games and Virtual Worlds for Serious Applications, Coventry, UK, 36–42 (2009a)

Charles, T., Bustard, D.W., Black, M.M.: Game inspired tool support for e-learning processes. Electron. J. e-Learn. **7**(2), 101–110 (2009b)

Charles, T.: ELEGANT: Enhanced e-learning engagement using game absorption techniques, PhD Thesis, University of Ulster (2010)

Connell, J.P., Spencer, M.B., Aber, J.L.: Educational risk and resilience in African-American youth: context, self, action, and outcomes in school. Child Dev. **65**, 493–506 (1994)

Csikszentmihalyi, M.: Flow, The Psychology of Optimal Experience. Harper Perennial, New York (1991)

Dillenbourg, P.: What do you mean by collaborative learning? In: Dillenbourg, P. (ed.) Collaborative-Learning: Cognitive and Computational Approaches, pp. 1–19. Elsevier, Oxford (1999)

Dillenbourg, P., Baker, M., Blaye, A., O'Malley, C.: The evolution of research on collaborative learning. In: Spada, E., Reiman, P. (eds.) Learning in Humans and Machine: Towards an Interdisciplinary Learning Science, pp. 189–211. Elsevier, Oxford (1996)

Eccles, J.S., Wigfield, A., Schiefele, U.: Motivation to succeed. In: Damon, W., Eisenberg, N. (eds.) Handbook of Child Psychology: Social, Emotional, and Personality Development, Vol. 3, pp. 863–932. Wiley, New York (1998)

Gamification Encyclopedia.: http://gamification.org/. Accessed 2 June 2011

Garris, R., Ahlers, R., Driskell, J.: Games, motivation, and learning: A research and practice model. Simulat. Gaming **33**(4), 441–467 (2002)

Gee, J.P.: Good Video Games and Good Learning: Collected Essays on Video Games. Peter Lang, New York (2007)

Ginsburg, G.S., Bronstein, P.: Family factors related to children's intrinsic/extrinsic motivational orientation and academic performance. Child Dev. **64**, 1461–1474 (1993)

Greenagel, F.: The illusion of e-learning: why we're missing out on the promise of technology. http://www.guidedlearning.com/illusions.pdf. Accessed 2 June 2011 (2002)

Harter, S.: Effectance motivation reconsidered: Toward a developmental model. Hum. Dev. **21**, 34–64 (1978)

Harter, S., Connell, J.P.: A model of the relationship among children's academic achievement and their self-perceptions of competence, control, and motivational orientation. In: Nichols, J. (ed.) The Development of Achievement Motivation, pp. 219–250. JAI, Greenwich, CT (1984)

Kelly, H., Howell, K., Glinert, E., Holding, L., Swain, C., Burrowbridge, A., Roper, M.: How to build serious games. Commun. ACM **50**(7), 44–49 (2007)

Koster, R.: Theory of Fun for Game Design. Paraglyph Inc, Frederick, MD (2004)

Lee, J.J., Hammer, J.: Gamification in education: What, how, why bother? Acad. Exch. Q. **15**(2), 1–5 (2011)

Malone, T.W., Lepper, M.R.: Making learning fun: a taxonomy of intrinsic motivations for learning. In: Snow, R.E., Farr, M.J. (eds.) Aptitude, Learning and Instruction: Cognitive and Affective Process Analysis, Vol. 3, pp. 223–253. Lawrence Erlbaum, Hillsdale, NJ (1987)

Michael, D., Chen, S.: Serious Games: Games That Educate, Train, and Inform. Course Technology Inc, Boston, MA (2005)

Mitchell, A., Savill-Smith, C.: The use of computer and video games for learning. Learning and Skills Development Agency. http://www.m-learning.org/knowledge-centre/research. Accessed 2 June 2011 (2004)

Oblinger, D.G.: Growing up with Google: What it means to education. Emerg. Technol. Learn. **3**, 11–29 (2008)

O'Brien, H.L., Toms, E.G.: What is user engagement? A conceptual framework for defining user engagement with technology. J. Am. Soc. Inf. Sci. Technol. **59**(6), 938–955 (2008)

Prensky, M.: The motivation of gameplay. On the Horiz. **10**(1), 5–11 (2002)

Prensky, M. Digital Game-Based Learning. Paragon House Publishers, St Paul, MN (2007)

Quinn, C.: Engaging Learning. Pfeiffer, San Francisco, CA (2005)

Salen, K., Zimmerman, E.: Rules of Play: Game Design Fundamentals. MIT Press, Cambridge, MA (2003)

Shaffer, D., Squire, K., Halverson, R., Gee, J.P.: Video games and the future of learning. Phi Delta Kappa **87**(2), 105–111 (2005)

Sheldon, L.: The Multiplayer Classroom: Designing Coursework as a Game. Course Technology PTR, Florence, KY (2011)

Skinner, E.A, Belmont, M.J.: Motivation in the classroom: Reciprocal effects of teacher behavior and student engagement across the school year. J. Educ. Psychol. **85**(4), December, 571–581 (1993)

Skinner, E.A, Zimmer-Gembeck, M.J, Connell, J.P.: Individual differences and the development of perceived control. Monogr. Soc. Res. Child Dev. **63**(2–3, Serial No. 254) (1998)

Squire, K., Jenkins, H.: Harnessing the power of games in education. Insight **3**(5), 7–33 (2004)

Steinberg, L., Elmen, J.D, Mounts, N.S.: Authoritative parenting, psychosocial maturity, and academic success among adolescents. Child Dev. **60**, 1424–1436 (1989)

Sweetser, P., Wyeth, P.: GameFlow: A model for evaluating player enjoyment in games. Comput. Entertain. **3**(3), Article 3A (2005)

Ulicsak, M., Wright, M.: Games in education: serious games. A Futurelab Literature Review, http://media.futurelab.org.uk/resources/documents/lit_reviews/Serious-Games_Review.pdf. Accessed 2 June 2011 (2010)

Wishart, J.: Cognitive factors related to user involvement with computers and their effects upon learning from an educational computer game. Comput. Educ. **15**(1–3), 145–150 (1990)

Yee, N.: Motivations for play in online games. CyberPsychol. Behav. **9**(6), 772–775 (2006)

Zepke, N., Leach, L.: Improving student engagement: Ten proposals for action. Active Learn. High. Educ. **11**(3), 167–177 (2010)

Chapter 22
What Computing Students Can Learn by Developing Their Own Serious Games

Matt Smith

22.1 Introduction

Computer games require many different aspects of computing science theory and practice to come together, and the sophistication of the game determines the range. The motivational benefits of computer games (i.e. as interesting 'subjects' for study compared with 'boring' traditional software case study systems such as banking or databases) have been exploited for computing student learning of computing concepts (for example see Smith et al., 2008, where mobile phone game software was used as a case study for several computing topics, including software testing). However, once one asks students to develop their own computer games, additional issues relating to design, programming (implementation) and testing of complex, interactive, multimedia software systems come into play. An example of a progression of game development programming projects for different semesters or years of teaching might include: simple number guessing games (guess a number from 1 to 10, and the computer says if the answer is right or wrong), simple card games requiring 'arrays' of cards to be created and shuffled and dealt, 2D arcade and platform games, up to interactive 3D games (now possible in 4–5 week projects through use of game development environments such as Unity – see Unity Technologies, 2011). For undergraduate computing students, setting *serious* games as the team objective (rather than simply games for entertainment) further bring into play key issues about the importance of the users of the final computer system and the learning that the computer game is intended to support. For example recent projects set to fourth year computing students at ITB (Institute of Technology Blanchardstown, Dublin, Ireland) include 3D games to promote the learning of fire safety and also campus building layouts for new staff and students induction. Serious games very effectively bring into focus issues of usability, universal design, and the importance of evaluating software from the user's point of view as much as, if not more than, the range and quality of the technical features of the software.

M. Smith (✉)
Department of Informatics, Institute of Technology Blanchardstown,
Dublin 15, Republic of Ireland
e-mail: matt.smith@itb.ie

M. Ma et al. (eds.), *Serious Games and Edutainment Applications*,
DOI 10.1007/978-1-4471-2161-9_22, © Springer-Verlag London Limited 2011

22.2 Educational Context

Clearly serious games researchers and developers are pursuing an educational agenda – we aim to improve the effectiveness, and perhaps enjoyment, of educational experiences through exploiting the positive and distinctive features that computer games offer. However, just because a computer game is involved, there is not necessarily any additional educational quality in the software product, or of user (student) experience when using the software, or any lasting educational benefit to the user after using the product. The central thesis pursued in this chapter relates to the benefits for computing students resulting from themselves becoming serious games developers. As a part of this we need to explore and argue issues and principles relating the quality of the learning resulting from users' (students') experiences with serious games. Papert (1993b, cited by Kafai, 2006) created two terms to help make clear the difference between 'instructionist' serious games created by educational technologists, and 'constructionist' serious games created by students themselves. Our argument follows Papert's constructionist concept.

Applied computing is sometimes described as a solution looking for a problem. When discussing serious games, key elements are the student, the serious game, and the domain of learning which the game is intended to help the student with learning. This is illustrated in Fig. 22.1.

If there is a computer game then it must have been developed by a software development team.[1] Serious computer games are developed by educational technology teams. Therefore there is a group of developers with expertise in the domains of computing and education, there is the serious game they are developing, and finally there is the student learning about the domain embodied in the serious game.

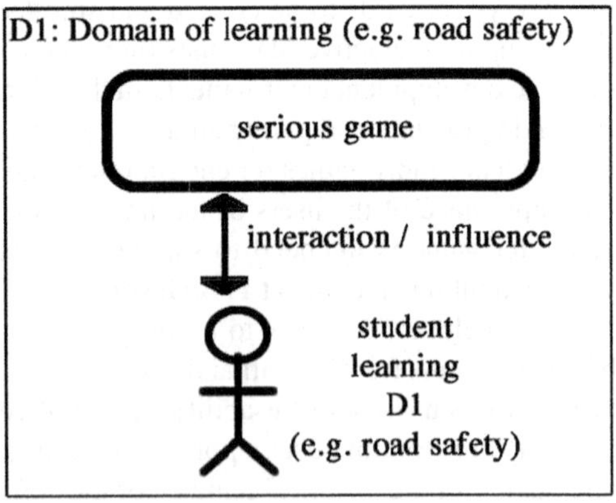

Fig. 22.1 Student influenced through interaction with serious game

[1] There are many roles to be played in software development, and more for educational software development, we'll refer to the developers as teams; although it is possible (although a challenge) for an individual to take on all roles as the developer.

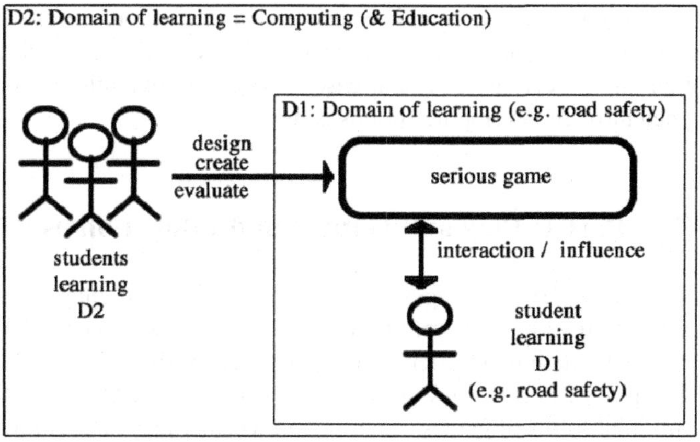

Fig. 22.2 Student educational technologist team creates serious game

As shall be argued later, part of the 'richness' of Enquiry-Based Learning (EBL) for students creating serious games related to them having to take on board the full range of aspects of D2 (Expertise in Computing and Education). This includes a role as an educator, as well as that of a software (game) developer. Therefore we can redraw the framework of the two domains with the student team in the role as serious game developers, as illustrated in Fig. 22.2. This represents a complex and rich learning scenario, which the student software development team must become aware of and manage. Not illustrated, but implied, is also the software development 'life cycle' – the process that students go through, in their work to design, create an evaluate an effective serious game.

22.3 Organisation of This Chapter

The chapter is structured as follows:

- Review Part 1: cultural concepts and definitions of fun, games and education-game relationships
- Review Part 2: constructivist educational research
- Review Part 3: an exploration of situated learning and Enquiry-Based Learning, and the benefits researchers claim for such teaching-learning approaches
- Review Part 4: the development of the field of computer supported learning from early days to recent work and serious games
- Analysis, from a computing student educational perspective, of what a serious games is as a software system, and the requirements for the process of designing, creating and evaluating serious games systems
- A proposal for a progressive approach to using computer games modification as a way to encourage school-aged students to develop an interest in mathematics and

computing, to support K-12[2] learning goals and also to encourage more students into considering technological development as a career and degree subject.
- Description and reflection of several cases studies of computing students who have learned through developing serious games

22.4 Review Part 1: Play and Games, and Education as a Game

English is one of the few languages with different words for 'play' and 'game'; although such a distinction is marred by the fact that both words can play the role of verb or noun, although more often 'play' is used as a verb, and 'game' as a noun (Frasca, 2007, p. 38). Frasca goes on to state that Lalande (1928) was the first to categorise different forms of games, according to whether they end with winners or losers, or their goal is less structured play with no end goal. Some game research originated from more traditional fields of study such as narratology and drama (for example see Bal, 2009, and Laurel, 1993), however the limitations or inappropriateness of a narrative approach to understanding interactive and dynamic games has led to proposals for studies in 'ludology' (originally Huizinga [1938] 1950, and more recently Frasca, 1999, 2003, and Juul, 1999). In many cases the general term 'game studies' is beginning to be used for research in these areas (for example see Mäyrä, 2008). Such disciplines generally agree on definitions and differentiations of 'play' as an activity with no immediately useful objective apart from the pleasure experienced, while 'game' is a form of play with a result defining winning or losing. Frasca (1999) coins the terms 'paidea' and 'ludus' for these definitions, to avoid the ambiguities associates with the different roles game and play can take in English. It is interesting that there is agreement that the presence or formation of rules is recognised as a common feature of 'play' – it is not the rules that distinguish play from game, but whether there can be a 'winner'.

In addition to becoming accepted as legitimate to support education, computer games are beginning to be argued as a new art form in their own right. As argued by Koster (2005) and Muzyka (quotations cited by Griffin, 2011), currently computer games are struggling for acceptance as legitimate, and are being challenged due to such uncomfortable issues as graphic violence and the social interactions (such as solicitation, and dangerous driving) that players simulate in games. For example see Bulletstorm (Electronic Arts, 2011) and Grand Theft Auto (Rockstar Games, 1997). Zeschuk argues that a key issue with the fledgling attempts to legislate regarding video game content is that:

> Folks who criticise games in a judiciary process like legislature make the mistake that games are for kids ... The word 'game' probably gives them the wrong impression ... They are not familiarizing themselves with what they are criticizing. If you only know hearsay, how can you form an opinion. (Zeschuk, quotation appearing in Griffin, 2011)

[2] K-12 refers to the range of free education in the USA, from around 4 years-old ('K' for Kindergarten) to 12th grade (around 18 years-old).

Censorship of games is neither new, nor restricted to computer games. DiMaggio (2001) writes about the Hungarian censorship of the board game 'Monopoly', and its substitution with a communist, politically correct game 'Economise Wisely!'. Koster argues that the current questionable status of computer games in society is similar to that of many art forms in the past:

> ... painting was once a blasphemous act that robbed reality of its essence. Dance was seen as wantonness incapable of expressing any higher emotions. The novel was self-indulgent gothic nonsense ... film was ... unworthy of adult attention. Jazz was devil music... And Shakespeare himself was no more than a bit player and sometime scribbler for the theatre in the bad part of town. Proper women weren't allowed because their reputations would be ruined ... We learned better. (Koster, 2005, p. 218)

While serious computer games have become a popular topic in recent years, the idea of people learning important lessons or knowledge through playing games is not new. In the early parts of Frasca's (2007) PhD dissertation, having discussed the use of strategy games such as Go and Chess and their relationship with military strategic training, he goes on to describe several examples of politically motivated educational games produced around 1900 by members of the British suffragette movement arguing for women to gain voting rights. He cites Crawford describing how card games such as 'Suffragette' (1907) and board games such as 'Prank-a-Squith' (1909) brought the 'message of the cause ... into domestic circles where more rabid propaganda might not have been welcomed.'(Crawford, 2002, p. 235)

Despite the history of games to support learning, Schell (2008) suggests that cultural obstacles continue to be present, challenging the legitimacy of games for education, due to arguments along the lines that '...education is serious, but games are not; therefore games have no place in education' (p. 43). This echoes Schechner's (1988) observation 'In the West, play is a rotten category, tainted by unreality, inauthenticity, duplicity, make-believe, looseness, fooling around, and inconsequentiality' (cited by Pearce, 2009, p. 3). Such cultural views of the lack of value of play were perhaps originally observed and described in Huizinga's seminal work: '[play] a free activity standing quite consciously outside 'ordinary' life as being 'not serious,' but at the same time absorbing the player intensely and utterly. It is an activity connected with no material interest, and no profit can be gained by it.' (Huizinga, 1938, cited by Pearce, 2009). Therefore, it is perhaps not surprising that we, as serious games researchers and developers, find some cultural resistance regarding the benefits or legitimacy of encouraging students to 'play', if no profit is believed to come from such activity. Frasca describes his dismay at Huizinga's and others denigration of 'play' as being of little or no value. He counters one component of such arguments by suggesting that, for young children at least, play is ordinary life. Prensky (2001) quotes an instructional technologist professor as complaining 'The problem with edutainment is that there is too much –tainment and not enough edu-' (Prensky, 2001, p. 375)

Likewise, serious games developers may find resistance from the student (players) in the form of distrust of the explicit attempts to 'hijack' an enjoyable play-experience for an educational agenda. In their teacher's guide for the second-level serious game 'The Business Game' Pixel Learning see the need to address teachers' potential misgivings about the term 'game': 'It is recognised that the term 'game' may have, for some, negative connotations in relation to education. The authors would seek to reassure teachers ...[The Business Game is] very much an educational product ...' (PIXEL Learning, 2005, p. 7)

However, Schell makes an effective argument that most formal educational systems *are* games:

> Students (players) are given a series of assignments (goals) that must be handed in (accomplished) by certain due dates (time limits). They received grades (scores) as feedback repeat as assignments (challenges) get harder and harder, until the end of the course when they are faced with a final exam (boss monster), which they can only pass (defeat) if they have mastered all the skills in the course (game). (Schell, 2008, p. 43)

Schell asks the question 'So, why doesn't education feel more like a game?' He answers the question by listing many positive features of games that traditional education lacks, including: surprises, projection, pleasures, community, a bad 'interest curve'. Schell (2008, p. 248) talks about 'interest curves', a similar concept to Krug's (2000) 'reservoir of goodwill'. In both cases the concept is of the client/audience member/player/website visitor starts off with some emotional mental state (feelings of interest in the game, feelings towards a website, etc.) and their experiences (good or bad) change their feelings for better or worse. In other words Schell is arguing something which would probably be supported by many reflecting upon their own schooling, that the quality of interest and enjoyment of the typical school child's experience is much lower in the classroom than compared to interest and enjoyment when playing games (whether computer games or other kinds).

Dille and Platten (2007, p. 71) argue that the 'core compulsion' for game players is the effectiveness of the system of rewards and punishments. It is interesting that they specially equate the loss of a 'life' with loss of player's time and progress. One potential disadvantage of serious games to support many educational agendas is that playing games is time consuming; and formal educational systems have existing challenges for fitting a large set of curriculum goals into limited classroom schedules. However, most children and adults voluntarily spend much of their time playing games, *outside* of any classroom. The issue of how many hours some people spent playing computer games has led to investigation into issues of the existence of some form of 'addiction' to video games. Schell (2008, p. 451) writing about potential bad influences of computer games on players cites a study by Yee (2002) which attempted to define and analyse 'unhealthy' game playing practices, and their causes. Yee describes finding a mixture of pull and push factors including psychological (pull) benefits from the games, and games as an escape from unpleasant real world issues (push factors).

Given Schell's arguments of formal educational as a game, a recent conversation with a third-level lecturer in mathematics (McGuinness, 2011) highlighted another parallel between features of education and games, relating to the reward of 'unlock-codes'. McGuinness has developed a series of interactive e-learning spreadsheets to support the learning of mathematics by first year undergraduate business students. Students are advised to first attempt several simple pen-and-paper exercises to develop an initial understanding of a topic, before then solving more complicated problems making use the interactive e-learning system. He found that many students using the e-learning system were having difficulties due to misconceptions about basic concepts, because they had failed to attempt the pen-and-paper exercises as preparation. McGuinness is now planning to redevelop his e-learning system to require students to have to enter an 'unlock-code' before being able to use the system to solve a problem for a given topic. The system will first display an introductory pen-and-paper problem to the student, which they would have to solve and whose answer would act as the unlock-code. Since the system dynamically generates problems and solutions, each time a student wishes to use the system they will be presented with a unique (or at least very rarely repeated) problem, so students would be unable to avoid having to complete the pen-and-paper exercise through sharing of unlock-codes. This e-learning system feature closely parallels many multi-level games (for example see the Aqua Energizer game by Uselab, 2001) which display an unlock-code after each level has been completed, so that players can only jump directly to later levels if they've already completed the earlier ones. This is the reward of 'time' to the player, who no longer has to spend time working through all the early parts of a game to get to the part they are currently attempting to master.

Mäyrä (2008) presents a framework of game studies in the form of three inseparable spheres of enquiry (1) the player, (2) the game, (3) the study of the contexts of player and game. Mäyrä explicitly argues that the more general concept of 'context' is appropriate for the third sphere of enquiry, rather than more narrowly defined 'relationships' between player and game. Mäyrä warns that 'Game, players and their interactions are too complex and interesting in their diversity to allow for all-powerful simplifications' (p. 10).

22.5 Review Part 2: Constructivist Learning Theories

The educational approach underlying the work described and arguments made in this chapter are that of the constructivist school of education. As Papert (1993a, p. 179) states 'Learning is not separate from reality'. Not all learning takes place in a classroom. Not all learning is planned or structured through an intended curriculum or agenda. For example, informal learning by community members at computing centres (for example see Cook and Smith, 2004) demonstrates that both at an individual level, and at a community or societal level, significant benefits can result from simply the provision of a building, welcoming staff and modest computing facilities.

Many computer games exhibit features that actively support the user in becoming confident they can play the game up to their level of competence, and that they can improve their level of competence by playing at a level slightly exceeding what they have succeeded in doing before. Mahyuddin et al. (2006, p. 61, citing

Bandura, 1986) define self-efficacy as '... the beliefs about one's capabilities to learn or perform behaviours at designated levels'. Many computer games present one or more screens of 'instructions' describing how to play the game. Computer games often offer a 'training' or 'practice' level, with the explicit goal of supporting user's learning and demonstration of the basic controls required to play the game. Most computer games offer a sequence of progressively more challenging 'levels', whereby the first level is simple and achievable by players with few skills or limited strategy beyond the basic input methods required to play the game. Each new level is a little harder than the previous one, the challenge increasing through speed or number or categories or behaviour of the game agents and objects. Many serious games are targeted at the K-12 educational range, and most members of this target group would have exposure (and therefore confidence) in playing.

There is general agreement of the relationship between students' self-efficacy and their academic performance (for example see Mahyuddin et al., 2006; Zimmerman, 2000; Schunk, 1989). In related work, 'comfort with studying computing' was found to be the best predictor of success in a computing course, above mathematical ability (Wilson, 2002). Zimmerman discusses research that demonstrates how educational interventions targeted to help students increase their self-efficacy, led to increases in self-efficacy, increased commitment to attaining the goals, and corresponding increases in academic performance. Given these research results, and computer game developers' work in supporting student self-efficacy in game playing confidence, it is not surprising that K-12 students have high self-efficacy with regards to playing and being able to perform well at computer games. Such results provide a strong motivation to explore computer game self-efficacy successes and attempt to implement such strategies into serious games, with hopefully corresponding high measures of student self-efficacy, academic performance and commitment to achieving goals.

To try to place some of these concepts in an educational perspective, one needs to return to modern concepts of individual- (Piaget, 1952) and social- constructivism (Vygotsky, 1962). Vygotskian theory argues the crucial role of social interactions, leading educational researchers to investigate issues surrounding social mediation (for example see Engestrom, 1996, cited by Verenikina, 2003) to better learn effective educational interventions. Much has been written about the Vygotsky's ZPD (Zone of Proximal Development) concept (for example see Verenikina, 2003). Teaching-learning events (interventions) 'scaffold' the learner when working on tasks they are not (fully) able to complete by themselves yet, i.e. when they are working in their ZPD. Verenikian cites Wells (1999, citing Mercer and Fisher, 1993) as defining criteria for scaffolding teaching-learning events including (a) the event helps learners complete a task they could not manage on their own; (b) the event is intended to bring the learner to the level of competence where they will be able to complete the task unaided. This approach views ZPD scaffolding as having the main goal of helping transfer responsibility of the desired task completion from teacher to student. Students are already are self-efficious with regard to be able to achieve successful results playing computer games, therefore, if a learning task is in the form of a computer game, and the game includes the kinds of training and support features of games described above, then it might be expected that such a situation would be likely to increase students' belief that they will be able to accomplish the learning task.

Juul (2010) presents stereotypes of 'hardcore' computer game players versus 'casual' computer game players. Juul categorised game players according to four dimensions, each dimension mapping to a sliding scale. The four dimensions were: (a) fiction preference; (b) game knowledge; (c) time investment; and (d) attitude towards difficulty. Juul suggested that for each dimension, hardcore gamers were at the opposite end of the scale compared to casual gamers. He summarises the stereotypes as follows:

> The stereotypical casual player has a preference for positive and pleasant fictions, has player few video games, is willing to commit small amounts of time and resources toward playing video games, and dislikes difficult games; The stereotypical hardcode player has a preference for emotionally negative fictions like science fiction, vampires, fantasy and war, has played a large number of video games, will invest large amounts of time and resources toward playing video games, and enjoys difficult games. (Juul, 2010, p. 29)

Serious games designers should probably be targeting their games at casual gamers, since serious games usually aim to be appealing to an mixed audience of personality types – typically a serious game would be targeted at a specific school-child's age group, or a group of undergraduate students studying a particular subject, or a group of adults to be trained in a particular skill- or knowledge-set. While Juul actually found that having initially engaged with a game, casual players often invest much time and effort into playing the game, although playing it in ways different to that of hardcode gamers (for example, many short periods of time playing, rather than a small number of 'marathon' gaming sessions lasting many hours). So perhaps the advice is that serious games should be made to 'appear' as if they are casual games, to make it more likely that a wide range of users (students) will attempt the game, although in reality the serious game itself might also be able to benefit from features of non-casual games too.

22.6 Review Part 3: Situating Learning Through Enquiry

When there are specific intended academic learning outcomes, Laurillard (1993, 2002) argues for the importance of 'situated learning':

> academic learning must be situated in the domain of the objective, and learning activities must match that domain; learning environments must be designed with features that afford the learning of precepts . . . academic teaching must help students reflect on their experience of the world in a way that produces the intended way of representing it (Laurillard, 2002, p. 24)

Grabinger and Dunlap (1995) coined the term REAL for 'Rich Environments for Active Learning'. The goals for REAL match with many of those for Enquiry/Problem-Based Learning, including the following (although the REAL approach goes further, to require an active community of teachers and learners, beyond any single computing e-learning system):

- learning within authentic contexts
- encourage the growth of learner responsibility, initiative, decision making
- encourage ownership over the acquired knowledge

So, for example, if we want our undergraduate computing students to learn to work as members of real world software development teams, then we should attempt to 'situate' software development educational experiences in the context of teams and real world-style problems. We argue that this seems to be a close match with the goals, methods and benefit of team-based Enquiry-Based Learning (EBL) approaches. Much work has been undertaken in recent years in the fields of Problem-based and other Enquiry-based approaches to structure and drive more independent student learning. Generally such approaches involve organising students into teams, and requiring the student teams to solve 'problems' over a period of time. Students gain many important 'soft skills' such as communication, working with others, and time management. EBL drives student learning by having them design and develop solutions to complex (non-trivial, real world) problems, that require them to bring together many different aspects of their chosen domain of learning, to solve a task. In recent years such EBL approaches have begun to be used in technical subjects such as engineering and computing science. A computer game is a very appealing deliverable to ask a team of computing students to develop, since they already have a clear idea of what the software system does, and the importance of the user interface.

Hutchings (2009, p. 12) sums up the benefits of EBL stating that 'what we discover, we retain', and that through EBL students 'acquire their knowledge by means of a process of active learning'. Therefore, EBL would very much be a constructivist educational approach. Savery (2006) attempts to define Enquiry-Based Learning (EBL) and also to differentiate different terms and forms of EBL, such as Problem-Based Learning and Project-Based Learning etc. PBL has several defining characteristics (the first three are from Savery, 2006, p. 15):

(i) The tutor has a role as 'facilitator'
(ii) Learners are to be self-directed and self-regulated
(iii) Ill-structured problems provide the driving force for enquiry
(iv) Students work in teams
(v) 'Learning does not operate within boundaries of a subject or parts of a subject' (Hutchings and O'Rourke, 2004, p. 176) – i.e. learning for ill-defined, real-world style problems is by necessity interdisciplinary

Savery states that the key different between EBL and PBL is that in PBL the tutor/facilitator provides no supporting information relating the problem, whereas in EBL the tutor is 'both a facilitator of learning … and a provider of information' (p. 16). In general the claim benefits of EBL include:

- Improved written and oral communication skills
- Improved team-working skills, and eventually team-leading skills
- Confidence of how to go about tackling ill-defined problems, and able to identify learning needs and identify resources to support the required learning
- Development of ability to undertake 'deep' learning approaches focused on acquiring learning required to solve a problem
- Ability to plan a project of work, including clearly defined phased of designing a solution, 'selling' the solution to a client, planning and undertaking the work, evaluating the work, and the reporting on the work completed and evaluation in written reports and through oral presentations

Clearly EBL (perhaps in combination with other educational methods during the years of a degree) has much to offer in helping students become the articulate, problem-seeking individuals that academic institutions would be happy to graduate and commercial organisations would be happy to employ. Savery (2006) suggests some of the follow as costs or risks related to the introduction of EBL:

- Students new to the learning method require 'significant instructional scaffolding', and institutions need to develop 'extensive tutor-training programs' (Savery, 2006, p. 15)
- Typically at second level and undergraduate level, the 'instruction day is divided into specific blocks of time and organised around subjects' (p. 18) – clearly fragmenting students concentration, location, and groupings several times each day reduces opportunities for team collaborations in general, and for teams to focus and make progress on a single problem requiring anything significant number of hours
- EBL requires a fundamental change to the design of the traditional curricula (for example see Savery's argument, 2006, p. 14) and EBL must be the 'pedagogical base in the curriculum and not part of a didactic curriculum'. Such a change requires 'buy-in' at departmental, and probably institutional management levels – in this situation introducing EBL at third level may be theoretically easier than second level, due to many country's national curriculum requirements at second level compared to the relative independence of third level courses and institutions

Another potential problem when considering adopting an EBL approach, is that much EBL case studies and early successes were from its adoption in the teaching and assessment of *medical students*. Hutchings and O'Rourke (2004) warn that the methods and argued benefits of EBL are mostly based on medical teaching case studies, and that care should be taken to suitable *adapt* approaches for different disciplines. Donnelly (2004) describes a study where a PBL course was perceived as too busy and over assessed – her response was to halve the number of problems (from two to just one), and to reduce the number of components of work required to be delivered for the problem. Part of the 'learning curve' for educators moving from didactic teaching-learning-assessment approaches seems to be the need to reduce the number of tasks and assessments required from the students, moving towards a small number of 'rich' problems, each requiring students to bring together several sets of knowledge and skills that might have been previously individually assessed learning outcomes.

Hutchings describes how the problem is central to the reconciliation of the educator's 'responsibility to enlighten' with the EBL goal of the learner who 'takes possession of the process of discovery' (Hutchings, 2009, p. 12). The design of the problem is the responsibility of the educator, and therefore creating appropriate and high quality problems is essential for EBL to be successful. Huchings goes on to describe the importance of the role of the educator as 'facilitator' to 'guide, support and encourage students to develop their own learning' (p. 35), and the dangers of non-expert facilitators (de-motivation of students/lack of respect) or expert facilitators (who must carefully balance the extent to which their offer their subject expertise as a 'resource' to students). The educator must act 'as a book' containing knowledge that must be 'sought after'.

Other resources, in additional to the tutor, include library resources. McLoughlin (2005, p. 190) cites several other studies all reporting increase demand for library resources, including cases where students began to complain about insufficient library resources to support their EBL.

All-in-all, EBL is certainly not a 'miracle cure' than can be simply dropped into a course and a teacher/lecturer/tutor told to go ahead and deliver. In order to maximise the chances of successful introduction of EBL there needs to be significant preparation by the organisation, by the teaching staff, and careful re-evaluation of curriculum and assessment structures, as well as careful planning for resource issues such as effects on timetabling and room requirements, library contents and access etc.

Savery (2006) emphasises the importance of ill-structured problems, warning that 'when the expected outcomes are clearly defined, there is less need or incentive for the learner to set his/her own parameters' (p. 16). Mauffette et al. (2004, p. 13) cite Paris and Turner (1994) who argue that students are motivated by academic tasks with the following characteristics:

- Freedom to choose among alternatives
- Challenge that is moderately difficult
- Control over the task (i.e. students perception that they have control over what to do)
- Collaboration through peer commitment

Mauffette et al. in their document suggest additional features of good problems including: clear descriptions written in short and simple sentences, the open-endedness of the problem being appropriate for level of student (more directed for first years, more open-ended for fourth years). Finally Mauffette et al. emphasise the importance of the students' perceptions of the *relevance* of the problem to their future careers, i.e. a problem that is likely to highly motivate students is one that describes a 'situation that students might actually encounter . . . [as] a practitioner in this situation' (p. 18). A good example of this is illustrated in the work of Hutchings and O'Rourke (2004) who describe how they tried to create motivational problems in the discipline of literary studies; they found effective strategies included asking students to present proposals for a radio broadcast or writing a booklet for the Open University required students to consider 'complex issues of audience, intention and rhetoric' (p. 179), and were effective ways to help students view a problem in the literary field as relevant to an activity someone (perhaps them!) might have to undertake in the real-world. Assessment is always an important, and contentious, issue for undergraduate education. Bowe (2005, p. 103) reports that his team viewed assessment a broad way encompassing both the views of Angelo (1995) and Margolis (2001) – that assessment plays many roles including measuring student achievement, a method for educators to transparently communicate their aims and their desired changes to be searched for in learners. One must also acknowledge the important role that assessment methods play in motiving students and influencing their 'strategic' approaches in formal learning contexts. Issues of assessment for EBL include:

- Student perceptions of unfairness of group assessment not reflecting their individual contributions
- A reduced portion of assessment for subjects relates to the traditional theoretical content, since some is now allocated for team-working and communication skills

A summary of Bowe's (2005) descriptions of his team's successful improvements in assessment methods for EBL is as follows:

- Some 'group' products result in the same marks going to all team members
- Some 'individual' assessments (usually from tutor evaluation) award different grades to each individual
- A student 'induction' including discussion of the assessment strategies
- A wide range of assessment methods (oral, report, tutor evaluation, student-peer assessment, unseen final written exam)
- Different assessment criteria for team members versus team 'chair'
- A progression from more highly weighted 'process' grades, towards equal 'process' and 'product' assessments by the end of the year

A summary of Macdonald's (2005) descriptions of his assessment approach for EBL is as follows:

- Macdonald (2005, p. 85) cites Biggs'(2003) arguments for assessment design, that requires criterion, rather than norm, referenced assessment, adopting a much more holistic and divergent approach, involving significant peer and self-assessment, all features which enquiry and problem-based curricula increasingly reflect.

A common approach to tackle assessment issues in EBL (and other teaching) approaches is some method of 'Constructive alignment' (Biggs, 1999); often in the form of a two-dimensional matrix of learning outcomes against problem assessment methods.

22.7 Review Part 4: Computer Supported Learning and Intelligent Tutors

One early publication challenging academics in what is now the field of 'serious games' was Malone's (1981) magazine article, the title of which asked 'What makes computer games fun?'. He went on to ask 'How can the same things that make computer games captivating be used to make learning with computers more interesting and enjoyable?'. Around the same time a range of research and development was under way by people like Burton and Brown (1982) into educational games such as 'How the West Was Won', a.k.a. 'West' (cited in Collins, 1988). As can be seen from Fig. 22.3, despite limited graphical multimedia capabilities, interactive and 'intelligent' educational games were possible as far back as the 1980s.

The West game offered a lot to the student learner, including an interactive 'snakes and ladders' style game, where each player tries to reach the final 'town' (end of the board) first. Each player chooses mathematical operators to combine the three numbers provided by the 'spinners' (top right of the screen) to achieve either the highest number of steps possible, or sometimes more strategically, to land on a specific position to benefit from bonus steps. In addition to providing a serious game, the West system also provided a 'cognitive coach', which analysed

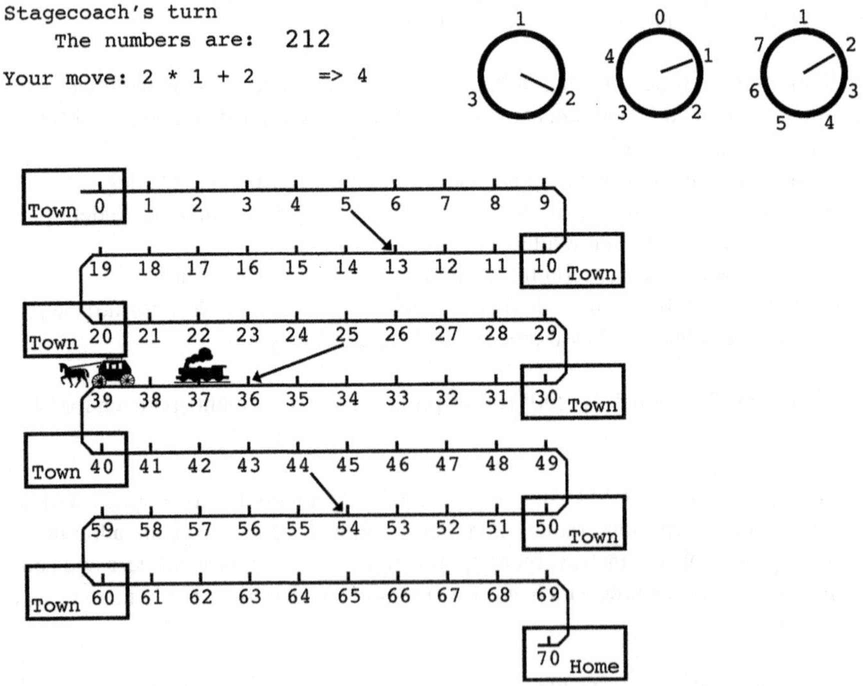

Fig. 22.3 Screenshot of game 'How the West Was Won' (from Burton and Brown, 1982, reproduced by Collins, 1988)

each player's strategies, and gave them timely 'hints' after poor moves, suggesting a strategic combination of numbers the student seems unaware of, and offering them the chance to retake their turn to implement the recommended strategy.

Much of the educational theories and techniques built around Vygotskian social constructivism assume (a) young children are the learners and (b) a human teacher is observing, interacting with, engaging in dialogue with the leaners. Serious games may be targeted at older children or adult learners, and in many cases serious game may be designed for such learners to work alone. This raises the question (challenge!) of how to embed the positive benefits of scaffolding and social constructivism in e-learning systems without an active, present, human educator. One direction e-learning researchers have followed is that of 'intelligent tutors'. It should not be forgotten that computer programs can do much more than simply facilitate game play by users (students). As previously described, the West system also offered a form of coaching. The computer's modelling of student beliefs (and perhaps misconceptions) allows for a wide range of rich interactions and interventions between computer system and user. Such 'intelligent tutors' can be explicit in their interactions, or the intervention may not be noticed by the user (student). Examples of explicit learning interventions by intelligent tutors can take many forms, for example, recommendations of how pairs of students might work together on a range of topics, based on analyses of their respective strengths and weaknesses in their learner models (Bull and Smith, 1997).

Vygotsky writes about the importance of intersubjectivity – the shared understanding between teacher and student – as important for effective and appropriate cognitive scaffolding dialogue interactions. The application of Artificial Intelligence (AI) techniques from the field of User Modelling to educational settings is generally termed 'Learner Modelling', and involves the computer system attempting to create an accurate model of what it believes the student 'knows', and/or a record of the actions, utterances and problem solving strategies the student has applied within the e-learning system. Achieving shared understanding is a challenging task for humans teachers,[3] as nicely illustrated in Verenikina's (2003) case study about a trainee teacher 'Marcia', who attempts to scaffold without fully achieving intersubjectivity first. However, any e-learning system's computer 'tutor' will need to create and maintain an accurate learner model on which to base effective intervention decisions. While AI has progressed in many directions over the last few decades, computer dialogue and learner action history analysis is a complex challenge, and reliable results are beyond computer programs except for simple analyses. Once approach to address this problem is through the approach of 'inspectable' learner models. An inspectable model is where the e-learning system

[3] In fact some intelligent computer systems have been developed specifically to assist human teachers in designing how to apply or embed pedagogic and andragogic (Knowles, 1970, cited by Davenport and Davenport, 1985) theories for particular scenarios. For example see Smith et al. (2004) for an example of an intelligent system that guides educators through a process of analysis and advice for planning how to design educationally effective dialogue elements in learning situations.

reveals its learner model to the student, and the student is able to identify (what they believe to be) inaccuracies in the model. There are various approaches to resolve disagreements between the e-learning system's learner model and the student's beliefs about their own knowledge and actions. Such interactions about the inspectable leaner model results in the student engaging in reflective metacognition – which itself helps students take an abstract step above the specific problem at hand, and can help lead to advances through their Vygotskian ZPD. Brna et al. (2011) have been investigating various approaches to the use of learner models to promote reflective metacognition in learners. More specifically Bull et al. (1995) have investigated inspectable learning models, and how students engage in highly reflective metacognition when interacting with a system and its beliefs about them; and of course the system then has a more reliable model of the learner's knowledge and strategies, on which to base educationally effective interventions.

22.8 Products and Processes – Serious Games as Software Systems to Be Developed

Mäyrä (2008, p. 162) suggests several different methodological approaches to game studies, including humanities methods, social science methods, reflective game playing as a method, and game software design as a method. Computer games are complex, interactive, multimedia software systems, and in order to create effective computer games much has to be learned by computing students, both about the product (i.e. the game software system) and the process of software design, development and evaluation. The previously mentioned suffragette card and board games must have taken much time and effort to design, prototype and develop. For modern game developers, the further requirement of technological implementation is also required; i.e. that of transferring the game design from ideas or paper designs into an interactive, multimedia computer system. A core argument we make is that the EBL 'problem' of designing and implementing a serious computer game is a sufficiently large and rich problem as to require a team of students to attempt it, and to drive their self-directed learning according to the particular choices and design decisions they make.

Mauffette et al. (2004) found EBL situations required students to address 'complex issues of audience, intention and rhetoric' – this sums up one of the key reasons to ask computing students to develop *serious* computer games, rather than general (entertainment) computer games. Issues of the user (Mauffette et al.'s 'audience') are brought much more explicitly into design and evaluation components of a serious game development project, since fundamentally a serious game aims to 'transform' the user in a particular way. The transformation is of course the knowledge and skills the game aims to help the user to learn.

As illustrated in Fig. 22.2 previously, there are two categories of student to consider when discussion a team of computing students asked to develop a serious game. There is the team of computing students, there to learn about the domain of computing (D2). Second, there are the students for whom the serious game is intended, they are to learn the domain (D1) of the goal of the serious game (for example, children to learn about road safety). Mäkila et al. argue the benefits of game development to computing students. The goal of requiring computing undergraduate students to develop computer games is not specially that their game development skills improve (although of course they do), but the desirable 'side effects' that result when students go through and complete the process of game software development projects. Such benefits include (Mäkila et al., 2009, p. 7):

- Synthesis of many skills required ('mixing pot for various study subjects')
- Pragmatic teaching approach – students learn advanced issues when they have to apply them to a project they are working on, as opposed to trying to learn about issues theoretically
- Student motivation – real game projects motivate students much more than trivial, non-challenging software projects
- General applicability – since game development is one of the most challenging software development domains, what students learn developing games transfers to many other domains of software engineering, especially multimedia software development, which has become very important in most modern computing systems
- Visible results – the game software 'product' makes demonstration of student achievement visibly explicit, for example in terms of whether requirements have been met and the quality of their decisions and solutions

The benefits of the last item above (Visible Results) should not be underestimated. One key challenge when educating undergraduates is helping them learn to critically reflect and evaluate their own work (ideally before submitting a final version). Such critical evaluation is part of the culture shock for students progressing from second-level to third-level (undergraduate) studies, since simply 'doing what was asked' no longer becomes unambiguous or sufficient for high grades. The issue of developing a serious game brings the targeted end-user (a student learning D1) explicitly the attention of the computing student development team, and they begin to see the need to think about, model, evaluate in the context of, the D1 students for whom the serious game is intended. Questions such as 'What is the goal of this software?' and 'How well does this system produced meet its goals' naturally are framed in the context, and with explicit references to the end user student. The result is (hopefully!) a rich and abstract dialogue, both between the students themselves, and between computing lecturer and computing students.

In addition to issues of the design and evaluation of the product (the serious game software system), issues about the processes involved in the software development project arise. A single student working on a simple software project (e.g. write a computer program to find the mean of a set of numbers) raises few (if any) issues of project lifecycle stages, planning of project stages, estimation of the duration of task, measurement of actual project progress against a project plan etc. However, a team of computing students, working over 4 or 5 weeks on a large software project (e.g.

a serious game), raises all of these issues. Most computing degrees include some learning and assessment about software project management, theoretical 'life-cycle' models, and perhaps even some theory about teams, leadership, and the documentation and chairing of meetings. An EBL approach whereby a team of students is given a major software development project suddenly 'situates' such project management concepts in the real world. Previous theory-based teaching and learning about projects and teams appears not to be sufficient, and, as highlighted by Savery (2006, p. 15) 'significant instructional scaffolding' is required to support students entry into EBL teaching and learning situations.

22.9 Case Study 1: EBL Game Development

This case study is based on a final year (year 4) BSc (Hons) Computing one-semester subject in game development. The course involved students working in teams (of 5 students per team) to design and develop two interactive 3D computer games. The first game was a serious game, over a period of 4 weeks. The second game was an entertainment game, over a period of 6 weeks. The teams were heterogeneous, in that they each included students with different computing backgrounds (due to a set of visiting overseas students during that academic year, as part of an EU Erasmus student-exchange programme). Figure 22.4 shown a screen from one teams' serious game – the aim of this game was to help a college visitor or new staff or student member learn the layout of a campus building, and be able to locate a

Fig. 22.4 Interactive building navigation game – library area

particular room or staff office location, or room type (e.g. where is Mr. John Doe's office, or where are the toilets on this floor).

The more technically sophisticated solution (involving real time 'path finding' from visitors location to desired room) was clearly less user-friendly than the other team's 'hard-coded' solution, which offered much smoother camera fly-throughs from the building entrance to each room. The specification of what was required clearly highlighted the need for the final system to be easy to use by non-technical people, and so (upon reflection) the student team offering the technically more advanced solution conceded that their solution included flaws in terms of user-friendliness.

Students were asked to complete anonymous feedback forms having completed the subject. Since student numbers were small (one group of less than 20 studens), and the number of returned forms was smaller (less than 10), the results cannot be used quantitatively, however, some interesting reflections emerge, that might motivate a detailed future study. Questions were asked about a range of issues relating to the course:

- Q1: all but one student indicated that they were more confident about working in teams
- Q2: all students indicated they emerged from the experience with increased belief of the importance of management for computer systems projects
- Q3: all students indicated they emerged from the experience more confident about being part of a computer systems development team in the future
- Q4: all but one student indicated they emerged from the experience more convinced about the usefulness of holding and documenting regular meetings of software development team members
- Q5: all but one student indicated that they felt that they had achieved more than they would have working individually in traditional teaching/learning mode
- Q6: student views were approximately equally spread between agreement and disagreement with the statement 'the Problem 2 task was less focussed than the Problem 1 task, because the Problem 1 task was focussed on helping the user learn something'

From these answers, in general students seemed to benefit from the EBL and situated software development outcomes hoped for in the design of the course. The split of answers to Question 6 about whether the serious game task was more focused than the entertainment game (problem 2) suggests either that the benefits of setting a serious game were not achieved, or that students were not aware of any of the benefits of tackling a serious game. The very fact that the issues of usability were conceded would suggest that students certainly took on board issues of the final user in terms of the evaluation of the effectiveness of their submitted software system.

Figure 22.5 illustrates one of the ways in which a serious game makes explicit issues of usability and software quality evaluation. The figure is a screenshot of the game, in which the user has requested guidance to find a particular room in a

Fig. 22.5 Interactive building navigation game – Recommended path for visitor passing through a wall

building. The game system used a path-finding algorithm to create a path from the user's current position in the building to the desired location, and indicated the path with a sequence of connected coloured straight lines, for the user to follow using the first-person controls (mouse and keyboard to select direction to move). In the figure we can see path of the generated path from as the striped line from the bottom right corner into a wall to the right of some double doors. We have added the arrow to the screen shot, to help indicate the weaknesses of this suggested path, since the arrow indicates where the recommend user path to follow travels *through the wall*, rather than through a *door*! Although the sophistication of the real time path-finding algorithm was a good demonstration of understanding and application of related degree subjects in Artificial Intelligence and computer programming, clearly suggesting a path through a wall falls down in terms of the quality of this serious game to help a user find the route through a building to locate a particular room. The student team submitting this serious game were happy to admit, once it was pointed out, that this was a weakness of their solution compared with less sophisticated, but more correct and user friendly alternatives. While it would have been nice for the student team to have undertaken their own game evaluation, and come to the same conclusions (and addressed the problem), this case study still demonstrates how having a serious game as the deliverable for students to construct, provides a clear framework in which general dialogue and quality evaluation metrics can be discussed and argued within. Whereas, were the game for entertainment rather than educational purposes, trade-offs between usability could have been argued versus the 'added-value' of dynamic path-finding in the game-playing entertainment user experience.

Unstructured suggestions and recommendations from students included:

- Positive feedback items included:
  - o Blogs in problem 2, rather than a 'monolithic' software design document
  - o The structure of 2 problems (game assignments) was about right (3 would not give enough time for each problem)
  - o The structure of a first shorter problem (game), followed by a second longer problem (game) was supported by student feedback comments
- general comments included:
  - o students found the subject very time consuming when compared with other classes which were more traditionally lecture based, with individual coursework assignments
  - o Students recommended the semester be organized into a short period (perhaps 2 weeks) of traditional teaching, before the longer period for EBL team-based game development. The argument for this suggested structure was that all students had to 'pick up' a new technology – none of the students from either college had previously developed games using the Unity 3D game system (Unity Technologies, 2011)[4]

From personal communications with students (Smith, 2011b), some students do believe that entertainment games are less favourably perceived as evidence of employee suitability for non-games computing employers. Since there is much evidence that students able to develop high quality computer games must demonstrate so many desirable, generic computer science skills and knowledge, an interesting follow-up study might be to survey computing employers about how true this student perception is. PIXEL Learning (2011) quote the Financial Times business analysis of the future of US corporate e-learning as follows:

> The potential (for games-based learning) is huge and remains largely untapped. For example, in educational applications alone International Data Corporation, the IT market research company, predicts that about 40 per cent of the US corporate e-learning market will use simulations by 2008 and estimates the market will be worth $10.8bn (£6bn) by 2007. (Financial Times, 2005)

Therefore, if would seem reasonable to argue that yet another benefit to computing students of learning to develop serious games is that it is becoming (or has perhaps now become) a legitimate business computing career.

---

[4] Although despite this recommendation for a more traditionally 'taught' component, all students succeeded in 'picking up' the new technology in the EBL structure, and all students achieved a high standard of work and learning by the end of the semester. Their argument was perhaps more one of the individual student time required to learn in the EBL structure, rather than its effectiveness.

22.10 Case Study 2: Children's Road Safety Game

This case study is based on a second year undergraduate, year-long student team project subject, for a digital media bachelor of arts degree. While the students are not learning to be computer programmers, they are still computing students with computer systems development skills. One team of three students chose to design, develop and evaluate an interactive multimedia computer game to help children just starting primary school (around 5 years of age) learn several road safety issues.

The team took on board issues of educational design as part of their system development life cycle. Before fully committing their software design to implementation, they undertook a 'wizard of Oz' style evaluation (for example see Dix et al., 1997, p. 210) with the co-operation of a local crèche. In this style of evaluation a human performs the actions the computer would take. When there is some computer prototype interface developed, the 'wizard' human can be in another room, and so give the impression that user(s) of the computer system are communicating with the computer program to be tested. However, when only pen-and-paper prototypes are available (as was the case at this stage – printed copies of the animation 'storyboard' were used, as shown in Fig. 22.6), the human 'wizard' sits in the room with the user(s) and shows or describes the actions the computer would take depending on choices the user(s) suggest. The results of this evaluation were informative, and surprising. The findings from the target user age group members of the evaluation group (5–6 year olds) can be summarized as follows, the children:

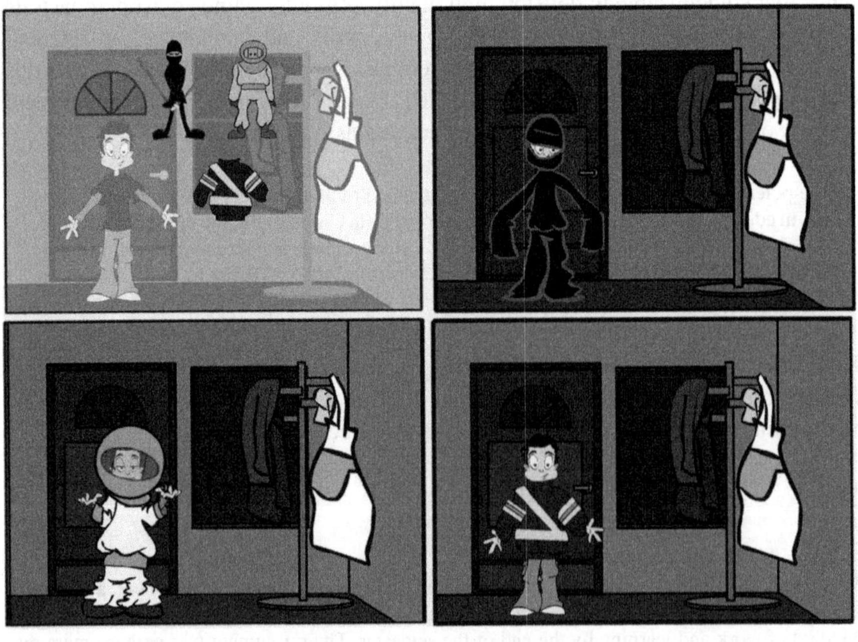

Fig. 22.6 Road safety game (interaction storyboard frames)

- did not know the 'safe cross code' (the nationally advertised song and procedure for how to safety cross the road),
- remembered little after the session (except the fun 'ninja' cartoon outfit),
- did not understand WHY some answers were right or wrong (for example, why a jacket with highly reflective strips around the arm, waist and diagonally across the shoulders front and back was the 'correct' clothing to wear when walking outside at night)

As a direct result of the evaluation, the crèche staff immediately began an educational programme to teach the 'safe cross code' to the children in their care; since they too were surprised that these primary school attending children had not learnt this road safety message already. The student serious game development team then had useful feedback to take back to their project, resulting in several design improvements to take on board what they had learnt.

This case study demonstrates how the EBL approach of asking teams of students to tackle a complex, real world problem, encourages them to accept the challenge, engage with the task and become the 'problem seekers' that demonstrate the kinds of independent learning third level education aims to promote, and potential employers seek in during their interview processes. This group of students investigated software and game development life cycles, and found the importance of prototyping, and evaluation. In computer games development a core concept is that of 'play-testing', for example see Fullerton (2008, chapter 9, Playtesting), and Schell (2008), chapter 7, The Game Improves Through Iteration).

Taking a serious games approach to education, we can look at one of the findings from the storyboard evaluation, and see how an identified educational goal might be achieved through a serious game. One finding was that some children did not understand WHY some answers were right or wrong for questions relating to what kinds of clothing to wear when going outside. The educational goal in this case is to help the children learn several relationships between different things they wear and how easy (or not) it is for others (especially road users) to see them under different lighting conditions. Several rules would seem to suggest themselves that we would want the children to learn:

- some clothes and materials are easier to see than others
  - corollary: some clothes and materials are harder to see
- it is harder to see people when it is dark, raining, foggy etc.
  - corollary: it is easier to see people in bright daytime conditions
- when it is dark outside:
  - light coloured clothes are easier to see
    - corollary: dark clothes are harder to see
  - reflective material is easy to see by motorists
    - corollary: it is hard to see people/things which are not reflective

- when it is bright in the day time
  - o brightly coloured materials are easy to see (such as hi-visibility 'fluorescent-style' yellow)
    - ▪ corollary: drab colours are harder to see
  - o contrasting colours and shades are easier to see
    - ▪ corollary: clothes of similar colours/shades are harder to see

So how can learning and understanding of these rules be supported through an educational game? A fundamental aspect of successful serious game is that the knowledge and skills we wish the student to learn are core to successful gameplay. So an educational game about choosing clothes and materials to be more visible must be at the core of such an educational game. There happens to already exist a children's game that is all about seeing people: 'hide and seek'. So one educational game to address this learning goal would be to create a real world or computer game based around hide and seek, where the student can in some way CHOOSE the items the 'hiders' are wearing, in order to make it easier to spot them. We propose[5] the following serious computer game that would embody these ideas:

> Game Concept: DRESSUP-AND-GO-SEEK: The aim of the game is to find all the other children in the scene. Before the children go and hide, the player can choose different items of clothing, and accessories such as stickers, belts, armbands, hats etc. from which the hiding children have to choose. The game 'levels' involve different locations, and also different times of day and weather conditions. At night-time the player has a torch, which they can shine around the screen to help them spot reflective materials.

22.11 Case Study 3: Student Project Choice: Why Choose to Develop a Serious Game if a Purely Entertainment Game Is Also an Option?

This case study is based on informal analysis and reflections from a recently taught multimedia programming undergraduate one-semester subject. In addition to other assessment methods, each student was required to choose an original project on which to work, and were given the choice of the design and develop either an entertainment game or a serious game. As part of the introduction to the subject students had explored and extended several simple examples of each type of game. The game project contributed 50% of the grade awarded for the subject (based on a combination of software quality, documentation quality and demonstration-defence to the lecturer), and the duration of this project almost the entire semester (12 weeks).

[5] The author believes that this is an original game idea. A search revealed no similar safety-oriented games. One game 'Costume Quest' (THQ, 2010) involves children dressing up to go trick-or-treating, however, this is an entertainment game, and the only safety aspect seems to be having to put on a safety helmet at a building site location.

A total of 34 student project submissions were received. A fifth of the students chose a serious game (7/34). Of those choosing to develop a serious game, almost half were non-Irish computing students (3/7). All three non-Irish students chose languages as the topic for their serious game. Half the Irish students (2/4) chose an Irish language serious game.

Personal reflection (in additional to conversations with the students throughout the semester during weekly labs, Smith, 2011b), suggest several interesting candidates for student's project choice motivations. We now argue several reasons why, for some students, a 'serious' game is more appealing from a computing student perspective. We suggest the following categories of student motivation for such a choice:

- motivation 1: serious game appealing since student sees themselves as an 'experienced user'
  - Students of computing have experience of education in general (whether recent, or in the past), so the goal of a serious game 'to support learning' is familiar to them.
- motivation 2: entertainment games are an unfamiliar application genre
  - Some students have little previous experience of playing entertainment computer games, and therefore for them, being asked to develop an entertainment computer game requires them to design and create something with which they are not familiar. Such students might include older students who have recently changed career direction and who have chosen to re-train as computing professionals, or perhaps students from backgrounds where they had little access to computers and computer games before attending college). For these students a serious game is simply a particular style of e-learning application, and all students (certainly by their second year of a degree) have some experience of educational contexts.
- motivation 3: student views themselves as a 'domain expert' of a subject their serious game will teach
  - Students can choose a topic in which they have some expertise, for example a second language they speak, or a skill such as playing a musical instrument, or simply choosing a basic learning goal for children such as simple mathematics or word/letter associations with pictures. Through choosing an educational domain in which the computing student is knowledgeable, they being the task of software design with increased confidence in their likely success. i.e. a higher self-efficacy than might otherwise have been the case.
- motivation 4: serious game computer project perceived as a more 'legitimate' entry on student's employment portfolio/resume
  - Increasingly undergraduates are being strategic about their choices of project topics (where such choice is permitted), since they wish to maximize the contribution their undergraduate courseworks and projects can make to their

job application 'portfolio'. One motivation (Smith, 2011b – informal summary of conversations over several years with students about software project choice factors) for computing students to select serious games over entertainment games for projects is their belief that entertainment games are less favourably perceived as evidence of employee suitability for non-games computing employers

- motivation 5: strategic choice since serious game perceived as 'easier' than entertainment game project
  - Many people, including computing students, initially view all e-learning systems as basic 'quiz' type systems. Given this view, a quiz game initially appears much simpler to program than an interactive multimedia 'entertainment' game involving moving objects, collision detection etc.

22.12 A Progressive Programme to Introduce K-12 Students to Game Development

Two young teenagers (aged 12 and 14, nephews of the author's wife) showed great interest in the author's Unity 3D (Unity Technologies, 2011) game editor when he was working with a 3D car driving game. Although neither studying computing, nor ever having written a computer program, after 5 minutes introduction, the teenagers were happily editing various physics parameters (e.g. superfast top speeds, half normal gravity, superfast breaking and acceleration) to give their car interesting behaviours. Many introductory computer programming courses for first year undergraduate computing students start very gently with 'hello world' text display programs, however, as this anecdote demonstrates, motivated students are happy to dive straight into physics computer code (for example, Unity JavaScript and C#) when it supports their ability to change and gain control of a fun 3D game. As Kafai (2006) points out, many modern computer games provide 'level editors' and even 'character editors', and so game players are beginning to become modifiers and creators (i.e. designers) of aspects of the computer games they play. The use of 'modding' existing games rather than coding computer programs from scratch, for undergraduate students, has been suggested and described by previous researchers (for example see El-Nasr and Smith, 2006).

The following is a proposed progressive sequence of game related activities, that could be the basis for an educational programme for K-12 students, and even first year undergraduates, to bring students from no previous programming or game development experience up to the level of being able to design and program their own complete games from scratch. This is partly due to the recent availability of powerful and sophisticated GUI-based game development systems such as Unity. The suggested progression is as follows:

1. students play complete, provided game
2. students edit non-behavioural character settings, such as hair, clothes, choice of character gender/age/body shape/face characteristics
   - initially have few choices, and choices are one from several
   - then more choices can be offered, and 'parameters' can be set, such as moving GUI (Graphical User Interface) sliders to vary a value in graduations, rather than simply turning an option on or off, or making a multiple-choice decision
3. students can change game 'world' objects
   - object properties can be changed, such as colours/materials/size
   - objects inside buildings can moved/added/deleted, such as chairs/doors/lamps/beds etc.
   - outdoors objects can be moved/added/deleted, such as whole buildings/geographic objects such as hills, trees, rivers, lakes, bridges etc.
4. students can change game 'world' geography
   - e.g. edit rooms in a building/duplicate or delete buildings/add geographic objects such as hills, trees, rivers, lakes, bridges etc.
5. students can create new interactive game content (e.g. pick–ups) choosing from existing behaviours
6. students create new game behaviours
   - the behaviour may be game response to pick-ups, or may be input events causing a newly created animation of an object to play (for example students might use a motion capture system such as the Kinect (Microsoft Corporation, 2011) to record a new 'dance' move, and code the logic for which input action to trigger the playing of the move)
   - they can associate them with new or existing game content
   - some form of visual language could be provided for this logic design, such as the Blender game logic editing (Blender Foundation, 2011) or Lego Mindstorms logic programming (Lego Group, 2011) – this stage requires students to understand 'events' (such as proximity to an object, or a total number of collected objects reaching a target value, or a countdown timer reaching zero, or the relationship between two (matching, or not) cards selected by a player) and functions to respond to those events with a particular behaviour
7. students create new game world's geography from scratch
   - but using the logic from an existing game, and either existing objects or new ones
8. students modify the logic of an existing game
9. students create new the complete game logic from scratch

K-12 students are computer literature. More than that, they are perhaps the first generation to accept, and event expect, to be able to modify and 'personalise' the computing 'spaces' they visit online (Chatfield, 2010, p. 154, quoting Wortley, Director of the UK's Serious Games Institute, see also Champion, 2011, p. 38, and Prensky, 2006, chapter 16). The proposed progression attempts to support this confidence (self-efficacy) of digital personalisation (changes that are purely cosmetic) through to modding the game environments (new objects with new behaviours), incrementally assisting the student as far as they wish, or need to develop. As El-Nasr and Smith (2006) discovered, students through modding can create new games with very different experiences and behaviours from the original (for example, pp. 5–7, they describe students who created Tertris and football games through modding of the Warcraft III first person shooter game engine!). Kafai (2006) describes the benefits to students who creates games to teach younger children mathematics operations on fractions.

22.13 Learning to Teach Computing Students – Another Domain of Learning

There is a further domain of learning, an abstract level above that of the students. As lustrated in Fig. 22.7, the higher education teacher is learning (or improving their learning) of teaching computing students. Ramsden's book is entitled '*Learning* to

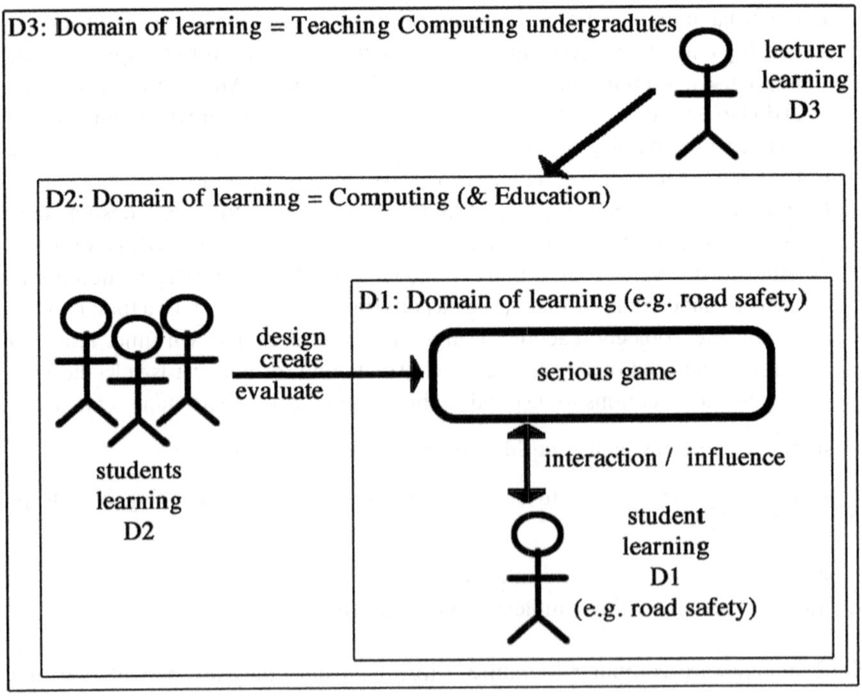

Fig. 22.7 Lecturer as reflective teacher – learning to teach computing

teach in Higher Education', and its message it that we don't know the implications of our teaching actions unless we take the effort to investigate them. Since who we teach (our students) and, although perhaps more slowly, what we teach (our academic disciplines) are changing over time, then we must continue to actively reflect and ask questions about the actual results of our teaching. He concludes '. . . a recognition that today's knowledge, however valuable, represents a partial and transitory perspective on reality. It must, like its progenitors, be superseded' (Ramsden, 1992, p. 267).

We would strongly support Ramsden's proposition that '. . . education will benefit if those who teach enquire into the effects of their activities on students' learning' (1992, p. 5); and it is that light that the review and investigative work in this chapter has been undertaken.

22.14 Conclusions

We have made an argument that there are many advantages to the setting, or at least offering, computing students' software development projects with the goal of their designing, developing and evaluation of serious games. One set of advantages are the computing science demands of serious games, in that students must apply and demonstrate a broad application of computing concepts and skills to successfully create a high quality serious game. A second set of advantages relate to student motivation; we have explored several different reasons why some students prefer to choose to develop a serious game, rather than an entertainment game. A third set of advantages are those resulting from an EBL style of learning, whereby teams of students improve project management, planning and communication skills, as they work together on a complex problem, and communicate their work and results to each other and to teachers. Kafai's discussion of constructionist approaches to student game making defines 'technological fluency' as involving 'not only knowing how to use new technological tools but also knowing how to make things of significance with those tools and most important, develop new ways of thinking based on the use of those tools' (2006, p. 39). This is the outcome for computing undergraduates that motivates the work described in this chapter. It should be noted, however, that the EBL-style teaching, learning and assessment methods described in this chapter required significant staff training, and development of additional learning resources (on teams and team leadership, project management). To date running and assessing such classes in EBL mode, while educationally satisfying, continues to be much more work for the teaching staff involved than traditional lecture-exam approaches; and with ever increasing demands for college 'efficiencies' the long term benefits to students are under threat due to short term budgetary and workload decisions by governments and educational institutions. If society wishes to benefit from innovations in teaching and learning, it must accept that there may be additional costs associated with the additional benefits.

The degree of artistic and engineering knowledge about computer games, and educational computer systems, appears to be coming of age, from hit or miss quality of individuals in the early days of the field, towards the development of structured approaches and a vocabulary and critical framework for the quality and categorization of such systems. There seems to be a great potential for improvement of the school learning experience (i.e. building upon analyses such as Schell's 'interest curves'). The promise of what serious games can offer is that, hopefully, in the future, the quality of learners' experiences will be closer to the enjoyment and interest they have with challenging computer games, rather than the rather lower enjoyment of traditional chalk-and-talk memory and regurgitation classroom teaching methods – why cannot most of our children's learning experiences be 'fun'?

In a recent conversation (Smith, 2011a) a final year computing undergraduate student spoke about the difference between a recent job interview (during their fourth year) and an interview the previous year. The student explained that in both interviews they had been asked to talk about their experiences of working in teams. The student explained how much more he had to talk about in his second interview, and how interested the interviewer was, because of his experiences of working in a heterogeneous software development team in a computer game development EBL structured subject. This student went on to state that since team-working skills seemed important to every job he was applying for, he recommended that final year computing students' year-long projects be pair- or team- based, again to give students more experience of large scale software projects and teamwork, both for the lessons learned and also as content to write about on their CVs (resumés) and to talk about during job interviews.

One contribution serious games are making to the entire field of computer games, is to explicitly demonstrate potential positive benefits to users of computer games (i.e. educational gains). Another contribution is that, since many serious games are aimed at supporting adult learners, they contribute evidence to society that games are not just for kids. Finally, given societal acceptance that worthwhile and non-trivial benefits can result from players of serious games, arguments for worthwhile and non-trivial benefits from other kinds of games (or games not labelled 'serious') become much easier to make and to communicate to society, and to the decision making groups within society such as the legislators. Of course, Koster (2005) maintains the argument that all games are serious, it's just that what user learn from games may or may not be intentionally aligned with some educational curriculum. . .

Frasca states his goal as to 'provide a framework for understanding . . . how players construct meaning while playing games' (2007, p. 20). An argument can be made that in order to develop effective serious computer games, the fields of ludology and game studies need to be supported and to progress, since serious games developers wish the change that occurs when students player serious games to be (in entirety, or at least to include) the *desired* educational outcomes motivating the development of the serious game in the first place.

Serious games provide a wonderful mechanism for motivating and encouraging students to spend time and effort improving their understanding in order to progress through a game. Our goal as serious games researchers and developers must be to help develop the theoretical foundations to understand and promote the design and development of serious games that lead to the desired educational goals. Serious games may not be the answer to all educational goals, but as we learn more about how to take a more 'game-centric' approach to our educationally design, it is likely that the quantity, range and quality (educational and fun) of games to support learning will continue to increase significantly in the foreseeable future.

References

Angelo, T.A.: Reassessing (and Defining) Assessment, AAHE Bull. **48**(3), 7 (1995). Cited in Bowe (2005, p. 103)

Bal, M.: Narratology: Introduction to the Theory of Narrative, 3rd edn. University of Toronto Press, Canada (2009)

Bandura, A.: Social Foundations of Through and Action: A Social Cognitive Theory. Prentice-Hall, NJ (1986). Cited by Mahyuddin et al. (2006)

Biggs, J.: Teaching for Quality Learning at University. Open University Press, Milton Keynes (1999)

Biggs, J.: Teaching for Quality Learning at University (Second Edition). SRHE/Open University Press, Milton Keynes (2003)

Blender Foundation: The Blender Open Source 3D Editing Application. The Blender Foundation, Netherlands. URL (last visited April 2011): www.blender.org (2011)

Bowe, B.: Chapter 11. Assessing problem-based learning: Case study of a physics problem-based learning course. In: Barrett, T., Mac Labhrainn, I., Fallon, H. (eds.) Handbook of Enquiry and Problem Based Learning. CELT, NUI Galway, Ireland (2005)

Brna, P., Bull, S., Dimitrova, V.: Learner Modelling for Reflection (LeMoRe). URL (last visited April 2011): www.eee.bham.ac.uk/bull/lemore/ (2011)

Bull, S., Smith, M.: A pair of student models to encourage collaboration. In: proceedings of 6th International Conference on User Modelling, Sardinia, Italy (1997)

Bull, S., Pain, H., Brna, P.: Mr Collins: A collaboratively constructed, inspectable student model for intelligent computer assisted language learning. Instr. Sci. **23**(1–3), 65–87 (1995)

Burton, R.R., Brown, J.S.: An investigation of computer coaching for informal learning activities. In: Sleeman, D.S., Brown, J.S. (eds.) Intelligent Tutoring Systems (pp. 69–98). Academic, New York (1982)

Champion, E.: Playing with the Past, Human-Computer Interaction Series, DOI 10.1007/978-1-84996-501-9_5. Springer, London (2011)

Chatfield, T.: Fun Inc. – Why Games are the 21st Century's Most Serious Business. Virgin Books, London (2010)

Collins, A.: Cognitive Apprenticeship and Instructional Technology. Technical Report, BBN Labs, MA (1988)

Cook, J., Smith, M.: Beyond formal learning: Informal community eLearning. Comput. Educ. **43**, 2 (2004)

Crawford, E.: The Women's Suffragette Movement: A Reference Guide 1866–1928. Cited by Frasca 2007. Taylor and Francis Group, New York (2002)

Davenport, J., Davenport, J.A.: A Chronology and Analysis of the Andragogy Debate. Adult Educ. Quart. **35**(3), 152–159 (1985)

Dille, F., Platten, J.Z.: The Ultimate Guide to Video Game Design Writing and Design. Watson-Guptil Publications, New York (2007)

DiMaggio, P.: The Twenty-First Century Firm: Changing Organization in International Perspective. Princeton University Press, Princeton, NJ (2001)

Dix, A., Finlay, J., Abowd, G., Beale, R.: Human-Computer Interaction, 2nd edn. Pearson Education, London (1997)

Donnelly, R.: Investigating the Effectiveness of Teaching 'Online Learning' in a Problem-based Learning Classroom Environment. In: Savin-Baden, M., Wilkie, K. (eds.) Challenging Research into Problem-Based Learning (pp. 50–64). Open University Press, Milton Keynes (2004)

Electronic Arts: Bulletstorm Computer Game. EA Game, Redwood City, CA (2011)

El-Nasr, M.S., Smith, B.K.: Learning Through Game Modding. ACM Comput. Entertain. **4**(1) (2006)

Financial Times: Financial Times, September 2005, London, UK (2005)

Frasca, G.: Ludology meets Narratology: Similitude and Differences Between (video) Games and Narrative. Finnish Version Originally Published in Parnasso 3, pp. 365–371 (1999)

Frasca, G.: Simulation versus narrative: Introduction to ludology. In: Wolf, M.J.P., Perron, B. (eds.) The Video Game Theory Reader (pp. 221–223), Routledge, London (2003)

Frasca, G.: Play the Message: Play, Game and Videogame Rhetoric. Unpublished PhD dissertation. IT University of Copenhagen, Denmark (2007)

Fullerton, T.: Game Design Workshop: A Playcentric Approach to Creating Innovative Games, 2nd edn. Morgan Kaufmann, San Francisco, CA (2008)

Giffin, J.: Bullets, beats and bleeding hearts (Life and Culture, p. 12). In: The Irish Times, Wednesday 9 March 2011, Dublin, Ireland (2011)

Grabinger, R., Dunlap, C.: Rich environments for active learning. Assoc. Learn. Technol. J. **3**(2), 5–34 (1995)

Huizinga, J.: Homo Ludens: A Study of the Play-Element in Culture. Translation of the original: (1950), Roy Publishers, New York (1938). Cited by Pearce C (2009)

Hutchings, W.: Enquiry-Based Learning: Definitions and Rationale. Report from Centre for Excellence in Enquiry-Based Learning, University of Manchester, UK (2009)

Hutchings, W., O'Rourke, K.: Medical studies to literary studies: Adapting paradigms of problem-based learning process for new disciplines. In: Savin-Baden, M., Wilkie, K. (eds.) Challenging Research into Problem-Based Learning (pp. 50–64). Open University Press, Buckingham (2004)

Juul, J.: A Clash between Game and Narrative. English Translation of Unpublished Masters thesis, University of Copenhagen, 1999 (1999)

Juul, J.: A Casual Revolution: Reinventing Video Games and their Players. The MIT Press, Cambridge, MA (2010)

Kafai, Y.B.: Playing and making games for learning: Instructionist and constructionist perspectives for game studies. Games Cult. **1**(1), 36–40 (2006)

Knowles, M.S.: The Modern Practice of Adult Education: Andragogy Versus Pedagogy. Association Press, New York (1970). Cited in Davenport and Davenport: (1985)

Koster, R.: A Theory of Fun. Paraglyph Press, Scottsdale, AZ (2005)

Krug, S.: Don't Make Me Think – A Common Sense Approach to Webs Usability. QUE. Indianapolis, IN (2000)

Lalande, A.: Vocabulaire technique et critique de la philosophie. Librairie Félix Alcan, Paris, France (1928). Cited by Frasca (2007)

Laurel, B.: Computers as Theatre. Addison-Wesley, London (1993)

Laurillard, D.: Rethinking University Teaching: A Framework for the Effective Use of Educational Technology. Routledge, New York (1993)

Laurillard, D.: Rethinking University Teaching: A Conversational Framework for the Effective Use of Educational Technologies, 2nd edn. Routledge, London (2002)

Lego Group: Lego Mindstorms Robot Programming. Lego Group, Denmark. URL (Last visited April 2011): mindstorms.lego.com (2011)

Macdonald, R.: Chapter 9. Assessment strategies for enquiry and problem based learning. In: Barrett, T., Mac Labhrainn, I., Fallon, H. (eds.) Handbook of Enquiry and Problem Based Learning. CELT, NUI Galway, Galway (2005)

Mahyuddin, R., Elias, H., Cheong, L.S., Muhamad, M F Noordin, N., Abdullah, M.C.: The Relationship between Students' Self Efficacy and their English Language Achievement. J. Educ. Educ. **21**, 61–71 (2006)

Mäkila, T., Hakonen, H., Smed, J., Best, A.: Three Approaches Towards Teaching Game Production. In: Kankaanranta, M., Neittaanmäki, P. (eds.) Design and Use of Serious Games. Springer, Berlin, German (2009)

Malone, T.: What makes computer games fun? BYTE **6**, 258–277 (1981)

Margolis, E. (ed.): The Hidden Curriculum in Higher Education. Routledge, New York (2001) Cited in Bowe (2005, p. 103)

Mauffette, Y., Kandlbinder, P., Soucisse, A.: The Problem in Problem-based Learning is the Problems: But do they Motivate Students? In: Savin-Baden, M., Wilkie, K. (eds.) Challenging Research into Problem-based learning (pp. 50–64). Open University Press, Buckingham (2004)

Mäyrä, F.: An Introduction to Game Studies. Sage, Thousand Oaks, CA (2008)

McGuinness, C.: Personal communications with the author. March 2011, Institute of Technology Blanchardstown, Dublin, Ireland. URL (last visited March 2011): colmmcguinness.org/live/fs.htm (2011)

McLoughlin, J.: Chapter 18. Co-ordinating and Managing PBL Programmes – Challenges and Strategies. In: Barrett, T., Mac Labhrainn, I., Fallon, H. (eds.) Handbook of Enquiry & Problem Based Learning. CELT, NUI Galway, Galway (2005)

Microsoft Corporation: Xbox Kinect. Microsoft Corporation, WA, USA. URL (last visited April 2011): www.xbox.com/en-IE/Kinect (2011)

Muzyka: Quotation appearing in Griffin (2011) (2011)

Papert, S. (1993a) Mindstorms: Children, Computers, and Powerful Ideas, 2nd edn. Harper Collins, New York

Papert, S. (1993b) The Children's Machine: Rethinking School in the Age of the Computer. Cited by Kafai. Basic Books, New York (2006)

Pearce, C.: Communities of Play. MIT Press, Cambridge, MA (2009)

Piaget, J.: The Origins of Intelligence in Children (Trans., Cook, M.). International Universities Press, New York (1952)

PIXEL Learning: Teacher's Guide & Resource Pack. PIXEL Learning Limited, UK. URL (last visited March 2011): www.thebusiness-game.com (2005)

PIXEL Learning: Evidence that using Games-based eLearning (G-beL) can lead to significant benefits for learners and organisations (White Paper). PIXEL Learning Limited, UK. (last visited March 2011): www.pixellearning.com (2011)

Prensky, M.: Digital Game-Based Learning. Paragon House, St. Paul, MN (2001)

Prensky, M.: Don't Bother Me Mom – I'm Learning. Paragon House, St. Paul, MN (2006)

Ramsden, P.: Leaning to Teach in Higher Education. Routledge, London (1992)

Rockstar Games: Grand Theft Auto Computer Game. Rockstar Games, New York (1997)

Savery, J.R.: Overview of problem-based learning: Definitions and distinctions. Interdiscip. J. Prob. Based Learn. **1**, 1 (2006)

Schechner, R.: Playing. Play Cult. **1**, 1 (1988). Cited in Pearce C (2009)

Schell, J.: The Art of Game Design – A Book of Lenses. Morgan Kaufmann, Burlinton, MA (2008)

Schunk, D.H.: Self-efficacy and achievement behaviours. Educ. Psychol. Rev. **1**, 173–208 (1989)

Smith, A.: Personal communications with the author. April 2011, Institute of Technology Blanchardstown, Dublin, Ireland (2011a)

Smith, M.: Personal communications with undergraduates in recent years. Institute of Technology Blanchardstown, Dublin, Ireland (2011b)

Smith, M., Cook, J., Oliver, M.: Learning Through Dialogue (LTD): A toolkit to support the process of planning for effective use of dialogue in learning. In: Proceedings of ED-MEDIA 2004,

World Conference on Educational Multimedia, Hypermedia and Telecommunications, Lugano, Switzerland (2004)

Smith, M., Gallery, R., McSweeney, D.: SECASE: An EU project creating multimedia learning materials for the teaching of software engineering. ED-TECH 2008, IT Dundalk, Ireland, June 2008 (2008)

THQ: Costume Quest (computer game). THQ Incorporated (computer game publisher). CA, USA. URL (last visited April 2011): www.thq.com (2010)

Unity Technologies: The Unity 3D game engine. Developed and distributed by Unity Technologies, USA. URL (last visited March 2011): www.unity3d.com (2011)

Uselab: Aqua Energizer computer game. Published by Miniclip.com. URL (last visited March 2011): www.miniclip.com/games/aqua-energizer/en/ (2001)

Verenikina, I.: Understanding Scaffolding and the ZPD in Education Research. In: AARE-2003, Proceedings of Australian Association of Research in Education (2003)

Vygotsky, L.S.: Thought and Language. MIT Press, CA (1962)

Wells, G.: Dialogic Inquiry: Towards a Sociocultural Practice and Theory of Education. Cambridge University Press, New York (1999)

Wilson, B.C.: A Study of Factors Promoting Success in Computer Science Including Gender Differences. Comput. Sci. Educ. **12**(1–2), 141–164 (2002)

Yee, N.: Ariadne – Understanding MMORPG Addiction. October 2002. www.nickyee.com/hub/additiction/home.html (2002)

Zeschuk, G.: Quotation appearing in Griffin (2011) (2011)

Zimmerman, B.J.: Self-efficacy: An essential motive to learn. Contemp. Educ. Psychol. **25**, 82–91 (2000)

Chapter 23
Social Interactive Learning in Multiplayer Games

Vanessa Camilleri, Leonard Busuttil, and Matthew Montebello

23.1 Unlearning What We Have Become

Learning in the 21st century has changed. The motivation for learning has changed. 30 years ago people were aspiring for production line environment; a vision which accounted for stability, for all things known and planned. Now society in general is aspiring for work which hasn't yet even been invented. Whereas some time ago, employers were happy with people struggling along a linear productivity chain, now employers have recognized that creativity, innovation and lateral ideas are some of the ingredients for a successful enterprise. Society hungers for people who can imagine, and who can think of problems and consequently plan for adequate solutions before they arise.

Society is no longer the product of the mass evolution. Every individual within society has a voice and wishes to carry that voice far and away, striking a meaningful chord somewhere – loud enough to achieve a ripple across the community. And yet, we are still stuck in an educational system which might preach 'Future' but which does otherwise. So where have the changes started? How did we get here? What are the main drivers which predict specific behavioural changes and most importantly where is all this going to lead us?

These questions are rather generalised variations of some of the philosophical underpinnings grounding our society values. However we want to attempt to trace the changes back to when they started having a significant impact the way society learns and interacts through a communication process. We are viewing this process in light of elements which are embodied in the fundamentals of entertainment and adapt these to 21st century learning skills.

If we were to propose a definition for 'a digital game' to someone with no pre-defined knowledge of what a game is, we might encounter an extraordinary challenge in trying to explain the intricate nature of the cognitive mesh of emotions and behaviour which are stimulated in humans owing to the technical foundations

V. Camilleri (✉)
University of Malta, Msida, Malta
e-mail: vanessa.camilleri@um.edu.mt

M. Ma et al. (eds.), *Serious Games and Edutainment Applications*,
DOI 10.1007/978-1-4471-2161-9_23, © Springer-Verlag London Limited 2011

and the heuristics which hold the game structure together. We might try to give a definition to a game such as an activity which one engages in, and which produces diversity or amusement; but that is really not being very accurate and rather quite vague. So once again in order to provide an answer we need to ask questions, such as 'How are digital games being represented? Who are THE gamers today? What are the essential elements that drive games in today's ever-increasing parallel domain which so frequently runs in parallel to real life?'

When we speak of games there are many different genres and so many forms of expression within the games. For the purpose of this chapter, we have decided to focus mostly on Massively Multiplayer Online Games (MMOGs) and Massively Multiplayer Online Role Playing Games (MMORPGs) to attempt a characterisation of the components which make them so popular in an attempt to design similar social interactive games for learning and education.

This chapter will first look at elements of social learning in relation to a number of learning theorists. These elements are most often viewed as the raw building blocks of complex learning systems where communities of practice play a vital role. The aim is that of introducing the concepts of social interactive systems before we look at games, and most particularly MMOGs and MMORPGs and thus merging the two to come up with common elements of design which are of particular importance to the motivation factor in learning decisions.

23.2 Learning Socially – What Does It Mean?

A number of learning theories have focused primarily on the learner as the 'sole' interpreter of information surrounding him/her. Through pedagogic applications we most often tend to focus on 'learner-centric' techniques as if the learner existed in a world of his/her own. However research trends are currently indicating that when individuals communicate their learning is enhanced (Chou and Min, 2009). Additionally when individuals perceive that they are communicating with a real person, even if embodied as a virtual avatar, learning is indeed augmented (Hamlen, 2011). One can possibly relate this to the fact that human activity is inherently based on interactivity within the social context. Communication which has evolved over the years is the result of the need for interaction which persons feel towards each other. Vygotsky's work (1978), entitled *Zone of Proximal Development*, has been interpreted many times over as the foundations of the socio-constructivist perspective where the learner solves problems not as an isolated individual but in his/her cultural surroundings and context. This also has leverage on a number of other perspectives which show the learner as part of a wider collection of mass participants, within this agglomeration of information. An interesting research study by Hrastinski (2009) presents a facet of online participation which is not simply resident on real time interactions such as talking or chatting, but belongs to more complex tasks whereby the ultimate goal and meaning of the online activity may be representative of a wider social activity.

This is also in line with other more modern theories of learning based on fundamental social models. According to Nonaka and Takeuchi (1995) knowledge is built internally through social and shared experiences and it is then externalised through various forms of expression. Traditionally many learning theories were built around the notion that the gain of knowledge should be focused solely on the learner and that's when learner-centered metaphors gained more momentum. However it is certainly not the case for many of today's research trends, where even Personalised Learning Environments (PLEs) are seen as more than just dependent on the learner represented as an isolated cell. Learning, in these instances, occurs as a just-in-time activity built around similar shared experiences, interactions and relations – something which the traditional online environment represented by learning management systems most frequently does not seem to sustain. Other social learning theories which impinge on the actual meaning of learning which occurs as a result of an activity which is based upon sharing and collaborating with a number of individuals, use externalised frameworks to help shed light on some of the complexity of the learning implications within these theories. One such theory, the social presence theory, explains the important role which media plays in influencing community concepts and interpretation of the facts – the Time, Interaction, Performance theory (TIP) (Chou and Min, 2009) then uses the same media concepts to explain how facts acquired and influenced by media in a community are then translated into knowledge. This is especially interesting when viewed from the perspective of games and gaming when one tries to analyse the various social media online games, as well as other forms of digital games and the popularity which has been gained through the environment which facilitates such interactions.

23.3 Learning in a Community – How Does It Happen?

Previously we explored the concept that Social learning occurs within a community setting or environment, and now we wish to reflect on the dynamics of learning within a community. Lave and Wenger (1991) followed in Vygotsky's steps by elaborating more on the processes through which individuals use the 'communal' knowledge to construct their own meanings and interpretations of the world around them.

Wenger (1998) defines communities of practice as a group of people, engaged in a common activity sharing common denominating factors which will lead them to accomplish a common goal. According to Lave and Wenger (1991), knowledge is not actually something which is inherent and which belongs solely to the individual. It becomes more of a shared practice so that learning becomes a participatory process lying at the core of the community into which the activity is spun. When one tries to apply this theory to multiplayer online games then it all starts to make sense. All the forums, wikis, and blogs which exist and which discuss THE one individual game, all aim to set up a community – and learning is an activity which is churned out from this community. Now if we try to put this theory into context we can see *newbies* entering the multiplayer online game, and they go through the process of inserting themselves in a community. This is not done by simply registering with the community. Insertion happens as a result of active engagement which then helps them master their practice and also facilitates the transmission of some of the skills acquired in the 'mastery' process to other newbies. It becomes a fantastic cycle of learning which is dependent solely on the individuals' engagement with the rest of the community. It almost feels like a thick mesh where the more individuals join in, then the stronger the community becomes hence increasing the game's popularity. This can be seen as a commercial or marketing strategy to sell more games and make money. The end result is that whatever it is, it works.

In terms of learning theories, communities of practice make a lot of sense because they are built around the concept of sharing (Oikita et al., 2007). One has the ability to push and pull information from the community with a unique existential purpose whilst at the same time the information is being moulded in line with the community influences. It thus becomes an extension to the social learning theories, in a more tangible aspect because each community pursues a unique goal and that goal drives all the learning which takes place inside it. This is also defined by Wenger (1998) as 'Reification'. One has to add that communities of practice do not by default preclude learning communities. Communities of practice may indeed stop at the external shell layer, without probing in-depth. These communities are transformed into learning communities of practice when 'deeper' learning is achieved; when one moves from the cathartic to the more exciting level of engagement when the interactions within the group lead to a more complex and critical level of contribution.

Communities of practice are also used within learning environments to churn experts from apprentices. Metaphorically speaking, a community of practice becomes a piggy-back ride, where the more expert individuals carry the less experienced ones on their backs for some time, so that the latter can observe, whilst immersing themselves into the ideas which drive the community – an 'enculturation' move where the individuals, consciously and cognitively are moving to procreate more experts in the area, so that they can work together towards a common solution. Such tight knit knowledge-building capacity is unfortunately not seen very frequently in schools where in the majority of cases the driving factor within the classroom community resides solely in the teacher who is also considered as the only 'master' guiding the group.

Many theories focusing on the application of communities of practice have been employed within work organisations and strategic management. What is interesting to note is that many of these theories have become embodied into the communities which have evolved naturally as a consequence of the development of games. The most popular digital online games which exist currently are symbiotically dependent on the communities of practice which are dispersed across the cyberspace. One cannot exist without the other – popular games thrive through the input from their followers and the followers need the challenge which the online games are offering. This then becomes much more than simply solving a quest or completing a mission – this becomes the social construction of the meaning which is given in context, which in this case is attributed to the game. In this chapter we have not explored in-depth any of the complexity theories which may impinge on the setting up of communities of practice. Indeed external factors such as culture, time and space may play an important role as well as the ease of emergence of the learning community in a context which allows flexibility in the design of the structure utilised to achieve the common goal. One aspect of this goal is to instantiate *happiness* and *pleasure* in sought after experience which contributes to the overall positive rapport within the same community.

23.4 The Game Experience – When Does It Occur?

In the previous sections, we have mostly looked at the social experiences which impinge on learning. Recent trends have implied that social experiences are often conducive to fun, and that most often entertainment happens in groups – never in isolation (Papert, 1998). This led to a huge spark in research in education with trends moving towards the direction of digital educational games, hitting at some past disastrous results. A few years ago, digital games which were included in the classroom practice were thought of as boring with activities mostly of the type drill and practice (Gee, 2008b). A recent, as yet unpublished study held in one of the schools in Malta, has shown students aged 15 who classified themselves as gamers, preferring to opt out of having games as part of their classroom practice, indicating as well that games should be played at home and not in the classroom. Of course these indicative statements do not come without the pre-required eyebrow-raising retributions which would demand explanations of such bland statements. If games are equivalent to fun, but the educational games we are designing have this permanent stigma that they are so boring that individuals would rather do without them than having to go through them, then we are seriously (no pun intended) bungling our jobs.

The questions we need to start asking ourselves, are more of a logistical nature. We now know the common elements which make up a game, or more precisely a digital game, and these are the agglomeration of experiences, which lead to a change in our emotions, thus helping us express ourselves in a manner which offers us some form of entertainment (Michael and Chen, 2005). But do we know the tangible elements which bind together the most popular games on the planet? Which are the most common games on the planet in the 2011 era, and why? By far the most spoken about, with the largest wiki in the world related to one specific subject is the MMORPG World of Warcraft (2011), but that doesn't mean that the first person shooter game, Call of Duty – Black Ops, or Halo (Gamespot, 2011) is lagging far behind.

One common denominator which we are looking for in our quest for games design is the social factor. We want to bring out the element which has its implications in online learning and merge it with the elements which are primarily bound to games, provided that the common factor remains the social dimension. We can therefore categorise games which are denominated by the social instances, under three broad headings.

- The Massively Multiplayer Online and Online Role Playing Games (MMOG/MMORPG)
- The classic Video Games
- The emergent Social Media Games

MMOPGs/MMORPGs use the online environment to provide gamers with a unique and immersive 3D world experience. The most popular genre is the fantasy with about 75% of 400 registered MMORPGs, where each world poses no boundaries to the limits of the imagination (MMORPG, 2011). Other genres include historical, sci-fi, sports and those which deal with real life scenarios. One of the highest rated, most popular MMORPG with a subscriber population which, according to the developing company Blizzard Entertainment, has over more than 12 million players globally, is 'World of Warcraft'. The developing company also reports that the latest release 'World of Warcraft. Cataclysm', has reached sales of more than 4.7 million copies in its first month. These staggering results confirm WoW as one of the most popular, if not the most popular MMORPG currently. However the question which arises is 'What makes this game popular?' With those figures, then one asks what makes it really top the bill.

The *classic video game* uses a game controller for user interactivity and feedback is displayed on a video device. There are various types of digital video games, although the greatest commercial traffic is by far registered with the casual games. Casual games are characterised by a set of rules which make them more user oriented and less demanding on the users' critical cognitive skills. Such games can range from platform games (2D and 3D), to sci-fi first person shooters as well as action, adventure, historical, and sports. The difference between the classic video games and the MMORPGs lies essentially in the real time interaction which can be established through the communities as they are connected over the Internet. Although a number of video games are now offering the multiplayer capabilities, they also have different game consoles which allow improved quality interface optimising the gaming experience. Examples of game consoles include the Microsoft Xbox, Nintendo Wii, Nintendo DS, and Sony Playstation, amongst others. The most popular ranked casual video games currently include Halo:Reach which is played on Xbox360, Tactics Ogre on PSP, DeadSpace 2 on PS3, Ghost Trick: Phantom Detective Review on DS, Call of Duty: Black Ops on Wii and PC, Vanquish on Xbox360.

Other video game categories include core games, mini games, serious games and educational games. Core games use the same differing and dedicated game consoles as the casual games but the nature of their game play includes a more in-depth cognitive involvement on the gamers' behalf. This means that these genres of games might not appeal to the casual gamer. The other category of serious games, go beyond entertainment and usually aim to offer a learning experience in an environment which allows gamers to be immersed in specific worlds. Although they might not be classified as strictly educational game, these genres of games may include role-playing and simulations to enhance the visual and interactive experience for the gamer. Education games may have different categories, including drill and practice, frame games, and mini games.

The other broad heading which merges the social element with the games refers to the *social media games* which have added on to their rise in popularity through the phenomenon of the growth of social media networks such as Facebook. Amongst the most popular social media games currently according to the Baribeau (2011), one finds *Cityville* (with an astounding 21,270,241[1] daily active users) followed closely by *Monopoly Millionaires* topping the charts, as well as games such as online *Scrabble* and *Yoville*, a lightweight virtual world game, both played through the interactive multiplayer features offered by the social media platform, Facebook. Car Town, another game built and designed around social mechanics, reported gamers enjoying 'the competitive nature of racing cars against [their] friends' (Baribeau, 2011).

Although games such as Farmville (average of 50 million monthly active users (Mack, 2011)) and Cityville can be played at the individual level, the feature which makes the gamer more successful at the game is his/her ability to acquire resources and help from his/her 'neighbour' via Facebook. Thus one would receive a number of messages of friends who enlist the help of other friends in order to acquire a new patch of strawberries, cattle or other farm-related provisions as well as build new roads or a brand-new town hall.

One very interesting feature which emerges from the popularity these games have acquired lies in their astounding simplicity. Games such as scrabble have been around for ages, people have played them in the comfort of their own homes, on the sofa, with family and friends. Now these games are accessible anywhere anytime as long as you have an Internet connection, and what's even more important is that no one needs to learn new rules of the game. And who wants to play against a computer when one can measure up to one's friends across the social network? Therefore the recipe of success of these social media games may be attributed to three major criteria: simplicity, accessibility and connections with friends. Another simplistic feature is the ease of play or lack of determinate skills needed to play the game and play the game with a degree of success. Gamers report that amongst the most important skills one needs to show is patience and perseverance, as well as abiding by the time-based rules which are imposed by these social media games. Most often activities associated with social media game boomers such as Farmville and Cityville are those of waiting for the assets to mature, whilst tending to them at the click of the button. This increases accessibility of the game extending it to all levels of abilities removing barriers associated to age, physical impairments and gender. It might be interesting to observe the number of males versus females which such games attract. Although the discrepancy expectancy might differ we might be treated to some pretty surprising statistics.

[1] Figures as registered through the Inside Social Games metric service on the 3rd March 2011; Available online: http://www.insidesocialgames.com/.

We have interviewed a number of gamers, all aged in 18–20 who have pocketed their fair share of hours at gaming and the first question which we asked was directed to THEIR definition of a game. In their opinions games are activities which are fun to do – nothing too complex about the matter – youths today want to do something fun which they cannot do in reality. And in their own words, games, when fun to pursue and when used as social activities become addictive – playing no longer becomes a secondary choice, it becomes the main focus. McGonigal (2011) in her search for this answer to explain this 'mass exodus' as more gamers are joining the 'virtual' reality and are finding refuge in a world which is parallel to the one which we inhabit, also corroborates this version of the definition of games. Although there are many multiple facets to games, and these include rewards, competitions, virtual environments, photorealism, and graphics what makes a game enticing to many gamers, is this 'voluntary participation' which helps them consciously decide to join a community with specific goals, using set rules and receiving feedback.

The gamers we interviewed were very adamant on stressing the importance of multiplayer features – it is an element which many in their community look for. People are no longer interested in playing AI, people want to measure up to people. People want to share, to communicate, people want to be immersed but they don't want to do it alone. That is the power which multiplayer games have invested in.

It has to be observed that a few years ago video and computer games exhibited essentially single player modes where the gamer had to measure up to the computer's artificially inserted neurons. These digital games enticed with their graphics and interactivity, possibly captivating their audience with the levels of challenge which were adapted according to the levels of ability achieved – all done solo. The way digital games have been evolving is that they are now *transforming the digital game from an instrument of perceived isolation into a medium for socialisation.* This evolution hasn't necessarily created a mutant which has removed the essentials of what made games work in the 1980s (McGonigal, 2011) but it has kept the characteristics which offer the gamers enough challenge in order to keep them to the edge of their capabilities – that thin red line that exists between 'too easy – too difficult' – Csìkszentmihàlyi (1991) describes this as the 'flow experience', or rather an experience which makes the gamer feel extremely good – thus inducing him to want more.

The game experience is therefore triggered when a gamer knowingly and voluntarily accepts to partake in an operation with set rules, which are standardised for the community – whether he/she decides to socialise through the game then that is up to the preference of the gamer. So we've got statistics – plenty of huge figures that show that people are *game to the Game* (pun intended). According to a report from the Entertainment Software Association (2011) the average adult gamer has been playing video games for the past 12 years with an amazing figure of 64% of gamers who choose to play games with other gamers in person. Mary Ulicsak, Martha Wright and Sue Cranmer from Futurelab (2010, p. 5), as per this report, have asserted that video gaming is indeed bringing out the potential of getting more families together in an environment which is fun to share amongst all family members. This report also shows figures for top selling video games in 2009, with games like Call of Duty and WII games topping the video game charts, whilst The SIMS, World of Warcraft, and Spore, topping the computer game charts. All of these are multiplayer games, fostering collaboration and strategy building.

McGonigal (2011) elaborates more on these facts and figures, and in answer to her previous question on the people's quest for happiness she mentions one very important aspect which lies at the very core of the matter. Our gamers mentioned it indirectly and it seems so obvious when you think about it. Ever since the birth and the ascent of man, our species have evolved as social animals – the sense of belonging swathing them in its warmth. So when a world tragedy or disaster hits, then the rest of the world population feels the need to step in and fulfil a purpose in its role as a member in the global community. The gaming experience triggers all these emotions and places them in a virtual environment – what is unreal at the individual level becomes real, people can really start helping to save the world, albeit if it is a virtual one and that is what makes this experience truly unique.

23.5 The Two Faces of Design – Why Do It?

So if a unique experience, whether it is complex or simplistic, is what makes a game successful, we need to figure out how to design a game... not just any Game, but THE Game...the game that target people will become immersed in and therefore enjoy. There is a huge dilemma...how do we design a serious game which attracts these massive number of gamers, who are already out there playing amazing games, and how do we design a game which imparts educational skills? Most often the term educational game is boring... at the mere mention of the word, our gamers, sitting through the interview, grimace. What is amazing is that many of these massively popular games which are so well liked by gamers around the globe some of whom actually become addicted to them, are in themselves quite educational and involve higher cognitive ability skills, which classroom practice is hard to match with. Take World of Warcraft for example, or SimCity, or Civilisation IV/V. These are all considered as strategy building games where the power of the community within the world becomes very strong as gamers are on a continuous quest to solve particular missions, such as solving all the *cataclysmatic* problems in 'Azeroth', or building a city, or going through ancient civilisations right up to the space age, building an empire which will take the virtual world by storm. The skills the gamers are required to amass from these games are all very complex and also an important feature of the design of these games but these are kept transparent from the user.

Gee (2008b) mentions that an essential part of the design within games is the notion that within video games there is no distinct demarcation between learning and assessment. The gamers are all the time learning what it takes to survive or succeed within this virtual environment and they are being assessed continuously. If they fail, then the system tells them immediately that they have failed and to try again. According to our gamers, when this happens, and it does happen rather frequently, and they are in a multiplayer environment, it adds so much more to all the fun of the game. Whereas in a normal classroom setting, failure is seen as something which is not only embarrassing in itself but also a cause for demotivation, inside the realm of the video game it is seen as a necessary measure in order to rise up to the challenge and move to another more complex level – and what adds fun to it is that 'you can even get the support of your friends' (Gamers, anonymous, (2010, November) Personal Interview). That in itself is a fantastic mirage, because so much educational research and learning theories have been dedicated to the quest of coming up with solutions, ideas and tools to be able to do this. And now we can see that this is already being done in these video games.

So, what's next? The video games are already on the market and inside the people's homes. Their characteristics can somehow be identified as well. The learning also seems to be happening because according to researchers, such as Barab et al. (2009), Aldrich (2009b), Charsky (2010), Hayes and Games (2009), video and computer games imply the kind of social and collaborative learning on which most of the learning theories which we have discussed above seem to be based upon. What seems to be missing is the context – applying curricular design and practice to the digital games, and we believe that we need to create the right context ourselves. We also need to design this context in the frame of mind of our audience and that means we have to target the right users for the specific game. Oblinger (2006) warns against designing games which might not be effective, and which might not really target the needs of the audience WITHIN the educational realm. We cannot produce a game just because games tend to be effective. There are so many of these games and most are not successful. It is only a few which make it to the top.

So the first principle of good game design is DESIGN with PEOPLE in mind. We will design games for an audience and therefore we need to talk to the audience to see what they really want.

The second principle of game design which Aldrich (2009b) mentions is that of thinking BIG when designing games – one thinks big in terms of skills and not just content. Creating a game in which the gamer is subjected to seeing a screen adding up numbers, might not be the right product for a teenage audience – for audiences of any age come to think of it. Skills such as adaptation, learning to survive, and applying real life models are big skills which many people have to use in real life. And what's even nicer is that in the gaming world these skills are still being mirrored. We see the concept of adaptation emerge in WoW or SuperMarioBros amongst the top popular games which struck gold in 2010, learning to survive in Call of Duty, Halo and WoW. Applying real life models seems to have struck it big with Farmville and Cityville, despite the extremely simple game playing skills needed. Aldrich also mentions applying economic, value and governing models, budgeting, communication, conceptual dead reckoning, and conflict management, all represented in games such as Civilisation IV and V or EVOKE.[2]

The third principle which struck a chord with Reeves and Read (2009) is that of DESIGNING the game design. 'Games are not meant to just happen'… gamer

[2] EVOKE was developed by the World Bank Institute, the learning and knowledge arm of the World Bank Group, and directed by alternate reality game master Jane McGonigal. [Online] Accessed 2001: http://blog.urgentevoke.net/2010/01/27/about-the-evoke-game/

conflict preventions, the design of Mods (customisable elements of the game user interface), the continuous feedback ensure that the gamers' experience is both unique and at the same time encapsulated within the game parameters.

In addition Reeves and Read (2009) also included 10 key ingredients in their lists of what makes great games. We have adopted these and got the educational paradigm to fit into these. After all, we have already concluded that digital games are already applying the basic learning theories.

1. Self Representation; many games and worlds use self representation embodied in an avatar; gamers are required to have this character alter-ego which can be as realistic or fantastic as the rules of the game allow. In this context, it is this alter-ego that has to make decisions, and most often gamers report, a kind of symbiotic relationship with this avatar who has to survive and succeed in the game.

2. 3D Environments; our gamers have in fact stated that they play games to do stuff which cannot be done in reality. In education there are many instances when the context and the environment doesn't permit the physical manipulation of objects, or time or space. For this reason, simulations and role-playing in games, would do a wonderful job of fulfilling the need of the gamer to reach more fantastic levels as the game proceeds.

3. Narrative: de Freitas and Oliver (2006) describe the concept of using narrative in an educational context, in a way which allows for immersion into the game. They describe this as 'Diegesis' which is represented very clearly when watching a movie. When the movie is narrated the audience sees the movie from the external thus not really partaking as one of the characters. When the movie becomes the narrative or the story, then the audience moves towards immersion. In the educational context, the authors surmise that this becomes a very critical factor in supporting the 'reflective' process of learning. This, we believe to be the distinguishing trait between mere presence in the world vs. education in context. de Freitas and Maharg (2001) discuss the transformation of learning in the digital age as a reconstruction of learning in terms of experiences and apprenticeships – becoming immersed in the narrative of a digital game contributes to enhancing learning experience.

4. Feedback: This is one of the essential elements of game design. Many game designers today (McGonigal, 2011), Aldrich (2009b), Reeves and Read (2009), Gee (2008a) all speak about the importance of continuous feedback for game design. The element of success or failure is measured and tested continuously and it doesn't really matter if the gamer fails the first time. Most gamers take this as a challenge and they need to rise up to the occasion and prove their worth. It is what essentially motivates the gamer to go on. During our interviews with our gamers they emphasised that the kind of feedback which drives them to get back on track after a failure is the feedback which can actually get them addicted to playing more and wanting more. This is another important design factor in the educational context; overcoming any failures of learning is paramount to the learning experience itself.

5. Reputations, Ranks and Levels: During the interviews, our gamers were very clear about their ideas – 'Reputation can make or break within a game. . .and even beyond, especially when gamers know you on a personal and real level'. Gamers look up to expert gamers with great awe and aim to not only follow in their steps but

also take over and achieve the highest rank or level position. This element of game design is, according to Crawford (1997), tantamount to proving oneself in terms of skills or abilities. In the classroom we get an inkling of people's fear of failure and we can see the decrease of the motivation in proving oneself during certain tasks. Digital computer games, bring this out naturally and this should be another important design factor in education.

6. Marketplace and Economies: One of the characteristics most often exhibited by multiplayer games is the concept of trading, acquisition and/or selling thus replicating the economy scale according to the magnitude and complexity of the game. Second Life, is a classic example of how the economies are running in virtual worlds when compared to the real life. People are not only working hard over in Second Life, but their commercial value has also risen. Educational implications? Many... including the reaped benefits – the scorepoints in terms of the assets or currencies. If we take Farmville or Cityville as other two examples of the game market place then we really see that such an economy-driven environment is masking an increased drive for engagement.

7. Competition with rules that are explicit: The same drive for engagement can be said to apply for competitions in games. People and gamers are constantly competing, and when this happens against people they know then it becomes even more fun. McGonigal (2011) describes how competing gamers are in reality socialising. She describes the social networking game *Lexolous* registering more than 5 million gamers connected through facebook, and the fun bickering between people who are close to each other, brings out the element of competition which instead of being considered as another barrier to social connectivity, is being considered as a fun way to spend time with someone. She takes the examples that many gamers are reporting having fun with their 'moms' playing this game, or rather *winning* the game. We ask, what if these competitive driven games are made use of explicitly for the curriculum and used beyond the classroom walls?

8. Teams: Multiplayer games are just that... social connectivism is just that. All the big game designers are doing just that. The emergence of social communities in large-scale projects which we are seeing across the Internet is enough proof to sustain that it is as Aldrich (2009b) describes the users who are the writers and the editors and not the professionals/McGonigal (2011) refers to a recently coined term – crowdsourcing[3] a classic example of which lies in Wikipedia. Crowdsourcing really and truly is what lies at the backbone of Web2.0; the Web which we inhabit currently. When one converts all the work which can be seen on Wikipedia and which is the product of a voluntary collaborative effort, by the mass, one would end with a 100 million hours of accumulation of human thought... and that is quite a substantial amount of human collective power. The community becomes a team, whose global effort can impinge greatly on the world. In education, collaboration fosters support in learning. Apprenticeship roles identified earlier as occuring in a

[3] Crowdsourcing is a term coined by Jeff Howe (2006) to describe the "outsourcing of the job to the crowd" (McGonigal, 2011)

community of practice surrounding the game is just one of the roles which one can assume within a team, in order to contribute to the team's global thinking effort. MMO's and MMORPG's which offer a persistent multiplayer environment are further enhanced in their organisation of BIG skills (Aldrich, 2009b) through the setting up of small teams with specific learning goals and attainment targets. Teamwork fosters an environment which leads to improved ranking, leveling and reputation building. In a group, we find our strength.

9. Parallel Communication Systems: We can also refer to these as multimodal communication systems, which are reflected in many game systems' multiple channels of communication. Interviewed gamers report that they have great fun even when playing multiplayer games with visuals which are not so amazing as long as the communication channels are in place. Therefore some popular games include voice support, and allow for public and private conversations. One feature the interviewed gamers highlighted was the similarity between the real world communication and the communication found in WoW. Through sound communication one feels a certain sense of belonging to the community and this appeals to the emotions of the gamers. This parallel channel of communication is also a medium which adds on to the fun of the game in a collaborative environment. During the interview the gamers provided anecdotes about games which they were playing and whose major fun elements were multiplied through the added voice communication channels.

10. Positive Stress Factors: McGonigal (2011) reports a study, which takes into consideration the psychological implications of 'fun'. The study indicates, that people tend to have better and more positive fun the harder the work which they do. The more pressure they feel in a game, the more positive the frame of mind of the person undergoing this 'positive stress' is. This positive stress provokes a positive emotion which the human brain perceives. Time constraints is one such factor which can be identified as a positive stress factor.

However when it comes to designing games, categorising them into 10 broad categories might be slightly simplistic. We do think that there are many other additional factors which need to be taken into consideration.

Big games don't just happen. Epic IS designed; it's not born out of a spontaneaous collective frenzy. We think that all digital game categories need to be epic to achieve a productive level of success. They need to overwhelm people with positive stress; designed for the flow of the experience; designed to make people happy.

One element which McGonigal mentions quite frequently and which other big game designers also mention is the involvement of the people. The modern Web (Web2.0) has proven that people have something to say and they are saying it. When designers empower people with voice, then they add the key ingredient of success. Games make use of this key ingredient through interactivity, through feedback, through the multiple communication channels. People want to compete against their friends, or against strangers, but most of all people crave for communication and for establishing links which would make them feel part of something bigger. Co-op, a term used frequently by gamers to define collaboration and cooperation, thus no longer becomes an option. It is the voice of the people which speaks in this case, and this voice can transform each individual into a collective mass, pushing each other, creating a sense of urgency to solve a problem, achieve a mission, or resolve a quest.

23.6 Practicing Ideals – Where Do We Go from Here?

Seely Brown (2011) described gamers as 'incredibly talented learners' – for many gamers if there is no learning involved in the game then it is no fun. Such a statement seems so paradoxical – so we try to analyse this in terms of the games which are so popular by mass demand and which most of our gamers have also mentioned. World of Warcraft (WoW), the MMORPG, is a classic example. MMORPGs are essentially persistent, networked and interactive games with a clearly established target which pre-empts gamers to connect and collaborate with other gamers through the social network which is established. Learning within the game framework becomes a social status acquisition within the world as more 'guilds' or communities are established. MMORPG (2011) reports an astounding formation of 2,578 registered guilds for 400 MMORPGs. Guilds remove the concept of single player, and emphasise the team. It is the strength of the collaborative effort of each individual player which places guilds at different strata of the game. It is also probably that which drives to 'addiction' within the game. Each player assumes responsibility for his/her own learning, in order to contribute to the levelling up of their team.

In addition we see today's generations, as people who embrace change. These games are supporting this need for change. A few years back, status quo was held as the stable environment. We were taught during an age which embraced an industry which was static, we didn't need change. Therefore we were taught to sit at desks and be productive, whilst reproducing that which teachers and books delivered. So what happened is that pretty like what happens during evolution, the traits of younger generations started changing to be able to escape from that reality and become immersed in a reality which offered a promise of something better… and this brought about change and learning. The human mutant, was crying out to learn, but opposed to being dictated what to learn. And we can still see it happening now, unfortunately. So when we asked gamers what they would include if they were to design their own games, they didn't see learning as an essential component. They equated learning with teaching or instructing and not the learning which occurs during games. Instead they saw change as the essential component; they saw accessibility; they saw networking; they saw fun. Learning is completely transparent and inherent. It was and will be considered as part of the strategies they have to conceive for more experimentation. We think that that in itself is such a fantastic way to learn. Seely Brown (2011) was during his interview discussing passion, and the way in which guilds in WoW excel through experimentation of new techniques in a concerted group effort. So to take the example of an athlete who is competing at a professional level, much of the excellence which is achieved at a personal level is in reality a group or team effort. What happens is that the athlete is within a team of people who train/play together, they compete against each other, they take time to analyse where challenges are, what each is doing right or wrong, most often coordinated by a team leader such as a coach. What drives these people with such passion is the healthy perspective of competition as one strives to perform better – as McGonigal (2011) also mentions, each tiny result triggers more happiness.

Whilst outlining his visions for the future of education and schooling, Gee (2008b), during an interview, emphasised that what is on next is the collaborative way forward where the intelligence of the group, outdoes the intelligence of the single smartest individual within the group. Another way forward is that of paving the ground for innovation, or rather creating opportunities where one doesn't necessarily apply the standard solutions but each individual would have the freedom within the group to experiment new ways to bring about change which might or might not provide the right solution. When the moves are wrong, when the proposals fail, then the group takes the time to reflect and understand why. This is the way forward for innovation. This is what the major education influencers are proposing today and this is one of the major components which game designers need to work with.

To this extent, we were recently going through a review for LittleBigPlanet2. LittleBigPlanet offers a great gaming concept to all those who are interested in not only playing games, but also creating games. Being Sony's adopted baby, it is aimed for PS3 or Playstation Portable users. However it has risen to popularity ever since its inception in 2008 through the added contribution of the gaming community. The game is two-fold; the gamer first creates the levels and the challenges – in essence, the game, and is then able to upload and share the self-created game levels with the rest of the world community as gamers share, compete and play at the different levels created by themselves. In just 2 years, LittleBigPlanet, acquired more than 3 million sales, BAFTA (British Academy of Film and Television Arts) awards and over 5 million of user-generated game levels (LittleBigPlanet2 Review, 2011). When this started out, the game was quite a risk in itself. No-one was sure, back in 2008, that a gaming community who would want to be so participative in the game creation itself, existed. However the success was also in part attributed by the fact that that the game's target audience are part of that new generation who are intent on bringing about change – creation itself thus becomes the new name of the game. So 2 years on, and the game developers have thought it best to comply with the change and take their audience – their gamers – up another level – ergo LittleBigPlanet2. They have inserted greater challenges in the game level creations, improved user accessibility for more AI in the game levels and reaching out for more flexibility within the robust structure which was initially offered for the first game in the series. Gamers are guided but at the same time the parameters are wide enough so that they can be as flexible in their own creations as they can, provided they remain within the 'rules' of the game. And that is another ingredient which works, which is already being taken up to some extent in a series of games, notably multiplayer games (this can be seen in the customisation of WoW mods) and will probably be taken up by other game developers in the near future. People want to interact but not just in terms of what the objects can do within the game world. People want to be able to create those objects themselves, test them out and if they fail, then they retry – and if one does that with other gamers then the game is also spiced up with some fun as well.

If we now take a moment to look back on the elements which we have previously discussed in terms of a proposed framework for the design of games in education we always come back to this continuum, one end of which represents the classroom and the other end of which represents games. Throughout this continuum we have learning. We might have learning which is reflected into didactics – where most frequently we have a passive listener who interprets the facts given, regurgitating them onto an exam paper when possible. We also have the other learner at the end of the continuum – one who is totally self-directed and most often passionate and motivated in his/her quest for learning within the game world.

Traditionally we were used to a predominant male figure in games, with a certain predisposition to lack of sleep, possibly lack of hygiene and totally immersed in a world of his own. These last couple of years have seen the evolution of a new breed of gamers. Now there is hardly any distinction between the sexes, or between cultures. We have seen this new breed metamorphose from the uncommunicative singular individual to a social dynamic group – where co-op becomes a term which is familiar amongst all gamers wishing to achieve a certain status. We are seeing families using games to strengthen ties, people of all ages playing across their social networks, communities emerging as more voices are being heard, and reach a climax by becoming more active in the game through game element creation and/or modification according to their own competitive stances.

The continuum thus uses games as a representation of the community-based learning which happens within the group structure. Paradoxically this is exactly what should be happening within the classroom – one might therefore argue that there is no continuum to pursue. However, what happens in practice, as is so often the case, is different.

So when it comes to framework design for games and serious games, we are not proposing a framework for the classroom, but for a target audience – for individuals who are already exposed to the ideals set forth by the games. Extending the portability of these games to the classroom is another matter, because this will no longer be dependent on the motivation or lack thereof on behalf of the students, but it will solely reside within the responsibility of the institution to do so. In the meantime one can offer best practice solution characteristics which would need to be included in the design of games – education included – contributing to a high scale motivational factor.

And yet we also want to integrate theoretical frameworks which facilitate deeper cognition and acquisition of skills. In this case we want to use games not just to teach content. That has been done and dealt with. Papert (1998) describes such games as 'Edutainment' and refers to these as 'Shavian Reversals', or rather the concept in genetics, which explains how an offspring discards the strong genes and retains the weak ones. In this example, between a marriage of education and games, the offspring 'Edutainment' would discard the elements of good game design and retain those elements of the curriculum, which are rather weak in terms of good educational practice. Most often the content represented in these games is rather fragmented and decontextualised – pretty much what happens inside a classroom where the learners are learning bits of broken down data, for the mere purpose of integrating within the school system.

Gee (2008a) discusses the difference between learning 'content' and learning 'skills'. It is interesting to note that Aldrich (2009a), McGonigal (2011), de Freitas and Maharg (2001) all refer to learning in games as a skill acquisition rather than targeting content. One might therefore surmise that although the content supplied needs to be planned and programmed within curricular activities, this takes on a rather secondary role when planning the design of the actual game.

de Freitas and Maharg (2001) discuss the framework for game design in terms of the paradigm shift towards social and collaborative interactions, where learning becomes an experiential activity. In this way they propose two sets of theoretical frameworks for games; one proposes the diegesis or rather the narrative of the game for immersion into the game world, whilst the other proposes the transactional aspect of learning through collaborative problem solving. Of course one doesn't exclude the other, they complement each other as they run in parallel.

As can be seen in the Fig. 23.1 below, we have designed a model with the elements which intersect in a sequence. Although this is a rather simplistic reduction of some of the best practice game design elements, in this diagram we can show, how the initial narrative which is at the underlying foundation for good game practices intersects with the possibility of offering gamers an enhanced 'flow experience' through the actual participation in the game creation. In these first two elements, we have included the concept of diegesis, as the game's narrative has the potential of enhancing the immersion experience for the gamer. Related to this, is the possibility of enhancing the learner experience by adding experiential activities which allow not only for changes within the game structure, but also the optimised experience as the gamer innovates, tries, succeeds or fails independently of pre-determined activities. It is within this realm that the gamer constructs his/her learning processes. This cannot be activated unless there is constant feedback. McGonigal (2011) surmises how games which are 'epic', are constantly demanding hard work from the gamers, they are constantly challenging them and constantly guiding them into what is successful and what is not. Just like the athletes in Seely Brown's comparative analysis (2011) we have people who try out new ideas, get feedback, analyse, reflect, repurpose, and retry until they achieve the mastery which they task upon themselves as they are driven by passion for a quest. Still, feedback without reflection becomes a diluted essence. This requires a stronger tie than the individual can provide. As Gee

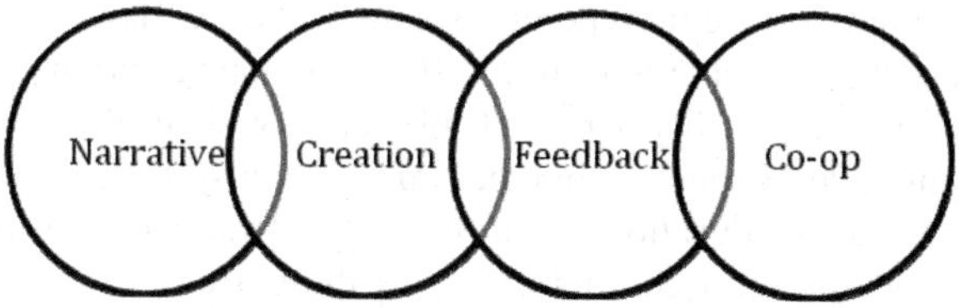

Fig. 23.1 Elements which work together for concerted game design

(2008b) mentioned the intelligence of the group outdoes the smartest of any individual within the group. There becomes a symbiotic relationship where each member thrives upon to conquests of the others and each member is driven by the responsibility towards the group and its members to excel, and within this group there is the competitive balance for survival and mastery.

Charsky (2010) describes this competition as a 'victory condition'. McGonigal (2011) describes the emotional peaks achieved during 'Epic Wins' when the competitor strives to achieve the final glory – the harder the challenge, the greater the competition, the greater the happiness level attained. When multiplayers are included in the game, then the competition becomes more challenging, the work increases, the motivation is enhanced and suddenly the ultimate goal is not so easy to achieve. Suddenly the 'flow experience' as described by Csìkszentmihàlyi and Rathunde (1992) becomes enhanced as the passion driving the gamer increases. So the gamer craves the need to learn more because that is the ultimate way of achieving mastery and status within the community. Throughout this chapter, we have also discussed the emotions which pertain to the community, stimulated by the sense of belonging which heightens the significance of responsibility within the collective.

Charsky (2010) discusses fidelity, or rather the real world representation of artefacts within the game world. We believe that this is another important characteristic of game design which comes together in the element of creation. When a gamer is actually 'doing' something, he/she is carrying out a task or an activity which most often cannot be recreated in real life. However the experience needs to be as close to situated reality as possible – as part of the 'diegesis' effect described by de Freitas and Maharg (2001), for an enhanced immersive experience which contributes to a realistic higher order cognitive activity as the gamer rises up to the challenge which is presented.

We have also discussed 'co-op' or rather cooperation in the game world. We have in fact mentioned the social emergence capabilities of multiplayer games. Our own gamers emphasised that they only played certain digital games because it was fun communicating with friends, because it was a way in which to extend their play to a more augmented or simulated environment which they cannot live through in real life, but which they could live as their avatars in an environment which has no boundaries or division but where group effort is what finally triumphs. To do this, we also need to consider a factor which hasn't yet been given much importance in the research we have come across – and that is accessibility. Many researchers assume that people have access to all consoles, however our gamers have indeed mentioned that beyond game characteristics they take in consideration what they have direct access to. Studies show that gamers might in the end prefer to play using one specific type of console or the PC (Essential Facts about the Computer and Video Game Industry, 2010)– one popular driving factor which WoW exhibits is its accessibility across all platforms without the added need of special console units. Pretty much as in other information systems business models, effective game design for education requires the added value of distribution practices, identifying target market needs and supplying those needs.

23.7 The Final Level

When we started out, it was with the premise that schools are not really following the 21st century trends. Sir Ken Robinson (2001) speaks a lot about the mass standardisation of our schooling system. He refers to it as a 'killer for creativity'. The paradox is that globally people are changing. Companies are evolving into innovative enterprises; each looking for THE idea which will strike gold. So company CEO's, managers and entrepreneurs are pushing to get people who can help them find this idea, solve a problem – and not just any problem but a first class problem – before it even crops up. On the other hand, we have schools, that seem to be taking this shift in mentality in their own stride – much too slowly when compared to what's happening in the world. So we have institutions, teachers, and even parents who are propagating a system which they were used to seeing some 20 or 30 years ago. But this has changed – it is becoming the paradigm shift. People like Gee (2008a), deFreitas and Maharg (2011), Oblinger (2006), Seely Brown (2011), Barab et al. (2009), amongst others are talking about this *transformational learning*, which goes beyond the facts and figures given in textbooks. All these do not contribute to create problem-solvers, or thinkers. Instead the facts and the figures and the textbooks will promote people who are very able to reproduce the data which has been supplied. That is no longer the priority in today's world.

What the world is looking for instead, are individuals with the abilities to think creatively, and collectively whilst working in a concerted effort towards supplying a higher order thinking contribution within a community. Gee (2008a) reflects on how communities demand rather highly skilled challenges from its individual members. Most often in schools, we are almost afraid of demanding work from our learners. We feel a kind of pressure to water down the challenges, to avoid pressures of any kind, and most often to try and reduce their mental efforts. It almost feels like we, as teachers, and as part of a larger institution are making and taking all the decisions of what the learners need to learn and when. Games do it differently. Games provide constant challenges, continuous assessment, just-in-time learning. It is ironic how inside a classroom, the terms 'assessment' and 'tests' bring out the doom and gloom. Inside a digital game world, 'assessment' and 'testing' is what makes a game fun…'where's the fun if you don't lose?' or 'how can you achieve an epic win without a challenge?' Gamers start out by playing the game, they get a vision of the game and then they learn because they feel the need to; they learn because they are driven by passion and motivation. When we think of the inclusion of games to motivate learners then we are not thinking in the correct order. Games don't just motivate because they are any kind of games. When games motivate they do so within a specific context which helps gamers see the targets and provides them with the right environment, at the right time, and with the right conditions for pursuing those targets.

So when we think back on our previous questions such as 'what makes games big?' we have now built a nice structure providing some answers. Big games are those that can satisfy the 21st century gamers' needs; fundamental needs such as creation and production, fidelity, feedback and communication.

Gamers want to be as much producers as consumers of products. They have now, as communities, mastered the games, and therefore the next logical step is for them to become part of the cycle of game creators. They also want to achieve that which cannot be achieved in real life. They don't want any limitations on their possibilities. They crave for the freedom to experiment – to reach a higher level experience through deeper immersion. They want to be tested all the time, because that is the only way that they achieve greater 'happiness' – greater *epic* wins in the game. They want just-in-time learning, where they learn when they need and what they need. This is also part of the experimentation, part of the freedom which they crave for. Gamers also want the fun part – and this is mostly achieved through communication. The social network which is built within the game world is an inherent part of the success of the most popular games which we have seen emerging in 2010 and which are predicted to achieve higher levels of success in 2011. Gamers have a voice and they want to be heard. They want to feel they belong to a group, to a community, which is also offering them added responsibilities within the group. The gamers in a community are both mentors and trainees, they guide and they learn together. Big games are big, because they follow what their gaming audience needs and wants. The next step for education is to take up all that is fundamentally good in big games, spice it up with demanding content, and let the rest work itself out. The paradigm shift is not just about the inclusion of multiplayer games – it's a whole new way of thinking seen from a parallel world.

References

Aldrich, C.: Learning Online with Games, Simulations, and Virtual Worlds. Wiley, Chichester/GB (2009a)

Aldrich, C.: The Complete Guide to Simulations and Serious Games: How the Most Valuable Content Will be Created in the Age Beyond Guttenberg to Google. Wiley, Chichester/GB (2009b)

Barab, S., Scott, B., Siyahhan, S., Goldstone, R., Ingram-Goble, A., Zuiker, S.: Transformational play as a curricular scaffold. J. Sci. Educ. Technol. **18**, 305–320 (2009)

Baribeau, T.: Cities, Cars, and Board Games Leading This Week's List of Fastest-Growing Facebook Games by DAU. Inside Social Games: Tracking Innovation at the Convergence of Games and Social Platforms. http://www.insidesocialgames.com/2011/03/02/cities-cars-and-board-games-leading-this-week%E2%80%99s-list-of-fastest-growing-facebook-games-by-dau/ (2011). Accessed

Charsky, D: From edutainment to serious games: A change in the use of game characteristics. Games Cult. **5**, 177–198 (2010)

Chou, S., Min, H.: The impact of media on collaborative learning in virtual settings:The perspective of social construction. Comput. Educ. **52**, 417–431 (2009)

Crawford, C.: The Art of Computer Game Design. University Vancouver Library, Vancouver (1997)

Csìkszentmihàlyi, M.: Flow: The Psychology of Optimal Experience. HarperCollins, New York (1991)

Csìkszentmihàlyi, M., Rathunde, K.: The measurement of flow in everyday life: Toward a theory of emergent motivation. In: Jacobs, J. (ed.) Nebraska Symposium on Motivation, 1992: Developmental Perspectives on Motivation, Current Theory and Research in Motivation, Vol. 40, pp. 57–97. University of Nebraska Press, Lincoln, NE, xiii, 299 pp (1992) de Freitas, S., Mharg, P.: Modelling learning experiences. In: de Freitas, S., Mharg, P. (eds.) Digital Games and Learning, pp. 1–41. Continuum International Publishing Group, London (2001)

de Freitas, S., Oliver, M.: (2006) How can exploratory learning with games and simulations within the curriculum be most effectively evaluated? Comput. Educ. **46**, 249–264.

Entertainment Software Association: Essential Facts about the Computer and Video Game Industry. Entertainment Software Association. http://www.theesa.com/facts/pdfs/ESA_Essential_Facts_2010.PDF (2011). Accessed 2011

Gee, J.: 'Learning and games.' The ecology of games: Connecting youth, games, and learning. In: Salen, K. (ed.) TheJohn D. and Catherine T. MacArthur Foundation Series on Digital Media and Learning, pp. 21–40. The MIT Press, Cambridge, MA. doi:10.1162/dmal.9780262693646.021 (2008a)

Gee, J.P.: Big Thinkers: James Paul Gee on Grading with Games. (Edutopia, Interviewer) (2008b)

Hamlen, K.R.: Children's choices and strategies in video games. Comput. Hum. Behav. **27**, 532–539 (2011)

Hayes, B., Games, I.: Making computer games and design thinking: A review of current software and strategies. Games Cult. doi: 10.1177/1555412008317312 (2009). Accessed 2011

Howe, J.: The Rise of Crowdsourcing. Wired. 14.06. http://www.wired.com/wired/archive/14.06/crowds.html. Accessed Feb 2011 (2006, June)

Hrastinski, S.: A theory of online learning as online participation. Comput. Educ. **52**, 78–82 (2009)

Lave, J., Wenger, E.: Situated Learning: Legitimate Peripheral Participation. Cambridge University Press, Cambridge (1991)

LittleBigPlanet 2 review:. GamesTM: http://www.gamestm.co.uk/reviews/littlebigplanet-2-review/ (2011). Accessed Feb 2011

Mack, D.: Top 25 Facebook games for March 2011. Inside social games: Tracking innovation at the convergence of games and social platforms. http://www.insidesocialgames.com/ (2011). Accessed 2011

McGonigal, J.; Reality Is Broken. Joanthan Cape, London (2011)

Michael D, Chen, S.: Serious Games. Cengage Learning, Inc, Boston, MA (2005)

MMORPG: MMORPG Gamelist – All Listed Games. MMORPG. http://www.mmorpg.com/gamelist.cfm/show/all/sCol/genreUC/sOrder/asc (2011). Accessed 2011

Nonaka, I., Takeuchi, H.: The Knowledge Creating Company: How Japanese Companies Create the Dynamics of Innovation. Oxford University Press, New York (1995)

Oblinger, D.: Games and learning: Digital games have the potential to bring play back to the learning experience. Educ. Q. **3**, 5–7 (2006)

Oikita S, Bailenson, J., Schwartz, D.L.: The mere belief of a social interaction improves learning. Twenty-ninth meeting of the Cognitive Science Society. Nashville, TN (2007)

Papert, S.: Does easy do it? Children, Games and Learning. Game Dev. Mag. 88 (1998)

Reeves, B., Read, J.: Total Engagement: Using Games and Virtual Worlds to Change the Way People Work and Businesses Compete. Harvard Business Press, Boston, MA (2009)

Reviews – Game Spot: http://www.gamespot.com/ (2011). Accessed 2011

Robinson, K.: Out of Our Minds: Learning to Be Creative. Wiley, Oxford (2001)

Seely Brown, J.: Digital Media – New Learners Of The 21st Century. Episode: Extended Interview: Dr. John Seely Brown. PBS Video (2011)

Vygotsky, L.S.: Mind in Society: The Development of Higher Psychological Processes, xi, 159 pp. Harvard University Press, Cambridge, MA (1978)

Wenger, E.: Communities of Practice: Learning, Meaning, and Identity. Cambridge University Press, New York (1998)

World of Warcraft. Blizzard Entertainment: World of Warcraft: http://www.worldofwarcraft.com/index.xml (2011). Accessed 2011

Index

A

Achievement emotions, 246, 250, 252
Adoption model, 291–307
Adventure games, 172, 172, 286, 311–312, 315–316, 317, 320, 325, 405
Adventure initiative games, 125–129, 131, 138
Alternative input devices, 6
Assessment, 5, 9, 12, 16, 20, 79–80, 91, 103, 109, 113, 122, 135, 142–144, 153, 175, 179, 191, 203, 225–241, 306, 330–331, 336, 341, 343–344, 401, 429–431, 444, 457–459, 464, 470, 475, 489, 499

C

Casual game, 405, 455, 486
Commercial-Off-The-Shelf (COTS) games, 4–5, 291–299, 302–307
Computer based assessment, 229–230, 233, 239
Computing undergraduate education, 463, 475–476
Constructivist learning theories, 453–455
Control-value theory, 246, 250–253, 256, 266–267
Cooperative learning, 61, 63–64, 66–68, 70–74, 76–77, 80
Course performance, 402–404, 410
Course structure, 5, 372–373, 375–376, 381–386, 388–392
Cultural heritage, 4, 153–155, 159

D

Development life cycle, 347–351, 366, 468, 469
Discussion board, 5, 372–386, 388–392
Dungeons and Dragons, 5, 329–346

E

Economic models, 37, 39–40
Educational games, 4–5, 31, 34, 37, 40, 54, 61, 64, 66, 67–68, 73, 80, 113, 169, 190, 198, 246, 248, 273, 287, 330, 426, 451, 460, 470, 485–486, 489
Edutainment applications, 3, 6
Emotion, 245–252, 257–259, 263–264, 266–267, 493
Enquiry-based learning, 5, 449, 456
Evaluation of serious game, 475
Experiential education, 125–131, 134, 138–139, 143, 153
Experimental studies, 65–66, 437–439

F

Flow theory, 61–62, 64, 66, 71–74, 80
Formal logic, 4

G

Game design, 4–5, 10–11, 13–20, 26, 33, 47–48, 50–51, 53, 62–64, 66, 68, 70–71, 74, 76, 80, 92, 104, 111–112, 114, 134, 139, 143, 151, 172–173, 190, 198–201, 203–205, 207, 215, 220, 225, 227, 246, 248–249, 296, 312–313, 330–332, 346, 349–350, 402, 409, 420–421, 427, 462, 490–493, 495–498
Game-enhanced learning, 425–444
Game engines, 12, 109, 116, 121, 246, 259, 292, 350–351, 356, 360, 367, 474
Game play experience, 46, 51
Games-based learning, 86, 88, 132, 347, 467
Gamification, 4–5, 9–13, 20, 399–421, 426

H

Haptic devices, 152–154, 157–158
Health and safety training, 4, 107–122

M. Ma et al. (eds.), *Serious Games and Edutainment Applications*,
DOI 10.1007/978-1-4471-2161-9, © Springer-Verlag London Limited 2011

I

Immersion, 4, 9, 11, 15, 17, 65–66, 69, 73, 76, 78–80, 157, 200, 204, 239, 299, 312, 315, 399, 427–428, 491, 497, 500
Intelligent tutors, 5, 16, 156, 169–170, 179, 245, 460–461

L

Learning context, 5, 198–199, 202–205, 207, 212–217, 219–221, 250, 276, 393, 404, 459
Learning impacts of serious games, 55
Learning languages, 179, 319, 345
Learning levels, 46–51, 53
Learning math, 30, 79, 329–333, 336, 339–345
Learning physics, 252
Learning SQL, 367

M

Massively Multi-Player Online Role-Playing Game (MMORPG), 65, 292, 296, 304, 306, 358, 482, 485–486, 493–494
Mobile devices, 4, 85–90, 102, 128, 134–137, 140, 142, 149, 198
Mobile education, 85–104
Mobile entertainment, 137
Mod, 5, 351
Multiplayer games, 5, 61, 73–74, 352, 481–500
Multisensory learning, 150, 154
Museum, 5, 155, 199, 213–221

N

Narrative, 5, 12, 18–20, 46–47, 74, 78–79, 153, 172, 180, 190, 201, 218, 273–287, 309–325, 331, 344, 450, 491, 497

O

Origin of serious games, 45

P

Pedagogical effectiveness, 46
Pervasive serious games, 6
Player behaviour, 4, 85–104
Psychology, 4, 6, 9, 11, 85–86, 90–91, 97–98, 103, 131, 171, 174, 180, 182, 185–186, 247–248, 250, 266, 297, 330, 399–421
Puzzle, 5, 200–201, 249, 273–274, 279–281, 283–287, 336, 402, 405

R

Re-contextualized games, 197–221

S

Science festival, 5, 199, 205
Scientific inquiry skills, 170, 185
Second life, 5, 12, 292, 295–296, 369–394, 492
Serious games assessment, 45–56
Serious games design, 16, 19, 455
Serious games market, 25
Simulation, 4–5, 16, 26–27, 29–30, 33, 40, 54, 76, 78–79, 86–87, 107, 109, 111, 114, 116, 118–120, 122, 126, 152, 205, 230–231, 238, 240–241, 248, 276, 287, 296, 306, 313–314, 331, 371, 399–401, 467, 486, 491
Situated learning, 63, 70, 80, 201, 449, 455
Social game, 4, 61, 64, 66, 68–80, 399–421, 487
Social interaction, 6, 9, 14–16, 19, 61, 63–70, 72–74, 77, 292, 399, 407, 427–428, 442, 450, 454
Social interactive learning, 5, 9, 15, 19–20, 156, 481–500
Social media, 6, 298, 303, 305, 407, 411, 454, 483, 486–487
Social studies, 5, 329, 332–333, 335–336, 341–343, 345
Storytelling, 286, 311–312, 332
Student engagement, 108, 299, 425–444

T

Transformative learning, 4, 46–47, 51–54, 56

V

Virtual Learning Environments (VLEs), 4, 149–150, 153–154, 164, 369–394, 440–441
Virtual worlds, 6, 10, 12–13, 15, 19, 76, 114, 118, 128–129, 149–164, 292–293, 295–296, 298, 311, 313–315, 321–322, 369–373, 376–385, 392–393, 487, 489, 492

W

Wiki, 295–296, 372–373, 376, 383, 385–387, 389, 391–392, 485

Z

Zone of proximal development, 71, 172, 180, 454, 482